# Professional Review Guide for the CCS-P Examination 2006 Edition

Patricia Schnering, RHIA, CCS
Toni Cade, MBA, RHIA, CCS, FHIMA
Anita Hazelwood, MLS, RHIA, FAHIMA
Carol Venable, MPH, RHIA, FHIMA
Irene Mueller, EdD, RHIA

**PRG Publishing, Inc.**
Professional Review Guides, Inc.

**Professional Review Guide for the CCS-P Examination, 2006 Edition**

Published by:
**PRG Publishing, Inc.**
**Professional Review Guides**
P. O. Box 528
St. Petersburg, Florida 33731
Phone: (727) 526-3163
FAX: (727) 526-4474
Toll Free: (888) 383-PRG1~or~ (888) 383-7741
E-mail: PJSPRG@aol.com
Web Page: http://www.prgpublishing.com



ISBN: 1-932152-30-X

Printed in the United States of America

Editors: Patricia Schnering, RHIA, CCS
Toni Cade, MBA, RHIA, CCS
Anita Hazelwood, MLS, RHIA, FAHIMA
Carol Venable, MPH, RHIA

## Disclaimer of Warranty

It is the authors' sincerest hope that each examination candidate using this review guide will pass the national examination. The authors suggest that students avail themselves of all resources possible including text books, class notes and independent study materials obtained during their educational process, attendance at examination review sessions, participation in study groups and the use of other examination review books.

The information and material contained in the book or the CD-ROM are provided "as is" without warranty of any kind, express or implied, including without limitation any warranty concerning the accuracy, adequacy or completeness of such information or material or the results to be obtained from using such information or material. Neither Professional Review Guides, Inc., PRG Publishing, Inc., the authors, or the distributor shall be responsible for any claim attributable to errors, omissions or other inaccuracies in the information or material contained in this book or the CD-ROM. And in no event shall Professional Review Guides, Inc., PRG Publishing, Inc., or the authors or distributors be liable for direct, indirect, special, incidental or consequential damages arising out of the use of such information or material.

# About the Authors

**Patricia J. Schnering, RHIA, CCS**
Patricia Schnering is the founder of PRG Publishing, Inc. and Professional Review Guides, Inc. She is a self-employed entrepreneur, working as author, editor and publisher for Professional Review Guides, Inc. and PRG Publishing Inc. Mrs. Schnering is a 1995 graduate of the Health Information Management program at St. Petersburg College in St. Petersburg, Florida. In 1998 she was certified as a CCS and in 1999 she received her RHIA certification. Her education includes a Baccalaureate degree from the University of South Florida in Tampa, Florida with a major in Business Administration. Since 1993, she has worked in Health Information Services supervisory positions, as a HIM consultant and as an adjunct HIM instructor at St. Petersburg College.

**Anita Hazelwood, MLS, RHIA, FAHIMA**
Anita Hazelwood is an Associate Professor in the Health Information Management Department at the University of Louisiana at Lafayette located in Lafayette, Louisiana. She has a Bachelor's degree in Medical Record Science, a Masters degree in Library Science and has been a credentialed Registered Health Information Administrator (RHIA) for 26 years.

Some of the courses that she teaches include: Coding and classification systems including ICD-9-CM and CPT coding; Reimbursement methodologies such as DRGs and RBRVS; Fraud and abuse; principles of health information management and Alternative delivery systems. She is also the Clinical Experience Coordinator.

Anita has actively consulted in hospitals, nursing homes, clinics, facilities for the mentally retarded and in other educational institutions. She has conducted numerous ICD-9-CM and CPT coding workshops throughout the state for hospitals and physician's offices.

On a professional level, Anita has been a member of the American Health Information Management Association (AHIMA) for several years. She is also a member of the Society for Clinical Coding (SCC) and served on the SCC board as Secretary in 1998. Anita has been the Internet Task Force Chairman for several years. She is a member of the AHIMA's Assembly on Education (AOE) and has served as Membership Chairman, a member of the Nominating Committee and on the Board of Directors.

Anita is a member of the Louisiana Health Information Management Association and was selected as its 1997 Distinguished Member.

**Irene Mueller, EdD, RHIA**
Irene Mueller is a 1992 graduate of the Health Information Administration (formerly Health Information Management) program at Western Carolina University in Cullowhee, NC, where she now serves as Program Director. She received her Master's degree in Library Science at Florida State University in 1974. In 2001, she earned her doctorate degree in Adult and Higher Education at Montana State University. Her experience in health information management includes outpatient coding, ten years as health information management educator (including serving as Program Director for HIT and HIA programs), and consulting experience for physician offices and small hospitals in Montana. She is a CAHIIM Panel Reviewer.

**Toni Cade, MBA, RHIA, CCS, FAHIMA**

Toni Cade is a graduate of the Health Information Management program at the University of Louisiana at Lafayette. Mrs. Cade also received her Master's degree in Business Administration (MBA). She is credentialed as a Registered Health Information Administrator (RHIA) and a Certified Coding Specialist (CCS). She has over 27 years experience and is listed in Marquis' Who's Who in Medicine and Health Care. Her HIM experience includes seven years in acute care hospital practice in a variety of positions, including Utilization Review Supervisor and Coding Supervisor. Mrs. Cade is currently employed as Associate Professor in the Health Information Management Department at the University of Louisiana at Lafayette in Lafayette, Louisiana. Her educational duties include teaching Prospective Payment Systems (i.e.: DRGs, RBRVS, RUGs, APGs/APCs), Medical Terminology, Performance Improvement, Utilization Review and Hospital Statistics. Mrs. Cade is the Management Internship Site Coordinator coordinating affiliation sites throughout the United States. She is also an independent consultant involved in providing educational workshops on coding (ICD-9-CM, CPT, Evaluation and Management Documentation Guidelines) and reimbursement (DRGs and APCs). Her consulting experience includes the performance of inpatient DRG audits and hospital charge analysis for attorneys in medical malpractice cases. She has served the Louisiana Health Information Management Association (LHIMA) in many capacities, including President. In 2003, she was awarded the LHIMA Distinguished Member Award. In 2004, she was awarded the LHIMA Outstanding Volunteer Award. She has also been a delegate to the American Health Information Management Association (AHIMA). She was nominated for the AHIMA Educator Award in 2004 and the Champion Award in 2005.

**Carol Venable, MPH, RHIA, FAHIMA**

Carol Venable is a Professor and Department Head of Health Information management at the University of Louisiana at Lafayette. She has a Bachelor's degree in Medical Record Science, a Master's degree in Public Health and Tropical Medicine and has been a credentialed Registered Health Information Administrator (RHIA) for over 28 years. Prior to teaching at ULL, Ms. Venable held the position of Director of Medical Records at Lafayette General Medical Center and has actively consulted in hospitals, nursing homes, clinics, home health agencies, educational institutions, physician's offices and facilities for the mentally retarded. She has written numerous articles and co-edited several coding publications. She has co-authored the books, *ICD-9-CM Diagnostic Coding and Reimbursement for Physician Services* and *ICD-10 Preview*. She was co-author of a chapter in the book, *Health Information: Management of a Strategic Resource, 2nd Edition*. She has been a member of the Louisiana Health Information Management Association and has served as President, President-elect, Treasurer, Delegate and a member of the Board of Directors as well as serving on various committees and projects. Carol has also been active in the American Information Management Association. She has served on the Item Writing Committee, Benchmarking the Best Practices in HIM Education Project, Council on Education and the Council on Certification's Roles and Functions Committee. She also serves as a member of the Panel of Accreditation Surveyors. In addition, Carol was awarded the Legacy Award by the American Health Information Management Association. She was elected to serve on the Assembly on Education's (AOE) Board of Directors and has served as chair of the Membership and Nomination Committees of the AOE. She also serves on the Editorial Review Board for the Educational Perspectives in Health Information Management, the journal of the Assembly on Education of the American Health Information Management Association.

# Acknowledgments

First and foremost, I would like to express my gratitude to all of the authors who have worked on the educational materials PRG Publishing has produced. They are seasoned professionals and excellent educators. They inspire me to work harder to produce better products. Each one of these educators presents a facet of HIM practice necessary to view the HIM arena as a whole.

There are very special people in my family who always knew I could do it when I wasn't sure I could. My husband, Bob, as always, continues to keep me grounded when I tend to spin off in space as I work on the books. My mother is my role model for perseverance leading to success. She embodies grace, courage, strength and endurance.

A special thanks to my daughter and friend, Holly Hiltz, for helping in a myriad of ways throughout the year – by taking phone calls, helping in the editing process and being a sounding board.

My thanks would not be complete without acknowledging all the HIM/HIT educators and students who support our efforts by purchasing PRG Publishing products. My reward is knowing that the materials you study here may assist you in preparing for the challenge of the examination. Thank you for the letters and words of encouragement.

Whichever credential you seek, I wish you the very best now and throughout your career.

Until we meet......

Patricia J. Schnering, RHIA, CCS

# Table of Contents

INTRODUCTION ........ 9

EXAM STUDY STRATEGIES AND RESOURCES ........ 15

CODING REVIEW ........ 29

CCS-P REVIEW MULTIPLE CHOICE QUESTIONS
- CLASSIFICATION SYSTEMS REGISTRIES AND INDEXING ........ 65
- MEDICAL BILLING AND REIMBURSEMENT SYSTEMS ........ 91
- MEDICAL SCIENCE ........ 109
- ICD-9-CM CODING ........ 127
- CPT-4 CODING ........ 157

CCS-P REVIEW Cases TO Code
- Medical Coding Cases ........ 215
- Answer Key to Cases ........ 463

CCS-P MOCK EXAMINATION
- Multiple Choice Questions ........ 487
- Answer key for Multiple Choice Questions ........ 506
- Coding Cases ........ 515
- Answer key for Coding Cases ........ 597

APPENDICES
- APPENDIX A - Pharmacology for Coding ........ 605
- APPENDIX B - Laboratory Testing ........ 611

Official ICD-9-CM Guidelines for Coding and Reporting ........ 617

Summary of ICD-9-CM Changes October 2005 ........ 669

# Introduction

This examination review guide represents a renewed effort to provide materials for HIM students and professionals. In reviewing the results of past examinations, we found that it would be beneficial for examination candidates to have additional practice in answering multiple choice questions. We have selected questions to cover the broad topic categories necessary in sitting for the CCS-P Certification Examination. Researching the questions as you study should increase your knowledge such that, when you encounter similar but different questions, you can arrive at the correct answer. We believe that this review material will jog your memory and build on information you have already gained through your education and professional experiences. This book provides you with a mix of coding questions and case exercises to both increase your coding skills and provide you with testing that mimics the exam format.

The beginning of this book offers suggestions for study and test taking strategies. The book is then divided into two additional sections. The first section is a coding review section containing multiple choice questions and coding case studies. The second section is a mock examination containing a Part I with sixty (60) multiple choice questions and a Part II with mock with cases to code. The back of the book contains appendices with information on pharmacology, laboratory testing and guidelines for ICD-9-CM coding.

| **Professional Review Guide for the CCS-P Examination Content Areas** | |
|---|---|
| CONTENT AREA | NUMBER OF QUESTIONS/CASES |
| Biomedical Sciences | 100 Questions |
| Anatomy and Physiology | |
| Medical Terminology | |
| Pathophysiology/Disease Process | |
| Pharmacology | |
| Clinical Classification Reimbursement Methodologies | |
| Classification Systems, Registries and Indexing | 80 Questions |
| Medical Billing and Reimbursement Systems | 52 Questions |
| ICD-9-CM Coding | 120 Questions |
| CPT Coding | 227 Questions |
| CCS-P Case Study Coding Review | 42 Cases |
| Mock Examinations | |
| Part I Mock Examination Question | 60 Questions |
| Part II Mock Examination Cases | 16 Cases |

The key to success on the exam is a thorough knowledge of CPT, HCPCS Level II and ICD-9-CM coding which can only be achieved through extensive use and familiarity with the code books. Having to use the code books to answer questions will help you increase speed in the use of both coding books.

This book is only one of many tools available to you to prepare. Use a variety of review methodologies (multiple choice questions, case studies, review of theory, mock exams, etc.) as an effective means of reviewing. These tools can help prepare you for the challenge of the 2006 coding exam.

The CCS-P examination is in a computer-based format. Carefully read your Candidate Handbook for the CCS-P Examination and continue to monitor AHIMA's web site to look for updated information on the examination format. Currently, the case studies are still being given to you in a paper format and you are expected to input your answer codes on a computerized form/screen on the computer screen.

Part I of the examination will have the sixty (60) multiple choice questions and the time constraint is sixty (60) minutes. You will be expected to answer the questions without use of your references and code books. Part II of the examination has a total of seventeen (17) cases to code using your CPT, HCPCS and ICD-9-CM code books. The time allotted for completing Part II of the examination is three hours (180 minutes).

| 2006 CCS-P Examination Content | |
|---|---|
| PART I | |
| Number of Multiple Choice Questions | 60 |
| Amount of time for questions | 60 minutes |
| Average time to answer each question | 1 minutes per question |
| PART II | |
| CPT E&M Chapter Cases | 6 |
| CPT Surgery Chapter Cases | 6 |
| CPT Medicine Chapter Cases | 3 |
| Case from remaining CPT Chapters and HCPCS Level II | 1 |
| Total number of cases | |
| Amount of time for Cases | 180 minutes |
| Average time to code each case | 10.59 minutes per case |
| Total time for Examination | 4 Hours |

Reminder: Monitor AHIMA's website for updates on the testing information.

**ABOUT THE COMPETENCIES FOR THE CCS-P EXAMINATION**

We suggest that you start by examining the competencies for the Certified Coding Specialist-Physician-based. They are listed as Domains and Task Statement Competencies which were created to reflect the necessary skill level for professional practice. A detailed list of the competencies is provided in the AHIMA Candidate Handbook for the CCS-P Examination.

It is the responsibility of American Health Information Management Association's (AHIMA) Council on Certification (COC) to assess what job tasks are frequently executed by newly certified practitioners. Additionally, the COC determines the job tasks that are critical to the practice--in other words, which job tasks that, if done incorrectly, could create a negative impact. The Task Statements are also referred to as the test specifications.

The process of identifying those critical job functions was accomplished by conducting a job analysis. The objective was to determine how the practice is evolving and to develop the test specifications and a certification examination to correspond with changes that are occurring in the field. The data that were collected as a result of this research provided the essential elements that were necessary to establish the test specifications for the certifying exam. The COC is responsible for developing and administering the certification examination and determining the eligibility of applicants to write the exam. The task statements for the Certified Coding Specialist-Physician-based are grouped into four Domains. These Domains are divided further into task statements. Weights for each Domain are assigned; however, weights were not assigned to the task statements. Each weight correlates to the degree of emphasis, or importance, given to each Domain statement as it relates to the current health information practice. The table displays the domains you will be responsible for on the examination.

| **CCS-P Examination Content with Percentage Questions by Domain** | | | |
|---|---|---|---|
| Domains | | Number of Questions | Percentage of Exam |
| Domain 1: | Health Information Documentation | 10 | 16% |
| Domain 2: | Coding | 25 | 42% |
| Domain 3: | Reimbursement Methods and Regulatory Guidelines | 12 | 20% |
| Domain 4: | Data Quality | 13 | 22% |
| **TOTAL** | | 60 | 100% |

These examination questions test your knowledge on three cognitive levels: recall (RE), application (AP) and analysis (AN). The recall level tests your memory of basic facts like being able to identify terms, methods, and procedures. The application level tests your ability to interpret data and information, to be able to apply concepts and principles, recognize relationships among data and calculate mathematical problems. The analysis level measures your ability to: solve specific problems by evaluating, comparing and selecting appropriate solutions for action; evaluate information and perform multiple calculations to assemble various elements into a total picture. The following table shows the number of questions by domain and cognitive level.

| **CCS-P Examination Content with Number of Questions by Cognitive Level** | | | | |
|---|---|---|---|---|
| Domains | Number of Questions | | | Total |
| | RE | AP | AN | |
| Domain 1: Health Information Documentation | 2 | 6 | 2 | 10 |
| Domain 2: Diagnostic Coding Guidelines | 5 | 7 | 13 | 25 |
| Domain 3: Procedural Coding Guidelines | 2 | 8 | 2 | 12 |
| Domain 4: Regulatory Guidelines and Reporting Requirements for Inpatient Hospitalizations | 2 | 8 | 3 | 13 |
| **TOTAL** | 11 | 29 | 20 | 60 |

Source: AHIMA Candidate Handbook for the CCS and CCS-P Examinations

As you can see from the table above, the examination is skewed toward application and analysis type questions. A total of 49 out of 60 questions are at the application and analysis level.

## Content and Insights

Now, let's take a look at the past. Before the CCS-P examination was in effect, information was gathered on the applicants for the CCS examination. AHIMA found that a "typical" examination applicant was a first time examination taker with the some of the traits listed in the first of the tables below. It came as no surprise that the success of the applicant had a strong relationship to the number of years of experience in coding

The first table gives some generalizations about the "typical" CCS test taker. And the second table shows some historical CCS-P exam success factors.

**CCS Applicant Generalizations**

| ***Applicant*** | ***Factor*** | ***Percentage*** |
|---|---|---|
| Age | over 40 years old | 59% |
| Coding Experience | 6 years or more | > 50% |
| Other Credentials | none | 55% |
| Education | high school or two-year college education | 76% |
| Work Place | HIM Department in a hospital | 72% |

**Success Factors for CCS Candidates**

| **Factor** | **Pass Rate** |
|---|---|
| Taking test for the first time | 64% |
| AHIMA credential | 80% |
| College education | 68% |
| Consultants | 85% |
| Working in HIM Department | 70% |

Coding experience: The pass rate increases in percentage with years of coding experience.

It is interesting to note that 80% of those successful exam applicants have an AHIMA credential and that as the number of years of coding experience increases so does the rate of exam success. Although the minimum requirement for eligibility to sit for the exam is a high school diploma or equivalent educational background, it is strongly recommended that you have at least one to two years of experience in coding.

One would assume that many of the same types of characteristics would be true of the CCS-P candidate. They would have experience in outpatient coding, probably do not have other credentials and work in an outpatient setting.

In addition, it would also follow that the success factors for the CCS-P Candidates would be similar. They would tend to be first time examination taker, have another AHIMA credential, and work in HIM departments either in the inpatient or outpatient arena.

Whatever your background or experience, we wish you the very best of luck in your quest for certification.

# Study Strategies and Resources

## STUDY STRATEGIES AND RESOURCES

### How to Use this Book

We suggest you answer the multiple choice questions and code the case studies in the review section of the book before taking the mock examination. It will give you a base line to begin your CCS-P Examination preparation. Your strengths and weaknesses will become more apparent, allowing you to plan your study time more effectively and focus on your problem areas.

After working through the review questions and case studies in the book, take the mock examination. It will provide you an opportunity to assess your speed in answering multiple choice questions and in coding cases.

### Study Strategies

Preparing for a major examination is similar to preparing for a marathon athletic event. The time allotted for the examination is a total of four hours. One suggestion is to use your study process to slowly build up your concentration time until you can focus your energy for several hours at a time. This is like the runner who begins jogging for 30 minutes and builds up to one hour, then one and a half hours, etc., and gradually increases the endurance time to meet the demands of the race. This strategy could work for you.

Everyone has his/her particular study style. Some people prefer to study alone while others work best in a group. Regardless of your preference, we strongly recommend that you take advantage of studying with a group at least some of the time. Studying with others can prove very helpful when working through your areas of weakness. Each member of the study team will bring strengths and weaknesses to the table and all can benefit from the collaboration. Even if you are a solitary learner, you may occasionally want to work with a group on those topics you find more challenging. If you do not have easy access to a study group for the examination, you may want to study with other HIM professionals over the Internet. The HIM community of practice CoP on the Internet would be a great avenue to find others who are in the same position.

Theoretically, material learned thoroughly after one study session will fade predictably with time. After one day, the average person retains only 80% of what was learned; ultimately he/she will remember about 30% of the material originally learned. That is why you are relearning information that you acquired over a period of years. Your aim is to achieve maximum recall through effective review.

Make your study process a systematic review of all coding topic categories followed by achieving mastery of strategically selected subjects within the topic categories. To facilitate this effort, we recommend that you design a ten-week study program. Plan on spending an average of 10 to 12 hours per week studying. The idea is to study smart, not to bulldoze through tons of material in a haphazard way.

***First, you must get organized***.

You must be deliberate about making sure that you develop and stick to a regular study routine. Find a place where you can study, either at home or at the library.

How you schedule your study time during the week is an individual decision. However, we recommend that you avoid all-nighters and other unreasonably long study sessions. The last thing you want to do is burn yourself out by working too long and too hard at one time. Try to do a little bit at a time and maintain a steady pace that is manageable for you.

***Second, develop your individual study program***.

Write the exam topics and subjects in a list. Outline the chapters in your coding textbooks and review the sections in your code books. Pinpoint your weakest subjects. Pause at each chapter outline and recall basic points. Do you draw a blank, recall them more or less, or do you feel comfortable with your recall? By using this approach, you can see where you stand.

***Then, weigh the importance of each subject***.

How are the topics emphasized in the examination competencies, textbooks, professional journal articles, coding guidelines and coding books? Take a look at the top DRGs and APCs. Try to pick out concepts that would make good examination questions.

***Make a list of the topics in the order that you plan to study them***.

Avoid trying to make a head-on attack by giving equal time and attention to all topics. Use the outline you have made to identify your weakest topics. Determine which topics you believe will require a significant amount of study time and which will only require a brief review. Your list will give you a clear mental picture of what you need to do and will keep you on track.

There are three additional advantages to a list. One, it builds your morale as you steadily cross off items that you have completed as you monitor your progress. Two, glancing back at the list from time to time serves to reassure you that you are on target. And three, you can readily see that you are applying your time and effort where they are most needed.

Keep the list conspicuously in view. Carefully plan your pre-exam study time and stick to your plan. Go to the exam like a trained and disciplined runner going to a marathon event!

**A Summary of Tips for Organizing Your Time and Materials**

1. Review the major CPT and ICD-9-CM coding topic categories and determine which areas you are strong in and which areas you need improvement in.

2. Set up a realistic study schedule. Customize the sample schedule provided in this book to meet your needs.

3. Spend more time and energy studying your areas of weakness. Remember, every question counts toward that passing grade.

4. Organize and review all of the following items:
   a. AHIMA Candidate Handbook for the CCS and CCS-P Examinations
   b. Official Coding Guidelines
   c. outpatient coding guidelines
   d. coding text books and any coding course syllabi, outlines, class notes and tests
   e. coding books
   f. *Coding Clinic* from the past 3-4 years
   g. *CPT Assistant* from the past 3-4 years
   h. professional journal articles on documentation, reimbursement and coding issues
   i. list of pertinent web sites for research and review

5. Enter valuable coding information directly into your code books. You will not be allowed to have loose materials in your books. However, any information that is permanently attached or written into the code book is acceptable.

6. One of the best ways to study for an examination is to take tests. Practice answering questions and working coding cases as much as possible. Time yourself so that you become accustomed to taking, on the average, less than one minute per each multiple choice question and around an average of thirteen to fourteen minutes for coding cases. Work with your watch in front of you. When working coding cases, be sure to follow the coding procedures that will be used in the examination. These procedures are listed in the Candidate Handbook from AHIMA.

7. Carefully read the Candidate Handbook from AHIMA. If anything in the handbook is not clear, seek assistance from AHIMA. You are held accountable for the important information, deadlines and instructions addressed in this material. This is especially important this year. In addition, since the CCS-P Examination will be in an electronic format, as more information about the examination becomes available, AHIMA will be adding that information on their website (AHIMA.org).

**Sample Study Schedule**

| | |
|---|---|
| Week 1 | Gather and review HCPCS/CPT and ICD-9-CM coding materials: Coding books, Journals, CPT Assistant (published quarterly by the AMA), Coding Clinics, etc.<br>Use this review guide by studying the coding review section and answering the questions in the Medical Science Chapter |
| Week 2 | Use your references to review Health Information Documentation in Domain I of the competencies for the CCS-P exam.<br>Review the ICD-9-CM Coding Clinics.<br>Review ICD-9-CM Coding conventions in your coding references (i.e. a coding text book or the front of your code book.<br>Review ICD-9-CM Coding Guidelines (For your convenience they are in the back of this book.<br>Answer the questions in the Classification and Indexing Chapter in this book. |
| Week 3 | Use your references to review Coding Competencies in Domain II.<br>Review the ICD-9-CM *Coding Clinics* (published by AHA).<br>Answer the questions in the ICD-9-CM Coding Chapter in this review guide. |
| Week 4 | Use your references to review Reimbursement Methods and Regulatory Guidelines in Domain III.<br>Review the CPT Evaluation and Management Guidelines in your coding materials (i.e. a coding text book, the *CPT Principles of Coding* and/or *the CPT Assistant).*<br>Answer the questions in the Billing and Reimbursement Chapter in this book. |
| Week 5 | Use your references to review Data Quality Competencies in Domain IV.<br>Review the CPT Coding rules using your coding materials (i.e. a coding text book or in the *CPT Assistant).*<br>Review the CPT Surgery section and remaining CPT sections including using modifiers using your coding materials (i.e. a coding text book, *CPT Principles of Coding* and *Understanding Modifiers).*<br>Answer the questions in the CPT Coding Chapter of this review guide. |
| Week 6 | Use your references to review ICD-9-CM and CPT Coding areas in which you are weak.<br>Work on the Study Cases in this review guide. |
| Week 7 | Use your references to review ICD-9-CM and CPT Coding areas in which you are weak<br>Work on the Study Cases in this review guide. |
| Week 8 | Use your references to review ICD-9-CM and CPT Coding areas in which you are weak.<br>Take the Mock Examination Part I |
| Week 9 | Use your references to review ICD-9-CM and CPT Coding areas in which you are weak.<br>Take the Mock Examination Part II |
| Week 10 | Do an overall coding review and look over areas that you feel you need for a final review. |

## STUDY RESOURCES

Don't spend time trying to memorize something you do not understand. The main issue is to understand the materials so you can use the knowledge in a practical way. Search for additional information that will help make the subject clear to you. There are four basic sources of information: books, people, educational programs/colleges and internet resources.

**Books and other written resources.**

- A different textbook may use another style of presentation that you are more receptive to and may be all you need to gain a better insight into the subject. It can offer a fresh point of view, provide relief from boredom, and encourage critical thinking in the process of comparing the texts. . There are a variety of books and workbooks available to use in studying for your coding certification.
- Periodical literature in the field provides well written articles that may open up the subject to you and turn your study into an adventure in learning. AHIMA publishes authoritative and insightful information on every aspect of coding. In addition to the ongoing coding articles in the Journal of AHIMA, Advance for Health Information Professionals has a special series of articles called "CCS Prep!". The journal, For the Record, has articles on coding in each issue. Sometimes an article can help put the subject material into practical perspective and pull it together so that you gain a deeper understanding. Don't forget to use the *Coding Clinics* and *CPT Assistant* to refresh your memory and learn more about specific coding guidelines. HIM Journals will help you keep updated on new information on coding issues that may be incorporated into the exams.
- Take advantage of the local college library by using reserved materials specifically set aside for HIM student study purposes.

**Your HIM community**

- Interaction with others can be truly beneficial in keeping you motivated and on track.
- Professional contacts can also be helpful in your study effort. Most people in our field are eager to share their knowledge and are flattered by appeals for information. Schedule a conference with the director of the HIM/Coding program at your local college. These educators may have current information and resources you are not aware of. Talking to those who have recently taken the examination can also be of great assistance.
- Collaboration with other test applicants can reveal fresh viewpoints, stimulate thought by disagreement, or at least let you see that you are not alone in your quest. Organize study groups and set aside specific times to work together. This interaction can be truly beneficial in keeping you motivated and on task.

**Classes, workshops, and seminars and Coding Teleconferences** present opportunities to learn and review the subject matter in a new light and keep you updated on changes. Take advantage of any coding review sessions available in your area.

**Internet Resources**

- Use the internet to connect with others who are preparing for the examination. AHIMA is on line for members. Using the coding Communities of Practice (CoP) on AHIMA's web site is an excellent way to get connected with professionals and peers. You may find other examination applicants to work with by using e-mail.
- Sample question and cases are available on AHIMA's website for you to use as test examples.
- There are innumerable resources for coding and reimbursement on the internet. Just be aware that you may want to verify the information as it is only as good as the source.

## Some Suggested Study Resources Include

1. **MANDATORY**: AHIMA *Candidate Handbook for the CCS and CCS-P Examinations*

2. **MANDATORY**: ICD-9-CM Code Book including updates from October 2005

3. **MANDATORY**: CPT Code Book, 2006 Edition

4. **MANDATORY HCPCS** Level II Code Book, 2006 Edition

5. *Coding Clinic* for ICD-9-CM (past issues from the last 3 to 4 years)

6. *ICD-9-CM Coding Handbook*, 2006 Edition by Faye Brown

7. "Official ICD-9-CM Guidelines for Coding and Reporting" – available online at: http://www.ahacentraloffice.com (also provided in the back of this book)

7. "Documentation Guidelines for Evaluation and Management Services", *CPT Assistant* (May 1995) as well as information in other *CPT Assistant* issues

8. Professional journal articles on coding
   *Journal of AHIMA*
   *Advance for Health Information Professionals*
   *For the Record*

9. Medical Dictionaries    Check for latest edition.
   *Dorland's Illustrated Medical Dictionary*. Philadelphia PA. W. B. Saunders
   *Mosby's Medical Dictionary*. St. Louis MO. Mosby
   *Steadman's Medical Dictionary*. Baltimore MD. Williams & Wilkins
   *Steadmans Concise Medical & Allied Health Dictionary*. Baltimore MD. Williams & Wilkins
   *Tabers Cyclopedic Medical Dictionary*. Philadelphia PA. F. A. Davis

10. Coding class/seminar/workshop notes and tests

11. Study groups/partners

12. On-the-job experience

13. Examination review sessions

14. Review books written for the CCS-P examinations

15. Various online computer resources (for online coding practice sites as well as those for information and internet interaction with others visit the following examples)
    **MANDATORY**: www.AHIMA.org
    www.CMS.hhs.gov
    www.ICD-9-CM.org

Those marked **MANDATORY** will be essential for you to have in order to prepare for the examination.

**Contact Information for Resources for CCS-P Examination Review Studies**

*CPT Code Book 2006*
American Medical Association (AMA) Phone: (800) 621-8335 Fax: (312) 464-5600
INGENIX ICD-9-CM Phone: (800) 464-3649
5032 W. Amelia Earhart Drive Salt Lake City, UT 84116

*Documentation Guidelines for E & M Coding*
Published May 1995 and revised November 1997
American Medical Association (AMA) and HCFA
Printed in the *CPT Assistant* May 1995 and November 1997.
Online at: http://www.cms.hhs.gov/medlearn/emdoc.asp
This web site is part of the Centers for Medicare and Medicaid Services website:
http://www.cms.hhs.gov/

*CPT Assistant*
American Medical Association: Phone: (800) 621-8335 Fax: (312) 464-5600

*HCPCS II, Code Book 2006 Edition*
American Medical Association: Phone: (800) 621-8335

*Official ICD-9-CM Guidelines for Coding and Reporting*
Central Office on ICD-9-CM of the American Hospital Association (AHA)
Phone: (312) 422-3000 or it can be accessed online at the
Web site for National Center for Health Statistics (NCHS) http://www.cdc.gov/nchs

*Coding Clinic for ICD-9-CM*
American Hospital Association: Phone: (312) 422-3000

*Step-By-Step Medical Coding,* by Carol Buck
Elsevier Saunders 11830 Westline Industrial Drive St. Louis Missouri 63146
Phone: (800) 545-2522

*ICD-9-CM Coding Handbook* by Faye Brown – 2006 Edition
American Hospital Association (AHA) American Hospital Publishing, Inc.
Books Division 737 N. Michigan Ave. Chicago, IL 60611-25615
Phone: (800) 242-2626 FAX: (312) 951-8491

*ICD-9-CM Code Book* with October 2005 updates
Channel Publishing, Ltd. P. O. Box 70723 Reno, NV 89570 Phone: (800) 248-2882
INGENIX ICD-9-CM Phone: (800) 464-3649
5032 W. Amelia Earhart Drive Salt Lake City, UT 84116

**AHIMA Resources for Coding**

AHIMA has developed a series of coding resources. We have listed some of the latest available titles here.

To place an order: call: **1-(800) 335-5535.**
You may contact AHIMA at the following address
**AHIMA Association Publishing and Fulfillment Services**
**P. O. Box 75438 Chicago, IL 60675-5438**

Also, visit the AHIMA Web page at: **http://www.ahima.org** for the candidate handbook and additional resources/information about the certification examinations.

*Basic CPT/HCPCS Coding*
Gail. I. Smith, MA, RHIA, CCS-P

*Basic ICD-9-CM Coding, 2006 Edition*
Lou Anne Schraffenberger, RHIA

*Clinical Coding Workout: Practice Exercises for Skill Development*
Rita Scichilone, MHSA, RHIT, CCS, CCS-P
Ann Zeisset, RHIT, CCS, CCS-P
Mary Stanfill, RHIA, CCS, CCS-P
Sue Hull, RHIA, CCS

*CPT/HCPCS Coding and Reimbursement for Physician Services*
Lynn Kuehn, MS, RHIA, CCS-P and Lavonne Wieland, RHIT

*Effective Management of Coding Services*
Lou Ann Schraffenberger, MBA, RHIA, CCS, Editor

*ICD-9-CM Diagnostic Coding and Reimbursement for Physician Services, 2006 Edition*
Carol Venable, MPH, RHIA and Anita C. Hazelwood, MLS, RHIA, FAHIMA

*Reimbursement Methodologies for Healthcare Services*
Lolita M. Jones, RHIA, CCS, Editor

The following HIM text books will give you an overall view of the Health Information Management:

*Health Information Management Technology, an Applied Approach*
Merida L. Johns, PhD, RHIA, Editor

*Health Information Management: Concepts, Principles, and Practice*
K. M. LaTour, MA, RHIA, and S. Eichenwald, MBA, RHIA, CHIMS, Editors

*Applying Inpatient Coding Skills under Prospective Payment*
Vickie L. Rogers, MS, RHIA and Ann M. Zeisset, RHIT, CCS, CCS-P

## THE DAY BEFORE AND THE MORNING OF THE EXAM

1) **Know the exam location.**
   If there are several testing sites, make sure you have the correct directions to the correct center. Going to the wrong address for a test and then having to hustle to get to the right testing center is very stressful.

2) **Avoid studying the night before the exam.**
   Last minute studying tends to increase your anxiety level. However, you may want to allocate a small amount time to review any information that you feel you must look at one more time.

3) **Organize in advance all the materials you need to take with you to the exam.**
   Review the candidate handbook carefully and be sure to have all the items that are required, especially the admission card, proof of identity and your code books.

4) **Get a good night's sleep.**
   Taking a four hour test with little rest the night before may prevent you from having the energy and stamina you need to complete the exam.

5) **Have a healthy meal before your exam.**
   Four hours is a long time to go on an empty stomach. Try to eat a meal for instance, cereal and fruit, bagel and fruit or juice or a meal with protein like cheese and crackers or eggs and toast. You need something to give you energy to keep going. Take a healthy snack bar to much on if you get hungry and need to take a short break at the testing center.

5) **Dress comfortably**.
   Plan for possible variations in room temperature. Dressing in layers may prove helpful if the room is too cold or hot for you.

6) **Arrive Early.**
   Allow yourself plenty of time so that you may arrive at the test site early.
   Take a practice drive. If necessary, spend the night before the examination in a hotel or motel near the exam test site if it is a great distance from your home.

## TAKING THE EXAMINATION

You have stuck to your study schedule and have conditioned yourself to be in the best physical and mental shape possible. Now comes the "moment of truth": the examination pops up on the screen before your eyes. Every paratrooper knows that in addition to having a parachute, one must know how to open it. You have mastered the major topics; you have the parachute. Now, you need to utilize good test taking techniques to apply the knowledge you have gained; open the parachute!

### Section 1 of the Examination (60 multiple choice questions):

1) **Taking the Practice Test.** Prior to starting the exam, you will be given a chance to practice taking an examination on the computer. Time will be allotted for this practice test; however, you may quit the practice test and begin the actual exam when you are comfortable with the computerized testing process.

2) **Read all directions and questions carefully.** Try to avoid reading too much into the questions. Be sensible and practical in your interpretation. Read ALL of the possible answers, since the first one that looks good may not be the best one.

3) **Scan the screen quickly for general question format.** Like the marathon runner, pace yourself for the distance. A good rule of thumb is 1 to 1.5 minutes per each multiple choice question. You may wish to keep the timer displayed on the computer to check your schedule throughout the exam. For example, at question 30, about one half hour will have elapsed, etc.

4) **Coming Back to Questions.** Some people answer all questions that they are certain of first. Then go back through the exam a second time to answer any questions they were uncertain about. Others prefer not to skip questions, but make their best choice on encountering each question and go on. Both can be good approaches; choose the one that works best for you. You can "mark" questions that you have left unanswered and/or those questions you may want to review. Before you sign off of the exam or run out of time, you have the ability to go back to those questions for a final review.

5) **Answer all the questions.** There are no penalties for guessing, but entering no answer is definitely a wrong answer.

6) **Process of Elimination.** Use deductive reasoning and the process of elimination to arrive at the most correct answer. Some questions may have more than one correct answer. You will be asked to select the "best" possible answer based on the information presented.

7) **Determine What Is Being Asked.** If the question is written in a scenario format, first identify the question being asked and then review the entire question for the information needed to determine the correct answer.

8) **Use all the time available to recheck your answers.** However, avoid changing your answers unless you are absolutely certain it is necessary. Second-guessing yourself often results in a wrong answer.

9) **You <u>must</u> pass the multiple choice question part of the examination** as well as the coding portion in order to receive your certification. All of that practice in taking multiple choice exams will pay off here.

**Section 2 of the Examination: Part II Sections A and B (Coding Scenarios)**

1) **Taking the Practice Test.** Prior to starting the exam, you will be given a chance to practice taking an examination on the computer. Time will be allotted for this practice test; however, you may quit the practice test and begin the actual exam when you are comfortable with the computerized testing process.

2) **Follow the procedures given for coding the test cases.** Do not use hospital, regional, or insurance standards that may differ from those used in the national examination directions. The test will be scored using the coding procedures given.

3) **Read all abstracts completely**. Identify the qualifying words and statements.

4) **Try to avoid reading too much into the information given**. Be sensible and practical in your interpretation. Points are deducted for inappropriate codes.

5) **Carefully review ancillary reports.** Ancillary reports may or may not contain information that is pertinent to the coding of the case. Do not assign codes for abnormal findings listed on ancillary reports unless the physician documents clinical significance.

6) **Only the codes themselves are considered in scoring**. Narrative descriptions will be ignored in scoring the examination. Carefully check the answer form to verify that you have entered the codes for a given case abstract into the space provided for that case.

7) **Use all the time available** to recheck your codes and make sure your answer form has been filled in correctly. However, avoid changing your answers unless you are absolutely certain it is necessary. Second guessing yourself often results in a wrong answer.

8) **The first code for inpatient cases should be the principal diagnosis.** Then list any additional diagnoses that are appropriate. The additional diagnoses do not need to be in any special order.

9) **The first code for outpatient cases should be the primary diagnosis.** Then list any additional diagnoses that are appropriate. The additional diagnoses do not need to be in any special order.

10) **Again, you <u>must</u> pass both Part I and Part II** of the examination in order to receive your certification.

**After the Examination**

A huge advantage to taking the computerized exam is that before you leave the testing center, you will be able to get your final test score instead of having to wait up to six weeks to receive the score by mail.

After taking the examination, it is time to reclaim your life and focus on your career. Plan a special reward for yourself at some point after the exam. Schedule a family vacation or a relaxing weekend get-away. Just find some way of being good to yourself. You certainly deserve it! You have worked hard, so relish your success.

**PAT'S EXAM EXPERIENCE**

The CCS examination was a moment of truth for me. Some people asked me what I was going to do if I failed the examination. Now there is something to give you nightmares - to co-author an exam review book and then FLUNK the exam! That was when I decided to borrow a line from the movie *True Lies*, "fear is not an option," and adapted it for my own motto -- "failure is not an option."

There were many days and nights when I doubted that I had what it takes. When I felt really fearful and uncomfortable, I made myself look back over the years of going to classes and all of the coding practice. I had completed all the courses required. I had studied hard and long in each one of them. I had made good grades. In fact, I graduated with honors. I was studying virtually every day to prepare for the exam. What more could I do? ABSOLUTELY NOTHING!!! Therefore, if I had done the best I could and I was doing the best I could, then, the worry was just taking up space in my head.

I told myself there was no way I could fail the exam. This was a routine that I had to repeat, sometimes several times a day when the doubt would creep in. Positive attitudes can and will make the pre-test jitters disappear. If you feel you can't do this, tell yourself that you have done it and that this is just one more test! I had prepared myself - I had done taken many, many, many tests successfully before. This one is JUST ONE MORE!

The night before the test, I tried to study just a little, but I just could not concentrate. I gave up trying to cram more information into my head and went to bed.

The next morning at the testing center, I had coffee while we waited for the room to be prepared. One of the students milling around commented that she had failed the CCS examination before and hoped to pass it this time. I was really nervous then, because this person had over 10 years of experience next to my measly experience. There were a lot of very nervous people there.

I had to remind myself to keep thinking: "I think I can. I think I can." I tried my best not to panic. After waiting what seemed like forever to start the exam, we were finally told to open the booklet for Part I and begin. I panicked at the first question. I could not understand what it asked. I had to stop, take a deep breath and relax. I went to the next question, and was able to answer it quickly. I went back to the first question and it looked simple! I found myself going down the page breezing along and answering the questions. Then, I gasped as I thought, "What if I am not going fast enough?" I stopped, looked at the question number, checked the time and figured that I was answering them in about one minutes each. Right on schedule. So, I calmed myself down and got back to business.

When I took the examination, it was still paper and pencil with fill in the answer bubbles. About halfway through the exam, I had another thought: "What if I am putting the answers in the wrong answer bubble?" After catching my breath, I looked at the question number and checked the answer bubble. Both were the same. I told myself to just relax and do the work at hand. Before I knew it, I had answered all the questions. I even had enough time to go back and review the ones I was not sure about.

One of the most difficult parts of the exam is the length of time sitting. I did take one break in the middle of the exam to use the restroom and walk around for a minute to clear my head.

Part I was the easy part. I was very adept at taking multiple choice question exams. Part II with the coding cases was my hardest section. I found that I wasn't completing the cases in 13 to 14 minutes, so I needed to speed up to finish the exam. It was really hard for me not to mull over each case.

When the exam was over, I was relieved, to say the least. For months it had been hanging over my head and now IT WAS OVER! I left not knowing if I had passed the examination or not. But, no matter what the results were, I had done the best I could and I was still a winner! Do the best you can and you will past the exam too. YOU CAN DO IT!

Affirmation: "I can handle anything on the exam - one question at a time." ~ Kathy DeAngelo, 1995

# Coding Review

Anita Hazelwood, MLS, RHIA, FAHIMA

| Sample 10 Step Outpatient ICD-9-CM coding process: |
|---|
| Never Code Only From the Index. Always Consult the Tabular List<br>Coding must accurately reflect provider's diagnostic statement as well as coding rules. |
| **General Conventions** are summarized earlier in this section of the book.<br>**Indentations** are used for all subterms below the term to which they apply. |
| **Caution** is advised in following the several levels of indentations of subterms. |
| 1. **Main Term** (conditions) are boldface type and are followed by the code number. |
| **Qualified Diagnosis** is a working diagnosis that is not yet proven or established. Do not code diagnoses with terms such as *suspected, rule out, ruled out, possible, probably, questionable*, etc. Code the sign(s) and/or symptom(s) that are documented. |
| **Special Main Terms** should be reviewed and considered. See list on in text.<br>**See Condition** indicates a descriptive term was looked up rather than the condition.<br>**See** directs the coder to a more specific term.<br>**See Also** refers to an index entry that may provide additional information. |
| 2. **(Non-essential Modifiers) do not have to be included in the diagnostic statement**<br>These subterms clarify or qualify the main term and are enclosed in parentheses. |
| 3. **Essential Modifiers / Subterms that <u>must be</u> included in the dx statement** are indented below the main term in alphabetical order (except "with" and "without").<br>They clarify the main term listing alternative sites, etiology, or clinical status. |
| 4. **Select Preliminary Code** before turning to the Tabular List. |
| 5. **Locate Preliminary Code** number and review the code descriptions.<br>**See Category** refers to the Tabular List category (three-digit code). |
| 6. **Includes Notes** appear with 3-digit categories and further define or add clarification.<br>**Excludes Notes** direct the coder to another location for proper code assignment.<br>**Return to the Index of Diseases** for other possible code selections if the code description in the Tabular List does not appear to fit the condition or reason for visit. |
| **NEC or "not elsewhere classified"** identifies codes to be assigned when information needed to assign a more specific code cannot be located in the code book.<br>**NOS or "not otherwise specified"** indicates that the code lacks specificity and the provider should be asked for a more specific diagnosis before assigning a code. |
| 7. **Assign 4th or 5th Digit** if one is available. Instructional notes about additional digits are found below the category or subcategory description. |
| 8. **Use Additional Code** indicates a second code is required to add necessary detail. |
| 9. **Primary Diagnosis** is the most significant condition for which services and/or procedures were provided and is sequenced first.<br>**Secondary Diagnosis** coexists with the primary diagnosis, has the potential to affect treatment of the primary condition, and is a condition being actively managed.<br>***Code First Underlying Condition*** indicates the code is to be sequenced as a secondary code. The code, title, and instructions are italicized. |
| 10. **Record Final Code(s).** |

# OUTPATIENT PROCEDURE CODING REVIEW

CMS – Center for Medicare and Medicaid Services (formerly HCFA- Health Care Financing Administration) administers Medicare and Medicaid.

HCPCS (Healthcare Common Procedural Coding System)

- is a coding system describing the physician and non-physician patient services covered by the government's Medicare and Medicaid programs
- was designed by CMS and is used primarily to report reimbursable services rendered to the patient
- has three (3) levels of HCPCS codes for ambulatory (outpatient) patients

LEVEL I - CPT (Current Procedural Terminology) is a coding system developed by the American Medical Association (AMA) to convert descriptions of medical, surgical, and diagnostic services rendered by health care providers into five-digit numerical codes. The codes are updated annually by AMA.

The CPT coding system:

- provides uniform language to accurately designate medical, surgical, and diagnostic services
- provides effective means of reliable, nationwide communication between physicians, patients, and third party payers
- allows for ability to compare reimbursements for procedures

Justification for listing of a procedure:

- The procedure is commonly performed by physicians nationally.
- The procedure must be consistent with modern medical practice.

LEVEL II -National Codes

- updated annually by CMS
- 5 digit alphanumeric codes

LEVEL III -CMS Program Memorandum AB-02-113, July 31, 2002 states:

"All unapproved local procedures and modifier codes must be discontinued by December 31, 2002, for Medicare carriers and by March 31, 2003 for Medicare fiscal Intermediaries;"

Remember: You won't be using any local codes for the examination.

## Rules for Coding CPT

1. Determine the service to be provided by analyzing the statement provided by the physician.

2. Identify the main term(s) in the Alphabetic Index.
   To locate a code in the index, the coder should first look up the procedure or service provided. If the procedure is not listed, look under the organ involved, the condition, synonym or eponym. Follow the guidance of the index in locating the code most accurately describing the service.

3. Write down or note the code number(s) found for the term.
   - If a single code number is given, locate the code in the body of the CPT book. Verify the code and its description against the statement assuring they match.
   - If two or more codes separated by a comma are given, locate each code in the body of the CPT. Read the description of each and select the appropriate code matching the statement.
   - If a range of codes is given locate the range of codes in the body of the CPT. Review the description of each entry prior to selecting a code.

4. NEVER code from the Alphabetic Index - look up the codes to verify accuracy.

5. Read all notes that apply to the code selected.
   Notes may appear at the beginning of a section, subsection or directly under the code description. Notes are utilized throughout the CPT requiring special attention and review by the coder. Some of these notes define terms, such as simple, intermediate, and complex wound repair. Other notes provide specific coding instruction, applicable to specific codes.

6. Select the appropriate modifier, if applicable to complete the code description.

7. Code multiple procedures from highest resource intensive to lowest (most complicated to least).

## Common Errors that Prevent Payment to Physician

1. No documentation or incomplete documentation for services billed
2. Missing signatures
3. Consistently assigning the same level of services
4. Billing of a consult instead of an office visit
5. Using invalid codes in the bill due to use of old coding resources/forms
6. Unbundling procedure codes
7. Not listing the chief complaint
8. Abbreviations that are misinterpreted
9. Billing of services included in global fee as a separate professional fee
10. Not using a modifier or use of in inappropriate modifier for accurate payment of a claim

## CPT Code Book Format Information

Guidelines: provide specific instructions about coding for each section. The guidelines contain definitions of terms, applicable modifiers, explanations of notes, subsection information, unlisted services, special reports information and clinical examples.

Sections: there are eight major areas into which all CPT codes and descriptions are categorized. CPT codes are arranged in numerical order in each section. The first 6 sections are comprised of 5-digit numerical codes. The codes in the last two sections, Category II and Category III Codes, are comprised of 5-digit codes: 4 numbers and a letter.

Evaluation and Management
Anesthesia
Surgery
Radiology
Pathology/Laboratory
Medicine
Category II Codes
Category III Codes

Category II Codes are optional tracking codes used to measure performance.

Category III Codes are temporary codes for emerging technology, services and procedures. These codes can be used for data collection purposes or possibly in the FDA approval process. If a Category III code is available, this code must be reported instead of a Category I unlisted code.

Subsections, subheadings, categories, and subcategories: divide the sections into smaller units, based on anatomy, procedure, condition, description or approach.

Symbols Used in CPT Coding: The following symbols are special guides that help the coder compare codes and descriptors with the previous year's CPT edition or that provide additional coding guidance.

● Bullet – used to indicate a new procedure or service code added since the previous edition of the CPT manual.

▲ Triangle – indicates that the code has been changed or modified since the last CPT manual edition.

\+ A plus sign is used to indicate an add-on code.

⦸ is used to identify a modifier -51 exempt code

►◄ A right and left triangle indicate the beginning and end of the text changes.

Modifiers: two-digit numbers added to CPT codes to supply more specific information about the services provided.

Special Reports: detailed reports that include adequate definitions or descriptions of the nature, extent, and need for the procedure and the time, effort and equipment necessary to provide the service.

## CPT Code Book Format Information

Continued:

Unlisted procedures: are procedures that are considered unusual, experimental or new and do not have a specific code number assigned. Unlisted procedure codes are located at the end of the subsections or subheads and may be used to identify any procedure that lacks a specific code.

CPT Index: located at the back of the CPT manual and arranged alphabetically.
To locate terms in the alphabetical index, look under the

- Service/procedure
- Anatomic site/body organ
- Condition/disease/problem
- Synonym
- Eponym (procedure named after someone)
- Abbreviation (ex: CBC)

Notations:

- "see": sends you to a more appropriate section
- "see also": cross-reference to refer to another main term

CPT Appendices in back section of the CPT manual:

- Appendix A: lists all modifiers with complete explanations for use
- Appendix B: contains a complete list of additions to, deletions from, and revisions of the previous year's edition
- Appendix C: provides clinical examples of Evaluation and Management (E&M) Procedures
- Appendix D: contains a listing of the CPT add-on codes
- Appendix E: contains a list of modifier -51 exempt codes
- Appendix F: contains a list of modifier -63 exempt codes
- Appendix G: Summary of CPT codes that include moderate (conscious) sedation
- Appendix H: Alphabetic index of performance measures by clinical condition or topic
- Appendix I: Genetic testing code modifiers
- Appendix J: Electro diagnostic medicine listing of sensory, motor and mixed nerves
- Appendix K: Product pending FDA approval
- Appendix L: Vascular families

## General E&M Coding Guidelines

1. Determine place of service: ex. office, emergency room or nursing home.

2. Determine type of service: consult, admission, newborn.

3. Determine patient status: new unless seen in last 3 years by the physician or another physician of the same specialty in the same group.

4. Determine 3 key components:
   1. History - problem focused, expanded problem focused, detailed, comprehensive
   2. Physical examination - problem focused, expanded problem focused, detailed, comprehensive
   3. Medical decision making - straightforward, low, moderate, high
   - New patients: require all 3 key components
   - Established patients: usually require 2 of the 3 key components
   - Some codes are based on time: critical care, prolonged services

5. Read Critical Care guidelines carefully. Watch for the procedures which are included in the codes.

6. Read Inpatient Neonatal and Pediatric Critical Care Services and intensive (non critical) low birth weight serices guidelines carefully. Watch for procedures that are inclusive in this area.

7. Be sure to read the coding guidelines for E&M coding carefully.

8. Review definition for "consultations" and determine when consult codes are more appropriate than office visit codes.

9. There are specific codes used for hospital observation services (initial care, discharge services) and codes for same day admissions and discharges.

10. When a patient is admitted as an inpatient on the same day services are provided at another site (office, ER, observation etc.), only the inpatient services are reported. The E&M services provided in these outpatient settings can be used to determine level of inpatient services provided.

11. Preventive Care codes are based on the patient's age.

## Some Additional Areas of Interest when coding with CPT

**Abortion**

Incomplete Abortions and Miscarriages are alternate terms for missed and spontaneous abortions.
Spontaneous abortion that occurs during any trimester and is completed surgically, assign 59812
Missed abortion that occurs during the first trimester, assign 59820
Induced abortion, which combines curettage and evacuation, assign 59851
Induced Abortion Evacuation, code 59841
Abortion by dilation and curettage, code 59840. Code 58120 is used for a nonobstrecal D&C.

**Angioplasty**

Determination of the site and whether it is open or percutaneous.
Open transluminal angioplasty of renal or other visceral arteries, aortic, iliac, femoral-popiteal, brachiocephalic, tibioperoneal trunk and branches, or venous sites code from 35450-35460
Percutaneous transluminal angioplasty of renal or other visceral arteries, aortic, femoral-popiteal, brachiocephalic or venous sites code from 35470-35476
PTCA: Percutaneous transluminal coronary angioplasty assign code appropriately from 92982 and 92984
Percutaneous transluminal angioplasty of the peripheral arteries and visceral arteries:

- 75962-75968 (Radiology Section) for the radiological supervision and interpretation

Codes 92980 and 92981 for stent placement include the PTCA and thus the PTCA is not coded separately.

**Appendectomy**

There are several codes that are used to describe appendectomies: open surgical appendectomy (including incidental) , laparoscopic appendectomy, appendectomy done for a ruptured appendix and appendectomy done for a specified purpose at the time of other major surgery.

**Auditory**

Simple mastoidectomy also called a transmastoid antrotomy (69501)
Complete mastoidectomy includes a myringotomy with drain insertion (69502)
Apicetomy is the excision of the tip of the petrous bone. This is often performed with a radical mastoidectomy (69530). It would be inappropriate to code 69511 in addition.
Tympanostomy (requiring insertion of ventilating tube)
Code 69436, Typanostomy (requiring insertion of ventilating tube) general anesthesia and 69433, Tympanostomy (requiring insertion of ventilating tube), local or topic anesthesia are used for "insertion of tubes"
Removal of impacted cerumen from one or both ears – use code 69210

## Some Additional Areas of Interest when coding with CPT

Continued

**Bronchoscopy & Biopsy**

Surgical bronchoscopy includes a diagnostic bronchoscopy.
Code appropriate endoscopy for each anatomic site examined.
Endobronchial biopsy, code 31625
Review for types of specimen collection:

- Biopsy forceps used to remove tissue.
- Bronchial brush used to obtain surface cells.
- Suction used to remove foreign bodies of mucous cells.
- Cell washings used to exfoliate cells from crevices.
- NOTE: Cell washings or brushings are not biopsies.

Transbronchial biopsy is performed by positioning the scope in the bronchus nearest to the lesion. A hole is punctured through the bronchus into the lung tissue where the lesion is located. The lesion is then biopsied. Transbronchical lung biopsy is reported with code 31628
Transbronchial needle aspiration biopsy (31629)
Catheter aspiration of tracheobronchial tree at bedside (31725)
Lymph node sampling, needle biopsies, and pleural flaps included in 32480-32500

**CABG**

To report combined arterial-venous grafts, it is necessary to report 2 codes:

1. The appropriate combined arterial-venous graft code (33517-33523); and
2. The appropriate arterial graft code (33533-33536).

Procurement of the saphenous vein graft is included in the description of the work for 33517-33523 and is not reported separately.
Procurement of an upper extremity artery is reported separately.

**Casting and Strapping**

Services in the musculoskeletal system include the application or removal of the first cast or traction device only. Subsequent replacement of casts, traction devices or removals are reported using codes from the 29000-29750 series of codes.
The codes in the 29000-29750 series of codes have very specific guidelines directing the use of the codes.

**Endoscopy**

Codes specify: the instrument used, the purpose and site of application.
Dx endoscopy is coded only if a surgical procedure was not done. Surgical endoscopy always includes a diagnostic endoscopy.
Code as far as the scope is passed
Stomach endoscopy is included with UGI endoscopy - not separately
Multiple codes may be necessary to cover one endoscopic episode.
Removal of gastrostomy tube by endoscopy, code 43247
Colonoscopy: first determine the route the procedure follows (via colostomy, colotomy, or rectum)
Colonoscopy with dilation of rectum or anorectum, code 45999
Biliary endoscopy (47550) is only used with 47420 or 47610.
EGDs are coded to 43235-43259.

## Some Additional Areas of Interest when coding with CPT

Continued

### Eye & Ocular

Preliminary iridectomy is not coded separately if performed as part of a cataract extraction or prior to lens extraction. It is included in the code for the lens extraction.

Code for extraction based on the type of procedure performed:

- ICCE: Intracapsular extraction
- ECCE: Extracapsular extraction
- Anterior chamber intraocular lens
- Posterior chamber intraocular lens

Do not code medication injections used in conjunction with cataract surgery. Injections are considered part of the procedure.

Cataract removal includes the following in codes 66830-66984

DO NOT CODE THE FOLLOWING PROCEDURES SEPARATELY: anterior capsulotomy, enzymatic zonulysis, iridectomy, iridotomy, lateral canthotomy, pharmacological agents, posterior capsulotomy, viscoelastic agents, subconjunctival and subtenon injections.

### Female Genital System

Code 57452-57461 are used to report various cervical colposcopic procedures.

Code 57454 describes colposcopy with single or multiple biopsies.

Code 58150 describes total abdominal hysterectomy with or without removal of tube(s) or ovary(s).

Code 58611 is an add on code that describes tubal ligation or transection when done at the time of cesarean delivery or intra-abdominal surgery.

### Fractures/Dislocations

- Treatment of fractures/dislocations may be open or closed.
- Closed treatment means that the fracture or dislocation site is not surgically opened. It is used to describe procedures that treat fractures by three methods: without manipulation, with manipulation and with or without traction.
- Open treatment implies that the fracture is surgically opened and the fracture is visualized to allow treatment.
- Skeletal fixation is neither open nor closed treatment. Usually pins are placed across the fracture usually using x-ray guidance.
- Manipulation is used to indicate the attempted reduction or restoration of a fracture or dislocation.

### Genitourinary

Many of the procedures in the urinary system are performed endoscopically – cystoscopy, urethroscopy, cystourethroscopy, ureteroscopy, pyeloscopy, and renal endoscopy.

Most cystourethroscopy codes are unilateral. When a cysto is performed bilaterally modifier -50 should be appended.

Codes in the 52320-52355 series include the insertion and removal of a temporary stent during diagnostic or therapeutic cystourethroscopic intervention(s).

Cystourethroscopy with removal of a self-retaining/indwelling ureteral stent, planned or staged during the associated normal postoperative follow-up period of the original procedure, is reported by means of code 52310 or 52315 with the -58 appended as appropriate.

Be careful to differentiate between codes for ureteral and urethral procedures

## Some Additional Areas of Interest when coding with CPT

Continued

### GI Biopsy

Code only the biopsy if a single lesion is biopsied but not excised.

Code only the biopsy and list only one time if multiple biopsies are done (from the same or different lesions) and none of the lesions are excised.

Code only the excision if a biopsy of a lesion is taken and the balance of the same lesion is then excised.

Code both the biopsy & excision if both are performed and if the biopsy is taken from a lesion different from that which is excised; AND the code for the excision does not include the phrase "with or without biopsy". If such a phrase is in the code narration, then a separate biopsy code should not be used.

Surgical endoscopy always include a diagnostic endoscopy.

Modifier -59 may be used to explain unusual circumstances when coding both biopsy and removal of a different lesion.

### Hernia Repair

- Hernia repair codes are categorized by type (inguinal, femoral, etc)
- Hernias are further categorized as "initial" or "recurrent" based on whether or not the hernia has required previous repair.
- Age and clinical presentation (reducible versus strangulated)
- Code 49568 is used only with incisional or ventral hernia repairs.

### Immunizations

Codes 90465-90474 are used to report the administration of vaccines/toxoids.

Codes 90476-90749 identify the vaccine product alone.

If a combination vaccine code is provided (MMR) it is not appropriate to report each component of the combination vaccine separately.

When the physician provides face-to-face counseling of the patient and family during the administration of a vaccine, report codes 90465-90468.

Do not append modifier -51 to the vaccine/toxoid product codes 90476-90749.

## Some Additional Areas of Interest when coding with CPT

Continued

**Integumentary**

Three types of repairs: Add lengths of repairs together and use one code for repairs of the same location and same type

- Simple: superficial wound involving skin and/or subcutaneous tissues and requiring simple suturing
- Intermediate**:** involving skin, subcutaneous tissues, and fascia or muscle, and requiring layer closure. May also be used when a single closure requires intensive debridement.
- Complex: repairs requiring reconstructive surgery, time consuming or complicated closures, or skin grafts

Debridement is coded separately: when gross contamination requires cleaning, when appreciable amounts of devitalized or contaminated tissue are removed and when debridement is carried out separately without primary closure

Lesion size is best found on the operative report.

Benign or malignant lesion(s): Code each lesion excised separately, simple closure after excision of lesion(s) is included in the code

Advancement Flap codes include excision of tissues, including lesions.

Free skin grafts:

Identify by size and location of the defect (recipient area) and the type of graft; includes simple debridement of granulations or recent avulsion

Use 15000 for initial wound preparation

Repair of donor site requiring skin graft or local flaps is to be added on as an additional procedure.

Report excision of lesion(s) separately.

Excisional biopsy is used when the entire lesion, whether benign or malignant is removed

Breast lesion excisions performed after being identified by pre-op radiological marker (localization wires) code 19125 and 19126

Placement of needle localization wires prior to biopsies, excisions, and other breast procedures use additional codes 19290 and 19291

**Laryngoscopy**

Many of the codes used to report laryngoscopies include the use of an operating microscope. Therefore, code 69990, Microsurgical techniques, requiring the use of operating microscope (List separately in addition to code primary procedure) would not be used with any codes which include the use of the microscope.

**Maternity Care and Delivery**

Antepartum care or services provided above the normally expected care (as defined in the CPT book) should be coded separately

Medical problems complicating labor and delivery management may require additional resources and should be identified by using E&M codes in addition to the codes for maternity care.

For surgical complications of pregnancy, see services in the surgery section.

If a physician provides all or part of the antepartum and/or postpartum patient care but does not perform delivery due to termination of pregnancy by abortion or referral to another physician for delivery, see the antepartum and postpartum care codes 59425-59426 and 59430.

Patients who have had previous cesarean delivery and now present with the expectaion of a vaginal delivery are coded using codes 59610-59622. If the patient has a successful vaginal delivery after a previous cesarean delivery (VBAC), use codes 59610-59614. If the attempt is unsuccessful and another cesarean delivery is carried out, use codes 59618-59622.

## Some Additional Areas of Interest when coding with CPT

Continued

**Nasal Hemorrhage**

Was it anterior or posterior?

- If anterior, was the hemorrhage simple or complex?
- If posterior, was the control of hemorrhage an initial or subsequent procedure?

Anterior nasal hemorrhage - has likely occurred if the physician inserts gauze packing or anterior packing or performs cauterization.

Posterior nasal hemorrhage - has likely occurred if the physician inserts nasal stents, tampons, balloon catheters, or posterior packing, or if the patient is taken to the OR for ligation of arteries to control bleeding.

Nosebleed subsequent to initial one. (30906) (Not pertinent for a nosebleed that occurred one year from the last nosebleed.)

**Neurology/Spine Surgery**

The spinal and spinal cord injection codes reflect the specific spinal anatomy such as subarachnoid or epidural, the level of the injection (cervical, thoracic, lumbar, or sacral) and the types of substances injected such as anesthetic steroids, antispasmodics, phenol, etc.).

Injection of contrast material during fluoroscopic guidance is included in the codes 62263-62264, 62270-62273, 62280-62282, 62310-62319, and 0027T. The fluoroscopic guidance itself is reported by code 76005. There are several notes under code 76005 that the coder should read carefully.

Code 62263 describes treatment involving injections of various substances over a multiple day period. Code 62263 is not reported for each individual injection but is reported once to describe the entire series of injections/infusions.

Code 62264 describes multiple treatments performed on the same day.

Other codes in this section refer to laminectomies, excisions, repairs and shunts. A basic distinction among the codes is the condition such as herniated disk as well as the approach used such as anterior or posterior or costovertebral.

Lumbar punctures (62270) are also called spinal taps and are used to obtain cerebrospinal fluid by inserting a needle into the subarachnoid space in the lumbar area.

When coding surgery on the spine, there are many sets of guidelines for the coder to review including those at the beginning of the subsection as well as throughout the subsection.

Co-surgery is common in spinal surgeries. When two surgeons work together both as primary surgeons each surgeon should report his/her distinct operative work by adding modifier-62 to the procedure code and any associated add-on codes for that procedure as long as both surgeons continue to work together as primary surgeons.

Additional codes for coding procedures on the spine and spinal cord are found in the nervous system subsection of the surgery section.

Spinal instrumentation is used to stabilize the spinal column during repair procedures. There are two types: segmental and nonsegmental.

- Segmental instrumentation involves attachment at each end of the spinal area and at least one intermittent fixation.
- Nonsegmental instrumentation is the use of a device attached only at each end.

## Some Additional Areas of Interest when coding with CPT

Continued

**Pacemakers**

1. Is it permanent or temporary?
2. What was the approach (transverse or thoracotomy)?
3. What type of device (electrodes and/or pulse generator)?
4. Where were the electrodes placed (atrial, ventricle, or both)?
5. Is this a revision, removal, or a replacement?
6. Was revision of the skin pocket done?

**Sentinel Nodes**

Sentinel Nodes procedures utilizes Isosulfan blue dye. After absorption of dye, the physician can visualize the node(s). Code 38792 is used for identification of sentinel node. For excision of sentinel node, see 38500-38542.

Usually 4 injections are performed around the primary lesion.

Use appropriate lymph node excision codes to report the excision.

A second sentinel node from a different lymphatic chain excised from a separate incision, report the excision and add modifier -59.

Lymphoscintigraphy code 78195

Injection for gamma probe node detection with imaging code 38790

**Thyroid**

Recall the thyroid has two lobes, one on each side of the trachea, the procedure may only be unilateral (60220), but it is still considered to be a total lobectomy.

Thyroidectomy may be:

- Total or Complete (60240) removing both lobes and the isthmus; it is not necessary to list the code twice.
- Subtotal (60210) removing one lobe, isthmus and part of opposite lobe.
- Partial removing one lobe and the removal of a portion of one lobe.

Thyroidectomy with neck dissection (60252 and 60254). Do not assign these codes if an isolated lymph node is excised or biopsied.

**Tonsillectomy and Adenoidectomy**

Separate codes describe: tonsillectomy and adenoidectomy; tonsillectomy alone, whether primary or secondary; adenoidectomy alone, primary; adenoidectomy alone, secondary.

Separate codes are reported for procedures performed on patients under age 12, and age 12 or older.

A primary procedure is one in which no prior tonsillectomy or adenoidectomy has been performed. A secondary procedure is one that is performed to remove residual or regrowth of tonsil or adenoid tissue.

**Wound Exploration**

Wound exploration codes (20100-20103) are used when a repair of a penetrating wound requires enlargement of the existing defect for exploration, cleaning and repair.

If the wound does not need to be enlarged, then only repair codes from the integumentary section are used.

# Classification Systems, Registries and Indexing

Anita Hazelwood, MLS, RHIA, FAHIMA

# Classification Systems, Registries and Indexing

*Anita Hazelwood, MLS, RHIA, FAHIMA*

1. Robert Thompson was seen in the outpatient department with a chronic cough and the record states, "rule out lung cancer". What should be coded as the patient's diagnosis?
   A) chronic cough
   B) observation and evaluation without need for further medical care
   C) diagnosis of unknown etiology
   D) lung cancer

REFERENCE: Abdelhak, p 241
ICD-9-CM Official Guidelines for Coding and Reporting, 2005

2. Which of the following is a valid ICD-9-CM principal diagnosis code?
   A) V27.2 Outcome of delivery, twins, both live born
   B) V30.00 Single live born, born in hospital
   C) E867 Accidental poisoning by gas distributed by pipeline
   D) M9010/0 Fibroadenoma, NOS

REFERENCE: Brown, p 208, 241, 289, 310-311

3. A physician performed an outpatient surgical procedure on the eye orbit of a Medicare patient. Upon searching the CPT codes and consulting with the physician, the coder is unable to find a code for the procedure. The coder should assign
   A) an unlisted Evaluation and Management code from the E&M section
   B) an unlisted procedure code located in the eye and ocular adnexa section
   C) a HCPCS Level Two (alphanumeric) code
   D) an ophthalmological treatment service code

REFERENCE: CPT (2006), p 48-49
Principles of CPT Coding, p 26
Smith, p 22

4. A system of preferred terminology for naming disease processes is known as a
   A) set of categories
   B) classification system
   C) medical nomenclature
   D) diagnosis listing

REFERENCE: Abdelhak, p 230
Johns, p 292
LaTour and Eichenwald, p 737

5. A patient who is taking the drug Antivert may be diagnosed with:
   A) dizziness
   B) urinary tract infection
   C) arthritis
   D) congestive heart failure

REFERENCE: Shannon, p 957-958

6. Which of the following is not included as a part of the minimum data maintained in the MPI?
   A) principal diagnosis
   B) patient medical record number
   C) full name (last, first and middle)
   D) date of birth

REFERENCE: Abdelhak, p 185
Johns, p 783
LaTour and Eichenwald, p 172, 243

7. In reviewing the medical record of a patient admitted for a left herniorrhaphy, the coder discovers an extremely low potassium level on the laboratory report. In examining the physicians' orders, the coder notices that intravenous potassium was ordered. The physician has not listed any indication of an abnormal potassium level or any related condition on the discharge summary. The best course of action for the coder to take is to
   A) confer with the physician and ask him/her to list the condition as a final diagnosis if he/she considers the abnormal potassium level to be clinically significant
   B) code the record as is
   C) code the condition as an abnormal blood chemistry
   D) code the abnormal potassium level as a complication following surgery

REFERENCE: Abdelhak, p 250-251
Brown, p 24

8. A coder notes that a patient is taking prescription Pilocarpine. The final diagnoses on the discharge summary are: congestive heart failure and diabetes mellitus. The coder should query the physician about adding a diagnosis of:
   A) arthritis
   B) glaucoma
   C) bronchitis
   D) laryngitis

REFERENCE: Shannon, p 1257

9. The patient is diagnosed with congestive heart failure. A drug of choice is:
   A) Ibuprofen
   B) Oxytocin
   C) Haloperidol
   D) Digoxin

REFERENCE: Shannon, p 491

10. The following clinical documentation is on the patient's medical record:

> Physical Examination:
> Physician notes distended abdomen and excessive weight gain in the last three weeks.
> Patient appears to be short of breath.
> Vital signs: T: 98.6
> Laboratory results: Show decreased serum albumin level
> Nurses' Notes: Abdominal girth measured daily; output monitored; daily weight taken.
> Procedures: Paracentesis x3
> Medications: Hydrodiuril
> Final diagnosis: Cirrhosis of the liver

The coder might query the physician to ask if the following condition could be added to the discharge summary:
A) acute pericarditis
B) lymphoma
C) Helicobacter pylori gastritis
D) ascites
REFERENCE: Rubin, p 425
Shannon, p 765

11. The local safety council requests statistics on the number of head injuries occurring as a result of skateboarding accidents during the last year. To retrieve this data, you will need to have the correct:
A) CPT code
B) Standard Nomenclature of Injuries codes
C) E codes and ICD-9-CM codes
D) HCPCS level II codes
REFERENCE: Brown, p 310
Schraffenberger (2006), p 257
Principles of ICD-9-CM Coding, p 56

12. A patient was admitted with severe abdominal pain, elevated temperature, and nausea. The physical examination indicated possible cholecystitis. Acute and chronic pancreatitis secondary to alcoholism was recorded on the face sheet as the final diagnosis. The principal diagnosis is
A) alcoholism
B) abdominal pain
C) cholecystitis
D) acute pancreatitis
REFERENCE: Coding Clinic, Second Quarter, 1990, p 4
Brown, p 41

13. The use of radioactive sources placed into a tumor-bearing area to generate high intensity radiation is termed:
A) stereotactic radiation treatment
B) proton beam treatment
C) brachytherapy
D) external beam radiation
REFERENCE: Principles of CPT Coding, p 337-339
Buck, p 329, 332

14. In general, all three key components (history, physical examination, and medical decision making) for the E/M codes in CPT should be met or exceeded when
    A) the patient is established
    B) a new patient is seen in the office
    C) the patient is given subsequent care in the hospital
    D) the patient is seen for a follow-up inpatient consultation

REFERENCE: CPT Book (2006), p 6-7

15. A direction to "Code first underlying disease" should be considered
    A) only when coding the inpatient records
    B) a mandatory instruction
    C) mandatory dependent upon the code selection
    D) a suggestion only

REFERENCE: Coding Clinic, January-February, 1986, p 9
Brown, p 12-13
Schraffenberger (2006), p 28
Hazelwood and Venable, p 22
Principles of ICD-9-CM Coding, p 19

16. According to the UHDDS, a procedure that is surgical in nature, carries a procedural or anesthetic risk or requires special training is defined as a
    A) principle procedure
    B) significant procedure
    C) operating room procedure
    D) therapeutic procedure

REFERENCE: Brown, p 47
Schraffenberger (2006), p 49, 54

17. The "cooperating party" responsible for maintaining the ICD-9-CM Disease classification is the
    A) Centers for Medicare and Medicaid Services (CMS)
    B) National Center for Health Statistics (NCHS)
    C) American Hospital Association (AHA)
    D) American Health Information Management Association (AHIMA)

REFERENCE: Abdelhak, p 231-232

18. An encoder which prompts the coder to answer a series of questions and choices based on the documentation in the medical record is called a (n):
    A) logic-based encoder
    B) automated codebook
    C) grouper
    D) automatic code assignment

REFERENCE: LaTour and Eichenwald, p 269

19. A patient is admitted with shortness of breath and hemoptysis. A chest X-ray revealed patchy infiltrates in the left lung and possible pneumonia. On the third day of hospitalization a bronchoscopy with biopsy was done which revealed a small cell carcinoma of the left upper lobe of the lung. A metastatic lesion in the brain was detected. The principal diagnosis is the
   A) metastatic brain carcinoma
   B) small cell lung carcinoma
   C) hemoptysis
   D) pneumonia

REFERENCE: Brown, p 19-20
Schraffenberger (2006), p 56

20. Jane Moore was admitted to the ambulatory care unit of the hospital for a planned cholecystectomy for cholelithiasis. Shortly before surgery, Jane developed tachycardia, and the surgery was canceled. After a thorough work-up for the tachycardia, Jane was discharged. This outpatient admission should be coded in the following sequence
   A) V code for canceled surgery, tachycardia, cholelithiasis
   B) Tachycardia, V code for canceled surgery, cholelithiasis
   C) Cholelithiasis, V code for canceled surgery
   D) Cholelithiasis, V code for canceled surgery, tachycardia

REFERENCE: Brown, p 54-55
Schraffenberger (2006), p 46

21. A patient has a total abdominal hysterectomy with bilateral salpingectomy. The coder selected the following codes:

| | |
|---|---|
| 58150 | Total abdominal hysterectomy (corpus and cervix), with or without removal of tube(s) with or without removal of ovary(s) |
| 58700 | Salpingectomy, complete or partial unilateral or bilateral (separate procedure) |

   This type of coding would be referred to as
   A) upcoding
   B) unbundling
   C) maximizing
   D) optimization

REFERENCE: Buck, p 101, 117
Smith, p 48-49

22. Code 402, Hypertensive Heart Disease would appropriately be used in which of the following situations?
   A) Left heart failure with benign hypertension
   B) Congestive heart failure; hypertension
   C) Hypertensive cardiovascular disease with congestive heart failure
   D) Cardiomegaly with hypertension

REFERENCE: Brown, p 266-267
Hazelwood and Venable, p 139
Schraffenberger (2006) p123-124
Principles of ICD-9-CM Coding, p 214-219

23. A patient is admitted to your hospital 6 weeks post myocardial infarction with severe chest pains. The correct code would be
   A) 414.8 Chronic MI
   B) 410.1x Acute MI
   C) 412 Old MI
   D) 413.0 Angina

REFERENCE: Brown, p 255-256
Hazelwood and Venable, p 142
Schraffenberger (2006), p 129
Principles of ICD—9-Coding, p 322

24. Which of the following is classified as a poisoning in ICD-9-CM?
   A) Syncope due to Contac pills and a three martini lunch
   B) Digitalis intoxication
   C) Reaction to dye administered for pyelogram
   D) Idiosyncratic reaction between various drugs

REFERENCE: Brown, p 337-338
Hazelwood and Venable, p 254-255
Schraffenberger (2006), p 247-248
Principles of ICD-9-CM Coding, p 322

25. Susan Dawn is status post mastectomy (six weeks) due to carcinoma of the breast. She is admitted to the outpatient clinic for chemotherapy. What is the correct sequencing of the codes?
   A) V58.1 chemotherapy; 174.9 malignant neoplasm of breast
   B) V58.1 chemotherapy; V10.3 personal history of neoplasm of the breast
   C) V67.00 follow-up exam after surgery; V58.1 chemotherapy
   D) V10.3 personal history of neoplasm of the breast; V58.1 chemotherapy

REFERENCE: Coding Clinic, 2nd Quarter, 1990, p 7
Brown, p 300-301
Hazelwood and Venable, p 86-87
Schraffenberger (2006), p 76-77

26. Which of the following is coded as an adverse effect in ICD-9-CM?
   A) Mental retardation due to intracranial abscess
   B) Rejection of transplanted kidney
   C) Tinnitus due to allergic reaction after administration of ear drops
   D) Non-functioning pacemaker due to defective soldering

REFERENCE: Brown, p 337
Hazelwood and Venable, p 251
Schraffenberger (2006), p 243-244

27. A service provided by a physician whose opinion or advice regarding evaluation and/or management of a specific problem is requested by another physician is referred to as
   A) a referral
   B) a consultation
   C) risk factor intervention
   D) concurrent care

REFERENCE: CPT (2005), p 14
Principles of CPT Coding, p 62-64
Smith, p 173

28. A patient with leukemia is admitted for chemotherapy five weeks after experiencing an acute myocardial infarction. How will the MI be coded?
   A) MI with 5th digit 1 - initial episode of care
   B) MI with 5th digit 2 - subsequent episode of care
   C) History of MI
   D) Chronic MI

REFERENCE: Brown, p 255-256
Hazelwood and Venable, p 142
Schraffenberger (2006), p 128-129

29. The most widely-discussed and debated unique patient identifier is the:
   A) patient's date of birth
   B) patient's first and last names
   C) patient's social security number
   D) Unique Physician Identification Number (UPIN)

REFERENCE: Abdelhak, p 81
LaTour and Eichenwald, p 131

30. The Central Office on ICD-9-CM which publishes *Coding Clinic* is maintained by the
   A) National Center for Health Statistics
   B) Centers for Medicare and Medicaid Services
   C) American Hospital Association
   D) American Health Information Management Association

REFERENCE: Abdelhak, p 232
Schraffenberger (2005), 2nd Edition, p 12

31. A nomenclature of codes and medical terms which provides standard terminology for reporting physicians' services for third party reimbursement is
   A) Current Medical Information and Terminology (CMIT)
   B) Current Procedural Terminology (CPT)
   C) Systematized Nomenclature of Pathology (SNOP)
   D) Diagnostic and Statistical Manual of Mental Disorders (DSM)

REFERENCE: Abdelhak, p 233
Schraffenberger (2005) 2nd Edition, p 7-8
LaTour and Eichenwald, p 264-265

32. The Level II (national) codes of the HCPCS coding system are maintained by the
   A) American Medical Association
   B) CPT Editorial Panel
   C) local fiscal intermediary
   D) Centers for Medicare and Medicaid Services

REFERENCE: Abdelhak, p 232
Schraffenberger (2005) 2nd Edition, p 8
Johns, p 303

33. A patient is admitted in alcohol withdrawal suffering from delirium tremens. The patient is a chronic alcoholic and cocaine addict. Which of the following is the principal diagnosis?
   A) alcoholic withdrawal
   B) chronic alcoholism
   C) cocaine dependence
   D) delirium tremens

REFERENCE: Brown, p 113
Schraffenberger (2006), p 108

34. A patient is admitted with pneumonia. Cultures are requested to determine the infecting organism. Which of the following, if present, would alert the coder to ask the physician whether or not this should be coded as gram-negative pneumonia?
   A) Pseudomonas
   B) Clostridium
   C) Staphylococcus
   D) Listeria

REFERENCE: Brown, p 87

35. The Level I (CPT) codes of the HCPCS coding system are maintained by the
   A) American Medical Association
   B) American Hospital Association
   C) local fiscal intermediary
   D) Centers for Medicare and Medicaid Services

REFERENCE: Abdelhak, p 232
Schraffenberger (2005) 2nd Edition, p 7
Johns, p 303

36. A physician excises a 3.1 cm malignant lesion of the scalp which requires full thickness graft from the thigh to the scalp. In CPT, which of the following procedures should be coded?
   A) Full thickness skin graft to scalp only
   B) Excision of lesion; Full-thickness skin graft to scalp
   C) Excision of lesion; Full-thickness skin graft to scalp; Excision of skin from thigh
   D) Code 15000 for surgical preparation of recipient site; Full-thickness skin graft to scalp

REFERENCE: CPT Assistant, Vol. 7, #9, September 1997, p 1-3
Smith, p 61

37. A patient is seen by a surgeon who determines that an emergency procedure is necessary. Identify the modifier that may be reported to indicate that the decision to do surgery was made on this office visit.
   A) -25
   B) -55
   C) -57
   D) -58

REFERENCE: CPT (2006), p 423-425
Smith, p 170

38. A patient develops difficulty during surgery and the physician discontinues the procedure. Identify the modifier that may be reported by the physician to indicate that the procedure was discontinued.
    A) -52
    B) -53
    C) -73
    D) -74

REFERENCE: CPT (2006), p 423-425
Smith, p 40

39. A patient has major surgery and sees the surgeon 10 days later for an unrelated E&M service. Indicate the modifier that should be attached to the E&M code for the service provided.
    A) -24
    B) -25
    C) -59
    D) -79

REFERENCE: CPT (2006), p 423-425
Smith, p 168-169

40. A barrier to widespread use of automated code assignment is
    A) inadequate technology
    B) poor quality of documentation
    C) resistance by physicians
    D) resistance by HIM professionals

REFERENCE: LaTour and Eichenwald, p 269

41. In assigning E&M codes, three key components are used. These are
    A) history, examination, counseling
    B) history, examination, time
    C) history, nature of presenting problem, time
    D) history, examination, medical-decision making

REFERENCE: CPT (2006), p 2
Principles of CPT Coding, p 38
Smith, p 155

42. Mrs. Jones has an appendectomy on November 1. She was taken back to surgery on November 2 for evacuation of a hematoma of the wound site. Identify the modifier that may be reported for the November 2 visit.
    A) -58
    B) -76
    C) -78
    D) -79

REFERENCE: CPT (2006), p 423-425
Smith, p 42

43. A pregnant patient was admitted to the hospital with uncontrolled diabetes mellitus. She is a type I diabetic and was brought under control and subsequently discharged. The following code was assigned:

| | |
|---|---|
| 648.03 | Other current condition in the mother classifiable elsewhere but complicating pregnancy, childbirth of the puerperium, diabetes mellitus |

Which of the following describe why the coding is in error?

A) the incorrect 5th digit was used
B) the condition should have been coded as gestational diabetes because she is pregnant
C) an additional code describing the diabetes mellitus should be used
D) only the code for the diabetes mellitus should have been used

REFERENCE: Brown, p 214
Schraffenberger (2006), 187-188
Principles of ICD-9-CM Coding, p 154

44. A secondary data source that houses and aggregates extensive data about patients with a certain diagnosis is a:

A) disease index
B) master patient index
C) disease registry
D) admissions register

REFERENCE: LaTour and Eichenwald, p 243

45. After reviewing the following excerpt from CPT, code 27646 would be interpreted as:

| | |
|---|---|
| 27645 | radical resection of tumor, bone; tibia |
| 27646 | fibula |
| 27647 | talus or calcaneus |

A) 27646 radical resection of tumor, bone; tibia and fibula
B) 27646 radical resection of tumor, bone; fibula
C) 27646 radical resection of tumor, bone; fibula or tibia
D) 27646 radical resection of tumor, bone; fibula, talus or calcaneus

REFERENCE: Smith, p 18-19
Principles of CPT Coding, p 23

46. A patient was admitted to the hospital with hemiplegia and aphasia. The hemiplegia and aphasia were resolved before discharge and the patient was diagnosed with cerebral thrombosis. What is the correct coding and sequencing?

A) hemiplegia; aphasia
B) cerebral thrombosis
C) cerebral thrombosis; hemiplegia; aphasia
D) hemiplegia; cerebral thrombosis; aphasia

REFERENCE: Brown, p 264
Hazelwood and Venable, p 148
Schraffenberger (2006), p 137

47. A 36-year old woman was admitted to the hospital for an obstetrical delivery of her third child. During the admission, a sterilization procedure was performed for contraceptive purposes. The V25.2 code for sterilization would be:
   A) assigned as a principal diagnosis
   B) assigned as a secondary diagnosis
   C) not assigned since this was the patient's third child
   D) not assigned since it is the same admission as the delivery

REFERENCE: Brown, p 220
Schraffenberger (2006), p 277

48. According to ICD-9-CM, which one of the following is not a mechanical complication of an internal implant?
   A) erosion of skin by pacemaker electrodes
   B) inflammation of urethra due to indwelling catheter
   C) leakage of breast prosthesis
   D) IUD embedded in uterine wall

REFERENCE: Brown, p 348
Hazelwood and Venable, p 266
Schraffenberger (2006), p 251
Principles of ICD-9-CM Coding, p 327-328

49 Given the following diagnosis: "Carcinoma of axillary lymph nodes and lungs, metastatic from breast". What is the primary cancer site(s)?
   A) axillary lymph nodes
   B) lungs
   C) breast
   D) both A & B

REFERENCE: Brown, p 293
Hazelwood and Venable, p 92
Schraffenberger (2006), p 84

50. In the diagnosis, "first, second, and third degree burns of the chest wall," a code is required for
   A) the first degree burn only
   B) the second degree burn only
   C) the third degree burn only
   D) for each of the first, second and third degree burns

REFERENCE: Brown, p 332
Hazelwood and Venable, p 242
Schraffenberger (2006), p 238
Principles of ICD-9-CM Coding, p 316-317

51. When is it appropriate to use category V10, history of malignant neoplasm?
   A) primary malignancy recurred at original site and adjunct chemotherapy is directed at the site.
   B) primary malignancy has been eradicated and no adjunct treatment is being given at this time.
   C) primary malignancy eradicated and the patient is admitted for adjunct chemotherapy to primary site
   D) primary malignancy is eradicated; adjunct treatment is refused by patient even through there is some remaining malignancy

REFERENCE: Brown, p 460-461
Schraffenberger (2006), p 76-77, 274-275

52. According to CPT, in which of the following cases would an established E&M code be used?
    A) A home visit with a 45 year old male with a long history of drug abuse and alcoholism. The man is seen at the request of Adult Protective Services for an assessment of his mental capabilities.
    B) John and his family have just moved to town. John has asthma and requires medication to control the problem. He has an appointment with Dr. You and will bring his records from his previous physician.
    C) Tom is seen by Dr. X for a sore throat. Dr. X is on call for Tom's regular physician, Dr. Y. The last time that Tom saw Dr. Y was a couple of years ago.
    D) A 78 year old female with weight loss and progressive agitation over the past two months is seen by her primary care physician for drug therapy. She has not seen her primary care physician in 4 years.

REFERENCE: CPT (2006), p 1
Buck, p 29
Principles of CPT Coding, p 39-41
CPT Assistant, Vol 8, #10, October 1998
Smith, p 154

53. In order to use the inpatient CPT consultation codes, the consulting physician must:
    A) order diagnostic tests
    B) document his findings in the patient's medical record
    C) communicate orally his opinion to the attending physician
    D) use the term "referral" in his report

REFERENCE: CPT (2006), p 14
Principles of CPT Coding, p 63
Buck, p 55-57
Smith, p 173

54. The attending physician requests a consultation from a cardiologist. The cardiologist takes a detailed history, performs a detailed examination and utilizes moderate medical decision-making. The cardiologist orders diagnostic tests and prescribes medication. He documents his findings in the patient's medical record and communicates in writing with the attending physician. The following day the consultant visits the patient to evaluate the patient's response to the medication, to review results from the diagnostic tests him and discuss treatment options. What codes should the consultant report for the two visits?
    A) an initial inpatient consult and a follow-up consult
    B) an initial inpatient consult for both visits
    C) an initial inpatient consult and a subsequent hospital visit
    D) an initial inpatient consult and initial hospital care

REFERENCE: Principles of CPT Coding, p 66-67

55. According to the American Medical Association, medical decision-making is measured by all of the following except:
    A) number of diagnoses/management options
    B) amount and complexity of data reviewed
    C) risk of complications
    D) specialty of the treating physician

REFERENCE: CPT (2006), p 7
Principles of CPT Coding, p 49-50
Smith, p 162-163

56. CPT provides Level I modifiers to explain all of the following situations except:
   A) when face-to-face services provided by a provider are greater than usually required for the highest level of E&M service for a given category
   B) when one surgeon provides only postoperative services
   C) when a patient sees a surgeon for follow-up care after surgery
   D) when the same laboratory test is repeated multiple times on the same day

REFERENCE: CPT (2006), p 423-425
Principles of CPT Coding, p 479-499

57. The best place to ascertain the size of an excised lesion for accurate CPT coding is the:
   A) discharge summary
   B) pathology report
   C) operative report
   D) anesthesia record

REFERENCE: Principles of CPT Coding, p 134
Smith, p 50

58. According to guidelines for CPT coding, the major factor to consider when determining whether or not to code lysis of adhesions is
   A) the type of surgery performed
   B) the complexity involved in lysing the adhesions
   C) the anatomical site that is being operated upon
   D) there is no factor because lysis of adhesions is never coded

REFERENCE: Principles of CPT Coding, p 213-214

59. In relation to bone grafts, an autograft
   A) refers to donor bone obtained from a bone bank
   B) is cancellous or bone cortex from the patient's own body
   C) is made of synthetic material
   D) is a whole piece of bone cortex from either a bone bank or the patient's own body

REFERENCE: Principles of CPT Coding, p 141-142

60. In regard to quality of coding, the degree to which the same results (same codes) are obtained by different coders or on multiple attempts by the same coder refers to
   A) reliability
   B) validity
   C) completeness
   D) timeliness

REFERENCE: Abdelhak, p 250
LaTour and Eichenwald, p 257

61. In regards to quality of coding, the degree to which the codes selected accurately reflect the diagnoses and procedures refer to:
   A) reliability
   B) validity
   C) completeness
   D) timeliness

REFERENCE: Abdelhak, p 250
LaTour and Eichenwald, p 256-257

62. The coding supervisor notices that the coders are routinely failing to code all possible diagnoses and procedures for a patient encounter. This indicates to the supervisor that there is a problem with:
   A) reliability
   B) validity
   C) completeness
   D) timeliness

REFERENCE: Abdelhak, p 250
LaTour and Eichenwald, p 257

63. When coding free skin grafts, which of the following is not an essential item of data needed for accurate coding?
   A) recipient site
   B) donor site
   C) size of defect
   D) type of repair

REFERENCE: Buck, p 147
Smith, p 60-61

64. In CPT, Category III codes include
   A) codes to describe emerging technologies
   B) codes to measure performance
   C) codes for use by non-physician practitioners
   D) codes for supplies, drugs, and durable medical equipment

REFERENCE: CPT (2006), p 417
Buck, p 15-16
Smith, p 2-3

65. In the ICD-9-CM classification system, shooting pain in the right eye due to the presence of an intact, correctly positioned permanent contact lens would be coded as:
   A) a current injury
   B) a late effect
   C) a mechanical complication of an internal prosthetic device
   D) an abnormal reaction of the body to the presence of an internal prosthetic device

REFERENCE: Brown, p 348
Hazelwood and Venable, p 267
Schraffenberger (2006), p 252

66. In the ICD-9-CM classification system, severe shock due to third degree burns sustained in an industrial accident would be coded as
   A) a current injury
   B) a late effect
   C) a mechanical complication of an internal prosthetic device
   D) an abnormal reaction of the body to the presence of an internal prosthetic device

REFERENCE: Brown, p 334

67. In the ICD-9-CM classification system, a non-functioning pacemaker due to the disintegration of the electrodes (leads) would be coded as
   A) a current injury
   B) a late effect
   C) a mechanical complication of an internal prosthetic device
   D) an abnormal reaction of the body to the presence of an internal prosthetic device

REFERENCE: Brown, p 348
Hazelwood and Venable, p 266-267
Schraffenberger (2006) p 251
Principles of ICD-9-CM Coding, p 327-328

68. In the ICD-9-CM classification system, an esophageal stricture due to a burn received in a house fire several years ago would be coded as:
   A) a current injury
   B) a late effect
   C) a mechanical complication of an internal prosthetic device
   D) an abnormal reaction of the body to the presence of an internal prosthetic device

REFERENCE: Brown, p 326-327
Hazelwood and Venable, p 50
Schraffenberger (2006), p 265

69. Dizziness and blurred vision following ingestion of prescribed Allegra and a glass of wine at dinner would be reported as a (an):
   A) poisoning
   B) adverse reaction to a drug
   C) late effect of a poisoning
   D) late effect of an adverse reaction

REFERENCE: Brown, p 338
Hazelwood and Venable, p 254
Schraffenberger (2006), p 248
Principles of ICD-9-CM Coding, p 322

70. Tachycardia after taking a correct dosage of prescribed Lortab would be reported as a (an):
   A) poisoning
   B) adverse reaction to a drug
   C) late effect of a poisoning
   D) late effect of an adverse reaction

REFERENCE: Brown, p 337
Hazelwood and Venable, p 251
Schraffenberger (2006), p 243-244

71. Blindness due to an allergic reaction to Ampicillin administered six years ago would be reported as a (an):
   A) poisoning
   B) adverse reaction to a drug
   C) late effect of a poisoning
   D) late effect of an adverse reaction

REFERENCE: Brown, p 343
Hazelwood and Venable, p 253-254
Schraffenberger (2006), p 247

72. The patient underwent bypass surgery for life threatening coronary artery disease. With the aid of extracorporeal circulation, the right internal mammary artery was taken down to the left anterior descending artery and saphenous vein grafts were brought from the aorta to the diagonal, the right coronary artery and the posterior descending artery. What is the correct ICD-9-CM coding for this procedure?
   A) single internal mammary artery bypass; aortocoronary artery bypass of 3 vessels
   B) aortocoronary bypass of three coronary arteries
   C) aortocoronary bypass of four coronary arteries
   D) single internal mammary artery bypass; aortocoronary bypass of 3 vessels, extracorporeal circulation

REFERENCE: Brown, p 277-279
Schraffenberger (2006), p 141-142

73. The method of calculating errors in a coding audit that allows for benchmarking with other hospitals and permits the reviewer to track errors by case type is the:
   A) record method
   B) benchmarking method
   C) code method
   D) focused review method

REFERENCE: Schraffenberger (2005) 2$^{nd}$ Edition, p 198

74. This code represents a HCPCS Level II National Code:
   A) W0166
   B) 99281
   C) J7030
   D) 66690

REFERENCE: Abdelhak, p 234
Johns, p 303

75. A radiologist is asked to review a patient's CT scan that was taken at another facility. The modifier -26 attached to the code indicates that the physician is billing for what component of the procedure?
   A) professional
   B) technical
   C) global
   D) confirmatory

REFERENCE: Buck, p 98, 317
Smith, p 137

76. When coding neoplasms, topography means
   A) cell structure and form
   B) site
   C) variation from normal tissue
   D) extent of the spread of the disease

REFERENCE: Abdelhak, p 269

77. According to CPT, antepartum care includes all of the following except:
A) initial and subsequent history
B) physical examination
C) monthly visits up to 36 weeks
D) routine chemical urinalysis

REFERENCE: Buck, p 262
Smith, p 114
Principles of CPT Coding, p 243-244

78. The cancer committee at Wharton General Hospital wants to compare long-term survival rates for pancreatic cancer by evaluating medical versus surgical treatment of the cancer. The best source of this data is:
A) disease index
B) operation index
C) master patient index
D) cancer registry abstracts

REFERENCE: Abdelhak, p 264-265
LaTour and Eichenwald, p 244

79. A list or collection of clinical words or phrases with their meanings is a:
A) data dictionary
B) language
C) medical nomenclature
D) clinical vocabulary

REFERENCE: LaTour and Eichenwald, p 262-263

80. The main difference between concurrent and retrospective coding is:
A) when the coding is done
B) what classification system is used
C) the credentials of the coder
D) the involvement of the physician

REFERENCE: Schraffenberger (2005) 2nd Edition, p 26

Answer Key for Classification Systems, Registries and Indexing

ANSWER EXPLANATION

*NOTE: Explanations are provided for those questions that require mathematical calculations and questions that are not clearly explained in the references that are sited.*

1. A

2. B M codes and E codes are never principal diagnosis codes and, in fact, are optional for coding. V-codes to describe the outcome of delivery are always secondary codes on the mother's chart.

3. B

4. C

5. A Antivert is used for the management of nausea and dizziness associated with motion sickness and in vertigo associated with diseases affecting the vestibular system.

6. A

7. A A coder should never assign a code on the basis of laboratory results alone. If findings are clearly outside of normal range and the physician has ordered additional testing or treatment, it is appropriate to consult with the physician as to whether a diagnosis should be added or whether the abnormal finding should be listed.

8. B Pilocarpine is used to treat open-angle and angle-closure glaucoma to reduce intraocular pressure

9. D Digoxin is used for maintenance therapy in congestive heart failure, atrial fibrillation, atrial flutter and paroxysmal atrial tachycardia. Ibuprofen is an anti-inflammatory drug. Oxytocin is used to initiate or improve uterine contractions at term and Haloperidol is used to manage psychotic disorders.

10. D

11. C HCPCS codes (Levels I and II) would only give the code for any procedures that were performed and would not identify the diagnosis code or cause of the accident. The correct name of the nomenclature for athletic injuries is the Standard Nomenclature of Athletic Injuries and is used to identify sports injuries. It has not been revised since 1976.

12. D

13. C

14. B All three key components (history, physical examination, and medical decision making) are required for new patients and initial visits. At least two of the three key components are required for established patients, subsequent visits, and follow-up consultations.

Answer Key for Classification Systems, Registries and Indexing

| | ANSWER | EXPLANATION |
|---|---|---|
| 15. | B | |
| 16. | B | |
| 17. | B | |
| 18. | A | |
| 19. | B | |
| 20. | D | There are V codes which indicate various reasons for canceled surgery. Review codes V64.0, V64.1, V64.2 and V64.3. As usual, the principal diagnosis is always the reason for admission, in this case, the cholelithiasis. The contraindication (the tachycardia) should also be coded. |
| 21. | B | |
| 22. | C | In order to use category 402 there must be a cause and effect relationship shown between the hypertension and the heart condition. "With" does not show this relationship nor does the fact that both conditions are listed on the same chart. The term "hypertensive" indicates a cause and effect relationship. |
| 23. | B | An acute MI is considered to be anything under 8 weeks duration from the time of initial onset. A chronic MI is considered anything over 8 weeks with symptoms. An old MI is considered anything over 8 weeks with NO symptoms. |
| 24. | A | A reaction due to mixing drugs and alcohol is coded as a poisoning. |
| 25. | A | The patient is admitted for chemotherapy (V58.1) and since the breast cancer is still actively being treated, it is still coded as current. |
| 26. | C | Mental retardation is a late effect, rejection of the kidney is a complication, and non-functioning pacemaker is a mechanical complication. |
| 27. | B | |
| 28. | B | |
| 29. | C | |
| 30. | C | |
| 31. | B | |
| 32. | D | |
| 33. | D | |
| 34. | A | |

Answer Key for Classification Systems, Registries and Indexing

| | ANSWER | EXPLANATION |
|---|---|---|
| 35. | A | |
| 36. | B | |
| 37. | C | |
| 38. | B | |
| 39. | A | |
| 40. | B | |
| 41. | D | |
| 42. | C | |
| 43. | C | |
| 44. | C | |
| 45. | B | |
| 46. | B | |
| 47. | B | |
| 48. | B | |
| 49. | C | |
| 50. | C | |
| 51. | B | |
| 52. | C | |
| 53. | B | |
| 54. | C | The first visit would be an inpatient consult. Because the physician continued to treat the patient and participate in his care all subsequent visits are considered as subsequent hospital care and are no longer consults. |
| 55. | D | |
| 56. | C | Modifier -21 may be used when the services that a physician provides are greater than those identified in the highest level of E&M visit. Modifier -55 is used by a physician who only provides postoperative services. Modifier -91 is used when a laboratory test is repeated multiple times on the same day. CPT code 99024 is used to report a follow-up visit after surgery. |

Answer Key for Classification Systems, Registries and Indexing

| | ANSWER | EXPLANATION |
|---|---|---|
| 57. | C | |
| 58. | B | |
| 59. | B | |
| 60. | A | |
| 61. | B | |
| 62. | C | |
| 63. | B | |
| 64. | A | |
| 65. | D | |
| 66. | A | |
| 67. | C | |
| 68. | B | |
| 61. | A | |
| 70. | B | |
| 71. | D | |
| 72. | D | The procedure described includes 1 internal mammary artery which is not considered an aortocoronary bypass. There were three aortocoronary bypasses – aorta to diagonal, aorta to right coronary artery and aorta to the posterior descending artery. The description states that extracorporeal circulation was used. |
| 73. | A | |
| 74. | C | HCPCS Level I codes are 5 digit (numeric) codes found in the CPT book. HCPCS Level II National Codes are alphanumeric starting a letter A-V. HCPCS Level III Local Codes are alphanumeric starting with a letter W-Z. Level III codes were eliminated as of December 31, 2003. |

| ANSWER | | EXPLANATION |
|---|---|---|
| 75. | A | With CPT radiology codes, there are three components that have to be considered. These are the professional, technical and global components. The professional component describes the services of a physician who supervises the taking of an X-ray film and the interpretation with report of the results. The technical component describes the services of the person who uses the equipment, the film and other supplies. The global component describes the combination of both professional and technical components. If the billing radiologist's services include only the supervision and interpretation component, the radiologist bills the procedure code and adds the modifier -26 to indicate that he did only the professional component of the procedure. |
| 76. | B | |
| 77. | C | |
| 78. | D | |
| 79. | D | |
| 80. | A | |

REFERENCE LIST

Abdelhak, Mervat; Grostick, Sara; Hanken, Mary Alice; Jacobs, Ellen.
*Health Information: Management of a Strategic Resource 2nd Edition.*
W.B. Saunders. Philadelphia, PA., 2001.

Brown, Faye.
*ICD-9-CM Coding Handbook for 2006.* American Hospital Association. Chicago, IL. 2005.

Buck, Carol J.
Step-*by-Step Medical Coding 2005 Edition. W.* B. Saunders. Philadelphia, PA., 2005.

*Coding Clinic.* American Hospital Association. Chicago, IL.

Hazelwood, Anita C. and Venable, Carol A. *ICD-9-CM Diagnostic Coding and Reimbursement for Physician Services 2006.* American Health Information Management Association. Chicago, IL. .

Introduction to the ICD-9-CM Coding Book.

Johns, Merida. *Health Information Management Technology An Applied Approach.* American Health Information Management Association. Chicago, IL, 2002.

LaTour, Kathleen and Eichenwald, Shirley. *Health Information Management: Concepts, Principles and Practice*. American Health Information Management Association. Chicago, IL, 2002

*Physicians' Current Procedural Terminology: CPT (2005), Professional Edition.* American Medical Association. Chicago, IL. 2004.

*Principles of CPT Coding, 4th Edition*. American Medical Association. Chicago, IL. 2005.

*Principles of ICD-9-CM Coding 3rd Edition,* American Medical Association. Chicago, IL. 2005.

Rubin, Emanuel. *Essential Pathology*. 3rd Edition. Lippincott Williams and Wilkins. Philadelphia, PA., 2001.

Schraffenberger, Lou Ann. *Effective Management of Coding Services*, 2nd Edition. American Health Information Management Association. Chicago, IL. 2005.

Schraffenberger, Lou Ann. *Basic ICD-9-CM Coding.* American Health Information Management Association. Chicago, IL, 2005.

Shannon, Margaret T. et al. *Health Professionals Drug Guide 2004*. Prentice Hall. Upper Saddle River, New Jersey, 2004.

Smith, Gail. *Basic CPT/HCPCS Coding 2004.* American Health Information Management Association. Chicago, IL. 2004.

# Medical Billing and Reimbursement Systems

Toni Cade, MBA, RHIA, CCS, FAHIMA

# Medical Billing and Reimbursement Systems

*Toni Cade, MBA, RHIA, CCS, FAHIMA*

1. Under the RBRVS, each HCPCS/CPT code contains three (3) components, each having assigned relative value units. These three (3) components are
   A) geographic index, wage index and cost of living index
   B) fee-for-service, per diem payment and capitation
   C) conversion factor, CMS weight and hospital specific rate
   D) physician work, practice expense and malpractice insurance expense

REFERENCE: Abdelhak, p 243

2. A patient was seen by Dr. Zachary. The charge for the office visit was $125. The Medicare beneficiary already met his deductible. The Medicare fee schedule amount is $100. Dr. Zachary does not accept assignment. The office manager will apply a practice termed as "balance billing", which means that the patient is
   A) financially liable for the Medicare fee schedule amount
   B) financially liable for charges in excess of the Medicare fee schedule
   C) not financially liable for any amount
   D) is financially liable for the entire charge for the office visit

REFERENCE: LaTour, p 315

3. The _______________ is a statement received from the fiscal intermediary or carrier indicating the amount the provider was paid.
   A) remittance advice
   B) advance beneficiary notice
   C) attestation statement
   D) acknowledgement notice

REFERENCE: Abdelhak, p 241
LaTour, p 315

4. A (an) ________________________contracts with the CMS to process claims for Medicare Part B (physicians') services
   A) Quality Improvement Organization (QIO)
   B) Medicare carriers
   C) Medicare fiscal intermediaries
   D) International Standards Organization (ISO)

REFERENCE: LaTour, p 311

5. The ________________________________ refers to a statement sent to the healthcare provider and the patient to clarify which services were provided, amount of charges incurred and amount of payments made by the health plan.
   A) explanation of benefits
   B) remittance advice
   C) healthcare claims transaction
   D) coordination of benefits

REFERENCE: LaTour, p 315

6. Currently, payment to the physician for outpatient surgery performed on a Medicare patient is based upon which prospective payment system?
   A) DRGs
   B) APGs
   C) RBRVS
   D) ASCs

REFERENCE: Abdelhak, p 244

7. Which of the following best describes the situation of a provider who agrees to accept assignment for Medicare Part B services?
   A) the provider is reimbursed at 15 percent above the allowed charge
   B) the provider is paid according to the Medicare Physician Fee Schedule (MPFS) plus 10 percent
   C) the provider can not bill the patients for the balance between the MPFS amount and the total charges
   D) the provider is a nonparticipating provider

REFERENCE: Green, p 48, 80

8. Hospitals use the _______ billing form and physician offices use the ________ billing form
   A) HCFA (CMS) 1500; UB-92
   B) UB-92; UB-92
   C) HCFA (CMS) 1500; HCFA 1500
   D) UB-92; HCFA (CMS) 1500

REFERENCE: Abdelhak, p 235

9. This means that the service or procedure is justified by the patient's symptoms and/or medical condition according to accepted standards of medical practice.
   A) peer review
   B) optimization
   C) benchmarking
   D) medical necessity

REFERENCE: Abdelhak, p 241

10. If the Medicare approved payment amount is $128.00 for a proctoscopy, what is the total Medicare approved payment amount for a doctor who does not accept assignment, applying the limiting charge for this procedure?
  A) $ 140.80
  B) $ 143.00
  C) $ 192.00
  D) $ 147.20

REFERENCE: Green, p 394-395

11. In a global payment methodology, all of the following are part of the "technical" components EXCEPT
  A) radiological equipment
  B) physician services
  C) radiological supplies
  D) support services

REFERENCE: LaTour, p 302

12. A Medicare patient has arthroscopic lysis of adhesions and shaving of the articular cartilage of the right knee. The codes are:
  29884-RT Arthroscopy, knee, surgical, with lysis of adhesions (separate procedure), right
  29877-RT Arthroscopy, knee, surgical, debridement/shaving of articular cartilage, right

| Comprehensive Codes | Component Codes |
|---|---|
| 29877 | 20610, 27570, 29870, 29871, 29874, 29875, 29884 |

  The Medicare CCI (Correct Coding Initiative) edits indicate that code 29877 is not a component code for 29884, but code 29884 is a component code for 29877. The correct code(s) to be reported on this claim is (are)
  A) 29884-RT and 29877-RT
  B) 29884-RT
  C) 29877-RT
  D) neither code

REFERENCE: Jones (2001), p 28, 51, 235

13. The hospital outpatient prospective payment system for Medicare applies to all of the following, EXCEPT, for
  A) physician reimbursement of observation services
  B) facility reimbursement for outpatient clinic visits
  C) facility reimbursement for emergency department visits
  D) facility reimbursement for hospital-based outpatient surgery

REFERENCE: Jones (2001), p 35

14. The Correct Coding Initiative (CCI) edits contain a listing of codes under two columns titled, "comprehensive codes" and "component codes". According to the CCI edits when a provider bills Medicare for a procedure that appears in both columns for the same beneficiary on the same date of service
    A) code only the component code
    B) do not code either one
    C) code only the comprehensive code
    D) code both the comprehensive code and the component code

REFERENCE: Jones (2001), p 51

15. This payment system replaced the customary, prevailing, and reasonable (CPR) charge payment system for physician services provided to Medicare patients. It is based upon relative value units.
    A) Medicare fee schedule
    B) pre-certification
    C) consolidated billing
    D) ancillary packaging

REFERENCE: Jones (2001), p 500

16. All of the following items are packaged under the Medicare outpatient prospective payment system, EXCEPT for
    A) medical visits
    B) supplies
    C) anesthesia
    D) recovery room

REFERENCE: Johns, p 377

17. The physician must sign a (an) ______________________________ according to Medicare reimbursement regulations. This must be signed by the physician at the time of appointment to the medical staff to ensure that the physician is aware of the serious consequences of misconduct in reporting diagnoses and procedures for hospital inpatients.
    A) attestation statement
    B) waiver of liability
    C) advance beneficiary notice
    D) acknowledgment statement

REFERENCE: Abdelhak, p 241

18. The most important consideration when selecting an outside coding contracting company to help a facility optimize their reimbursement is
    A) the cost to the hospital
    B) turnaround time of the audit findings from the company
    C) whether the review occurs before or after billing
    D) qualifications of the coders who work for the company

REFERENCE: Abdelhak, p 256

19. The limiting charge is a percentage limit on fees specified by legislation that the non-participating physician may bill Medicare beneficiaries above the fee schedule amount. The limiting charge is
    A) 10%
    B) 15%
    C) 20%
    D) 50%

REFERENCES: Jones (2001), p 499
Green, p 394-395

Use the following case scenario to answer questions #20 – #24.

| |
|---|
| A Medicare patient is seen in the physician's office.<br>The total charges for this office visit is $250.<br>The patient has not paid his deductible yet under Medicare Part B.<br>The Medicare fee schedule amount for this service is $200. |

20. The patient is financially liable for the deductible amount under Medicare Part B which is
    A) $500
    B) $100
    C) $110
    D) $800

REFERENCE: Jones (2001), p 174, 176, 495, 505

21. If this physician is a participating physician who accepts assignment for this claim, the total amount he will receive is
    A) $200
    B) $250
    C) $100
    D) $175

REFERENCE: Jones (2001), p 174, 176, 495, 505

22. If this physician is a non-participating physician who does <u>not</u> accept assignment for this claim, the total amount he will receive is
    A) $250
    B) $200
    C) $230
    D) $100

REFERENCES: Jones (2001), p 174, 176, 495, 505
Green, p 39-395

23. If this physician is a participating physician who accepts assignment for this claim, the total amount of the patient's financial liability (out of pocket expense) is
    A) $200
    B) $128
    C) $230
    D) $100

REFERENCE: Jones (2001), p 174, 176, 495, 505

24. If this physician is a non-participating physician who does not accept assignment for this claim, the total amount of the patient's financial liability (out of pocket expense) is
    A) $134
    B) $200
    C) $230
    D) $104

REFERENCE: Jones (2001), p 174, 176, 495, 505

25. In the managed care industry, there are specific reimbursement concepts, such as "capitation". All of the following statements are true in regards to the concept of "capitation", <u>EXCEPT</u> for
    A) Each service is paid based upon the actual charges.
    B) Providers are at full financial risk for capitated services.
    C) Capitation means paying a fixed amount per person.
    D) Capitation puts a lid on payments per person that otherwise might change under a fee-for-service system.

REFERENCE: Jones (2001), p 153

26. This document is published by the Office of Inspector General (OIG) every year. It details the OIG's focus for Medicare fraud and abuse for that year. It gives health care providers an indication of general and specific areas that are targeted for review. It can be found on the Internet on CMS' website.
    A) The OIG's Evaluation and Management Documentation Guidelines
    B) The OIG's Model Compliance Plan
    C) The Federal Register
    D) The OIG's Workplan

REFERENCE: Abdelhak, 636

27. The AR (Accounts Receivable) List shows:
    A) cases that have not yet been paid
    B) the amount the hospital was paid
    C) cases that have been paid
    D) denials that have been returned to the hospital

REFERENCE: Abdelhak, 241

28. In employer-sponsored health plans, employees may select their health plan
    A) during the contract period
    B) at the beginning of each fiscal year
    C) during the open enrollment period
    D) on the first day of any month

REFERENCE: Valerius, p 331

29. Which modifier indicates that a signed ABN is on file?
    A) AB
    B) GA
    C) GY
    D) GZ

REFERENCE: Valerius, p 372

30. Under Medicare Part B, all of the following statements are true and are applicable to non-participating physician providers, EXCEPT for
   A) providers must file all Medicare claims
   B) non-participating providers have a higher fee schedule than that for participating providers
   C) fees are restricted to charging no more than the "limiting charge" on non-assigned claims
   D) collections are restricted to only the deductible and co-insurance due at the time of service on an assigned claim

REFERENCE: Green, p 394-395

31. The office form used by healthcare providers that states the diagnoses and services rendered to the patient during the current encounter is called a/an
   A) superbill
   B) explanation of benefits
   C) rebill
   D) clinical abstract

REFERENCES: Schraffenberger 2nd Ed, p 237-238, 306
Green, p 66-67, 286

32. This information is published by the Centers of Medicare and Medicaid Services to outline diagnoses considered medically necessary for a certain test or procedure. The ICD-9-CM and CPT/HCPCS codes are listed in the memoranda.
   A) LCD (local coverage determinations)
   B) CCI (correct coding initiatives)
   C) OSHA (occupational safety and health administration)
   D) PEPP (payment error prevention program)

REFERENCES: Schraffenberger 2nd Ed, p 299
Green, p 290

33. The term "hard coding" refers to
   A) HCPCS/CPT codes that are coded by the coders
   B) HPCS/CPT codes that appear in the hospital's Chargemaster and will be included automatically on the patient's bill
   C) ICD-9-CM codes that are coded by the coders
   D) ICD-9-CM codes that appear in the hospital's Chargemaster

REFERENCE: Schraffenberger 2nd Ed, p 234-235

34. This is the amount <u>collected</u> by the facility for the services it bills
   A) costs
   B) charges
   C) reimbursement
   D) contractual allowance

REFERENCES: Schraffenberger 2nd Ed, p 278

35. Assume the patient already met his/her deductible and that the physician is a Medicare participating (PAR) provider. The physicians' standard fee for the services provided is $120.00. Medicare's PAR fee is $60.00. How much reimbursement will the physician receive from Medicare?
    A) $120.00
    B) $ 60.00
    C) $ 48.00
    D) $ 96.00

REFERENCES: Green, p 394-395

36. This accounting method attributes a dollar figure to every input required to provide a service
    A) cost
    B) charge
    C) reimbursement
    D) contractual allowance

REFERENCE: Schraffenberger 2nd Ed., p 278

37. This is the amount the facility <u>actually bills</u> for the services it provides
    A) costs
    B) charges
    C) reimbursement
    D) contractual allowance

REFERENCE: Schraffenberger 2nd Ed, p 278

38. This is the <u>difference</u> between what is charged and what is paid
    A) costs
    B) charges
    C) reimbursement
    D) contractual allowance

REFERENCE: Schraffenberger 2nd Ed, p 278

39. When appropriate, under the outpatient PPS, a hospital may use this CPT code in place of, but not in addition to, a code for a medical visit or emergency department service:
    A) CPT Code 99291 (critical care)
    B) CPT Code 99358 (prolonged evaluation and management service)
    C) CPT Code 35001 (direct repair of aneurysm)
    D) CPT Code 50300 (donor nephrectomy)

REFERENCE: Jones (2005), p 34-35

40. To monitor timely claims processing in a hospital, a summary report of "patient receivables" is generated frequently. Aged receivables can negatively affect a facility's cash flow; therefore, to maintain the facility's fiscal integrity, the HIM manager must routinely analyze this report
    A) remittance advice
    B) periodic interim payments
    C) DNFB (discharged, no final bill)
    D) charge master

REFERENCE: LaTour, p 625

41. Assume the patient already met his/her deductible and that the physician is a nonparticipating Medicare provider but does accept assignment. The standard fee for the services provided is $120.00. Medicare's PAR fee is $60.00 and Medicare's nonPAR fee is $57.00. How much reimbursement will the physician receive from Medicare?
   A) $120.00
   B) $60.00
   C) $57.00
   D) $45.60

REFERENCES: Green, p 394-395

42. This program, formerly CHAMPUS (Civilian Health and Medical Program-Uniformed Services), provides coverage for the dependents of armed forces personnel and retirees receiving care outside a military treatment facility.
   A) TRICARE
   B) CHAMPVA
   C) Indian Health Service
   D) Workers Compensation

REFERENCE: Johns, p 341, 352

43. Under Medicare Part B, to "accept assignment" means that the provider or supplier
   A) will be able to collect his/her total charges
   B) agrees to charge no more than 15% (limiting charge) over the allowed charge from the fee schedule
   C) accepts, as payment in full, the allowed charge from the fee schedule
   D) agrees to charge no more than 10% (limiting charge) over the allowed charge from the fee schedule

REFERENCE: Johns, p 394

44. Assume the patient already met his/her deductible and that the physician is a nonPAR physician who does not accept assignment. The physician's standard fee is $120.00. Medicare's nonPAR fee is $57.00. How much reimbursement will the physician receive from Medicare?
   A) $0.00
   B) $120.00
   C) $57.00
   D) $65.55

REFERENCES: Green, p 394-395

45. In the above situation, how much can the physician charge the Medicare beneficiary?
   A) $120.00
   B) $57.00
   C) $65.55
   D) $19.95

REFERENCES: Green, p 394-395

46. If the physician's standard fee for a service is $210.00 and the Medicare PAR fee is $115.00, what is the limiting charge for a nonparticipating (nonPAR) provider?
   A) $241.50
   B) $109.25
   C) $132.25
   D) $125.63

REFERENCES: Green, p 394-395

47. In calculating the fee for a physician's reimbursement, the three relative value units are each multiplied by
    A) geographic practice cost indices
    B) national conversion factor
    C) usual and customary fees for the service
    D) the cost of living index for the particular region

REFERENCES: Green, p 273-274

48. Medicare usually pays for what percentage of the allowed charge?
    A) 100 percent
    B) 50 percent
    C) 75 percent
    D) 80 percent

REFERENCE: Valerius, p 374

49. If a participating provider's usual fee for a service is $700.00 and Medicare's allowed amount is $450.00, what amount is written off by the physician?
    A) none of it is written off
    B) $250.00
    C) $340.00
    D) $391.00

REFERENCE: Valerius, p 373-374

Use the tables below to answer the following questions (#50-#52).

| SAMPLE RVUs | | | | |
|---|---|---|---|---|
| CPT Code | Description | Work RVU | Practice Expense RVU | Malpractice Expense RVU |
| 99203 | Office Visit | 1.34 | 0.64 | 0.05 |
| 99204 | Office Visit | 2.00 | 0.96 | 0.06 |
| 55650 | Vesiculotomy | 22.04 | 30.03 | 2.95 |
| 33400 | Valvuloplasty, aortic valve | 23.55 | 32.51 | 3.07 |
| 43800 | Pyloroplasty | 17.66 | 23.00 | 4.07 |

| SAMPLE GPCIs | | | |
|---|---|---|---|
| City | Work GPCI | Practice Expense GPCI | Malpractice Expense GPCI |
| San Francisco | 1.067 | 1.299 | 1.32 |
| New Orleans | 1.000 | .945 | 1.240 |
| New York City | 1.264 | 1.668 | 1.31 |
| Seattle | 1.648 | 1.465 | 1.09 |

Note: The conversion factor is $37.3374

50. The Medicare Physician Fee Schedule amount associated with this office visit for a new patient with a detailed history and examination, and low-complexity decision making in New Orleans is:
    A) $60.00
    B) $65.50
    C) $70.00
    D) $75.00

REFERENCE: Valerius, p 225-226

51. Using the previous tables, in which city would a physician receive the highest reimbursement for a valvuloplasty?
    A) San Francisco
    B) New Orleans
    C) New York City
    D) Seattle

REFERENCE: Valerius, p 225-226

52. Using the previous tables, in which city would a physician receive the lowest reimbursement for a valvuloplasty?
    A) San Francisco
    B) New Orleans
    C) New York City
    D) Seattle

REFERENCE: Valerius, p 225-226

Answer Key for Medical Billing and Reimbursement Systems

1. D

2. B

3. A

4. B

5. A

6. C

7. C The Medicare Physician Fee Schedule (MPFS) amounts are 5% higher for participating (PAR) providers than for non-participating (nonPAR) providers. Only nonPAR physicians are subject to the "limiting" charge.

8. D

9. D

10. D The limiting charge is 15% above Medicare's approved payment amount for doctors who do <u>not</u> accept assignment. ($128.00 X 1.15 = $147.20)

11. B

12. C CPT code 29884 is an integral component of code 29877; therefore code 29884 can not be reported with code 29877 for this patient. Only code 29877 is reported with the modifier –RT. The fact that code 29884 also specifies that it is a "separate procedure" indicates that this procedure code is commonly carried out as an integral component of a total service or procedure and therefore the codes designated as "separate procedure" should not be reported in addition to the code for the total procedure or service for which it is considered an integral component.

13. A

14. C

15. A

16. A

17. D

18. D

19. B

20. C The annual deductible for Medicare Part B services (which includes physician services) is $110.

21. A If a physician is a participating physician who accepts assignment, he will receive the lesser of "the total charges" or "the Medicare fee schedule amount". In this case the Medicare fee schedule amount is less; therefore, the total received by the physician is $200.00.

22. C If a physician is a non-participating physician who does not accept assignment; he may collect a maximum of 15% (the limiting charge) over the Medicare fee schedule amount. In this case, the Medicare fee schedule amount is $200.00. 15% over this amount is $30.00; therefore, the total that he can collect is $230.00.

23. B The Medicare fee schedule amount is $200.00. The patient must pay the deductible of $110.00. Of the remaining $90.00, the patient is responsible for 20% ($18.00). Medicare will pay 80% ($72.00). Therefore the total financial liability for the patient is $128.00 ($110.00 + $18.00).

24. A If a physician is a non participating physician who does not accept assignment; he my collect a maximum of 15% (the limiting charge) over the Medicare fee scheduled amount. In this case the Medicare fee schedule amount is $200.00. Fifteen percent over this amount is $30.00; therefore the total that he can collect is $230.00. The patient must pay the deductible of $110.00. The patient is responsible for 20%. Medicare will pay 80% ($96.00). Therefore the total financial liability for the patient is $134.00 (110.00+$24.00). Since the physician does <u>not</u> accept assignment, he can balance bill (and collect from the patient) the difference between the Medicare approved amount and the total charges, up to the limiting charge amount.

25. A

26. D

27. A

28. C

29. B GA indicates that a waiver of liability is on file. GZ indicates that an item or service is expected to be denied. GY indicates that an item is statutorily excluded.

30. B Under Medicare Part B, Congress has mandated special incentives to increase the number of health care providers signing PAR (participating) agreements with Medicare. One of those incentives includes a 5% higher fee schedule for PAR providers than for NonPAR (non-participating) providers.

31. A

32. A Local coverage determinations (LCDs) were formerly called local medical review policies (LMRPs)

33. B

34. C

35. C The physician receives 80% of the MPFS amount ($48.00) from Medicare.

36. A

37. B

38. D

39. A When a patient meets the definition of critical care, the hospital must use CPT Code 99291 to bill for outpatient encounters in which critical care services are furnished. This code is used instead of another E&M code.

40. C

41. D The Medicare nonPAR fee is 5% less than the Medicare PAR fee, which is $57.00 ($60.00 x .95 = $57.00).
The physician then receives 80% ($57.00 x .80) of the nonPAR fee, which is $45.60 form Medicare. He will also collect 20% from the patient which is $11.40.

42. A

43. C

44. A A non-participating physician who does not accept assignment receives no money directly from Medicare. The patient receives $45.60 (80% of $57.00) from Medicare.

45. C The physician can charge 115% of the fee listed in Medicare's fee schedule for nonPAR physicians. In this situation that would be 115% of $57.00 or $65.55). The patient's total out of pocket expense is $19.95. Medicare reimbursed the patient $45.60.

46. D

| | | |
|---|---|---|
| Physician's standard fee | $210.00 | |
| Medicare fee | $115.00 | |
| Medicare nonPAR fee | $109.25 | (115.00 x .95) |
| Limiting charge | $125.63 | (109.25 x 1.15) |

47. A

48 . D

49. B The participating physician agrees to accept Medicare's fee as payment in full, therefore the physician would collect $450.00.
The remainder ($700.00 - $450.00 = $250.00) is written off.

50. D The CPT code that is to be reported is 99203 based on the key elements.

(W RVU + PE RVU + M RVU) x conversion factor = payment

| | | |
|---|---|---|
| Work RVU = 1.34 | PE RVU = 0.64 | Malpractice RVU = 0.05 |
| Work GPCI = 1.00 | PE GPCI = .945 | Malpractice GPCI = 1.240 |
| 1.34 x 1 = 1.34 | 0.64 x .945 = .6048 | .05 x 1.240 = .062 |

(1.34 + .6048 + .062) x 37.3374
2.0068 x 37.3374 = $74.92 or $75.00

51. D The physician practicing in Seattle would receive the highest reimbursement.

| | | |
|---|---|---|
| Valvuloplasty | | Work RVU = 23.55 |
| | | PE RVU = 32.51 |
| | | Malpractice RVU = 3.07 |
| San Francisco | | 23.55 x 1.067 = 25.1278 |
| | | 32.51 x 1.299 = 42.2304 |
| | | 3.07 x 1.32 = 4.0524 |
| | Total: | 71.4106 x 37.3374 = $2,666.28 |
| New Orleans | | 23.55 x 1.000 = 23.55 |
| | | 32.51 x .945 = 30.7219 |
| | | 3.07 x 1.240 = 3.8068 |
| | Total: | 58.0787 x 37.3374 = $2,168.50 |
| New York City | | 23.55 x 1.264 = 29.7672 |
| | | 32.51 x 1.668 = 54.2266 |
| | | 3.07 x 1.31 = 4.0217 |
| | Total: | 88.0155 x 37.3374 = $3,286.26 |
| Seattle | | 23.55 x 1.648 = 38.8104 |
| | | 32.51 x 1.465 = 47.6271 |
| | | 3.07 x 1.09 = 3.3463 |
| | Total: | 89.7838 x 37.3374 = $3,352.29 |

The physician practicing in Seattle would receive the highest reimbursement.

52. B See calculations above. The physician practicing in New Orleans would receive the lowest reimbursement.

REFERENCE LIST

Abdelhak, Mervat; Grostick, Sara; Hanken, Mary Alice; Jacobs, Ellen, *Health Information: Management of a Strategic Resource*, 2nd Edition. W. B. Saunders, Philadelphia, PA. 2001.

CMS' website: http://cms.hhs.gov/paymentsystems/ (this website provides links to pages containing official informational materials on all of the Medicare payment systems and coding files.

Federal Register, Department of Health and Human Services-Center for Medicare and Medicaid Services. Vol. 65 No. 68. Medicare Program, "*Prospective Payment System for Hospital Outpatient Services; Final Rule*." Friday, April 7, 2000.

Green, Michelle A and Rowell, JoAnn C. *Understanding Health Insurance: A Guide to Billing and Reimbursement, 8th Edition. Thomson-Delmar Learning, 2006*

Johns, Merida L, *Health Information Management Technology: An Applied Approach* American Health Information Management Association, Chicago, IL. 2002.

Jones, Lolita, *Reimbursement for Hospital Outpatient Services.* American Health Information Management Association. Chicago, IL. 2005.

Jones, Lolita, *Reimbursement Methodologies for Healthcare Services.* American Health Information Management Association. Chicago, IL. 2001.

LaTour, Kathleen and Eichenwald, Shirley, *Health Information Management: Concepts, Principles, and Practice.* American Health Information Management Association. Chicago, IL. 2002.

Schraffenberger, Lou Ann, et al, *Effective Management of Coding Services.* American Health Information Management Association. Chicago, IL. 2005.

Valerius, Joanne, Bayes, Nenna and Newby, Cynthia, *Medical Insurance: A Guide to Coding and Reimbursement, 2nd Edition*, McGraw-Hill, 2005

# Medical Science

Irene L. E. Mueller, EdD, RHIA

# Medical Science

*Irene L. E. Mueller, EdD, RHIA*

According to the breakdown of content for both the RHIA and RHIT exams, medical science type questions have been included in Domain I, Health Care Data. In many instances Medical Science knowledge is virtually a prerequisite in order to be able to work with clinical classification systems such as ICD-9-CM and CPT.

1. The cause of aplastic anemia is
   A) acute blood loss
   B) bone marrow failure
   C) chronic blood loss
   D) inadequate iron intake

2. The most common cause of dementia in the United States is
   A) Autism
   B) Alzheimer Disease
   C) Alcohol abuse
   D) Anxiety disorder

3. Dr. Zambrano ordered a CEA test for Mr. Logan. Dr. Zambrano may be considering a diagnosis of
   A) cancer
   B) carpal tunnel syndrome
   C) cardiomyopathy
   D) congestive heart failure

4. The prevention of illness through vaccination occurs due to the formation of
   A) helper B cells
   B) immunosurveillance
   C) mast cells
   D) memory cells

5. A bee stung little Bobby. He experiences itching, erythema and respiratory distress caused by laryngeal edema and vascular collapse. In the emergency department, Bobby is diagnosed with
   A) allergic rhinitis
   B) allergic sinusitis
   C) anaphylaxic shock
   D) asthma

6. Which one of the following is NOT a function of helper T-cells?
   A) producing antibodies
   B) stimulating immune system as a whole
   C) stimulating macrophages to attack antigen
   D) stimulating plasma cells

7. A patient's history includes the following documentation:
   - Small ulcers (chancres) appeared on the genitalia and disappeared after four to six weeks
   - Elevated temperature, skin rash and enlarged lymph nodes

   Which of the following procedures will be used to initially diagnose the patient?
   A) bone marrow test
   B) chest x-ray
   C) serology test
   D) thyroid scan

8. What cells produce histamine in a Type I hypersensitivity reaction?
   A) Lymphocyte
   B) Macrophages
   C) Mast cells
   D) Neutrophils

9. Which one of the following cells produces antibodies?
   A) A-cells
   B) Cytotoxic T-cells
   C) Helper T-cells
   D) Plasma cells

10. Which of the following conditions is <u>NOT</u> a risk associated with essential hypertension?
    A) Age
    B) Cigarette smoking
    C) Low dietary sodium intake
    D) Obesity

11. A patient, who is HIV positive, has raised lesions, red or purple in color, on the genitals and groin. What is the stage of his disease process?
    A) ARC (AIDS related complex)
    B) Incubation period
    C) Initial infection
    D) Full blown AIDS

12. Each of the following pertains to COPD <u>EXCEPT</u>
    A) pneumonia
    B) chronic bronchitis
    C) emphysema
    D) smoking

13. Which of the following is a lethal arrhythmia?
    A) Atrial fibrillation
    B) Bradycardia
    C) Atrial tachycardia
    D) Ventricular fibrillation

14. The drug used to treat patients during the manic phase of bipolar disease is
    A) lithium carbonate
    B) lasix
    C) lanoxin
    D) lorazepam

15. A vision-related pathology that is caused by diabetes is
    A) retinal detachment
    B) retinoblastoma
    C) retinopathy
    D) rhabdomyosarcoma

16. Penicillin is effective in the treatment of all the following diseases <u>EXCEPT</u>
    A) Legionnaire's disease
    B) Lyme disease
    C) Strep throat
    D) Syphilis

17. Which step in viral replication shuts down host metabolism?
    A) Biosynthesis
    B) Uncoating
    C) Lysis
    D) Adsorption

18. A diagnostic test for meningitis usually involves
    A) blood cultures
    B) cerebrospinal fluid analysis
    C) stool C & S
    D) testing urine

19. Which disease listed below is a malignancy of the lymphatic system?
    A) Cystic fibrosis
    B) Hodgkin's disease
    C) Leukemia
    D) Von Willebrand's disease

20. Jane was diagnosed with bladder carcinoma. Her cancer was staged as T2, N0, M0. This means that Jane's cancer is a/an
    A) carcinoma in situ
    B) invasive tumor invading the detrusor muscle
    C) invasive tumor invading the lamina propria
    D) noninvasive papillary tumor

21. Which of the following autoimmune diseases affects tissues of the urinary system?
    A) Goodpasture syndrome
    B) Hashimoto disease
    C) Myasthenia gravis
    D) Rheumatoid arthritis

22. Pain is a symptom of which of the following conditions?
    A) First degree burn (superficial)
    B) Second degree burn (partial thickness)
    C) Third degree burn (full thickness)
    D) A and B

23. A 75 year old patient has a sore tongue with tingling and numbness of the hands and feet. She has headaches and is fatigued. Following diagnostic workup, the doctor orders monthly injections of vitamin B12. This patient mostly likely has which of the following conditions?
   A) Aplastic anemia
   B) Autoimmune hemolytic anemia
   C) Pernicious anemia
   D) Sickle cell anemia

24. Which one of the following is NOT a pathophysiological factor in anemia?
   A) Excessive RBC breakdown
   B) Lack of RBC maturation
   C) Loss of bone marrow function
   D) Loss of spleen function

25. Most viral diseases are transmitted directly from person to person. Which of the diseases listed below is a viral disease that is transmitted by way of a mosquito vector?
   A) Meningitis
   B) Streptococcus
   C) Mononucleosis
   D) Encephalitis

26. Necrosis extending down to the underlying fascia is characteristic of a decubitus ulcer in stage
   A) One
   B) Two
   C) Three
   D) Four

27. Scabies, a highly contagious condition that produces intense pruritus and rash, is caused by
   A) head lice
   B) itch mites
   C) ringworm
   D) jock itch

28. A physician prescribes a diuretic for his patient. He could be treating any of the following disorders <u>EXCEPT</u>
   A) mitral stenosis
   B) congestive heart failure
   C) pneumonia
   D) pulmonary edema

29. All of the following are examples of direct transmission of a disease <u>EXCEPT</u>
   A) contaminated foods
   B) coughing or sneezing
   C) droplet spread
   D) physical contact

30. Which of the following is the most deadly type of skin cancer?
    A) Squamous cell carcinoma
    B) Oat cell carcinoma
    C) Malignant melanoma
    D) Basal cell carcinoma

31. John Palmer was in a car accident and sustained severe chest trauma resulting in a tension pneumothorax. Manifestations of this disorder include all of the following EXCEPT
    A) bradycardia
    B) dyspnea
    C) hypertension
    D) severe hypoxemia

32. Cancer derived from connective tissue is classified as a/an
    A) adenoma
    B) carcinoma
    C) lipoma
    D) sarcoma

33. Sex-linked genetic diseases
    A) are transmitted during sexual activity
    B) involve a defect on a sex chromosome
    C) occur equally between males and females
    D) occur only in males

34. A stapedectomy is the procedure that cures
    A) atherosclerosis.
    B) multiple sclerosis
    C) otosclerosis.
    D) scoliosis.

35. What key event occurs in the transition between compensated and uncompensated congestive heart failure?
    A) Increase pulmonary pressure
    B) Increase renal blood flow
    C) Decreased collateral blood flow
    D) Loss of kidney function

36. Which of the following sequences correctly depicts the flow of blood through the heart to the lungs?
    A) Right atrium, right ventricle, lungs, pulmonary artery
    B) Right atrium, right ventricle, pulmonary artery, lungs
    C) Right ventricle, right atrium, lungs, pulmonary artery
    D) Right ventricle, right atrium, pulmonary artery, lungs

37. Diastole occurs when
    A) cardiac insufficiency is present
    B) the atria contracts
    C) the ventricles contract
    D) the ventricles fill

38. The most fatal type of lung cancer is
    A) adenocarcinoma
    B) large cell cancer
    C) small cell cancer
    D) squamous cell cancer

39. Gas exchange in the lungs takes place at the
    A) alveoli
    B) bronchi
    C) bronchioles
    D) trachea

40. Oxygen is carried in the blood
    A) bound to hemoglobin
    B) in the form of carbonic acid
    C) plasma
    D) serum

41. Which of the following anatomical parts is involved in both the respiratory and digestive systems?
    A) Trachea
    B) Pharynx
    C) Nasal cavity
    D) Larynx

42. A disease of the ear that causes vertigo is
    A) labyrinthitis
    B) mastoiditis
    C) Meniere disease
    D) A and C

43. A properly functioning "sodium pump" will
    A) actively transport potassium out of the cell
    B) actively transport potassium into the cell
    C) passively transport sodium out of the cell
    D) actively transport sodium into the cell

44. A pathological diagnosis of transitional cell carcinoma is made. The examined tissue was removed from the
    A) esophagus
    B) pleura
    C) bladder
    D) oral cavity

45. Most carbon dioxide is carried in the
    A) blood as CO2 gas
    B) blood bound to hemoglobin
    C) blood plasma in the form of carbonic acid
    D) red blood cells

46. The key diagnostic finding for typical pneumonia is a/an
    A) abnormal blood electrolytes
    B) lung consolidation-x-ray
    C) elevated WBC
    D) positive sputum culture

47. The presence of fluid in the alveoli of the lungs is characteristic of
    A) COPD
    B) Crohn's disease
    C) pneumonia
    D) tuberculosis

48. Full-blown AIDS sets in as
    A) HIV virus concentration decreases
    B) immunity to HIV increases
    C) helper T-cell concentration decreases
    D) CD4 receptors increase

49. Which of the following best describes tuberculosis?
    A) An ordinary lung infection
    B) An acute bacterial infection of the lung
    C) A chronic, systemic disease whose initial infection is in the lungs
    D) A viral infection of the lungs

50. The result of a patient's Papanicolaou smear is reported as class IV. This indicates the examined cells are
    A) conclusively malignant
    B) abnormal-malignancy strongly suggested
    C) atypical-no malignancy evident
    D) atypical-malignancy suggested

51. Mary Mulholland has diabetes. Her physician has told her about some factors that put her more at risk for infections. Which of the following factors would probably NOT be applicable?
    A) Increased glucose in body fluids
    B) Increased blood supply
    C) Hypoxia
    D) A & C

52. Most of the digestion of food and absorption of nutrients occurs in the
    A) ascending colon
    B) esophagus
    C) small intestine
    D) stomach

53. The Phalen wrist flexor test is a noninvasive method for diagnosing
    A) carpal tunnel syndrome
    B) Down syndrome
    C) severe acute respiratory syndrome
    D) Tourette syndrome

54. Ulcerations of the small intestine are characteristic of
    A) appendicitis
    B) Crohn's disease
    C) Grave disease
    D) diverticulitis

55. The patient's pathology report revealed the presence of Reed-Sternberg cells. This is indicative of
    A) Hodgkin lymphoma
    B) leukemia
    C) non-Hodgkin lymphoma
    D) sarcoma

56. Colorectal cancer usually arises from
    A) cells of the muscularis
    B) cells of the serosa
    C) diverticula
    D) polyps

57. Which of the following is NOT a diagnostic or screening test for colorectal cancer?
    A) CEA blood test
    B) Sigmoidoscopy
    C) Stool occult blood
    D) Upper GI X-Ray

58. Which of the following is <u>NOT</u> an identified risk factor for colorectal cancer?
    A) Alcohol use
    B) Cancer elsewhere in body
    C) Obesity
    D) High fiber diet

59. In general, excessive RBC breakdown could result in
    A) high bilirubin levels
    B) elevated BUN
    C) Crohn's disease
    D) peptic ulcers

60. The most common blood borne infection on the United State is
    A) helicobacter pylori
    B) hepatitis A
    C) hepatitis C
    D) hemophilia

61. The first stage of alcoholic liver disease is
    A) alcoholic hepatitis
    B) cirrhosis
    C) fatty liver
    D) jaundice

62. Portal hypertension can contribute to all of the following EXCEPT
   A) ascites
   B) dilation of blood vessels lining intestinal tract
   C) esophageal varices
   D) kidney failure

63. Which of the following is a liver function test?
   A) AST (SGOT)
   B) BUN
   C) ECG
   D) TSH

64. Which of the following is a risk factor involved in the etiology of gall stones?
   A) Being overweight
   B) Being an adolescent
   C) Low fat diets
   D) Presence of peptic ulcer

65. A serum potassium level of 2.8 would indicate
   A) Addison's disease
   B) anemia
   C) diabetic ketoacidosis
   D) hyperkalemia

66. A procedure performed with an instrument that freezes and destroys abnormal tissues (including seborrheic keratoses, basal cell carcinomas, and squamous cell carcinomas) is
   A) cryosurgery
   B) electrodesiccation
   C) phacoemulsification
   D) photocautery

67. Which of the organs listed below has endocrine and exocrine functions?
   A) Kidney
   B) Liver
   C) Lung
   D) Pancreas

68. Which of the following is an effect of insulin?
   A) Decreases glycogen concentration in liver
   B) Increases blood glucose
   C) Increases the breakdown of fats
   D) Increases glucose metabolism

69. A sweat test was done on a patient with the following symptoms: frequent respiratory infections, chronic cough and foul smelling bloody stools. Which of the following diseases is probably suspected?
   A) Cystic breast disease
   B) Cystic fibrosis
   C) Cystic lung disease
   D) Cystic pancreatic disease

70. Which of the following disease manifestations is NOT associated with a myocardial infarction?
   A) Severe pain, relieved by Nitroglycerine
   B) Intractable indigestion
   C) Sympathetic nerve induced sweating
   D) Clammy skin due to peripheral vasoconstriction

71. Diabetic microvascular disease occurs
   A) as a direct result of elevated serum glucose
   B) as a result of elevated fat in blood
   C) due to damage to nerve cells
   D) only in Type I diabetics

72. Lean build, lack of family history, early age of onset and insulin dependency are all characteristics of
   A) Type I diabetes
   B) Type II diabetes
   C) Type III diabetes
   D) Type IV diabetes

73. An elevated serum amylase would be characteristic of
   A) acute pancreatitis
   B) gall bladder disease
   C) post-renal failure
   D) pre-renal failure

74. Clinical manifestations of this disease includes: polydipsia, polyuria, weight loss and hyperglycemia. Which of the following tests would be ordered to confirm the disease?
   A) Fasting blood sugar
   B) Glucagon
   C) Glucose tolerance test
   D) Postprandial blood sugar

75. Common kidney stone treatments that allow small particles to be flushed out of the body naturally include all of the following EXCEPT
   A) extracorporeal shock wave lithotripsy
   B) fluid hydration
   C) ureteroscopy and stone basketing
   D) using medication to dissolve the stone

76. Which of the following best summarizes the formation of urine?
   A) Unwanted substances are selectively transported into urine
   B) Wanted substances are selectively removed from urine
   C) Only waste products are selectively added to the urine as it forms
   D) Wanted substances are selectively transformed into urine

77. The patient has no visible bleeding but remains anemic. Her physician is concerned about possible gastrointestinal bleeding. Which of the following tests might be ordered?
   A) DEXA scan
   B) Guaiac smear test
   C) Pap smear test
   D) Prostatic specific antigen test

78. Which of the following tests is NOT part of a liver panel?
   A) Albumin
   B) Alkaline phosphatase
   C) Bilirubin
   D) Creatinine

79. Maria Giovanni is in the hospital recovering from surgery. Based on her symptoms, her doctors are concerned about the possibility that she has developed a pulmonary embolism. Which of the following procedures will provide the definitive diagnosis?
   A) Chest x-ray
   B) Lung scan
   C) Pulmonary angiography
   D) None of the above

80. Foaming urine due to excess protein in the urine is a symptom of which of the following diseases?
   A) Acute glomerulonephritis
   B) Bladder cancer
   C) Peptic ulcer
   D) Prostate cancer

81. Which of the following is a congenital condition that is the most severe neural tube defect?
   A) Meningocele
   B) Myelomeningocele
   C) Spina bifida occulta
   D) Severe combined immunodeficiency

82. Which of the following tubes conveys sperm from the seminal vesicle to the urethra?
   A) Ejaculatory duct
   B) Epididymis
   C) Prostate
   D) Vas deferens

83. The most common type of vaginitis is
   A) bacterial
   B) protozoan
   C) viral
   D) yeast

84. Five to ten percent of the patients with an inherited defect of the BRCA1 or BRCA2 gene are at risk for developing
   A) brain carcinoma
   B) breast carcinoma
   C) bronchial carcinoma
   D) none of the above

85. A patient with this type of anemia will have red blood cells that microscopically appear hypochromic and microcytic.
   A) Aplastic
   B) Folic acid
   C) Iron deficiency
   D) Vitamin B12

86. _________ is usually the first symptom of benign prostate hyperplasia.
   A) Abdominal pain
   B) Burning pain during urination
   C) Difficulty in urinating
   D) Pelvic pain

87. The hypothalamus, thalamus, and pituitary gland are all parts of the
   A) brain stem
   B) cerebellum
   C) cerebrum
   D) limbic system

88. Which of the following best summarizes the prognosis for cervical cancer?
   A) All stages have extremely high cure rates
   B) All stages have extremely poor cure rates
   C) Cure rate is high only when conization of cervix occurs
   D) Virtual 100% cure rate if cervical intraepithelial neoplasia

89. Sudden Infant Death Syndrome (SIDS) risk factors include
   A) mother is younger than 20
   B) smoking during pregnancy
   C) being a male
   D) all of the above

90. Decrease in blood pressure, salivation and heart rate are examples of
   A) sympathetic nervous system responses
   B) parasympathetic nervous system responses
   C) automatic nervous system responses
   D) higher brain function

91. Photophobia or visual aura preceding a headache is characteristic of
   A) malnutrition
   B) classic migraines
   C) mastitis
   D) myasthenia gravis

92. Grave Disease
   A) is an autoimmune disease
   B) most commonly affects males
   C) usually can not be treated
   D) usually affects the elderly

93. "Pill-rolling" tremor is a characteristic symptom of
   A) epilepsy
   B) Guillain Barre syndrome
   C) myasthenia gravis
   D) Parkinson's disease

94. Rheumatoid arthritis typically affects the
   A) intervertebral disks
   B) knees and elbows
   C) small joints of the hands and feet
   D) weight bearing joints

95. Henry experienced sudden sharp chest pain that he described as heavy and crushing. His pain and past medical history caused Dr. James to suspect that Henry was having a myocardial infarction. Which of the following tests is a more specific marker for a MI?
   A) CK-MB
   B) LDH1
   C) AST
   D) Troponin I

96. Bone mass density is a useful diagnostic test for
   A) osteoarthritis
   B) osteomyelitis
   C) osteoporosis
   D) rheumatoid arthritis

97. A patient is on Coumadin therapy. Which of the following tests is commonly ordered to monitor the patient's Coumadin levels?
   A) Bleeding time
   B) Blood smear
   C) Partial thromboplastin time
   D) Prothrombin time

98. A toxic goiter has what distinguishing characteristic?
   A) Iodine deficiency
   B) Parathyroid involvement
   C) Presence of muscle spasm
   D) Thyroid hyperfunction

99. How can Grave disease be treated?
   A) Antithyroid drugs
   B) Radioactive iodine therapy
   C) Surgery
   D) All of the above

100. Fractures occur in patients with osteoporosis due to
   A) falling from loss of balance
   B) fibrous joint adhesions tearing apart small bones
   C) loss of bone mass
   D) tendency to fall from lack of joint mobility

Answer Key for Medical Science

1. B
2. B
3. A
4. D
5. C
6. A
7. C
8. C
9. D
10. C
11. D
12. A
13. D
14. A
15. C
16. A
17. A
18. B
19. B
20. B
21. A
22. D
23. C
24. D
25. D
26. C
27. B
28. C
29. A
30. C
31. C
32. D
33. B
34. C
35. D
36. B
37. D
38. C
39. A
40. A
41. B
42. D
43. B
44. C
45. D
46. B
47. C
48. C
49. C
50. B
51. B

Answer Key for Medical Science

52. C
53. A
54. B
55. A
56. D
57. D
58. D
59. A
60. C
61. C
62. D
63. A
64. A
65. C
66. A
67. D
68. D
69. B
70. A
71. A
72. A
73. A
74. C
75. C
76. B
77. B
78. D
79. C
80. A
81. B
82. A
83. A
84. B
85. C
86. C
87. D
88. D
89. D
90. B
91. B
92. A
93. D
94. C
95. D
96. C
97. D
98. D
99. D
100. C

REFERENCE LIST:


American Medical Association Encyclopedia of Medicine
Published by: AMA
Chicago, IL

Boyd's Introduction to the Study of Disease
Published by: Lea & Febiger
Philadelphia, Pa

Essentials of Human Diseases and Conditions, 3rd Ed.
Published by: Elsevier Saunders
St. Louis, MO

The MERCK MANUAL of Diagnosis and Therapy
Published by: Merck & Co., Inc.
Rathway, NJ

Mosby's Medica, Nursing, & Allied Health Dictionary
Published by: Mosby
St. Louis, MO

Pathology for the Health-Related Professions
Published by: W. B. Saunders Company
Philadelphia, PA

Taber's Cyclopedic Medical Dictionary
Published by: F. A. Davis Company
Philadelphia, PA

# ICD-9-CM Coding

Carol Venable, MPH, RHIA, FAHIMA

# ICD-9-CM CODING

*Carol Venable, MPH, RHIA, FAHIMA*

In the multiple choice questions in Part I of the computerized examination, you will not be using your coding book. All necessary information needed to answer the questions will be provided in the question, in the answer keys or as an exhibit. You will use your knowledge of coding guidelines and conventions to select the most correct choice.

Rather than providing everything you need to answer our questions, we want you to use your code books to answer the questions. We believe that it is imperative that you use your code book in the questions. In this way, you gain knowledge and refresh your knowledge of the coding guidelines and how they are applied. This practice using the code book will also help in increasing your speed in looking up the codes when you are coding the cases in Part II of the examination.

Some resources and references for ICD-9-CM coding include:

Basic ICD-9-CM coding (2006)
Lou Ann Schraffenberger, Lou Ann, CCS, CCS-P
American Health Information Management Association (AHIMA)

*ICD-9-CM Coding Handbook*, (2006)
Brown, Faye
American Hospital Association, Chicago, IL

*Coding Clinic*
American Hospital Association, Chicago, IL

*Step by Step Coding, 2005 Edition*
Buck, Carol
W. B. Saunders, Philadelphia, PA

Also, there is a complete line of coding textbooks and reference books available from AHIMA.

You can contact them by phone at: 312-223-1100 or order on line at their web site: www.ahima.org.

**Last, but not least, make sure that you refer to the AHIMA Candidate Handbook to review directions and any specific coding information concerning the examination.**

Infectious and Parasitic Diseases

1. Patient is admitted with a left ankle fracture. Patient also has AIDS with Kaposi's sarcoma of the skin.
   A) 042, 176.0, 824.8
   B) 824.8, 176.0, V08
   C) 176.1, 824.8, V08
   D) 824.8, 042, 176.0

Reference: Brown, p 91-92, 315, 319-320
Schraffenberger, p 70

2. Septicemia due to methicillin resistant staphylococcus aureus. Patient also was admitted with septic shock and decubitus ulcer of the sacrum.
   A) 038.19, 785.59, 707.0,
   B) 038.11, V09.0, 707.03, 995.92, 785.52
   C) 707.0, 038.11, 785.59
   D) 038.11, 755.59, 995.92

Reference: Brown, p 85-87, 188-189
Schraffenberger, p 65-66

3. Nephropathy due to tuberculosis (confirmed histologically) of the kidney.
   A) 016.05, 583.81
   B) 583.81, 016.0
   C) 016.0, 583.81
   D) 016.01, 583.81

Reference: Brown, p 85, 174
Schraffenberger, p 65

4. A patient is admitted with fever and severe headache. Diagnostic workup revealed viral meningitis. Patient also has asthma with acute exacerbation and hypertension, both of which are treated.
   A) 047.9, 780.6, 784.0, 493.90, 401.9
   B) 047.8, 493.92, 401.1
   C) 047.9, 493.92, 401.9
   D) 780.6, 784.0, 047.9, 493.90, 401.9

Reference: Brown, p 83, 127, 146, 266-267
Schraffenberger, p 111-112, 122-123 150-151

5. Nurse Jones suffers a needle stick and presents for HIV testing. She sees her physician for the test results and counseling.
   A) V72.6, 795.71
   B) 795.71, V65.8
   C) V08, V72.6, V65.44
   D) V73.89, V65.44, V01.79, V01.79

Reference: Brown, p 91
Schraffenberger, p 70

6. Right arm paralysis due to poliomyelitis that patient suffered as a child.
   A) 045.11, 342.81
   B) 138, 344.41
   C) 344.40, 138
   D) 138, 342.81

Reference: Brown, p 84-85
Schraffenberger, p 67

Neoplasms

7. Patient is admitted for chemotherapy for treatment of breast cancer with liver metastasis. Patient had a mastectomy 4 months ago.
   A) 197.7, V10.3
   B) 174.9, 197.7
   C) V58.11, V10.3, 197.7
   D) V58.11, 174.9, V45.71 197.7

Reference: Brown, p 289-290, 293-294, 299-302
Schraffenberger, p 76-77, 84-87

8. Patient with a history of malignant neoplasm of the lung is admitted with seizures. Work up revealed metastasis of the lung cancer to the brain.
   A) 780.39, V10.11, 198.3
   B) 162.9, V10.11, 198.3, 780.39
   C) 198.3, 780.39, V10.11
   D) 198.3, 780.39, 162.9

Reference: Brown, p 289-290, 293-294
Schraffenberger, p 76-77, 85-87

9. Patient is admitted to the hospital for treatment of dehydration following chemotherapy as treatment for ovarian cancer.
   A) 276.51, 183.0
   B) 183.0, 276.51
   C) 276.51, 183.0
   D) 183.0, 276.51

Reference: Brown, p 300-301
Schraffenberger, p 81-83

10. Malignant melanoma, skin of back.
   A) 173.5, 86.4
   B) 172.5, 86.4
   C) 173.5, 86.3
   D) 172.5, 86.3

Reference: Brown, p 287
Schraffenberger, p 81-82

11. Patient is admitted with abdominal pain. Needle biopsy of the liver reveals secondary malignancy of the liver. Primary site is unknown at time of discharge.
   A) 197.7, 199.10
   B) 197.7, 789.00
   C) 197.7, 199.1
   D) 197.7, 199.01

Reference: Brown, p 293-294
Schraffenberger, p 76-77

12. Patient with a history of cancer of the colon and status post colostomy is admitted for closure of the colostomy. Patient is also being treated for chronic obstructive pulmonary disease and diastolic heart failure.
   A) 153.2, 496, 482.30
   B) V55.3, 496, V10.05: 428.30
   C) V55.3, 496, V10.05: 428.0
   D) V55.3, 492.8, 428.30

Reference: Brown, p 145, 300
Schraffenberger, p 76-77, 274-277

Endocrine, Nutritional, and Metabolic Disorders and Immunity Disorders

13. Female, 68 years old was admitted with Type I diabetes mellitus with a diabetic ulcer of the left heel.
   A) 250.80, 707.14
   B) 707.14, 250.80
   C) 250.81, 707.0
   D) 250.82, 707.14

Reference: Brown, p 95-96, 98, 190
Schraffenberger, p 91-94, 198

14. Sixty seven year old is admitted with acute dehydration secondary to nausea and vomiting that is due to acute gastroenteritis. Patient is treated for dehydration.
   A) 558.9, 787.01, 276.51
   B) 558.9, 787.01, 276.5
   C) 276.51, 787.01, 558.9
   D) 276.51, 558.9

Reference: Brown, p 37
Schraffenberger, p 44, 94-95

15. Hyperthyroidism with exophthalmic goiter.
   A) 242.02
   B) 242.00
   C) 242.01
   D) 242.11

Reference: ICD-9-Code book

16. Aplastic anemia secondary to chemotherapy administered for multiple myeloma.
   A) 284.8, 203.00, E933.1
   B) 203.00, 284.8, E933.1
   C) 284.9, 203.00, E933.1
   D) 203.01, 284.8, E933.1

Reference: Brown, p 121, 300
Schraffenberger, p 96, 161

17. Male patient admitted with gastrointestinal hemorrhage resulting in acute blood loss anemia. Source of bleed unknown.
    A) 285.9, 578.1
    B) 578.1, 285.1
    C) 578.9, 285.1
    D) 578.9, 280.0

Reference: Brown, p 120-121, 157
Schraffenberger, p 44, 97-98, 162-163

18. Severe malnutrition.
    A) 263.9
    B) 261
    C) 262
    D) 263.8

Reference: Brown, p 101

<u>Diseases of the Blood and Blood-Forming Organs</u>

19. Thrombocytopenia, purpura
    A) 287.4
    B) 287.8
    C) 287.9
    D) 287.30

Reference: Schraffenberger, p 99

20. Sickle cell anemia with crisis
    A) 282.61
    B) 282.62
    C) 282.63
    D) 282.69

Reference: Brown, p 122
Schraffenberger, p 98

21. Sickle cell pain crisis
    A) 282.62
    B) 282.60
    C) 282.5
    D) 282.42

Reference: Brown, p. 122
Schraffenberger, p. 98

22. Anemia, neutropenia, and thrombocytopenia
    A) 285.9, 288.0, 287.5
    B) 288.0, 287.5, 285.9
    C) 284.8
    D) 285.29

Reference: Brown, p. 121

23. Anemia due to end stage renal disease, patient treated for anemia.
   A) 285.8
   B) 285.21, 585
   C) 285.2, 585
   D) 285.9

Reference: Brown, p 121
Schraffenberger, p 98

24. Pernicious anemia
   A) 280.9
   B) 280.8
   C) 281.1
   D) 281.0

Reference: Brown, p 119
Schraffenberger, p 97-98

Mental Disorders

25. Mild mental retardation due to old viral encephalitis.
   A) 319, 049.8
   B) 317, 326
   C) 317, 047.8
   D) 317, 139.0

Reference: Brown, p 84
Schraffenberger, p 87

26. Anxiety with depression
   A) 300.11, 311
   B) 300.4
   C) 309.28
   D) 300.00, 311

Reference: Brown, p 109

27. Delirium tremens with alcohol dependence
   A) 291.0, 303.90
   B) 303.91, 291.0
   C) 291.3, 303.90
   D) 291.0, 303.00

Reference: Brown, p 113
Schraffenberger, p 108

28. Latent schizophrenia, chronic with acute exacerbation.
   A) 295.52
   B) 295.55
   C) 295.54
   D) 295.53

Reference: Brown, p 107
Schraffenberger, p 105-106

29. Chronic paranoia due to continuous cocaine dependence.
   A) 301.0, 305.61
   B) 297.1, 304.21
   C) 297.1, 305.61
   D) 297.1, 301.0
Reference: Brown, p 113
Schraffenberger, p 104-105

30. Attention deficit disorder with hyperactivity
   A) 314.2
   B) 314.8
   C) 314.00
   D) 314.01
Reference: ICD-9-CM Code Book

Diseases of the Nervous System and Sense Organs

31. A five-year-old female is admitted to ambulatory surgery with chronic otitis media.
   A) 382.95
   B) 381.3
   C) 382.9
   D) 381.89
Reference: Schraffenberger, p 115-116

32. Patient is a type II diabetic with a diabetic cataract.
   A) 250.51, 366.42
   B) 250.50, 366.41
   C) 250.52, 366.41
   D) 366.41, 250.50
Reference: Brown, p 97, 135
Schraffenberger, p 114-115

33. Epilepsy and paraplegia as residuals of a head injury suffered five years ago.
   A) 345.90, 344.1, 907.0
   B) 345.91, 344.1, 907.0
   C) 959.01, 345.90, 344.1
   D) 345.81, 344.2, 907.0
Reference: Brown, p 128
Schraffenberger, p 112-113

34. Alzheimer's disease with dementia
   A) 331.0, 294.8
   B) 294.8
   C) 331.0, 294.10
   D) 331.0
Reference: Brown, p 106
Schraffenberger, p 105-106

35. Communicating hydrocephalus.
    A) 331.2
    B) 331.3
    C) 331.4
    D) 331.3, 294.11

Reference: ICD-9-CM code book

36. Carpal tunnel syndromel.
    A) 354.1
    B) 354.2
    C) 354.3
    D) 354.0

Reference: Brown, p 131

<u>Diseases of the Circulatory System</u>

37. Patient admitted with carotid artery disease and acute cerebral infarction with left hemiparesis, dysphagia and aphasia. Dysphagia and aphasia have resolved by discharge, but residual hemiparesis remains.
    A) 433.11, 342.90
    B) 433.11, 434.91, 342.90, 784.3, 787.2
    C) 436, 342.90, 784.3, 787.2
    D) 434.91, 342.90

Reference: Brown, p 263-264
Schraffenberger, p 136-138

38. Hypertensive kidney disease, congestive heart failure and acute systolic heart failure.
    A) 404.93
    B) 404.11, 428.0, 428.21
    C) 403.90, 428.0, 428.21
    D) 404.91

Reference: Brown, p 267
Schraffenberger, p 123-126

39. Acute inferior wall myocardial infarction with unstable angina. Patient also has coronary artery disease and atrial fibrillation.
    A) 410.41, 411.1, 414.01, 427.31
    B) 410.41, 414.00, 411.1, 427.31
    C) 410.40, 414.00, 427.31
    D) 410.41, 414.01, 427.31

Reference: Brown, p 255-256, 258
Schraffenberger, p 127-128, 134-135

40. Patient with a diagnosis of aortic valve stenosis and mitral valve regurgitation is admitted for aortic valve replacement. Patient is also under treatment for congestive heart failure.
    A) 396.2, 398.91
    B) 424.1, 424.0, 428.0
    C) 396.2, 428.0
    D) 424.1, 424.0, 428.0

Reference: Brown, p 260-261
Schraffenberger, p 120, 132-135

41. Atherosclerotic peripheral vascular disease of the lower leg with claudication.
   A) 440.20
   B) 440.21
   C) 444.22
   D) 443.9

Reference: Brown, p 269-270
Schraffenberger, p 130-132

<u>Diseases of the Respiratory System</u>

42. Patient presents to the outpatient department for a chest x-ray. Physician order lists the following reasons for the chest x-ray: fever and cough, rule out pneumonia. Radiologist reports the chest x-ray is positive for pneumonia.
   A) 486
   B) 780.6, 786.2, V72.5
   C) 780.6, 786.2
   D) V72.5, 780.6, 786.2

Reference: Brown, p 141
Schraffenberger, 148-150

43. Aspiration pneumonia with pneumonia due to staphylococcus aureus. Patient also has emphysema.
   A) 507.0, 482.9, 496
   B) 507.0, 482.41, 496
   C) 507.0, 491.21
   D) 507.0, 482.41, 492.8

Reference: Brown, p 143
Schraffenberger, p 148-150

44. Acute respiratory failure due to congestive heart failure.
   A) 518.81, 428.0
   B) 518.81, 428.1
   C) 428.0, 518.81
   D) 428.0, 518.80

Reference: Brown, p 148-150
Schraffenberger, p 151-154

45. Hypertrophic tonsillitis.
   A) 463
   B) 474.00
   C) 474.02
   D) 463

Reference: ICD-9-CM code book

46. Chronic obstructive pulmonary disease with an exacerbation of acute bronchitis.
   A) 491.22
   B) 496, 466.0
   C) 466.0, 496
   D) 491.22, 466.0

Reference: Brown, p 145-146
Schraffenberger, p 147-148

47. Extrinsic asthma with status asthmaticus
    A) 493.11
    B) 493.90
    C) 493.01
    D) 493.81

Reference: Brown, p. 146
Schraffenberger, p. 150-154

48. Exacerbation of myasthenia gravis resulting in acute respiratory failure.
    A) 358.00, 518.81
    B) 518.81, 358.01
    C) 358.00, 581.82
    D) 518.82, 358.00

Reference: Brown, p 148-150
Schraffenberger, p 151-154

Disease of the Digestive System

49. Patient admitted to the hospital for repair of ventral hernia. Surgery is cancelled after chest x-ray revealed lower lobe pneumonia. Patient is placed on antibiotics to treat the pneumonia.
    A) 553.20, 486, V64.1
    B) 486, 553.20, V64.1
    C) 486, 553.20
    D) 553.20, 486, 54.11

Reference: Brown, p 54-55, 142, 164
Schraffenberger, p 46, 148-150

50. Gastric ulcer with hemorrhage resulting in acute blood loss anemia.
    A) 531.20, 285.1
    B) 285.1, 531.20
    C) 531.40, 280.0
    D) 531.40, 285.1

Reference: Brown, p 119-121, 158
Schraffenberger, p 97-98, 159-160

51. Diverticulitis large bowel with abscess.
    A) 562.10
    B) 562.11
    C) 562.11, 569.5
    D) 562.10, 569.5

Reference: Brown, p 160
Schraffenberger, p 166

52. Acute and chronic cholecystitis with cholelithiasis.
    A) 574.00, 574.10, V64.41
    B) 574.00, 574.10
    C) 574.00
    D) 574.00, V64.41

Reference: Brown, p 162-163
Schraffenberger, p 155

53. Bleeding esophageal varices with alcoholic liver cirrhosis and portal hypertension. Patient is alcohol dependent.
    A) 456.20, 571.2, 303.90
    B) 571.2, 456.20, 303.90, 280.0
    C) 572.3, 571.2, 303.90, 456.20
    D) 303.90, 456.20, 303.90

Reference: Brown, p 50, 111-113, 158
Schraffenberger, p 107

54. Patient is admitted for work up for melena. Laboratory results reveal chronic blood loss anemia. Crohn's disease of the descending colon.
    A) 578.1, 555.1
    B) 555.1
    C) 555.2, 578.1
    D) 555.1, 578.1

Reference: Brown, p 119-122
Schraffenberger, p 97-98, 161

<u>Diseases of the Genitourinary System</u>

55. Acute urinary tract infection due to E. coli.
    A) 599.0, 041.4
    B) 599.0
    C) 041.4, 599.0
    D) 590.2, 041.4

Reference: Brown, p 87
Schraffenberger, p 170-171

56. Patient presents with complaint of gross hematuria. Diagnosis of benign prostatic hypertrophy is made.
    A) 600.01
    B) 600.00
    C) 600.00, 599.7
    D) 600.01, 599.7

Reference: Brown, p 177-178
Schraffenberger, p 171

57. Male patient presents to the ER in acute renal failure; also being treated for hypertension
    A) 410.00, 586
    B) 401.9, 584.9
    C) 585.9, 401.1
    D) 584.9, 401.9

Reference: Brown, p. 174

58. Hemorrhagic cystitis.
    A) 595.9
    B) 595.9, 041.4
    C) 595.8,
    D) 596.7

Reference: Brown, p 171
Schraffenberger, p 170-171

59. Urethral calculus.
    A) 594.1
    B) 594.0
    C) 594.2
    D) 594.3

Reference: ICD-9-CM code book

60. End-stage kidney disease which resulted from malignant hypertension
    A) 403.01
    B) 585.9, 401.0
    C) 403.00
    D) 401.0, 585.9

Reference: Brown, p. 173-175
Schraffenberger, p 169-170

<u>Obstetrics</u>

61. Vaginal delivery of a full term live born infant.
    A) 650, V27.0
    B) 648.91, V27.0
    C) 650, 648.91, V27.0
    D) 650. V27.0, 73.59, 66.32

Reference: Brown, p 207-208, 210-211, 218-220
Schraffenberger, p 185-186

62. Incomplete abortion complicated by excessive hemorrhage.
    A) 634.12
    B) 634.12, 285.1
    C) 634.11
    D) 634.91

Reference: Brown, p 225-227
Schraffenberger, p 177-181

63. Obstructed labor due to breech presentation; single liveborn delivered via Cesarean section.
    A) 660.52
    B) 660.01, 652.21, V27.0
    C) 660.01, V27.0
    D) 660.51, 652.21

Reference: Brown, p 207-208, 211-212
Schraffenberger, p 186-188, 191, 193-194

64. Delivery of a single newborn at 43 weeks gestation; manually assisted delivery.
    A) 650, V27.0
    B) 645.22, V27.0
    C) 644.21, V27.0
    D) 645.21, V27.0

Reference: Brown, p 207-212
Schraffenberger, p 182-188

65. Female, 26 weeks pregnancy is treated for a fractured distal radius and ulna.
    A) 813.44
    B) 648.93, 813.44
    C) 813.44, V22.2
    D) V22.2, 813.44

Reference: Brown, p 204, 207
Schraffenberger, p 183, 187-188

66. Patient diagnosed with tubal pregnancy.
    A) 633.20
    B) 633.11
    C) 633.00
    D) 633.10

Reference: Brown, p. 230-231
Schraffenberger, p. 183

Diseases of the Skin and Subcutaneous Tissue

67. Abscess with cellulitis of the abdominal wall. Culture is positive for staph aureus.
    A) 682.8, 041.11
    B) 682.2, 041.11
    C) 682.2 707.8
    D) 682.2

Reference: Brown, p 188-189
Schraffenberger, p 197-198

68. Scar contracture skin of hand as a late effect of burn
    A) 701.4
    B) 709.2
    C) 906.8
    D) 709.2, 906.6

Reference: ICD-9-CM code book

69. Chronic ulcers of the calf and back.
    A) 707.12, 707.8
    B) 707.8, 707.8
    C) 707.8
    D) 707.12

Reference: Brown, p 187-188, 190
Schraffenberger, p 198, 200-201

70. Dermatitis due to prescription topical antibiotic cream used as directed by physician.
    A) 692.4
    B) 692.3, E930.9
    C) 692.3
    D) 692.3, E930.1

Reference: Brown, p 187
Schraffenberger, p 198

71. Boil, left face.
   A) 680.0
   B) 680.1
   C) 680.8
   D) 680.9

Reference: Brown, p 187

72. Abscessed pilonidal cyst.
   A) 685.1
   B) 685.09
   C) 685.0
   D) 685.11

Reference: Brown, p 187

<u>Diseases of the Musculoskeletal System and Connective Tissue</u>

73. Pathological fracture of the femur due to metastatic bone cancer. Patient has a history of lung cancer.
   A) 198.5, 733.14, V10.11
   B) 733.14, 198.5, V10.11
   C) 821.00, 198.5, V10.11
   D) 821.00, 162.2, 162.9

Reference: Brown, p 198-199
Schraffenberger, p 76-77

74. Herniated lumbar intervertebral disc with paresthesia.
   A) 722.11
   B) 839.20
   C) 722.10, 839.20
   D) 722.10

Reference: Brown, p 195-196
Schraffenberger, p 204-205

75. Pyogenic arthritis of the hip due to Group A Streptococcus
   A) 716.95, 041.01
   B) 715.95, 041.01
   C) 711.05, 041.01
   D) 711.05

Reference: Brown, p 196
Schraffenberger, p 203-204

76. Bunion left foot and hammertoe right foot; Keller procedure and hammer toe repair performed.
   A) 727.1, 735.4
   B) 727.1, 735.3
   C) 727.2, 735.3
   D) 727.1, 735.5

Reference: ICD-9-CM code book

77. Malunion of humeral fracture (original injury occurred one year ago).
   A) 812.20
   B) 733.82, 905.2
   C) 733.81, 905.2
   D) 733.94, 905.2

Reference: Schraffenberger, p 204-205

78. Recurrent internal derangement of the left knee.
   A) 715.96
   B) 718.36
   C) 836.2
   D) 715.36

Reference: Brown, p 197

<u>Congenital Anomalies</u>

79. Liveborn infant, born in hospital, cleft palate and lip.
   A) 749.20, 27.54, 27.62
   B) 749.20
   C) V30.00, 749.20
   D) V30.00

Reference: Brown, p 235-236
Schraffenberger, p 208-209, 211

80. Newborn, born in hospital with Tetralogy of Fallot
   A) 745.8
   B) V30.01, 746.09
   C) 745.4
   D) V30.00, 745.2

Reference: Brown, p 235-236

81. Newborn infant transferred to Happy Valley Hospital for treatment of esophageal atresia.
   A) V30.00
   B) 750.3
   C) V30.00, 750.3
   D) 750.3, V30.00

Reference: Brown, p 235-236
Schraffenberger, p 208-209

82. Cervical spinal bifida with hydrocephalus
   A) 741.4
   B) 741.5
   C) 741.01
   D) 741.91

Reference: Brown, p 235-236
Schraffenberger, p 209-210

83. Clubfoot.
   A) 754.70
   B) 754.71
   C) 736.71
   D) 736.79

Reference: Brown, p 235-236
Schraffenberger, p 212-213

84. Full-term infant, born in hospital. Diagnosed with polycystic kidneys.
   A) 753.12
   B) V30.00, 753.12
   C) V30.00
   D) 753.12, V30.00

Reference: Brown, p 236-237
Schraffenberger, p 208,-212

<u>Certain Conditions Originating in the Perinatal Period</u>

85. Full term newborn, born in hospital. Mother is addicted to cocaine, however, infant tested negative.
   A) V30.00, 760.75
   B) 797
   C) V30.00, 779.5
   D) V30.00

Reference: Brown, p 241, 244-246
Schraffenberger, p 215-217

86. Pre-term infant born via Cesarean section admitted to Children's Hospital for severe birth asphyxia.
   A) V30.01, 765.10, 768.5
   B) 765.10, 768.5, V30.01
   C) 768.5, 765.10
   D) 768.5

Reference: Brown, p 243
Schraffenberger, p 217

87. Neonatal jaundice in preterm infant born in hospital.
   A) V30.00, 774.2
   B) 774.2
   C) V30.00
   D) V27.00, 774.2

Reference: Brown, p 241-242
Schraffenberger, p 208-209

88. One week old infant admitted to the hospital with diagnosis of urinary tract infection contracted prior to birth. Urine culture positive for E.coli.
   A) V30.00, 599.0
   B) 599.0, 041.4
   C) V30.00, 599.0, 041.4
   D) 771.82, 599.0, 041.4

Reference: Brown, p 83, 245-246
Schraffenberger, p 217

89. Infant of diabetic mother.
    A) 775.1
    B) V30.00
    C) 775.0
    D) 250.00

Reference: Brown, p 241-242, 246-247

90. Full-term infant born in hospital. Birth complicated by cord compression that affected newborn.
    A) V30.00, 762.5
    B) V30.00
    C) 762.6
    D) 762.6, V30.00

Reference: Brown, p 241-242, 246
Schraffenberger, p 215-216

<u>Symptoms, Signs, and Ill-defined Conditions</u>

91. Patient admitted with abdominal pain. Discharge diagnosis is listed as: abdominal pain due to gastroenteritis or diverticulosis.
    A) 789.00
    B) 562.10, 558.9
    C) 789.00, 558.9, 562.10
    D) 558.9, 562.10, 789.00

Reference: Brown, p 75-77
Schraffenberger, p 56-58, 223-224

92. Lung mass.
    A) 518.89
    B) 786.6
    C) 793.1
    D) 786.9

Reference: Brown, p 75-77
Schraffenberger, p 219-221

93. Patient complains of vertigo; physician orders CT of brain.
    A) 780.4
    B) V72.5
    C) V72.5, 780.4
    D) 780.4, V72.5

Reference: Brown, p 75-77
Schraffenberger, p 219-221

94. Patient presents to the emergency room with ascites.
    A) 789.30
    B) 789.40
    C) 789.5
    D) 782.3

Reference: Brown, p 76-77
Schraffenberger, p 219-221

95. Patient admitted with fever due to bacteremia.
   A) 780.6, 790.7
   B) 038.9
   C) 780.6
   D) 790.7

Reference: Brown, p 75-77
Schraffenberger, p 219-221

96. Urinary retention.
   A) 788.21
   B) 788.1
   C) 788.20
   D) 788.29

Reference: Brown, p 75-77
Schraffenberger, p 219-221

<u>Injury and Poisoning</u>

97. Fracture of the medial malleolus due to fall down steps.
   A) 824.1, E880.9
   B) 824.0, E880.9
   C) 824.0
   D) 824.1, E880.1

Reference: Brown, p 309-311, 315-319
Schraffenberger, p 229-230, 257-258

98. Closed head injury, patient was a passenger in a motor vehicle involved in a head on collision with another motor vehicle.
   A) 959.01, E812.1
   B) 959.09, E812.2
   C) 959.01, E813.2
   D) 959.09, E813.1

Reference: Brown, p 309-312
Schraffenberger, p 229-230, 257-260, 268-269

99. Gunshot wound to abdomen with moderate laceration of liver. Patient was assaulted with a pistol.
   A) 864.00, E965.1
   B) 864.10, E965.0
   C) 864.01, E965.1
   D) 864.13, E965.0

Reference: Brown, p 309-312
Schraffenberger, p 233-237, 259-260

100. Patient was admitted with third degree burn of upper back which involved 20% of his body surface. There was an explosion and fire at his home.
   A) 942.25, 948.02, E890.2
   B) 942.44, 948.21, E895
   C) 942.34, 948.22, E890.3
   D) 942.24, 949.3, E897

Reference: Brown, p. 331-334
Schraffenberger, p 238-239

101. Third degree burn to thigh and second degree burn to foot.
   A) 945.36, 945.22, E924.0
   B) 945.22, 945.36, E924.0
   C) 945.22, E924.0
   D) 945.29, 945.09, E924.0

Reference: Brown, p 331-334
Schraffenberger, p 238-239, 259-260

102. Laceration of left wrist with injury to radial nerve as a result of an accident by broken glass.
   A) 881.02
   B) 881.12, E920.8
   C) 955.3, E920.8
   D) 881.12, 955.3, E920.8

Reference: Brown, p 309-312, 323
Schraffenberger, p 235-237, 241-242, 259-260

103. Female, 76 years old, admitted with tachycardia due to Theophylline toxicity.
   A) 785.0, E942.1
   B) 995.2, E942.1
   C) 785.0, E944.1
   D) 995.2, E944.1

Reference: Brown, p 337-342
Schraffenberger, p 243-249

104. Patient suffered seizure as a result of taking prescribed Phenergan. Patient took medication with beer.
   A) 780.39, 980.0, E860.0
   B) 967.8, 980.0, 780.39, E852.8, E860.0
   C) 967.8, 780.39, E852.8
   D) 780.39, E852.8, E860.0

Reference: Brown, p 343, 337-340
Schraffenberger, p 247-249

105. Pain in hip due to displaced hip prosthesis.
   A) 996.49
   B) 996.77
   C) 719.45
   D) 996.49, 719.45

Reference: Brown, p 199-200
Schraffenberger, p 250-253

106. Post operative hemorrhage resulting in acute blood loss anemia.
   A) 997.72, 285.1
   B) 999.1, 285.1
   C) 998.11, 285.1
   D) 998.11

Reference: Brown, p 349-350
Schraffenberger, p 252-254

V-Codes

107. Admission for colostomy takedown.
   A) V44.3
   B) 536.8
   C) V55.3, 536.8
   D) V55.3

Reference: Brown, p 63-66
Schraffenberger, p 271, 272, 283

108. Pre-operative EKG for patient that is to be admitted for elective cholecystectomy for chronic cholecystitis and cholelithiasis. EKG reveals atrial flutter.
   A) 574.10
   B) V72.81, 51.23
   C) V72.81, 574.10, 427.32
   D) 427.32

Reference: Brown, p 63, 68
Schraffenberger, p 292-293

109. Screening examination for lung cancer.
   A) V72.9
   B) 162.9
   C) V72.5
   D) V76.0

Reference: Brown, p 68-69
Schraffenberger, p 293-294

110. Patient admitted for observation for head injury following a fall. Patient also suffered a minor laceration to the forehead. Head injury was ruled out.
   A) V71.4, 873.42, E888.9
   B) 873.42, E888.9
   C) 850.0, 873.42, E888.9
   D) V71.4, E888.9

Reference: Brown, p 66-67
Schraffenberger, p 265, 291-292

The following questions are to be answered without using your coding book

111. Elderly man was admitted through the emergency department for severe urinary retention. Upon study, it was determined that his hypertension was uncontrolled (215/108). Prior medical records show admission 8 weeks ago for the same problem. As per conditions on previous admission, his BPH is complicated by acute cystitis. He is noncompliant with medications. Medication for the hypertension was immediately started and his hypertension was quickly brought under control.

| | |
|---|---|
| 600.00 | Benign Prostatic Hypertrophy without urinary obstruction |
| 600.01 | Benign Prostatic Hypertrophy with urinary obstruction |
| 600.3 | Cyst of the Prostate |
| 595.0 | Acute Cystitis |
| 595.9 | Cystitis unspecified |
| 788.20 | Retention of urine, unspecified |
| 401.9 | Hypertension, unspecified |
| 401.0 | Hypertension, malignant |
| V15.81 | Noncompliance with medical treatment |

A) 600.01, 595.0, 788.20, 401.9, V15.81
B) 600.3, 595.0, 401.0, V15.81
C) 600.00, 595.9, 788.20, 401.9, V15.81
D) 600.3, 595.0, 788.20, 401.0, V15.81

Reference: Brown, p 63-66, 177-178, 266
Schraffenberger, p 122-126, 171, 274-276

112. Thirty-two year old female known HIV positive was admitted with lesions of the anterior trunk. Excisional biopsies of the skin lesions were positive for Kaposi's sarcoma. Further examination revealed thrush.

| | |
|---|---|
| 042 | Human Immunodeficiency Virus (HIV) Disease |
| 795.71 | Nonspecific serological evidence of HIV |
| 176.0 | Kaposi's sarcoma of skin |
| 686.00 | Pyoderma, unspecified |
| 112.0 | Candidiasis of the mouth |
| 528.9 | Other and unspecified disease of the oral soft tissue |

A) 042, 686.00, 112.0
B) 042, 176.0, 112.0
C) 795.71, 176.0, 528.9
D) 795.71, 686.00, 528.9

Reference: Brown, p 91-92
Schraffenberger, p 67-70, 200, 235-237

113. A female patient was admitted with uncontrolled Type II Diabetes. Patient also had an abscessed diabetic ulcer of the foot. Culture and sensitivity of abscess shows growth of staphylococcus aureus, methicillin resistant. Patient was started on the appropriate antibiotic. Patient is on oral as well as injectional insulin for control of diabetes.

| | |
|---|---|
| 041.11 | Staphylococcus aureus |
| 041.19 | Other staphylococcus |
| 250.82 | Diabetes mellitus with specified manifestation Type II uncontrolled |
| 250.83 | Diabetes mellitus with specified manifestation Type I, uncontrolled |
| 682.7 | Abscess of foot, except toes |
| 682.8 | Abscess of other specified site |
| 707.15 | Ulcer of other part of foot |
| 707.8 | Chronic ulcer of other specified sites |
| 707.00 | Decubitus ulcer, unspecified site |
| V09.0 | Infection with organisms resistant to penicillins |

A) 250.83, 682.82, V09.0
B) 682.7, 682.7, 707.15, 041.19
C) 682.8, 041.19, 250.82, 707.00
D) 250.82, 682.7, 707.15, 041.11, V09.0

Reference: Brown, p 87-88, 95-98, 187-188, 190
Schraffenberger, p 64-65, 92-94, 197-198, 200-201, 274

114. Patient was admitted from the nursing home in acute respiratory failure that was due to congestive heart failure. Chest x-ray also showed pulmonary edema. Patient was intubated and placed on mechanical ventilation and expired the day after admission.

| | |
|---|---|
| 428.0 | Congestive heart failure, unspecified |
| 428.1 | Left heart failure |
| 428.20 | Systolic heart failure, unspecified |
| 518.81 | Acute respiratory failure |
| 518.84 | Acute and chronic respiratory failure |
| 518.4 | Acute edema of lung, unspecified |

A) 428.1, 518.84, 518.4
B) 428.20, 428.0, 518.81, 518.4
C) 518.81, 428.0, 96.71
D) 482.0, 518.4

Reference: Brown, p 148-150, 152-153
Schraffenberger, p 132-135, 152-154

115. The patient has hypertensive heart disease and nephrosclerosis with chronic kidney failure. The patient had placement of arteriovenous fistula in his left wrist to prepare for the hemodialysis.

| | |
|---|---|
| 404.92 | Hypertensive heart and kidney disease with chronic kidney disease |
| 404.93 | Hypertensive heart and kidney disease with heart failure and chronic kidney disease |
| 585.9 | Chronic kidney disease unspecified |
| V56.0 | Extracorporeal dialysis |

A) 404.93, 585
B) 404.92
C) 404.93
D) 404.92, 585

Reference: Brown, p 174-176
Schraffenberger, p 122-126

116. The patient has had abnormal heavy uterine bleeding and abdominal pain. There was bright red blood in the vagina and the right adnexa was enlarged. The woman was admitted. Right follicular ovarian cyst. Acute blood loss anemia.

| | |
|---|---|
| 620.0 | Follicular cyst of the ovary |
| 285.1 | Acute post hemorrhagic anemia |
| 280.0 | Chronic blood loss anemia |

A) 620.0, 285.1
B) 620.0, 280.0

Reference: Brown, p 121
Schraffenberger, p 172-173

117. Jane Doe is six weeks post mastectomy for carcinoma of the breast. She is admitted for chemotherapy. What is the correct sequencing of the codes?

A) V58.11 (chemotherapy), 174.9 (malignant neoplasm of the breast), V45.71 (acquired absence of breast)
B) V58.1 (chemotherapy), V10.3 (personal history of malignant neoplasm of breast), V45.71 (acquired absence of breast)
C) V67.0 (follow-up exam after surgery), V58.11 (chemotherapy)
D) V10.3 (personal history of malignant neoplasm of breast)

Reference: Brown, p 299-302
Schraffenberger, p 76-77, 274-276

118. The patient was admitted due to increasingly severe pain in his right arm, shoulder and neck for the past 6 weeks. MRI tests showed herniation of the C5-C6 disc. The patient is currently being treated for COPD and CAD with a history of a PTCA.

| | |
|---|---|
| 722.0 | Displacement of cervical intervertebral disc without myelopathy |
| 722.1 | Displacement of thoracic or lumbar intervertebral disc without myelopathy |
| 492.8 | Other emphysema |
| 496 | Chronic airway obstruction, not elsewhere classified |
| 414.01 | Coronary atherosclerosis of native coronary vessel |
| 414.00 | Coronary atherosclerosis unspecified vessel native or graft |
| V45.82 | Percutaneous transluminal coronary angioplasty status |

A) 722.0, 492.8, 414.01, V45
B) 722.1, 496, 414.01, V45.82
C) 722.1, 492.8, 414.00
D) 722.0, 496, 414.01, V45.82

Reference: Brown, p 145-146, 195-196, 259-260
Schraffenberger, p 130-132, 151-152, 204, 281-282

119. A 75-year-old man is admitted to your facility with acute cerebral embolism with infarction. He had hemiplegia and dysphagia. Physical therapy was given for the hemiplegia. Dysphagia was resolved at the time of discharge

| | |
|---|---|
| 434.11 | Cerebral embolism with cerebral infarction |
| 342.90 | Hemiplegia, unspecified, affecting unspecified side |
| 787.2 | Dysphagia |
| V57.1 | Physical therapy |

A) 434.11, 342.90, V57.1
B) 434.11, 342.90, 787.2
C) 434.11, 342.90
D) 434.11, 342.90, 787.2, V57.1

Reference: Brown, p 263-264
Schraffenberger, p 136-138

120. Patient is admitted to St. Mary's Hospital with hyperthermia, tachycardia, hypoxemia and altered mental status. Urinalysis is positive for E. coli and blood cultures are negative. Patient is immediately started on broad spectrum IV antibiotics. Physician documents urosepsis as the final diagnosis. The coder should

A) report 599.0 (urosepsis), and 041.4 (E. coli)
B) report 038.42 (septicemia due to E. coli) and 995.91 (SIRS)
C) report 038.42 (septicemia due to E. coli), 599.0 (urosepsis) and 995.91 (SIRS)
D) confer with physician for reporting 038.9 (septicemia) based upon the clinical findings with 041.4 (E. coli) and 995.91 (SIRS)

Reference: Brown, p 85-87
Schraffenberger, p 65-67, 389-392

ANSWER KEY for ICD-9-CM Coding

1. D
2. B
3. A
4. C
5. D
6. C
7. D
8. C
9. A
10. B
11. C
12. B
13. A
14. D
15. B
16. A
17. C
18. B
19. D
20. B Pain is a symptom that is integral to the sickle cell crisis and therefore, is not coded.
21. A
22. C
23. B
24. D
25. D
26. B
27. A
28. C
29. B
30. D
31. C
32. B
33. A
34. C
35. B
36. D
37. A
38. C
39. D
40. A
41. B
42. A
43. D
44. C
45. B
46. A

47. C
48. B
49. A
50. D
51. C
52. A
53. C
54. B The physician should be asked if the blood loss should be added as a discharge Diagnosis.
55. A
56. C
57. D
58. A
59. C
60. A
61. A
62. C
63. B
64. D
65. B
66. D
67. B
68. D
69. A
70. B
71. A
72. C
73. B
74. D
75. C
76. A
77. C
78. B
79. C
80. D
81. B
82. C
83. A
84. B
85. D
86. C
87. A
88. D
89. C
90. A
91. C
92. B

ANSWER KEY for ICD-9-CM Coding

93. A
94. C
95. D
96. C
97. B
98. A
99. D
100. C
101. A
102. D
103. C
104. B
105. A
106. C
107. D
108. C
109. D
110. A
111. A
112. B
113. D
114. C
115. B
116. A
117. A
118. D
119. C
120. D

## REFERENCES


*ICD-9-CM Coding Handbook with answers, 2006 Edition*
Author: Faye Brown
Publisher: American Hospital Association (AHA)

*Basic ICD-9-CM Coding, 2006 Edition*
Author: Lou Anne Schraffenberger, MBA, RHIA, CCS, CCS-P
Publisher: American Health Information Management Association (AHIMA)

*ICD-9-CM Code Book with October 2005 updates*
Channel Publishing, Ltd.
INGENIX

# CPT-4 Coding

Anita Hazelwood, MLS, RHIA, FHIMA

# CPT-4 Coding

*Anita Hazelwood, MLS, RHIA, FHIMA*

Evaluation and Management

1. Patient is admitted to the hospital with acute abdominal pain. The attending medical physician requests a surgical consult. The consultant agrees to see the patient and conducts a comprehensive history and physical examination. The physician ordered lab work to rule out pancreatitis along with an ultrasound of the gallbladder and abdominal x-ray. Due to the various diagnosis possibilities and tests reviewed a moderate medical decision was made.
   A) 99244
   B) 99222
   C) 99254
   D) 99204

REFERENCE: Step-By-Step, p 55-57
Principles of CPT Coding, p 66
Smith, p 173-174

2. An established patient returns to the physician's office for follow up on his hypertension and diabetes. The physician takes the blood pressure and references the patient's last three (3) glucose tests. The patient is still running above normal glucose levels so the physician decides to adjust the patient's insulin. An expanded history and physical examination was performed.
   A) 99213
   B) 99232
   C) 99202
   D) 99214

REFERENCE: Step-By-Step, p 50
Principles of CPT Coding, p 53
Smith, p 172

3. Patient arrives in the Emergency Room via a medical helicopter. The patient has sustained multiple life threatening injuries due to a multiple car accident. The patient goes into cardiac arrest ten (10) minutes after arrival. An hour and thirty minutes of critical care time is spent trying to stabilize the patient.
   A) 99285; 99288; 99291
   B) 99291; 99292
   C) 99291; 99292; 99285
   D) 99282

REFERENCE: Step-By-Step, p 60-61
Principles of CPT Coding, p 71-77
Smith, p 175

4. The physician provided services to a new patient who was in a rest home for an ulcerative sore on the hip. A problem focused history and physical examination was performed and a straightforward medical decision was made.
   A) 99304
   B) 99325
   C) 99324
   D) 99334

REFERENCE: Step-By-Step, p 67
Principles of CPT Coding, p 82-83
Smith, p 177

5. The physician provided the initial care of a critically ill neonate and two days of subsequent care to the critically ill neonate. Services were provided in the neonatal intensive care unit. Code for all care provided.
   A) 99295
   B) 99295; 99298; 99298
   C) 99295; 99296
   D) 99295; 99296; 99296

REFERENCE: CPT Book, 2006
Principles of CPT Coding, p 75
Smith, p 175-176
Step by Step, p 63

6. Services were provided to a patient in the Emergency Room after the patient twisted her ankle stepping down from a curb. The emergency room physician ordered x-rays of the ankle that came back negative for a fracture. A problem focused history and physical examination was performed and ankle strapping was applied. A prescription for pain was given to the patient. Code the emergency room visit only.
   A) 99201
   B) 99282
   C) 99281
   D) 99211

REFERENCE: Step-by-Step, p 60-61
Principles of CPT Coding, p 68-69
Smith, p 174

7. An established patient was seen in her primary physician's office. The patient fell at home and came to the physician's office for an examination. Due to a possible concussion the patient was sent to the hospital to be admitted as an observation patient. A detailed history and examination was performed and the medical decision was low complexity. The patient stayed overnight and was discharged the next afternoon.
   A) 99214; 99234
   B) 99214; 99218; 99217
   C) 99218
   D) 99218; 99217

REFERENCE: CPT Book, 2006
Principles of CPT Coding, p 54
Smith, p 172
Step by Step, p 51-52

8. An out of town patient presents to a walk-in clinic to have a prescription refilled for a nonsteroidal anti-inflammatory drug. The physician performs a problem-focused history and physical examination with a straightforward decision.
   A) 99211
   B) 99201
   C) 99212
   D) 99202

REFERENCE: Step-By-Step, p 49
Principles of CPT Coding, p 53
Smith, p 172

9. An office consultation is performed for a postmenopausal woman who is complaining of spotting in the past six (6) months with right lower quadrant tenderness. A detailed history and physical was performed with a low complexity medical decision.
   A) 99242
   B) 99243
   C) 99273
   D) 99263

REFERENCE: Step-By-Step, p 55-57
Principles of CPT Coding, p 65
Smith, p 173

<u>Anesthesia</u>

10. Upper abdominal ventral hernia repair
    A) 00832
    B) 00750
    C) 00752
    D) 00830

REFERENCE: Step-By-Step, p 82-92
Principles of CPT Coding, p 303-305

11. Total hip replacement
    A) 01210
    B) 01402
    C) 01230
    D) 01214

REFERENCE: Step-By-Step, p 82-92
Principles of CPT Coding, p 303-305

12. Vaginal hysterectomy
    A) 00846
    B) 00944
    C) 00840
    D) 01963

REFERENCE: Step-By-Step, p 92
Principles of CPT Coding, p 303-305

13. Placement of vascular shunt in forearm
    A) 01844
    B) 01850
    C) 00532
    D) 01840

REFERENCE: Step-By-Step, p 92
Principles of CPT Coding, p 303-305

14. Decortication of left lung
    A) 01638-LT
    B) 00542-LT
    C) 00546-LT
    D) 00500-LT

REFERENCE: Step-By-Step, p 92
Principles of CPT Coding, p 303-305

15. Total shoulder replacement
    A) 01760
    B) 01630
    C) 01402
    D) 01638

REFERENCE: Step-By-Step, p 92
Principles of CPT Coding p 303-305

16. Cesarean section
    A) 00855
    B) 01961
    C) 00946
    D) 01960

REFERENCE: Step-By-Step, p 92
Principles of CPT Coding, p 303-305

17. Procedures on bony pelvis
    A) 00400
    B) 01170
    C) 01120
    D) 01190

REFERENCE: Step-By-Step, p 92
Principles of CPT Coding, p 303-305

18. Corneal transplant
    A) 00144
    B) 00140
    C) 00147
    D) 00190

REFERENCE: Step-By-Step, p 92
Principles of CPT Coding, p 303-305

Surgery - Integumentary System

19. Patient presents to the hospital for skin grafts due to previous third degree burns. The burn eschar of the back was removed. Once the eschar was removed, the defect size measured 10 cm x 10 cm. A skin graft from a donor bank was placed onto the defect and sewn into place as a temporary wound closure.
    A) 15000, 15170
    B) 15300
    C) 15000, 15200
    D) 15000, 15300

REFERENCE: Step-By-Step, p 150
Principles of CPT Coding, p 141-143
Smith, p 60
CPT Changes: An Insider's View, 2006

20. Patient presents to the operating room for excision of 4.5 cm malignant melanoma of the left forearm. A 6 cm x 6 cm rotation flap was created for closure.
    A) 14021-LT
    B) 11606; 14020-LT
    C) 14300-LT
    D) 11606; 15100

REFERENCE: Step-By-Step, p 139, 145-146
Principles of CPT Coding, p 140-141
Smith, p 60

21. Female patient has a percutaneous needle biopsy of the left breast lesion in the lower outer quadrant. Following the biopsy frozen section results, the physician followed this with an excisional removal of the same lesion.
    A) 19100; 19125
    B) 19100; 191200-LT
    C) 19120-LT
    D) 19100; 19120; 19120

REFERENCE: Step by Step, p 157-158
Smith, p 63-64

22. Patient presents to the Emergency Room with lacerations of right lower leg that involved the fascia. Lacerations measured 5.0 cm and 2.7 cm.
    A) 11406; 11403
    B) 12034
    C) 12032; 12031
    D) 12032

REFERENCE: Step by Step, p 143-145
Principles of CPT Coding, p 138-140
Smith, p 54-55

23. Ten sq cm epidermal autograft to the face from the back.
    A) 15110
    B) 15115
    C) 15110, 15115
    D) 15120

REFERENCE: CPT Book 2006
CPT Changes: An Insider's View, 2006

24. Non-human graft for temporary wound closure. Patient has a 5 cm defect on the scalp.
    A) 15335
    B) 15400
    C) 15420
    D) 15430

REFERENCE: CPT Book 2006
CPT Changes: An Insider's View, 2006

25. Patient is admitted for a blepharoplasty of the left lower eyelid and a repair for a tarsal strip of the left upper lid.
    A) 67917-E1, 15822-E2
    B) 67917-E1, 15820-E2
    C) 67917-E1
    D) 67917-E1, 15823-E2

REFERENCE: CPT Assistant, January 2005, p 46

26. Patient presents to the Emergency Room with lacerations sustained in an automobile accident. Repairs of the 3.3 cm skin laceration of the left leg that involved the fascia, 2.5 cm and 3.0 cm lacerations of the left arm involving the fascia and 2.7 cm of the left foot, which required simple sutures, were performed. Sterile dressings were applied.
    A) 12032; 12032; 12031; 12002
    B) 12002, 12002
    C) 12034, 12002
    D) 13150; 12032, 12032, 12001

REFERENCE: Step-By-Step, p 143-145
Principles of CPT Coding, p 138-140
Smith, p 54-55

27. Patient presents to the operating room for excision of three (3) lesions. The 1.5 cm and 2.0 cm lesions of the back were excised with one excision. The 0.5 cm lesion of the hand was excised. The pathology report identified both back lesions as squamous cell carcinoma. The hand lesion was identified as seborrheic keratosis.
    A) 11604; 11420
    B) 11402; 11420; 11403
    C) 11403; 11642; 11462
    D) 11602; 11402

REFERENCE: Step-By-Step, p 138-139
Principles of CPT Coding, p 136
CPT Assistant, Nov. 2002, p 5-6, 8
Smith, p 49-51

28. Patient presents to the radiology department where a fine needle aspiration of the breast is performed utilizing computer tomography.
    A) 19120
    B) 19102
    C) 17260
    D) 10022, 76360

REFERENCE: CPT Assistant, November 2002, p 2-3
Step by Step, p 130

29. Patient presents to the operating room where a 3.2 cm malignant lesion of the shoulder was excised and repaired with simple sutures. A 2.0 cm benign lesion of the cheek was excised and was repaired with a rotation skin graft.
    A) 11604, 11442, 14040, 12001
    B) 14040, 11604
    C) 15000, 15120
    D) 17264, 17000, 12001

REFERENCE: CPT Assistant, November 2002, p 5-8
CPT Assistant, August 2002, p 5
CPT Assistant, July 1999, p 3-4
Step by Step, p 139, 145-146
Smith, p 49-51, 60

30. Patient was admitted to the hospital for removal of excessive tissue due to massive weight loss. Liposuction of the abdomen and bilateral thighs was performed.
    A) 15831
    B) 15831; 15833; 15833
    C) 15877; 15879; 15879
    D) 15839

REFERENCE: CPT Assistant, May 2001, pg 11
Step by Step, p 152

<u>Surgery - Musculoskeletal</u>

31. Patient presents to the hospital with ulcer of the right foot. Patient is taken to the operating room where a revision of the right metatarsal head is performed.
    A) 28104-RT
    B) 28111-RT
    C) 28288-RT
    D) 28899-RT

REFERENCE: CPT Book 2006

32. Patient presents to the Emergency Room following a fall. X-rays were ordered for the lower leg and results showed a fracture of the proximal left tibia. The emergency room physician performed a closed manipulation of the fracture with skeletal traction.
    A) 27532-LT
    B) 27536-LT
    C) 27530-LT
    D) 27524-LT

REFERENCE: Step-By-Step, p 165-168
Principles of CPT Coding, p 153-154
Smith, p 68

33. Trauma patient was rushed to the operating room with multiple injuries. Open reduction with internal fixation of intertrochanteric femoral fracture; open reduction of the tibial and fibula shaft with internal fixation was performed.
    A) 27245; 27759
    B) 20690
    C) 27248; 27756
    D) 27244; 27758

REFERENCE: Step-By-Step, p 165-168
Principles of CPT Coding, p 153-154
Smith, p 68

34. Open I&D of a deep abscess of the cervical spine.
   A) 22010
   B) 22015
   C) 10060
   D) 10140

REFERENCE: CPT Book 2006
CPT Changes: An Insider's View, 2006

35. Patient presents to the Emergency Room following an assault. Examination of the patient reveals blunt trauma to the face. Radiology reports that the patient suffers from a fracture to the frontal skull and blow out fracture of the orbital floor. Patient is admitted and taken to the operating room where a periorbital approach to the orbital fracture is employed and an implant is inserted.
   A) 21407; 21275
   B) 21387; 61330
   C) 21390
   D) 61340; 21401

REFERENCE: Step-By-Step, p 165-168
Smith, p 68

36. Patient presents with a traumatic partial amputation of the second, third, and fourth fingers on the right hand. Patient was taken to the operating room where completion of the amputation of three (3) fingers was performed with direct closure.
   A) 26910-F6; 26910-F7; 26910-F8
   B) 26843-RT
   C) 26951-F6, 26951-F7, 26951-F8
   D) 26550-RT

REFERENCE: CPT Book, 2006

37. Patient is brought to the Emergency Room following a shark attack. The paramedics have the patient's amputated foot. The patient is taken directly to the operating room to reattach the patient's foot.
   A) 28800
   B) 28200; 28208
   C) 28110
   D) 20838

REFERENCE: CPT Book, 2006

38. Patient presents to the hospital with a right index trigger finger. Release of the trigger finger was performed.
   A) 26060-F7
   B) 26055-F6
   C) 26170-F6
   D) 26110

REFERENCE: CPT Book, 2006

39. Patient had been diagnosed with a bunion. Patient was taken to the operating room where a simple resection of the base of the proximal phalanx along with the medial eminence was performed. Kirschner wire was placed to hold the joint in place.
    A) 28292
    B) 28290
    C) 28293
    D) 28298

REFERENCE: CPT Assistant, December 1995, p 5-7
Smith, p 178
Principles of CPT Coding, p 167-171

<u>Surgery - Respiratory</u>

40. Patient has a bronchoscopy with endobronchial biopsies of three sites.
    A) 31625, 31625, 31625
    B) 31625
    C) 31622, 31625
    D) 31622, 31625, 31625, 31625

REFERENCE: CPT Assistant, June 2004, p 11

41. Patient presents to the surgical unit and undergoes unilateral endoscopy partial ethmoidectomy and maxillary antrostomy.
    A) 31254; 31256
    B) 31201; 31225
    C) 31290; 31267
    D) 31233; 31231

REFERENCE: Step-By-Step, p 189-190
CPT Assistant, January 1997, p 4-6
Principles of CPT Coding, p 176
Smith, p 74-75

42. Patient has been diagnosed with metastatic laryngeal carcinoma. Patient underwent subtotal supraglottic laryngectomy with radical neck dissection.
    A) 31540
    B) 31367
    C) 31365
    D) 31368

REFERENCE: Step-By-Step, p 197-198

43. Patient was involved in an accident and has been sent to the hospital. During transport the patient develops breathing problems and upon arrival to the hospital an emergency transtracheal tracheostomy was performed. Following various x-rays the patient was diagnosed with traumatic pneumothorax and a thoracentesis was performed.
    A) 31603; 31612
    B) 31610; 32000
    C) 31603; 32002
    D) 31603; 32000

REFERENCE: Step-By-Step, p 199-201

44. Patient with laryngeal cancer has a tracheoesophageal fistula created and has a voice box inserted.
A) 31611
B) 31580
C) 31395
D) 31502
REFERENCE: CPT Book, 2006

45. Upper lobectomy of the right lung with repair of the bronchus.
A) 32480
B) 32486
C) 32320
D) 32480, 32501
REFERENCE: Step-By-Step, p 204

46. Patient with a deviated nasal septum that was repaired by septoplasty.
A) 30400
B) 30620
C) 30520
D) 30630
REFERENCE: Step-By-Step, p 194

47. Lye burn of the larynx repaired by laryngoplasty.
A) 31588
B) 16015
C) 31360
D) 31540
REFERENCE: CPT Book, 2006

48. Bronchoscopy with multiple transbronchial right upper and right lower lobe lung biopsy with fluroscopic guidance.
A) 31628-RT; 76000-RT
B) 31717-RT, 31632-RT
C) 32405-RT
D) 31628-RT; 31632-RT
REFERENCE: CPT Assistant, March 1999, p 3.
Principles of CPT Coding, p 178-181
CPT Changes: An Insider's View, 2005
Step by Step, p 189
Smith, p 80

49. Patient has recurrent spontaneous pneumothorax which has resulted in a chemical pleurodesis by thoracoscopy.
A) 32650
B) 32005; 32601
C) 32605
D) 32960
REFERENCE: Principles of CPT Coding, p 181-183
Step by Step p 189

50. Laryngoscopic stripping of vocal cords for leukoplakia of the vocal cords
   A) 31535
   B) 31540
   C) 31541
   D) 31570

REFERENCE: Principles of CPT Coding, p 177-178
Smith, p 78
Step by Step, p 189

<u>Surgery - Cardiovascular System</u>

51. Patient returns to the operating room following open-heart bypass for exploration of blood vessel to control postoperative bleeding in the chest.
   A) 35820
   B) 20101
   C) 35761
   D) 35905

REFERENCE: CPT Coding Book 2006

52. Patient undergoes construction of apical aortic conduit with and insertion of a single ventricle ventricular assist device.
   A) 33400
   B) 33975
   C) 33977
   D) 33975, 33404

REFERENCE: CPT Assistant, January 2004, p 28

53. Patient presents to the operating room where a CABG x 3 is performed using the mammary artery and two sections of the saphenous vein.
   A) 33534; 33511
   B) 33534; 33518; 33511
   C) 33535
   D) 33533; 33518

REFERENCE: Step-By-Step, p 219
Principles of CPT Coding, p 195-197
Smith, p 85

54. Patient complains of recurrent syncope following carotid thromboendarterectomy. Patient returns two weeks after initial surgery and undergoes repeat carotid thromboendarterectomy
   A) 33510
   B) 35301
   C) 35201
   D) 35301; 35390

REFERENCE: CPT Assistant Winter, 1993, p 3

55. Patient is admitted with alcohol cirrhosis and has a TIPS procedure performed.
   A) 35476, 36011, 36481
   B) 37183
   C) 37182
   D) 37140

REFERENCE: CPT Assistant, December 2003, p 1-3

56. Eighty year old patient has carcinoma and presents to the operating room for placement of a tunneled implantable centrally inserted venous access port.
   A) 36558
   B) 36571
   C) 36561
   D) 36493

REFERENCE: Principles of CPT Coding, p 203-205
CPT Assistant February 1999, p 1-5
CPT Assistant November 1999, p 19-20
CPT Changes: An Insider's View 2005
Smith, p 88

57. Patient presents to the operating room and undergoes an endovascular repair of an infrarenal abdominal aortic aneurysm utilizing a unibody bifurcated prosthesis.
   A) 34800; 34813
   B) 34802
   C) 34804
   D) 35081

REFERENCE: Principles of CPT Coding, p 198-201
CPT Assistant, September 2002, p 4;
CPT Assistant, February 2003, p 2-4, 16
Step by Step, p 225-226

58. The physician punctures the left common femoral to examine the right common iliac.
   A) 36245
   B) 36246
   C) 36247
   D) 36140

REFERENCE: CPT Book 2006

59. Patient has a history of PVD for many years and experiences chest pains. The patient underwent Doppler evaluation that showed a common femoral DVT. Patient is now admitted for thromboendartectomy.
   A) 35371
   B) 35372
   C) 35456
   D) 35256

REFERENCE: Step-By-Step, p 226

60. Patient presents to the hospital with a diagnosis of femoral artery atherosclerotic disease. The patient is taken to the operating room and undergoes an aortofemoral popliteal bypass.
   A) 35551
   B) 35651
   C) 35556
   D) 35656

REFERENCE: CPT Code Book 2006

Surgery - Hemic/Lymphatic Systems and Mediastinum and Diaphragm

61. Patient has breast carcinoma and is now undergoing sentinal node biopsy. Patient was injected for sentinel node identification and two deep axillary lymph nodes showed up intensely. These two lymph nodes were completely excised. Path report was positive for metastatic carcinoma.
    A) 38525; 38790
    B) 38589
    C) 38308; 38790
    D) 38525; 38792

REFERENCE: CPT Assistant, November, 1998 p 15-16
CPT Assistant, July 1999, p 6-12
Step by Step, p 289-290

62. Patient has a history of hiatal hernia for many years, which has progressively gotten worse. The decision to repair the hernia was made and the patient was sent to the operating room where the repair took place via the thorax and abdomen.
    A) 39545
    B) 39530
    C) 39502
    D) 39503

REFERENCE: Step-By-Step, p 279

63. Patient has a bone marrow aspiration of the iliac crest and of the tibia.
    A) 38220, 38220-59
    B) 38231
    C) 38230
    D) 38220

REFERENCE: CPT Assistant, January 2004, p 26
Step by Step, p 289

64. Trauma patient is rushed to the operating room with multiple injuries. The patient had his spleen removed due to massive rupture with repair of lacerated diaphragm.
    A) 38115; 39501
    B) 38120; 39599
    C) 38102; 39540
    D) 38100; 39501

REFERENCE: Step-By-Step, p 280-281, 289

65. Laparoscopic retroperitoneal lymph node biopsy
    A) 38570
    B) 38780
    C) 49323
    D) 38589

REFERENCE: Step-By-Step, p 289-290

66. Excision mediastinal cyst
    A) 11400
    B) 39200
    C) 17000
    D) 39400

REFERENCE: Step-By-Step, p 281

67. Patient diagnosed with cystic hygroma of the axilla, which was excised.
    A) 38555
    B) 11400
    C) 38550
    D) 38300
REFERENCE: CPT Code Book 2006

68. Laparoscopy with multiple biopsies of retroperitoneal lymph nodes.
    A) 38570
    B) 38571
    C) 38570-22
    D) 38572
REFERENCE: CPT Book 2006

69. Cannulation of the thoracic duct.
    A) 38794
    B) 36810
    C) 36260
    D) 38999
REFERENCE: CPT Code Book 2006

70. Patient has been on the bone marrow transplant recipient list for three months. A perfect match was made and the patient came in and received peripheral stem cell transplant.
    A) 38231
    B) 38230
    C) 38241
    D) 38240
REFERENCE: Step-By-Step, p 289

Surgery - Digestive System

71. Laparoscopic gastric banding.
    A) 43842
    B) 43843
    C) 43770
    D) 43771
REFERENCE: CPT Book 2006
CPT Changes: An Insider's View, 2006

72. Patient presents with a history of upper abdominal pain. Cholangiogram was negative and patient was sent to the hospital for ERCP. During the procedure the sphincter was incised and a stent was placed for drainage.
    A) 43260; 43262; 43624
    B) 43262; 43269
    C) 43267
    D) 43262; 43268
REFERENCE: CPT Assistant, Spring 1994, p 5-7

73. Patient presents to the emergency room with right lower abdominal pains. Emergency room physician suspects possible appendicitis. Patient was taken to the operating room where a laparoscopic appendectomy was performed. Pathology report was negative for appendicitis.
   A) 44950
   B) 44950; 49320
   C) 44970
   D) 44901

REFERENCE: Principles of CPT Coding, p 214-215

74. Morbid obese patient comes in for vertical banding of the stomach.
   A) 43848
   B) 43659
   C) 43842
   D) 43999

REFERENCE: CPT Assistant, May 1998, p 5-6

75. Patient was discharged two (2) days following total abdominal hysterectomy. Upon return to the surgeon's office for follow-up the physician discovered the patient had pain in the surgical wound. Upon further investigation it was discovered that the patient had fallen and it was feared that the patient ruptured the internal sutures. Patient returned to the hospital for exploratory surgery and suture of the abdominal wall wound.
   A) 12031
   B) 20102
   C) 49900
   D) 49002

REFERENCE: CPT Code Book 2006

76. Injection snoreplasty for treatment of palatal snoring.
   A) 42299
   B) 42145
   C) 42999
   D) 40899

REFERENCE: CPT Assistant, December 2004, p 19

77. Patient arrives to the hospital and has her esophagogastric junction sutured endoscopically.
   A) 43410
   B) 43415
   C) 43502
   D) 0008T

REFERENCE: CPT Assistant, February 2001, p 5-6

78. Young child presents with cleft lip and cleft palate. This is the first attempt of repair, which includes major revision of the cleft palate, and unilateral cleft lip repair.
   A) 42200; 40701
   B) 42225; 40700
   C) 42220; 40720
   D) 42215; 40700

REFERENCE: CPT Code Book, 2006

79. Patient has a history of chronic alcohol abuse with portal hypertension. Patient has been vomiting blood for the past three (3) days and presented to his physician's office. Patient was sent to the hospital for evaluation and an EGD was performed. Biopsy findings showed gastritis, esophagitis and bleeding esophageal varices, which were injected with sclerosing solution.
    A) 43235; 43244; 43204
    B) 43239; 43244
    C) 43239; 43243
    D) 43239; 43243; 43204

REFERENCE: Step-By-Step, p 276
Principles of CPT Coding, p 220-222
Smith, p 92-94

80. Patient is admitted for contact laser vaporization of the prostate. The physician performed a TURP and transurethral resection of the bladder neck at the same time.
    A) 52648
    B) 52648, 52450, 52500
    C) 52450, 53500
    D) 52648, 52450

REFERENCE: CPT Assistant, July 2005, p 15

<u>Surgery - Urinary System</u>

81. Patient comes to the hospital with a history of right flank pain. Urine tests are negative. Radiology examination reveals that the patient has renal cysts. Patient is now admitted for laparoscopic ablation of the cysts.
    A) 50541
    B) 50390
    C) 50280
    D) 50920

REFERENCE: CPT Assistant, November 1999, p 25
CPT Assistant, May 2000, p 4
CPT Assistant, October 2001, p 8
CPT Assistant, January, 2003, p 19
CPT Changes: An Insider's View, 2000

82. Patient has extensive bladder cancer. She underwent a complete cystectomy with bilateral pelvic lymphadenectomy and creation of ureteroileal conduit.
    A) 51575; 50820
    B) 50825; 51570; 38770
    C) 51595
    D) 51550; 38770

REFERENCE: CPT Code Book 2006

83. Patient presents to the hospital with right ureteral calculus. Patient is taken to the operating room where a cystoscopy with ureteroscopy is performed to remove the calculus.
    A) 52353
    B) 52310
    C) 51065
    D) 52352

REFERENCE: Step-By-Step, p 271-274
Principles of CPT Coding, p 230-233

84. Female with six (6) months of stress incontinence. Outpatient therapies are not working and the patient decides to have the problem fixed. Laparoscopic urethral suspension was completed.
   A) 51992
   B) 51990
   C) 51840
   D) 51845

REFERENCE: CPT Assistant, November 1999, p 26
CPT Assistant, May 2000, p 4
CPT Changes: An Insider's View 2000

85. Patient has ovarian vein syndrome and has ureterolysis performed.
   A) 58679
   B) 58660
   C) 52351
   D) 50722

REFERENCE: Step By Step, p 273

86. Male patient has been diagnosed with benign prostatic hypertrophy and undergoes a transuretheral destruction of the prostate by radiofrequency thermotherapy.
   A) 52648
   B) 53852
   C) 52601
   D) 53850

REFERENCE: CPT Assistant, November, 1997, p 20
CPT Assistant, April, 2001, p 4

87. Nephrectomy with resection of 1/2 of the ureter.
   A) 50220
   B) 50234
   C) 50230; 50650
   D) 50546

REFERENCE: Step-By-Step, p 272-273

88. Male with urinary incontinence. Sling procedure was performed six months ago and now returned for a revision of the Sling procedure.
   A) 53449
   B) 53442
   C) 53440
   D) 53431

REFERENCE: CPT Book, 2006

89. Excision of 2.5 cm bladder tumor with cystoscopy.
   A) 51550
   B) 51530
   C) 52235
   D) 51060

REFERENCE: Step-By-Step, p 273-274
Principles of CPT Coding, p 230-233

90. Closure of ureterocutaneous fistula.
   A) 50930
   B) 50920
   C) 57310
   D) 50520
REFERENCE: CPT Code Book 2006

Surgery - Male Genital System

91. Removal of nephrostomy tube with fluoroscopic guidance.
   A) 50387
   B) 50389
   C) 99212
   D) 99213
REFERENCE: CPT Book 2006
CPT Changes: An Insider's View, 2006

92. Patient has been diagnosed with prostate cancer. Patient arrived to the operating room where a therapeutic orchiectomy is performed.
   A) 54560
   B) 54530
   C) 55899
   D) 54520
REFERENCE: CPT Assistant, October 2001, p 8

93. Patient undergoes laparoscopic orchiopexy for intra-abdominal testes.
   A) 54650
   B) 54699
   C) 54692
   D) 55899
REFERENCE: CPT Assistant, November 1999, p 27
CPT Assistant, May 2000, p 4
CPT Assistant, October 2001, p 8
CPT Changes: An Insider's View, 2000

94. Scrotal wall abscess drainage.
   A) 55100
   B) 55150
   C) 54700
   D) 55110
REFERENCE: CPT Code Book 2006

95. Hydrocelectomy of spermatic cord.
   A) 55500
   B) 55000
   C) 55041
   D) 55520
REFERENCE: CPT Assistant, October, 2001, p 8

96. Patient has been followed by his primary care physician for elevated PSA. Patient underwent prostate needle biopsy in the physician office two weeks ago and final pathology was positive for carcinoma. Patient is admitted for prostatectomy. Frozen section of the prostate and one lymph node is positive for prostate cancer with metastatic disease to the lymph node. Prostatectomy became a radical perineal with bilateral pelvic lymphadenectomy.
   A) 55845
   B) 55815
   C) 55815; 38562
   D) 38770

REFERENCE: Smith, p 108-109

97. Male presented to operating room for sterilization by bilateral vasectomy.
   A) 55200
   B) 55400
   C) 55250
   D) 55450

REFERENCE: CPT Assistant, June 1998, p 10
CPT Assistant, July 1998, p 10

98. Laser destruction of penile condylomas.
   A) 54057
   B) 17106
   C) 17270
   D) 54055

REFERENCE: CPT Code Book 2006
Smith, p 108

99. First stage repair for hypospadias with skin flaps.
   A) 54300
   B) 54308; 14040
   C) 54322
   D) 54304

REFERENCE: CPT Code Book 2006

100. Priapism operation with spongiosum shunt.
   A) 54450
   B) 54352
   C) 54430
   D) 55899

REFERENCE: CPT Code Book 2006

Surgery - Female Genital System

101. Patient was admitted to the hospital with sharp pelvic pains. A pelvic ultrasound was ordered and the results showed a possible ovarian cyst. The patient was taken to the operating room where a laparoscopic destruction of two (2) corpus luteum cysts was performed.
A) 49321
B) 58925
C) 58561
D) 58662
REFERENCE: Step-By-Step, p 257-260
Principles of CPT Coding, p 240

102. Patient was admitted with a cystocele and rectocele. An anterior colporrhaphy was performed.
A) 57250
B) 57260
C) 57240
D) 57110
REFERENCE: Principles of CPT p 237
Step by Step, p 253

103. Patient has a Bartholin's gland cyst that was marsupilizated.
A) 54640
B) 10060
C) 58999
D) 56440
REFERENCE: CPT Code Book, 2006

104. Patient is at a fertility clinic and undergoes intrauterine embryo transplant.
A) 58679
B) 58322
C) 58323
D) 58974
REFERENCE: CPT Code Book 2006

105. Patient has been diagnosed with carcinoma of the vagina and she has a radical vaginectomy with complete removal of the vaginal wall.
A) 57107
B) 57110
C) 51707
D) 57111
REFERENCE: Step-By-Step, p 252

106. Patient has been diagnosed with uterine fibroids and undergoes a total abdominal hysterectomy with bilateral salpingo-oophorectomy.
A) 58200
B) 58150
C) 58262
D) 58150; 58720
REFERENCE: Step-By-Step, p 256
Principles of CPT Coding, p 238-239

107. Hysteroscopy with D&C and polypectomy
   A) 58563
   B) 58558
   C) 58120; 58100; 58555
   D) 58558; 58120
REFERENCE: Step-By-Step, p 255
Principles of CPT Coding, p 239
Smith, p 113

108. Laparoscopic tubal ligation utilizing Endoloop.
   A) 58670
   B) 58615
   C) 58671
   D) 58611
REFERENCE: Step-By-Step, p 259
Principles of CPT Coding, p 239-240

109. Laser destruction extensive herpetic lesions of the vulva.
   A) 17106
   B) 17004
   C) 56515
   D) 56501
REFERENCE: CPT Code Book, 2006

110. Patient undergoes hysteroscopy with excision uterine fibroids
   A) 58545
   B) 58140
   C) 58561
   D) 58140; 49320
REFERENCE: Step-By-Step, p 255-257
Principles of CPT Coding, p 239
Smith, p 113

Surgery - Maternity Care and Delivery

111. Attempted vaginal delivery in a previous cesarean section patient, which resulted in a repeat cesarean section.
   A) 59409
   B) 59612
   C) 59620
   D) 59514
REFERENCE: Step-By-Step, p 262-263
Principles of CPT Coding, p 244-246

112. Patient is admitted to the hospital following an ultrasound at 25 weeks when revealed fetal pleural effusion. A fetal thoracentesis was performed.
   A) 59074
   B) 32000
   C) 32002
   D) 76815
REFERENCE: CPT Assistant, May 2004, p 3-4
Principles of CPT Coding, p 242

113. Patient in late stages of labor arrives at the hospital. Her OB physician is not able to make the delivery and the house physician delivers the baby vaginally. Primary care physician resumes care after delivery. Code the delivery.
A) 59409
B) 59612
C) 59620
D) 59400
REFERENCE: Step-By-Step, p 262-263
Principles of CPT Coding, p 243-246

114. Patient is 24 weeks pregnant and arrives in the emergency room following an automobile accident. No fetal movement or heart beat noted. Patient is taken to the OB ward where prostaglandin is given to induce abortion.
A) 59200
B) 59855
C) 59821
D) 59410
REFERENCE: Principles of CPT Coding, p 249
Step by Step, p 264

115. Patient is 6 weeks pregnant and complains of left sided abdominal pains. Patient is suspected of having an ectopic pregnancy. Patient has a laparoscopic salpingectomy with removal of the ectopic tubal pregnancy.
A) 59120
B) 59200
C) 59121
D) 59151
REFERENCE: Step-By-Step, p 263
Principles of CPT Coding, p 242

116. Cesarean delivery with antepartum and postpartum care.
A) 59610
B) 59514
C) 59400
D) 59510
REFERENCE: Step-By-Step, p 262
Principles of CPT Coding, p 243-246

117. A pregnant patient has an incompetent cervix which was repaired using a vaginal cerclage.
A) 57700
B) 57531
C) 59320
D) 53902
REFERENCE: Principles of CPT Coding, p 243

118. A D&C is performed for postpartum hemorrhage.
A) 59160
B) 58120
C) 58558
D) 58578
REFERENCE: Step-By-Step, p 264

119. Hysterotomy for hydatidifom mole and tubal ligation.
A) 58285; 58600
B) 58150; 58605
C) 51900; 58605
D) 59100; 58611
REFERENCE: Principles of CPT Coding, p 240
Step by Step, p 263

120. D&C performed for patient with diagnosis of incomplete abortion at 8 weeks.
A) 59812
B) 59820
C) 58120
D) 59160
REFERENCE: Principles of CPT Coding, p 248

Surgery - Endocrine System

121. Patient comes in for a percutaneous needle biopsy of the thyroid gland.
A) 60000
B) 60270
C) 60699
D) 60100
REFERENCE: CPT Assistant, June 1997, p 5

122. Laparoscopic adrenalectomy, complete.
A) 60650
B) 60650-50
C) 60659
D) 60540
REFERENCE: CPT Book 2006

123. Left carotid artery excision for tumor of carotid body.
A) 60650
B) 60600
C) 60605
D) 56321
REFERENCE: Step-By-Step, p 290

124. Patient undergoes total thyroidectomy with parathyroid autotransplantation.
A) 60240; 60512
B) 60520; 60500
C) 60260; 60512
D) 60650; 60500
REFERENCE: Step-By-Step, p 290-291

125. Unilateral partial thyroidectomy
A) 60252
B) 60210
C) 60220
D) 60520
REFERENCE: Step-By-Step, p 290-291

Surgery - Nervous System

126. Patient comes in through the emergency room with a wound that was caused by an electric saw. Patient is taken to the operating room where two (2) ulna nerves are sutured.
   A) 64837
   B) 64892; 69990
   C) 64836; 64837
   D) 64856; 64859

REFERENCE: Step-By-Step, p 297

127. Laminectomy and excision of intradural lumbar lesion.
   A) 63272
   B) 63267
   C) 63282
   D) 63252

REFERENCE: CPT Book 2006

128. Patient comes in for steroid injection for lumbar herniated disk. Marcaine and Aristocort were injected into the L2-L3 space.
   A) 64520
   B) 64483
   C) 62311
   D) 64714

REFERENCE: CPT Assistant, September 1997, p 10
Principles of CPT Coding, p 265
Smith, p 121

129. Patient with Parkinson's disease is admitted for an insertion of a brain neurostimulator pulse generator with one electrode array.
   A) 61885
   B) 61850; 61863
   C) 61888
   D) 61867; 61870

REFERENCE: CPT Assistant, April 2001, p 8-9
CPT Assistant, June 2000, p 4, 12
Principles of CPT Coding, p 261

130. Patient has rhinorrhea which requires repair of the CSF leak with craniotomy.
   A) 63707
   B) 63709
   C) 62100
   D) 62010

REFERENCE: CPT Changes: An Insider's View 2002

131. Patient has metastatic brain lesions. Patient undergoes stereotactic radiosurgery gamma knife of two lesions.
   A) 61533
   B) 61500
   C) 61793; 61793
   D) 61793

REFERENCE: CPT Assistant, April 2004, p 15
Principles of CPT Coding, p 257-258

132. Patient has right sacroiliac joint dysfunction and requires a right S2-S3 paravertebral facet joint anesthetic nerve block.
   A) 62311
   B) 64475
   C) 64483
   D) 64520

REFERENCE: CPT Assistant, November 1999, p 33, 37
CPT Assistant, February 2000, p 4
CPT Assistant, September 2004, p 3
CPT Changes: An Insider's View 2000
Smith, p 121
Principles of CPT Coding, p 270-274

133. Patient requires repair of a 6 cm meningocele.
   A) 63700
   B) 63709
   C) 63180
   D) 63702

REFERENCE: CPT Code Book 2006

134. Patient comes in through the emergency room with a laceration of the posterior tibial nerve. Patient is taken to the operating room where the nerve requires transposition and suture.
   A) 64856
   B) 64831; 64832; 64876
   C) 64840; 64874
   D) 64834; 64859; 64872

REFERENCE: Step-By-Step, p 297

<u>Surgery - Eye and Ocular Adnexa</u>

135. Patient returns to the physician's office complaining of obscured vision. Patient has had cataract surgery 6 months prior. Patient requires laser discission of secondary cataract.
   A) 66821
   B) 64831
   C) 67835
   D) 66830

REFERENCE: Smith, p 124-125

136. Patient undergoes enucleation of left eye and muscles were reattached to an implant.
   A) 65135-LT
   B) 65105-LT
   C) 65730-LT
   D) 65103-LT

REFERENCE: Principles of CPT Coding, p 279

137. Patient suffers from strabismus and requires surgery. Recession of the lateral rectus (horizontal) muscle with adjustable sutures was performed.
   A) 67340; 67500
   B) 67314; 67320
   C) 67332; 67334
   D) 67311; 67335

REFERENCE: CPT Book, 2005
CPT Assistant, Summer 1993, p 20
CPT Assistant, March 1997, p 5
CPT Assistant, November 1998, p 1
CPT Assistant, September 2002, p 10
Smith, p 126

138. Radial keratotomy.
   A) 92070
   B) 65855
   C) 65767
   D) 65771

REFERENCE: CPT Book, 2006

139. Correction of trichiasis by incision of lid margin.
   A) 67840
   B) 67830
   C) 67835
   D) 68740

REFERENCE: CPT Book, 2006

140. Patient undergoes ocular resurfacing construction utilizing stem cell allograft from a cadaver.
   A) 67320
   B) 66999
   C) 68371
   D) 65781

REFERENCE: CPT Assistant, May 2004, p 9-11
Principles of CPT Coding, p 281

141. Aphakia penetrating corneal transplant.
   A) 65755
   B) 65730
   C) 65750
   D) 65765

REFERENCE: Principles of CPT Coding, p 280

142. Lagophthalmos correction with implantation using gold weight.
   A) 67912
   B) 67911
   C) 67901
   D) 67121

REFERENCE: CPT Assistant, May, 2004, p 12

143. Lacrimal fistula closure.
A) 68760
B) 68761
C) 68700
D) 68770
REFERENCE: CPT Book, 2006

<u>Surgery - Auditory</u>

144. Patient comes into the office for removal of impacted ear wax.
A) 69210
B) 69200
C) 69222
D) 69000
REFERENCE: Principles of CPT Coding, p 293

145. Patient with a traumatic rupture of the ear drum repaired the tympanoplasty with incision of the mastoid. Repair of ossicular chain not required.
A) 69641
B) 69646
C) 69642
D) 69635
REFERENCE: CPT Book, 2006

146. Patient came in for excision of a middle ear lesion.
A) 11440
B) 69540
C) 69552
D) 69535
REFERENCE: CPT Book, 2006

147. Patient with chronic otitis media requiring eustachian tube catheterization.
A) 69400
B) 69424
C) 69421
D) 69405
REFERENCE: CPT Book, 2006

148. Modified radical mastoidectomy
A) 69511
B) 69505
C) 69635
D) 19180
REFERENCE: CPT Book, 2006

149. Decompression internal auditory canal.
A) 69979
B) 69915
C) 69970
D) 69960
REFERENCE: CPT Book, 2006

150. Myringoplasty
   A) 69620
   B) 69635
   C) 69610
   D) 69420
REFERENCE: CPT Assistant, March 2001, p 10

151. Insertion of cochlear device inner ear.
   A) 69711
   B) 69949
   C) 69930
   D) 69960; 69990
REFERENCE: CPT Book, 2006

152. Patient with Bell's Palsy requiring a total facial nerve decompression.
   A) 64742
   B) 64771
   C) 69955
   D) 64864
REFERENCE: CPT Book, 2006

153. Drainage of simple external ear abscess.
   A) 69000
   B) 69100
   C) 10060
   D) 69020
REFERENCE: CPT Assistant, October 1997, p 11
CPT Assistant, October 1999, p 10

Radiology

154. Administration of initial oral radionuclide therapy for hyperthyroidism.
   A) 78015
   B) 77402
   C) 78099
   D) 79005
REFERENCE: Step-By-Step, p 331

155. Patient comes into the outpatient department at the local hospital for an MRI of the cervical spine with contrast. Patient is status post automobile accident.
   A) 72156
   B) 72142
   C) 72149
   D) 72126
REFERENCE: Step-By-Step, p 319

156. Obstetric patient comes in for a pelvimetery with placental placement.
   A) 74710
   B) 76946
   C) 76805
   D) 76825
REFERENCE: CPT Code Book 2006

157. Patient comes into his physician office complaining of wrist pain. Physician sends the patient to the hospital for an arthrography. Code complete procedure.
A) 73115
B) 73100
C) 73110
D) 25246; 73115
REFERENCE: Step-By-Step, p 319

158. Patient has carcinoma of the breast and undergoes proton beam delivery of radiation to the breast with a single port.
A) 77523
B) 77432
C) 77520
D) 77402
REFERENCE: Step-By-Step, p 329
Principles of CPT Coding, p 336

159. CT Scan of the head with contrast.
A) 70460
B) 70542
C) 70551
D) 70470
REFERENCE: Step-By-Step, p 319
Principles of CPT Coding, p 314

160. Patient undergoes x-ray of the foot with three (3) views.
A) 73620
B) 73610
C) 73630
D) 27648; 73615
REFERENCE: Step-By-Step, p 319

161. Radiologist provides fluoroscopic guidance for facet joint injection.
A) 71023
B) 76003
C) 76001
D) 76005
REFERENCE: CPT Assistant, November 1999, p 32, 34, 41
CPT Assistant, January 2000, p 1
CPT Assistant, February 2000, p 6
CPT Assistant, August 2000, p 8
CPT Assistant, September 2002, p 11
CPT Assistant, September, 2004, p 5
CPT Changes: An Insider's View 2000

162. Pregnant female comes in for a complete fetal and maternal evaluation via ultrasound.
A) 76856
B) 76805
C) 76811
D) 76810
REFERENCE: Step-By-Step, p 322
Principles of CPT Coding, p 330

163. Ultrasonic guidance for the needle biopsy of the liver. Code the complete procedure.
   A) 47000; 76942
   B) 47000; 76938
   C) 47000; 76999
   D) 47000; 76003
REFERENCE: Step-By-Step, p 322

<u>Pathology and Laboratory</u>

164. What code is used for a culture of embryos less than four days?
   A) 89251
   B) 89272
   C) 89268
   D) 89250
REFERENCE: CPT Assistant, April 2004, p 2
CPT Assistant May 2004, p 16
CPT Assistant June, 2004, p 9
CPT Changes, An Insider's View, 2004
Principles of CPT Coding, p 368

165. Basic metabolic panel and total bilirubin.
   A) 80048; 82247
   B) 80053
   C) 80100
   D) 82239; 80400; 80051
REFERENCE: Step-By-Step, p 338-338
Smith, p 148
Principles of CPT Coding, p 347

166. Huhner test and semen analysis.
   A) 89325
   B) 89258
   C) 89399
   D) 89300
REFERENCE: CPT Assistant, November 1997, p 36
CPT Assistant, July 1998, p 10
CPT Assistant, October 1998, p 1
CPT Assistant, April 2004, p 3
Principles of CPT Coding, p 368

167. Chlamydia culture.
   A) 87110
   B) 87106
   C) 87118
   D) 87109; 87163
REFERENCE: Step-By-Step, p 344

168. Partial thromboplastin time utilizing whole blood.
   A) 85732
   B) 85730
   C) 85245
   D) 85245
REFERENCE: Step-By-Step, p 343
Smith, p 149

169. Pathologist bills for gross and microscopic examination of medial meniscus.
   A) 88300
   B) 88302; 88311
   C) 88325
   D) 88304
REFERENCE: Step-By-Step, p 345-346
Principles of CPT Coding, p 367

170. Cytopathology of cervical Pap smear with automated thin layer preparation utilizing computer screening and manual rescreening under physician supervision.
   A) 88175
   B) 88148
   C) 88160; 88141
   D) 88161
REFERENCE: Step by Step, p 345
CPT Assistant, July 2003, p 9
CPT Assistant, March 2004, p 4
CPT Changes: An Insider's View, 2003
CPT Changes: An Insider's View, 2006

171. Pathologist performs a postmortem examination including brain of an adult. Tissue is being sent to the lab for microscopic examination.
   A) 88309
   B) 88025
   C) 88099
   D) 88028
REFERENCE: Step by Step, p 345

172. Clotting Factor VII/
   A) 82530
   B) 85240
   C) 85362
   D) 85230
REFERENCE: Step by Step, p 343
Smith, p 149

173. IV push of one anti-neoplastic drug.
   A) 96401
   B) 96409
   C) 96411
   D) 96413
REFERENCE: Principles of CPT Coding, p 456-458

174. One-half (1/2) hour of IV chemotherapy by infusion followed by IV push of a different drug.
   A) 96413
   B) 96413, 96411
   C) 96413, 96409
   D) 96409, 96411

REFERENCE: Principles of CPT Coding, p 456-458

175. Caloric vestibular test using air.
   A) 92543, 92700
   B) 92543, 92543
   C) 92700
   D) 92543

REFERENCE: CPT Assistant, November 2004, p 10

Medicine Section

176. Patient presents to the emergency room with chest pains. The patient is admitted as a twenty-three (23) hour observation. The cardiologist orders cardiac workup and the patient undergoes left heart catheterization via the left femoral artery with visualization of the coronary arteries and left ventriculography. The physician interprets the report. Code the heart catheterization.
   A) 36245; 93514; 93545; 93540; 93555
   B) 93524; 93545; 93542; 93555; 93556
   C) 93510; 93545; 93543; 93555; 93556
   D) 93511; 93539; 93541; 93545; 93555

REFERENCE: Step-By-Step, p 234-237
Smith, p 191-192
Principles of CPT Coding, p 424-427

177. Mother brings her one (1) year old in for the influenza split virus vaccine. Physician discusses merits of the vaccine with the mother.
   A) 90658; 90472
   B) 90657; 90465
   C) 90703
   D) 90657

REFERENCE: Step-By-Step, p 353-358
CPT Assistant, April 2005, p 2-3
CPT Changes: An Insider's View 2005
Principles of CPT Coding, p 382-388
Smith, p 184-185

178. Patient with hematochromatosis had a therapeutic phlebotomy performed on an outpatient basis.
   A) 99195
   B) 36522
   C) 36514
   D) 99199

REFERENCE: CPT Assistant, June 1996, p 10

179. A Medicare patient undergoes PTCA with drug eluting stent placement in the left anterior descending artery and angioplasty only in the right coronary artery.
   A) 92996; 92980
   B) 92982-RC, G0290
   C) 93510; 92980; 92981
   D) 92982; 92996, G0290

REFERENCE: Step-By-Step, p 229-230
CPT Assistant, April 2005, p 14
Smith, p 189
Principles of CPT Coding, p 417-421

180. Transesophageal echocardiography (TEE) with probe placement, image, and interpretation and report.
   A) 93307
   B) 93303; 93325
   C) 93312; 93313; 93314
   D) 93312

REFERENCE: CPT Assistant, December 1997, p 5
CPT Assistant, January 2000, p 10
Principles of CPT Coding, p 422

181. Which code listed below would be used to report an esophageal electrogram during an EPS.
   A) 93600
   B) 93615
   C) 93612
   D) 93616

REFERENCE: CPT Assistant, April 2004, p 9
Smith, p 192
Principles of CPT Coding, p 428-433

182. Cardioversion of cardiac arrhythmia by external forces.
   A) 92961
   B) 92950
   C) 92960
   D) 92970

REFERENCE: CPT Assistant, Summer 1993, p 13
CPT Assistant, November 1999, p 49
CPT Assistant, June 2000, p 5
CPT Assistant, November 2000, p 9
CPT Assistant, July 2001, p 11
CPT Changes: An Insider's View 2000
Principles of CPT Coding, p 415-416

183. Osteopathic manipulative treatment to three body regions.
   A) 98926
   B) 98941
   C) 97110
   D) 97012

REFERENCE: Step-By-Step, p 372
Principles of CPT Coding, p 467

184. Patient presents to the Respiratory Therapy Department and undergoes a pulmonary stress test. CO2 production with O2 uptake with recordings were also performed.
   A) 94450
   B) 94620
   C) 94656
   D) 94621

REFERENCE: CPT Assistant, November 1998, p 35
CPT Assistant, January 1999, p 8
CPT Assistant, August, 2002, p 10
Principles of CPT Coding, p 439

185. IV infusion of chemotherapy for three hours.
   A) 96422, 96423, 96423
   B) 96409, 96411
   C) 96413, 96415, 96415
   D) 96413, 96413, 96413

REFERENCE: Step-By-Step, p 369-370
Principles of CPT Coding, p 456-459
CPT Changes: An Insider's View 2006
Smith, p 195

---

For the following questions, you will be utilizing the codes provided for the scenarios. You will need to code appropriate ICD-9-CM and CPT-4 codes

186. Patient presents to the hospital for debridement of a diabetic ulcer of the left ankle. The patient has a history of recurrent ulcers. Medications taken by the patient are Diabeta and the patient was covered in the hospital with Insulin sliding-scales. The ulcer was debrided down to the bone.

| | |
|---|---|
| 250.70 | Diabetes with peripheral circulatory disorders, type II, or unspecified |
| 250.71 | Diabetes with peripheral circulatory disorders, type I |
| 250.80 | Diabetes with other specified manifestations, type II, or unspecified |
| 250.81 | Diabetes with other specified manifestations, type I |
| 707.06 | Decubitus ulcer, ankle |
| 707.09 | Decubitus ulcer other site |
| 11043 | Debridement, skin, subcutaneous tissue and muscle |
| 11044 | Debridement, skin, subcutaneous tissue, muscle and bone |

   A) 250.81, 707.06, 11044
   B) 250.71, 11043
   C) 250.80, 707.06, 11044
   D) 250.81, 250.70, 707.09, 11044

REFERENCE: Step by Step p 132
Principles of CPT Coding, p 128
Brown, p 95-97

187. Patient presents to the Emergency Room department following a fall from a tree. X-rays were ordered for the left upper arm which showed a fracture of the humerus shaft. The emergency room physician performed a closed reduction of the fracture and placed the patient in a long arm spica cast. Code the diagnoses and procedures, excluding the x-ray.

| | |
|---|---|
| 812.21 | Fracture humerus, shaft, closed |
| 812.31 | Fracture, humerus, shaft, closed |
| E884.9 | Other fall from one level to another |
| 24500 | Closed treatment of humeral shaft fracture; without manipulation |
| 24505 | Closed treatment of humeral shaft fracture; with manipulation, with or without skeletal traction |
| 24515 | Open treatment of humeral shaft fracture with plate/screws, with or without cerclage |
| 29065 | Application, cast; shoulder to hand (long arm) |
| LT | Left side |

A) 812.21, E884.9, 24505-LT
B) 812.21, 24515-LT
C) 812.21, E884.9, 24505-LT, 29065
D) 812.31, 24500-LT

REFERENCE: Step by Step, p 165-168
Principles of CPT Coding, p 153-154
Smith, p 68
Brown, p 317

188. Patient was admitted with hemoptysis and underwent a bronchoscopy with transbronchial lung biopsy. Following the bronchoscopy the patient was taken to the operating room where a left lower lobe lobectomy was performed without complications. Pathology reported large cell carcinoma of the left lower lobe.

| | |
|---|---|
| 162.5 | Malignant neoplasm of the lower lobe of the lung |
| 162.8 | Malignant neoplasm of other parts of bronchus or lung |
| 162.9 | Malignant neoplasm of the bronchus and lung, unspecified |
| 31625 | Bronchoscopy with biopsy, with or without fluroscopic guidance |
| 31628 | Bronchoscopy with transbronchial lung biopsy, with or without fluoroscopic guidance |
| 32405 | Biopsy, lung or mediastinum, percutaneous needle |
| 32440 | Removal of lung, total pneumonectomy |
| 32480 | Removal of lung, other than total pneumonectomy, single lobe (lobectomy) |
| 32484 | Removal of lung, other than total pneumonectomy, single segment (segmentectomy) |

A) 162.9, 31625
B) 162.5, 31628, 32480
C) 162.9, 32405, 32484
D) 162.8, 32440

REFERENCE: Principles of CPT Coding, p 183-184
Smith, p 80
CPT Assistant, June 2001, p 10
CPT Assistant, September 2004, p 9
CPT Assistant, June 2002, p 10
CPT Changes: An Insider's View 2004

189. Patient was admitted for right upper quadrant pain. Workup included various x-rays that showed cholelithiasis. Patient was taken to the operating room where a laparoscopic cholecystectomy was performed. During the procedure the physician was unable to visualize through the ports and an open cholecystectomy was elected to be performed. Intraoperative cholangiogram was performed. Pathology report states acute and chronic cholecystitis with cholelithiasis.

| | |
|---|---|
| 574.00 | Calculus of gallbladder with acute cholecystitis without obstruction |
| 574.10 | Calculus of gallbladder with other cholecystitis without obstruction |
| 789.01 | Abdominal pain of the right upper quadrant |
| V64.41 | Laparoscopic procedure converted to open procedure |
| 47605 | Cholecystectomy with cholangiography |
| 47563 | Laparoscopy, surgical; cholecystectomy with cholangiography |

A) 789.01, 574.10, 47563
B) 789.01, 574.00, 574.10, 47563, 47605
C) 574.00, 574.10, V64.41, 47605
D) 574.00, 47563, 47605

REFERENCE: Brown, p 161
Hazelwood and Venable, p 43, 175
Principles of CPT Coding, p 224-225

190. Patient came to the hospital from a local nursing home for a PEG tube placement via EGD. Patient had dysphagia and dominant hemiplegia due to prior CVA.

| | |
|---|---|
| 434.91 | Acute, but ill-defined, cerebrovascular disease |
| 438.21 | Late effect of CVA with hemiplegia affecting dominant side |
| 438.81 | Late effect of CVA with apraxia |
| 438.82 | Late effect of CVA with dysphagia |
| 787.2 | Dysphagia |
| 43219 | Esophagoscopy, rigid or flexible with insertion of plastic tube or stent |
| 43246 | Upper gastrointestinal endoscopy of esophagus, stomach, and either the duodenum and/or jejunum with directed placement of percutaneous gastrostomy tube |
| 43750 | Percutaneous placement of gastrostomy tube |
| 44372 | Small intestine endoscopy, enteroscopy beyond second portion of duodenum with placement of percutaneous jejunostomy tube |

A) 438.81, 43219
B) 438.82, 438.21, 43246
C) 434.91, 787.2, 344.41, 44372
D) 434.91, 43750

REFERENCE: Step-By-Step, p 276
Principles of CPT Coding, p 220
Brown, p 263-264
Hazelwood and Venable, p 148

191. Patient presents to the Emergency Room complaining of right forearm/elbow pain after racquetball last night. Patient states that he did not fall, but overworked his arm. Past medical history is negative and the physical examination reveals the patient is unable to supinate. A four view x-ray of the right elbow is performed and is negative. The physician signs the patient out with right elbow sprain. Prescription of Motrin is given to the patient.

| | |
|---|---|
| 841.2 | Sprain of radiohumeral joint |
| 841.8 | Sprain of other specified sites of the elbow and forearm |
| 841.9 | Sprain of unspecified site of the elbow and forearm |
| E927 | Overextertion and strenuous movements |
| E928.9 | Unspecified accident |
| 73040 | X-ray of shoulder, arthrography radiological supervision and interpretation |
| 73070 | X-ray of elbow, two views |
| 73080 | X-ray of elbow, complete, minimum of three views |
| 99281 | E/M visit to Emergency Room - problem focused history, problem focused exam, straightforward medical decision. |
| 99282 | E/M visit to Emergency Room - expanded problem focused history, expanded problem focused exam, medical decision of low complexity |

A) 841.8, 73080
B) 841.9, E928.9, 99281, 73070
C) 841.2, 73080, 99282, 73040
D) 841.9, E927, 99281, 73080

REFERENCE: CPT Code Book 2006
Brown, p 310-312
Smith, p 138-139, 174

192. A Medicare patient presents with internal derangement of the right knee. Postoperative diagnosis is torn medial meniscus and chondromalacia of the lateral compartment. Procedures performed included a diagnostic arthroscopy, partial medial meniscectomy and a chondroplasty.

| | |
|---|---|
| 715.36 | Osteoarthritis, localized, not specified whether primary or secondary, lower leg |
| 717.0 | Old bucket handle tear of medial meniscus |
| 717.3 | Other and unspecified derangement of medial meniscus |
| 717.7 | Chondromalacia of patella |
| 717.9 | Unspecified internal derangement of knee |
| 836.0 | Tear of medial cartilage or meniscus of knee, current |
| 836.1 | Tear of lateral cartilage or meniscus of knee, current |
| 29870 | Arthroscopy, knee, diagnostic, with or without synovial biopsy (separate procedure) |
| 29877 | Arthroscopy, knee, surgical, with debridement/shaving of articular cartilage (chondroplasty) |
| 29879 | Arthroscopy, knee, surgical, with abrasion arthroplasty (including chondroplasty where necessary) or multiple drilling or micro fracture |
| 29880 | Arthroscopy, knee, surgical, with meniscectomy (medial AND lateral, including any meniscal shaving) |
| 29881 | Arthroscopy, knee, surgical, with meniscectomy (medial OR lateral, including any meniscal shaving) |
| G0289 | Arthroscopy, knee, surgical, for removal of loose body, foreign body, debridement/shaving of articular cartilage (chondroplasty) at the time of other surgical knee arthroscopy in a different compartment of the same knee |
| RT | Right side |

A) 717.3, 717.7, 29881-RT, 29877, G0289
B) 836.1, 715.36, 29870, 29881-RT, 29877
C) 836.0, 717.7, 29881-RT, G0289
D) 717.9, 717.0, 717.7, 29880, 29879

REFERENCE: Step by Step, p 181-182
Principles of CPT Coding, p 173-174
Smith, p 71

193. Chronic nontraumatic rotator cuff tear. Arthroscopic subacromial decompression with mini-open rotator cuff repair.

| | |
|---|---|
| 726.10 | Disorders of bursae and tendons in shoulder region, unspecified |
| 727.61 | Complete rupture of rotator cuff, nontraumatic |
| 840.4 | Sprains and strains of rotator cuff (capsule) |
| 23410 | Repair of ruptured musculotendinous cuff (e.g., rotator cuff); open, acute |
| 23412 | Repair of ruptured musculotendinous cuff (e.g. rotator cuff) open; chronic |
| 29821 | Arthroscopy, shoulder, surgical; synovectomy, complete |
| 29823 | Arthroscopy, shoulder, surgical; debridement, extensive |
| 29826 | Arthroscopy, shoulder, surgical; decompression of subacromial space with partial acromioplasty, with or without coracoacromial |
| 29827 | Arthroscopy, shoulder, surgical; with rotator cuff repair |

A) 840.4, 726.10, 29823
B) 727.61, 29826, 23412
C) 840.4, 29826, 29821
D) 727.61, 23410

REFERENCE: Principles of CPT Coding, p 173-174
Smith, p 71

194. The patient is on vacation and presents to a physician's office with a lacerated finger. The physician repairs the laceration and gives a prescription for pain control and has the patient follow up with his primary physician when he returns home. The physician fills out the superbill as a problem focused history and examination with straightforward medical decision making. Also checked is a laceration repair for a 1.5 cm finger wound.

| | |
|---|---|
| 99201 | New Patient office visit with a problem focused history, problem focused examination and straightforward medical decision making |
| 99212 | Established patient office visit with a problem focused history, problem focused examination and straightforward medical decision making |
| 12001 | Simple repair of superficial wounds of scalp, neck, axillae, external genitalia, trunk and/or extremities (including hands and feet); 2.5 cm or less |
| 13131 | Repair, complex, forehead, cheeks, chin, mouth, neck, axillae, genitalia, hands and/or feet; 1.1 cm to 2.5 cm |

A) 99212; 13131
B) 12001
C) 99212; 12001
D) 99201; 12001

REFERENCE: Step by Step, p 49, 143-145
Smith, p 54-56, 172

195. A 69 year old established female patient presents to the office with chronic obstructive lung disease, congestive heart failure and hypertension. The physician conducts a comprehensive history and physical examination and makes a medical decision of moderate complexity. Physician admits the patient from the office to the hospital for acute exacerbation of CHF.

| | |
|---|---|
| 428.0 | Congestive Heart Failure, unspecified |
| 402.91 | Hypertensive heart disease, with congestive heart failure |
| 401.9 | Essential hypertension, unspecified |
| 401.1 | Essential hypertension, benign |
| 496 | Chronic obstructive pulmonary disease |
| 99212 | Established office visit for problem focused history and exam, straightforward medical decision making |
| 99214 | Established office visit for a detailed history and exam, moderate medical decision making |
| 99222 | Initial hospital care for comprehensive history and exam, moderate medical decision making |
| 99223 | Initial hospital care for comprehensive history and exam, high medical decision making |

A) 402.91; 496; 99214
B) 428.0; 496; 401.1; 99223
C) 428.0; 496; 401.9; 99222
D) 402.91; 496; 401.1; 99212

REFERENCE: Step by Step, p53
Brown, p 266-267
Smith, p 172-173

196. Established 42 year old patient comes into your office to obtain vaccines required for his trip to Sri Lanka. The nurse injects intramuscularly the following vaccines: Hepatitis A and B vaccines, cholera vaccine, and yellow fever vaccine. As the coding specialist, what would you report on the CMS 1500 form?

A) Office visit, hepatitis A and B vaccine, cholera vaccine and yellow fever vaccine
B) Office visit, intramuscular injection; HCPCS Level II codes
C) Office visit; administration of two or more single vaccines; vaccine products for hepatitis A and B, cholera, and yellow fever
D) Administration of two or more single vaccines; vaccine products for hepatitis A and B, cholera, and yellow fever.

REFERENCE: Step by Step, p 353-358
Smith, p 184-185

197. Patient presents to the operating room where the physician performed, using imaging guidance, a percutaneous breast biopsy utilizing a rotating biopsy device.

| | |
|---|---|
| 19000 | Puncture aspiration of cyst of breast |
| 19103 | Biopsy of breast; percutaneous, automated vacuum assisted or rotating biopsy device, using imaging guidance |
| 19120 | Excision of cyst, fibroadenoma, or other benign or malignant tumor, aberrant breast tissue, duct lesion, nipple or areolar lesion (except 19140), open, male or female, one or more lesions |
| 19125 | Excision of breast lesion identified by preoperative placement of radiological marker, open; single lesion |
| 19295 | Image guided placement, metallic localization clip, percutaneous, during breast biopsy (List separately in addition to code for primary procedure) |

A) 19103
B) 19125; 19295
C) 19120
D) 19000

REFERENCE: CPT Assistant, Jan 2001, page 10-11
Step by Step, p 157
Smith, p 63-64

198. Facelift utilizing the SMAS flap technique

| | |
|---|---|
| 15788 | Chemical peel, facial; epidermal |
| 15825 | Rhytidectomy; neck with platysmal tightening (platysmal flap, P-flap) |
| 15828 | Rhytidectomy; cheek, chin, and neck |
| 15829 | Rhytidectomy; superficial musculoaponeurotic system (SMAS) flap |

A) 15825
B) 15788
C) 15829
D) 15828

REFERENCE: Step by Step Coding, p 152

199. Patient presents to the operating room for a secondary Achilles tendon repair.

| | |
|---|---|
| 27599 | Unlisted procedure, femur or knee |
| 27650 | Repair, primary, open or percutaneous, ruptured Achilles tendon |
| 27654 | Repair, secondary, Achilles tendon, with or without graft |
| 27698 | Repair, secondary, disrupted ligament, ankle, collateral (e.g., Watson-Jones procedure) |

A) 27599
B) 27654
C) 27650
D) 27698

REFERENCE: CPT Code Book, 2006

200. Tracheostoma revision with flap rotation.

| | |
|---|---|
| 31613 | Tracheostoma revision; simple, without flap rotation |
| 31614 | Tracheostoma revision; complex, with flap rotation |
| 31750 | Tracheoplasty; cervical |
| 31830 | Revision of tracheostomy scar |

A) 31830
B) 31750
C) 31614
D) 31613

REFERENCE: Step by Step, p 199-201

201. Patient complains of frequent temporal headaches and the physician suspects temporal arteritis. Patient underwent temporal artery biopsy.

| | |
|---|---|
| 784.0 | Headache |
| 446.5 | Temporal arteritis |
| 37600 | Ligation; external carotid artery |
| 37609 | Ligation or biopsy, temporal artery |
| 37615 | Ligation, major artery (e.g., post-traumatic, rupture); neck |

A) 784.0; 37615
B) 784.0; 37609
C) 446.5; 37600
D) 446.5; 37609

REFERENCE: CPT Code Book 2006

202. Blood transfusion of 3 units of packed red blood cells.

| | |
|---|---|
| 36430 | Transfusion, blood or blood components |
| 36455 | Exchange transfusion; blood, other than newborn |
| 36460 | Transfusion, intrauterine, fetal |

A) 36430
B) 36430; 36430; 36430
C) 36460
D) 36455

REFERENCE: CPT Code Book 2006

203. Two year old patient returns to the hospital for cleft palate repair where a secondary lengthening procedure takes place.

| | |
|---|---|
| 40720 | Plastic repair of cleft lip/nasal deformity; secondary, by recreation of defect and reclosure |
| 42145 | Palatopharyngoplasty |
| 42220 | Palatoplasty for cleft palate; secondary lengthening procedure |
| 42226 | Lengthening of palate, and pharyngeal flap |

A) 40720
B) 42220
C) 42226
D) 42145
REFERENCE: CPT Code Book 2006

204.Tonsillectomy on a 14 year old.

| | |
|---|---|
| 42820 | Tonsillectomy and adenoidectomy; under age 12 |
| 42821 | Tonsillectomy and adenoidectomy; age 12 or over |
| 42825 | Tonsillectomy, primary or secondary; under age 12 |
| 42826 | Tonsillectomy, primary or secondary; age 12 or over |

A) 42820
B) 42821
C) 42825
D) 42826
REFERENCE: Principles of CPT Coding, p 213

205. Laparoscopic repair of umbilical hernia.

| | |
|---|---|
| 49580 | Repair umbilical hernia, under age 5 years, reducible |
| 49585 | Repair umbilical hernia, age 5 years or over, reducible |
| 49659 | Unlisted laparoscopy procedure, hernioplasty, herniorrhaphy, herniotomy |
| 49999 | Unlisted procedure, abdomen, peritoneum and omentum |

A) 49580
B) 49999
C) 49585
D) 49659
REFERENCE: Step By Step, p 279
Smith, p 99

206. Excision of simple internal and external hemorrhoids.

| | |
|---|---|
| 46221 | Hemorrhoidectomy, by simple ligature (e.g., rubber band) |
| 46255 | Hemorrhoidectomy, internal and external, simple |
| 46260 | Hemorrhoidectomy, internal and external, complex or extensive |
| 46945 | Ligation of internal hemorrhoids; single procedure |

A) 46255
B) 46945
C) 46221
D) 46260
REFERENCE: CPT Code Book, 2006

207. Ureterolithotomy completed laparoscopically.

| | |
|---|---|
| 50600 | Ureterotomy with exploration or drainage (separate procedure) |
| 50945 | Laparoscopy, surgical ureterolithotomy |
| 52325 | Cystourethroscopy; with fragmentation of ureteral calculus |
| 52352 | Cystourethroscopy, with urethroscopy and/or pyeloscopy; with removal or manipulation of calculus (ureteral catheterization is included) |

A) 52352
B) 52325
C) 50600
D) 50945

REFERENCE: CPT Assistant, November 1999, p 26
CPT Assistant, May 2000, p 4
CPT Assistant, October 2001, p 8
CPT Changes: An Insider's View, 2000

208. Patient undergoes partial nephrectomy for carcinoma of the kidney.

| | |
|---|---|
| 50220 | Nephrectomy, including partial ureterectomy, any open approach including rib resection |
| 50234 | Nephrectomy with total ureterectomy and bladder cuff; through same incision |
| 50240 | Nephrectomy, partial |
| 50340 | Recipient nephrectomy (separate procedure) |

A) 50234
B) 50220
C) 50340
D) 50240

REFERENCE: Step-By-Step, p 272-273

209. Patient presents to the operating room for fulguration of bladder tumors. The cystoscope was inserted and entered the urethra which was normal. Bladder tumors measuring approximately 1.5 cm were removed.

| | |
|---|---|
| 50957 | Ureteral endoscopy through established ureterostomy, with or without irrigation, instillation, or ureteropyelography, exclusive of radiologic service; with fulguration and/or incision, with or without biopsy |
| 51530 | Cystotomy; for excision of bladder tumor |
| 52214 | Cystourethroscopy, with fulguration of trigone, bladder neck, prostatic fossa, urethra, or periurethral glands |
| 52234 | Cystourethroscopy, with fulguration (including cryosurgery or laser surgery) and/or resection of small bladder tumor(s) (0.5 up to 2.0 cm) |

A) 52234
B) 50957
C) 52214
D) 51530

REFERENCE: Step by Step, p 273-274

210. Excision of Cowper's gland.

| | |
|---|---|
| 53220 | Excision or fulguration of carcinoma of urethra |
| 53250 | Excision of bulbourethral gland (Cowper's gland) |
| 53260 | Excision or fulguration; urethral polyp(s), distal urethra |
| 53450 | Urethromeatoplasty, with mucosal advancement |

A) 53250
B) 53450
C) 53260
D) 53220
REFERENCE: CPT Code Book 2006

211. Placement of Double-J stent.

| | |
|---|---|
| 52320 | Cystourethroscopy (including ureteral catheterization); with removal of ureteral calculus |
| 52330 | Cystourethroscopy; with manipulation, without removal of ureteral calculus |
| 52332 | Cystourethroscopy with insertion of indwelling ureteral stent (e.g. Gibbons or double-J type) |
| 52341 | Cystourethroscopy, with treatment of ureteral stricture (e.g. balloon dilation, laser electrocautery, and incision) |

A) 52341
B) 52320
C) 52330; 52332
D) 52332
REFERENCE: Principles of CPT Coding, p 231-232

212. Closure of traumatic kidney injury.

| | |
|---|---|
| 13100 | Repair, complex trunk, 1.1 cm to 2.5 cm |
| 50400 | Pyeloplasty (Foley Y-pyeloplasty), plastic operation on renal pelvis, with or without plastic operation on ureter, nephropexy, nephrostomy, pyelostomy or ureteral splinting; simple |
| 50500 | Nephrorrhaphy, suture of kidney wound or injury |
| 50520 | Closure of nephrocutaneous or pyelocutaneous fistula |

A) 50520
B) 13100
C) 50500
D) 50400
REFERENCE: CPT Code Book 2006

213. Litholapaxy, 3.0 cm calculus.

| | |
|---|---|
| 50590 | Lithotripsy, extracorporeal shock wave |
| 52317 | Litholapaxy, simple or small (less than 2.5 cm) |
| 52318 | Litholapaxy, complicated or large (over 2.5 cm) |
| 52353 | Cystourethroscopy, with ureteroscopy and/or pyeloscopy; with lithotripsy |

A) 52353
B) 50590
C) 52318
D) 52317
REFERENCE: CPT Code Book 2006

214. Patient presented to the operating room where an incision was made in the epigastric region for a repair of ureterovisceral fistula.

| | |
|---|---|
| 50520 | Closure of nephrocutaneous or pyelocutaneous fistula |
| 50525 | Closure of nephrovisceral fistula, including visceral repair; abdominal approach |
| 50526 | Closure of nephrovisceral fistula including visceral repair; thoracic approach |
| 50930 | Closure of ureterovisceral fistula (including visceral repair) |

A) 50526
B) 50930
C) 50520
D) 50525

REFERENCE: CPT Code Book 2006

215. Amniocentesis.

| | |
|---|---|
| 57530 | Trachelectomy, amputation of cervix (separate procedure) |
| 57550 | Excision of cervical stump, vaginal approach |
| 59000 | Amniocentesis, diagnostic |
| 59200 | Insertion of cervical dilator (separate procedure) |

A) 59000
B) 59200
C) 57550
D) 57530

REFERENCE: Step-By-Step, p 263
Principles of CPT Coding, p 242

216. Excision of thyroid adenoma.

| | |
|---|---|
| 60100 | Biopsy thyroid, percutaneous core needle |
| 60200 | Excision of cyst or adenoma of thyroid, or transection of isthmus |
| 60210 | Partial thyroid lobectomy, unilateral; with or without isthmusectomy |
| 60280 | Excision of thyroglossal duct cyst or sinus |

A) 60210
B) 60200
C) 60280
D) 60100

REFERENCE: CPT Code Book 2006

217. Patient is admitted to the hospital with facial droop, left sided paralysis. CT Scan of the brain shows subdural hematoma. Burr holes were performed to evacuate the hematoma.

| | |
|---|---|
| 432.1 | Non-traumatic subdural hematoma |
| 852.20 | Subdural hemorrhage following injury without mention of open intra-cranial wound, unspecified state of unconsciousness |
| 61150 | Burr hole(s) or trephine; with drainage of brain abscess or cyst |
| 61154 | Burr hole(s) with evacuation and/or drainage of hematoma, extradural or subdural |
| 61156 | Burr hole(s); with aspiration of hematoma or cyst, intracerebral |
| 61314 | Craniectomy or craniotomy for evacuation of hematoma, infratentorial; extradural or subdural |

A) 852.20; 61156
B) 432.1; 61314
C) 432.1; 61154
D) 852.20; 61150

REFERENCE: Step by Step Coding, p 292
Brown, p 316

218. Spinal tap.

| | |
|---|---|
| 62268 | Percutaneous aspiration, spinal cord or syrinx |
| 62270 | Spinal puncture, lumbar diagnostic |
| 62272 | Spinal puncture, therapeutic, for drainage of cerebrospinal fluid (by needle or catheter) |
| 64999 | Unlisted procedure, nervous system |

A) 62272
B) 64999
C) 62268
D) 62270

REFERENCE: Principles of CPT Coding, p 264-265
Step by Step Coding, p 295-296

219. Injection of anesthesia for nerve block of the brachial plexus.

| | |
|---|---|
| 64413 | Injection, anesthetic agent; cervical plexus |
| 64415 | Injection, anesthetic agent; brachial plexus, single |
| 64510 | Injection, anesthetic agent; stellate ganglion (cervical sympathetic) |
| 64530 | Injection, anesthetic agent; celiac plexus, with or without radiologic monitoring |

A) 64415
B) 64413
C) 64530
D) 64510

REFERENCE: Principles of CPT Coding, p 270
Step by Step, p 297

220. Repair of retinal detachment with vitrectomy

| | |
|---|---|
| 67040 | Vitrectomy, mechanical, pars plana approach; with endolaser panretinal photocoagulation |
| 67105 | Repair of retinal detachment, one or more sessions; photocoagulation, with or without drainage of subretinal fluid |
| 67108 | Repair of retinal detachment; with vitrectomy, any method, with or without air or gas tamponade, focal endolaser photocoagulation, cryotherapy, drainage of subretinal fluid, scleral buckling, and/or removal of lens by same technique |
| 67112 | Repair of retinal detachment; by scleral buckling or vitrectomy, on patient having previous ipsilateral retinal detachment repair(s) using scleral buckling or vitrectomy techniques |

A) 67112
B) 67105
C) 67108
D) 67040

REFERENCE: CPT Assistant, October 2002, p 8
Principles of CPT Coding, p 282-283

221. SPECT bone imaging.

| | |
|---|---|
| 76075 | Dual energy x-ray absorptiometry (DXA), bone density study, one or more sites; axial skeleton (e.g. hips, pelvis, spine) |
| 76977 | Ultrasound bone density measurement and interpretation, peripheral site(s), any method |
| 78300 | Bone and/or joint imaging; limited area |
| 78320 | Bone and/or joint imaging; tomographic (SPECT) |

A) 76977
B) 78320
C) 76075
D) 76977

REFERENCE: CPT Code Book 2006
CPT Assistant, June 2003, p 11

222. Vitamin B-12.

| | |
|---|---|
| 82180 | Ascorbic acid (Vitamin C), blood |
| 82607 | Cyanocobalamin (Vitamin B-12) |
| 84590 | Vitamin A |
| 84591 | Vitamin, not otherwise specified |

A) 84590
B) 82180
C) 84591
D) 82607

REFERENCE: Step by Step Coding, p 342
Smith, p 148-149

223. Hepatitis C antibody.

| | |
|---|---|
| 86803 | Hepatitis C antibody |
| 86804 | Hepatitis C antibody; confirmatory test (e.g. immunoblot) |
| 87520 | Infectious agent detection by nucleic acid (DNA or RNA); hepatitis C, direct probe technique |
| 87522 | Infectious agent detection by nucleic acid (DNA or RNA); hepatitis C, quantification |

A) 86804
B) 86803
C) 87522
D) 87520

REFERENCE: Step by Step Coding, p 343

224. Creatinine clearance.

| | |
|---|---|
| 82550 | Creatine Kinase (CK), (CPK); total |
| 82565 | Creatinine; blood |
| 82575 | Creatinine; clearance |
| 82585 | Cryofibrinogen |

A) 82550
B) 82565
C) 82575
D) 82585

REFERENCE: Step by Step Coding, p 342

225. Comprehensive electrophysiologic evaluation (EPS) with induction of arrhythmia.

| | |
|---|---|
| 93618 | Induction of arrhythmia by electrical pacing |
| 93619 | Comprehensive electrophysiologic evaluation with right atrial pacing and recording, right ventricular pacing and recording, His bundle recording, including insertion and repositioning of multiple electrode catheters, without induction or attempted induction of arrhythmia |
| 93620 | Comprehensive electrophysiologic evaluation including insertion and repositioning of multiple electrode catheters with induction or attempted induction of arrhythmia; with right atrial pacing and recording, right ventricular pacing and recording, His bundle recording |
| +93623 | Programmed stimulation and pacing after intravenous drug infusion (List separately in addition to code for primary procedure) |
| 93640 | Electrophysiologic evaluation of single or dual chamber pacing cardioverter-defibrillator leads including defibrillation threshold evaluation (induction of arrhythmia, evaluation of sensing and pacing for arrhythmia termination) at time of initial implantation or replacement |

A) 93618; 93620
B) 93620
C) 93640; 93623
D) 93619; 93620

REFERENCE: Step-By-Step, p 238
CPT Assistant, Summer 1994, p 12
CPT Assistant, August 1997, p 9
CPT Assistant, October 1997, p 10
CPT Assistant, July 1998, p 10
CPT Changes: An Insider's View 2002 & 2003

226. Patient presents to the hospital for a two view chest x-ray for a cough. The radiology report comes back negative. What would be the correct codes to report to the insurance company?

| | |
|---|---|
| 786.2 | Cough |
| 786.3 | Hemoptysis |
| V72.5 | Radiology examination |
| 71010 | Radiologic examination, chest; single view, frontal |
| 71020 | Radiologic examination, chest, two views, frontal and lateral |
| 71035 | Radiologic examination, chest, special views |

A) V72.5; 71020
B) 786.2; 71020
C) V72.5; 71035
D) 786.2; 786.3, 71010

REFERENCE: Brown, p 487

227. Patient presents to the hospital for a 3 view x-ray of the right shoulder. The diagnosis is shoulder pain and the radiology report states the patient has a dislocated shoulder. What would be the correct codes to report to the insurance company?

| | |
|---|---|
| 719.41 | Shoulder pain |
| 831.00 | Closed dislocation shoulder, unspecified |
| 831.01 | Closed dislocation shoulder, anterior |
| 73020 | Radiologic examination, shoulder; one view |
| 73030 | Radiologic examination, shoulder; complete, minimum of two views |
| 73060 | Radiologic examination; humerus, minimum of two views |

A) 831.00; 73060-RT
B) 719.41; 73020-RT
C) 831.01; 73030-RT
D) 831.00; 73030-RT

REFERENCE: Brown, p 487

Answer Key for CPT-4 Coding

1. C
2. A
3. B
4. C
5. D
6. C
7. D
8. B
9. B
10. C
11. D
12. B
13. A
14. B
15. D
16. B
17. C
18. A
19. D
20. C
21. C
22. B
23. B
24. C
25. B
26. C
27. A
28. D
29. B
30. C
31. D
32. A
33. D
34. A Codes 10060 and 10140 are used for I&Ds of superficial abscesses.
35. C
36. C
37. D
38. B
39. A
40. B
41. A
42. D
43. C
44. A
45. D
46. C
47. A
48. D
49. A
50. B
51. A

Answer Key for CPT-4 Coding

52. B
53. D
54. B
55. C
56. C
57. C
58. A
59. A
60. B
61. D
62. B
63. A
64. D
65. A
66. B
67. C
68. A
69. A
70. D
71. C
72. D
73. C
74. C
75. C
76. A
77. D
78. D
79. C
80. A
81. A
82. C
83. D
84. B
85. D
86. B
87. A
88. B
89. C
90. B
91. B
92. D
93. C
94. A
95. A
96. B
97. C
98. A
99. D
100. C
101. D
102. C

103. D
104. D
105. D
106. B
107. B
108. C
109. C
110. C
111. C
112. A
113. A
114. B
115. D
116. D
117. C
118. A
119. D
120. A
121. D
122. A
123. C
124. A
125. B
126. C
127. A
128. C
129. A
130. C
131. C
132. B
133. D
134. C
135. A
136. B
137. D
138. D
139. B
140. D
141. C
142. A
143. D
144. A
145. D
146. B
147. D
148. B
149. D
150. A
151. C
152. C
153. A

Answer Key for CPT-4 Coding

154. D
155. B
156. A
157. D
158. C
159. A
160. C
161. D
162. C
163. A
164. D
165. A
166. D
167. A
168. B
169. D
170. A
171. B
172. D
173. B
174. B
175. C Code 92543 is for use when an irrigation substance is used.
176. C
177. B
178. A
179. B
180. D
181. B
182. C
183. A
184. D
185. C
186. C
187. A Casting is included in the surgical procedure.
188. B
189. C
190. B
191. D
192. C Diagnostic arthroscopy of the right knee was performed. In the medical compartment, a partial medial meniscectomy was performed. In the lateral compartment, a chondroplasty was performed.
193. B Code both the arthroscopic procedure and the open procedure. Both need to be reported because there were two separate procedures.
194. D
195. C According to CPT guidelines, when a patient is admitted to the hospital on the same day as an office visit, the office visit is not billable. Code rules do not allow the use of 402.91 because the scenario given does not state that the patient has hypertensive heart disease.

196. D According to the CPT coding guidelines for vaccines, only a separate identifiable Evaluation and Management code may be billed in addition to the vaccine. In this scenario, the patient was seen only for his vaccines. This guideline immediately eliminates all the other answers.
197. A
198. C
199 B
200. C
201. B
202. A Report this code only once no matter how many units were given.
203. B
204. D
205. D
206. A
207. D
208. D
209. A
210. A
211. D
212. C
213. C
214. B
215. A
216. B
217. C Codes starting with 852 are considered to be traumatic injuries. No injury was stated in the case, so 432.1 - non-traumatic subdural hematoma would be the appropriate code.
218. D
219. A
220. C
221. B
222. D
223. B
224. C
225. B
226. B
227. D

Coding References

*Basic CPT/HCPCS Coding, 2005 Edition*
Author: Gail Smith Publisher: AHIMA

*CPT Assistant*
Publisher: American Medical Association

*CPT Changes: An Insider's View*
Publisher: American Medical Association

*HCPCS Medicare's National Level II Codes (2006)*
Publisher: American Medical Association

*Health Information: Management of a Strategic Resource,* 2nd edition
Author: M. Abdelhak, et al Publisher: W. B. Saunders

*ICD-9-CM Coding Handbook* with Answers, 2006 Revised Edition
Author: Faye Brown Publisher: American Hospital Association

*ICD-9-CM Coding and Reimbursement for Physician Services*
Authors: Anita Hazelwood and Carol Venable Publisher: AHIMA 2006

*Physician's Current Procedural Terminology CPT-2006*
Publisher: American Medical Association

*Principles of CPT Coding*
Publisher: American Medical Association

*Step by - Step - Medical Coding, 2005 edition*
Author: Carol Buck Publisher: W. B. Saunders

# CCS-P Case Study Coding Review

## CCS-P CODING INSTRUCTIONS

Refer to your AHIMA Candidate handbook for updated coding instructions for part II of the CCS-P Certification Examination. Visit AHIMA online at www.AHIMA.org for additional information on the electronic testing process.

These guidelines are from the 2005 Candidate Handbook. We assume that they will be very similar to the 2006 guidelines for coding the cases in Part II of the CCS-P exam.

1. Record up to four ICD-9-CM diagnoses and six CPT and/or HCPCS Level II procedural codes in the spaces provided at the end of the coding cases. Don't forget that points are deducted for inappropriate codes.
2. Select diagnoses, conditions, problems, or other reasons for care that require ICD-9-CM coding in a physician-based encounter/visit either in a physician's office, clinic, outpatient area, emergency room, ambulatory surgery, or other ambulatory care setting, apply ICD-9-CM instructional notations and conventions and current approved "Basic Coding Guidelines for Outpatient Services" and Diagnostic Coding and Reporting Requirements for Physician Billing" (*Coding Clinic for ICD-9-CM*, Fourth Quarter, 1995). In addition, the latest updated Coding Guidelines for Outpatient Services are in the back of this book.
3. Sequencing is not required for diagnoses or procedures.
4. Modifiers and linking diagnoses to procedures are tested in Part I of the examination only and are not required for the coding cases.
5. To assign codes to secondary diagnoses, apply the following directions:
    - Code and report chronic diseases as many times as the patient is receiving treatment and care for the condition(s).
    - Code all documented conditions that co-exist at the time of the visit and that require or affect patient care, treatment, or management.
    - Do not code conditions previously treated and no longer existing.
6. Code for professional services only and only for the designated physician for each individual case.
7. Assign CPT codes and/or HCPCS Level II codes for all appropriate procedures.
8. Assign CPT codes for anesthetic procedures listed in the anesthesia section only if applicable.
9. Assign CPT codes for medical procedures based on current CPT guidelines.
10. Confirm Evaluation and Management (E&M) codes based on the information provided for each case. *For the purposes of this examination, the level of key components have been given so you will not be expected to assign the level of history, examinations, and medical decision making.*
11. Assign CPT codes for radiologic and laboratory procedures listed in the radiology and laboratory sections only when applicable.
12. Assign HCPCS Level II National (alphanumeric) codes as appropriate.
13. Do not assign:
    - HCPCS Level III Local codes
    - ICD-9-CM E codes
    - ICD-9-CM M codes
    - ICD-9-CM, Volume 3, procedure codes

## Case Study 1

**Office Visit**
**Face Sheet**

| | |
|---|---|
| Patient's Name | Leon Kane |
| Date of Visit: | January 26, 2006 |
| Age: | 55 |
| Sex: | Male |
| Insurance: | Self Pay |

## Case Study 1
## Office Visit

This is a 55-year-old male returning to the office for palpitations. The patient reports what he describes as his "heart flipping about" and then experiences some pain. The episode lasted for just a few seconds. He states it is more likely to occur when he is stressed out. He has not noticed any association with exercise. He is quite concerned about the possibility of this being related to his heart. No other cardiovascular complaints. He also complains of excessive thirst and fatigue.

Allergies: None

Medications: None

Blood pressure is 100/60, and pulse 77. He is a well-developed, well-nourished male in no acute distress.

| | |
|---|---|
| Neck: | Supple. No JVD or bruit. |
| Lungs: | Clear to auscultation. |
| Heart: | Rate & Rhythm Regular<br>EKG was done which revealed normal sinus rhythm. |
| Abdomen: | No masses detected. |

IMPRESSION AND PLAN:

1. Palpitations. Blood was drawn for cholesterol profile, which was sent to an outside lab. Stress test will be ordered for next week.
2. Rule out diabetes. Blood was drawn for glucose levels.
3. Fatigue. Blood was drawn for thyroid profile.
4. Patient is to follow-up in two weeks to discuss the stress test and all lab results.

| | |
|---|---|
| History: | Expanded Problem Focused |
| Examination: | Expanded Problem Focused |
| Medical Complexity: | Low |

# Case Study 1

EKG RESULTS

A twelve-lead EKG machine was hooked up to a 55-year-old patient with leads place in proper protocol. The vent. rate was 62 BPM, PR interval was 156, QRS duration was 72, and P-R-T axes were 49, 50, and 49 respectively.

IMPRESSION:
1. Normal Sinus Rhythm
2. Normal EKG

**Case Study 1**
**Answer Sheet**

| DIAGNOSES | ICD-9-CM CODES | | | | | |
|---|---|---|---|---|---|---|
| DX 1 | | | | . | | |
| DX 2 | | | | . | | |
| DX 3 | | | | . | | |
| DX 4 | | | | . | | |

| PROCEDURES | CPT CODES | | | | | | MODIFIERS (If Applicable) | |
|---|---|---|---|---|---|---|---|---|
| PR 1 | | | | | | - | | |
| PR 2 | | | | | | - | | |
| PR 3 | | | | | | - | | |
| PR 4 | | | | | | - | | |
| PR 5 | | | | | | - | | |
| PR 6 | | | | | | - | | |

## CASE STUDY 2

### Emergency Room Visit

### Face Sheet

| | |
|---|---|
| Patient's Name: | Patience Cooper |
| Date of Visit: | January 14, 2006 |
| Age: | 80 |
| Sex: | Female |
| Insurance: | Medicare |

## CASE STUDY 2

DATE OF ADMISSION: 1-14-06

HISTORY:

This elderly female was brought to the Emergency Room today when she was out with some friends and developed nausea and vomiting. She also developed diarrhea last night. She has a slight fever and appears to be somewhat dehydrated. She has been started on an IV.

PAST MEDICAL HISTORY:

She has had the usual childhood diseases. She has a history of arthritis. History of cataract extraction of the left eye.

ALLERGIES: No apparent allergies.
MEDICATIONS: She is on no medications.
SOCIAL HISTORY: She is a widow who lives alone.

PHYSICAL EXAMINATION:

| | |
|---|---|
| General: | Well developed, well nourished female in no acute distress. Blood pressure is 100/74, pulse 70, temperature of 101, respiration 18. |
| Head: | Normocephalic. |
| Eyes: | There is an opacity, right eye. Aphakia in the left. |
| Neck: | Supple. No bruits. |
| Skin: | Negative. |
| Chest: | Few scattered rhonchi. |
| Heart: | Normal rhythm. No murmurs appreciated. |
| Abdomen: | Slightly distended with tenderness. Bowel sounds present. |
| Extremities: | Negative. |

IMPRESSION:
1. Gastroenteritis
2. Slight dehydration
3. Arthritis

The patient was discharged in good condition. No further nausea and vomiting. Patient was given a prescription for Flagyl 500 mg t.i.d. for 10 days.

LABORATORY EXAMINATION

Special Laboratory Examination: Stool.
Results: Stool shows moderate amount of Giardia Lamblia Cysts.

| | |
|---|---|
| History: | Expanded Problem Focused |
| Examination: | Expanded Problem Focused |
| Medical Decision: | Low |

**Case Study 2**
**Answer Sheet**

| DIAGNOSES | ICD-9-CM CODES | | | | | |
|---|---|---|---|---|---|---|
| DX 1 | | | | . | | |
| DX 2 | | | | . | | |
| DX 3 | | | | . | | |
| DX 4 | | | | . | | |

| PROCEDURES | CPT CODES | | | | | MODIFIERS (If Applicable) | | |
|---|---|---|---|---|---|---|---|---|
| PR 1 | | | | | | - | | |
| PR 2 | | | | | | - | | |
| PR 3 | | | | | | - | | |
| PR 4 | | | | | | - | | |
| PR 5 | | | | | | - | | |
| PR 6 | | | | | | - | | |

## <u>Case Study 3</u>

**Office Visit**

**Face Sheet**

| | |
|---|---|
| Patient's Name: | Lois Graham |
| Date of Visit: | January 30, 2006 |
| Age: | 40 |
| Sex: | Female |
| Insurance: | Government |

## Case Study 3
### Office Visit

HISTORY OF PRESENT ILLNESS: This is a first visit for this 40-year-old female. She is complaining of abnormal vaginal discharge and bleeding on and off for approximately three weeks. She denies any trauma. Patient is sexually active and her LMP was a month ago. Period has not started this month. She denies any chest pain, shortness of breath, or urinary problems.

PAST MEDICAL HISTORY: Usual childhood diseases.
Two vaginal deliveries, one in 1977 and 1986.

ALLERGIES: None known.

MEDICATIONS: Birth control pills.

SOCIAL HISTORY: She does not smoke or drink. She is very active with jogging every day and playing tennis. She is married and lives with her husband and two children.

FAMILY HISTORY: Father died of an aneurysm seven years ago; mother is in good health. No history of breast or cervical cancer in the family.

PHYSICAL EXAMINATION:

| | |
|---|---|
| Vital Signs: | BP 120/70; Pulse 85; Respirations 20. Height 5' 5", Weight 135 lb. Well developed, well-nourished female in no acute distress. |
| HEENT: | Pupils equal, round and reactive to light and accommodation. Extraocular muscles are intact: Trachea is midline. |
| Neck: | Thyroid not palpable. No jugular distention. Carotid pulses are present bilaterally. |
| Breasts: | No masses, tenderness or nipple discharge. |
| Lungs: | Clear to auscultation and percussion. |
| Heart: | Normal sinus rhythm. No murmurs appreciated. |
| Abdomen: | No masses or tenderness noted. No hernias appreciated. No enlargement of the liver or spleen. |
| Pelvic: | Vaginal examination reveals no lesions or masses. Discharge is noted and a sample was collected and sent to an outside laboratory for testing. No bleeding noted. External genitalia is normal. No lesions noted on cervix. Uterus is not enlarged. |
| Urinary: | Urethral meatus is normal. No masses noted for urethra or bladder. |

PLAN: Patient is to follow up in one week for lab results. Patient will be scheduled for abdominal x-ray tomorrow.

| | |
|---|---|
| History: | Detailed |
| Examination: | Detailed |
| Medical Decision: | Low Complexity |

**Case Study 3**
**Answer Sheet**

| DIAGNOSES | ICD-9-CM CODES | | | | | |
|---|---|---|---|---|---|---|
| DX 1 | | | | . | | |
| DX 2 | | | | . | | |
| DX 3 | | | | . | | |
| DX 4 | | | | . | | |

| PROCEDURES | CPT CODES | | | | | MODIFIERS (If Applicable) | | |
|---|---|---|---|---|---|---|---|---|
| PR 1 | | | | | | - | | |
| PR 2 | | | | | | - | | |
| PR 3 | | | | | | - | | |
| PR 4 | | | | | | - | | |
| PR 5 | | | | | | - | | |
| PR 6 | | | | | | - | | |

## CASE STUDY 4

### Office Visit

### Face Sheet

| | |
|---|---|
| Patient's Name: | Myles Springs |
| Date of Visit: | January 18, 2006 |
| Age: | 17 |
| Sex: | Male |
| Insurance: | Self Pay |

## Case Study 4
## Office Visit

HISTORY OF PRESENT ILLNESS: This is a recheck for a persistent toothache. Patient is a 17-year-old male with a bad tooth who was seen four days ago and started on Penicillin and Percocet. He has run out of Percocet and his mother has not gotten him in to see the dentist. He has persistent pain.

PHYSICAL EXAMINATION:

| | |
|---|---|
| HEENT: | The left lower second molar is viewed and found to be decaying with a large open cavity on the medial posterior aspect. He has persistent severe pain; however, there is no significant inflammation of the gingiva, no active purulent discharge. |
| Head: | Normocephalic. |
| Lungs: | Clear. |

IMPRESSION: Odontalgia with dental decay.
Patient was given a new prescription for Percocet and an appointment with a dental clinic for care.

| | |
|---|---|
| History: | Problem Focused |
| Examination: | Problem Focused |
| Medical Decision: | Straightforward |

**<u>Case Study 4</u>**
**Answer Sheet**

| DIAGNOSES | ICD-9-CM CODES | | | | | |
|---|---|---|---|---|---|---|
| DX 1 | | | | . | | |
| DX 2 | | | | . | | |
| DX 3 | | | | . | | |
| DX 4 | | | | . | | |

| PROCEDURES | CPT CODES | | | | | MODIFIERS (If Applicable) | | |
|---|---|---|---|---|---|---|---|---|
| PR 1 | | | | | | - | | |
| PR 2 | | | | | | - | | |
| PR 3 | | | | | | - | | |
| PR 4 | | | | | | - | | |
| PR 5 | | | | | | - | | |
| PR 6 | | | | | | - | | |

## CASE STUDY 5

### Office Visit

### Face Sheet

| | |
|---|---|
| Patient's Name: | Turk Joseph |
| Date of Visit: | January 8, 2006 |
| Age: | 25 |
| Sex: | Male |
| Insurance: | Prudential |

## Case Study 5
## Office Visit

HISTORY OF PRESENT ILLNESS:
This is a first time visit for this 25 year old male who cut his right hand while opening a can. He is being seen on an emergency basis in the office due to the patient presenting with a lacerated hand. Patient stated that he cut his right hand and just came to the closest physician. The wound does not involve any deep structures. Fingers do not have a decrease in movement.

PAST MEDICAL HISTORY: Noncontributory.

MEDICATIONS: None.

PHYSICAL EXAMINATION:

| | |
|---|---|
| General: | Healthy appearing male in mild distress.<br>BP 130/75, Pulse 88, Respirations 16. |
| Skin: | Warm and dry. No lesions noted. |
| Lungs: | Clear to auscultation and percussion. No decreased breath sounds noted. |
| Extremities: | Normal range of motion times four. The dorsum part of the right hand has a 1.5-cm laceration which is superficial with no deep structure involvement. |

The right hand was prepped with Betadine and anesthetized with 1% plain Xylocaine. The wound was irrigated with saline and explored. No evidence of foreign body or deep structure involvement. The wound was closed with interrupted sutures. A sterile dressing was applied.

IMPRESSION:
Right hand laceration. The patient was given a prescription for Erythromycin to prevent infection and he is to take Tylenol for pain.

Follow-up in office in three weeks for suture removal.

| | |
|---|---|
| History: | Expanded problem |
| Examination: | Expanded problem |
| Medical Decision: | Straightforward |

**<u>Case Study 5</u>**
**Answer Sheet**

| DIAGNOSES | ICD-9-CM CODES | | | | | |
|---|---|---|---|---|---|---|
| DX 1 | | | | . | | |
| DX 2 | | | | . | | |
| DX 3 | | | | . | | |
| DX 4 | | | | . | | |

| PROCEDURES | CPT CODES | | | | | MODIFIERS (If Applicable) | | |
|---|---|---|---|---|---|---|---|---|
| PR 1 | | | | | | - | | |
| PR 2 | | | | | | - | | |
| PR 3 | | | | | | - | | |
| PR 4 | | | | | | - | | |
| PR 5 | | | | | | - | | |
| PR 6 | | | | | | - | | |

## CASE STUDY 6

**Office Visit**

**Face Sheet**

| | |
|---|---|
| Patient's Name: | Dorothy Belle |
| Date of Visit: | January 6, 2006 |
| Age: | 50 |
| Sex: | Female |
| Insurance: | Commercial |

## Case Study 6
## Office Visit

HISTORY OF PRESENT ILLNESS:

Patient presents to the office with a two day history of a sore throat. Patient is also experiencing fever and difficulty with swallowing.

PAST HISTORY:

Patient has a history of asthma not under current management. Appendectomy two months ago. No known allergies.

PHYSICAL EXAMINATION:

| | |
|---|---|
| General: | Alert and oriented. In no acute distress.<br>T: 100.9; P: 128; R: 18; B/P: 102/60 |
| Throat: | Tonsillar swelling with pharyngeal erythema. |
| Ears/Nose: | Normal. |
| Respiratory: | No respiratory distress. |
| Abdomen: | Surgical incision healing well. |

Throat culture for strep screen taken and sent to an outside lab. Report came back positive.

IMPRESSION: Acute Tonsillitis
Patient was given a prescription for Amox 400-mg p.o.

To return in one week.

| | |
|---|---|
| History: | Expanded Problem Focused |
| Examination: | Expanded Problem Focused |
| Medical Decision: | Low |

**<u>Case Study 6</u>**
**Answer Sheet**

| DIAGNOSES | ICD-9-CM CODES | | | | | |
|---|---|---|---|---|---|---|
| DX 1 | | | | . | | |
| DX 2 | | | | . | | |
| DX 3 | | | | . | | |
| DX 4 | | | | . | | |

| PROCEDURES | CPT CODES | | | | | MODIFIERS (If Applicable) | | |
|---|---|---|---|---|---|---|---|---|
| PR 1 | | | | | | - | | |
| PR 2 | | | | | | - | | |
| PR 3 | | | | | | - | | |
| PR 4 | | | | | | - | | |
| PR 5 | | | | | | - | | |
| PR 6 | | | | | | - | | |

## CASE STUDY 7

### Emergency Room Visit

### Face Sheet

| | |
|---|---|
| Patient's Name: | Steven Tam |
| Date of Visit: | January 16, 2006 |
| Age: | 7 |
| Sex: | Male |
| Insurance: | Government |

## Case Study 7
## Emergency Room Report

HISTORY OF PRESENT ILLNESS:
This is a seven-year-old boy who was brought to the Emergency Room by his parents. He has been running an elevated temperature for the past twelve hours; the high was 103. He also complains of stomach pains and vomiting. The parents are very concerned.

PAST MEDICAL HISTORY: Negative.

ALLERGIES and Medications: None.

SOCIAL HISTORY: Patient lives with his parents. Attends elementary school where he is in the first grade.

PHYSICAL EXAMINATION:

| | |
|---|---|
| General: | Well-developed, well-nourished child who is lethargic and pale. His temperature is 101. Pulse 110. Respirations 28. BP 99/72. |
| HEENT: | Eyes are normal. There is a minimal amount of inflammation of the tonsils. Ears, nose, and mouth are normal. |
| Neck: | Supple. |
| Skin: | Negative. |
| Chest: | Lungs sounds are normal. |
| Heart: | Normal rhythm with no murmurs appreciated. |
| Abdomen: | Diffuse tenderness. No masses or organomegaly noted. |
| Neurological: | Normal. |
| Extremities: | Normal. |

EXAMINATIONS:
Abdominal x-ray was normal.
Labs normal except for UA which was positive for E. Coli > 100,000.

IMPRESSION: Acute pyelonephritis.

DISPOSITION: Discharged with Bactrim and will follow up with his physician.

| | |
|---|---|
| History: | Expanded Problem Focused |
| Examination: | Expanded Problem Focused |
| Medical Decision: | Low |

**Case Study 7**
**Answer Sheet**

| DIAGNOSES | ICD-9-CM CODES | | | | | |
|---|---|---|---|---|---|---|
| DX 1 | | | | . | | |
| DX 2 | | | | . | | |
| DX 3 | | | | . | | |
| DX 4 | | | | . | | |

| PROCEDURES | CPT CODES | | | | | MODIFIERS (If Applicable) | | |
|---|---|---|---|---|---|---|---|---|
| PR 1 | | | | | | - | | |
| PR 2 | | | | | | - | | |
| PR 3 | | | | | | - | | |
| PR 4 | | | | | | - | | |
| PR 5 | | | | | | - | | |
| PR 6 | | | | | | - | | |

**Code the Diagnoses using ICD-9-CM Codes and Code the Emergency Room Physician Visit with CPT E&M Code(s)**

## CASE STUDY 8

### Emergency Room Report

### Face Sheet

| | |
|---|---|
| Patient's Name: | Nancy Jean |
| Date of Visit: | January 16, 2006 |
| Age: | 40 |
| Sex: | Female |
| Insurance: | Commercial |

**Case Study 8**
**Emergency Room Report**

DATE OF ADMISSION: 1-16-06

CHIEF COMPLAINT: Severe headaches, nausea and vomiting.

HISTORY:
This 40-year-old female was seen in the Emergency Room on 1/16/06 for complaints of headaches, neck pain, nausea and vomiting, with the possibility of viral meningitis. At the time, my impression was that it probably was a viral syndrome. A spinal tap was done by the hospital anesthesiologist to rule out viral meningitis. The spinal tap was unremarkable. A CT scan of the head was also performed by the hospital anesthesiologist and was also unremarkable.

PAST MEDICAL HISTORY: Noncontributory.
Allergies: None.
Medications: None.
Social History: Noncontributory.

PHYSICAL EXAMINATION:
General: At present, examination reveals her to be in moderate distress due to her headaches.
HEENT: Markedly photophobia. No gross lesions noted. Pupils round and reactive. Trachea midline.
Chest: Lungs clear to auscultation and percussion.
Heart: Murmurs not noted.
Abdomen: Soft, no organomegaly.
Neurological: Examination includes the cranial nerve, motor, sensory, gait and station, deep tendon reflexes, and cerebellum, which were unremarkable. No nuchal rigidity noted. No Brudzinski or Kernig's signs.
Extremities: All pulses palpable.

PROCEDURE: Spinal tap & CT of Head performed by hospital anesthesiologist.

LABORATORY RESULTS: CSF showed 1 WBC and 1 RBC, glucose 33, protein 27.

IMPRESSION:
1. Viral Syndrome
2. Headaches

Patient is discharged from the Emergency Room and is to follow up with her physician.
A prescription of Demerol 50 mg p.o. q.d. was given.

| | |
|---|---|
| History: | Expanded Problem Focused |
| Examination: | Expanded Problem Focused |
| Medical Decision: | Moderate |

**Case Study 8**
**Answer Sheet**

| DIAGNOSES | ICD-9-CM CODES | | | | | |
|---|---|---|---|---|---|---|
| DX 1 | | | | . | | |
| DX 2 | | | | . | | |
| DX 3 | | | | . | | |
| DX 4 | | | | . | | |

| PROCEDURES | CPT CODES | | | | | MODIFIERS (If Applicable) | | |
|---|---|---|---|---|---|---|---|---|
| PR 1 | | | | | | - | | |
| PR 2 | | | | | | - | | |
| PR 3 | | | | | | - | | |
| PR 4 | | | | | | - | | |
| PR 5 | | | | | | - | | |
| PR 6 | | | | | | - | | |

## CASE STUDY 9

### Emergency Room Visit

### Face Sheet

| | |
|---|---|
| Date of Service: | 01/29/06 |
| Age: | 53 |
| Sex: | Female |
| Admitting Diagnosis: | Abdominal pain |
| Discharge Diagnoses: | Abdominal pain<br>Hemoptysis<br>Nausea and vomiting |
| Disposition: | Home |

## Case Study 9

### Emergency Room Visit

DATE OF VISIT: 01/29/06

CHIEF COMPLAINT: Vomiting of blood.

HISTORY OF PRESENT ILLNESS: This female was seen in the Emergency Room today due to severe abdominal pain, nausea, and vomiting of blood. The patient does have a history of cholithiasis with common bile duct obstruction. Cholecystectomy was done approximately three weeks prior to this admission without any complications.

PAST MEDICAL HISTORY: Cholecystectomy three weeks ago.

ALLERGIES: None.

MEDICATIONS: None.

SOCIAL HISTORY: Patient smokes 1/2 pack per day.

REVIEW OF SYSTEMS:

| | |
|---|---|
| Cardiovascular System: | No dyspnea or pain. |
| Gastrointestinal: | Severe abdominal pain with nausea and vomiting of blood. |
| Genitourinary: | No dysuria. |

PHYSICAL EXAMINATION:

| | |
|---|---|
| General: | Well nourished, well developed female. |
| HEENT: | Pupils are equal, round and reactive to light and accommodation. Extraocular muscles are intact. |
| Neck: | No masses or thyroidomegaly. |
| Chest: | Clear to auscultation bilaterally. |
| Heart: | Regular rate and rhythm. |
| Abdomen: | Soft, non tender. No masses. Bowel sounds are present. There is a scar present secondary to cholecystectomy. |
| Neurological: | Normal |
| Extremities: | Normal |

LABORATORY FINDINGS:
CBC 10/32; WBC 14; Na 140, K+ 4.5, Glu 115, BUN 2.0, Creatinine 0.5.

RADIOLOGY FINDINGS: Upper Abdominal and Gallbladder Ultrasound is normal.

PLAN:
Patient is discharged in stable condition and will follow up with her physician.
She is to contact the Emergency Room if further symptoms occur.

| | |
|---|---|
| History: | Expanded problem focused |
| Physical: | Expanded problem focused |
| Medical Decision Making: | Moderate Decision |

## Case Study 9

### Radiology Report

DATE: 01/29/06

PROCEDURE: Upper Abdominal and Gallbladder Ultrasound

The liver is normal in size, contour, and echogenicity. The pancreas is normal in size. Both kidneys are normal in size, shape and position. The common bile duct is normal.

**Case Study 9**
**Answer Sheet**

| DIAGNOSES | ICD-9-CM CODES | | | | | |
|---|---|---|---|---|---|---|
| DX 1 | | | | . | | |
| DX 2 | | | | . | | |
| DX 3 | | | | . | | |
| DX 4 | | | | . | | |

| PROCEDURES | CPT CODES | | | | | MODIFIERS (If Applicable) | | |
|---|---|---|---|---|---|---|---|---|
| PR 1 | | | | | | - | | |
| PR 2 | | | | | | - | | |
| PR 3 | | | | | | - | | |
| PR 4 | | | | | | - | | |
| PR 5 | | | | | | - | | |
| PR 6 | | | | | | - | | |

# CASE STUDY 10

## Ambulatory Surgery

## Face Sheet

| | |
|---|---|
| DATE OF ADMISSION: | 1-16-06 |
| AGE: | 45 |
| SEX: | Female |
| ADMITTING DIAGNOSIS: | Carpal tunnel syndrome, left wrist |
| DISCHARGE DIAGNOSIS: | Carpal tunnel syndrome, left wrist<br>Type I Diabetes Mellitus<br>Hypertension |
| PROCEDURE: | Decompression of medial nerve, left wrist |
| DISPOSITION: | Home |

## Case Study 10

### History and Physical

DATE OF ADMISSION: 1-16-06

ADMITTING DIAGNOSIS: Carpal tunnel syndrome left wrist

HISTORY OF PRESENT ILLNESS:
This patient has been complaining of left wrist pain for approximately one year. She has been receiving physical therapy for six months and it does not seem to be helping. She is a transcriptionist and does repetitive computer work. She has been wearing bilateral wrist supports which have helped to some extent.

PAST MEDICAL HISTORY:
The patient has a history of T&A; hysterectomy two years ago; history of Type I Diabetes Mellitus and hypertension. She does not complain of chest pain or shortness of breath.

ALLERGIES: No apparent allergies.

MEDICATIONS: Patient takes Humulin 70/30 and Zestril.

SOCIAL HISTORY: Noncontributory.

PHYSICAL EXAMINATION:

| | |
|---|---|
| General: | This is a well developed, well nourished female in no acute distress. |
| Head: | Normocephalic. |
| Neck: | Supple. No masses. Carotid pulse is palpable. Trachea is in midline. |
| Skin: | Negative. |
| Chest: | Clear to auscultation and percussion. |
| Heart: | No murmurs, gallops, or rubs. |
| Abdomen: | Negative. |
| Extremities: | Left wrist has weakness. Unable to touch thumb and little finger together. There is a prominent mass on the palmar aspect of the left wrist. |

PLAN:
Patient will be seen at the ambulatory surgery center for carpal tunnel surgery.

## Case Study 10

### Operative Report

| | |
|---|---|
| Date of Operation: | 1-16-06 |
| Preoperative Diagnosis: | Carpal tunnel syndrome left wrist |
| Postoperative Diagnosis: | Carpal tunnel syndrome left wrist |
| Operation: | Decompression of medial nerve, left wrist |
| Surgeon: | E.B. Mannion, MD |
| Anesthesia: | Bier block |
| Estimated Blood Loss: | Less than 500 cc |

PROCEDURE:
Under Bier block anesthesia, preparation was done with Betadine scrub, Betadine solution and sterile draping was done. Curvilinear incision was made based on the lunar side of the longitudinal wrist crease and carried up to the proximal flexor wrist crease. This was carried through subcutaneous tissue. Range retractors were inserted. The median nerve was visualized using the microscope at the proximal edge of the transverse carpal ligament. The nerve was protected and using curved dissecting scissors, the transverse carpal ligament was sectioned under direct vision. The nerve was quite compressed. After the ligament had been sectioned, the wound was closed with interrupted 5-0 nylon sutures and sterile dressings were applied. The patient tolerated the procedure well and circulation to the extremity was intact at the completion of the procedure.

## Case Study 10

**Progress Notes:**

Patient was taken to the operating room for carpal tunnel repair. Patient tolerated the procedure well. No apparent complications are noted. Patient will be discharged when stable and to follow up in my office in two weeks.

## Case Study 10

**Orders:**

1. Standard post-operative orders.
2. Discharge patient from Recovery Room when stable.
3. Vital signs q 15 minutes x 4; then q 30 x 2; then q 1 hr until discharge.
4. Tylenol 500 mg q 4 for pain.
5. Discharge when patient is stable.

**<u>Case Study 10</u>**
**Answer Sheet**

| DIAGNOSES | ICD-9-CM CODES | | | | | |
|---|---|---|---|---|---|---|
| DX 1 | | | | . | | |
| DX 2 | | | | . | | |
| DX 3 | | | | . | | |
| DX 4 | | | | . | | |

| PROCEDURES | CPT CODES | | | | | MODIFIERS (If Applicable) | | |
|---|---|---|---|---|---|---|---|---|
| PR 1 | | | | | | - | | |
| PR 2 | | | | | | - | | |
| PR 3 | | | | | | - | | |
| PR 4 | | | | | | - | | |
| PR 5 | | | | | | - | | |
| PR 6 | | | | | | - | | |

# CASE STUDY 11

## Ambulatory Surgery

## Face Sheet

| | |
|---|---|
| Date of Service: | 01/19/06 |
| Age: | 61 |
| Sex: | Male |
| Admitting Diagnosis: | Dyspepsia<br>Dysphagia |
| Discharge Diagnoses: | Candidal esophagitis<br>Acute and chronic gastritis<br>Helicobacter |
| Procedure: | Esophagogastroduodenoscopy with biopsies |

## Case Study 11

### History and Physical

DATE OF ADMISSION: 1-19-06

ADMITTING DIAGNOSIS: Dyspepsia and Dysphagia.

HISTORY OF PRESENT ILLNESS:
This gentleman has been complaining of dyspepsia for the past month. Now has developed difficulty in swallowing. Patient was treated conservatively with Riopan. With the difficulty in swallowing we will proceed with an esophagogastroduodenoscopy.

PAST MEDICAL HISTORY:
History of basal cell carcinoma of the back, hypertension now not treated, diabetes.

ALLERGIES: None.

MEDICATIONS: Riopan and Glucotrol.

SOCIAL HISTORY: Patient does not smoke, alcohol is minimal.

PHYSICIAL EXAMINATION:

| | |
|---|---|
| General: | This is an obese male. Vital signs are within normal limits. |
| HEENT: | Extraocular movements are intact. No evidence of cataracts. Dysphagia and dyspepsia. |
| Neck: | Without bruits, masses or adenopathy. |
| Chest: | Clear to auscultation bilaterally without any crackles or wheezes. |
| Heart: | Regular rate and rhythm. No murmurs or gallops. |
| Abdomen: | Without hernias, masses or hepatosplenomegaly. Bowel sound present in all four quadrants. |
| Neurological: | Normal. |
| Extremities: | Unremarkable. |

PLAN:
Patient will be admitted to one day surgery for an Esophagogastroduodenoscopy.

## Case Study 11

### Operative Report

| | |
|---|---|
| Date of Operation: | 1-19-06 |
| Preoperative Diagnosis: | 1. Dyspepsia<br>2. Dysphagia |
| Postoperative Diagnosis: | 1. Candidal esophagitis, biopsies taken for confirmation.<br>2. Upper GI endoscopy was otherwise unremarkable. Gastric biopsies were taken to exclude Helicobacter pylori infection |
| Operation: | Esophagogastroduodenoscopy |
| Surgeon: | Rodney Verne, MD |
| Assistant: | V. G. Smith, MD |
| Anesthesia: | Demerol 50 mg intravenous, Versed 6 mg intravenous |
| Instrument: | Olympus video gastroscope |

PROCEDURE:
The risks and benefits of the procedure were explained to the patient and informed consent was obtained. The patient was placed in the left lateral decubitus position. Flexible video endoscope was gently advanced through the circopharyngeus into the esophagus. There are typical changes of candidal esophagitis in the mid and distal esophagus. Photographs and biopsies were taken. The GE junction was located at 38 cm from the incisors. Retroflexed views in the cardia showed no fundic mass.

The endoscope was placed in the forward viewing position and advanced from the greater curvature to the antrum and there was no evidence of ulceration or mass. The pylorus was patent. The duodenal bulb is non-deformed and free of ulceration. Post-bulbar duodenum is unremarkable. The endoscope was then withdrawn back into the stomach. Gastric biopsies were taken to exclude Helicobacter pylori and the procedure was terminated. The patient tolerated the procedure well without evident complications.

RECOMMENDATIONS:
1. Await results of pathologic findings.
2. Diflucan therapy 100 mg daily x three weeks for treatment of Candidiasis.
3. The patient will follow up with her primary physician.

## Case Study 11

### Pathology Report

| | |
|---|---|
| Date: | 1-19-06 |
| Physician: | Rodney Verne, MD |
| Preoperative Diagnosis: | Dyspepsia/dysphagia |
| Surgical Procedure: | EGD |
| Postoperative Diagnosis: | Candidal, esophagitis |
| Specimen(s): | 1. Esophageal biopsy<br>2. Gastric biopsy |
| GROSS: | There are two containers. |

Container number one, labeled "biopsy esophagus", consists of fragments of gray-white soft tissue. In aggregate, these measure .3 x .3 x .2 cm and are submitted in cassette "1".

Container number two, labeled "biopsy gastric", consists of two fragments of gray-tan soft tissue in aggregate .3 x .2 x .2 cm. Submitted in cassette "2".

GROSS AND MICROSCOPIC EXAMINATION:

Biopsy of esophagus: Esophagitis

COMMENT:
Special stain for fungal organisms is positive with fungal elements consistent with candidal esophagitis.

Gastric biopsies: Acute and chronic gastritis

COMMENT:
Special stain for Helicobacter organism is strongly positive.

## Case Study 11

**Progress Notes:**

01/19/06: Patient has a history of dyspepsia and dysphagia for a month. Taken to endoscopy room where an esophagogastroscopy was performed. Biopsies showed esophagitis, acute and chronic gastritis with Helicobactor present. Patient tolerated the procedure well.

---

**Orders:**

1. Standard postoperative orders
2. Vital signs q 15 minutes x 4; then q 30 x 2; then q 1 until discharge.
3. Start on soft diet.
4. Discharge when patient is stable.

**<u>Case Study 11</u>**
**Answer Sheet**

| DIAGNOSES | ICD-9-CM CODES | | | | | |
|---|---|---|---|---|---|---|
| DX 1 | | | | . | | |
| DX 2 | | | | . | | |
| DX 3 | | | | . | | |
| DX 4 | | | | . | | |

| PROCEDURES | CPT CODES | | | | | MODIFIERS (If Applicable) | | |
|---|---|---|---|---|---|---|---|---|
| PR 1 | | | | | | - | | |
| PR 2 | | | | | | - | | |
| PR 3 | | | | | | - | | |
| PR 4 | | | | | | - | | |
| PR 5 | | | | | | - | | |
| PR 6 | | | | | | - | | |

# CASE STUDY 12

## Emergency Room Visit

## Face Sheet

| | |
|---|---|
| Date of Service: | 01/28/06 |
| Age: | 65 |
| Sex: | Female |
| Admitting Diagnosis: | Nose bleed |
| Discharge Diagnosis: | Recurrent nosebleed |
| Disposition: | Home |

## Case Study 12

**Emergency Room Visit**

DATE OF SERVICE: 01/28/06

HISTORY OF PRESENT ILLNESS:
Patient presents to the Emergency Room with a history of waking up with her nose bleeding. This is the second occurrence of epistaxis that she has had. She states that the bleeding has resolved. Denies that she takes any aspirin.

PHYSICAL EXAMINATION:

| | |
|---|---|
| HEENT: | Normal tympanic membranes. The examination of the nares shows evidence of former bleeding site, it is now resolved. Oropharynx is normal. |
| Neck: | Supple, no bruits. |
| Lungs: | Clear. |

IMPRESSION: Recurrent nosebleed.

The patient is to return her primary physician if bleeding reoccurs.

| | |
|---|---|
| History: | Problem focused |
| Physical: | Problem focused |
| Medical Decision Making: | Straightforward |

**Case Study 12**
**Answer Sheet**

| DIAGNOSES | ICD-9-CM CODES | | | | | |
|---|---|---|---|---|---|---|
| DX 1 | | | | . | | |
| DX 2 | | | | . | | |
| DX 3 | | | | . | | |
| DX 4 | | | | . | | |

| PROCEDURES | CPT CODES | | | | | MODIFIERS (If Applicable) | | |
|---|---|---|---|---|---|---|---|---|
| PR 1 | | | | | | - | | |
| PR 2 | | | | | | - | | |
| PR 3 | | | | | | - | | |
| PR 4 | | | | | | - | | |
| PR 5 | | | | | | - | | |
| PR 6 | | | | | | - | | |

## CASE STUDY 13

### Monthly Nursing Home Assessment

### Face Sheet

| | |
|---|---|
| Patient's Name: | John Henning |
| Date of Visit: | January 1, 2006 |
| Age: | 75 |
| Sex: | Male |
| Insurance: | Medicare |

## Case Study 13
## Monthly Nursing Home Assessment

DATE: 01/08/06

This patient has been in the nursing home for the past six months and is being evaluated on a monthly basis. He has a previous history of left-sided cerebrovascular accident with right-sided paralysis. The patient has been demented since his stroke and has been seen by a psychiatrist who diagnosed psychosis and placed him on Risperidone and Lorazepam. Patient will open his eyes to name only. Does not answer any questions. He has been having swallowing problems but has not developed any signs of choking.

| | |
|---|---|
| GENERAL: | BP 125/78, P 78, Weight 108 with a loss of 5 lb. since last month. |
| HEENT: | Laxity of the lower jaw; cataracts bilaterally. |
| Lungs: | Clear to auscultation and percussion. |
| Heart: | Normal sinus rhythm. There is a 2/6 heart murmur. |
| Abdomen: | No mass, organomegaly, tenderness. |
| CNS: | The patient responds to name only; right-sided paralysis due to old CVA. |
| Skin: | Normal. |

IMPRESSION:
1. Old left-sided cerebrovascular accident with right-sided paralysis
2. Malnutrition with weight loss
3. Psychosis

PLAN:
1. Speech pathologist to evaluate
2. Calorie count
3. The patient is a DNR

| | |
|---|---|
| History: | Detailed |
| Examination: | Detailed |
| Medical Decision: | Moderate complexity |

**Case Study 13**
**Answer Sheet**

| DIAGNOSES | ICD-9-CM CODES | | | | | |
|---|---|---|---|---|---|---|
| DX 1 | | | | . | | |
| DX 2 | | | | . | | |
| DX 3 | | | | . | | |
| DX 4 | | | | . | | |

| PROCEDURES | CPT CODES | | | | | MODIFIERS (If Applicable) | | |
|---|---|---|---|---|---|---|---|---|
| PR 1 | | | | | | - | | |
| PR 2 | | | | | | - | | |
| PR 3 | | | | | | - | | |
| PR 4 | | | | | | - | | |
| PR 5 | | | | | | - | | |
| PR 6 | | | | | | - | | |

## CASE STUDY 14

### Skilled Nursing Facility Visit

### Face Sheet

| | |
|---|---|
| Patient Name: | Cora Wilkinson |
| Date of Visit: | January 15, 2006 |
| Age: | 68 |
| Sex: | Female |
| Insurance: | Medicare |

## <u>Case Study 14</u>
## Skilled Nursing Facility Visit

Date of Visit: January 15, 2006

HISTORY OF PRESENT ILLNESS:
This is a follow up visit for this 68-year-old female. She was admitted to Oakdale Nursing Home 10 days ago with cellulitis of the left foot. She was placed in Oakdale for IV Therapy of her cellulitis. She is recovering well and the infection is about gone. She has a history of Type I diabetes.

Allergies: None
Medications: Insulin 70/30, IV Vancomycin

REVIEW OF SYSTEMS: Normal.

PHYSICAL EXAMINATION:

| | |
|---|---|
| General: | Well-developed, well-nourished female in no acute distress. BP 128/75. Pulse: 80, regular and strong. Respirations: 12, unlabored and regular. Temperature: Normal. Height: 5 foot. |
| HEENT: | Normal. No lesions noted. |
| Skin: | Left foot shows slight reddening on the upper surface. Infection had decreased significantly. All other areas are normal. |

PLAN:
Patient is doing well and will be taken off IV Vancomycin.
She will be discharged home tomorrow and will be given a prescription for Penicillin.
She is to follow up in my office in one week.

| | |
|---|---|
| History: | Problem focused |
| Examination: | Problem focused |
| Medical Decision: | Straightforward |

**Case Study 14**
**Answer Sheet**

| DIAGNOSES | ICD-9-CM CODES | | | | | |
|---|---|---|---|---|---|---|
| DX 1 | | | | . | | |
| DX 2 | | | | . | | |
| DX 3 | | | | . | | |
| DX 4 | | | | . | | |

| PROCEDURES | CPT CODES | | | | | MODIFIERS (If Applicable) | | |
|---|---|---|---|---|---|---|---|---|
| PR 1 | | | | | | - | | |
| PR 2 | | | | | | - | | |
| PR 3 | | | | | | - | | |
| PR 4 | | | | | | - | | |
| PR 5 | | | | | | - | | |
| PR 6 | | | | | | - | | |

**PROVIDE ICD-9-CM DIAGNOSES CODES AND CPT PROCEDURE CODE(S) ONLY**

## CASE STUDY 15

### Inpatient Face Sheet

| | |
|---|---|
| Admit Date: | 01/01/06 |
| Discharge Date: | 01/04/06 |
| Sex: | Female |
| Age: | 27 |
| Disposition: | Home |

Admitting Diagnoses:
1. Diarrhea, rule-out infectious colitis, viral gastroenteritis, inflammatory bowel disease
2. Dehydration
3. Pregnancy
4. Thyroid Goiter

Discharge Diagnoses:
1. Enteritis due to Clostridium difficile
2. Dehydration
3. Thyroid Goiter
4. Pregnancy

Procedures:
1. Colonoscopy with biopsies

**Case Study 15**
**Discharge Summary**

Admitted: 01/01/06
Discharged: 01/04/06

DISCHARGE DIAGNOSES:
1. Infectious Enteritis
2. Dehydration
3. Pregnant
4. Thyroid Goiter

PROCEDURE PERFORMED: Colonoscopy on 1/3/06.

HISTORY:
This is a 27 year-old pregnant female who is complaining of severe diarrhea with bowel movements every 10 minutes with watery stools and incontinence. This began early this morning. She does not feel it is caused by something she ate. She is also complaining of cramps and nausea. She is unable to keep liquids down.

PAST MEDICAL HISTORY: Positive for goiter.

PAST SURGICAL HISTORY: Negative

PHYSICAL EXAMINATION:
Vital Signs: Blood pressure 110/60, temperature 98.6, pulse 88, respirations 16.
Neck: Thyroid goiter
Heart: Regular rate and rhythm.
Lungs: Clear to auscultation. No rales or rhonchi, or wheezing.
Abdomen: Soft with good bowel sounds. No pain or masses. No hepatosplenomegaly. Some lower abdominal tenderness.
Extremities: Within normal limits.

LABORATORY:
Hematology as of 1/1/06 showed white blood count of 8,000, red blood cells 4.05, hemoglobin 12.9, hematocrit 39.3.
On 1/3/06, the white blood count was 6,000, red blood cells 3.70, hemoglobin 12.3 and hematocrit 35.1.

Urinalysis on 1/1/06 showed yellow-clear urine.
Chemistry levels on 1/1/06 showed sodium 139, potassium 3, chloride 110, glucose 104, BUN 8, creatinine 0.5, total protein 6.8, Albumin 3.9, Globulin 2.9. Anion gap ratio 1.3. Calcium 9.3. Total bilirubin 0.2.

Chemistry profile on 1/3/06 showed a sodium of 142, potassium 4, chloride 107, CO2 22, glucose 85, BUN 3, creatinine 0.7, magnesium 1.6. HcG quantitative at 6,320, approximately 6-7 weeks. Stool culture was positive for Clostridium difficile and she was started on intravenous antibiotics.

## Case Study 15
## Discharge Summary

Continued:

RADIOLOGY:
Transabdominal and transvaginal obstetrical sonogram shows a normal single viable intrauterine pregnancy at 4.9 weeks gestational age.

HOSPITAL COURSE:
The patient was admitted with diarrhea to rule out underlying cause. Dr. Blessed, saw her for pregnancy with gastrointestinal disturbance.

Recommendations were intravenous hydration and close monitoring. She was given Phenergan suppository for nausea and vomiting. The patient responded well to the treatment regime.

The patient was discharged in good condition. Activity and diet as tolerated. She will follow up with me as needed and will follow up with Dr. Blessed as instructed. The patient has been advised to have the goiter evaluated as an outpatient.

## Case Study 15
## History and Physical

CHIEF COMPLAINT:
This 27 year-old white female complains of severe diarrhea with bowel movements every 10 minutes and fecal incontinence as well as nocturnal bowel movements. She complains of cramps with nausea and vomiting. She denies chronic diarrhea.

PAST MEDICAL HISTORY: Thyroid goiter.

PAST SURGICAL HISTORY: Negative

SOCIAL HISTORY: Non-smoker, non-drinker

FAMILY HISTORY: Negative for colitis or colon cancer

ALLERGIES: None known

MEDICATIONS: None

REVIEW OF SYSTEMS:

| | |
|---|---|
| Cardiovascular: | Within normal limits. |
| Pulmonary: | Within normal limits. |
| Gastrointestinal: | Nausea and vomiting. Denies excessive aspirin or antacid use. Denies dysphagia, gallbladder disease, liver disease or pancreatitis. No history of peptic ulcer disease. |

PHYSICAL EXAMINATION:

| | |
|---|---|
| Vital Signs: | Her temperature is 98.6, pulse 88, respiratory rate 16, blood pressure 110/60, weight 130, height 5 feet, 7 inches. |
| Neck: | Thyroid goiter |
| Heart: | Regular rate. No murmurs |
| Lungs: | Clear to auscultation. No rales, rhonchi or wheezing. |
| Abdomen: | Soft. Good bowel sounds. No pain or masses. No hepatosplenomegaly. Some lower abdominal tenderness. |
| Rectal: | No stool. No masses. |
| Extremities: | Within normal limits. |

IMPRESSIONS:
1. Severe diarrhea and dehydration secondary to infectious colitis versus clostridium difficile infection versus viral gastroenteritis versus inflammatory bowel disease, less likely.
2. Thyroid goiter

PLAN:
1. IV hydration
2. Blood cultures
3. Stool cultures
4. Await CBC with differential to determine whether the patient needs IV antibiotics.

## Case Study 15
## Procedure Note

| | |
|---|---|
| Date: | 1/3/06 |
| Preoperative Diagnosis: | Refractory severe diarrhea with negative stool cultures |
| Postoperative Diagnosis: | 1. No active colitis<br>2. No pseudomembranes noted<br>3. Normal terminal ileum that was visualized<br>4. Internal hemorrhoids |
| Procedure: | Colonoscopy to the terminal ileum with random biopsies |
| Surgeon: | Robert Blessed, MD |
| Indications: | Refractory severe diarrhea with negative stool cultures. |

DESCRIPTION OF PROCEDURE:
Following informed consent the patient was brought to the endoscopy suite and given IV sedation. Colonoscope was inserted into the rectum and advanced to the left colon and beyond the splenic flexure, maneuvered through the hepatic flexure and moved down the ascending colon to the cecum. The appendiceal orifice was visualized. The ileocecal valve was entered and approximately 10 cm of terminal ileum were visualized and photographed and was within normal limits. The scope was withdrawn form the right colon, pulled back to the transverse, descending, sigmoid and rectum; all adequately visualized and there was no active colitis and no pseudomembranes noted. There were no masses palpable or mucosal abnormalities. Random rectosigmoid biopsies were obtained and the scope was withdrawn.

**PATHOLOGY REPORT**

SPECIMENS: Tissue rectosigmoid biopsy

DIAGNOSIS:
Histologically unremarkable fragments of superficial colonic mucosa. No evidence of significant inflammation; no evidence of dysplasia.

## Case Study 15

**PROGRESS NOTES:**

1/1: Admit Note: Severe diarrhea, cramping and nausea in a 27 year-old pregnant female. Patient is dehydrated due to the severe diarrhea. She is admitted for treatment and work up of gastrointestinal symptoms. Patient was unaware she was pregnant so will have OB follow her also.

1/2:
S: Diarrhea less frequent, still complains of intestinal cramping
O: Responding slowly to medications, vital signs good, blood cultures negative
A: Still with GI symptoms and dehydration
P: Will schedule colonoscopy to rule out colitis. Continue with IV hydration and repeat stool culture.

1/3:
S: Feels better, still some cramping
O: Stool positive for C. difficile
A: Tolerated colonoscopy, normal colon
P: Discontinue IVs, change to p.o. antibiotics

1/4:
S: Feels good, no diarrhea or cramping
O: Labs within normal limits, vitals stable, tolerating full diet and activity
A: Okay from GI standpoint. Will follow thyroid goiter as an outpatient
P: Discharge home

## Case Study 15

**ORDERS:**

1/1:
1. Admit patient to medical floor
2. Vital signs q. shift
3. Phenergan suppository for N/V
4. Blood and stool cultures
5. IV hydration
6. CBC, WBC, Chemistry profile
7. Pregnancy Test

1/2:
1. Transabdominal and transvaginal sonogram
2. Continue IV hydration
3. Colonoscopy in morning
4. Repeat stool culture

1/3:
1. Discontinue IVs, switch to p.o. antibiotics
2. Advance diet

1/4:
1. Discharge home

**Case Study 15**
**Answer Sheet**

| DIAGNOSES | ICD-9-CM CODES | | | | | |
|---|---|---|---|---|---|---|
| DX 1 | | | | . | | |
| DX 2 | | | | . | | |
| DX 3 | | | | . | | |
| DX 4 | | | | . | | |

| PROCEDURES | CPT CODES | | | | | MODIFIERS (If Applicable) | | |
|---|---|---|---|---|---|---|---|---|
| PR 1 | | | | | | - | | |
| PR 2 | | | | | | - | | |
| PR 3 | | | | | | - | | |
| PR 4 | | | | | | - | | |
| PR 5 | | | | | | - | | |
| PR 6 | | | | | | - | | |

**PROVIDE ICD-9-CM CODES FOR DIAGNOSES AND CPT CODES FOR PROCEDURE(S)**

## CASE STUDY 16

### Inpatient Face Sheet

| | |
|---|---|
| Admit Date: | 01/10/06 |
| Discharge Date: | 01/08/06 |
| Sex: | Female |
| Age: | 62 |
| Disposition: | Home |

ADMITTING DIAGNOSES:
1. Abdominal pain
2. Hypertension

DISCHARGE DIAGNOSES:
1. Acute and chronic cholecystitis and cholelithiasis
2. Hypertension
3. Hypokalemia
4. Urinary Tract Infection with E.coli

PROCEDURE:
1. Laparoscopic cholecystectomy

## Case Study 16
## Discharge Summary

Admitted: 01/10/06
Discharged: 01/08/06

ADMITTING DIAGNOSIS:
1. Abdominal pain
2. Hypertension

DISCHARGE DIAGNOSES:
1. Acute cholecystitis with cholelithiasis
2. Hypertension
3. Hypokalemia
4. Urinary tract infection

PROCEDURES:
Laparoscopic cholecystectomy by Dr. Haley

HISTORY OF PRESENT ILLNESS:
See History and Physical

HOSPITAL COURSE:
Patient was admitted and given IV antibiotics and Demerol for pain. HIDA scan revealed complete blockage of the cystic duct, for which Dr. Haley performed a laparoscopic cholecystectomy without difficulty. Patient did very well post-operatively. Began ambulating post-op day one, and advanced to full diet on day two. She remained afebrile. Her potassium dropped to 2.7 and she was given IV potassium supplement with improvement.

LABORATORY DATA:
Admission chest x-ray was normal.
Hemoglobin and hematocrit 13.5/40 with post op H/H at 12.1/37.
White count on admission was 16,000 with drop to 7,900 following surgery and IV antibiotics.
Differential and platelets were normal.
Glucose 100, Na 135, BUN 9, SGOT 28.
Pathology report revealed gangrenous cholecystitis and cholelithiasis.

The patient was discharged on the fourth day post-operative.

She will resume her previous medications as prescribed.

She is also to take Cipro 500 mg. b.i.d. for one week.

Regular diet and activity as tolerated.

She will follow up with Dr. Haley for staple removal in one week and follow up with me in two weeks.

## Case Study 16
## History and Physical

REASON FOR ADMISSION: Abdominal pain and vomiting

HISTORY OF PRESENT ILLNESS: This is a 62 year-old woman with a history of back pain who is having increased epigastric abdominal pain with nausea for the past four days. She states the abdominal pain has since radiated to her back. She denies fever, chills, vomiting or change in bowel habits.

ALLERGIES: Penicillin and Morphine

PAST MEDICAL HISTORY: Hypertension, herniated lumbar and cervical discs requiring laminectomies, anxiety and status post hysterectomy, reason unknown.

CURRENT MEDICATIONS: Procardia, Estrace, Relafen, Zantac and Quinine

SOCIAL HISTORY: Remote smoking history, social alcohol

REVIEW OF SYSTEMS:

| | |
|---|---|
| General: | Well-developed, well-nourished woman in no acute distress |
| Vital Signs: | Stable, slightly febrile |
| Integument: | Slightly dry, decreased turgor |
| HEENT: | Clear, throat clear |
| Neck: | Supple |
| Chest: | A few rhonchi, otherwise clear to auscultation |
| Cardiac: | Regular rate and rhythm, no clicks, murmurs or gallops |
| Abdomen: | Soft, tender in the right upper quadrant with no rebound or guarding. Normoactive bowel sounds |
| Rectal: | Heme negative with normal tone |
| Extremities: | No cyanosis or clubbing. Trace pedal edema |
| Neurological: | No deficits |
| Breasts: | Soft, symmetrical without discharge or masses |
| Genitalia: | Deferred |

LABORATORY DATA:
Urinalysis shows positive bacteria, positive nitrates. Culture and sensitivity positive for E. coli.
White blood count 16,000, hemoglobin 13.5, hematocrit 40, platelet count 171,000. Sodium 135, Potassium 3.2, amylase 44.
Ultrasound of the gallbladder shows a 1.5-cm gallstone.
The hepatobiliary scan is positive for obstruction.
Electrocardiogram shows normal sinus rhythm with left anterior hemiblock, no acute ST-T changes.

ASSESSMENT:
1. Cholecystitis
2. Urinary tract infection

PLAN:
1. Start intravenous Ancef
2. Give patient pain control for gallbladder colic
3. Have surgery evaluate for acute abdomen

## Case Study 16
**Procedure Note**

| | |
|---|---|
| DATE OF PROCEDURE: | 1/4/06 |
| PREOPERATIVE DIAGNOSIS: | Acute cholecystitis |
| POSTOPERATIVE DIAGNOSIS: | Acute and chronic cholecystitis with lithiasis |
| PROCEDURE: | Laparoscopic cholecystectomy |
| SURGEON: | Dr. Hailey |
| ANESTHESIA: | General endotracheal anesthesia |
| ANESTHESIOLOGIST: | Patricia Miller, MD |

DESCRIPTION OF PROCEDURE:
Under general endotracheal anesthesia with the patient in the supine position, the abdomen was prepped with Betadine and draped. The oral gastric tube and Foley catheter were inserted. An infraumbilical incision was made. A versus needle was inserted and the abdomen was insufflated to 15 millimeters of mercury with carbon dioxide. A 10-11 millimeter trocar was inserted and zero degree laparoscope was inserted. A 5 millimeter trocar was placed three finger breadths below the right costal margin in the anterior axillary line two finger breadths below the right costal margin in the mid clavicular line and three finger breadths below the xiphoid in the midline. The gallbladder was elevated superiorly and adhesions from the gallbladder to the hepatic flexure and omentum were reflected inferiorly. Dissection was carried out at the neck of the gallbladder and cystic duct. Silver clip was placed on the neck of the gallbladder to prevent stones from migrating down the cystic duct. The cystic duct was ligated times two with #0 chromic endoloop approximately 4 millimeters from its junction with the common duct and a sliver clip was placed between these two loops. The cystic artery was doubly sliver clipped and divided. The gallbladder was removed from the liver fossa utilizing a hook cautery, placed in an endopouch and retrieved through the umbilicus. During the course of the procedure, the abdomen was irrigated copiously with a solution of heparinized saline and Ancef. Once hemostasis was assured, air was evacuated and trocars were removed. Umbilical fascial defect was closed with a figure of eight suture of #0 Vicryl. The skin was closed with subcuticular #3-0 Vicryl. Steri-strips were applied. The patient tolerated the procedure well. The patient was transferred to the Recovery Room in satisfactory condition.

PATHOLOGY REPORT:

| | |
|---|---|
| Specimen: | Gallbladder |
| Microscopic Diagnosis: | Acute and chronic gangrenous cholecystitis and cholelithiasis |

## Case Study 16

**PROGRESS NOTES:**

1/3: Admit note: This is a 62 year-old female who is admitted for evaluation of acute abdominal pain with nausea. The pain and nausea began four days ago and is now radiating to her back. Patient is started on antibiotics and Demerol for pain.

1/4:
S: Complaining of abdominal pain and decreased appetite
O: HIDA scan positive for blockage of cystic duct secondary to gall stones. H/H okay at 13.5/40 and WBCs at 16,000. UA positive for E.coli; coverage with existing IV antibiotics
A: Cholecystitis with cholelithiasis
P: Patient is schedule for Laparoscopic Cholecystectomy

1/5:
S: Complaining of minimal pain at incision sites
O: H/H stable at 12.1/37, WBCs 7,900. Pathology positive for gangrenous acute and chronic cholecystitis and cholelithiasis
A: Good post-op course. Tolerating soft diet
P: Advance diet, continue, IV fluids and antibiotics, repeat UA

1/6:
S: Feels good, hungry
O: K+ decreased to 2.7, add KCL to IV for replacement. Afebrile, vital signs stable, incisions clean and dry. Repeat UA clear
A: Progressing well
P: Advance to full diet, repeat K+ level following replacement. Change to p.o. medications when IVs finished

1/7:
S: Wants to go home
O: Electrolytes within normal limits, vitals stable, afebrile, incisions healing
A: Good post op course
P: Plan discharge

1/8:
S: No complaints
O: Vitals stable, bowel sounds present
A: Ready for discharge
P: Discharge home

**ORDERS**:

1/3:
1. Admit patient
2. IV Ancef and Demerol for pain
3. UA and culture if positive
4. Liquid diet
5. HIDA scan
6. CXR and EKG
7. CBC, WBC, Chem Profile
8. Continue with home meds

1/4:
1. Prep for Laparoscopic Cholecystectomy

1/5:
1. Repeat labs
2. Continue current IV medications
3. Advance to regular diet in morning

1/6:
1. Replace K+ with KCL added to IV fluids
2. When IV fluids finished, switch to p.o. Cipro 500-mg b.i.d.

1/8:
1. Discharge home

**Case Study 16**
**Answer Sheet**

| DIAGNOSES | ICD-9-CM CODES | | | | | |
|---|---|---|---|---|---|---|
| DX 1 | | | | . | | |
| DX 2 | | | | . | | |
| DX 3 | | | | . | | |
| DX 4 | | | | . | | |

| PROCEDURES | CPT CODES | | | | | MODIFIERS (If Applicable) | | |
|---|---|---|---|---|---|---|---|---|
| PR 1 | | | | | | - | | |
| PR 2 | | | | | | - | | |
| PR 3 | | | | | | - | | |
| PR 4 | | | | | | - | | |
| PR 5 | | | | | | - | | |
| PR 6 | | | | | | - | | |

## PROVIDE ICD-9-CM CODES FOR DIAGNOSES

## CASE STUDY 17

### Inpatient Face Sheet

| | |
|---|---|
| Admit Date: | 1/06/2006 |
| Discharge Date: | 1/10/2006 |
| Sex: | Female |
| Age: | 64 |
| Disposition: | Home |

Admitting Diagnoses:
1. Neutropenic sepsis
2. Status post chemotherapy for non-Hodgkin's lymphoma
3. Hypertension

Discharge Diagnoses:
1. Pancytopenia with neutropenic sepsis secondary to chemotherapy
2. Non-Hodgkin's lymphoma
3. Hypoalbuminemia
4. Hypertension

## Case Study 17
## Discharge Summary

Admitted: 1/06/2006
Discharge: 1/10/2006
ADMISSION DIAGNOSES:
1. Neutropenic sepsis
2. Status post chemotherapy for non-Hodgkin's lymphoma
3. Hypertension

DISCHARGE DIAGNOSES:
1. Pancytopenia with neutropenic sepsis secondary to chemotherapy
2. Non-Hodgkin's lymphoma
3. Hypoalbuminemia
4. Hypertension

HISTORY: This is a 64 year-old female with non-Hodgkin's lymphoma, currently undergoing chemotherapy. The patient was evaluated by Oncology in follow-up and found to be neutropenic as well as febrile.

PHYSICAL EXAMINATION:

| | |
|---|---|
| Vital Signs: | Blood pressure 132/90. Temperature was 102. |
| HEENT: | Dry oral mucous membranes. No thrush or herpetic lesions. |
| Neck: | Supple, no adenopathy. |
| Lungs: | Clear. |
| Heart: | Slightly tachycardiac, no murmur. |
| Abdomen: | Soft, non tender. |
| Extremities: | Pulses bilateral. Decreased muscle tone. |

LABORATOY DATA: Chemistries revealed total protein 5.8, albumin 2.4. Calcium 7.3, 7.6. The follow-up chem-7 revealed CO2 of 25, chloride 111.
Admission white blood cell count was 0.1, hemoglobin 11.2, hematocrit 32.8, red cell indices were normal. The platelet count was 14,000. The last blood count revealed white blood cell count of 3,500. The hemoglobin was 11.4, hematocrit 34.3, red cell indices remained normal. The urinalysis was pale in color and clear with trace protein noted, nitrite negative, leukocyte esterase negative. The urine culture showed no growth. Blood culture showed no growth.

RADIOLOGY: The chest x-ray showed no acute process.

HOSPITAL COURSE: The patient was admitted after follow-up with her oncologist. She was found to be febrile and neutropenic, rule out sepsis. The patient was admitted and placed in isolation. Cultures were obtained and the patient was placed on IV Fortaz as well as IV Gentamicin. The patient had pancytopenia with drop in her platelet count and the patient was given platelet transfusion, and blood transfusions as well as IV fluids for dehydration. The patient had a mild reaction to the transfusion and was given IV steroids as well as Benadryl. The patient was started on Neupogen injections on 1/7/06. The patient again received platelet and blood transfusion on 1/7/06 and additional platelet transfusion on 1/9/06. The patient's white blood cell count was increasing and she was less clinically septic. IV antibiotics were converted to oral Cipro. Her isolation was discontinued and she remained afebrile. The patient's platelets counts continued to be low. However, this will be managed as an outpatient.

DISCHARGE INFORMATION: Medications: Floxin 400 mg twice daily. Mycostatic swish and swallow 5 cc 3 times daily. Patient is discharged in improved condition. Diet and activity as tolerated. The patient will follow-up with me in my office in one week.

## Case Study 17
## History and Physical

CHIEF COMPLAINT: Neutropenic sepsis.

HISTORY OF PRESENT ILLNESS:
This is 64 year-old white female with a known history of non-Hodgkin's lymphoma. The patient has been treated with chemotherapy and, on evaluation by Oncology, was found to be febrile and neutropenic. She was felt to be clinically septic. There was also evidence of significant neutropenia. The patient was admitted to the Oncology floor for antibiotic therapy, monitoring of her blood counts, medications to raise her white and hemoglobin counts and to be placed in reverse isolation.

PAST MEDICAL HISTORY: Non-Hodgkin's lymphoma, and hypertension.

SOCIAL HISTORY: Non-smoker, no alcohol use.

FAMILY HISTORY: Positive for cancer and heart disease.

REVIEW OF SYSTEMS: Negative

PHYSICAL EXAMINATION:

| | |
|---|---|
| Vital Signs: | Blood pressure 132/90, respirations 28, temperature 102. |
| HEENT: | Negative except for dry oral mucous membranes. No thrush or herpetic lesions. |
| Neck: | Supple, no carotid bruit. No evidence of adenopathy. |
| Lungs: | Clear. |
| Cardiac: | Slightly tachycardic, but no murmur. |
| Abdomen: | Soft, non tender, positive bowel sounds. |
| Extremities: | Bilateral pulses. Poor muscle tone. No evidence of deep venous thrombosis or cellulitis. |

ASSESSMENT:
1. Neutropenic sepsis, status post chemotherapy
2. Non-Hodgkin's lymphoma

PLAN:
1. Admit and place in reverse isolation
2. Intravenous hydration
3. Intravenous antibiotics
4. Continue present medications
5. Follow blood counts

# Case Study 17

**Progress Notes**

1/6: Admit Note: Patient with non-Hodgkin's lymphoma admitted to isolation for neutropenic sepsis secondary to chemotherapy.

1/7:
S: "Feel better today"
O: Vital signs stable, WBCs 0.1, platelets 14,000, temperature 101.3, blood and urine cultures negative
A: Responding to antibiotics, still dehydrated
P: Continue IV fluids and antibiotics. Transfuse platelets and PRBCs. Begin neupogen injections

1/8:
S: No complaints
O: Vitals stable, temp 99.8, transfusion reaction last night requiring IV steroids and Benadryl
A: Continued improvement, responded well to steroids and Benadryl for transfusion reaction
P: Continue current meds, transfuse PRBCs and platelets tomorrow.

1/9:
S: "I feel great"
O: WBC at 3500, platelets at 14,000, afebrile, vitals stable
A: Less clinically septic, tolerated transfusions well with no adverse reaction
P: Discontinue isolation, change antibiotics to p.o. Discontinue IV fluids

1/10:
S: "I want to go home"
O: Afebrile, platelets still low
A: Ready for discharge, will manage platelets as an outpatient
P: Discharge home

## Case Study 17

**Orders:**

1/6:
1. Admit to reverse isolation
2. IV fluids at 83cc/hr with IV Fortaz and Gentamicin
3. Urine and blood cultures
4. Chemistry profile
5. CBC, WBC
6. Type and cross 4 units
7. PA and lateral CXR
8. Vitals q shift

1/7:
1. Begin daily neupogen injections
2. Transfuse 2 units PRBCs and platelets

1/8:
1. Continue with current treatment

1/9:
1. Transfuse 2 units PRBCs and platelets
2. Discontinue isolation
3. Discontinue IV fluids when finished and switch to p.o. antibiotics

1/10:
1. Discharge home

**Case Study 17**
**Answer Sheet**

| DIAGNOSES | ICD-9-CM CODES | | | | | |
|---|---|---|---|---|---|---|
| DX 1 | | | | . | | |
| DX 2 | | | | . | | |
| DX 3 | | | | . | | |
| DX 4 | | | | . | | |

| PROCEDURES | CPT CODES | | | | | MODIFIERS (If Applicable) | | |
|---|---|---|---|---|---|---|---|---|
| PR 1 | | | | | | - | | |
| PR 2 | | | | | | - | | |
| PR 3 | | | | | | - | | |
| PR 4 | | | | | | - | | |
| PR 5 | | | | | | - | | |
| PR 6 | | | | | | - | | |

**PROVIDE ICD-9-CM CODES FOR DIAGNOSES AND CPT CODES FOR PROCEDURE(S)**

## CASE STUDY 18

### Inpatient Face Sheet

| | |
|---|---|
| Admit Date: | 1/11/06 |
| Discharge Date: | 1/15/06 |
| Sex: | Female |
| Age: | 50 |
| Disposition: | Home |

Admit Diagnoses:
1. Right upper lobe lesion
2. Asthmatic bronchitis
3. Depression

Discharge Diagnoses:
1. Non-small cell carcinoma right upper lobe
2. Metastasized to hilar and thoracic lymph nodes
3. Chronic obstructive pulmonary disease
4. Depression

Procedures:
1. Flexible bronchoscopy
2. Right upper lobe lobectomy

## Case Study 18
## Discharge Summary

Admitted: 1/11/06
Discharged: 1/15/06

DISCHARGE DIAGNOSES:
1. Non-small-cell carcinoma right upper lobe of lung with metastasis to hilar and thoracic lymph nodes
2. Chronic obstructive pulmonary disease
3. Depression

PROCEDURES PERFORMED:
1. Flexible bronchoscopy
2. Right upper lobe lobectomy

HISTORY OF PRESENT ILLNESS.
This is a 50 year old female with a 3 cm lesion in the right upper lobe. She had an episode of bronchitis in January. Subsequent chest x-ray revealed a lesion in the right upper lobe. A CAT scan of the chest was performed and the presence of the lesion in the right upper lobe was confirmed.

HOSPITAL COURSE:
The patient underwent flexible bronchoscopy with right upper lobectomy on January 11, 2006. The findings were a 3-cm lesion in the right upper lobe with metastasis to the lymph nodes. The patient tolerated the procedure well. Vital signs remained stable. There was minimal chest tube drainage. She was advanced to a regular diet the second post-operative day.

LABORATORY DATA: Routine laboratory work on admission showed a potassium of 4.0, BUN 10, creatinine 0.6. WBCs 8.8, hemoglobin 13.7 and hematocrit 38.2. Platelet count 288,000. The urinalysis was negative. PT was 10.1. Discharge laboratory was unchanged with the exception of BUN 12, creatinine 0.9. Hemoglobin 11.3 and hematocrit 34.2

EKG: Sinus rhythm

IMAGING: The pre-operative chest x-ray showed a 3.0 cm suspicious nodule in the right upper lobe with chronic obstructive pulmonary disease. Post operative chest x-ray showed good expansion of the right middle and lower lobes.

The patient was discharged on the fourth post-operative day in satisfactory condition. Regular diet as tolerated. She is to limit activity for the next three weeks. She will follow up in my office in one week.

Discharge medications include: Vicodin 1 tablet P.O. q 4h. prn. for pain. Elavil 150-mg h.s., Ventolin 2 puffs q.i.d.

## <u>Case Study 18</u>
## History and Physical

CHIEF COMPLAINT: Right upper lobe lesion.

HISTORY OF PRESENT ILLNESS:
This is a 50 year old female with a 3 cm lesion in the right upper lobe. She had an episode of bronchitis in January. Subsequent chest x-ray revealed a lesion in the right upper lobe. A CAT scan of the chest was performed and the presence of the lesion in the right upper lobe was confirmed. The patient is admitted at this time for a bronchoscopy and right thoracotomy.

REVIEW OF SYSTEMS:
Patient denies hematemesis, melena and angina pectoris. There are no complaints of syncope, claudication, or edema.

| | |
|---|---|
| HEENT: | No masses, pupils equal, round, reactive to light. No oral cavity lesions. No evidence of JVD, thyroid is not enlarged. No carotid bruits. |
| Chest: | Symmetrical. |
| Lungs: | Clear to auscultation and percussion. No wheezing. |
| Heart: | No murmurs, no gallops, regular rhythm. |
| Abdomen: | No masses, no organomegaly. |
| Extremities: | No cyanosis, clubbing or edema. Good peripheral pulses. |

PAST MEDICAL HISTORY:
She has asthmatic bronchitis and has been hospitalized twice in the past for bronchitis. Patient is currently treated for depression. She has no history of diabetes mellitus, hypertension, myocardial infarction or neurological deficits. She has had no surgeries.

MEDICATIONS: Elavil 150-mg h.s., Ventolin 2 puffs q.i.d.

ALLERGIES: None known

SOCIAL HISTORY: She smokes two packs of cigarettes per day and has smoked for 30 years.

FAMILY HISTORY: Noncontributory

IMPRESSION:
1. Right upper lobe lesion
2. Rule out bronchogenic carcinoma
3. Rule out benign lesion
4. Asthmatic bronchitis
5. Depression

PLAN: Patient is admitted for bronchoscopy and right thoracotomy with right upper lobectomy. The procedures and the risks involved were fully explained to the patient and all questions answered and an informed consent was signed by the patient.

## Case Study 18
## Operative Report

| | |
|---|---|
| DATE OF OPERATION: | 1/11/06 |
| PREOPERATIVE DIAGNOSIS: | Right Upper Lobe Lesion |
| POSTOPERATIVE DIAGNOSIS: | Carcinoma of the right upper lobe with metastasis to hilar and thoracic lymph nodes |
| SURGEON: | Heather Schoonover, M.D. |
| OPERATIVE PROCEDURE: | 1. Flexible bronchoscopy<br>2. Right upper lobe lobectomy |

INDICATIONS: Female patient with a 3-cm lesion centrally located in the right upper lobe.

FINDINGS:
The bronchoscopy was negative. On thoracotomy there was a 3-cm lesion centrally located in the right upper lobe. There were positive nodes in the hilar and thoracic lymph nodes.

DESCRIPTION OF PROCEDURE:
Under general anesthesia the flexible bronchoscope was introduced through both lumen of the endotracheal tube. The carina was normal. Both the right and left bronchial trees were visualized down to the subsegmental level. There was no evidence of endobronchial lesions. The bronchoscopy was negative.

After prepping and draping the operative area a right posterolateral thoracotomy was made. The incision was deepened through the skin, subcutaneous tissue and latissimus dorsi muscle. The serratus anterior muscles were retracted anteriorly and the chest was entered through the fifth intercostal space. On exploration of the right lung there was a 3-cm lesion centrally located in the right upper lobe. A right total lobectomy was performed based upon the above findings. Surrounding lymph nodes were inspected and biopsies were obtained from both the hilar and surrounding thoracic nodes.

Frozen section was positive for non-small cell carcinoma. The bronchial resection margin was negative for tumor. The inferior pulmonary ligament was taken all of the way up to the inferior pulmonary vein. The bronchial stump was checked up to a pressure of 35mmHg and there was no air leak. Hemostasis was again secured. A chest tube was placed through a separate stab wound and secured to the skin with 0 silk. The incision was closed using #2 Vicryl pericostal sutures, #1 Vicryl for the latissimus dorsi muscle, 2-0 Vicryl for the subcutaneous tissue and staples for the skin.

The estimated blood loss was less than 200 cc. The patient tolerated the procedure very well and was taken to the recovery room in good condition with stable vital signs.

## Case Study 18

**PROGRESS NOTES**:

1/11: Admit Note: A 50 year-old female found to have a 3 cm lesion in the right upper lobe. She is admitted at this time for flexible bronchoscopy and right thoracotomy.

1/12: S: Complains of incisional pain
O: Vital signs stable, labs within normal limits, minimal chest tube drainage
A: Post op CXR shows good expansion of right middle and lower lobes
P: Patient doing well from surgical standpoint, will remove chest tube in a.m.

1/13: S: Less pain, depressed with diagnosis
O: Vital remain stable, afebrile, good lung sounds
A: Progressing nicely
P: Advance to full diet, increase ambulation

1/14: S: Feels better today
O: Afebrile, vital signs stable, labs look good
A: Incisions clean and dry with no redness
P: Possible discharge tomorrow

1/15: S: Ready to go home
O: Discharge labs and CXR within normal limits
A: Incisions healing well
P: Discharge patient

---

**ORDERS**:

1/11: 1. Admit patient
2. Have consents signed for flexible bronchoscopy and right thoracotomy
3. Place pre-op diagnostics on chart

1/12: 1. Ambulate patient
2. Repeat CXR
3. Repeat labs

1/13: 1. Advance to full diet
2. Increase ambulation

1/14: 1. No new orders

1/15: 1. Discharge patient

**Case Study 18**
**Answer Sheet**

| DIAGNOSES | ICD-9-CM CODES | | | | | |
|---|---|---|---|---|---|---|
| DX 1 | | | | . | | |
| DX 2 | | | | . | | |
| DX 3 | | | | . | | |
| DX 4 | | | | . | | |

| PROCEDURES | CPT CODES | | | | | | MODIFIERS (If Applicable) | |
|---|---|---|---|---|---|---|---|---|
| PR 1 | | | | | | - | | |
| PR 2 | | | | | | - | | |
| PR 3 | | | | | | - | | |
| PR 4 | | | | | | - | | |
| PR 5 | | | | | | - | | |
| PR 6 | | | | | | - | | |

**PROVIDE CODES FOR DIAGNOSES AND CPT CODES FOR PROCEDURE(S)**

## CASE STUDY 19

### Inpatient Face Sheet

| | |
|---|---|
| Admit Date: | 1/15/06 |
| Discharge Date: | 1/17/06 |
| Sex: | Female |
| Age: | 46 |
| Disposition: | Home |

Admitting Diagnoses:

Herniated cervical disc
Neck and right arm pain
Asthma

Discharge Diagnoses:

Herniated C7-T1 disc
Radiculopathy secondary to above
Asthma
Respiratory distress secondary to morphine

Procedure:

Cervical fusion, anterior
Excision of C7-T1

## Case Study 19
## History and Physical

CHIEF COMPLAINT: Neck and arm pain

HISTORY OF PRESENT ILLNESS:
This 46-year-old female is referred by her primary care physician, Dr. Adrianna Rose, due to neck and right arm pain that she attributes to a whip lash type injury sustained during a fall while using her roller blades in March of last year. She has been treated medically by her PCP without resolution of her symptoms. She was seen by Dr. Alexander Warren who ordered EMG nerve conduction velocity testing and subsequent MRI. Patient describes her pain as radiating into the right shoulder, down the back of the arm with pain in the fingers. The pain is all on the right side and is made worse by moving her neck. Patient denies any other pain.

PAST MEDICAL HISTORY:

MEDICATIONS: Flexeril and Vicodin for pain and occasional inhaler for asthma.

ALLERGIES: None known

OPERATIONS: Appendectomy in 1979

REVIEW OF SYSTEMS:

| | |
|---|---|
| Vital Signs: | Temperature 98.7, pulse 73, respirations 18, blood pressure 117/78 |
| HEENT: | Unremarkable |
| Neck: | Decreased range of motion due to pain |
| Heart: | Regular rate and rhythm |
| Lungs: | Clear |
| Abdomen: | Soft, non-tender |
| Extremities: | Decreased grip on the right as compared to the left. |

SOCIAL HISTORY:
Single, non-drinker, non-smoker. Lives with two teen-aged children.

FAMILY HISTORY: Non-contributory

ASSESSMENT:
Review of MRI demonstrates herniated disc on the right at C7-T1
C8 radiculopathy secondary to C7-T1 herniated disc.

PLAN: Diskectomy

## Case Study 19
## Procedure Note

DATE: 1/15/06

PREOPERATIVE DIAGNOSIS: C7-T1 herniated disk, right

POSTOPERATIVE DIAGNOSIS: C7-T1 herniated disk, right

PROCEDURE: C7-T1 microdiskectomy and fusion with Allograft and premier plate system.

SURGEON: Dr. Stephanie Waldron

ASSISTANT: Dr. Norma Millard

ANESTHESIA: General

INDICATIONS: The patient is a 46-year-old female with neck and right arm pain, found to have a large herniated disk.

DESCRIPTION OF PROCEDURE: The patient was inducted with general anesthesia and placed supine on the operating table. The neck was prepped and draped in the usual manner. A transverse skin incision was made low in the neck from the sternocleidomastoid to the midline. The platysmas was cut sharply. Dissection was carried down to the space between carotid sheath laterally, esophagus and trachea medially. Prevertebral fascia was opened. Appropriate level was identified by x-ray. Longus colli muscles were cauterized, elevated and retracted. Then, posts were drilled in the body of C7 and T1 and the disk spaced was distracted. It was opened initially with a #15 blade and interspace rongeurs. Microscope was brought into the field and a dissection was carried down to the posterior longitudinal ligament and the dura was exposed transversely. Herniated fragment was found in the right lateral gutter.

A foraminotomy was carried out giving exposure to the initial part of the C8 nerve. Once this was accomplished, and it felt to be well decompressed, the wound was irrigated out. An allograft was fashioned with slightly more height on the left than on the right, as this is where some extra bone was removed. This was tapped into place, the posts were removed, the holes were waxed and an appropriate size 25-mm fusion premier plate was put into place and screwed into place. The compression devise was used to give some compression on the bone. Once this was accomplished, the wound was irrigated and closed with 3-0 coated Vicryl in the platysma and 4-0 coated Vicryl in the skin.
The patient tolerated the procedure well without complications.

ESTIMATED BLOOD LOSS: 100 CC.

## Case Study 19

### Progress Notes

1/15: Admit note: Patient admitted with complaint of neck pain radiating to the right arm. MRI revealed a herniated C7-T1 disc. Patient is admitted for elective diskectomy. The procedure, alternative therapy and the accompanying risks have been discussed and she desires the procedure.

1/15: Operative Note:

| | |
|---|---|
| Pre-op: | C7-T1 HNP |
| Post-op: | Same |
| Operation: | C7-T1 diskectomy |
| Surgeon: | Dr. Waldron |
| Assistant: | Dr. Millard |
| Anesthesia: | General |

Patient was given Morphine post operatively in the Recovery Room. Patient immediately suffered respiratory distress as a result of the Morphine. Narcan was administered with immediate results. Patient was observed for an additional 2 hours post recovery with no further adverse effects. She was transferred to the floor alert and oriented with no further signs of complications.

1/15:
S: Patient feeling well, only complaint of incisional pain.
O: Respiratory rate normal with no signs of distress.
A: Neurological stable.
P: Patient advised of allergy to Morphine and instructed to never allow administration of Morphine.

1/16:
S: No complaints
O: Afebrile, vital signs stable
A: Upper extremity strength good, sutures intact without redness
P: Discharge tomorrow

1/17: Discharge Note: Patient admitted on 1/15/06 for elective diskectomy C7-T1. Patient tolerated surgery well. Patient developed respiratory distress as a result of Morphine given post operatively in the Recovery Room. Respiratory distress quickly reversed with administration of Narcan. Patient's vital signs and laboratory values were within normal limits throughout hospitalization. Incision is healing well with sutures intact. Patient is stable from a neurological standpoint with good upper extremity strength. She is to follow up with me in three weeks. Activity as tolerated, however, she is to do no lifting. Discharge home in good condition.

## Case Study 19

**Orders:**

1/15: Pre-operative Orders:

1. Admit to Dr. Rose
2. Complete following tests two days pre-op:
   - CBC
   - C/C UA
   - PT/PTT
   - Type and Screen
   - Chem basic
   - Chest x-ray
   - EKG
3. Pre-op per anesthesia
4. Start I.V. 1000CC D5LR prior to surgery
5. Bilateral Thigh High TED Hose
6. NPO

1/15: PACU Standing Orders

1. Vital signs every 5 minutes for 15 minutes, then every 15 minutes until discharged from PACU.
2. Oxygen via nasal cannula at 3-5L/Minute
3. May discontinue oxygen when stable
4. Check operative site every 30 minutes
5. Maintain I.V. with D5LR 500cc while in PACU
6. Discharge from PACU when discharge criteria met

1/16:

1. Incentive spirometer q 2 hours.

1/17:

1. D/C home
2. F/U 3 weeks

**Case Study 19**
**Answer Sheet**

| DIAGNOSES | ICD-9-CM CODES | | | | | |
|---|---|---|---|---|---|---|
| DX 1 | | | | . | | |
| DX 2 | | | | . | | |
| DX 3 | | | | . | | |
| DX 4 | | | | . | | |

| PROCEDURES | CPT CODES | | | | | MODIFIERS (If Applicable) | | |
|---|---|---|---|---|---|---|---|---|
| PR 1 | | | | | | - | | |
| PR 2 | | | | | | - | | |
| PR 3 | | | | | | - | | |
| PR 4 | | | | | | - | | |
| PR 5 | | | | | | - | | |
| PR 6 | | | | | | - | | |

**PROVIDE ICD-9-CM CODES FOR DIAGNOSES AND CPT CODES FOR PROCEDURE(S)**

## CASE STUDY 20

### Inpatient Face Sheet

| | |
|---|---|
| Admit Date: | 1/14/06 |
| Discharge Date: | 1/15/06 |
| Sex: | Female |
| Age: | 24 |
| Disposition: | Home |
| Admitting Diagnosis: | Pre-term Labor |
| Discharge Diagnosis: | Pre-term Labor |

## Case Study 20
## Labor and Delivery History and Physical

History: Patient is a 24-year-old female, gravida 2, para 0, Abortus 0, who had her prenatal care at the Women's Clinic. She presented to Labor and Delivery with the complaint of abdominal pain and cramps. Her membrane is intact.

LMP: 05/20/05. EGA of 31.4 weeks. Ultrasound at 6 weeks. No complications during this pregnancy.

PAST MEDICAL HISTORY: Non-contributory

PAST SURGICAL HISTORY: None

MEDINCE: None during pregnancy

ALLERGIES: No known allergies

PRE-NATAL LABS: Rh +, Rubella BL, VDRL NR, GC -, Chlamydia -, Pap -, AB Screen 0, Hepatitis Screen -, Diabetic Screen 153

PHYSICAL EXAM:

| | |
|---|---|
| Vital signs: | BP 135/82, Temp. 98.4, Pulse 102, Resp. 21, FHTs 145 |
| General: | No acute diseases |
| HEENT: | No asymmetry |
| Neck: | No asymmetry |
| Heart: | Regular rate and rhythm |
| Lungs: | Clear to auscultation bilaterally |
| Abdomen: | Soft, non-tender, non-distended, + bowel sounds |
| Extremities: | No edema |
| Neuro: | No deficits |
| Cervix | 1/th |
| Presenting Part | VTX/FFN + |

Impression: 24-year-old G2P000 at 31.4 weeks with PTL.

Plan:
1. Admit
2. U/S

| | |
|---|---|
| History: | Detailed |
| Examination: | Detailed |
| Medical Decision: | Low complexity |

## Case Study 20

**Progress Notes:**

1/14: Admit note: Patient admitted to Labor and Delivery with pre-term labor at 31.4 weeks gestation. Patient immediately started on MgSo4.

S: Patient denies HA/CP/SOB/CTX/RUQ pain
O: VS 121/73, P 87, FHT: 135-141, + accelerations
A: 24-year-old at 31.4 weeks with PTL
P: Follow Mg levels, perform US

1/15: S: Patient reports that pain is completely gone
O: PE, WNL. FHT: 150's, + accels, - decels.
A: PTL with Mg tocolysis, US indicates fetus at 1698 gm, cervix closed
P: DC today, strict bed rest with BRP, Follow up at clinic in one week.

---

**Orders:**

1/14:

1. Admit to L&D with PTL at 31.4 weeks
2. CBC and Clean Catch UA
3. MgSo4 per protocol – 5 Gm loading dose/then 2 gms/hr
4. Fetal Monitor
5. US
6. Strict bed rest
7. Clear liquid diet

1/15:

1. DC MgSo4
2. Transfer to antepartum
3. If patient remains stable throughout the day, may discharge this evening.

**<u>Case Study 20</u>**
**Answer Sheet**

| DIAGNOSES | ICD-9-CM CODES | | | | | |
|---|---|---|---|---|---|---|
| DX 1 | | | | . | | |
| DX 2 | | | | . | | |
| DX 3 | | | | . | | |
| DX 4 | | | | . | | |

| PROCEDURES | CPT CODES | | | | | MODIFIERS (If Applicable) | |
|---|---|---|---|---|---|---|---|
| PR 1 | | | | | | - | |
| PR 2 | | | | | | - | |
| PR 3 | | | | | | - | |
| PR 4 | | | | | | - | |
| PR 5 | | | | | | - | |
| PR 6 | | | | | | - | |

**PROVIDE ICD-9-CM CODES FOR DIAGNOSES AND CPT CODES FOR PROCEDURE(S)**

## CASE STUDY 21

### Inpatient Face Sheet

| | |
|---|---|
| Admit Date: | 1/10/06 |
| Discharge Date: | 1/15/06 |
| Sex: | Male |
| Age: | 55 |
| Disposition: | Home with Home Health Care |

Admitting Diagnoses:
1. Diabetic ulcer
2. Uncontrolled diabetes
3. Chronic renal failure
4. Pneumonia

Discharge Diagnoses:
1. Diabetic ulcer
2. Uncontrolled diabetes with peripheral circulatory disease
3. Pneumonia
4. Anemia
5. Chronic renal failure

Procedure:
1. Excisional debridement decubitus ulcer

## Case Study 21
## Discharge summary

Admitted: 1/10/06
Discharged: 1/15/06

ADMITTING DIAGNOSIS:
1. Diabetic ulcer
2. Uncontrolled diabetes
3. Chronic renal failure
4. Pneumonia

DISCHARGE DIAGNOSIS:
1. Diabetic ulcer
2. Uncontrolled diabetes with peripheral circulatory disease
3. Pneumonia
4. Anemia
5. Chronic renal failure

PROCEDURE:
1. Excisional debridement decubitus ulcer

HISTORY:
This is a 55 year-old male who was admitted through the Emergency Room for elevated blood sugars, a necrotic heel ulcer of the left foot. The patient was admitted for control of his blood sugars and treatment of the heel ulcer.

PAST MEDICAL HISTORY:
This patient has a long history of type I diabetes, chronic renal failure, coronary artery disease with history of CABG, peripheral vascular disease with subsequent below knee amputation of the right leg.

HOSPITAL COURSE:
The patient was admitted to the hospital and started on intravenous antibiotic therapy. The patient was placed on sliding scale insulin therapy as well as wound care for the heel necrosis. The patient's left heel ulcer was debrided of all necrotic tissue on 1/11/06. There was no cellulitis of the foot; however, there were multiple areas of skin break down on the foot. The patient had no feeling in his left foot, secondary to severe diabetic neuropathy. The patient was continued on local wound care and antibiotic therapy. The patient's renal failure was monitored and fluids restricted. The patient's chest x-ray was positive for left lower lobe pneumonia. Sputum culture was not ordered as the patient was already on intravenous antibiotic therapy for the skin ulcer.

## Case Study 21
## Discharge Summary

Continued:

LABORATORY DATA:
Hemoglobin 9.4, hematocrit 29.6, WBC 8,600, platelet count 336,000. Urinalysis was normal except for a small amount of bacteria, and proteinuria. Sodium was 130, potassium 4.1, chloride 92, CO2 32, glucose 270, BUN 53 and creatinine 3.2.

DISCHARGE MEDICATIONS:
70/30 insulin in the morning and 20 units in the evening
Cardizem CD 180 mg once daily
Imdur 60 mg once a day
Lasix 80 mg once a day
Pepcid 20 mg twice a day
Paxil 10 mg three times a day
Nitrostat prn.
Patient is prescribed Floxin once daily times seven days

The patient was felt to have reached maximum benefit of hospitalization and was discharged home in fair condition. He will be followed by home health care for wound care and monitoring of his diabetes as well as chronic renal failure. He is to continue with an 1800 ADA diet. His activity is limited due to his wheelchair. He is to have no weight bearing on his left foot. He will follow up in my office in ten days.

## Case Study 21
**History and Physical**

CHIEF COMPLAINT: Diabetic ulcer left foot, elevated blood sugars.

HISTORY OF PRESENT ILLNESS:
This is a 55-year-old white male who presented to the Emergency Room because of high blood sugars. This patient has a long history of Type I diabetes. He also has chronic renal failure due to his diabetes. This gentleman also has a history of coronary artery disease, CABG and myocardial infarction in 1996. He has diabetic peripheral vascular disease with a history of below the knee amputation of his right leg. He presently has an open necrotic area on the left foot, most likely due to PVD.

PAST MEDICAL HISTORY:
He denies hypertension, shortness of breath. Significant past history is detailed above.

PAST SURGICAL HISTORY: See above

ALLERGIES: None known

MEDICATIONS:
70/30 insulin in the morning and 20 units in the evening, Cardizem CD 180 mg once daily, Imdur 60 mg once a day, Lasix 80 mg once a day, Pepcid 20 mg twice a day, Paxil 10 mg three times a day, Nitrostat as needed.

SOCIAL HISTORY:
Patient lives with his wife. He does not smoke or drink. Patient is disabled due to his chronic illness.

FAMILY HISTORY: Non-contributory

PHYSICAL EXAMINATION:

| | |
|---|---|
| Vital Signs: | Temperature 97.7, pulse 77, respirations 20, blood pressure 146/62 |
| HEENT: | Unremarkable |
| Neck: | Carotid bruit. The neck is supple |
| Heart: | Regular rate and rhythm |
| Lungs: | Clinically clear |
| Abdomen: | Soft, non-tender, no organomegaly |
| Extremities: | Right below the knee amputation. There is a necrotic area on the left heel and an open ulcer on the left foot |

## Case Study 21
## History and Physical

Continued:

DIAGNOSTIC DATA:
The patient's labs that have been done show a hemoglobin of 9.4, hematocrit of 29.6, white blood count 8.6, platelet count 336,000. Urinalysis is abnormal with 25-50 RBCs, 50-100 WBCs, small amount of bacteria, glycosuria, and proteinuria. Chemistry: sodium 130, potassium 4.1, chloride 92, CO2 31, anion gap is 11, glucose 260. BUN 53 and creatinine 3.2. Blood cultures and urine cultures have been ordered. The patient has been started on Floxin 400 twice a day. He had a CT scan of the head which is negative.

His EKG reveals right bundle branch block with right axis deviation, bifascicular block, right bundle branch block with left posterior fascicular block.

IMPRESSION:
1. Uncontrolled diabetes
2. Atherosclerotic cardiovascular heart disease
3. Diabetic peripheral vascular disease with left heel and foot ulcer and neuropathy
4. Carotid stenosis
5. Status post right below the knee amputation
6. End stage renal disease

## Case Study 21

### Progress Notes

1/10: Admit Note: 55 year old diabetic male admitted for elevated blood sugars and necrotic heel ulcer of left foot. Patient has a long history of Type I diabetes, PVD with BKA right in 1995. Patient has CRF, not yet requiring dialysis.

1/11:
- S: Complains only of chest pain from coughing
- O: Glucose under better control with sliding scale coverage, last accucheck is 203, renal stable, BUN 57 and creatinine 3.8
- A: Foot ulcers debrided at bedside of necrotic tissue
- P: Continue IV antibiotics and wound care for ulcers

1/12:
- S: Feeling better
- O: BS at 189, BUN/Creatinine at 54/3.6, CXR shows clearing of infiltrates
- A: Foot healing nicely, respiratory status improving
- P: Continue current treatment plan

1/13
- S: No complaints
- O: BS leveling, now at 160. Renal status is stable
- A: Patient is improving, foot ulcer is healing well
- P: DC IV fluids when completed and start on P.O. meds

1/14:
- S: Patient is ready to go home
- O: Wounds look good, BS now in good control, renal status stable
- A: Patient can be discharged tomorrow, reaching maximum medical improvement
- P: Will plan discharge tomorrow

1/15: Discharge note: Patient will be followed by home health care for wound care and monitoring of diabetes and renal failure.

## Case Study 21

**Orders:**

1/10:
1. Admit patient
2. CBC, WBC, Chem profile, CXR, EKG
3. IV antibiotics
4. Sliding scale insulin, accuchecks q 2 hr
5. Whirlpool therapy for ulcers

1/11:
1. Debridement tray at bedside
2. Continue with wound care treatment

1/12:
1. Adjust sliding scale
2. Repeat labs and CXR

1/13:
1. DC IVs when finished
2. Switch to Floxin 400 mg twice daily

1/14:
1. Repeat labs

1/15:
1. Discharge home with home health care

**Case Study 21**
**Answer Sheet**

| DIAGNOSES | ICD-9-CM CODES | | | | | |
|---|---|---|---|---|---|---|
| DX 1 | | | | . | | |
| DX 2 | | | | . | | |
| DX 3 | | | | . | | |
| DX 4 | | | | . | | |

| PROCEDURES | CPT CODES | | | | | MODIFIERS (If Applicable) | | |
|---|---|---|---|---|---|---|---|---|
| PR 1 | | | | | | - | | |
| PR 2 | | | | | | - | | |
| PR 3 | | | | | | - | | |
| PR 4 | | | | | | - | | |
| PR 5 | | | | | | - | | |
| PR 6 | | | | | | - | | |

**PROVIDE ICD-9-CM CODES FOR DIAGNOSES AND CPT CODES FOR PROCEDURE(S)**

## CASE STUDY 22

### Inpatient Face Sheet

| | |
|---|---|
| Admit Date: | 1/27/06 |
| Discharge Date: | 1/30/06 |
| Sex: | Female |
| Age: | 72 |
| Disposition: | Home |

Admitting Diagnosis:
1. Chest pain, rule out acute coronary artery disease

Discharge Diagnoses:
1. Coronary Artery Disease
2. Unstable Angina
3. Atrial Fibrillation
4. Secondary Degree AV Block
5. Status Post Percutaneous Transluminal Coronary Angioplasty

Procedures:
1. Diagnostic left heart catheterization, Percutaneous transluminal coronary angioplasty, Coronary angiograms

## Case Study 22
## Discharge Summary

Admitted: 1/27/06

Discharged: 1/30/06

ADMITTING DIAGNOSES
1. Chest Pain, rule out acute coronary artery disease

DISCHARGE DIAGNOSES:
1. Chest pain, acute intermediate coronary syndrome
2. History of arteriosclerosis of the native coronary vessels
3. Atrial fibrillation
4. Second degree atrioventricular block

PROCEDURE PERFORMED:
1. Left heart catheterization, selective coronary angiography, percutaneous transluminal coronary angioplasty.

HOSPITAL COURSE:
This is a 72 year-old female with a history of coronary artery disease, status post percutaneous transluminal coronary angioplasty several months ago. She came in with acute intermediate coronary syndrome. A myocardial infarction was ruled out. In view of these events, it was decided to perform a diagnostic heart catheterization and possible percutaneous transluminal coronary angioplasty versus bypass surgery.

A diagnostic heart catheterization was performed and showed the following: the left main coronary artery was open, the left anterior descending artery was open, there was a previous stent in the circumflex system which had no obstruction. There was a totally occluded distal right coronary artery. There was some collateral circulation filling the right coronary artery. In view of this, it was felt that the patient would benefit from percutaneous transluminal coronary angioplasty, so the patient received IV Heparin, ReoPro and intracoronary Nitroglycerin and we were able to open the distal right coronary artery with balloon angioplasty.

The patient began ambulation the day after the above procedure. The patient is stable at discharge. Discharge to home on Atenolol 25 mg once a day, Monopril 10 mg once a day and aspirin. She will follow a low cholesterol, low fat diet. She is to follow up in my office in one week.

## Case Study 22
**History and Physical**

CHIEF COMPLAINT: Chest pain.

HISTORY OF PRESENT ILLNESS:
This is a 72-year-old white female with a history of coronary artery disease, status post percutaneous transluminal coronary angioplasty and stent implantation last summer, who has been taking Tenormin 50 mg once a day, Monopril 10 mg once a day, one aspirin a day and nitroglycerin prn. She experienced an episode of palpitation and lightheadedness last night, and this morning she started having chest pain. The patient called 911 and the EMS staff found her with a very fast rhythm, heart rate of 160 per minute accompanied with atrial fibrillation. She denied any prior history of palpitations and denies chest pains prior to this episode. The patient denies diabetes mellitus or high blood pressure. She denies history of myocardial infarction in the past. She has a strong family history of coronary artery disease. She denies alcohol or smoking.

PAST MEDICAL HISTORY: The past history is only pertinent for coronary artery disease and low HDL, post menopausal.

PAST SURGICAL HISTORY: History of back surgery

ALLERGIES: Sulfa

REVIEW OF SYSTEMS: See history of present illness. Patient denies paroxysmal nocturnal dyspnea, orthopnea, leg swelling, fatigue or loss of consciousness.

PHYSICAL EXAMINATION:

| | |
|---|---|
| General Appearance: | Patient is alert, cooperative and in no acute distress. |
| Vital Signs: | Her heart rhythm is in regular. Telemetry shows a second degree atrioventricular block, Mobitz type I, with beats 2 and 4, 2:3 conduction. No electrocardiogram evidence of ischemia. |
| Head and Neck: | Neck is supple. No jugular venous distention, no carotid bruits. |
| Lungs: | Clear |
| Heart: | Irregular rate and rhythm. No murmur, gallop or rub. |
| Abdomen: | Soft, non-tender. Bowel sounds present. No tenderness on rebound. |
| Extremities: | No cyanosis or edema. Bilateral peripheral pulses. |

ASSESSMENT:
1. Prolonged chest pain, rule out acute coronary artery disease
2. Mobitz type I second degree atrioventricular block
3. Coronary artery disease, status post stent implantation eight months ago

PLAN:
1. Admit to telemetry. Obtain cardiac enzymes and serial electrocardiograms
2. Hold Tenormin and place on Norvasc and nitrates
3. Cardiac catheterization and electrophysiology study

## Case Study 22
## Procedure Note

Date: 1/27/06

Procedure: Left Heart Catherization
Selective Coronary Angiography
PTCA of Distal Right Coronary Artery

Pre Operative Diagnosis: Unstable angina r/o CAD

Post Operative Diagnosis: CAD

Surgeon: Anthony C. Stamper, MD

Procedure Note:

A diagnostic left heart catheterization was performed and showed the following: the left main coronary artery was open, the left anterior descending artery was open, there was a previous stent in the circumflex system which had no obstruction. There was a totally occluded distal right coronary artery. There was some collateral circulation filling the right coronary artery. In view of this, it was felt that the patient would benefit from percutaneous transluminal coronary angioplasty, so the patient received IV Heparin, ReoPro and intracoronary Nitroglycerin and we were able to open the distal right coronary artery with balloon angioplasty. There was no clot formation or dissection. The patient returned to the floor in stable condition.

## Case Study 22
## Progress Notes

1/27: S: Chest pain
O: EKG and enzymes negative for AMI
A: Unstable angina, probable coronary occlusion
P: Heart Cath. and possible PTCA

1/28: S: Patient feels great, no chest pain
O: Labs within normal limits, EKG stable; patient ambulating
A: CAD
P: Observe a few more days

1/29: S: No chest pain, wants to go home
O: Vitals stable, heart sounds good, regular rhythm
A: Patient is stable, continues to do well
P: Plan discharge for a.m.

1/30: S: "Never felt better"
O: CXR clear, labs and vitals within normal limits
A: Patient stable for discharge
P: Discharge now

---

**Orders**

1/27:
1. Admit patient to telemetry
2. Vitals q4 hr.
3. Prepare for Left Heart Catheterization and possible PTCA
4. Continue home medications
5. Serial EKGs
6. Cardiac enzymes
7. Cardiac diet
8. Hold Tenormin, place on Norvasc and IV nitrates

1/28: 1. Ambulate

1/29: 1. Discontinue all IVs

1/30: 1: Discharge patient

**Case Study 22**
**Answer Sheet**

| DIAGNOSES | ICD-9-CM CODES | | | | | |
|---|---|---|---|---|---|---|
| DX 1 | | | | . | | |
| DX 2 | | | | . | | |
| DX 3 | | | | . | | |
| DX 4 | | | | . | | |

| PROCEDURES | CPT CODES | | | | | MODIFIERS (If Applicable) | | |
|---|---|---|---|---|---|---|---|---|
| PR 1 | | | | | | - | | |
| PR 2 | | | | | | - | | |
| PR 3 | | | | | | - | | |
| PR 4 | | | | | | - | | |
| PR 5 | | | | | | - | | |
| PR 6 | | | | | | - | | |

**PROVIDE ICD-9-CM CODES FOR DIAGNOSES AND CPT CODES FOR PROCEDURE(S)**

## CASE STUDY 23

### Inpatient Face Sheet

| | |
|---|---|
| Admit Date: | 1/24/06 |
| Discharge Date: | 1/31/06 |
| Sex: | Female |
| Age: | 70 |
| Disposition: | Home |

Admitting Diagnoses:
1. Acute abdominal pain, rule out diverticular disease
2. History of hypertension

Discharge Diagnoses:
1. Perforated sigmoid colon secondary to diverticulitis
2. Dense intra-abdominal adhesions
3. Hypertension
4. Post-operative atelectasis
5. Acute pharyngitis
6. Small bowel defect requiring resection

Procedures Performed:
1. Hartmann's procedure, lysis of adhesions, small bowel resection, colostomy
2. Flexible sigmoidoscopy

## Case Study 23
## Discharge Summary

Admitted: 1/24/06

Discharged: 1/31/06

ADMITTING DIAGNOSES:
1. Acute abdominal pain, probably due to diverticular disease
2. History of hypertension

DISCHARGE DIAGNOSIS:
1. Perforated sigmoid colon secondary to diverticulitis
2. Dense intra-abdominal adhesions
3. Hypertension
4. Pulmonary atelectasis, persistent post operative
5. Acute pharyngitis

PROCEDURES:
1. Hartmann's procedure, lysis of adhesions, small bowel resection
2. Flexible sigmoidoscopy

HISTORY OF PRESENT ILLNESS:
This is a 70 year-old white lady who had, on the day of admission undergone an outpatient colonoscopy. The physician was unable to advance the scope past the sigmoid colon and felt she had a perforated bowel secondary to diverticulitis. She has had a history of numerous episodes of diverticulitis.

PAST MEDICAL HISTORY: Hypertension, hysterectomy, appendectomy

MEDICATIONS ON ADMISSION: Inderal-LA and aspirin

ALLERGIES: None known

PHYSICAL EXAMINATION:
Reveals an elderly white lady with tenderness in the left lower quadrant of the abdomen.

LABORATORY DATA:
The admission laboratory data were within normal limits with the exception of low hematocrit of 34, hemoglobin 11.8 and elevated globulin 3.9. Post-operatively, white count was over 19,000, transiently returning to normal in two days. The hemoglobin dropped to 10.1 with hematocrit of 29.7.

RADIOLOGY REPORTS:
Gastrografin enema findings were suggestive of perforation at the level of the rectosigmoid, at a point where the patient had extensive diverticula.

## Case Study 23
## Discharge Summary

Continued:

Chest x-ray revealed pneumomediastinum and subcutaneous emphysema but no pneumothorax. There was air in the retroperitoneum. The follow-up chest x-rays showed nasogastric tube in satisfactory position with decreased subcutaneous emphysema within the neck and decreased pericardial air collection since the prior study, and development of small bilateral effusions on 1/28/06. The abdominal x-rays showed a large amount of free retroperitoneal air and air in the mediastinum.

HOSPITAL COURSE:
The patient was admitted and started on intravenous antibiotics with Unasyn and Tobramycin combination.

The patient was seen in consult by Gastrology who felt she probably had an acute sigmoid perforation secondary to diverticular disease. He felt she would benefit with Gastrografin enema, especially to determine whether she could be treated conservatively or not. The procedure was completed with the findings as mentioned above. It was felt she would require resection.

She was taken to the operating room where the above procedures were performed. The patient tolerated the procedure well under general anesthesia. The estimated blood loss was less than 100 cc with no replacement. The pathology report revealed diverticulosis with diverticulitis and perforation of the small bowel.

Postoperatively, the wound was healing nicely. The colostomy was noted to be viable. She was transferred to the surgical floor on 1/25/06. She was having the expected amount of abdominal discomfort post surgery. She also complained of sore throat and was started on Cepacol throat lozenges. The intravenous fluids and medications were continued.

The colostomy was not functioning over the first few days. There was minimal drainage from the nasogastric tube. Reglan was added. Breath sounds were decreased over the right lower lobe on 1/28/06. The chest x-ray revealed atelectasis. CXRs were done daily and the RLL was re-expanded on 1/30/06.

The colostomy began functioning on 1/29/06. Intravenous fluids were discontinued. Intravenous Lasix was given. Her diet was increased with toleration. Activity was increased and medications were changed to p.o.

The patient improved significantly in the next several days and she was stable enough to be discharged. She will be followed in the office in one week. She is discharged on Duricef 500-mg b.i.d. and Tylox one q.4h prn. Soft diet and activity as tolerated.

## Case Study 23
### History and Physical

CHIEF COMPLAINT: Abdominal pain

HISTORY OF PRESENT ILLNESS:
The patient is a 70 year-old white female who has undergone attempted colonoscopy this morning. There was difficulty in negotiating the sigmoid colon and the patient developed tenderness post-colonoscopy. Abdominal x-rays revealed free air as well as mediastinal air.

PAST MEDICAL HISTORY: Hypertension, hysterectomy, appendectomy

MEDICATIONS ON ADMISSION: Inderal-LA and aspirin

ALLERGIES: None known

PHYSICAL EXAMINATION:
Well developed, well nourished, seventy year-old white female in moderate distress.

REVIEW OF SYSTEMS:

| | |
|---|---|
| Cardiac: | Normal sinus rhythm |
| Pulmonary: | Clear |
| HEENT: | Within normal limits |
| Abdomen: | Soft with left lower quadrant pain and some distention |
| Extremities: | Bilateral pedal pulses |

Patient will be admitted for conservative management in hopes of avoiding surgery. She will receive intravenous antibiotic and bowel rest.

## Case Study 23
**Procedure Note**

DATE OF PROCEDURE: 1/24/06

PROCEDURE: Attempted full colonoscopy

SURGEON: Alexander Glenn, MD

INDICATION: Abdominal pain with history of diverticular disease

DESCRIPTION OF PROCEDURE:
With the patient in the left lateral position under direct luminal vision, a complete colonoscopy was attempted, but the Olympus colonoscope was only advanced up to 30 cm inside the sigmoid. The findings were as follows:

1. Rectum and anal canal: Internal hemorrhoids are seen in circumferential fashion, not bleeding at the time. No evidence of masses, lesions, angioma or polyps seen in the rectal area.

2. Rectosigmoid junction, sigmoid and descending colon: Extensive sigmoid diverticulosis with significant peridiverticulitis and spasm appreciated in a highly redundant sigmoid.

In view of the fact that the diverticular process was so extensive and the sigmoid extremely redundant, the advancement of the scope beyond this area was difficult and hence the procedure was terminated.

The patient returned to the floor in stable condition.

FINAL IMPRESSION:

1. Extensive sigmoid diverticulosis with diverticulitis and spasm
2. Redundant sigmoid
3. Internal hemorrhoids

## Case Study 23
## Procedure Note

DATE OF PROCEDURE: 1/24/06
PREOPERATIVE DIAGNOSIS: Perforated sigmoid colon
POSTOPERATIVE DIAGNOSIS:
1. Perforated sigmoid colon
2. Dense intra-abdominal adhesions

PROCEDURE:
1. Hartmann's procedure
2. Lysis of adhesions
3. Small bowel resection

SURGEON: Eric Worton, MD

FINDINGS: Moderately large perforation of the sigmoid colon approximately 2 cm in diameter with pelvic phlegmon. Dense intra-abdominal adhesions requiring extensive lysis taking 2 hours.

DESCRIPTION OF PROCEDURE:
The patient was taken to the operating suite and placed in the supine position. After adequate induction of general anesthesia the patient was prepped and draped in sterile fashion.

A midline incision was made and the abdomen was entered. Dense adhesions were encountered requiring extensive sharp dissection.

The area of transection in the proximal sigmoid was dissected out circumferentially. The mesentery was taken down between Kelly clamps. Rectosigmoid was mobilized. The distal sigmoid was dissected out circumferentially and a roticulator placed across this. A stapler was fired, the bowel was transected.

Small bowel adhesions were lysed. One area was extremely thin resulting in a serosal defect which required resection. An area in the mid jejunum was dissected out circumferentially both proximally and distally. The intervening mesentery was serially cross-clamped between Kelly clamps. The vessels were ligated with 2-0 silks. G.A. was fired across both sides. Functional end-to-end anastomosis was then performed.

The abdomen was irrigated with copious amounts of fluid. A Jackson-Pratt drain was placed in the pelvis.

Attention was then directed toward closure. The proximal defect was made in the left lower quadrant. Transected colon was brought out through the colostomy defect without difficulty. Upon adequate sponge, needle, lap, and instrument count the abdominal wound was closed with running #2 Prolene suture.

The subcutaneous tissue was irrigated with copious amounts of antibiotic solution. The cautery was utilized for hemostasis. The skin was loosely approximated. Jackson-Pratt drain was secured with 3-0 Nylon. A sterile dressing was applied and attention turned towards maturation of the colostomy.

The colon was secured to the fascia with three interrupted 3-0 Vicryl sutures. The colon was than transected and the colostomy matured in the usual fashion with interrupted 3-0 Vicryl sutures. The colostomy appliance was placed and the patient was taken to the recovery room having tolerated the procedure well.

## Case Study 23

**PROGRESS NOTES:**

1/24: Admit Note: Patient admitted following attempted colonoscopy. Physician was unable to advance the scope past the sigmoid colon and felt she had perforated bowel secondary to diverticulitis. This patient has a long history of diverticulitis. Laboratory data is within normal limits with the exception of H/H of 11.8/34. Patient was taken to surgery for resection of bowel. She tolerated the procedure well with minimal blood loss. The pathology report revealed diverticulitis and bowel perforation.

1/25:
S: Incisional pain
O: H/H dropped to 10.1/29.7, WBC 19,000, vital signs stable
A: Good post-operative course so far
P: Continue present treatment

1/26:
S: Less surgical pain
O: WBCs coming down, now at 14,000, vitals stable, incisions clean and dry
A: Continues to improve
P: Begin ambulation, maintain liquid diet

1/27:
S: Complaining of sore throat
O: WBCs normal, incisions healing nicely, colostomy still not functioning, but viable
A: Acute pharyngitis
P: Continue all meds; add Cepacol lozenges for sore throat

1/28:
S: Throat still sore, some surgical pain
O: Minimal NG drainage, decreased breath sounds RLL
A: Wound healing nicely, possible atelectasis
P: Get CXR to evaluate atelectasis

1/29:
S: Feels better, throat less sore
O: CXR shows persistent post op atelectasis RLL, colostomy beginning to function
A: Good post op course
P: Advance diet; remove NG tube, CXR daily

1/30:
S: More comfortable with NG tube out
O: CXR improved, RLL expanded, tolerating diet
A: Continues to improve, colostomy functioning nicely
P: Plan for discharge tomorrow

1/31:
S: Ready to go home
O: Wounds clean and dry, afebrile, tolerating diet
A: Good post op recovery
P: Discharge today

## Case Study 23

**ORDERS:**

1/24:
1. Admit patient and prep for bowel resection
2. Transfer to SICU following surgery
3. Follow unit protocol
4. Vitals q4h
5. IV Unasyn and Tobramycin

1/25:
1. Transfer to surgical floor
2. Continue all current meds and treatment
3. Cepacol throat lozenges for sore throat

1/26:
1. Portable CXR
2. Continue all orders

1/27:
1. CXR daily

1/28:
1. Advance diet

1/29:
1. Remove NG tube

1/30:
1. Discontinue IVs

1/31:
1. Discharge

## Case Study 23
## Answer Sheet

| DIAGNOSES | ICD-9-CM CODES | | | | | |
|---|---|---|---|---|---|---|
| DX 1 | | | | . | | |
| DX 2 | | | | . | | |
| DX 3 | | | | . | | |
| DX 4 | | | | . | | |

| PROCEDURES | CPT CODES | | | | | MODIFIERS (If Applicable) | | |
|---|---|---|---|---|---|---|---|---|
| PR 1 | | | | | | - | | |
| PR 2 | | | | | | - | | |
| PR 3 | | | | | | - | | |
| PR 4 | | | | | | - | | |
| PR 5 | | | | | | - | | |
| PR 6 | | | | | | - | | |

**PROVIDE ICD-9-CM CODES FOR DIAGNOSES AND CPT CODES FOR PROCEDURE(S)**

## CASE STUDY 24

### Inpatient Face Sheet

Admitted: 1/14/06

Discharged: 1/17/06

Sex: Female

Age: 35

Disposition: Home

Admitting Diagnosis:
1. Ovarian cyst

Discharge Diagnoses:
1. Ovarian cyst
2. Post operative blood loss
3. Urinary tract infection

Procedures:
1. Total abdominal hysterectomy
2. Bilateral salpingo-oophorectomy
3. Exploratory laparotomy

## Case Study 24
## Discharge Summary

Admitted: 1/14/06
Discharged: 1/17/06

DISCHARGE DIAGNOSES:
1. Ovarian cyst
2. Uterine adhesions
3. Urinary tract infection
4. Post operative anemia

PROCEDURES PERFORMED:
1. Exploratory laparotomy
2. Hysterectomy
3. Bilateral salpingo-oophorectomy

HISTORY:
This 35-year-old female has experienced pelvic pain for three months duration. Pelvic ultrasound revealed a right ovarian cystic mass. She was admitted for elective surgery.

PAST MEDICAL HISTORY:
Refer to History and Physical for complete history.

HOSPITAL COURSE:
Patient underwent exploratory laparotomy that revealed a benign cyst of the right ovary and adhesions of the uterus requiring hysterectomy and bilateral salpingo-oophorectomy. She tolerated the surgery without complication. Postoperative course was significant for postoperative anemia, requiring transfusion of PRBCs. She also was noted to have elevated temperature and cultures indicated a urinary tract infection. She was already on IV antibiotics post surgery that would also cover the UTI. She progressed well, in spite of the anemia and the UTI and was discharged in good condition on 1/17/06. She was given a prescription for antibiotics and iron pills. Activity as tolerated, however, no driving for two weeks. Diet as tolerated. She is to see me in three days for postoperative follow up and staple removal.

## Case Study 24
## History and Physical

CHIEF COMPLAINT: Pelvic pain

HISTORY OF PRESENT ILLNESS:
This 35-year-old gravida 3, para 3 has complained of pelvic pain for three months duration. Pelvic ultrasound revealed her right ovary to be enlarged with a large cystic mass. She is admitted today for elective exploratory laparotomy. The patient understands that she may require a hysterectomy and possible salpingo-oophorectomy.

PAST MEDICAL HISTORY: Negative, except for childbirth.

PAST SURGICAL HISTORY: No surgeries.

SOCIAL HISTORY: Non-smoker, non-drinker.

FAMILY HISTORY: Non-contributory.

ALLERGIES: Penicillin

MEDICATIONS: None

REVIEW OF SYSTEMS:
HEENT: Within normal limits
Neck: Supple. No lymphadenopathy
Heart: Regular rhythm, no murmurs
Lungs: Clear to auscultation
Abdomen: Soft. Good bowel sounds. Pelvic pain on palpation.
Rectal: Deferred
Extremities: Within normal limits.

IMPRESSION:
1. Ovarian cyst

PLAN:
1. Exploratory laparotomy

## Case Study 24
## Procedure Note

| | |
|---|---|
| Date of Procedure: | 1/14/06 |
| Preoperative Diagnosis: | Ovarian cyst, right |
| Postoperative Diagnosis: | Right ovarian cyst<br>Peritoneal adhesions |
| Surgeon: | Dr. Hollie Schoonover |
| Anesthesiologist: | Dr. Layne Allen |
| Procedure: | Exploratory laparotomy<br>Hysterectomy, Bilateral salpingo-oophorectomy |

DESCRIPTION OF PROCEDURE:
Following administration of general anesthesia, the patient's abdomen was prepped and draped in sterile manner. A midline incision was done below the umbilicus to the pubis symphysis and then taken down to the fascia. The muscles were separated and the peritoneum was cut taking care to avoid the bladder and bowel. There was a large cystic mass on the right ovary measuring 6 x 8 centimeters. Following lysis of adhesions, the right ovary and tube with the cyst intact were removed. The left tube and ovary were removed in similar fashion. On inspection of the uterus, it was noted to have extensive adhesions. The decision was made to perform a hysterectomy and this was carried out without complications. All bleeders were ligated using 0-Vicryl. The pelvic cavity was irrigated with saline. The abdomen was then closed using 2-0 Dexon and the skin was closed using staples. The patient tolerated the procedure and was discharged to the recovery room in good condition.

Estimated blood loss: 400cc

## Pathology Report

Specimens:

1. Uterus
2. Left ovary and fallopian tube
3. Right ovary and fallopian tube with cystic mass

Microscopic Diagnosis:

1. Uterus:
   Dense adhesions
   Mild chronic cervicitis
2. Left fallopian tube and ovary:
   Atrophic ovary with normal fallopian tube
3. Right fallopian tube and ovary:
   Normal right tube and benign cyst of the ovary

## Case Study 24

**Progress Notes:**

1/14: Patient admitted to surgical floor following exploratory laparotomy, hysterectomy and bilateral salpingo-oophorectomy. Patient tolerated the procedure well. Is fully awake and complains of moderate surgical pain. Patient will remain NPO until the evening meal and then will have a soft diet. Ambulate upon full recovery from anesthesia.

1/14:
S: Moderate pain.
O: Incision clean and dry, vital signs good. H/H 9.8/35.4. Was 12.9/42.3 on admission. Temp elevated to 101.2.
A: Probable post op anemia.
P: Monitor H/H, continue with present pain medication.

1/15:
S: Feels okay
O: Incision clean and dry, vitals good. H/H dropped to 8.10/32.2. Temp still elevated, 100.1
A: Possible occult infection
P: Will culture to r/o infection. Continue to monitor H/H.

1/16:
S: Complains of minor pain at operative site
O: Vital signs good. H/H at 10.9/39.8 after transfusion. Temperature 99.9
A: Urine culture revealed UTI. Treated with antibiotics. Ambulating freely, progressing well
P: Change to p.o. antibiotics, monitor H/H, probable discharge tomorrow

1/17:
S: Feels well, ready to go home
O: Incision healing well, vital signs good. H/H at 11.2/42.1. Temperature Normal.
A: Ready for discharge
P: Discharge home; follow up in office in one week

**Orders:**

1/14:
1. Admit patient to surgical floor from recovery
2. Standard post-operative orders
3. Vital signs q.6 hours

1/15:
1. Blood and urine cultures to rule out infection
2. Transfuse two units PRBCs
3. Continue with IV antibiotics

1/16:
1. Change IV antibiotics to p.o.
2. Continue to monitor H/H

1/17:
1. Discharge home

**Case Study 24**
**Answer Sheet**

| DIAGNOSES | ICD-9-CM CODES | | | | | |
|---|---|---|---|---|---|---|
| DX 1 | | | | . | | |
| DX 2 | | | | . | | |
| DX 3 | | | | . | | |
| DX 4 | | | | . | | |

| PROCEDURES | CPT CODES | | | | | | MODIFIERS (If Applicable) | |
|---|---|---|---|---|---|---|---|---|
| PR 1 | | | | | | - | | |
| PR 2 | | | | | | - | | |
| PR 3 | | | | | | - | | |
| PR 4 | | | | | | - | | |
| PR 5 | | | | | | - | | |
| PR 6 | | | | | | - | | |

## CASE STUDY 25

**Emergency Room Visit**

**Face Sheet**

| | |
|---|---|
| Date of Service: | 01/01/06 |
| Age: | 25 |
| Sex: | Female |
| Admitting Diagnosis: | Injury to left wrist |
| Discharge Diagnosis: | Sprain left wrist |
| Disposition: | Home |

## Case Study 25
## Emergency Room Visit

DATE OF SERVICE: 1/01/06

HISTORY OF PRESENT ILLNESS:
A 25-year-old female was at work today when a bread tray fell on her left wrist. She has persistent pain in the area which is exacerbated with moving the wrist and hand. She describes the pain as very severe.

PAST MEDICAL HISTORY: Noncontributory.

ALLERGIES: None.

PHYSICAL EXAMINATION:

| | |
|---|---|
| General: | Well-developed, well-nourished female in moderate distress. Vitals are stable. |
| Skin: | Warm and dry. |
| HEENT: | Unremarkable. |
| Chest: | Symmetrical. |
| Extremities: | The left wrist is tender and mildly swollen especially over the distal ulna with no gross deformity. Normal range of motion against resistance with moderate pain. No abrasions or lacerations. Normal distal neurosensory examination. The remainder of the extremity examination is within normal limits. |

Neurological: She is awake, alert, and oriented times three with no focal neurologic deficits.

RADIOLOGY EXAMINATION:
The patient was taken to the x-ray room where the wrist was x-rayed. No acute fractures appreciated in the AP and Lateral views.

IMPRESSION: Left wrist sprain.

The patient was placed in a padded splint and was given a prescription for Darvocet. She will follow up with her physician next week.

| | |
|---|---|
| History: | Expanded problem focused |
| Examination: | Detailed |
| Medical Decision Making: | Low Decision |

**Case Study 25**
**Answer Sheet**

| DIAGNOSES | ICD-9-CM CODES | | | | | |
|---|---|---|---|---|---|---|
| DX 1 | | | | . | | |
| DX 2 | | | | . | | |
| DX 3 | | | | . | | |
| DX 4 | | | | . | | |

| PROCEDURES | CPT CODES | | | | | MODIFIERS (If Applicable) | | |
|---|---|---|---|---|---|---|---|---|
| PR 1 | | | | | | - | | |
| PR 2 | | | | | | - | | |
| PR 3 | | | | | | - | | |
| PR 4 | | | | | | - | | |
| PR 5 | | | | | | - | | |
| PR 6 | | | | | | - | | |

| |
|---|
| **PROVIDE ICD-9-CM CODES FOR DIAGNOSES AND CPT CODE(S) FOR PHYSICIAN VISIT (E&M CODE)** |

## CASE STUDY 26

### Inpatient Face Sheet

| | |
|---|---|
| Admit Date: | 1/12/06 |
| Discharge Date: | 1/18/06 |
| Sex: | Female |
| Age: | 75 |
| Disposition: | Home |

Admitting Diagnoses:
1. Asthmatic bronchitis
2. Pneumonia
3. Supraventricular tachycardia
4. Chronic diastolic heart failure

Discharge Diagnoses:
1. Pneumonia
2. Asthmatic bronchitis
3. Supraventricular tachycardia
4. Chronic diastolic heart failure
5. Osteoarthritis

Procedures:
None

**Code E&M Visit for Dr. Magee's Initial Hospital Care**

| | |
|---|---|
| History: | Comprehensive |
| Examination: | Comprehensive |
| Medical Decision Making: | Moderate Complexity |

## Case Study 26

DISCHARGE SUMMARY

ADMTTED: 1/12/2006

DISCHARGED: 1/18/2006

ADMITTING DIAGNOSES:
1. Asthmatic bronchitis, rule out pneumonia.
2. Osteoarthritis.
3. Supraventricular tachycardia

DISCHARGE DIAGNOSES:
1. Pneumonia
2. Asthmatic bronchitis.
3. Osteoarthritis.
4. Supraventricular tachycardia.
5. Chronic diastolic heart failure

CHIEF COMPLAINT: Shortness of breath, history of asthma, possible pneumonia, fever.

HISTORY OF PRESENT ILLNESS: A 75 -year-old female presented to the emergency room with the above complaints. She had been treated as an outpatient by her primary care physician, Dr. Nicholas Magee. She failed to improve with Zithromax. The patient has a past history of bronchial asthma, supraventricular arrhythmia, and chronic diastolic heart failure. Her cardiologist is Dr. Benjamin William and her pulmonologist is Dr. Victoria Stamper. On 3/23/06, the patient had a cardiac catheterization with findings of minimal coronary artery disease.

PHYSICAL EXAMINATION: On exam today the patient is short of breath with congestion noted in the head and chest, expiratory wheezing, rales and rhonchi throughout. No edema. For complete physical details, please see history and physical.

HOSPITAL COURSE: The patient was admitted and given intravenous fluids, placed on telemetry monitoring, started on intravenous steroids, which were subsequently tapered; pan cultured, and had a pulmonary medicine consult. CT scan of the sinus showing pansinusitis and chest x-ray showing and pneumonia.

Consultation with Dr. Stamper of pulmonary medicine was performed.

RADIOLOGY REPORTS:
PA and lateral chest x-ray of January 12, showed left lower lobe pneumonia. CT scan of the sinuses taken on 1/13 showed pansinusitis. Follow-up PA and lateral chest x-ray on 1/15 showed clear, but hyperexpanded lungs compatible with the patient's clinical history of asthma, no evidence of focal consolidation pneumonia – compared to the chest x-ray of 1/13, which showed slight improvement of left lower lobe pneumonia and hiatal hernia.

LABORATORY DATA: On admission glucose 116, sodium 135, potassium 3.5, blood urea nitrogen 11, creatinine 1.4, calcium 8.4. On 1/15 glucose 125, sodium 137,

**Case Study 26**

DISCHARGE SUMMARY

Continued:

Potassium 3,9, blood urea nitrogen 19, creatinine 1.5, calcium 8.5. On admission white blood cell count was 22,300 with a hemoglobin 13.9, hematocrit 42.0, platelets 210,000. White blood cell count had decreased on 1/15 to 12,900 with hemoglobin of 12.7, hematocrit 37.7, platelets 266,000. Blood culture negative.

HOSPITAL COURSE: The patient presented with shortness of breath, cough and congestions, following outpatient care for respiratory infection. She has a history of asthma. She was admitted and placed on intravenous antibiotics, supplemental oxygen, nebulizer therapy with bronchodilators and intravenous steroids. She also was found to have sinusitis, pneumonia.

The patient was felt to have reached maximum medical improvement on 1/17 and was cleared for discharge. The patient was given the instructions and advice and will go home with the medications and the nebulizer treatments of Albuterol and saline four times a day.

DISCHARGE MEDICATIONS:

1. Levaquin 250 mg once a day for seven days.
2. Claritin 10 mg, one tablet daily.
3. Nasonex nasal spray, two sprays each nostril daily.
4. Potassium chloride spray, three or four times four times a day.
5. Lanoxin 0.125 mg daily
6. Lasix

## Case Study 26

History and Physical

ADMISSION DATE: 1/12/2006

CHIEF COMPLAINT: Shortness of breath, history of asthma, possible pneumonia, fever.

HISTORY: This 75 year old female presented to the emergency room with the above complaints. She was initially seen by her primary care physician Zithromax but failed to improve her symptoms. The patient was found to have possible infiltrate on chest x-ray, pyrexia and was admitted for further evaluation and treatment.

The past medical history includes bronchial asthma, history of supraventricular arrhythmia and palpitation.

PREVIOUS CONSULTANTS: Dr. Benjamin William and Dr. Victoria Stamper

PROCEDURES: On 04/23/2005, the patient had cardiac catheterization with findings of minimal coronary artery disease with recommendation for medical management.

PRESENT MEDICATIONS: The present medications include Lanoxin .25 milligrams daily, Nasonex nasal spray and Claritin D 24 hour tablet.

Additional medical history includes asthmatic bronchitis, and respiratory allergies.

PAST SURGERY: cataracts

SOCIAL HISTORY: The patient admits to cigarette smoking. She has never been married and has no children.

ALLERGIES: None known.

SYSTEMS REVIEW:

| | |
|---|---|
| INTEGUMENT: | Denies rashes, seborrhea or psoriasis. |
| HEENT: | Denies any problems chewing, tasting, hearing or swallowing. |
| RESPIRATORY: | Admits to shortness of breath, asthma and dyspnea on exertion |
| GASTROINTESTINAL: | Unremarkable |

FAMILY HISTORY: The family history includes two brothers and two sisters. One brother deceased. One brother has asthma. Parents are deceased. Mother died at age 82 from a stroke and father died at age 85 from a stroke.

## Case Study 26

History and Physical

Continued:

PHYSICAL EXAMINATION: The physical examination reveals a well nourished, well hydrated, Caucasian female with no complaints, alert and cooperative, mild respiratory stridor.

LUNGS: Full aeration, expiratory wheezing bilaterally.

CARDIOVASCULAR: S1 and S2 regular. No palpitations perceived at this time. No irregular rhythm noted on auscultation by this examiner. There is no jugular venous distention.

ABDOMEN: The abdomen is soft, nontender. No guarding, rebound or rigidity.

IMPRESSION AT THIS TIME: Asthmatic bronchitis, rule out pneumonia

RECOMMENDATION: Intravenous fluids, intravenous steroids, intravenous Levaquin, panculture, pulmonary medicine consult

CONDITION AT THIS TIME: Guarded.

## Case Study 26

CONSULTATION

DATE: 1/12/2006

REQUESTING PHYSICIAN: Dr. Magee

CONSULTING PHYSICIAN: Dr. Stamper

This is a 75-year-old female who has a longstanding history of asthma since the age of eight who was not doing well for the past few days with increased shortness of breath, cough and congestion. She saw Dr. Magee who gave her Zithromax, which did not help her symptoms. Then she developed increased fever, cough and congestion so she came to the emergency room where she was noted to have questionable pneumonia and bronchitis and bronchospasm. She was admitted to the hospital for further treatment.

PAST MEDICAL HISTORY: The past medical history is positive for longstanding asthma, COPD exacerbation requiring recurrent hospitalization, and history of allergic rhinitis. She also has a history of postnasal drip, chronic wheezing, shortness of breath, tachycardia

SOCIAL HISTORY: Past history of smoking. Doesn't abuse alcohol. She lives alone.

FAMILY HISTORY: Parents died of stroke in there eighties. One brother had asthma.

MEDICATIONS PRIOR TO ADMISSION: The patient's medications prior to admission included Vioxx 25 milligrams once a day, Ablution inhaler, Claritin 10 milligrams once a day, Serevent inhaler, Flonase inhaler and nasal spray.

ALLERGIES: None known
REVIEW OF SYSTEMS: Otherwise negative.

PHYSICAL EXAMINATION: Alert white female who is in acute distress, tachycardic and tachypneic, she is short of breath. Temperature 100.4, pulse 120, respirations 20, blood pressure 140/98, saturation 88 percent, on admission. Last vitals – temperature 97, pulse 99, respirations 20, blood pressure 150/80.

| | |
|---|---|
| HEENT: | Negative except some sinus tenderness and postnasal drip. |
| NECK: | No jugular venous distention. |
| LUNGS: | Bilateral diffuse rhonchi and wheezes. |
| HEART: | Regular rhythm, tachycardia, no gallops or murmur. |
| ABDOMEN: | The abdomen is soft, nontender. |
| EXTREMITIES: | No edema. |

## Case Study 26

CONSULTATION

Continued:

Chest x-ray was reviewed; there is no definite infiltrate except some basilar atelectasis, early infiltrate cannot be ruled out. Arterial blood gas – pH 7.45, pCO2 30, pO2 73 on two liters nasal cannula. White blood count 18.1, hemoglobin 13.9. Comprehensive metabolic panel essentially unremarkable. Bilirubin 1.67. Digoxin .49.

ASSESSMENT:

1. Bronchial asthma.
2. Bronchitis.
3. No definite pneumonia, however, cannot be ruled out.
4. Basilar atelectasis.
5. Tachycardia due to above.

RECOMMENDATION: Intravenous Solu-Medrol, intravenous antibiotics, oxygen, nebulizer treatment, sinus x-rays and follow closely.

**Case Study 26**
**Answer Sheet**

| DIAGNOSES | ICD-9-CM CODES | | | | | |
|---|---|---|---|---|---|---|
| DX 1 | | | | . | | |
| DX 2 | | | | . | | |
| DX 3 | | | | . | | |
| DX 4 | | | | . | | |

| PROCEDURES | CPT CODES | | | | | MODIFIERS (If Applicable) | |
|---|---|---|---|---|---|---|---|
| PR 1 | | | | | | - | | |
| PR 2 | | | | | | - | | |
| PR 3 | | | | | | - | | |
| PR 4 | | | | | | - | | |
| PR 5 | | | | | | - | | |
| PR 6 | | | | | | - | | |

**PROVIDE ICD-9-CM CODES FOR DIAGNOSES**

## CASE STUDY 27

### INPATIENT FACE SHEET

| | |
|---|---|
| Admit Date: | 1/25/06 |
| Discharge Date: | 1/02/06 |
| Age: | 78 |
| Sex: | Male |
| Disposition: | Home |

Admit Diagnoses:
1. Dyspnea, rule out pulmonary embolism.
2. History of deep venous thrombosis.
3. Chronic renal insufficiency.
4. Dizziness, possibly benign positional vertigo, rule out other causes.

Discharge Diagnoses:
1. Dyspnea on exertion, confirmed secondary to pulmonary embolism.
2. Mild congestive heart failure, chronic systolic.
3. History of chronic renal failure
4. Diabetes mellitus type I.
5. Diabetic neuropathy.

Procedure Performed:
None

## Case Study 27

DISCHARGE SUMMARY

ADMITTED: 1/25/06

DISCHARGED: 2/01/06

ADMITTING DIAGNOSES:
1. Dyspnea, rule out pulmonary embolism.
2. History of deep venous thrombosis.
3. Chronic renal insufficiency.
4. Dizziness, possibly benign positional vertigo, rule out other causes.

DISCHARGE DIAGNOSES:
1. Dyspnea on exertion, confirmed secondary to pulmonary embolism.
2. Mild congestive heart failure, chronic systolic.
3. History of chronic renal failure
4. Type I diabetes mellitus.
5. Diabetic neuropathy.
6. Chronic obstructive pulmonary disease.
7. Dizziness – etiology likely multifactorial, patient started on Meclezine

HISTORY: This is a 78-year-old gentleman with the above-mentioned medical problems who came to the emergency room at this time with light-headedness, dizziness, wooziness, drunk feeling, not sure of his steps. He was having increasing shortness of breath and does have a history of deep venous thrombosis and pulmonary emboli.

PERTINENT EXAM: Blood pressure 123/80, pulse rate 109, respirations 16, temperature 96.
HEENT: Unremarkable.
NECK: No jugular venous distention.
LUNGS: A few crepitations, no wheezing.
HEART: Regular. No murmur.
ABDOMEN: Distended, soft, nontender.
EXTREMITIES: 2-3 + edema.

LABORATORY: White blood cell account 11,500, left shift differential. Other counts were normal. Follow-up hemoglobin 11.1, hematocrit 32.9. Baseline INR normal. Chemistries – sodium 135, blood urea nitrogen 35, creatinine 1.8, alkaline phosphatase 80. AST/ALT levels initially normal. Follow-up blood sugar 198-200. Urinalysis – yellow and hazy appearance, microscopic blood noted, protein noted, nitrite negative, leukocyte esterase a small amount detected. Urine culture suggested a contaminated specimen.

Chest film revealed some prominent interstitial markings and possible congestive heart failure.

## Case Study 27

DISCHARGE SUMMARY

Continued:

Computed tomography brain scan – mild atrophy. Ventilation perfusion lung scan revealed an intermediate probability for pulmonary embolism. Electrocardiogram – sinus rhythm, sinus tachycardia. Arterial blood gases on two liters nasal cannula, pH 7.41, pC02 33.1, p02 98.8, bicarb 20.8 and saturation is 97.5%.

HOSPITAL COURSE: The patient admitted with increasing weakness, dyspnea and hypoxemia and dizziness at this time as well. There is no evidence of acute cerebrovascular accident. Computed tomography brain scan revealing chronic changes, nothing acute.

Ultimately the patient was found to have a pulmonary embolism and started on subcutaneous Lovenox injection, 1 mg/kg subcutaneous every twelve hours and then Coumadin started as well. Daily prothrombin time, INR evaluations were obtained and Coumadin doses were titrated accordingly. We were able to confirm the suspicion with a computed tomography scan and pulmonary angiogram. The patient was continued on anticoagulation, as well as treatment for heart failure with Ace inhibitor therapy. He had reached the maximal hospital benefit and was discharged 2/1/06.

MEDICATIONS ON DISCHARGE:
1. Humulin 75/25 15 units twice daily.
2. Xanax .25 mg three times a day.
3. Celexa 30 mg at hs.
4. Coumadin 10 mg daily.
5. Protonex 40 mg a day.
6. Prinivil 40 mg daily.
7. Meclezine

DIET: 1800 ADA, low fat, low salt.

OTHER THERAPEUTIC MEASURES: The patient reached maximum therapeutic benefit from his hospital admission. He was discharged with his medications and diet as listed.

ACTIVITY: As tolerated.

## Case Study 27

HISTORY & PHYSICAL

ADMITTED: 1/25/2006

CHIEF COMPLAINT: Dizziness, lightheadedness, and shortness of breath on exertion.

HISTORY OF PRESENT ILLNESS: This is 78-year-old gentleman who has a history of multiple medical problems. He came into the emergency room because he was feeling dizzy, lightheaded, woozy, and kind of drunk. He could not be sure of his steps. He has also been complaining of increased shortness of breath on exertion. He does have chronic dyspnea on exertion due to multiple medical problems including obesity, deep venous thrombosis; however, he feels that his symptoms are worse than before.

PAST MEDICAL HISTORY: His history is positive for multiple medical problems. He has history of hypertension, diabetes mellitus type I, deep venous thrombosis. He has been on Coumadin for quite some time because of deep venous thrombosis.

SOCIAL HISTORY: He smoked cigarettes but quit smoking 25 years ago. He does not drink alcohol. He is married, lives with his wife.

ALLERGIES: None.

REVIEW OF SYSTEMS: As mentioned earlier; other than that, is unremarkable. He does not have any chest pain, denies any shortness of breath on exertion. He has no cough, hemoptysis, fever or chills. No nausea or vomiting, abdominal pain, diarrhea, or urinary burning or hematuria at this time.

MEDICATIONS: Protonix 40 milligrams once a day, and insulin 75/25 Humalog 35 units in the morning and 35 units in the evening.

PHYSICIAL EXAMINATION:
GENERAL APPEARANCE: Elderly white gentleman who is in no respiratory distress, but gets short of breath on exertion.
VITAL SIGNS: Blood pressure 123/80 on admission, pulse 109, respirations 16, temperature 96, oxygen saturation 98%.

| | |
|---|---|
| HEENT: | Head, ears, eyes, nose, and throat was negative. |
| NECK: | No jugular venous distention. |
| LUNGS: | There are a few crepitations, no wheezing, rhonchi, or rales. |
| HEART: | Regular rhythm, no gallops or murmur. |
| ABDOMEN: | The abdomen is distended, soft, nontender. |
| EXTREMITIES: | There is 2-3 + edema. |

## Case Study 27

HISTORY & PHYSICAL

Continued:

LABORATORY DATA: The pertinent laboratories include on admission, urinalysis positive for white blood cells and 2+ bacteria. White blood cell count 11.5, hemoglobin 12.4. Comprehensive metabolic panel is unremarkable, except blood urea nitrogen 35, creatinine 1.8. Troponin I 0.05. Prothrombin time and partial thromboplastin time normal, partial thromboplastin time 54. D-dimer positive. Chest x-ray: Basal atelectasis, otherwise unremarkable. There is some interstitial marking. Computerized tomography scan of the brain was unremarkable. Urine culture: Multiple species, could be contaminant.

ASSESMENT:

1. Shortness of breath on exertion which could be related obesity, chronic obstructive pulmonary disease, asthma, bronchitis, rule out pulmonary emboli, especially with the history of deep venous thrombosis.
2. History of deep venous thrombosis and renal insufficiency.
3. Dizziness, rule out benign positional vertigo, orthostatic hypotension, rule out bleeding, cerebrovascular accident et cetera.

RECOMMENDATIONS:

1. Computerized tomography scan of brain.
2. Neurology consultation.
3. Orthostatic check of blood pressure and pulse.
4. Check complete blood count, chemistry, other laboratories.
5. Get pulmonary CT-angiogram to rule out pulmonary emboli.
6. Check oxygen saturation on exertion.
7. Give nebulizer treatment and oxygen, insulin, and other medications as before.

## Case Study 27

CONSULTATION

DATE: 1/26/2006

REQUESTING PHYSICIAN: Dr. Chase William

CONSULTING PHYSICIAN: Dr. Lynn Pagano

HISTORY OF PRESENT ILLNESS: The patient is a 78-year-old white male with history of diabetes mellitus type I, history of hypertension, who was admitted to the hospital with dizziness.

He denied any fall, any loss of consciousness, denied any slurring of the speech, he denied any weakness focally.

PAST MEDICAL HISTORY: Hypertension, diabetes mellitus type 1.

MEDICATIONS: He is on clonidine, Norvasc, Protonix, and insulin.

NEUROLOGICAL EXAMINATION:

GENERAL APPEARANCE: On examination, the patient is pleasant, awake, alert, oriented times three.

VITAL SIGNS: Temperature 98 degrees, blood pressure 133/74, pulse is 94 beats per minute.

HEENT: There is equal eye movement, reactive to light. No nystagmus, no carotid bruit. The left visual field is normal. No neck rigidity, no Kernig or Brudzinski sign.

CRANIAL NERVES: The cranial nerves are unremarkable. Palatal movement is intact with tongue midline. Corneal and gag reflexes are intact.

MOTOR SYSTEM: Normal tone and power, 5/5 in all four extremities proximally and distally. There is decreased pinprick and touch in bilateral upper and lower extremities distally, with decreased position and vibration. Deep tendon reflexes +2 in the lower extremities, +1 knee jerk, and absent ankle jerk, and absent ankle jerk. Plantar is both down going.

CEREBELLAR: Finger-to nose, heel-to-shin normal. Speech is clear, alert, with normal naming, normal comprehensions, normal reading.

**Case Study 27**

CONSULTATION

Continued:

LABORATORY DATA: Urinalysis: Hazy and many bacteria 2+, Chemistry: Sodium 135, potassium 4.8, blood urea nitrogen 35, creatinine 0.8, sugar 149, alkaline phosphatase 580, globulin 4.5. White blood cell count 11.5, hemoglobin 12.5, hematocrit 36.5, platelet count 268.

IMPRESSION:
The patient has hypertension, diabetes mellitus type I, with severe peripheral neuropathy with complaints of feeling dizziness, lightheaded, without any acute focal motor or sensory deficit, without any nystagmus:

1. Rule out benign positional vertigo.
2. Rule out cardiac arrhythmia versus gastrointestinal, which is unlikely.
3. Rule out orthostatic hypotension.

RECOMMENDATIONS:
1. Computerized tomography scan of the head.
2. Meclezine 25 milligrams p.o. b.i.d.
3. Physical therapy, occupational therapy for gait training.
4. Diabetic control
5. Check for orthostatic blood pressure every six hours.

## Case Study 27

**Answer Sheet**

| DIAGNOSES | ICD-9-CM CODES | | | | | |
|---|---|---|---|---|---|---|
| DX 1 | | | | . | | |
| DX 2 | | | | . | | |
| DX 3 | | | | . | | |
| DX 4 | | | | . | | |

| PROCEDURES | CPT CODES | | | | | MODIFIERS (If Applicable) | | |
|---|---|---|---|---|---|---|---|---|
| PR 1 | | | | | | - | | |
| PR 2 | | | | | | - | | |
| PR 3 | | | | | | - | | |
| PR 4 | | | | | | - | | |
| PR 5 | | | | | | - | | |
| PR 6 | | | | | | - | | |

**PROVIDE ICD-9-CM CODES FOR DIAGNOSES AND CPT CODES FOR PROCEDURE(S)**

## Case Study 28

### Inpatient Face Sheet

| | |
|---|---|
| Admit Date: | 1/25/06 |
| Discharge Date: | 1/29/06 |
| Sex: | Female |
| Age: | 35 |
| Disposition: | Home |

Admitting Diagnoses:
1. Induction of labor
2. Severe pre-eclampsia
3. Intrauterine growth retardation

Discharge Diagnoses:
1. Severe preeclampsia
2. Accelerated hypertension
3. Intrauterine growth retardation
4. Pre-term at 36 weeks

Procedure:
1. Primary low transverse C-section

## Case Study 28

### Discharge Summary

Admitted: 1/25/06

Discharged: 1/29/06

ADMITTING DIAGNOSES:
1. Induction of labor
2. Severe pre-eclampsia
3. IUGR

DISCHARGE DIAGNOSES:
1. Severe preeclampsia
2. Accelerated hypertension
3. IUGR

Patient is a 35 year-old, gravida 3 para 2, admitted for induction due to severe pre-eclampsia and late decelerations. She was admitted for induction and began on Pitocin. However, due to persistent late decelerations, patient underwent a primary low flap transverse Cesarean section with delivery of a 4 pound 12 ounce liveborn male with 6, 9 Apgars.

There were no postoperative problems other than accelerated hypertension, for which the patient was started on Apresoline and Aldomet. Last blood pressure reading was 180/90. Discharge hemoglobin and hematocrit were 11.3 and 32.4 and platelet count was 122. The platelet count had been as low as 94,000. The patient's magnesium levels when she was on magnesium ranged between 4.5 and 4.0, her electrolytes were normal, alkaline phosphatase 262 and 304. The hemoglobin and hematocrit on admission were 13 and 37, platelet count was 158,000. The PT and PTT were normal. The urinalysis was negative.

The patient was discharged in satisfactory condition with diet and activity as tolerated. Patient will continue to take Aldomet and Apresoline. I will see the patient in my office in one week for staple removal.

## Case Study 28

### History and Physical

HISTORY OF PRESENT ILLNESS:

The patient is a 35 year-old gravida 3 para 2, due date 1/25/06, who I saw in my office with blood pressure of 154/104, 150/98, 2+ protein. She was immediately sent to the hospital for admission for induction of labor.

ANTEPARTUM HISTORY:

She has had two vaginal deliveries in the past. Her ultrasound was consistent with dates. Her group B Strep was negative. She has a history of hypertension.

PAST MEDICAL HISTORY: Usual childhood diseases.

FAMILY HISTORY: Noncontributory

ALLERGIES: None known

PHYSICAL EXAMINATION:

| | |
|---|---|
| Vital Signs: | Blood pressure ranged from 154/90 to 168/104 |
| HEENT: | Within normal limits |
| Chest: | Clear to percussion and auscultation |
| Heart: | Normal sinus rhythm |
| Breasts: | Without masses or discharge |
| Abdomen: | Gravid |
| Extremities: | Without clubbing or cyanosis. There was +1 edema. Reflexes were +2. |
| Cervical: | Cervical examination revealed she was 1 cm. |

She was admitted and Pitocin was started. There was noted to be decreased variability and occasional late decelerations. The Pitocin was once again stopped. She began having contractions on her own with recurrent late decelerations. Oxygen was started. She was turned on her side and the late decels continued. Magnesium was started at 6 gm and then 1 gm an hour for the pre-eclampsia. There was no response to the medication; consequently the patient will undergo a primary low transverse C-section.

## Case Study 28

### Procedure Note

| | |
|---|---|
| Date: | 1/25/06 |
| PREOPERATIVE DIAGNOSES: | Intrauterine pregnancy 36 weeks, preeclampsia, fetal distress |
| POSTOPERATIVE DIAGNOSES: | Intrauterine pregnancy 36 weeks, severe preeclampsia, persistent late decelerations with intrauterine growth retardation |
| PROCEDURE: | Primary low transverse C-section |
| SURGEON: | Nicolas Todd, M.D. |
| ANESTHESIA: | Spinal |

The patient was taken to the operating room. After adequate level of spinal anesthesia, Foley catheter was inserted. She was prepped and draped in the usual sterile fashion.

A Pfannenstiel incision was made taken down through the subcutaneous tissue to the fascia. The fascia was scored and taken transversely. Rectus muscle was split. The peritoneum was opened.

The uterus was incised in a low transverse manner with delivery of 6-9 Apgar liveborn male. The cord was noted to be thin. The placenta was delivered. It was noted to be small. Uterus, tubes and ovaries were noted to be normal. The uterus was closed in two separate layers with running locked 0 chromic. Posterior peritoneum was closed with 0 chromic. The uterus was placed back into the abdomen; anterior peritoneum was closed with 0 chromic. The fascia was closed with running 0 Vicryl and the skin was closed with staples.

ESTIMATED BLOOD LOSS: 600 ccs

FLUIDS RECEIVED: Ringers Lactate

The patient tolerated the procedure well and left the recovery room in satisfactory condition.

## Case Study 28

**PROGRESS NOTES:**

1/25: Admit note: Gravida 3, para 2, 35 year old white female admitted for induction of labor due to severe preeclampsia. Patient was admitted directly from my office. She is at 36 weeks gestation by dates. There is evidence of IUGR also. Patient has had a benign prenatal course with the exception of hypertension. Patient was started on Pitocin without success. There were persistent late decelerations noted and patient was transferred to surgical suite for immediate C-section. Patient delivered a 4 pound, 12 ounce liveborn male infant.

1/26: S: Feels well, other than surgical pain
O: BP 160/95
A: Incision clean and dry, no redness or tenderness.
P: Continue BP meds, advance diet and activity

1/27: S: Feeling well
O: Good post op course, BP 168/104
A: Accelerated hypertension
P: Continue meds

1/28: S: No pain, ambulating
O: BP better, but still high at 150/98
A: Continues with elevated BP
P: Doing well, will discharge

1/29: S: Ready for home
O: Vitals stable, except BP, afebrile, incisions healing
A: Hypertension
P: Discharge, follow hypertension as outpatient

---

**ORDERS:**

1/25: 1. Admit patient to obstetrics
2. IV Pitocin for induction
3. Monitor BP q 15 min
4. CBC, WBC, Chem profile
5. Magnesium IV

1/25: 1. Prep for C-Section

1/26: 1. Continue IV fluids
2. Start patient on Apresoline and Aldomet for BP control
3. Advance diet

1/27: 1. Continue BP meds
2. Discontinue IVs

1/28: 1. Continue meds

1/29: 1. Discharge

## Case Study 28

**Answer Sheet**

| DIAGNOSES | ICD-9-CM CODES | | | | | |
|---|---|---|---|---|---|---|
| DX 1 | | | | . | | |
| DX 2 | | | | . | | |
| DX 3 | | | | . | | |
| DX 4 | | | | . | | |

| PROCEDURES | CPT CODES | | | | | | MODIFIERS (If Applicable) | |
|---|---|---|---|---|---|---|---|---|
| PR 1 | | | | | | - | | |
| PR 2 | | | | | | - | | |
| PR 3 | | | | | | - | | |
| PR 4 | | | | | | - | | |
| PR 5 | | | | | | - | | |
| PR 6 | | | | | | - | | |

**PROVIDE ICD-9-CM CODES FOR DIAGNOSES ONLY**

## CASE STUDY 29
### Inpatient Face Sheet

| | |
|---|---|
| Admit Date: | 1/13/06 |
| Discharge Date: | 1/16/06 |
| Sex: | Female |
| Age: | 86 |
| Disposition: | Home with Home Health Care |

Admitting Diagnoses:
1. Cellulitis, right lower extremity
2. Acute exacerbation of chronic obstructive pulmonary disease
3. Coronary artery disease
4. Hypothyroidism

Discharge Diagnoses:
1. Cellulitis right lower extremity
2. Acute exacerbation of chronic obstructive pulmonary disease
3. Coronary artery disease
4. Hypothyroidism
5. Gastroesophageal reflux disease
6. Depression
7. Degenerative joint disease

## Case Study 29
## Discharge Summary

Admitted: 1/13/06
Discharged: 1/16/06

DISCHARGE DIAGNOSES:
1. Cellulitis of the right lower extremity
2. Acute exacerbation of chronic obstructive pulmonary disease.
3. Coronary artery disease
4. Hypothyroidism
5. Gastroesophageal reflux disease
6. Depression
7. Degenerative joint disease

HISTORY OF PRESENT ILLNESS:
Please see admission history and physical examination. This is an 86 year old female with a 75 pack-year smoking history and severe chronic obstructive pulmonary disease who is seen for recurrent cellulitis in the right lower extremity which has not responded to outpatient oral antibiotic and diuretic treatment.

HOSPITAL COURSE:
She was treated with intravenous Lasix, Aldactone, potassium supplement, bronchodilator treatment, Solu-Medrol and intravenous Claforan. The inflammation of the right lower extremity resolved over the next few days. Her wheezing improved and at rest her lungs were clear. With minimal exertion she was noted to have wheezing and desaturation with O2 saturation dropping to 84% on room air. She was advised to have home oxygen therapy.
The edema of the lower extremities resolved and she will be continued on oral Lasix and Aldactone. The patient is discharged home with home health care to follow. Oxygen 2 liters via nasal cannula. Her condition is improved.

DISCHARGE MEDICATIONS:
1. Imdur 60 mg 1/2 tablet q a.m.
2. Synthroid 0.125 mg q.i.d.
3. Albuterol 2.5 mg plus Atrovent 500 mg via nebulizer q.3h.
4. K-Dur 20 mEq b.i.d.
5. Aldactone 25 mg b.i.d.
6. Lasix 80 mg q a.m. and noon
7. Flovent 220 4 puffs b.i.d. with aerochamber
8. Biaxin 250 mg b.i.d. times 3 days
9. Accolate 20 mg b.i.d.
10. Effexor XR 75 mg q.i.d. for depression

Diet: no added salt. Activity as tolerated. She will follow up in my office in 10 days.

## Case Study 29
## History and Physical

CHIEF COMPLAINT: Swelling, redness and heat of the right lower extremity.

HISTORY OF PRESENT ILLNESS:
Patient was seen in my office for swelling, erythema and heat of the right lower extremity and started on oral antibiotics and diuretics as an outpatient. She has not responded to outpatient treatment, therefore, is admitted for inpatient therapy.

PAST MEDICAL HISTORY:
Surgeries include thyroidectomy, total hip replacement, appendectomy. She also has severe COPD, hypothyroidism, peptic ulcer disease, diverticulosis, coronary artery disease, and mild congestive heart failure.

MEDICATIONS:
Current medications include Synthroid 0.125 mg q.i.d., Imdur 60 mg one-half tablet q.i.d., Azmacort 2 puffs q.i.d., potassium chloride 10 mEq t.i.d. , Aldactone 25 mg b.i.d., Lasix 80 mg b.i.d., Colace 100 mg b.i.d., Accolate 20 mg b.i.d., Albuterol 2.5 mg plus Atrovent 500 mcg nebulizer q.3h.

ALLERGIES: Iodine

FAMILY HISTORY: Noncontributory

SOCIAL HISTORY: Previous smoker, no tobacco currently. No alcohol.

REVIEW OF SYSTEMS:
History of gastroesophageal reflux disease, peptic ulcer disease, and osteoarthritis.

PHYSICAL EXAMINATION:

| | |
|---|---|
| Vital Signs: | Blood pressure 168/70, pulse 96, temperature 99.5, respirations 30. She is wheezing and appears dyspneic. |
| HEENT: | Unremarkable |
| Neck: | Thyroidectomy scar, carotids 2+. No JVD |
| Chest: | Wheezing bilaterally |
| Cardiovascular: | Regular rate and rhythm |
| Abdomen: | Benign |
| Extremities: | Pitting edema both lower extremities, right greater than left. Right anterior shin is hot, red and indurated |
| Neurologic: | Unremarkable |

**<u>Case Study 29</u>**
**History and Physical**

Continued:

LABORATORY DATA:
Electrolytes are normal. Potassium 4.1. White count 9.5, hemoglobin 12.5. Urinalysis is clear. Chest x-ray shows slight atelectasis in the right base, chronic obstructive pulmonary disease. No acute infiltrates nor congestive heart failure noted. Electrocardiogram shows sinus rhythm, right bundle branch block, nonspecific ST-T changes.

ASSESSMENT:
1. Cellulitis, right lower extremity.
2. Acute exacerbation of COPD
3. Coronary artery disease
4. Hypothyroidism
5. Degenerative joint disease
6. Gastroesophageal reflux disease

PLAN:
Admit for intravenous antibiotics, diuresis, and pulmonary rehab.

## Case Study 29

**PROGRESS NOTES**:

1/13: Admit Note: 86 year-old female was seen in my office one week ago with recurrent cellulitis of her right leg. She was placed on antibiotics and diuretics, however, has had no response to outpatient therapy. She is now admitted for aggressive treatment.

1/14: S: Complains only of leg pain and SOB
O: Afebrile, vital signs stable, wheezing with minimal exertion
A: Leg looks better, less redness. COPD is severe, will probably require home O2
P: Continue with present treatment

1/15: S: Feeling much better, able to ambulate some but easily tires
O: Labs within normal limits, vitals remain stable, still with SOB and wheezing on exertion
A: Leg has responded well to IV medications
P: DC IV and start on p.o. Biaxin

1/16: S: Patient desires discharge
O: Afebrile, vital signs stable
A: Leg looks much better
P: Discharge patient

---

**ORDERS:**

1/13: 1. Admit patient to service of Sarah Stamper, M.D.
2. IV Lasix and Claforan
3. Respiratory treatments
4. WBC, CBC, EKG, CXR

1/14: 1. Continue current treatment regime

1/15: 1. Increase ambulation
2. DC IV fluids
3. Biaxin 500 mg p.o. twice daily

1/16: 1. Discharge patient with Home Health Care

**Case Study 29**
**Answer Sheet**

| DIAGNOSES | ICD-9-CM CODES | | | | | |
|---|---|---|---|---|---|---|
| DX 1 | | | | . | | |
| DX 2 | | | | . | | |
| DX 3 | | | | . | | |
| DX 4 | | | | . | | |

| PROCEDURES | CPT CODES | | | | | MODIFIERS (If Applicable) | | |
|---|---|---|---|---|---|---|---|---|
| PR 1 | | | | | | - | | |
| PR 2 | | | | | | - | | |
| PR 3 | | | | | | - | | |
| PR 4 | | | | | | - | | |
| PR 5 | | | | | | - | | |
| PR 6 | | | | | | - | | |

**PROVIDE ICD-9-CM CODE(S) FOR DIAGNOSES ONLY**

## CASE STUDY 30

### Inpatient Face Sheet

| | |
|---|---|
| Admit Date: | 1/24/06 |
| Discharge Date: | 1/27/06 |
| Sex: | Male |
| Age: | 84 |
| Disposition: | Expired |

Admitting Diagnoses:
1. Pneumonia secondary to possible community-acquired Strep pneumoniae
2. Respiratory failure and hypoxia secondary to pneumonia
3. New onset atrial fibrillation
4. History of liver cirrhosis with splenomegaly and some ascites
5. History of myeloproliferative disorder

Discharge Diagnoses:
1. Respiratory failure
2. Streptococcus pneumonia
3. Atrial fibrillation
4. Alcoholic liver cirrhosis
5. Hepatorenal syndrome
6. Streptococcal septicemia
7. Septic shock
8. Urinary Tract Infection, E.coli
9. Uremia
10. Hypertension
11. Hypoglycemia

## Case Study 30

**Discharge Summary**
Admitted: 1/24/06
Expired: 1/27/06

ADMITTING DIAGNOSES:
1. Pneumonia secondary to possible community-acquired Strep pneumoniae
2. Respiratory failure and hypoxia secondary to pneumonia
3. New onset atrial fibrillation
4. History of liver cirrhosis with splenomegaly and some ascites
5. History of myeloproliferative disorder

DISCHARGE DIAGNOSES:

1. Septic shock with multi-organ failure
2. Streptococcal pneumoniae pneumonia and respiratory failure
3. Escherichia coli urosepsis
4. Hypoglycemia secondary to sepsis and cirrhosis of the liver
5. New onset atrial fibrillation
6. Hepatorenal syndrome

HISTORY OF PRESENT ILLNESS AND HOSPITAL COURSE:

The patient is an 84 year-old white male who is admitted to the hospital after complaining of shortness of breath, cough with productive sputum, fever and chills, and pain below the breast area. In the Emergency Room his temperature was 98.3, blood pressure was 140/80, pulse was 140. Patient was noted to be in atrial fibrillation with rapid ventricular rate and required Digoxin intravenous push and Procainamide and cardioversion. Patient went into respiratory failure with hypoxia, requiring intubation and ventilator assistance. Patient was also noted to be severely neutropenic and acidotic in acute renal failure. Patient was seen in the Emergency Room by cardiology for new onset of atrial fibrillation and cardioverted for this.

The patient's white blood cell count remained 1,700 the day after admission and his echocardiogram Doppler studies showed that he had a left ejection fraction of 60%, mild mitral regurgitation and tricuspid regurgitation. His prothrombin time was 12 and partial thromboplastic time was 41. His Bun and creatinine went up to 67/2.6 and his hemoglobin and hematocrit remains within normal limits. His calcium did drop to 7.8 along with a decreased albumin. His chest x-ray shows right-sided opacity secondary to his pneumonia. Blood cultures grew gram-positive cocci in chains.

## Case Study 30

### Discharge Summary

Continued:

Impression on 1/25/06 the patient was having Streptococcus pneumonia with multi-organ failure. The patient did have a history of cirrhosis of the liver and splenomegaly and pancytopenia. Patient was started on intravenous Dopamine and intravenous hydration because of decreased urine output and increasing renal functions and possible hepatorenal syndrome. The patient remained lethargic, responding to deep painful stimuli. The patient's urine grew Escherichia coli and blood cultures grew Streptococcal pneumoniae pneumonia. His white count increased to 23,900 with Neupogen. His BUN and creatinine went up to 86/4.4. The patient remained hypoglycemic and required D5 and D10 drips. The patient continued to be hypertensive in renal failure and acidotic.

In spite of the aggressive treatment and continued ventilator assistance the patient expired on 1/27/06.

## Case Study 30

### History and Physical

CHIEF COMPLAINT:
The patient was admitted through the Emergency Room after complaining of increased shortness of breath and productive cough.

HISTORY OF PRESENT ILLNESS:
Patient was well until two days prior to admission when he began having shortness of breath, productive cough, fever and chills. He also complained of pain beneath the breast area. The patient was brought to the Emergency Room by EMS. In the Emergency Room the patient's temperature was 98.3, blood pressure was 140/80, pulse was 140. Patient was in atrial fibrillation with rapid ventricular response and was treated with Digoxin 0.5 mg intravenous push and Procainamide. Patient also required cardioversion at 100-200 joules. The patient was also noted to be in acute respiratory distress with hypoxia requiring intubation and ventilator assistance. The patient's blood work revealed severe neutropenia, acidosis and renal failure.

At present the patient is sedated and most of the history is taken from the wife and from previous charts.

PAST MEDICAL HISTORY:
Includes cirrhosis of the liver, likely secondary to excessive alcohol intake. There is also a history of myeloproliferative disorder and a history of ascites. There is no prior history of atrial fibrillation, heart disease, diabetes, gastrointestinal disease or neurological symptoms.

SOCIAL HISTORY: History of excessive alcohol intake and former smoker.

FAMILY HISTORY: Strong history of colon cancer.

ALLERGIES: None known.

PHYSICAL EXAMINATION: Presently intubated, sedated and unresponsive.

| | |
|---|---|
| HEENT: | Pupils equal and reactive to light, non-icterus, non-pallor. Orally intubated. |
| Neck: | Supple, no lymphadenopathy, and no jugular venous distention. |
| Lungs: | No rales, no rhonchi |
| Heart: | S1 and S2, no murmur or gallop |
| Abdomen: | Distended, possible ascites present |
| Extremities: | Mild peripheral edema, no rash or ulcers noted |

## Case Study 30

### History and Physical

Continued:

LABORATORY DATA:
Blood gas revealed pH 7.33, pCO2 34 and pO2 of 51 and saturation of 86%. The patient's urinalysis is consistent with leukocyte esterase small amount, nitrite negative. His white blood cell count is 0.8, hemoglobin 10.6, hematocrit 31.8 and platelet count 79,000. His sodium is 137, potassium 4.2, chloride 102, glucose is 88, BUN 60, creatinine 2.3 and CPK is 63. Alkaline phosphatase 142, SGOT 185, bilirubin 1.8. Prothrombin time is 13, INR is 1.1 and partial thromboplastin time is 42.

IMPRESSION:
1. Pneumonia secondary to community acquired strep pneumoniae
2. Respiratory failure secondary to pneumonia
3. New onset atrial fibrillation
4. History of cirrhosis of the liver with splenomegaly and ascites
5. History of myeloproliferative syndrome with pancytopenia

PLAN:
1. Patient is admitted to Intensive care, intubated and on ventilator
2. Patient has already been started on broad spectrum intravenous antibiotic

## Case Study 30

**Progress Notes**:

1/24: Admit Note: Elderly white gentleman admitted through the Emergency Room in acute respiratory failure, pneumonia, sepsis and septic shock. He also has new onset of atrial fibrillation that required cardioversion in the E.R. The patient was intubated and placed on the ventilator. The patient required Digoxin and Procainamide IV push in the ER.

1/25: S: Unresponsive
O: Lethargic, responds to deep painful stimuli. UA positive for E.coli, blood positive for strep. BUN/creatinine 86/4.4, decreased urine output, BP 210/130
A: Sepsis, UTI, acute renal failure, multi-organ failure, prognosis grave
P: IV Dopamine and hydration, continue present vent settings

1/26: S: Unresponsive
O: White count increasing with Neupogen injections, renal labs worsening, patient less responsive now hypoglycemic
A: Respiratory and multi-organ failure, renal failure, hepatorenal syndrome
P: Prognosis is poor

1/27: S: Unresponsive
O: Patient rapidly declining
A: Poor prognosis
P: Continue supportive care

## Case Study 30

**Orders:**

1/24: 1. Admit patient to CCU
2. Follow CCU protocol
3. Respiratory services to maintain vent
4. Strict I&O

1/25: 1. IV Dopamine and hydration
2. Add Neupogen injections
3. Continue present vent settings
4. Repeat all labs

1/26 1. Add D5 and D10 drips for hypoglycemia
2. Continue all previous orders

## Case Study 30

**Answer Sheet**

| DIAGNOSES | ICD-9-CM CODES | | | | | |
|---|---|---|---|---|---|---|
| DX 1 | | | | . | | |
| DX 2 | | | | . | | |
| DX 3 | | | | . | | |
| DX 4 | | | | . | | |

| PROCEDURES | CPT CODES | | | | | MODIFIERS (If Applicable) | | |
|---|---|---|---|---|---|---|---|---|
| PR 1 | | | | | | - | | |
| PR 2 | | | | | | - | | |
| PR 3 | | | | | | - | | |
| PR 4 | | | | | | - | | |
| PR 5 | | | | | | - | | |
| PR 6 | | | | | | - | | |

**PROVIDE ICD-9-CM CODE(S) FOR DIAGNOSES ONLY**

## CASE STUDY 31

### Inpatient Face Sheet

| | |
|---|---|
| Admit Date: | 1/25/06 |
| Discharge Date: | 1/30/06 |
| Sex: | Female |
| Age: | 82 |
| Disposition: | Skilled Nursing Facility for Rehab |

Admitting Diagnoses:
1. Cerebral infarction
2. Hypertension
3. Atrial fibrillation
4. Osteoarthritis

Discharge Diagnoses:
1. Left middle cerebral artery occlusion with cerebral infarction
2. Atrial fibrillation
3. Mitral regurgitation
4. Urinary tract infection
5. Pacemaker in situ
6. Bilateral carotid artery disease
7. Hypertension
8. Osteoarthritis
9. Right hemiplegia

## Case Study 31

### Discharge Summary

Admitted: 1/25/06

Discharge: 1/30/06

DISCHARGE DIAGNOSES:
1. Left middle cerebral artery occlusion with cerebral infarction
2. Atrial fibrillation
3. Mitral regurgitation
4. Urinary tract infection
5. Pacemaker in situ
6. Bilateral carotid artery disease
7. Hypertension
8. Osteoarthritis

HISTORY OF PRESENT ILLNESS:
This an 82 year-old white female who was found on the floor at her home. She had right-sided weakness, stool incontinence and garbled speech. The CAT scan was positive for infarction with left basal ganglia hemorrhage.

HISTORY AND PHYSICAL: See H&P

MEDICATIONS: Lanoxin

ALLERGIES: Sulfa

PHYSICAL EXAMINATION:
Elderly white female, hypertensive 196/73. Pale subconjuntival and nail beds. Garbled speech with weakness on the right.

LABORATORY DATA:
The patient's admission laboratory data were within normal limits with the exception of hemoglobin 16.5, hematocrit 48.8; 100 mg of protein, a large amount of occult blood and 5 to 9 red blood cells on urinalysis; elevated globulin of 4.2, alkaline phosphatase 161, CPK 346. The Lanoxin was subtherapeutic at 0.6. Drug screening was negative. During hospitalization there was a transient mild leukocytosis of 14,700 and hemoglobin returned to normal. Sedimentation rate was elevated at 39 on 1/26/06. The PTT rose to therapeutic and vacillated throughout.

A repeat urinalysis revealed a large amount of leukocytes, continued occult blood and red blood cells up to 50+ with 20 to 29 white blood cells and moderate bacteria. Urine culture revealed Escherichia coli.

## Case Study 31

### Discharge Summary

Continued:

The sodium dropped as low as 126 but rebounded to 132 by 1/28/06. The globulin returned to normal. The albumin dropped slightly below normal. The alkaline phosphatase returned to normal. The CPK levels steadily decreased to 213 and 186 with CK-MB remaining within normal limits.

RADIOLOGY REPORTS:
The chest x-ray revealed cardiomegaly, several calcified granuloma in the right upper, mid and lower lung zones, left sided pacemaker in satisfactory position and no acute changes.

The CAT scan of the brain, non-contrast showed acute left middle cerebral artery infarction with hemorrhage within the left basal ganglia. A repeat CAT scan was unchanged.

A KUB showed nasogastric tube in satisfactory position, non-specific bowel gas pattern. A repeat KUB did reveal the nasogastric tube to be coiled in the stomach on 1/29/06.

A carotid duplex Doppler examination showed moderate bilateral carotid occlusive disease with plaquing at the right carotid bifurcation, left common carotid and carotid bifurcation but no evidence of flow-restricting lesion, stenosis of less than 35%, external carotid stenosis approaching 40% to 50%, antegrade vertebral artery blood flow bilaterally, no change since January of last year.

An echocardiogram revealed hypokinetic septal and apical wall motion, aortic valve sclerosis, mitral annular calcification, and moderate mitral regurgitation.

A electrocardiogram revealed pacemaker rhythm with rate of 58 per minute, left ventricular hypertrophy, ST-T abnormalities, Q waves in V1 and V2, diffuse T wave abnormalities, consistent with ischemia. The subsequent repeats showed atrial fibrillation with transient rapid ventricular response and premature ventricular contractions.

HOSPITAL COURSE:
The patient was admitted on 1/25/06. She was started on routine and Intensive Care Unit orders, neuro checks, Lanoxin, Decadron intravenously, multivitamins, intravenous hydration.

It was noted by neurological consult that the patient had two cerebrovascular accidents with the atrial fibrillation as the likely source. Anticoagulation was initiated cautiously after blood pressure was brought under control. Intravenous Nipride was begun for blood pressure control. Heparin was begun. Catapres was added for additional blood pressure control and Decadron was also added.

## Case Study 31

### Discharge Summary

Continued:

The patient remained afebrile other than intermittent temperatures of 100.

The patient was evaluated by speech pathology. She was noted to have severe receptive and fluent aphasia. Speech therapy will be initiated.

Nasogastric tube was inserted for administration of medications due to lack of poor oral intake and dysphagia with some aspiration potential noted on video swallow study. Following improvement in the patient's condition, nasogastric tube was removed and diet was adjusted. Dysphagia cleared by discharge.

The patient began to improve but remained aphasic and with right-sided hemiplegia. It was decided that she would require intensive rehab, so she was transferred to a rehab facility for continued physical, speech and occupational therapy. Patient is to be continued on pureed diet.

DISCHARGE MEDICATIONS:
Catapres TTS Patch 0.4 mg patch q weekly
Lanoxin 0.125 mg daily
Norvasc 5 mg daily
Multivitamins one daily
Floxin 200 mg q 12h times five days

## Case Study 31

### History and Physical

CHIEF COMPLAINT: Garbled speech and right sided weakness.

HISTORY OF PRESENT ILLNESS:
This 82 year-old white female was found on the floor by her neighbors and brought to the Emergency Room via EMS. A CAT scan of the brain was completed which revealed a left MCA infarct with hemorrhage into the left basal ganglia.

CURRENT MEDICATIONS: Lanoxin

PAST MEDICAL HISTORY:
Positive for hypertension, atrial fibrillation and degenerative osteoarthritis.

SOCIAL HISTORY: Non-smoker, occasional alcohol

PHYSICAL EXAMINATION:
Elderly white female who is in acute distress. She has garbled speech.

REVIEW OF SYSTEMS:

| | |
|---|---|
| Vital Signs: | Blood pressure 199/73, pulse 78, respiratory rate of 18, afebrile |
| HEENT: | Pupils equal and reactive to light, sclerae is not icteric. Subconjunctival is pale |
| Lungs: | Clear |
| Heart: | Regular sinus rhythm with an irregular rate |
| Abdomen: | Soft, benign. No organomegaly or mass to palpation |
| Extremities: | No edema, no varicosity. Nail beds are pale |
| Neuro: | Good DTR, negative Babinski |

IMPRESSION: Acute cerebrovascular accident

PLAN:
1. Admit to Intensive Care.
2. Serial electrocardiograms and cardiac enzymes.
3. Neuro checks q2h.
4. Carotid duplex.
5. Echo to heart. EEG

## Case Study 31

**Progress Notes:**

1/25: Admit Note: Patient admitted with left MCA infarction. Patient also has severe hypertension. Please see H&P for complete details.

1/26: S: Non-communicative
O: Sed rate elevated to 39, rest of lab data within normal limits. Carotid Doppler revealed bilateral occlusive disease, but not of any clinical significance
A: Patient still aphasic with right sided paralysis
P: Repeat CT of Brain and do KUB, ECHO

1/27: S: Remains aphasic
O: BP remains high, but slowly coming under control, NG tube in good position per KUB Repeat CT of brain unchanged for admission CT. ECHO revealed moderate mitral regurgitation
A: Patient is slowly improving
P: Transfer to neuro floor. Add Catapres for additional BP control

1/28: S: Feels better after transfer out of ICU
O: BP better controlled, Repeat UA positive for E.coli. Some strength returning on right. Sodium dropped to 126
A: UTI, hyponatremia, dysphagia clearing
P: Remove NG tube and advance diet. Start Cipro p.o. 500mg for UTI. Monitor sodium level

1/29: S: No new complaints
O: Labs improving, vitals stable
A: Tolerating advanced diet
P: Discharge planning for intensive rehab, patient agreeable

1/30: S: Ready for transfer to rehab
O: Patient's condition is stable. BP better controlled. Sodium level normal
A: Patient will continue with speech and physical therapy at Rehab center
P: Transfer patient

## Case Study 31

**Orders:**

1/25:
1. Admit to ICU
2. Neuro checks q 2h
3. Serial EKGs and cardiac enzymes
4. CXR
5. ICU protocol
6. Carotid Doppler
7. IV Decadron, Lanoxin, Nipride and fluids at 83cc/hr

1/26:
1. Repeat CT brain
2. KUB, ECHO
3. Continue present meds
4. Repeat UA

1/27:
1. Add Catapres
2. Have speech pathology evaluated

1/28:
1. Remove NG tube, advance diet
2. Cipro for UTI

1/29:
1. Case Management for discharge planning

1/30:
1. Transfer to Rehab

## Case Study 31

**Answer Sheet**

| DIAGNOSES | ICD-9-CM CODES | | | | | |
|---|---|---|---|---|---|---|
| DX 1 | | | | . | | |
| DX 2 | | | | . | | |
| DX 3 | | | | . | | |
| DX 4 | | | | . | | |

| PROCEDURES | CPT CODES | | | | | MODIFIERS (If Applicable) | | |
|---|---|---|---|---|---|---|---|---|
| PR 1 | | | | | | - | | |
| PR 2 | | | | | | - | | |
| PR 3 | | | | | | - | | |
| PR 4 | | | | | | - | | |
| PR 5 | | | | | | - | | |
| PR 6 | | | | | | - | | |

**PROVIDE ICD-9-CM CODE(S) FOR DIAGNOSES ONLY**

## CASE STUDY 32

### Inpatient Face Sheet

| | |
|---|---|
| Admit Date: | 1/10/06 |
| Discharge Date: | 1/06/06 |
| Sex: | Female |
| Age: | 79 |
| Disposition: | ACLF |

Admitting Diagnoses:

1. Syncope
2. Hypertension
3. Chronic Obstructive Pulmonary Disease
4. Hyperlipidemia
5. Congestive Heart Failure

Discharge Diagnoses;

1. Syncope, undetermined etiology
2. Chronic Obstructive Pulmonary Disease
3. Congestive Heart Failure
4. Hypertension
5. Hyperlipidemia

## Case Study 32

### Discharge Summary

ADMITTED: 1/10/06

DISCHARGED: 1/06/06

DISCHARGE DIAGNOSES:

1. Syncope, undetermined etiology
2. Malnourishment
3. CHF
4. COPD
5. Hypertension
6. Hyperlipidemia

PROCEDURES: None

HISTORY OF PRESENT ILLNESS:

Patient presented to the Emergency Department with complaint of weakness and feeling of passing out for two days duration. Patient was admitted to telemetry to rule out cardiac origin of syncope. Patient is also under current treatment for COPD, CHF, hypertension and hyperlipidemia.

HOSPITAL COURSE:

Patient was continued on home medications for treatment of chronic illnesses as documented above. Lab values were within normal limits, with the exception of low protein and albumin indicative of mild malnourishment. In addition, the lipids were elevated. Patient was started on Ensure to address the malnourishment and Pravacol was increased to 40 mg per day to bring the lipids under control. EKG and ECHO were insignificant in determining a cause of the syncope. The patient's hypertension, COPD and CHF remained under control while the patient was in the hospital. In light of not finding a cause of the syncope and the patient's weakened state from the malnourishment, it was recommended that she enter an ACLF temporarily until her strength returned and she was able to return to her own home. She was in agreement with this and arrangements were made for discharge to an ACLF. She is to follow a high protein, low fat diet and continue with Ensure. Activity as tolerated.

## Case Study 32

### History & Physical

CHIEF COMPLAINT: Weakness and syncope

HISTORY OF PRESENT ILLNESS:
This 79-year-old woman presented to the emergency room with complaints of weakness and syncope. She was accompanied by a friend who provided most of the current history. The friend states that the patient has had several episodes of "passing out" in the last two days. The patient has not fallen during these episodes so there has been no injury as a result of these syncopal episodes.

PAST MEDICAL HISTORY:
Significant for COPD for which she uses inhalers and nebulizer treatment. Also is treated for hypertension, CHF and high cholesterol. Patient has had a hysterectomy and cholecystectomy.

FAMILY HISTORY:
Mother deceased at 82 years of age with a myocardial infarction. Father deceased at 45 due to Coal Miners disease. Patient has no siblings.

SOCIAL HISTORY: 100 year pack smoking history, quit in 1995. No alcohol use.

MEDICATIONS: Lasix, Pravacol, Potassium and Cardizem

ALLERGIES: None known

PHYSICAL EXAMINATION: Blood pressure 110/75, pulse 88, respirations 18, temperature 98.2. Patient appears malnourished.

REVIEW OF SYSTEMS:

| | |
|---|---|
| HEENT: | Pupils equal and reactive to light. Pale conjunctiva. Moist mucous membranes. |
| NECK: | Supple without masses. |
| LUNGS: | Decreased breath sounds. |
| HEART: | Regular rate and rhythm. |
| ADOMEN: | Soft, nontender. Bowel sounds present. |
| EXTREMITIES: | No cyanosis or clubbing. |

IMPRESSION:

1. Syncope, etiology to be determined
2. Hypertension
3. COPD
4. Hyperlipidemia
5. CHF

PLAN:

1. Admit to telemetry
2. Continue with home meds

## Case Study 32

**Progress Notes:**

1/3: Admit Note: Patient admitted via Emergency Room to telemetry for syncope, undetermined etiology. Patient to continue with home meds for CHF, COPD, hypertension and hyperlipidemia.

1/4:
S: No syncope while here
O: EKG showed sinus rhythm with RBBB. ECHO WNL Chest x-ray, no CHF, known COPD. Hypertension under control. Vital signs good. Chem profile significant for low protein and albumin with HDL of 281.
A: No cardiac reason for syncope. Patient is malnourished.
P: Continue with current treatment. Add Ensure to diet as a supplement.

1/5:
S: No complaints. No further syncopal episodes
O: Rhythm remains unchanged. Condition stable.
A: Repeat labs within normal limits, except for protein and albumin which are still low.
P: Case management to arrange transfer to ACLF until patient can return home.

1/6: Discharge Note: No cardiac or chemical explanation for syncope. Patient to be discharged to an ACLF until she can return to her own home. Continue with dietary supplement in light of mild malnourishment.

---

**Orders:**

1/3:
1. Admit patient to service of Dr. James Mitchell, per Dr. Lyle Douglas, Emergency Room physician.
2. Place patient on telemetry
3. Chem profile, CBC
4. Continue with patient's home medications
5. EKG, Chest x-ray, ECHO

1/4.
1. Repeat labs
2. Provide patient with ensure
3. Case Management to assist with discharge plans

1/5:
1. Discontinue telemetry
2. Arrange transfer to ACLF tomorrow.

1/6:
1. Discharge today to ACLF

## Case Study 32

**Answer Sheet**

| DIAGNOSES | ICD-9-CM CODES | | | | | |
|---|---|---|---|---|---|---|
| DX 1 | | | | . | | |
| DX 2 | | | | . | | |
| DX 3 | | | | . | | |
| DX 4 | | | | . | | |

| PROCEDURES | CPT CODES | | | | | MODIFIERS (If Applicable) | | |
|---|---|---|---|---|---|---|---|---|
| PR 1 | | | | | | - | | |
| PR 2 | | | | | | - | | |
| PR 3 | | | | | | - | | |
| PR 4 | | | | | | - | | |
| PR 5 | | | | | | - | | |
| PR 6 | | | | | | - | | |

**PROVIDE ICD-9-CM CODES FOR DIAGNOSES AND CPT CODE(S) FOR PROCEDURE(S)**

## CASE STUDY 33

### Inpatient Face Sheet

| | |
|---|---|
| Admit Date: | 1/06/06 |
| Discharge Date: | 1/10/06 |
| Sex: | Male |
| Age: | 60 |
| Disposition: | Home with Home Health Care |

Admit Diagnoses:
1. Fracture right hip
2. Ascites
3. Decubitus ulcer

Discharge Diagnoses:
1. Intertrochanteric fracture right hip
2. Decubitus ulcer
3. Ascites in alcoholic liver cirrhosis
4. Hyperammonemia
5. Chronic obstructive pulmonary disease
6. Right lower quadrant abdominal mass, etiology unknown

Procedures:
1. Closed reduction with internal fixation of fracture right hip
2. Paracentesis

## Case Study 33

### DISCHARGE SUMMARY

ADMITTED: 1/06/06
DISCHARGED: 1/10/06

DISCHARGE DIAGNOSES:
1. Intertrochanteric fracture right hip
2. Severe COPD
3. Chronic alcoholic cirrhosis with massive ascites
4. Right lower quadrant abdominal mass, etiology unknown

PROCEDURES:
1. Closed reduction with internal fixation of fracture of right hip
2. Paracentesis

HOSPITAL COURSE:

This elderly gentleman had a fall at home resulting in an intertrochanteric fracture of the right hip. He was transported to the Emergency Room and placed in Buck's traction. The patient was typed and crossed for six units of blood. He received two units pre-operatively. On post-operative day two, he underwent paracentesis for removal of 2.5 liters of ascites. The post-operative course was complicated by a rise in ammonia. This came down with Lactulose. The patient also has two open areas, Stage II decubitus on his coccyx and buttock. The bases are clean and dry. These are being treated with Duoderm.

On the day of discharge his ammonia was 47. He is comfortable and ambulating with a walker. His abdomen is less tense. He is afebrile and vital signs are stable. The hip wound is healing. He is discharged on Percodan, and routine medications of Lasix 40 mg b.i.d., Aldactone 100 mg q.i.d. wit K-Dur 20 mEq in the morning and 10 mEq in the evening.

He is discharged on a low salt diet with moderate fluid restriction.
He will be seen by home health care. The patient will see me in my office in ten days and will undergo a colonoscopy in four to six weeks to investigate the abdominal mass.

# Case Study 33

## History and Physical

CHIEF COMPLAINT: Fell at home, presents now with hip pain

HISTORY OF PRESENT ILLNESS:
This is a 60 year-old male who fell at home this morning with immediate pain in the right hip. There was no loss of consciousness. In the Emergency Room he was found to have an intertrochanteric fracture. He is admitted to the hospital for definitive evaluation and treatment.

PAST MEDICAL HISTORY:
Significant for long standing alcoholic liver disease with cirrhosis and ascites. And he was found to have a right lower quadrant mass by his gastroenterologist.

ALLERGIES: Tylenol PM

MEDICATIONS:
Lasix 40 mg b.i.d., Aldactone 100 mg q.i.d. with K-Dur 10 mEq b.i.d., low salt diet, moderate fluid restriction to 1200 cc q.i.d.

SOCIAL HISTORY:
No alcohol in the past five years. One pack of tobacco per day. Patient is retired.

PHYSICAL EXAMINATION: Blood pressure 110/70, pulse 88, marked muscle wasting.

REVIEW OF SYSTEMS:

| | |
|---|---|
| HEENT: | Within normal limits. |
| Neck: | Supple, no adenopathy |
| Chest: | Clear |
| Abdomen: | Marked ascites, liver spans about 2-3 fingers below costal margin and is firm |
| Extremities: | Patient is in Buck's traction with foreshortening of the right leg |

LABORATORY DATA:
Random blood sugar 145, alkaline phosphatase 179. Bilirubin and SGOT are normal. The white blood cell count is 15,400, hemoglobin of 8.8 with a hematocrit of 26.2, MCV is 72, MCH is 23.9.

IMPRESSION:
1. Fall resulting in an intertrochanteric fracture right hip
2. Chronic cirrhosis
3. COPD, with tobacco dependency
4. Right lower quadrant abdominal mass, will work up

PLAN:
1. Type and cross 6 units, transfuse 2
2. Gastrointestinal consult regarding paracentesis
3. Closed reduction with internal fixation of fracture of right hip

## Case Study 33

### Procedure Note

| | |
|---|---|
| DATE OF PROCEDURE: | 1/06/06 |
| PREOPERATIVE DIAGNOSIS: | Intertrochanteric fracture, right hip |
| POSTOPERATIVE DIAGNOSIS: | Intertrochanteric fracture, right hip |
| SURGEON: | Alexander Warren, M.D. |
| ANESTHESIA: | Spinal |
| ANESTHESIOLOGIST: | Norma Jean, M.D. |
| ESTIMATED BLOOD LOSS: | 350 cc<br>No replacement |

DESCRIPTION OF PROCEDURE:
After satisfactory induction of spinal anesthesia with the patient lying on the fracture table, traction applied to the right lower extremity with internal rotation, reducing the fracture. The left leg abducted to allow the image intensifier to come into view in both AP and lateral positions.

Standard lateral incision was made taken through the skin and subcutaneous tissue, the fascia slit longitudinally. The vastus lateralis split longitudinally, coming along the proximal aspect of the femur. Guide wire inserted in good position, both AP and lateral. This was then reamed to accept the 95 mm barrel screw. A 135 degree four-hole plate was attached. The titanium cortical side screws were inserted. Good fixation was obtained.

The area was irrigated with saline and antibiotic solution. A medium set screw was put in place. Constavac drain was inserted through a separate puncture site. Vastus lateralis was closed with interrupted 0 Vicryl suture, the fascia with interrupted 0 Vicryl suture, the subcutaneous tissue with 00 Vicryl and the skin with staples. Neosporin, Adaptic, bulky 4 x 4s, ABDs and Mefix dressing applied.

The patient tolerated the procedure well and left the operating room in good condition.

## Case Study 33

**PROGRESS NOTES**

1/6: Admit Note: Patient is admitted via the Emergency Room after suffering a fall at home resulting in intertrochanteric fracture of the right femur. Patient was a former drinker, now has liver cirrhosis and ascites. Patient is also a smoker with COPD. Patient is admitted for definitive treatment of hip fracture. Admitting H/H is 10.8/37.2, will T&C six units and transfuse two prior to surgery.

1/7:
- S: Only complaint is surgical pain
- O: H/H is stable, will not require blood transfusions. Abdomen is very tense. Stable respiratory status. No shortness of breath and good lung sounds
- A: Ascites, stable from surgical standpoint
- P: Begin ambulation with minimal weight bearing, will do paracentesis tomorrow

1/8:
- S: No complaints
- O: Vital signs stable, afebrile, incision clean and dry, ammonia elevated
- A: Paracentesis with removal of 2.5 liters ascitic fluid
- P: Continue ambulation, give Lactulose for elevated ammonia

1/9:
- S: Doing well
- O: Vitals stable, ammonia level within normal limits, abdomen less tense, afebrile
- A: Good post operative recovery
- P: Will plan discharge for tomorrow

1/10: Patient to be discharged home with home health care

---

**ORDERS**:

1/6:
1. Admit patient
2. Continue Buck's traction
3. Prepare for surgery this afternoon
4. Cross and type six units, transfuse two prior to surgery
5. Respiratory treatments prior to surgery
6. CBC, WBC, Chem profile

1/7:
1. Incentive spirometer q 4 hr
2. Begin ambulation
3. Ammonia level

1/8:
1. Paracentesis tray to bedside
2. Lactulose for elevated ammonia level

1/9:
1. Continue with current orders

1/10:
1. Discharge home with home health care

**Case Study 33**
**Answer Sheet**

| DIAGNOSES | ICD-9-CM CODES | | | | | |
|---|---|---|---|---|---|---|
| DX 1 | | | | . | | |
| DX 2 | | | | . | | |
| DX 3 | | | | . | | |
| DX 4 | | | | . | | |

| PROCEDURES | CPT CODES | | | | | MODIFIERS (If Applicable) | | |
|---|---|---|---|---|---|---|---|---|
| PR 1 | | | | | | - | | |
| PR 2 | | | | | | - | | |
| PR 3 | | | | | | - | | |
| PR 4 | | | | | | - | | |
| PR 5 | | | | | | - | | |
| PR 6 | | | | | | - | | |

**PROVIDE ICD-9-CM CODES FOR DIAGNOSES ONLY**

## CASE STUDY 34

### Inpatient Face Sheet

| | |
|---|---|
| Admit Date: | 1/02/06 |
| Discharge Date: | 1/05/06 |
| Sex: | Female |
| Age: | 42 |
| Disposition: | Transfer to Psychiatric Facility |

Admitting Diagnoses:
1. Drug overdose
2. Diet controlled diabetes
3. Peripheral vascular disease

Discharge Diagnoses:
1. Accidental overdose of Haldol and Xanax
2. Diet controlled diabetes
3. Peripheral vascular disease

## Case Study 34
**Discharge Summary**

Admitted: 1/02/06
Discharged: 1/05/06

Discharge Diagnoses:
1. Accidental poisoning of Haldol and Xanax
2. Type II diabetes
3. Peripheral vascular disease
4. Depression

HISTORY:

This 42 year-old female was admitted to intensive care following overdose of Haldol and Xanax. Patient is currently treated for depression. See history and physical for complete details.

HOSPITAL COURSE:

This patient was admitted to the Intensive Care Unit following ingestion of Haldol and Xanax. Patient was given IV fluids and Narcan to counteract the overdose of medication. She responded well to the Narcan and the day following admission was more alert and less confused. She remained in the ICU for one additional day until she was transferred to the medical floor. Her laboratory results were within normal limits on transfer to the medical unit. The patient denied a suicide attempt, however, in light of her ongoing depression she is being transferred to the Psychiatric Facility for continued treatment.
Her condition from a medical standpoint was stable upon transfer.

## Case Study 34
### History & Physical

CHIEF COMPLAINT:
This patient was brought to my office by her friend who had stopped by her home because she was unable to reach her by phone. The friend states that the patient was exhibiting inappropriate behavior and told her that she had taken some pills. I sent the patient to the hospital as a direct admission because of her mental status changes and possible drug overdose.

HISTORY OF PRESENT ILLNESS:
Upon presentation to my office, the patient had become lethargic and was becoming difficult to arouse. She has a known history of depression and was treated with antidepressants. It is unknown at this time if she has overmedicated herself with the antidepressants. This patient has a history of peripheral vascular disease and diet controlled diabetes.

ALLERGIES: None

PAST MEDICAL HISTORY: As indicated above.

CURRENT MEDICATIONS: Haldol and Xanax

SOCIAL HISTORY: Lives alone. No tobacco or alcohol use.

REVIEW OF SYSTEMS;

| | |
|---|---|
| General. | Well-developed, somewhat unkempt woman. She is confused. Somewhat lethargic and difficult to arouse and then becomes combative. |
| Vital signs: | Temperature of 99.9, blood pressure 120/90. Pulse 118,. Respirations at 21. |
| HEENT: | Within normal limits. |
| NECK: | No lymphadenopathy. |
| CARDIAC: | Sinus tachycardia. |
| LUNGS: | Clear to auscultation. |
| ABDOMEN: | No masses, bowel sounds present |
| EXTREMITIES: | No cyanosis, edema or clubbing. |
| SKIN: | Unremarkable |

IMPRESSION:
1. Drug overdose, Haldol and Xanax
2. Peripheral vascular disease
3. Type II diabetes

PLAN:
1. Admit patient to intensive care.
2. Standing ICU orders
3. Drug screen

## Case Study 34

**Progress Notes:**

1/2: Admit Note: Patient admitted to intensive care for suspected drug overdose of Haldol and Xanax. Prescriptions had been issued two days ago. Multiple dosages were missing from the bottles and drug screen is positive for antidepressants. Patient has been under treatment for depression. Monitor patient in ICU.

1/3: S: Patient does not recall what brought her to the hospital.
O: Patient awake, less confused, vital signs improved, labs improving
A: Patient somewhat improved
P: Continue ICU monitoring and with current meds and IVs. Case Management to arrange transfer to Psychiatric Facility when medically stable.

1/4: S: Feels much better, but admits to feeling depressed. Denied suicide attempt.
O: Patient more alert today. Vital signs good. All labs WNL
A: Transfer out of ICU today
P: Transfer to Psych Hospital in the morning.

1/5: Discharge Note: Patient is medically stable for transfer to Psychiatric Facility following overdose of Haldol and Xanax.

## Case Study 34

**Orders:**

1/2:
1. Admit to ICU
2. Standing ICU orders
3. IV NS at 125cc/hr
4. Narcan IV
5. Accuchecks q 4 hours
6. Drug screen

1/3:
1. Decrease IV rate to 75cc/hr
2. Case Management for discharge planning

1/4:
1. Transfer to medical floor
2. DC IVs

1/5:
1. Transfer to Psychiatric Facility under the care of Dr. Sierra Seybolt

## Case Study 34
## Answer Sheet

| DIAGNOSES | ICD-9-CM CODES | | | | | |
|---|---|---|---|---|---|---|
| DX 1 | | | | . | | |
| DX 2 | | | | . | | |
| DX 3 | | | | . | | |
| DX 4 | | | | . | | |

| PROCEDURES | CPT CODES | | | | | MODIFIERS (If Applicable) | | |
|---|---|---|---|---|---|---|---|---|
| PR 1 | | | | | | - | | |
| PR 2 | | | | | | - | | |
| PR 3 | | | | | | - | | |
| PR 4 | | | | | | - | | |
| PR 5 | | | | | | - | | |
| PR 6 | | | | | | - | | |

**PROVIDE ICD-9-CM CODES FOR DIAGNOSES AND CPT CODE(S) FOR PROCEDURE(S)**

## CASE STUDY 35

### INPATIENT FACE SHEET

| | |
|---|---|
| Admit Date: | 1/09/06 |
| Discharge Date: | 1/23/06 |
| Age: | 79 |
| Sex: | Male |
| Disposition: | Home with Home Health Care |

Admission Diagnoses:

1. Acute bronchial asthma in exacerbation.
2. Hypoxemia, hypercapnia.
3. Suspected chronic obstructive pulmonary disease.
4. Rule out pulmonary embolism.
5. Hypertension.
6. Hyperlipidemia.

Discharge Diagnoses:

1. Acute bronchial asthma with acute exacerbation.
2. Tracheobronchitis.
3. Chronic hypoxemia.
4. Suspect underlying chronic obstructive pulmonary disease.
5. History of hypertension.
6. Hyperlipidemia.

Procedures Performed:

1. Broncoscopy with biopsies and lavage

## Case Study 35

### DISCHARGE SUMMARY

ADMITTED: 1/9/06

DISCHARGED: 1/23/06

DISCHARGE DIAGNOSES:
1. Acute bronchial asthma with acute exacerbation.
2. Tracheobronchitis.
3. Chronic hypoxemia.
4. Suspect underlying chronic obstructive pulmonary disease.
5. History of hypertension.
6. Hyperlipidemia.

ADMITTING DIAGNOSES:
1. Acute bronchial asthma in exacerbation.
2. Hypoxemia, hypercapnia.
3. Suspected chronic obstructive pulmonary disease.
4. Rule out pulmonary embolism.
5. Hypertension.
6. Hyperlipidemia.

PROCEDURE:
1. Bronchoscopy with lavage and biopsy

HISTORY OF PRESENT ILLNESS:
This is a 79-year-old male patient with above-mentioned medical problems who now presents with increasing shortness of breath, cough, wheezing and respiratory distress. He has been on multiple bronchodilators and inhaled steroids, including Flovent, nebulizer, Theophylline and a small dose of prednisone.

HOSPITAL COURSE:
This patient was admitted with increasing shortness of breath. He was not responding to outpatient medical therapy. He was placed on Albuterol nebulized respiratory treatment and started on a short course of pulse intravenous steroids, given mucolytics expectorants and continued on Theophylline. He was cultured and placed on intravenous Claforan initially, empirically; he was otherwise continued on treatment for hypertension. A therapeutic bronchoscopy was performed with evidence of thick, purulent mucous plugs widespread on both sides, some narrowing of the left lower lobe bronchus also noted with some inflammation. Biopsies were negative for malignancy. He was continued on Mucomyst at this point, nebulized respiratory treatments, chest physiotherapy and intravenous Solu-Medrol.

Following several days of aggressive treatment he started to improve and was less short of breath, bronchospasm was resolving and was discharged on December 23.

## Case Study 35

**DISCHARGE SUMMARY**

Continued

| | |
|---|---|
| PERTINENT EXAM: | Audible wheezing, coughed continuously, tachycardic, tachypneic, afebrile. |
| VITAL SIGNS: | Blood pressure stable. |
| HEENT: | Revealed postnasal drip. |
| NECK: | No jugular venous distention. |
| LUNGS: | Diffuse wheezing, rhonchi and rales. |
| HEART: | Regular. |
| ABDOMEN: | Soft. |
| EXTREMITIES: | No edema. |

REVIEW OF LABORATIORY DATA:
The bronchoscopy cytology revealed no malignancy. The arterial blood gases on room air – pH 7.48, pC02 36, p02 56, bicarb 26.4, and saturation 92.3%. Complete blood count – white blood cell count 9,800. Hemoglobin 15, hematocrit 47.1 and platelet count normal. Follow-up complete blood count remained stable. Chemistries – blood urea nitrogen 17, creatinine 1.4. Troponin I normal on a serial basis. Albumin 2.4 to 3.3. Liver functions normal. Theophylline level 19.2. Urinalysis – yellow and clear; microscopic blood noted, protein negative, nitrite negative, leukocyte esterase a small amount detected. Sputum revealed Candida. Urine culture – no growth. Sputum for Acid-fast bacilli – test still pending at this time although smears were negative. The chest revealed a new hazy opacity of the left mid lung, in the lower lung area, possibly fusion or atelectasis. This persisted on follow – up.

Electrocardiogram: sinus rhythm, sinus tachycardia. While on telemetry the patient was in sinus rhythm.

MEDICATIONS ON DISCARGE:

1. Prednisone 30 mg daily for four days, then 20mg daily for four days, then 10mg daily.
2. Flovent 220 mcg three puffs twice daily.
3. Albuterol treatments four times daily.
4. Norvasc 5mg daily.
5. Lasix 40mg half tablet daily.
6. Potassium 10meq daily.
7. Nasonex spray two puffs daily.
8. Theophylline 200mg twice daily.

ACITIVITY: As tolerated.

## Case Study 35

### HISTORY AND PHYSICAL

ADMISSION DATE: 1/09/2006

CHIEF COMPLAINT: Shortness of breath, wheezing, cough and chest congestion.

HISTORY OF PRESENT ILLNESS:
This is a 79-year-old male with multiple admissions for respiratory problems and exacerbation of asthma. Presented to the emergency room because of increasing shortness of breath, cough, wheezing and respiratory distress. Apparently he has been on multiple bronchodilators and inhaled steroids, including Flovent, nebulizer, Theophylline and a small dose of Prednisone a day. In spite of the outpatient treatment, his symptoms continued to worsen. He was admitted to the hospital for further treatment.

PAST MEDICAL HISTORY:
Past medical history is positive for long standing bronchial asthma with chronic exacerbation, steroid-dependent asthma. He also had history of tracheobronchitis, hypertension, and hyperlipidemia.

MEDICATIONS AT HOME:
Flovent 220 micrograms 2 puffs twice a day, but he is not using regularly. Nebulizer 4 times a day, Norvasc 5 milligrams once a day, Lasix 40 milligrams ½ tablet once a day, potassium 10 milliequivalent once a day, calcium t.i.d., Theophylline 200 milligrams b.i.d., and Prednisone 5 milligrams once a day.

ALLERGIES: None.

SOCIAL HISTORY: Does not smoke Never smoked.

REVIEW OF SYSTEMS:

| | |
|---|---|
| HEENT: | Revealed postnasal drip. |
| NECK: | No jugular venous distension. |
| LUNGS: | Bilateral diffuse wheezing, rhonchi and rales. |
| HEART: | Regular rhythm. |
| ABDOMEN: | Soft. |
| EXTREMITIES: | No edema. |
| GASTROINTESTINAL: | No gastritis, gastroesophageal reflux, occasional indigestion no ulcer. |
| RESPIRATORY: | As mentioned in the history. |
| CARDIAC: | History of hypertension, but no history of angina, coronary artery disease. Does not have any chest pain. He had an echocardiogram in 2001, which was normal with ejection fraction of 60 percent. |
| MUSCULOSKELETAL: | Negative |
| NEUROLOGIC: | Negative for stroke, transient ischemic attack, headache, dizziness or syncope. |
| GENITOURINARY: | Negative. The rest of review of systems is negative. |

## Case Study 35

### HISTORY AND PHYSICAL

Continued:

PHYSICAL EXAMINATION:
Elderly male who is in acute distress with audible wheeze. He coughs continuously. He is tachycardiac, tachypneic, afebrile. Vitals stable otherwise.

The labs, x-rays, etcetera, were reviewed.

IMPRESSION:

1. Acute bronchial asthma and exacerbation.
2. Severe hypoxemia, hypercapnia. Rule out due to chronic obstructive pulmonary disease, bronchospasm. Rule out other causes, like pulmonary embolism.

PLAN: Will give IV steroids, IV antibiotics, nebulizer treatment, and oxygen.
Get a spiral CT scan to rule out pulmonary emboli.
Continue other treatment, and will follow him closely.

## Case Study 35

**PROCEDURE REPORT**

DATE: 1/15/06

ENDOSCOPIST: Dr. Brandon Douglas

PROCEDURE: Bronchoscopy.

INDICATION: Left lower lobe collapse, due to mucous plug.

ANESTHESIA: Dr. Jeffrey Cottrell

DESCRIPTION OF PROCEDURE:

After the anesthesiologist anesthetized the patient, the Olympus bronchoscope was introduced through the bite block into the oral cavity. The upper airway was seen and wan unremarkable. Cords were sprayed with Xylocaine. The scope was passed through the cords into the trachea which was free of lesion. Carina was sharp. The scope was passed into the right mid stem bronchus. The upper lobe and middle lobe segments were seen. They are remarkable for thick purulent mucous plugging of all the bronchial segments. Aggressive lavage with saline and Mucomyst were done. In spite of that, mucous plugs were quite thick and it required manual removal of the mucous plugs through the scope. Subsequently the scope was withdrawn back to the left main stem, and left upper lobe and lingual lobe and sub segments were seen. They were also remarkable for severe mucous plugging which were removed manually. After complete evacuation of mucous plugs was done, bronchial segments were visualized again and there was some narrowing of left lower segment with some inflamed, swollen mucosa. Biopsies were done from that segment. Bronchial washings were done and sent for cytology and culture.

The patient tolerated the procedure well.

FINDINGS: Thick, purulent mucous pluggings were widespread on both sides. There was some narrowing of left lower lobe bronchus with inflamed, swollen mucosa with smooth margin.

SPECIMENS: Biopsies were done from left lobe bronchus. Washing were done. Bronchoscopic lavage was done using saline and Mucomyst, and all the mucous plugs were removed.

## Case Study 35

PATHOLOGY REPORT

DATE: 1/18/06

SPECIMEN TYPE: CYTO

SURGIACAL PATHOLOGY / CYTOPATHOLOGY REPORT

PRE – OP DIAGNOSIS: LEFT LOWER LOBE COLLAPSE: INFLAMED SWOLLEN BRONCHIAL MUCOSA LEFT LOWER LOBE

POST OP DIAGNOSIS LEFT LOWER LOBE COLLAPSE: INFLAMED SWOLLEN BRONCHIAL MUCOSA LEFT LOWER LOBE

SPECIMEN(S)

BRONCHIAL WASHING MATERIAL

GROSS DESCRIPTION
Received 8 cc of hemorrhagic fluid in the laboratory. 2 smears and 1 cell block are prepared for cytological evaluation.

MICROSCOPIC DESCRIPTION
Microscopic examination of the specimen reveals groups of and single appearing poorly preserved epithelial cells displaying nuclear enlargement, hyperchromasia, increased N/C bronchial columnar, metaplastic and reserve cells: pulmonary macrophages, mixed inflammatory cells, necrotic debris and fungal elements.

CYTOPATHOLOGICAL DIAGNOSIS

BRONCHIAL WASHING: POORLY PRESERVED DYSPLASTIC EPITHELIAL CELLS PRESENT. CANDIDA SPECIES IDENTIFIED.

## Case Study 35

SURGICAL PATHOLOGY / CYTOPATHOLOGY REPORT

PRE – OP Diagnosis: LEFT LOWER LOBE COLLAPSE: INFLAMED SWOLLEN BRONCHIAL MUCOSA LEFT LOWER LOBE

POST OP Diagnosis: LEFT LOWER LOBE COLLAPSE: INFLAMED SWOLLEN BRONCHIAL MUCOSA LEFT LOWER LOBE

SPECIMEN(S)

LUNG LEFT LOWER LOBE – BIOPSY X4

GROSS DESCRIPTION
The specimen consists of four fragments of tan tissue ranging from 0.1 up to 0.6 cm in greatest dimension. Entirely submitted.

MICROSCOPIC DIAGNOSIS

BIOPSY OF LEFT LOWER LOBE: MILD NONSPECIFIC CHRONIC BRONCHITIS WITH HYPERTROPHY OF THE SUBMUCOSAL GLANDS AND THICKENING OF THE SUBEPITHELIAL BASEMENT MEMBRANE.

NO TUMOR PRESENT.

FINAL DIAGNOSIS

BIOPSY OF LEFT LOWER LOBE:

MINUTE DETACHED FRAGMENT OF DYSPLASTIC EPITHELIUM.
MILD NONSPECIFIC CHRONIC BRONCHITIS WITH HYPERTROPHY OF SUBMUCOSAL GLANDS AND THICKENED SUBEPITHELIAL BASEMENT MEMBRANE.

## Case Study 35

**Answer Sheet**

| DIAGNOSES | ICD-9-CM CODES | | | | | |
|---|---|---|---|---|---|---|
| DX 1 | | | | . | | |
| DX 2 | | | | . | | |
| DX 3 | | | | . | | |
| DX 4 | | | | . | | |

| PROCEDURES | CPT CODES | | | | | MODIFIERS (If Applicable) | | |
|---|---|---|---|---|---|---|---|---|
| PR 1 | | | | | | - | | |
| PR 2 | | | | | | - | | |
| PR 3 | | | | | | - | | |
| PR 4 | | | | | | - | | |
| PR 5 | | | | | | - | | |
| PR 6 | | | | | | - | | |

**PROVIDE ICD-9-CM CODES FOR DIAGNOSES AND CPT CODE(S) FOR PROCEDURE(S)**

## CASE STUDY 36

### INPATIENT FACE SHEET

| | |
|---|---|
| ADMIT DATE: | 01/02/06 |
| DISCHARGE DATE: | 01/10/06 |
| AGE: | 47 |
| SEX: | M |
| DISPOSITION: | Home |

ADMISSION DIAGNOSES:
1. Low back pain.
2. L5-S1 radiculopathy.

DISCHARGE DIAGNOSIS:
1. Herniated nucleus pulposus right sided at L5-S1.

OPERATION/PROCEDURE:
1. Lumbar laminectomy at L5 and S1
2. Right sided L5-S1 micro-diskectomy.
3. Use of operating microscope.

## Case Study 36
## HISTORY & PHYSICAL

ADMISSION DATE: 01/02/2006

REASON FOR ADMISSION: The patient is a 47-year-old gentleman who presented with severe back pain.

HISTORY OF PRESENT ILLNESS:
The patient is a 47-year-old gentleman seen in my office in a severe state of pain. It was suspected that the patient had radiculopathy. The patient was sent for a MRI. The radiologist reported a very large disc herniation with right-sided disc protrusion and early extrusion of the disc material at L5-S1 with compression of the thecal sac.

MEDICATIONS PRIOR TO ADMISSION:
The patient's medications prior to admission included Tylenol #3, Decadron and Vicodin.

ALLERGIES: The patient has no known allergies.

SOCIAL HISTORY:
The patient is married and lives with his wife. The patient has a history of smoking one pack of cigarettes per day. The patient has a history of drinking alcoholic beverages occasionally.

REVIEW OF SYSTEMS:
The patient denied a history of chest pain. The patient denied a history of chest pressure. The patient denied a history of chest tightness. The patient denied a history of difficulty breathing.

PHYSICAL EXAMINATION:

| | |
|---|---|
| VITAL SIGNS: | The patient's vital signs on admission were stable. |
| NECK: | The neck was supple. There was no jugular venous distention. There were no carotid bruits. |
| LUNGS: | The lungs were clear to auscultation and percussion. There were no signs of consolidation. |
| HEART: | The heart was normal. |
| ADOMEN: | The abdomen was soft and non-tender. The bowel sounds were positive. |
| EXTREMITIES: | The examination of the extremities was negative for cyanosis, clubbing or edema. |
| NEUROLOGICAL: | The cranial nerves two through twelve appeared to be intact. The tone was normal. The power was five by five in the upper extremities. The power was decreased in the right lower extremity secondary to maybe being in pain. The sensation on the right side revealed only one plus at the knee and ankle jerks. The straight leg raising was positive. |

PLAN: Consultation with neurology and surgical consultation will be requested.

## Case Study 36

### CONSULTATION

REQUESTING PHYSICIAN: Dr. Rosie Wags
DATE: 01/02/06
CONSULTING PHYSICIAN: Dr. Zachary Service
CHIEF COMPLAINT: Right lower extremity pain.

HISTORY OF PRESENT ILLNESS: This is a 47-year-old gentleman who has a past medical history significant for bulging disc at L5-L1. The patient was having this pain and was ultimately relieved with medication, as well as chiropractic manipulation. The patient had magnetic resonance imaging done yesterday, which showed he had a bulging disc at L5-S1 on the right side. At the time of the examination, the patient is awake, alert and oriented x 4. He denied any lowered extremity weakness, but complained of right lower extremity pain at the L5-S1 nerve root distribution. He denied any bowel or bladder dysfunction.

PAST MEDICAL HISTORY: No significant past medical history.

MEDICATIONS: Vicodin, Tylenol #3, Soma, Decadron.

SOCIAL HISTORY: Smokes one pack of cigarettes per day. Denies any alcohol use.

REVIEW OF SYSTEMS: Completely reviewed and was negative.

PHYSICAL EXAMINATION: This is a 47-year-old gentleman lying in bed in no acute distress.
HEAD: Norma cephalic, traumatic.
ENT: Within normal limits.
NECK: Supple. No bruits are auscultated. No adenopathy.
CHEST: Clear to auscultation.
HEART: Regular rate and rhythm. No murmurs, rubs or gallops.
ABDOMEN: Positive bowel sounds, non-tender, no distended. No organomegaly.
EXTREMITIES: No cyanosis, edema or clubbing.
NEUROLOGIC: The patient is alert and oriented x 3. Cranial nerves II-XII are grossly intact. Pupils are equal, round and react to light and accommodation. Extraocular movements are intact. Cerebellar function is intact. Motor/sensory exam is intact.

There is negative Babinski. No pronator drift. Strength is 5/5 in all extremities in all ranges of motion. There was a positive straight-leg raise on the right. There was evidence of a decreased reflex knee jerk on the right, which was 1+. MRI scan of the lumbar spine revealed L5-S1 right-sided disc herniation.

IMPRESSION: Low back pain. L5-S1 radiculopathy.
RECOMMENDATIONS:

1. The patient is stable.
2. Continue current care.
3. Suggest an epidural steroid injection, as well as physical therapy at this time.

## Case Study 36

### Consultation

REQUESTING PHYSICIAN: Dr. Rosie Wags
DATE: 01/02/06
CONSULTING PHYSICIAN: Dr. Liza Gaige
REASON FOR CONSULTATION:
The patient is a 47-year-old gentleman who presented with lower back pain.

HISTORY OF PRESENT ILLNESS:
The patient is a 47-year-old gentleman whose past medical history was significant for a history of a bulging disc in 1994 at L5 and S1. He subsequently had a MRI that revealed L5 and S1, herniated disc. The patient was then admitted to the hospital for further management. A neurological consultation was then requested. At this time the patient is still having lower back pain with some pain radiating to the right lower extremity, all the way to the toes. The patient denied a history of chest pain. The patient denied a history of shortness of breath. There is no history of nausea or vomiting. The patient denied a history of dysphagia.

PAST MEDICAL AND SURGICAL HISTORY:
The patient has a history of a fall with lower back pain.

MEDICATIONS PRIOR TO ADMISSION:
The patient's medications prior to admission included Vicodin and Tylenol #3 and Soma and Decadron.

ALLERGIES: The patient has no known allergies.

SOCIAL HISTORY:
The patient has a history of smoking approximately one pack of cigarettes per day. The patient has a history of drinking alcoholic beverages occasionally.

PHYSICAL EXAMINATION:
GENERAL APPEARANCE: On examination the patient is awake, alert and oriented times three.

NEUROLOGICAL: Extraocular movements were intact. Pupils are equal, round and reactive to light and accommodation. There was no nystagmus. There were no carotid bruits. The visual fields were within normal limits. There was no Kernig sign. There was no Brudzinski sign. The cranial nerves two through twelve appeared to be intact. The tongue was midline. The corneal reflex was intact. The gag reflex was intact. Motor system revealed tone was normal. Power was five by five in left upper extremity and the right upper extremity. The power in the lower extremities was five by five distally but three plus to four by five because of the severe pain proximally. The sensory examination revealed normal pinprick, tough and temperature. Normal position. Normal vibration. The reflexes were plus one at the right knee jerk and ankle jerk. The straight leg raising was a stronger positive in the right lower extremity than in the left lower extremity. The patient can walk but with a limp. The patient cannot walk on heel and tiptoes.

## Case Study 36

### Consultation

Continued:

LABORATORY INVESTIGATIONS:
The Magnetic Resonance Imaging of the lumbar spine revealed L5-S1 central and right side herniated disc.

IMPRESSION:

1. Severe lower back pain.
2. Severe radicular pain mainly of the right lower extremity secondary to herniated disc.
3. L5-S1 radiculopathy.
4. Straight leg raising positive.
5. Right knee jerk plus one, decreased compared to the left knee jerk.

RECOMMENDATIONS:

1. Immediate lumbar laminectomy

## Case Study 36

**OPERATIVE REPORT**

DATE: 01/04/06

SURGEON: Dr. Liza Gaige

PREOPERATIVE DIAGNOSIS: Herniated nucleus pulposus right sided at L5-S1.

POSTOPERATIVE DIAGNOSIS: Herniated nucleus pulposus right sided at L5-S1.

OPERATION/PROCEDURE: Lumbar laminectomy at L5 and S1, Right sided.
L5-S1 micro-diskectomy.
Use of the leica microscope.

ASSISTANT: Dr. Jeff Cottrell

COMPLICATIONS: There were no complications.

ANESTHESIA: General endotracheal anesthesia.

ESTIMATED BLOOD LOSS: Less than 50cc.

INDICATIONS FOR THE PROCEDURE:
This is a young gentleman with intractable right sciatica of eight years duration who has failed conservative treatment. The patient is now being taken to surgery for decompression and removal of the disc. The risks of the surgery and the limitations of the surgery were explained to the patient and the patient's wife at length. They understand the risks and wish to proceed with procedure.

DESCRIPTION OF THE OPERATION:
Intravenous lines were started. Thigh high TED and compression boots were placed on the lower extremities. The patient received general endotracheal anesthesia. The patient was placed in the prone position resting on the Wilson frame. All the pressure points were appropriately padded. The area in the lumbar spine was shaved, prepped and draped in the usual sterile manner. An incision was made in the spinous process of L5 to S1 inclusive using the subperiosteal dissection. The lamina of right L5 and S1 were exposed. Intraoperative x-ray confirmed our level. Using the Anspach drill we thinned out the lamina arch to the level of the ligamentum flavum. The operative microscope was prepped and draped and brought into the field. The remainder of the procedure was performed using the microscope. We then proceeded to do the laminotomy of L5 on the right side of the inferior two thirds and superior two thirds of S1. This exposed the nerve root going out. The nerve root was retracted slightly medially. There was a large anterior compression of the nerve root pushing the nerve root posteriorly. Slightly moving the nerve root medially, we exposed the big rent in the angelus fibrosis, entered this big defect and the micro-diskectomy was performed.

## Case Study 36

### OPERATIVE REPORT

Continued:

There was a large disc herniation that had broken through the angelus and into the posterior part of the vertebral body of L5-S1. Once the diskectomy was performed, the wound was irrigated thoroughly using antibiotic solution. With a small nerve hook we went ahead and looked for any residual fragments and there were none. The wound was then irrigated thoroughly using a copious amount of antibiotic solution. The wound was closed in serial layers using #0-Vicryl in an interrupted fashion on the muscle and fascial layers. We used #2-0 Vicryl sutures to close the subcutaneous tissues. We used #2-0 Nurolon vertical and multi-locking sutures for the skin. All the sponge and needle counts were reported correct at the end of the procedure. The patient tolerated the procedure well. The patient was extubated in the operating room and was taken to the recovery room in stable condition moving all extremities.

---

SURGICAL PATHOLOGY REPORT

ACUTE HERNIATED DISC L5-S1

SPECIMENS(S)      DISC. NOS – L5-S1

GROSS DESCRIPTION

THE SPECIMEN CONSISTS OF MULTIPLE IRREGULAR FRAGMENTS OF FIBROCARTILAGINOUS TISSUE WEIGHING APPROXIMATELY 5 GRAMS IN AGGREGATE.

REPRESENTATIVE SECTIONS ARE SUBMITTED IN A SINGLE CASSETTE FOR DECALCIFICATION AND PROCESSING.

MICROSCOPIC DIAGNOSIS:
DEGENERATED FIBROCARTILAGINOIS TISSUE CONSISTENT WITH INTERVERTEBRAL DISC.
CLINICALLY HERNIATED DISC L5-S1

## Case Study 36

**Answer Sheet**

| DIAGNOSES | ICD-9-CM CODES | | | | | |
|---|---|---|---|---|---|---|
| DX 1 | | | | . | | |
| DX 2 | | | | . | | |
| DX 3 | | | | . | | |
| DX 4 | | | | . | | |

| PROCEDURES | CPT CODES | | | | | MODIFIERS (If Applicable) | | |
|---|---|---|---|---|---|---|---|---|
| PR 1 | | | | | | - | | |
| PR 2 | | | | | | - | | |
| PR 3 | | | | | | - | | |
| PR 4 | | | | | | - | | |
| PR 5 | | | | | | - | | |
| PR 6 | | | | | | - | | |

**PROVIDE ICD-9-CM CODES FOR DIAGNOSES AND CPT CODE(S) FOR PROCEDURE(S)**

## CASE STUDY 37

### INPATIENT FACE SHEET

Admit Date: 1/14/06

Discharge Date: 1/16/06

Age: 89

Sex: F

Disposition: Home

Admit Diagnoses:
Lower abdominal pain and nausea possibly due to partial small bowel obstruction.
History of colon resection for cancer with elevated CEA of 23.1. Rule out recurrence of cancer.

Discharge Diagnoses:

1. Diverticulosis
2. Benign colon polyp

Procedure:

1. Colonoscopy with polypectomy and biopsy.

## Case Study 37

### HISTORY AND PHYSICAL

ADMITTED: 1/14/06
CHIEF COMPLAINT: Abdominal pain, nausea and vomiting.

HISTORY OF PRESENT ILLNESS: This is an 89-year-old woman who has been complaining of abdominal pains, vomiting and nausea for several weeks. She is admitted at this time for further evaluation, including colonoscopy. The patient has a history of colon cancer with an elevated CEA, suggesting recurrence of cancer.

PAST HISTORY: The patient had colon resection June 2001 for colon cancer. She had her left lung resected in July 1995 for carcinoma. In addition, she has had coronary artery bypass graft in 1999 for severe coronary artery disease. She has known hypertension and osteoporosis with L1 compression fracture.

MEDICATIONS: Metoprolol 100 milligrams b.i.d., Cardizem 180 milligrams daily and Cardura.

ALLERGIES: No known allergies.

SOCIAL HISTORY: The patient is widowed and lives alone. She does not smoke cigarettes or drink alcohol.

FAMILY HISTORY: There is a strong family history of arteriosclerotic heart disease and myocardial infarction.

REVIEW OF SYSTEMS: The patient has had intermittent diarrhea over the past years, since the time of her colon surgery. She has had episodes where her abdomen becomes distended and hard.

PHYSICAL EXAMINATION:
GENERAL: On physical examination the patient is pleasant, alert, 89-year-old woman in no distress.
HEENT: Shows capillary reflexes. Her extraocular movements are normal. There is no pallor, icterus. Ears and throat are unremarkable. Neck is supple and free of masses. There is no jugular venous distension in the neck.
CHEST: Symmetrical.
LUNGS: Lung fields are clear.
HEART: Heart sounds are regular with no significant murmurs.
ABDOMEN: Firm. Bowel sounds are active. There is some diffuse low abdominal tenderness, most noted in the right lower quadrant. There is no rebound tenderness. There are no apparent masses.
EXTREMITIES: Show 2 plus edema.

ASSESSMENT: The patient is an 89-year-old woman with known colon cancer and recurrent episodes of abdominal pain and vomiting over the past several weeks. The case has been discussed with her Gastroenterologist, Dr. Angela Gaige. She is admitted at this time for continued intravenous fluid hydration, colonoscopy and diagnostic workup.

## <u>Case Study 37</u>

### CONSULTATION

| | |
|---|---|
| DATE: | 1/14/06 |
| REQUESTING PHYSICIAN: | Dr. Bronwyn Mills |
| CONSULTING PHYSICIAN: | Dr. David Clark |

REASON FOR CONSULTATION: Evaluation of patient with lower abdominal pain, nausea and vomiting.

HISTORY: This 89-year-old woman is referred for further evaluation of lower abdominal pain, nausea and vomiting. Her bowel movements are erratic and range from being constipated with no bowel movement for several days to loose bowel movements. She has lost about three pounds over the past month.

She underwent CT scan of the abdomen and pelvis on 1/24/06 revealing a dilated bile duct. Her liver enzymes, however, were normal and HIDA scan revealed no evidence of obstruction and thus it was felt that the dilation of the bile duct was physiologic and did not represent obstruction. She had a CEA of 23.1 on 1/23/06.

PAST MEDICAL HISTORY:
Colon resection for cancer of the colon in June 2001.
Coronary artery bypass graft in 1995.

MEDICATIONS IN THE HOSPITAL: Pepcid 20 mg IV q.12h.; nitroglycerin q.i.d.; atenolol 25 mg p.o. b.i.d.

ALLERGIES: None known

SOCIAL HISTORY: Cigarettes – smoked up until 1989.

FAMILY HISTORY: Negative for cancer.

PHYSICAL EXAMINATION:
GENERAL APPEARANCE: Pleasant cooperative woman, who appears to be in moderate distress due to her abdominal symptoms.

| | |
|---|---|
| HEENT: | Normocephalic, traumatic. No scleral icterus. |
| NECK: | Supple. No lymphadenopathy or thyromegaly. |
| LUNGS: | Clear. |
| HEART: | Regular rate and rhythm. No murmurs, rubs or gallops. |
| ABDOMEN: | Moderately tender and moderately distended in the lower abdomen. No hepatosplenomegaly. |
| RECTAL: | No masses. Firm stool. Negative for occult blood. |
| EXTREMITIES: | No cyanosis, clubbing or edema. |
| NEUROLOGIC: | Alert and oriented x 3. Grossly nonfocal. |

LABORATORY: 1/14/06, glucose 113, BUN 25, creatinine 1.3. The remainder of the CMP, amylase and lipase are within normal range. CBC within normal range.

## Case Study 37

**CONSULTATION**

Continued:

Abdominal series on 1/13/06 reveals possible partial small bowel obstruction and possible persistent pleural effusion.

IMPRESSION:
Lower abdominal pain and nausea possibly due to partial small bowel obstruction.
History of colon resection for cancer with elevated CEA of 23.1. Rule out recurrence of cancer.
Dilated common bile duct but normal liver enzymes and HIDA scan on recent admission suggesting no physiological obstruction.

PLAN:
Colonoscopy advised.
Repeat CEA.
Clear liquid diet.

## Case Study 37

### PROCEDURE NOTE

| | |
|---|---|
| Date of Procedure: | 1/15/06 |
| Preoperative Diagnoses: | Abdominal pain, nausea, vomiting, history of colon cancer |
| Postoperative Diagnoses: | Marked diverticulosis<br>Small internal hemorrhoid<br>Benign polyp |
| Surgeon: | Dr. David Clark |
| Procedure: | Colonoscopy with biopsy |

DESCRIPTION OF PROCEDURE:

Following IV sedation, the colonoscope was inserted into the rectum and advanced to the left colon and beyond to the splenic flexure and into the ascending colon and into the cecum. A five mm polyp at the level of previous anastomosis was removed with snare and additional biopsies were taken the sigmoid level. The patient tolerated the procedure well.

# Case Study 37

## Answer Sheet

| DIAGNOSES | ICD-9-CM CODES | | | | | |
|---|---|---|---|---|---|---|
| DX 1 | | | | . | | |
| DX 2 | | | | . | | |
| DX 3 | | | | . | | |
| DX 4 | | | | . | | |

| PROCEDURES | CPT CODES | | | | | MODIFIERS (If Applicable) | | |
|---|---|---|---|---|---|---|---|---|
| PR 1 | | | | | | - | | |
| PR 2 | | | | | | - | | |
| PR 3 | | | | | | - | | |
| PR 4 | | | | | | - | | |
| PR 5 | | | | | | - | | |
| PR 6 | | | | | | - | | |

# Case 38

## Office Visit

| | |
|---|---|
| Patient's Name: | Eunice Freeman |
| Date of Visit: | January 31, 2006 |
| Age: | 17 |
| Sex: | Female |
| Insurance: | Commercial |

## Case 38
## Office Visit

HISTORY OF PRESENT ILLNESS:
This is a first time visit for this 17 year old female who was referred to me from the Rosedale Hospital Emergency Room. The patient was seen in the Emergency Room on Sunday with neck and back discomfort due to an automobile accident. The patient was a restrained driver. The car received front-end damage that occurred at a moderate rate of speed. According to the Emergency Room report, there was no loss of consciousness. There is no evidence of hearing disorder, headaches, or blurry vision. No initial neurologic complaints. She is wearing a neck brace.

PAST MEDICAL HISTORY: Negative.

PHYSICAL EXAMINATION:

| | |
|---|---|
| Vital Signs: | Blood pressure: 120/70, Temp - normal. Pulse 68. Respiration 20. |
| General: | Well developed, well-nourished female in no acute distress, but has mild discomfort in the neck and lower back. |
| HEENT: | Pupils are equal and reactive. Fundoscopic is normal. Negative Battle sign. |
| Neck: | Mildly tender in the paracervical muscles, but no deformity is noted. No hematoma noted. |
| Back: | Lower back is minimally tender in the paralumbar muscles. |
| Chest: | The chest wall is nontender. |
| Lungs: | Clear bilaterally with no rales, rhonchi, or wheezes. |
| Abdomen: | Soft and nontender. |
| Extremities: | No clubbing, cyanosis, or edema. Range of motion is intact. |
| Neurological: | Cranial nerves II-XII are intact. Plantar reflexes are downward going bilaterally. |

MEDICAL DECISION:
Patient brought the x-rays taken in the Emergency Room and they were reviewed. C-Spine is unremarkable. Lumbosacral Spine shows evidence of transitional vertebral body with partial lumbarization of S1 with no evidence of acute fracture or subluxation.

IMPRESSION: Neck and lumbar back strain secondary to automobile accident.

She was given instructions for rest for the next 24 hours. Prescriptions for Darvocet N100 q.i.d., p.r.n. for pain and Robaxin 750 q.i.d. for spasms p.r.n.. She is to continue wearing the neck brace to help keep the neck area still. She is to follow up with me in one week.

| | |
|---|---|
| History: | Detailed |
| Examination: | Detailed |
| Medical Decision: | Low Complexity |

**Abswer Sheet**
**Case 38**

| DIAGNOSES | ICD-9-CM CODES | | | | | |
|---|---|---|---|---|---|---|
| DX 1 | | | | . | | |
| DX 2 | | | | . | | |
| DX 3 | | | | . | | |
| DX 4 | | | | . | | |

| PROCEDURES | CPT CODES | | | | | MODIFIERS (If Applicable) | | |
|---|---|---|---|---|---|---|---|---|
| PR 1 | | | | | | - | | |
| PR 2 | | | | | | - | | |
| PR 3 | | | | | | - | | |
| PR 4 | | | | | | - | | |
| PR 5 | | | | | | - | | |
| PR 6 | | | | | | - | | |

## Case 39

### Ambulatory Surgery

| | |
|---|---|
| Patient's Name: | Bonnie Bonn |
| Date of Visit: | January,6 2006 |
| Age: | 71 |
| Sex: | Female |
| Insurance: | Medicare |

## Case 39

### History and Physical

DATE OF ADMISSION: 1-6-06

HISTORY OF PRESENT ILLNESS:
This 71-year-old female has been hospitalized for symptomatic slow heart rate and atrial fibrillation. Echocardiogram did show evidence of enlarged left atrium and the patient has been taking Coumadin for over a month. Patient has also had electrocardioversion and was converted but did revert back into atrial fibrillation. Patient is not taking any medications for the complete AV block and it was felt and a pacemaker would be the best option for the patient.

PAST MEDICAL HISTORY: Noncontributory.

SOCIAL HISTORY: Patient is married and lives with her husband. Does not smoke or drink alcohol.

PHYSICAL EXAMINATION:

| | |
|---|---|
| General: | Well developed female in no acute distress. |
| HEENT: | Within normal limits. |
| Heart: | Complete AV block and atrial fibrillation. No murmurs noted. |
| Lungs: | Clear to auscultation. |
| Abdomen: | Soft, non-tender. |
| Urogenital: | Denies problems. |
| Extremities: | Within normal limits. Full range of motion. |

PLAN: Patient will be admitted for a pacemaker.

## Case 39

### Operative Report

Date of Operation: 1-6-06

Preoperative Diagnosis: AV Block
Atrial Fibrillation

Postoperative Diagnosis: AV Block
Atrial Fibrillation

Operation: Implantation of a DDIR mode-switching permanent pacemaker and leads.

Surgeon: David Pool, MD

Assistant: Kent David, MD

Anesthesia: Versed 6 mg IV, 1% Xylocaine

PROCEDURE:
The left infraclavicular area was prepped and draped in the usual manner and the area was infused with 1% Xylocaine. A pacemaker pocket was formed with the incision made parallel to the left clavicle, down to the level of the prepectoral fascia. The left subclavian vein was then easily cannulated and over a guide wire, two 7-French sheaths were passed without difficulty. Through these sheaths, a Medtronic model lead was fastened to the right ventricular apex and fixed into position. Through the other sheath, a Medtronic model lead was passed to the right atrial appendage and fixed into position. After adequate endocardiac anchoring was assured threshold testing on these leads were performed.

R waves measured 10.2 mV. Ventricular capture occurred down to an amplitude of 0.4 volts, and a pulse width of 0.5 msec, measuring a current of 0.7 MA. The 5-volt resistance was measured at 707 ohms. On the atrial lead, atrial fibrillation waves measured 1.5 to 3.8 mV. Atrial impedance measured 536 ohms. We could not test capture due to the presence of the atrial fibrillation. Once in these positions, the leads were anchored using the anchoring sleeves with two 2-Ethibond sutures, then a purse string suture was placed around the leads to prevent back bleeding.

The patient tolerated the procedure well without any complications.

## Case 39

**Progress Note:**

The patient was admitted for a permanent pacemaker for a complete AV block and atrial fibrillation. The patient was taken to the Operating Room where a pacemaker was inserted. No complications from the procedure were noted. The patient is to be discharged when discharge criteria has been met and will follow up in my office in a week.

**Physician Orders:**

Routine vital signs
Place on cardiac monitor until discharge
Diet as tolerated
Up with assistance
IVD5RL@83 cc/hr. Change to heparin lock with flush when tolerating p.o. fluids well
M.S. 4-10 mg IM for severe pain q 3-4 hr. p.r.n.
Discharge when patient is stable.

**Answer Sheet**
**Case 39**

| DIAGNOSES | ICD-9-CM CODES | | | | | |
|---|---|---|---|---|---|---|
| DX 1 | | | | . | | |
| DX 2 | | | | . | | |
| DX 3 | | | | . | | |
| DX 4 | | | | . | | |

| PROCEDURES | CPT CODES | | | | | MODIFIERS (If Applicable) | | |
|---|---|---|---|---|---|---|---|---|
| PR 1 | | | | | | - | | |
| PR 2 | | | | | | - | | |
| PR 3 | | | | | | - | | |
| PR 4 | | | | | | - | | |
| PR 5 | | | | | | - | | |
| PR 6 | | | | | | - | | |

## Case 40
**Ambulatory Care**
**Face Sheet**

| | |
|---|---|
| Date of Admission: | 1-16-06 |
| Date of Discharge: | 1-16-06 |
| Age: | 46 |
| Sex: | Female |
| ADMITTING DIAGNOSIS: | Nasal obstruction |
| DISCHARGE DIAGNOSES: | 1. Bilateral hypertrophic turbinates<br>2. Nasoseptal spur |
| PROCEDURE: | Functional internal nasal reconstruction |
| DISPOSITION: | Home |

## Case 40
## History and Physical

DATE OF ADMISSION: 1-16-06

ADMITTING DIAGNOSIS: Nasal obstruction

HISTORY OF PRESENT ILLNESS:
This patient has been complaining of nasal obstruction for several months. She also had a left nasal polyp and a Caldwell Luc done many years ago. She has been given antihistamines and decongestants, but have not rectified her condition.

PAST MEDICAL HISTORY:
Caldwell Luc many years ago. No other significant problems.

ALLERGIES: None.

MEDICATIONS: Antihistamine and decongestant

SOCIAL HISTORY:
Patient smokes 1/2 pack per day; alcohol - social. Hobbies include gardening, reading, and sailing.

PHYSICAL EXAMINATION:

| | |
|---|---|
| General: | Well developed, well nourished female in no acute distress. |
| HEENT: | Head is normocephalic. She has a spur on the right in the inferior turbinates bilaterally, which are obstructed and hypertrophic. |
| Chest: | Clear to auscultation and percussion. |
| Heart: | Normal rhythm. |
| Abdomen: | Negative. |
| Neurological: | Normal. |
| Extremities: | Normal. |

PLAN:
The patient will be admitted to one day surgery for functional intranasal surgery for bilateral hypertrophic turbinates and nasoseptal spur.

## Case 40
## Operative Report

Date of Operation: 1-16-06

Preoperative Diagnoses:
1. Bilateral hypertrophic turbinates
2. Nasoseptal spur

Postoperative Diagnoses: Same

Operation: Functional internal nasal reconstruction

Surgeon: Carlos Earl, III., MD

Anesthesia: General

Anesthesiologist: C.V. Wilkinson, MD

Estimated Blood Loss: Less than 500 cc.

Complications: None

PROCEDURE:
The patient was taken to the surgical suite and prepped and draped in the usual fashion. General anesthesia was given, both nasal cavities were packed and the anterior aspect of the septum and both inferior turbinates were infiltrated with 1% Xylocaine with 1:40,000 epinephrine solution.

The nose was inspected and the patient was found to have a septal spur on the right side which was obstructing her nasal passages. Both interior turbinates were hypertrophic.

An incision was made along the caudal end of the septum and was carried down to the perichondrium and dissected posteriorly and inferiorly. The second incision was then made 1.5 cm beyond the first one, and the mucoperichondrium on the opposite side was dissected posteriorly and inferiorly. The septal cartilage was not detached from the maxillary crest and the nasal process of the palatine bone on that side was removed. The vomer was fractured and left intact.

With the obstructing cartilaginous and bony portion corrected, the septal mucosa was placed back and was closed. A left inferior turbinoplasty was then carried out making an incision from the anterior superior aspect down to the anterior inferior. The turbinate bone was dissected medially and laterally and was removed. The nasal cavity was packed and attention was turned to the other side, where an incision was made and the turbinate bone was dissected medially and posteriorly. Some of the bone was removed.

Bilateral nasal splints were placed and bilateral nasal packing was placed inferiorly. The patient was transferred to the recovery room in satisfactory condition. No apparent complications noted.

## Case 40

**Progress Notes:**

01/16/06: Patient was taken to the operating room for functional internal nasal reconstruction. Patient tolerated the procedure well. Nasal packs are in place. No apparent complication from the surgery or anesthesia is noted. Patient will be discharged when stable and is to follow up in my office tomorrow.

---

**Orders:**

1. Standard postoperative orders.
2. Discharge patient from Recovery Room when stable.
3. Vital signs q 15 minutes x 4; then q 30 x 2; then q 1 hr until discharge.
4. Urinary catherization x 1 if patient unable to void.
5. Start on soft diet.
6. Check nasal packings prior to leaving for excessive bleeding.
7. Discharge when patient is stable.

**Case 40**
**Answer Sheet**

| DIAGNOSES | ICD-9-CM CODES | | | | | |
|---|---|---|---|---|---|---|
| DX 1 | | | | . | | |
| DX 2 | | | | . | | |
| DX 3 | | | | . | | |
| DX 4 | | | | . | | |

| PROCEDURES | CPT CODES | | | | | MODIFIERS (If Applicable) | | |
|---|---|---|---|---|---|---|---|---|
| PR 1 | | | | | | - | | |
| PR 2 | | | | | | - | | |
| PR 3 | | | | | | - | | |
| PR 4 | | | | | | - | | |
| PR 5 | | | | | | - | | |
| PR 6 | | | | | | - | | |

**Case 41**
**Ambulatory Surgery**
**Face Sheet**

| | |
|---|---|
| Patient's Name: | Bill Penn |
| Date of Visit: | January-19-06 |
| Age: | 40 |
| Sex: | Male |
| Insurance: | Commercial |

**Case 41**
**Ambulatory Surgery**
**History and Physical**

DATE OF ADMISSION: 01-19-06

CHIEF COMPLAINT: Left elbow pain.

HISTORY OF PRESENT ILLNESS:
The patient has been complaining of left elbow pain for approximately 6 months. MRI was positive for torn ulnar collateral ligament. Patient underwent left ulnar collateral ligament repair approximately 5 months ago. The patient has sharp pain in the elbow with ulnar nerve palsy. He denies feeling a pop in the elbow.

Allergies: None.
Medications: None.
Past surgical history: Left ulnar collateral ligament reconstruction.

PHYSICAL EXAMINATION:
General: Vital signs are within normal limits.
HEENT: Extraocular movements are intact.
Chest: Clear to auscultation bilaterally without any crackles or wheezes.
Extremities: Tender over the medial aspect of the elbow. Hitchhiker's test is positive. He has decreased sensation along the 5th finger and on the 4th finger, he is intact to light touch on the radial border. On the ulnar border, 2-point discrimination is intermittent.

PLAN: Patient will be admitted to local hospital for ulnar nerve transposition.

## Case 41

### Ambulatory Surgery
### Operative Report

| | |
|---|---|
| DATE OF OPERATION: | 01-19-06 |
| PREOPERATIVE DIAGNOSIS: | Left ulnar nerve entrapment |
| POSTOPERATIVE DIAGNOSIS: | Left ulnar nerve entrapment |
| PROCEDURE: | Ulnar nerve transposition |
| SURGEON: | Rodney Verne, MD |
| ASSISTANT: | V.G. Smith, MD |

PROCEDURE:
The patient was taken to the Operating Room where general anesthesia was administered without complications. The left arm was prepped and draped in the usual sterile manner.

The previous incision was used and dissected down. The medial cutaneous nerve was identified, protected and retracted out of harm's way. The ulnar nerve was identified proximally and the intermuscular septum was excised. The ulnar nerve was followed into the cubital tunnel and the tunnel was released. The ulnar nerve was encased in scar tissue over the ulnar collateral ligament reconstruction. We released the cubital tunnel and released the scar tissue at the ulnar nerve. We then followed the ulnar nerve down as it split into the flexor carpi ulnaris two heads. The FCU is split at four fingerbreadths below the joint surface. The inferior fascia is clearly identified and released. The superior fascia from the FCU is clearly identified and released.

The nerve was then stimulated and it did respond to the stimulation distal to the area of compression. Satisfied with the decompression, we then went to transport the nerve. The ulnar nerve is elevated using vessel loops and transposed anteriorly. After the nerve is transposed, a limited neurolysis is performed. After the neurolysis the fascicles are clearly seen to be intact. A sling is made using the fascia of the flexor wad and is tied down with ample room for the ulnar nerve.

The nerve is irrigated and the tourniquet is released. No excessive bleeding is noted. The subcu is closed with #1 and 2-0. Dry sterile dressing is applied. The patient tolerated the procedure well.

<u>**Case 41**</u>

**Ambulatory Surgery**
**Progress Notes and Orders**

## PROGRESS NOTES

Patient admitted to the ambulatory surgery suite where the patient was prepped for surgery. The patient received education on the procedure to be performed.

Taken to the operating room where an ulnar nerve transposition was performed and the patient returned to the room in satisfactory condition.

## ORDERS

Ancef 1 gm IVPB one hour pre-op
NPO
Clip, prep, scrub op site with Betadine Solution

<u>Postoperative Orders</u>

Discharge when alert and stable.
IV orders per anesthesia.
Tylenol #3 q 4 h p.r.n.

**<u>Case 41</u>**
**Answer Sheet**

| DIAGNOSES | ICD-9-CM CODES | | | | | |
|---|---|---|---|---|---|---|
| DX 1 | | | | . | | |
| DX 2 | | | | . | | |
| DX 3 | | | | . | | |
| DX 4 | | | | . | | |

| PROCEDURES | CPT CODES | | | | | MODIFIERS (If Applicable) | | |
|---|---|---|---|---|---|---|---|---|
| PR 1 | | | | | | - | | |
| PR 2 | | | | | | - | | |
| PR 3 | | | | | | - | | |
| PR 4 | | | | | | - | | |
| PR 5 | | | | | | - | | |
| PR 6 | | | | | | - | | |

## Case 42

### Ambulatory Surgery
### Face Sheet

| | |
|---|---|
| Patient's Name: | Georgia Phillips |
| Date of Visit: | January 17, 2006 |
| Age: | 52 |
| Sex: | Female |
| Insurance: | Medicare |

## Case 42

### History and Physical

DATE OF ADMISSION: 1-17-06

HISTORY OF PRESENT ILLNESS:
The patient has a history of bilateral breast cysts and in a follow-up mammogram a mass was discovered in the left breast. Patient also has some dimpling in the area demonstrated on mammogram in the upper outer quadrant.

PAST MEDICAL HISTORY: Patient has a history of mitral valve prolapse.

ALLERGIES: Demerol and Biaxin.

MEDICATIONS: V-Tabs prior to procedures for her mitral valve prolapse.

PHYSICAL EXAMINATION:

| | |
|---|---|
| Vital signs: | BP 146/80; Respiration's 17; Pulse 77; Temperature 99.0 |
| Skin: | Warm and dry. |
| Eyes: | The pupils are equal, round, reactive to light and accommodation. Sclera is clear. |
| Neck: | Supple. No masses, scars or bruits. |
| Lungs: | Clear to auscultation and percussion. |
| Heart: | Normal sinus rhythm. No murmurs or gallops. |
| Breasts: | Breasts are symmetrical. There is an area of slight skin retraction on the upper outer quadrant of the left breast. There is some thickness in the area. No other masses felt. No axillary lymphadenopathy. |
| Extremities: | Good distal pulses. |

Plan:
Patient will be brought to the Ambulatory Surgical Center for a left breast biopsy.

## Case 42

### Operative Report

| | |
|---|---|
| Date of Operation: | 1-17-06 |
| Preoperative Diagnosis: | Left Breast Mass |
| Postoperative Diagnosis: | Infiltrating ductal cell carcinoma left breast. |
| Procedure Performed: | Excision of left breast mass. |
| Surgeon: | Cheryl Bottom, MD |
| Assistant: | Jon Actor, MD |

PROCEDURE:
The patient was placed on the supine position where anesthesia was administered. The left breast was prepped and draped in the usual sterile manner.

A transverse incision was made along the mass and was carried down through the skin and subcutaneous tissue. A firm mass was identified and was sharply excised from the surrounding breast tissue. Bleeding was controlled with electrocautery.

The wound was closed using interrupted sutures of 3-0 Vicryl for the deep layer. The subcutaneous tissue was closed with interrupted suture of 3-0 Vicryl and the skin was closed 4-0 Monocryl. Dressing was applied. The patient tolerated the procedure well.

## Case 42

### Pathology Report

| | |
|---|---|
| Date: | 1-17-06 |
| Physician: | Cheryl Bottom, MD |
| Preoperative Diagnosis: | Left Breast Mass |
| Surgical Procedure: | Excision left breast mass |
| Postoperative Diagnosis: | Infiltrating ductal carcinoma |
| Specimen(s): | Left Breast Mass |

GROSS:

Received directly from the operating room is a 4 x 3 x 3 cm. ovoid pink-tam to yellow fibroadipose tissue which is firm.

GROSS AND MICROSCOPIC EXAMINATION:

Excisional biopsy of left breast:

Invasive ductal carcinoma, 2.3 cm, histologic grade 2, nuclear grade 2, mitotic grade 1. Focal lymph vascular space invasion is noted.
Diffuse fibrocystic changes are also noted.

## Case 42

**PROGRESS NOTES:**

Patient has a left breast mass and was taken to the Operating Room where an excisional biopsy of the mass was performed. Pathology report is pending final determination, but preliminary report is ductal carcinoma.

**PHYSICIAN ORDERS:**

Pre-Operative Orders

Diet: NPO
Consent to read: Excision left breast mass
Ancef 1 gm IV before surgery

Post-Operative Orders

Vicodin 1 q6h p.r.n.
Liquids as tolerated
Discharge when criteria is met

## Case 42

### Answer Sheet

| DIAGNOSES | ICD-9-CM CODES | | | | | |
|---|---|---|---|---|---|---|
| DX 1 | | | | . | | |
| DX 2 | | | | . | | |
| DX 3 | | | | . | | |
| DX 4 | | | | . | | |

| PROCEDURES | CPT CODES | | | | | MODIFIERS (If Applicable) | | |
|---|---|---|---|---|---|---|---|---|
| PR 1 | | | | | | - | | |
| PR 2 | | | | | | - | | |
| PR 3 | | | | | | - | | |
| PR 4 | | | | | | - | | |
| PR 5 | | | | | | - | | |
| PR 6 | | | | | | - | | |

# CCS-P Case Study

## *Answer Key*

## CCS-P Case Study Answer KEY

### Case 1

| Diagnoses | ICD-9-CM Codes | | | | | |
|---|---|---|---|---|---|---|
| DX 1 Palpitations | 7 | 8 | 5 | . | 1 | |
| DX 2 Fatigue | 7 | 8 | 0 | . | 7 | 9 |
| DX 3 Thirst | 7 | 8 | 3 | . | 5 | |
| DX 4 | | | | . | | |

| Procedures | CPT Codes | | | | | Modifier (If Applicable) | | |
|---|---|---|---|---|---|---|---|---|
| PR1 Office Visit | 9 | 9 | 2 | 1 | 3 | - | | |
| PR2 EKG - 12 Lead | 9 | 3 | 0 | 0 | 0 | - | | |
| PR3 Blood Draw | 3 | 6 | 4 | 1 | 5 | - | | |
| PR4 Lab Handling | 9 | 9 | 0 | 0 | 0 | - | | |
| PR5 | | | | | | - | | |
| PR6 | | | | | | - | | |

### Case 2

| Diagnoses | ICD-9-CM Codes | | | | | |
|---|---|---|---|---|---|---|
| DX 1 Giardiasis | 0 | 0 | 7 | . | 1 | |
| DX 2 Dehydration (volume depletion) | 2 | 7 | 6 | . | 5 | 1 |
| DX 3 Arthropathy, unspecified site | 7 | 1 | 6 | . | 9 | 0 |
| DX 4 | | | | . | | |

| Procedures | CPT Codes | | | | | Modifier (If Applicable) | | |
|---|---|---|---|---|---|---|---|---|
| PR1 ER Visit | 9 | 9 | 2 | 8 | 2 | - | | |
| PR2 | | | | | | - | | |
| PR3 | | | | | | - | | |
| PR4 | | | | | | - | | |
| PR5 | | | | | | - | | |
| PR6 | | | | | | - | | |

## CCS-P Case Study Answer KEY

### Case 3

| Diagnoses | ICD-9-CM Codes | | | | | |
|---|---|---|---|---|---|---|
| DX 1 Vaginal Discharge | 6 | 2 | 3 | . | 5 | |
| DX 2 Vaginal Bleeding | 6 | 2 | 3 | . | 8 | |
| DX 3 | | | | . | | |
| DX 4 | | | | . | | |

| Procedures | CPT Codes | | | | | Modifier (If Applicable) | | |
|---|---|---|---|---|---|---|---|---|
| PR1 Office visit | 9 | 9 | 2 | 0 | 3 | - | | |
| PR2 Lab handling | 9 | 9 | 0 | 0 | 0 | - | | |
| PR3 | | | | | | - | | |
| PR4 | | | | | | - | | |
| PR5 | | | | | | - | | |
| PR6 | | | | | | - | | |

### Case 4

| Diagnoses | ICD-9-CM Codes | | | | | |
|---|---|---|---|---|---|---|
| DX 1 Odontalgia | 5 | 2 | 5 | . | 9 | |
| DX 2 Dental Caries | 5 | 2 | 1 | . | 0 | 0 |
| DX 3 | | | | . | | |
| DX 4 | | | | . | | |

| Procedures | CPT Codes | | | | | Modifier (If Applicable) | | |
|---|---|---|---|---|---|---|---|---|
| PR1 Office Visit | 9 | 9 | 2 | 1 | 2 | - | | |
| PR2 | | | | | | - | | |
| PR3 | | | | | | - | | |
| PR4 | | | | | | - | | |
| PR5 | | | | | | - | | |
| PR6 | | | | | | - | | |

## CCS-P Case Study Answer KEY

### Case 5

| Diagnoses | ICD-9-CM Codes | | | | | |
|---|---|---|---|---|---|---|
| DX 1 Open wound of hand except finger(s) alone, without mention of complication | 8 | 8 | 2 | . | 0 | |
| DX 2 | | | | . | | |
| DX 3 | | | | . | | |
| DX 4 | | | | . | | |

-

| Procedures | CPT Codes | | | | | Modifier (If Applicable) | | |
|---|---|---|---|---|---|---|---|---|
| PR1 Office Visit, New Patinet | 9 | 9 | 2 | 0 | 2 | - | | |
| PR2 Office Visit - Emergency Basis | 9 | 9 | 0 | 5 | 8 | - | | |
| PR3 Suture Hand 1.5 cm | 1 | 2 | 0 | 0 | 1 | - | | |
| PR4 | | | | | | - | | |
| PR5 | | | | | | - | | |
| PR6 | | | | | | - | | |

### Case 6

| Diagnoses | ICD-9-CM Codes | | | | | |
|---|---|---|---|---|---|---|
| DX 1 Streptococcal Tonsillitis | 0 | 3 | 4 | . | 0 | |
| DX 2 | | | | . | | |
| DX 3 | | | | . | | |
| DX 4 | | | | . | | |

| Procedures | CPT Codes | | | | | Modifier (If Applicable) | | |
|---|---|---|---|---|---|---|---|---|
| PR1 Office Visit | 9 | 9 | 2 | 1 | 3 | - | | |
| PR2 Culture handling | 9 | 9 | 0 | 0 | 0 | - | | |
| PR3 | | | | | | - | | |
| PR4 | | | | | | - | | |
| PR5 | | | | | | - | | |
| PR6 | | | | | | - | | |

## CCS-P Case Study Answer KEY

### Case 7

| Diagnoses | ICD-9-CM Codes | | | | | |
|---|---|---|---|---|---|---|
| DX 1 Acute Pyelonephritis | 5 | 9 | 0 | . | 1 | 0 |
| DX 2 E. Coli | 0 | 4 | 1 | . | 4 | |
| DX 3 | | | | . | | |
| DX 4 | | | | . | | |

| Procedures | CPT Codes | | | | | Modifier (If Applicable) | | |
|---|---|---|---|---|---|---|---|---|
| PR1 Emergency Room Visit | 9 | 9 | 2 | 8 | 2 | - | | |
| PR2 | | | | | | - | | |
| PR3 | | | | | | - | | |
| PR4 | | | | | | - | | |
| PR5 | | | | | | - | | |
| PR6 | | | | | | - | | |

### Case 8

| Diagnoses | ICD-9-CM Codes | | | | | |
|---|---|---|---|---|---|---|
| DX 1 Unspecified viral infection | 0 | 7 | 9 | . | 9 | 9 |
| DX 2 Headaches | 7 | 8 | 4 | . | 0 | |
| DX 3 | | | | . | | |
| DX 4 | | | | . | | |

| Procedures | CPT Codes | | | | | Modifier (If Applicable) | | |
|---|---|---|---|---|---|---|---|---|
| PR1 Emergency Room Visit | 9 | 9 | 2 | 8 | 3 | - | | |
| PR2 | | | | | | - | | |
| PR3 | | | | | | - | | |
| PR4 | | | | | | - | | |
| PR5 | | | | | | - | | |
| PR6 | | | | | | - | | |

## CCS-P Case Study Answer KEY

### Case 9

| Diagnoses | ICD-9-CM Codes | | | | | |
|---|---|---|---|---|---|---|
| DX 1 Abdominal Pain Unspecified site | 7 | 8 | 9 | . | 0 | 0 |
| DX 2 Hematemesis | 5 | 7 | 8 | . | 0 | |
| DX 3 Nausea with Vomiting | 7 | 8 | 7 | . | 0 | 1 |
| DX 4 | | | | . | | |

| Procedures | CPT Codes | | | | | | Modifier (If Applicable) | |
|---|---|---|---|---|---|---|---|---|
| PR1 Emergency Room Visit | 9 | 9 | 2 | 8 | 3 | - | | |
| PR2 | | | | | | - | | |
| PR3 | | | | | | - | | |
| PR4 | | | | | | - | | |
| PR5 | | | | | | - | | |
| PR6 | | | | | | - | | |

### Case 10

| Diagnoses | ICD-9-CM Codes | | | | | |
|---|---|---|---|---|---|---|
| DX 1 Carpal Tunnel Syndrome | 3 | 5 | 4 | . | 0 | |
| DX 2 Type I Diabetes Mellitus, without mention of complication, not stated as uncontrolled | 2 | 5 | 0 | . | 0 | 1 |
| DX 3 Essential hypertension, unspecified | 4 | 0 | 1 | . | 9 | |
| DX 4 | | | | . | | |

| Procedures | CPT Codes | | | | | | Modifier (If Applicable) | |
|---|---|---|---|---|---|---|---|---|
| PR1 Decompression of Medial Nerve, Left Wrist | 6 | 4 | 7 | 2 | 1 | - | L | T |
| PR2 Operating Microscope | 6 | 9 | 9 | 9 | 0 | - | | |
| PR3 | | | | | | - | | |
| PR4 | | | | | | - | | |
| PR5 | | | | | | - | | |
| PR6 | | | | | | - | | |

## CCS-P Case Study Answer KEY

### Case 11

| Diagnoses | ICD-9-CM Codes | | | | | |
|---|---|---|---|---|---|---|
| DX 1 Candidal esophagitis | 1 | 1 | 2 | . | 8 | 4 |
| DX 2 Acute gastritis | 5 | 3 | 5 | . | 0 | 0 |
| DX 3 Atrophic gastritis | 5 | 3 | 5 | . | 1 | 0 |
| DX 4 Helicobacter pylori (bacterial infection) | 0 | 4 | 1 | . | 8 | 6 |

| Procedures | CPT Codes | | | | | Modifier (If Applicable) | | |
|---|---|---|---|---|---|---|---|---|
| PR1 Esophagogastroduodenoscopy with biopsies | 4 | 3 | 2 | 3 | 9 | - | | |
| PR2 | | | | | | - | | |
| PR3 | | | | | | - | | |
| PR4 | | | | | | - | | |
| PR5 | | | | | | - | | |
| PR6 | | | | | | - | | |

### Case 12

| Diagnoses | ICD-9-CM Codes | | | | | |
|---|---|---|---|---|---|---|
| DX 1 Epistaxis | 7 | 8 | 4 | . | 7 | |
| DX 2 | | | | . | | |
| DX 3 | | | | . | | |
| DX 4 | | | | . | | |

| Procedures | CPT Codes | | | | | Modifier (If Applicable) | | |
|---|---|---|---|---|---|---|---|---|
| PR1 Emergency Room Visit | 9 | 9 | 2 | 8 | 1 | - | | |
| PR2 | | | | | | - | | |
| PR3 | | | | | | - | | |
| PR4 | | | | | | - | | |
| PR5 | | | | | | - | | |
| PR6 | | | | | | - | | |

## CCS-P Case Study Answer KEY

### Case 13

| Diagnoses | ICD-9-CM Codes | | | | | |
|---|---|---|---|---|---|---|
| DX 1 CVA with paralysis | 4 | 3 | 8 | . | 2 | 0 |
| DX 2 Malnutrition | 2 | 6 | 3 | . | 9 | |
| DX 3 Weight Loss | 7 | 8 | 3 | . | 2 | 1 |
| DX 4 Psychosis | 2 | 9 | 8 | . | 9 | |

| Procedures | CPT Codes | | | | | Modifier (If Applicable) | | |
|---|---|---|---|---|---|---|---|---|
| PR1 Nursing Home Visit | 9 | 9 | 3 | 0 | 9 | - | | |
| PR2 | | | | | | - | | |
| PR3 | | | | | | - | | |
| PR4 | | | | | | - | | |
| PR5 | | | | | | - | | |
| PR6 | | | | | | - | | |

### Case 14

| Diagnoses | ICD-9-CM Codes | | | | | |
|---|---|---|---|---|---|---|
| DX 1 Other cellulitis and abscess, foot, except toes | 6 | 8 | 2 | . | 7 | |
| DX 2 Type I Diabetes Mellitus, without mention of complication, not stated as uncontrolled | 2 | 5 | 0 | . | 0 | 1 |
| DX 3 | | | | . | | |
| DX 4 | | | | . | | |

| Procedures | CPT Codes | | | | | Modifier (If Applicable) | | |
|---|---|---|---|---|---|---|---|---|
| PR1 Nursing Home Visit | 9 | 9 | 3 | 1 | 1 | - | | |
| PR2 | | | | | | - | | |
| PR3 | | | | | | - | | |
| PR4 | | | | | | - | | |
| PR5 | | | | | | - | | |
| PR6 | | | | | | - | | |

## CCS-P Case Study Answer KEY

### Case 15

| Diagnoses | ICD-9-CM Codes | | | | | |
|---|---|---|---|---|---|---|
| DX 1 Pregnancy with Clostridium Infection | 6 | 4 | 7 | . | 8 | 3 |
| DX 2 Pregnancy with Thyroid Goiter | 6 | 4 | 8 | . | 1 | 3 |
| DX 3 Pregnancy with Dehydration | 6 | 4 | 8 | . | 9 | 3 |
| DX 4 Enteritis due to Clostridium Difficile | 0 | 0 | 8 | . | 4 | 5 |

| Procedures | CPT Codes | | | | | Modifier (If Applicable) | | |
|---|---|---|---|---|---|---|---|---|
| PR1 Colonoscopy with biopsy | 4 | 5 | 3 | 8 | 0 | - | | |
| PR2 | | | | | | - | | |
| PR3 | | | | | | - | | |
| PR4 | | | | | | - | | |
| PR5 | | | | | | - | | |
| PR6 | | | | | | - | | |

### Case 16

| Diagnoses | ICD-9-CM Codes | | | | | |
|---|---|---|---|---|---|---|
| DX 1 Acute Cholecystitis with Cholelithiasis | 5 | 7 | 4 | . | 0 | 0 |
| DX 2 Chronic Cholecystitis with Cholelithiasis | 5 | 7 | 4 | . | 1 | 0 |
| DX 3 Urinary Tract Infection | 5 | 9 | 9 | . | 0 | |
| DX 4 E. Coli | 0 | 4 | 1 | . | 4 | |

| Procedures | CPT Codes | | | | | Modifier (If Applicable) | | |
|---|---|---|---|---|---|---|---|---|
| PR1 Laparoscopic Cholecystectomy | 4 | 7 | 5 | 6 | 2 | - | | |
| PR2 | | | | | | - | | |
| PR3 | | | | | | - | | |
| PR4 | | | | | | - | | |
| PR5 | | | | | | - | | |
| PR6 | | | | | | - | | |

## CCS-P Case Study Answer KEY

### Case 17

| Diagnoses | ICD-9-CM Codes | | | | | |
|---|---|---|---|---|---|---|
| DX 1 Septicemia NOS | 0 | 3 | 8 | . | 9 | |
| DX 2 SIRS | 9 | 9 | 5 | | 9 | 3 |
| DX 3 Non-Hodgkin's Lymphoma | 2 | 0 | 2 | . | 8 | 0 |
| DX 4 Infection following infusion | 9 | 9 | 9 | . | 3 | |
| Additional diagnosis: Dehydration | 2 | 7 | 6 | . | 5 | 1 |

| Procedures | CPT Codes | | | | | | Modifier (If Applicable) | |
|---|---|---|---|---|---|---|---|---|
| PR1 | | | | | | - | | |
| PR2 | | | | | | - | | |
| PR3 | | | | | | - | | |
| PR4 | | | | | | - | | |
| PR5 | | | | | | - | | |
| PR6 | | | | | | - | | |

### Case 18

| Diagnoses | ICD-9-CM Codes | | | | | |
|---|---|---|---|---|---|---|
| DX 1 Malignant Neoplasm Right Upper Lobe, Lung | 1 | 6 | 2 | . | 3 | |
| DX 2 Secondary Malignancy Thoracic Lymph Notes | 1 | 9 | 6 | . | 1 | |
| DX 3 Asthmatic Bronchitis | 4 | 9 | 3 | . | 2 | 0 |
| DX 4 Depression, NOS | 3 | 1 | 1 | . | | |

| Procedures | CPT Codes | | | | | | Modifier (If Applicable) | |
|---|---|---|---|---|---|---|---|---|
| PR1 Lobectomy of Right Upper Lobe | 3 | 2 | 4 | 8 | 0 | - | R | T |
| PR2 Flexible bronchoscopy | 3 | 1 | 6 | 2 | 2 | - | 5 | 9 |
| PR3 Biopsy lymph nodes | 3 | 8 | 5 | 0 | 0 | - | 5 | 1 |
| PR4 | | | | | | - | | |
| PR5 | | | | | | - | | |
| PR6 | | | | | | - | | |

## CCS-P Case Study Answer KEY

### Case 19

| Diagnoses | ICD-9-CM Codes | | | | | |
|---|---|---|---|---|---|---|
| DX 1 Displacement of cervical intervertebral disc without myelopathy | 7 | 2 | 2 | . | 0 | |
| DX 2 Dsypnea & Respiratory abnormality | 7 | 8 | 6 | . | 0 | 9 |
| DX 3 Opiates/Narcotics causing adverse effects in theurapeutic use | E9 | 3 | 5 | . | 2 | |
| DX 4 Asthma, unspecified type, without acute exacerbation | 4 | 9 | 3 | . | 9 | 0 |

Note: Although E codes are not coded on the examination, we wanted to remind you that all adverse effects must be coded as per coding guidelines. This may be covered in the multiple choice question in the first part of the examination also.

| Procedures | CPT Codes | | | | | | Modifier (If Applicable) | |
|---|---|---|---|---|---|---|---|---|
| PR Arthrodesis, anterior, including diskectomy; cervical | 2 | 2 | 5 | 5 | 4 | - | | |
| PR2 Laminotomy, foraminotomy and/or excision of herniated intervertebral disk, cervical | 6 | 3 | 0 | 2 | 0 | - | 5 | 1 |
| PR3 | | | | | | - | | |
| PR4 | | | | | | - | | |
| PR5 | | | | | | - | | |
| PR6 | | | | | | | | |

### Case 20

| Diagnoses | ICD-9-CM Codes | | | | | |
|---|---|---|---|---|---|---|
| DX 1 Threatened premature labor, antepartum | 6 | 4 | 4 | . | 0 | 3 |
| DX 2 | | | | . | | |
| DX 3 | | | | . | | |
| DX 4 | | | | . | | |

| Procedures | CPT Codes | | | | | | Modifier (If ARlicable) | |
|---|---|---|---|---|---|---|---|---|
| PR1 Initial hospital care | 9 | 9 | 2 | 2 | 1 | - | | |
| PR2 | | | | | | - | | |
| PR3 | | | | | | - | | |
| PR4 | | | | | | - | | |
| PR5 | | | | | | - | | |
| PR6 | | | | | | - | | |

## Case Study Answer Key

### Case 21

| Diagnoses | ICD-9-CM Codes | | | | | |
|---|---|---|---|---|---|---|
| DX 1 Diabetes mellitus, Type I with peripheral circulatory disorder, uncontrolled | 2 | 5 | 0 | . | 7 | 3 |
| DX 2 Diabetic ulcer | 7 | 0 | 7 | . | 1 | 4 |
| DX 3 Chronic renal failure | 5 | 8 | 5 | . | 9 | |
| DX 4 Pneumonia | 4 | 8 | 6 | . | | |

| Procedures | CPT Codes | | | | | Modifier (If Applicable) | | |
|---|---|---|---|---|---|---|---|---|
| PR 1 Excisional debridement | 1 | 1 | 0 | 4 | 2 | - | | |
| PR 2 | | | | | | - | | |
| PR 3 | | | | | | - | | |
| PR 4 | | | | | | - | | |
| PR 5 | | | | | | - | | |
| PR 6 | | | | | | - | | |

### Case 22

| Diagnoses | ICD-9-CM Codes | | | | | |
|---|---|---|---|---|---|---|
| DX 1 Coronary artery disease, native artery | 4 | 1 | 4 | . | 0 | 1 |
| DX 2 Unstable angina | 4 | 1 | 1 | . | 1 | |
| DX 3 Atrial fibrillation | 4 | 2 | 7 | . | 3 | 1 |
| DX 4 Second degree atrioventricular block | 4 | 2 | 6 | . | 1 | 3 |

| Procedures | CPT Codes | | | | | Modifier (If Applicable) | | |
|---|---|---|---|---|---|---|---|---|
| PR 1 PTCA, single vessel | 9 | 2 | 9 | 8 | 2 | - | R | C |
| PR 2 Left heart catheterization | 9 | 3 | 5 | 1 | 0 | - | | |
| PR 3 Coronary angiography | 9 | 3 | 5 | 4 | 5 | - | | |
| PR 4 Supervision and interpretation | 9 | 3 | 5 | 5 | 6 | - | | |
| PR 5 | | | | | | - | | |
| PR 6 | | | | | | - | | |

## Case Study Answer Key

### Case 23

| Diagnoses | ICD-9-CM Codes | | | | | |
|---|---|---|---|---|---|---|
| DX 1 Diverticulitis of colon | 5 | 6 | 2 | . | 1 | 1 |
| DX 2 Perforation of sigmoid | 5 | 6 | 9 | . | 8 | 3 |
| DX 3 Post-operative atelectasis | 9 | 9 | 7 | . | 3 | |
| DX 4 Atelectasis | 5 | 1 | 8 | . | 0 | |

| Procedures | CPT Codes | | | | | | Modifier (If Applicable) | |
|---|---|---|---|---|---|---|---|---|
| PR 1 Hartman's Procedure | 4 | 4 | 1 | 4 | 3 | - | | |
| PR 2 Lysis of adhesion | 4 | 4 | 0 | 0 | 5 | - | 2 | 2 |
| PR 3 Flexible sigmoidoscopy | 4 | 5 | 3 | 7 | 8 | - | 2 | 2 |
| PR4 Small bowel resection | 4 | 4 | 1 | 2 | 0 | - | 5 | 1 |
| | | | | | | - | | |
| | | | | | | - | | |

### Case 24

| Diagnoses | ICD-9-CM Codes | | | | | |
|---|---|---|---|---|---|---|
| DX 1 Ovarian cyst | 6 | 2 | 0 | . | 2 | |
| DX 2 Uterine adhesions | 6 | 2 | 1 | . | 5 | |
| DX 3 Acute blood loss anemia | 2 | 8 | 5 | . | 1 | |
| DX 4 Urinary tract infection | 5 | 9 | 9 | . | 0 | |
| Additional Diagnosis: Postoperative blood loss | 9 | 9 | 8 | . | 1 | 1 |

| Procedures | CPT Codes | | | | | | Modifier (If Applicable) | |
|---|---|---|---|---|---|---|---|---|
| PR 1 Hysterectomy with bilateral salpingo-oophorectomy | 5 | 8 | 1 | 5 | 0 | - | | |
| PR 2 | | | | | | - | | |
| PR 3 | | | | | | - | | |
| PR 4 | | | | | | - | | |
| PR 5 | | | | | | - | | |
| PR 6 | | | | | | - | | |

## Case Study Answer Key

### Case 25

| Diagnoses | ICD-9-CM Codes | | | | | |
|---|---|---|---|---|---|---|
| DX 1 Sprain, wrist, unspecified site | 8 | 4 | 2 | . | 0 | 0 |
| DX 2 | | | | . | | |
| DX 3 | | | | . | | |
| DX 4 | | | | . | | |

| Procedures | CPT Codes | | | | | | Modifier (If Applicable) | |
|---|---|---|---|---|---|---|---|---|
| PR 1 Application of short arm splint (forearm to hand) | 2 | 9 | 1 | 2 | 5 | - | L | T |
| PR 2 Evaluation and Management (ER visit) | 9 | 9 | 2 | 8 | 2 | - | | |
| PR 3 X-ray, wrist, two views | 7 | 3 | 1 | 0 | 0 | - | L | T |
| PR 4 | | | | | | - | | |
| PR 5 | | | | | | - | | |
| PR 6 | | | | | | - | | |

### Case 26

| Diagnoses | ICD-9-CM Codes | | | | | |
|---|---|---|---|---|---|---|
| DX 1 Pneumonia | 4 | 8 | 6 | . | | |
| DX 2 Asthmatic bronchitis | 4 | 9 | 3 | . | 9 | 2 |
| DX 3 Supraventricular tachycardia | 4 | 2 | 7 | . | 8 | 9 |
| DX 4 Chronic diastolic heart failure | 4 | 2 | 8 | . | 3 | 2 |
| Additional Diagnosis: Osteoarthritis | 7 | 1 | 5 | | 9 | 0 |

| Procedures | CPT Codes | | | | | | Modifier (If Applicable) | |
|---|---|---|---|---|---|---|---|---|
| PR 1 Initial hospital visit | 9 | 9 | 2 | 2 | 2 | - | | |
| PR 2 | | | | | | - | | |
| PR 3 | | | | | | - | | |
| PR 4 | | | | | | - | | |
| PR 5 | | | | | | - | | |
| PR 6 | | | | | | - | | |

## Case Study Answer Key

### Case 27

| Diagnoses | ICD-9-CM Codes | | | | | |
|---|---|---|---|---|---|---|
| DX 1 Pulmonary embolism | 4 | 1 | 5 | . | 1 | 9 |
| DX 2 Chronic systolic congestive heart failure | 4 | 2 | 8 | . | 2 | 2 |
| DX 3 Hypertensive renal disease with failure | 4 | 0 | 3 | . | 9 | 1 |
| DX 4 Type I diabetes | 2 | 5 | 0 | . | 6 | 1 |
| Additional Diagnosis: Diabetic neuropathy | 3 | 5 | 7 | | 2 | |

Both the diabetes code and the diabetic neuropathy must be used.

| Procedures | CPT Codes | | | | | - | Modifier (If Applicable) | |
|---|---|---|---|---|---|---|---|---|
| PR1 | | | | | | - | | |
| PR2 | | | | | | - | | |
| PR3 | | | | | | - | | |
| PR4 | | | | | | - | | |
| PR5 | | | | | | - | | |
| PR6 | | | | | | - | | |

### Case 28

| Diagnoses | ICD-9-CM Codes | | | | | |
|---|---|---|---|---|---|---|
| DX 1 Abnormality in fetal heart rate or rhythm, delivered, with or without mention of antepartum complication | 6 | 5 | 9 | . | 7 | 1 |
| DX 2 Pre-eclampsia or eclampsia superimposed on pre-existing hypertension, delivered, with or without mention of antepartum complication | 6 | 4 | 2 | . | 7 | 1 |
| DX 3 Malignant hypertension | 4 | 0 | 1 | . | 0 | |
| DX 4 Poor fetal growth, affecting management of mother, delivered, with or without mention of antepartum complication | 6 | 5 | 6 | . | 5 | 1 |
| Additional Diagnoses: Mother with single liveborn | V | 2 | 7 | . | 0 | |
| Early onset of delivery | 6 | 4 | 4 | . | 2 | 1 |
| Elderly Multigravida | 6 | 5 | 9 | . | 6 | 1 |

| Procedures | CPT Codes | | | | | - | Modifier (If Applicable) | |
|---|---|---|---|---|---|---|---|---|
| PR 1 Low cervical Cesarean section | 5 | 9 | 5 | 1 | 0 | - | | |
| PR 2 | | | | | | - | | |
| PR 3 | | | | | | - | | |
| PR 4 | | | | | | - | | |
| PR 5 | | | | | | - | | |
| PR 6 | | | | | | - | | |

## Case Study Answer Key

### Case 29

| Diagnoses | ICD-9-CM Codes | | | | | |
|---|---|---|---|---|---|---|
| DX 1 Cellulitis and abscess of leg, except foot | 6 | 8 | 2 | . | 6 | |
| DX 2 Acute exacerbation of chronic obstructive pulmonary disease | 4 | 9 | 1 | . | 2 | 1 |
| DX 3 Congestive heart failure, unspecified | 4 | 2 | 8 | . | 0 | |
| DX 4 Coronary atherosclerosis, of native coronary artery | 4 | 1 | 4 | . | 0 | 1 |

| Procedures | CPT Codes | | | | | Modifier (If Applicable) | | |
|---|---|---|---|---|---|---|---|---|
| PR1 | | | | | | - | | |
| PR2 | | | | | | - | | |
| PR3 | | | | | | - | | |
| PR4 | | | | | | - | | |
| PR5 | | | | | | - | | |
| PR6 | | | | | | - | | |

### Case 30

| Diagnoses | ICD-9-CM Codes | | | | | |
|---|---|---|---|---|---|---|
| DX 1 Acute respiratory failure | 5 | 1 | 8 | . | 8 | 1 |
| DX 2 Streptococcus pneumonia | 4 | 8 | 1 | . | | |
| DX 3 Atrial fibrillation | 4 | 2 | 7 | . | 3 | 1 |
| DX 4 Alcoholic liver cirrhosis | 5 | 7 | 1 | . | 2 | |

| Procedures | CPT Codes | | | | | Modifier (If Applicable) | | |
|---|---|---|---|---|---|---|---|---|
| PR1 | | | | | | - | | |
| PR2 | | | | | | - | | |
| PR3 | | | | | | - | | |
| PR4 | | | | | | - | | |
| PR5 | | | | | | - | | |
| PR6 | | | | | | - | | |

## Case Study Answer Key

### Case 31

| Diagnoses | ICD-9-CM Codes | | | | | |
|---|---|---|---|---|---|---|
| DX 1 Unspecified cerebral artery occlusion with cerebral infarction | 4 | 3 | 4 | . | 9 | 1 |
| DX 2 Urinary tract infection | 5 | 9 | 9 | . | 0 | |
| DX 3 Atrial fibrillation | 4 | 2 | 7 | . | 3 | 1 |
| DX 4 Mitral regurgitation, not otherwise specified | 4 | 2 | 4 | . | 0 | |
| Additional Diagnoses: | | | | | | |
| E. Coli (bacterial infection) | 0 | 4 | 1 | . | 4 | |
| Hyposmolality and/or hyponatremia | 2 | 7 | 6 | . | 1 | |
| Occlusion and stenosis fo precerebral arteries, multiple and bilateral, without mention of cerebral infarction | 4 | 3 | 3 | . | 3 | 0 |
| Hemiplegia, unspecified, affecting unspecified site | 3 | 4 | 2 | . | 9 | 0 |
| Essentiial Hypertension, unspecified | 4 | 0 | 1 | . | 9 | |
| Aphasia | 7 | 8 | 4 | . | 3 | |

| Procedures | CPT Codes | | | | | Modifier (If Applicable) | |
|---|---|---|---|---|---|---|---|
| PR1 | | | | | - | | |
| PR2 | | | | | - | | |
| PR3 | | | | | - | | |
| PR4 | | | | | - | | |
| PR5 | | | | | - | | |
| PR6 | | | | | - | | |

### Case 32

| Diagnoses | ICD-9-CM Codes | | | | | |
|---|---|---|---|---|---|---|
| DX 1 Syncope, and collapse | 7 | 8 | 0 | . | 2 | |
| DX 2 Malnourishment of mild degree | 2 | 6 | 3 | . | 1 | |
| DX 3 Congestive heart failure, unspecified | 4 | 2 | 8 | . | 0 | |
| DX 4 Chronic obstructive pulmonary disease | 4 | 9 | 6 | . | | |

| Procedures | CPT Codes | | | | | Modifier (If Applicable) | |
|---|---|---|---|---|---|---|---|
| PR1 | | | | | - | | |
| PR2 | | | | | - | | |
| PR3 | | | | | - | | |
| PR4 | | | | | - | | |
| PR5 | | | | | - | | |
| PR6 | | | | | - | | |

## Case Study Answer Key

### Case 33

| Diagnoses | ICD-9-CM Codes | | | | | |
|---|---|---|---|---|---|---|
| DX 1 Closed fracture of neck of femur, intertrochanteric section | 8 | 2 | 0 | . | 2 | 1 |
| DX 2 Decubitus ulcer, buttock | 7 | 0 | 7 | . | 0 | 5 |
| DX 3 Chronic obstructive pulmonary disease | 4 | 9 | 6 | . | | |
| DX 4 Alcoholic liver cirrhosis | 5 | 7 | 1 | . | 2 | |
| Additional Diagnosis: Decubitus ulcer, coccyx | 7 | 0 | 7 | | 0 | 9 |

| Procedures | CPT Codes | | | | | - | Modifier (If Applicable) | |
|---|---|---|---|---|---|---|---|---|
| PR1 Closed reduction, internal fixation femur | 2 | 7 | 2 | 4 | 4 | - | | |
| PR2 Paracentesis | 4 | 9 | 0 | 8 | 0 | - | 5 | 1 |
| PR3 Transfusions, whole blood | 3 | 6 | 4 | 3 | 0 | - | 5 | 1 |
| PR4 | | | | | | - | | |
| PR5 | | | | | | - | | |
| PR6 | | | | | | - | | |

### Case 34

| Diagnoses | ICD-9-CM Codes | | | | | |
|---|---|---|---|---|---|---|
| DX 1 Poisoning, Haldol | 9 | 6 | 9 | . | 2 | |
| DX 2 Accidental poisoning | E8 | 5 | 3 | . | 1 | |
| DX 3 Poisoning Xanax | 9 | 6 | 9 | . | 4 | |
| DX 4 Accidental poisoning | E8 | 5 | 3 | . | 2 | |
| Additional Diagnoses:<br>Depressive disorder<br>Type II diabetes<br>Peripheral vascular disease, unspecified | <br>3<br>2<br>4 | <br>1<br>5<br>4 | <br>1<br>0<br>3 | <br>.<br>.<br>. | <br><br>0<br>9 | <br><br>0<br> |

| Procedures | CPT Codes | | | | | - | Modifier (If Applicable) | |
|---|---|---|---|---|---|---|---|---|
| PR1 | | | | | | - | | |
| PR2 | | | | | | - | | |
| PR3 | | | | | | - | | |
| PR4 | | | | | | - | | |
| PR5 | | | | | | - | | |
| PR6 | | | | | | - | | |

**Case Study Answer Key**

## Case 35

| Diagnoses | ICD-9-CM Codes | | | | | |
|---|---|---|---|---|---|---|
| DX 1 Acute bronchial asthma with exacerbation | 4 | 9 | 3 | . | 2 | 2 |
| DX 2 Acute tracheobronchitis | 4 | 6 | 6 | . | 0 | |
| DX 3 Hypertension | 4 | 0 | 1 | . | 9 | |
| DX 4 Hyperlipidemia | 2 | 7 | 2 | . | 4 | |

| Procedures | CPT Codes | | | | | Modifier (If Applicable) | | |
|---|---|---|---|---|---|---|---|---|
| PR1 Bronchoscopy with closed (endoscopic) biopsy | 3 | 1 | 6 | 2 | 5 | - | | |
| PR2 Bronchial lavage | 3 | 1 | 6 | 2 | 4 | - | 5 | 1 |
| PR3 | | | | | | - | | |
| PR4 | | | | | | - | | |
| PR5 | | | | | | - | | |
| PR6 | | | | | | - | | |

## Case 36

| Diagnoses | ICD-9-CM Codes | | | | | |
|---|---|---|---|---|---|---|
| DX 1 Herniated lumbar intervertebral disc, without myelopathy | 7 | 2 | 2 | . | 1 | 0 |
| DX 2 | | | | . | | |
| DX 3 | | | | . | | |
| DX 4 | | | | . | | |

| Procedures | CPT Codes | | | | | Modifier (If Applicable) | | |
|---|---|---|---|---|---|---|---|---|
| PR1 Excision intervertebral disc | 6 | 3 | 0 | 3 | 0 | - | | |
| PR2 Operating microscope | 6 | 9 | 9 | 9 | 0 | - | | |
| PR3 | | | | | | - | | |
| PR4 | | | | | | - | | |
| PR5 | | | | | | - | | |
| PR6 | | | | | | - | | |

## Case Study Answer Key

### Case 37

| Diagnoses | ICD-9-CM Codes | | | | | |
|---|---|---|---|---|---|---|
| DX 1 Diverticulosis of colon | 5 | 6 | 2 | . | 1 | 0 |
| DX 2 Benign neoplasm colon | 2 | 1 | 1 | . | 3 | |
| DX 3 Personal history of colon cancer | V | 1 | 0 | . | 0 | 5 |
| DX 4 Osteoporosis, unspecified | 7 | 3 | 3 | . | 0 | 0 |

| Procedures | CPT Codes | | | | | Modifier (If Applicable) | | |
|---|---|---|---|---|---|---|---|---|
| PR1 Colonoscopy with removal of polyp | 4 | 5 | 3 | 8 | 5 | - | | |
| PR2 Colonoscopy with closed (endoscopic) biopsy of large intestine | 4 | 5 | 3 | 8 | 0 | - | 5 | 1 |
| PR3 | | | | | | - | | |
| PR4 | | | | | | - | | |
| PR5 | | | | | | - | | |
| PR6 | | | | | | - | | |

### Case 38

| Diagnoses | ICD-9-CM Codes | | | | | |
|---|---|---|---|---|---|---|
| DX 1 Neck strain | 8 | 4 | 7 | . | 0 | |
| DX 2 Lumbar back strain | 8 | 4 | 7 | . | 2 | |
| DX 3 | | | | . | | |
| DX 4 | | | | . | | |

| Procedures | CPT Codes | | | | | Modifier If Appicable) | | |
|---|---|---|---|---|---|---|---|---|
| PR 1 Office Visit | 9 | 9 | 2 | 0 | 3 | - | | |
| PR 2 | | | | | | - | | |
| PR 3 | | | | | | - | | |
| PR 4 | | | | | | - | | |
| PR 5 | | | | | | - | | |
| PR 6 | | | | | | - | | |

**Case Study Answer Key**

**Case 39**

| Diagnoses | ICD-9-CM Codes | | | | | |
|---|---|---|---|---|---|---|
| DX 1 Atroventricular block,complete | 4 | 2 | 6 | . | 0 | |
| DX 2 Atrial Fibrillation | 4 | 2 | 7 | . | 3 | 1 |
| DX 3 | | | | . | | |
| DX 4 | | | | . | | |

| Procedures | CPT Codes | | | | | | Modifier (If Applicable) | |
|---|---|---|---|---|---|---|---|---|
| PR 1 Insertion Pacemaker with dual leads | 3 | 3 | 2 | 0 | 8 | - | | |
| PR 2 | | | | | | - | | |
| PR 3 | | | | | | - | | |
| PR 4 | | | | | | - | | |
| PR 5 | | | | | | - | | |
| PR 6 | | | | | | - | | |

**Case 40**

| Diagnoses | ICD-9-CM Codes | | | | | |
|---|---|---|---|---|---|---|
| DX 1 Hypertrophy of nasal turbinates | 4 | 7 | 8 | . | 0 | |
| DX 2 Other diseases fo nasal cavity and sinuses | 4 | 7 | 8 | . | 1 | |
| DX 3 | | | | . | | |
| DX 4 | | | | . | | |

| Procedures | CPT Codes | | | | | | Modifier (If Applicable) | |
|---|---|---|---|---|---|---|---|---|
| PR 1 Nasal reconstruction | 3 | 0 | 5 | 2 | 0 | - | | |
| PR 2 Excision nasoseptal spur | 3 | 0 | 1 | 3 | 0 | - | 5 | 1 |
| PR 3 | | | | | | - | | |
| PR 4 | | | | | | - | | |
| PR 5 | | | | | | - | | |
| PR 6 | | | | | | - | | |

## Case Study Answer Key

## Case 41

| Diagnoses | ICD-9-CM Codes | | | | | |
|---|---|---|---|---|---|---|
| DX 1 Ulnar Nerve Entrapment | 3 | 5 | 4 | . | 2 | |
| DX 2 | | | | . | | |
| DX 3 | | | | . | | |
| DX 4 | | | | . | | |

| Procedures | CPT Codes | | | | | - | Modifier (If Applicable) | |
|---|---|---|---|---|---|---|---|---|
| PR 1 Ulnar nerve transposition | 6 | 4 | 7 | 1 | 8 | - | | |
| PR 2 | | | | | | - | | |
| PR 3 | | | | | | - | | |
| PR 4 | | | | | | - | | |
| PR 5 | | | | | | - | | |
| PR 6 | | | | | | - | | |

## Part II Section B Case 42

| Diagnoses | ICD-9-CM Codes | | | | | |
|---|---|---|---|---|---|---|
| DX 1 Malignant neoplasm of female breast, upper-outer quadrant | 1 | 7 | 4 | . | 4 | |
| DX 2 Mitral valve disorder | 4 | 2 | 4 | . | 0 | |
| DX 3 | | | | . | | |
| DX 4 | | | | . | | |

| Procedures | CPT Codes | | | | | - | Modifier (If Applicable) | |
|---|---|---|---|---|---|---|---|---|
| PR 1 Excision breast mass | 1 | 9 | 1 | 2 | 0 | - | | |
| PR 2 | | | | | | - | | |
| PR 3 | | | | | | - | | |
| PR 4 | | | | | | - | | |
| PR 5 | | | | | | - | | |
| PR 6 | | | | | | - | | |

# CCS-P

# Mock Examination

## CCS-P MOCK EXAMINATION

This mock examination follows the format and time constraints that are used in the certification examination. The mock examination contains 60 multiple choice questions and a total of 16 coding cases.

The CCS-P examination is in a computer-based format. Carefully read your Candidate Handbook for the CCS-P examination and continue to monitor AHIMA's web site to look for updated information on the examination format.

**Part I** of the CCS-P Mock Examination has 60 multiple choice questions. You are allotted 90 minutes to complete them. The timing you are striving for is about one minute to one and one half (1 to 1½) minutes per question so that you will be able to complete this part of the "real" examination in the 90 minutes allotted. These questions cover physician-based competencies, ICD-9-CM diagnostic coding, and CPT and HCPCS (Level II) procedural coding across all specialties.

**Part II** of the examination consists of 16 coding case testing your knowledge of ICD-9-CM Volumes 1-2 and HCPCS Level II (including E&M and all sections of CPT Coding). You are allowed 150 minutes to complete Part II of the examination. That gives you between 9 and 9 and one half (9 to 9½) minutes per case.

By following the time constraints on this mock examination, we hope you will get an idea of how much time you need and how much time is allotted for both the multiple choice questions and the cases to code on the CCS-P Certification Examination.

Scoring in the CCS-P Examination:

Points will be deducted for incorrect and/or unnecessary codes
Points will be deducted for any inappropriate codes
Sequencing the diagnoses and operative codes are not considered in scoring

Do not use facility, regional or insurance standards that differ from the procedures given for the examination.

NOTE: See procedures for coding that appear in Appendix B of the AHIMA Candidate Handbook for the CCS-P Examination.

## CCS-P MOCK EXAMINATION MULTIPLE CHOICE QUESTIONS

1. The Medicare Physician Fee Schedule is comprised of what three elements?
   A) relative value units for each service, geographic adjustment factor and national conversion factor
   B) national conversion factor, RBRVS and relative value units for each service
   C) geographic adjustment factor, RBRVS and relative value units for each service
   D) none of the above

2. Medicare patient had a benign lesion measuring 0.5 cm removed from his back at his physician's office.

| | |
|---|---|
| 11400 | Excision, benign lesion including margins, except skin tag (unless listed elsewhere), trunk, arms or legs, excised diameter 0.5 cm or less |
| 11600 | Excision, malignant lesion including margins, trunk, arms, or legs; excised diameter 0.5 cm or less |
| 17000 | Destruction (eg. laser surgery, electrosurgery, cryosurgery, chemosurgery, surgical curettement) all benign or pre-malignant lesions (eg. actinic keratosis) other than skin tags or cutaneous vascular proliferative lesions; first lesion |
| -57 | Decision for Surgery |

   A) 17000
   B) 11400-57
   C) 11600-57
   D) 11400

3. Patient was seen in the Emergency Department with lacerations on the left arm. Two lacerations, one 7 cm. and one 9 cm. were closed with layered sutures.

| | |
|---|---|
| 12002 | Simple repair of superficial wounds of scalp, neck, axillae, external genitalia, trunk and/or extremities (including hands and feet); 2.6 cm to 7.5 cm |
| 12004 | Simple repair of superficial wounds of scalp, neck, axillae, external genitalia, trunk and/or extremities (including hands and feet); 7.6 cm to 12.5 cm |
| 12035 | Layer closure of wounds of scalp, axillae, trunk and/or extremities (excluding hands and feet); 12.6 cm to 20.0 cm |
| 12045 | Layer closure of wounds of neck, hands, feet and/or external genitalia; 12.6 cm to 20.0 cm |

   A) 12045
   B) 12035
   C) 12002, 12004
   D) 12004

4. ORIF of the 4th digit on the left foot would be identified by what code?

| | |
|---|---|
| 28505 | Open treatment of fracture great toe, phalanx or phalanges, with or without internal or external fixation |
| 28510 | Closed treatment of fracture, phalanx or phalanges, other than great toe; without manipulation, each |
| 28525 | Open treatment of fracture, phalanx or phalanges, other than great toe, with or without internal or external fixation, each |
| T3 | Left foot, fourth digit |
| T8 | Right foot, fourth digit |
| -51 | Multiple Procedures |

A) 28505-51
B) 28525-T3
C) 28510-T8
D) 28525-51

5. A 10-year old boy who is an established patient comes into the office complaining of itching on his right leg. The itching has occurred for two days after a walk in the woods behind his home. The itching is constant. The skin of the right leg has patchy red areas with vesicular eruptions. Left leg appears to be normal. Vitals: BP 120/70, Pulse 77, Respirations 16. Skin: Right leg with patchy red areas with vesicular eruptions. Lungs: Clear. Heart: Regular rhythm. Gait is normal. Musculoskeletal System: Normal except for the right leg. Physician prescribes a topical corticosteroid cream. Diagnosis: Poison Oak. Patient is to return to office in two days for follow-up.

| | |
|---|---|
| 691.8 | Atopic dermatitis |
| 692.3 | Contact dermatitis and other eczema due to drugs and medicines in contact with skin |
| 692.6 | Contact dermatitis and other eczema due to plants (except food) |
| 99202 | New patient office visit for expanded problem focused history and exam, straightforward medical decision making |
| 99212 | Established patient office visit for a problem focused history and exam, straightforward medical decision making |
| 99213 | Established patient office visit for expanded problem focused history and exam, low medical decision making |

A) 691.8, 99202
B) 692.3, 99213
C) 692.6, 99213
D) 692.6, 99212

6. A patient who has been diagnosed with hypertension visits her physician on a monthly basis. The nurse conducted the blood pressure check under the physician's supervision. Code the office visit.
   A) 99211 Office or other outpatient visit for the evaluation and management of an established patient that may not require the presence of a physician
   B) 99201 Office or other outpatient visit for the evaluation and management of a new patient, problem focused history and examination, straightforward medical decision making
   C) 99203 Office or other outpatient visit for the evaluation and management of a new patient, detailed history and examination, low complexity medical decision making
   D) 99212 Office or other outpatient visit for the evaluation and management of an established patient, problem focused history and examination, straightforward medical decision making

7. Patient returns to the primary physician's office with a sore throat and headache. Physician checks the throat, neck area, ears and sinuses and concludes that the patient has the flu. Perform evaluation and management coding.
   A) 99203 Office or other outpatient visit for the evaluation and management of a new patient, detailed history and examination, low complexity medical decision making
   B) 99211 Office or other outpatient visit for the evaluation and management of an established patient, that may not require the presence of a physician
   C) 99201 Office or other outpatient visit for the evaluation and management of a new patient, problem focused history and examination, straightforward medical decision making
   D) 99212 Office or other outpatient visit for the evaluation and management of an established patient, problem focused history and examination, straightforward medical decision making

8. Patient is taken to the surgical suite and has a 5.0 cm x 3.0 cm lesion removed from the left thigh. Pathologist reports that it is squamous cell carcinoma. A split-thickness skin graft is obtained from the right thigh and placed over the defect.

| | |
|---|---|
| 11606 | Excision malignant lesion including margins, trunk, arms, or legs; excised diameter over 4.0 cm |
| 15000 | Surgical preparation or creation of recipient site by excision of open wounds burn eschar, or scar (including subcutaneous tissues) or incisional release of scar contracture first 100 sq. cm. |
| 15100 | Split thickness autograft, trunk, arms, legs; first 100 sq. cm. |
| 15220 | Full thickness graft, free, including direct closure of donor site, scalp, arms, and/or legs; 20 sq. cm or less |
| -51 | Multiple procedures |

   A) 11606, 15100-51
   B) 15220, 15000-51
   C) 15100, 15000-51
   D) 11606, 15220-51

9. Ambulatory Surgery patient has a laparoscopic ovarian cystectomy and hysteroscopy with D&C.

| | |
|---|---|
| 58555 | Hysteroscopy, diagnostic (separate procedure) |
| 58558 | Hysteroscopy, surgical; with sampling of endometrium and/or polypectomy, with or without D&C |
| 58661 | Laparoscopy, surgical; with removal of adnexal structures (partial or total oophorectomy and/or salpingectomy |
| 58662 | Laparoscopy, surgical; with fulguration or excision of lesions of the ovary, pelvic viscera, or peritoneal surface by any method |
| 58673 | Laparoscopy, surgical; with salpingostomy (salpingoneostomy) |
| -51 | Multiple procedures |

A) 58673, 58558-51
B) 58558, 58662-51
C) 58558, 58661-51
D) 58662, 58673-51

10. The physician performed a colonoscopy with biopsy of the ascending colon and a snare polypectomy of the descending colon. What would be coded?

| | |
|---|---|
| 45378 | Colonoscopy, flexible, proximal to splenic flexure; diagnostic |
| 45380 | Colonoscopy, flexible, proximal to splenic flexure; with biopsy, single or multiple |
| 45385 | Colonoscopy, flexible, proximal to splenic flexure; with removal of tumor(s), polyp(s), or other lesion(s) by snare technique |
| -51 | Multiple procedures |

A) 45378
B) 45385
C) 45380
D) 45380, 45385-51

11. Physician states in office visit notes that the lower end of the humerus has been fractured and that he performed an open reduction of the humerus with internal fixation. How would you code the fracture?
A) Code the fracture as an open fracture since the open reduction was performed
B) Code the fracture as an open fracture with the modifier -55 for postoperative management only
C) Code the fracture as a closed fracture since the coding rules state unless the physician states it as open; always assume the fracture to be closed
D) Code the fracture as an open fracture since the coding rules always assume the fractures to be open

12. Thrombectomy of venous bypass graft

| | |
|---|---|
| 35700 | Reoperation, femoral-popliteal or femoral (popliteal)-anterior tibial, posterior tibial, peroneal artery or other distal vessels, more than one month after original operation. (List separately in addition to code for primary procedure) |
| 35860 | Exploration for postoperative hemorrhage, thrombosis or infection; extremity |
| 35875 | Thrombectomy of arterial or venous graft (other than hemodialysis graft or fistula) |
| 35876 | Thrombectomy of arterial or venous graft (other than hemodialysis graft or fistula); with revision of arterial or venous graft |

A) 35875, 35700
B) 35860
C) 35875
D) 35876, 35700

13. A patient is admitted to the hospital for a suspected head injury following an automobile accident. In addition, the patient suffered a Colle's fracture, facial lacerations and contusions to both knees. The fracture was casted and the facial lacerations were sutured. Diagnostic studies were negative for head injury. The correct principal diagnosis for this case should be
A) Colle's fracture
B) facial lacerations
C) observation following other accident
D) contusions of the knee

14. Patient has a complex uroflowmetry with physician interpretation of the results.

| | |
|---|---|
| 51741 | Complex uroflowmetry (eg. calibrated electronic equipment) |
| -26 | professional component |
| -57 | decision for surgery |
| -77 | repeat procedure by another physician |
| -82 | assistant surgeon (when qualified resident surgeon not available) |

A) 51741-26
B) 51741-57
C) 51741-77
D) 51741-82

15. It would be appropriate to use code 69990 (use of operating microscope) as an additional procedure with which primary procedure listed below?
A) 49906 Free omental flap with microvascular anastomosis
B) 31561 Laryngoscopy, direct, operative, with arytenoidectomy; with operating microscope
C) 64905 Nerve pedicle transfer, first stage
D) 20955 Bone graft with microvascular anastomosis, fibula

16. Which of the following scenarios identifies a pathologic fracture?
    A) greenstick fracture secondary to a fall from a bed
    B) compression fracture of the skull after being hit with a baseball bat
    C) vertebral fracture with cord compression following car accident
    D) compression fracture of the vertebrae as a result of bone metastasis

17. Apply the proper modifier that indicates when a physician repaired a broken leg and a broken arm at the same operative session.

| | |
|---|---|
| 27766 | Open treatment of medial malleolus fracture, with or without with internal or external fixation |
| 25620 | Open treatment of distal radial fracture (eg. Colle or Smith type) or epiphyseal separation, with or without fracture of ulnar styloid, with or without internal or external fixation |
| -51 | Multiple procedure |
| -59 | Distinct procedural service |
| -62 | Two surgeons |
| -77 | Repeat procedure by another physician |
| -54 | Surgical care only |

A) 27766, 25620-59-51
B) 27766-62, 25620-62
C) 27666-77
D) 27766, 25620-54

18. Cesarean delivery with antepartum and postpartum care.

| | |
|---|---|
| 59400 | Routine obstetric care, including antepartum care, vaginal delivery, (with or without episiotomy and/or forceps) and postpartum care |
| 59510 | Routine obstetric care including antepartum care, cesarean delivery, and postpartum care |
| 59514 | Cesarean delivery only; |
| 59610 | Routine obstetric care including antepartum care, vaginal delivery (with or without episiotomy and/or forceps) and postpartum care, after previous cesarean delivery |

A) 59610
B) 59514
C) 59400
D) 59510

19. Assign the code(s) that would be appropriate if a patient is admitted to the hospital directly from the highest level physician's office visit.

| | |
|---|---|
| 99214 | Established patient, office visit, detailed history and exam, moderate complexity medical decision making |
| 99220 | Initial Observation care, comprehensive history and exam, high complexity medical decision making |
| 99223 | Initial hospital care, comprehensive history and exam, high complexity medical decision making |

A) 99214
B) 99220
C) 99223
D) 99214, 99223

20. Arthroscopic medial meniscectomy, minor synovectomy and articular cartilage debridement was performed. What is reported on the CMS (HCFA) 1500?
A) meniscectomy, medial and lateral
B) synovectomy, medial meniscectomy
C) medial meniscectomy, synovectomy, articular cartilage debridement
D) medial meniscectomy

21. Patient comes to the office for a cough. After the examination, the physician signs the patient out as having possible pneumonia. What do you code for this visit?

| | |
|---|---|
| 786.2 | Cough |
| 486 | Pneumonia, organism unspecified |

A) 486
B) not coded
C) 786.2
D) 786.2, 486

22. D&C for missed abortion, first trimester.

| | |
|---|---|
| 59820 | Treatment of missed abortion, completed surgically; first trimester |
| 59840 | Induced abortion, by dilation and curettage |
| 59850 | Induced abortion, by one or more intra-amniotic injections (amniocentesis-injections), including hospital admission and visits, delivery of fetus and secundines |
| 59855 | Induced abortion, by one or more vaginal suppositories (eg. Prostaglandin) with or without cervical dilation (eg. laminaria), including hospital admission and visits, delivery of fetus and secundines |

A) 59840
B) 59850
C) 59855
D) 59820

23. Chronic otitis media with bilateral myringotomy and tube insertion using local anesthesia.

| | |
|---|---|
| 381.00 | Acute nonsuppurative otitis media, unspecified |
| 381.05 | Acute allergic mucoid otitis media |
| 382.9 | Unspecified otitis media |
| 69400 | Eustachian tube inflation, transnasal; with catheterization |
| 69405 | Eustachian tube catheterization, transtympanic |
| 69420 | Myringotomy including aspiration and/or eustachian tube inflation |
| 69433 | Tympanostomy (requiring insertion of ventilating tube), local or topical anesthesia |
| -50 | Bilateral procedure |

A) 382.9, 69420-50
B) 382.9, 69433-50
C) 381.05, 69405-50
D) 381.00, 69400-50

24. Which of the following is coded as an adverse effect in ICD-9-CM?
A) tinnitus due to allergic reaction after administration of ear drops
B) mental retardation due to intracranial abscess
C) rejection of transplanted kidney
D) non-functioning pacemaker due to defective soldering

25. You are a biller for a radiology group and one of the radiologists submits for billing a 23 year old patient who has had an x-ray of the left forearm and right forearm.

| | |
|---|---|
| 73090 | Radiology examination; forearm, two views |
| 73221 | MRI, any joint of upper extremity; without contrast material(s) |
| -LT | Left side |
| -RT | Right side |
| -50 | Bilateral |
| -59 | Distinct procedure |

A) 73090-50
B) 73221
C) 73090-LT, 73090-RT
D) 73090, 73090-59

PLEASE
DO NOT
STAPLE
IN THIS
AREA

CARRIER

PICA

# HEALTH INSURANCE CLAIM FORM

PICA

## PATIENT AND INSURED INFORMATION

1. MEDICARE (Medicare #) ☐ MEDICAID (Medicaid #) ☐ CHAMPUS (Sponsor's SSN) ☐ CHAMPVA (VA File #) ☐ GROUP HEALTH PLAN (SSN or ID) ☐ FECA BLK LUNG (SSN) ☐ OTHER (ID) ☐

1a. INSURED'S I.D. NUMBER (FOR PROGRAM IN ITEM 1)

2. PATIENT'S NAME (Last Name, First Name, Middle Initial)

3. PATIENT'S BIRTH DATE MM | DD | YY SEX M ☐ F ☐

4. INSURED'S NAME (Last Name, First Name, Middle Initial)

5. PATIENT'S ADDRESS (No., Street)

6. PATIENT RELATIONSHIP TO INSURED Self ☐ Spouse ☐ Child ☐ Other ☐

7. INSURED'S ADDRESS (No., Street)

CITY STATE

8. PATIENT STATUS Single ☐ Married ☐ Other ☐ Employed ☐ Full-Time Student ☐ Part-Time Student ☐

CITY STATE

ZIP CODE TELEPHONE (Include Area Code) ( )

ZIP CODE TELEPHONE (INCLUDE AREA CODE) ( )

9. OTHER INSURED'S NAME (Last Name, First Name, Middle Initial)

10. IS PATIENT'S CONDITION RELATED TO:

11. INSURED'S POLICY GROUP OR FECA NUMBER

a. OTHER INSURED'S POLICY OR GROUP NUMBER

a. EMPLOYMENT? (CURRENT OR PREVIOUS) ☐ YES ☐ NO

a. INSURED'S DATE OF BIRTH MM | DD | YY SEX M ☐ F ☐

b. OTHER INSURED'S DATE OF BIRTH MM | DD | YY SEX M ☐ F ☐

b. AUTO ACCIDENT? PLACE (State) ☐ YES ☐ NO

b. EMPLOYER'S NAME OR SCHOOL NAME

c. EMPLOYER'S NAME OR SCHOOL NAME

c. OTHER ACCIDENT? ☐ YES ☐ NO

c. INSURANCE PLAN NAME OR PROGRAM NAME

d. INSURANCE PLAN NAME OR PROGRAM NAME

10d. RESERVED FOR LOCAL USE

d. IS THERE ANOTHER HEALTH BENEFIT PLAN? ☐ YES ☐ NO ***If yes***, return to and complete item 9 a-d.

**READ BACK OF FORM BEFORE COMPLETING & SIGNING THIS FORM.**

12. PATIENT'S OR AUTHORIZED PERSON'S SIGNATURE I authorize the release of any medical or other information necessary to process this claim. I also request payment of government benefits either to myself or to the party who accepts assignment below.

SIGNED ________________ DATE ________

13. INSURED'S OR AUTHORIZED PERSON'S SIGNATURE I authorize payment of medical benefits to the undersigned physician or supplier for services described below.

SIGNED ________________

## PHYSICIAN OR SUPPLIER INFORMATION

14. DATE OF CURRENT: MM | DD | YY ◀ ILLNESS (First symptom) OR INJURY (Accident) OR PREGNANCY(LMP)

15. IF PATIENT HAS HAD SAME OR SIMILAR ILLNESS. GIVE FIRST DATE MM | DD | YY

16. DATES PATIENT UNABLE TO WORK IN CURRENT OCCUPATION FROM MM | DD | YY TO MM | DD | YY

17. NAME OF REFERRING PHYSICIAN OR OTHER SOURCE

17a. I.D. NUMBER OF REFERRING PHYSICIAN

18. HOSPITALIZATION DATES RELATED TO CURRENT SERVICES FROM MM | DD | YY TO MM | DD | YY

19. RESERVED FOR LOCAL USE

20. OUTSIDE LAB? ☐ YES ☐ NO $ CHARGES

21. DIAGNOSIS OR NATURE OF ILLNESS OR INJURY. (RELATE ITEMS 1,2,3 OR 4 TO ITEM 24E BY LINE)

1. ___ . __
2. ___ . __
3. ___ . __
4. ___ . __

22. MEDICAID RESUBMISSION CODE ORIGINAL REF. NO.

23. PRIOR AUTHORIZATION NUMBER

| 24. A DATE(S) OF SERVICE From MM DD YY | To MM DD YY | B Place of Service | C Type of Service | D PROCEDURES, SERVICES, OR SUPPLIES (Explain Unusual Circumstances) CPT/HCPCS | MODIFIER | E DIAGNOSIS CODE | F $ CHARGES | G DAYS OR UNITS | H EPSDT Family Plan | I EMG | J COB | K RESERVED FOR LOCAL USE |
|---|---|---|---|---|---|---|---|---|---|---|---|---|
| 1 | | | | | | | | | | | | |
| 2 | | | | | | | | | | | | |
| 3 | | | | | | | | | | | | |
| 4 | | | | | | | | | | | | |
| 5 | | | | | | | | | | | | |
| 6 | | | | | | | | | | | | |

25. FEDERAL TAX I.D. NUMBER SSN EIN ☐ ☐

26. PATIENT'S ACCOUNT NO.

27. ACCEPT ASSIGNMENT? (For govt. claims, see back) ☐ YES ☐ NO

28. TOTAL CHARGE $

29. AMOUNT PAID $

30. BALANCE DUE $

31. SIGNATURE OF PHYSICIAN OR SUPPLIER INCLUDING DEGREES OR CREDENTIALS (I certify that the statements on the reverse apply to this bill and are made a part thereof.)

SIGNED DATE

32. NAME AND ADDRESS OF FACILITY WHERE SERVICES WERE RENDERED (If other than home or office)

33. PHYSICIAN'S, SUPPLIER'S BILLING NAME, ADDRESS, ZIP CODE & PHONE #

PIN# GRP#

(APPROVED BY AMA COUNCIL ON MEDICAL SERVICE 8/88)

***PLEASE PRINT OR TYPE***

APPROVED OMB-0938-0008 FORM CMS-1500 (12-90), FORM RRB-1500, APPROVED OMB-1215-0055 FORM OWCP-1500, APPROVED OMB-0720-0001 (CHAMPUS)

For questions 26-28 use the following scenario and the blank CMS 1500 form as a guide to answer the questions regarding Dr. Jones' billing.

> Patient was seen in the Emergency Room by Dr. Jones with complaints of right lower quadrant pain for 24 hours. No episodes of vomiting or diarrhea. Physical exam disclosed rebound tenderness over McBurney's point. Rest of history and examination was within normal limits. Lab was ordered and reported as: WBC 20.0, RBC 4.00, platelets 250,000. Patient was admitted to the hospital under my services with diagnosis of acute appendicitis. Later in the day the patient was taken to the operating room where a laparoscopic appendectomy was performed and the patient was discharged the next day to be seen in the office in one week.

Billing information:

| | |
|---|---|
| Level 3 hospital visit | $ 100 |
| Hospital discharge | $ 75 |
| Appendectomy | $1,500 |

Place of Service
11 Office
21 Inpatient Hospitalization
22 Outpatient - Hospital
23 Emergency Room

Type of Service
1 Medical
2 Surgical
5 Lab/Dialysis

| | |
|---|---|
| 99220 | Initial Observation day |
| 99223 | Initial hospital care |
| 99231 | Subsequent hospital care |
| 99238 | Hospital discharge day management |
| 99283 | Emergency Department visit |
| 44950 | Appendectomy |
| 44970 | Laparoscopy, surgical, appendectomy |
| 540.9 | Acute appendicitis without mention of peritonitis |
| 789.01 | Right lower quadrant abdominal pain |

26. What ICD-9-CM and CPT codes would you bill for the day of surgery?
    A) 789.02, 99231
    B) 789.02, 44950
    C) 540.9, 99231, 44970
    D) 540.9, 44970

27. What place of service code(s) would you use?
    A) 21
    B) 23
    C) 2
    D) 1, 22, 23

28. Using the CMS 1500 form, which sections of the form would you fill out if this was a Medicare patient with no secondary insurance?
    A) 1, 2, 3, 4, 5, 6, 7, 8, 9, 10, 11,12, 13,17, 21, 22, 24, 25, 26, 27, 28, 30, 31, 32, 33
    B) 1, 2, 3, 5, 6, 8, 10, 11, 12, 13, 14, 17, 18, 20, 21, 23, 24, 25, 27, 28, 30, 31, 32, 33
    C) 1, 2, 3, 8, 9, 10, 11, 12, 13, 17, 21, 24, 25, 28, 30, 31, 33
    D) 2, 3, 4, 5, 6, 8, 10, 13, 14, 15, 18, 20, 21, 24, 25, 30, 33

29. Dr. Absu removed two lesions from the thigh. One excision was made and the first lesion was 1.2 cm and the second lesion was 1.7 cm. Pathology Department reports both lesions to be non-malignant.

| | |
|---|---|
| 11401 | Excision, benign lesion including margins, except skin tag, trunk, arms, or legs; excised diameter 0.6 to 1.0 cm |
| 11402 | Excision, benign lesion including margins, except skin tag, trunk, arms, or legs; excised diameter 1.1 to 2.0 cm |
| 11403 | Excision, benign lesion including margins, except skin tag, trunk, arms, or legs; excised diameter 2.1 to 3.0 cm |
| -51 | Multiple procedures |
| -59 | Distinct procedural service |

A) 11401
B) 11402, 11402-51
C) 11402, 11403-59
D) 11403

30. Patient underwent a left heart cath via the femoral artery with left ventriculography with visualization of coronary arteries and mammary artery bypass. Saphenous vein graft to Diagonal patent. Saphenous vein graft - Right coronary artery patent. Left internal mammary artery to left anterior descending patent. Normal ventriculogram. Severe native coronary artery disease.

| | |
|---|---|
| 414.00 | Coronary atherosclerosis of unspecified type of vessel, native or graft |
| 414.01 | Coronary atherosclerosis of native coronary artery |
| 414.02 | Coronary atherosclerosis of autologous vein bypass graft |
| 414.03 | Coronary atherosclerosis of nonautologous biological bypass graft |
| 414.04 | Coronary atherosclerosis of artery bypass graft |
| 414.05 | Coronary atherosclerosis unspecified type of bypass graft |
| 93501 | Right heart catheterization |
| 93510 | Left heart catheterization, retrograde, from the brachial artery, axillary artery, or femoral artery; percutaneous |
| 93526 | Combined right heart catheterization and retrograde left heart catheterization |
| 93539 | Injection procedure during cardiac catheterization; for selective opacification of arterial conduits (eg. internal mammary), whether native or used for bypass |
| 93540 | Injection procedure during cardiac catheterization; for selective opacification of aortocoronary venous bypass grafts, one or more coronary arteries |
| 93543 | Injection procedure during cardiac catheterization; for selective left ventricular or left atrial angiography |
| 93544 | Injection procedure during cardiac catheterization; for aortography |
| 93545 | Injection procedure during cardiac catheterization; for selective coronary angiography (injection of radiopaque material may be by hand) |
| 93555 | Imaging supervision, interpretation and report for injection procedure(s) during cardiac catheterization; ventricular and/or atrial angiography |
| 93556 | Imaging supervision, interpretation and report for injection procedure(s) during cardiac catheterization; pulmonary angiography, aortography, and/or selective coronary angiography including venous bypass grafts and arterial conduits (whether native or used in bypass) |

A) 414.00, 414.05, 93526, 93540, 93543, 93544, 93545
B) 414.01, 414.04, 93510, 93539, 93543, 93545
C) 414.01, 93510, 93539, 93540, 93543, 93545; 93555; 93556
D) 414.04, 414.01, 93510

31. Codes from Chapter 11, Complications of Pregnancy, Childbirth, and the Puerperium should always be sequenced as primary tabulation when a pregnant female seeks medical attention, unless the physician documents that the pregnancy is not aggravating the condition or the condition is not aggravating the pregnancy.
   A) true
   B) false

32. Mitch was admitted directly from his physician's office for dehydration. Mitch has had gastroenteritis for several days that has resulted in dehydration and requires intravenous hydration. Mitch also has chronic renal failure and is at high risk for acute on chronic renal failure. Two days following admission Mitch develops acute renal failure. Mitch also has hypertension. What are the diagnosis codes?

| | |
|---|---|
| 276.50 | Volume depletion, unspecified |
| 276.51 | Dehydration |
| 401.90 | Essential Hypertension, unspecified |
| 403.91 | Hypertensive kidney disease, unspecified, with chronic kidney disease |
| 403.90 | Hypertensive kidney disease, unspecified without chronic kidney disease |
| 584.9 | Acute renal failure, unspecified |
| 585.9 | Chronic kidney disease, unspecified |
| 586 | Renal failure, unspecified |

   A) 584.9, 403.90, 276.51
   B) 276.51, 584.9, 403.91
   C) 403.91, 276.51
   D) 276.51, 586, 584.9, 401.9

33. The Alphabetic Index to Disease in the ICD-9-CM code book is ordered by main terms that usually identify
   A) surgical procedures
   B) disease conditions
   C) modifier descriptions
   D) anatomical sites

34. The type of anemia that is associated with an abnormal reduction of red blood cells due to the lack of bone marrow blood production is:
   A) Iron deficiency
   B) Pernicious
   C) Aplastic
   D) Blood loss

35. Aunt Elsie is brought to the hospital for increased confusion. She is subsequently diagnosed with Alzheimer's disease with dementia and cerebral atherosclerosis. Aunt Elsie is also treated for hypertension and hypothyroidism.

| | |
|---|---|
| 244.9 | Acquired hypothyroidism, unspecified |
| 294.10 | Dementia in conditions classified elsewhere without behavioral disturbance |
| 294.11 | Dementia in conditions classified elsewhere with behavioral disturbance |
| 331.0 | Alzheimer's disease |
| 401.9 | Essential Hypertension unspecified |
| 437.0 | Cerebral atherosclerosis |

A) 437.0, 294.10, 244.9, 401.9
B) 294.10, 401.9, 244.9
C) 331.0, 244.9, 401.9, 294.11
D) 331.0, 294.10, 437.0, 244.9, 401.9

36. Pathological fracture of the femur due to metastatic bone cancer. Patient has a history of lung cancer. Only the fracture was treated. The following conditions should be reported

| | |
|---|---|
| 162.9 | Primary malignancy lung and bronchus, unspecified |
| 198.5 | Secondary malignancy bone and bone marrow |
| 733.14 | Pathologic fracture neck of femur |
| 821.00 | Traumatic fracture femur unspecified part |
| V10.11 | Personal history of malignant neoplasm lung and bronchus |

A) 198.5; 733.14; V10.11
B) 733.14; 198.5; V10.11
C) 821.00; 198.5; V10.11
D) 821.00; 198.5; 162.9

37. In reviewing a medical record for coding purposes, the coder notes that the discharge summary has not yet been transcribed. In its absence, the best place to look for the patient's response to treatment and documentation of any complications which may have developed during this episode of care is in the
A) doctors' progress note section
B) operative report
C) history and physical
D) doctors' orders

38. A possible diagnosis for a patient with shortness of breath, orthopnea, pedal edema and treated with IV Lasix could be
   A) pneumonia
   B) pleural effusion
   C) COPD
   D) CHF

39. Absence of P-waves, symptoms of palpitations, dyspnea, dizziness and treatment with Digoxin, diuretics and cardioversion may indicate
   A) acute MI
   B) CHF
   C) atrial fibrillation
   D) respiratory failure

40. The physician has documented the final diagnoses as: acute myocardial infarction, COPD, CHF, hypertension, atrial fibrillation and status-post cholecystectomy. The following conditions should be reported

| | |
|---|---|
| 401.1 | Essential hypertension, benign |
| 401.9 | Essential hypertension, unspecified |
| 402.91 | Hypertension, heart disease, unspecified, with heart failure |
| 410.91 | Acute Myocardial Infarction, unspecified site, initial episode of care |
| 427.31 | Atrial fibrillation and flutter |
| 428.0 | Congestive Heart Failure, unspecified |
| 496 | Chronic Obstructive Pulmonary Disease |
| V45.79 | Other acquired absence of organ |

   A) 410.9, 496, 402.91, 427.31, V45.79
   B) 410.91, 496 , 428.0, 401.9, 427.31
   C) 410.91, 496, 428.0, 401.9, 427.31, V45.79
   D) 410.91, 496, 428.0, 401.1, 427.31

41. Which of the following is the term describing a woman who has delivered one child?
   A) primipara
   B) primigravida
   C) nulligravida
   D) paragravida

42. HPV or human papilloma virus is
   A) caused by the spirochete *Treponema pallidum*
   B) a vaginal inflammation that is caused by a protozoan parasite
   C) also known as genital warts
   D) characterized by painful urination and an abnormal discharge

43. Which diagnostic technique records the patient heart rates and rhythms over a 24-hour period?
   A) echocardiography
   B) electrocardiography
   C) Holter monitor
   D) Angiocardiography

44. The UHDDS definition of principal diagnosis is the
    A) complaint or condition that required the patient to be admitted to the hospital
    B) diagnosis that the physician feels was the most severe
    C) condition established after study to occasion the admission of the patient to the hospital
    D) condition that utilized the most resources

45. Which of the following would NOT be considered fraud?
    A) unbundling (exploding) codes
    B) offering a kickback
    C) misrepresenting a diagnosis to justify payment
    D) billing for services rendered

46. Employing the SOAP style of progress notes, choose the "assessment" statement from the following:
    A) patient states low back pain with sciatica is as severe as it was on admission
    B) patient moving about very cautiously, appears to be in pain
    C) adjust pain medication; begin physical therapy tomorrow
    D) sciatica unimproved with hot pack therapy

47. In determining when to report other diagnoses, the following guidelines will apply
    A) clinical evaluation or therapeutic treatment
    B) diagnostic procedures or increase nursing care and/or monitoring of patient
    C) extend the length of stay
    D) all of the above

48. This condition is described as both acute (subacute) and chronic and there are separate subterms in Volume II of the ICD-9-CM Code Book, apply the following instruction(s)
    A) code the acute condition only
    B) assign codes for both conditions
    C) assign codes for both and sequence the acute condition first
    D) assign codes for both and sequence the chronic condition first

49. You would expect to find documentation regarding the assessment of an obstetric patient's lochia, fundus, and perineum on the
    A) prenatal record
    B) labor record
    C) delivery room record
    D) postpartum record

50. Which of the following would be coded as a poisoning?
    A) Coumadin intoxication due to a cumulative effect
    B) idiosyncratic reaction to Artane
    C) interaction between Aldomet and a vasodilating agent
    D) reaction between Coumadin and an over the counter medication

51. The special form which plays the central role in planning and providing care at nursing, psychiatric and rehabilitation facilities is the
    A) interdisciplinary care plan
    B) medical history and review of systems
    C) interval summary
    D) problem list

52. Which of the following are considered late effects regardless of time?
   A) congenital defect
   B) non union
   C) non healing fracture
   D) poisoning

53. Four people were seen in your Emergency Department yesterday. Which one will be coded as a poisoning?
   - Robert – diagnosed with digitalis intoxication
   - Gary – had an allergic reaction to a dye administered for a pyleogram
   - David – developed syncope after taking Contac pills with a double scotch
   - Brian – had an idiosyncratic reaction between two properly administered prescription drugs

   A) Robert
   B) Gary
   C) David
   D) Brian

54. A patient with carcinoma of the prostate with metastasis to the bone and liver was admitted to the hospital following intertrochanteric fracture. An open reduction and internal fixation was performed to repair the fracture. The pathologist reported malignant neoplasm at the site of the pathological fracture. The principal diagnosis would be
   A) carcinoma of the prostate
   B) secondary bone metastases
   C) pathological fracture, neck of femur
   D) intertrochanteric fracture

55. Ketones in urine are indicative of what disease
   A) cirrhosis
   B) renal failure
   C) diabetes
   D) urinary tract infection

56. Serum glucose levels greater than 200 are associated with
   A) pancreatitis
   B) uncontrolled diabetes
   C) liver cirrhosis
   D) dehydration

57. A patient with a prior CVA and residual dysphagia was noted to have trouble swallowing while receiving lunch. The patient aspirated and immediately had difficulty breathing. Upon admission to the hospital, the patient was in respiratory failure, was intubated and placed on the ventilator. Chest x-ray revealed aspiration pneumonia. The principal diagnosis is:
   A) old CVA
   B) dysphagia
   C) aspiration pneumonia
   D) respiratory failure

58. ICD-9-CM codes are sequenced for third party payors based on definitions from the
A) UHDDS
B) Coding Clinic
C) CMS (HCFA) Coding Guidelines
D) Federal Register

59. Sedera had three babies in four years and she considered that more than enough. During her hospitalization for her third delivery, Sedera had a sterilization procedure performed. When the record is coded, the V-code for sterilization, V25.2 is
A) not used
B) used and sequenced as principal diagnosis
C) used and sequenced as a secondary diagnosis
D) the only code used

60. Patient is admitted for elective cholecystectomy for treatment of chronic cholecystitis with cholelithiasis. Prior to administration of general anesthesia, patient suffers cerebral thrombosis. Surgery is subsequently cancelled. Code and sequence the coding from the following codes.

| | |
|---|---|
| 434.00 | Cerebral thrombosis without mention of cerebral infarction |
| 574.10 | Calculus of gallbladder with other cholecystitis, without mention of obstruction |
| V64.1 | Surgery cancelled, contraindication |
| 997.02 | Iatrogenic cerebrovascular infarction or hemorrhage |
| 51.22 | Cholecystectomy |

A) 997.02, 574.10, 51.22
B) 574.10, 434.00, V64.1
C) 997.02, 434.00, V64.1
D) 434.00, V64.1

**ANSWER KEY CCS-P MOCK EXAMINATION MULTIPLE CHOICE QUESTIONS**

1. A The physician fee schedule is updated each April 15 and is composed of the three basic elements in answer A.

REFERENCE: Buck, p 569

2. D Modifier -57 Decision for Surgery would not be used in the scenario since the information provided does not specify whether this was a planned or spontaneous decision to have the lesion removed. This eliminates answers B and C. Answer A can be ruled out because the lesion was excised not destroyed.

REFERENCE: Principles of CPT Coding, p 133-134

3. B The sizes of the simple wound repairs of the same body area are added together in order to select the correct CPT code.

REFERENCES: Buck, p 144-145
Principles of CPT Coding, p 139-140

4. B

REFERENCE: Principles of CPT Coding, p 454

5. C Poison Oak codes to contact dermatitis due to plants. The level of history is expanded problem focused (2 history of present illness elements and 1 review of system element); the level of exam is problem focused (only affected body area); and the level of decision is low (level of risk: low; presenting problems: acute, uncomplicated; management options: prescription). Therefore, two of the three key components have been met: expanded problem focused history and low medical decision making.

REFERENCE: Principles of CPT Coding, p 39-49

6. A

REFERENCE: CPT Code Book

7. D The level of history is problem focused (1 history of present illness element); the level of exam is problem focused (single body area); and the level of medical decision is straightforward. Only two key components need to be met since patient is established.

REFERENCE: Principles of CPT Coding, p 39-49

8. A According to the CPT coding guidelines for grafts, code 15000 does not include the removal of lesions. Guidelines lead you to code the excision of lesion and the graft.

REFERENCE: Principles of CPT Coding, p 137-140

9. B

REFERENCE: Principles of CPT Coding, p 239-240

10. D When you have a polypectomy at one site and a biopsy at another site, both are to be coded.

REFERENCES: Principles of CPT Coding, p 215-217

11. C A fracture is always assumed "closed" unless otherwise stated by the physician.

REFERENCE: Brown, p 315

12. C
REFERENCE: Principles of CPT Coding, p 195-196

13. A Generally, the most severe injury is reported first.
REFERENCE: Buck p 511

14. A Modifier -26 professional component would be appropriate
REFERENCE: Principles of CPT Coding, p 442-483

15. C The use of code 69990 is only for procedures that do not have the microscope as an inclusive component.
REFERENCE: Principles of CPT Coding, p 177

16. D
REFERENCE: Brown, 198-199
Schraffenberger, p 204-205

17. A Modifier -51, multiple procedures would be appropriate, as would modifier -59, distinct procedural service.
REFERENCE: Principles of CPT Coding, p 485-486

18. D
REFERENCES: Buck, p 262
Principles of CPT Coding, p 244

19. C CPT guidelines states that when a patient is admitted from a physician's office to the hospital on the same day that you do not code an office visit.
REFERENCE: Principles of CPT Coding, p 58-59

20. D Minor synovectomy and articular debridement is included in the meniscectomy code.
REFERENCE: CPT Code Book

21. C Since a definitive diagnosis has not been established, code the symptoms/signs as opposed to the diagnosis
REFERENCES: Hazelwood and Venable, p 4-5
Brown, p 419

22. D
REFERENCE: Principles of CPT Coding, p 249

23. B Since the procedure is bilateral, either code twice or use the modifier -50
REFERENCES: Buck, p 301
Principles of CPT Coding, p 295

24. A
REFERENCES: Schraffenberger, p 229-232, 236-237, 251-252
Brown, p 43-44, 345

25. A Modifiers -LT and -RT are not appropriate since modifier -50 bilateral is the more definitive modifier
REFERENCE: CPT Code Book

26. D
REFERENCE: CPT Code Book

27. A Patient was in an inpatient hospital setting
REFERENCE: Green and Rowell, p 326

28. B
REFERENCE: Green and Rowell, p 64-67

29. D When two lesions are removed employing one excision; the lesions and the distance between the lesions are added together. One code is reported which now reflects the complete diameter of the two lesions.
REFERENCE: Principles of CPT Coding, p 136

30. C
REFERENCE: Principles of CPT Coding, p 424-427

31. A
REFERENCE: Buck, p 498

32. B
REFERENCES: Brown, p 173-174
Schraffenberger, p 124-125

33. B
REFERENCE: Buck, p 402-404

34. C
REFERENCE: Brown, p 121

35. D
REFERENCES: Brown, p 106, 263, 266-267
Schraffenberger, p 123-124, 136-138

36. B Only the pathologic fracture was treated therefore it needs to be sequenced first.
REFERENCE: Brown, p 63-64, 198-199, 289-290, 293-294

37. A The physician releasing the patient should write a final note of summary of the patient's course of treatment, stating the patient's condition at discharge, and instructions for the patient's activity, diet and medications as well as any follow up appointments or instructions. If a patient expires, the final notes describe the circumstances regarding the death, the findings, the cause of death, and whether or not an autopsy was performed.
REFERENCE: Abdelhak, p 93

38. D
REFERENCE: Merck Manual

39. C
REFERENCE: Merck Manual

40. B Category V45.7x, acquired absence of organ is intended to be used for patient care where the absence of organ affects treatment.
REFERENCES: Brown, p 69, 255-258, 260-261
Schraffenberger, p 123-124, 125-129, 132-133

41. A
REFERENCE: Merck Manual

42. C
REFERENCE: MercK Manual

43. C
REFERENCE: Merck Manual

44. C
REFERENCE: Brown, p 19

45. D
REFERENCE: Buck, p 576-578

46. D Progress note elements written in the acronym "SOAP" style are:
S- subjective, records what the patient states is the problem
O- objective, records what the practitioner identifies through the history, physical examination, and diagnostic tests
A- assessment, combines the subjective and objective into a conclusion
P- plan, what approach is going to be taken to resolve the problem
REFERENCE: Abdelhak, p 99-100

47. D
REFERENCE: Brown, p 22-25

48. C
REFERENCE: Brown, p 41-42

49. D The postpartum data records information about the condition of the mother after delivery and includes an assessment of the lochia and conditions of the breasts, fundus, and perineum.
REFERENCE: Abdelhak, p 96

50. D
REFERENCES: Schraffenberger, p 244-247
Brown, p 337-344

**ANSWER KEY CCS-P MOCK EXAMINATION MULTIPLE CHOICE QUESTIONS**

51. A The interdisciplinary care plan is the foundation around which patient care is organized. It contains input from the unique perspective of each discipline involved. It includes an assessment, statement of goals, identification of specific activities or strategies to achieve those goals, and periodic assessment of goal attainment.
REFERENCE: Abdelhak, p 93

52. B
REFERENCES: Schraffenberger, p 265-269
Brown, p 43

53. C The condition should be coded as a poisoning when there is an interaction of an over the counter drug and alcohol. Answers A, B & D are adverse effects of a correctly administered prescription drug.
REFERENCE: Brown, p 337-344

54. C
REFERENCE: Brown, p 198-199, 293-294, 299-300

55. C
REFERENCE: Merck Manual

56. B
REFERENCE: Merck Manual

57. D
REFERENCE: Brown, p 148-150

58. A The definitions in the UHDDS should be followed to sequence codes for reporting inpatient information to third party payers.
REFERENCE: Brown, p 19

59. C
REFERENCES: Schraffenberger, p 253
Brown, p 220

60. B
REFERENCES: Schraffenberger, p 48-54
Brown, p 54-55

## REFERENCES


Basic ICD-9-CM Coding, 2006
by Lou Ann Schraffenberger
American Health Information Management Association

CPT Code Book, 2006
American Medical Association

Health Information: Management of a Strategic Resource
by Mervat Abdelhak
W. B. Saunders

ICD-9-CM Code Book, with October 2005 updates
INGENIX
Channel Publishing

ICD-9-CM Coding Handbook, 2006
by Faye Brown
American Hospital Association

ICD-9-CM Diagnostic Coding and Reimbursement for Physician Services, 2006
by Anita Hazelwood and Carol Venable
American Health Information Management Association

Merck Manual
The Merck Publishing Group

Principles of CPT Coding
American Medical Association

Step by Step Coding, 2005 Edition
by Carol Buck
WB Saunders

Understanding Health Insurance, A Guide to Professional Billing
by Michelle Green and Jo Ann Rowell
Delmar Thompson Learning

# CCS-P Mock Examination

# Coding Cases

## CCS-P MOCK EXAMINATION
## CODING INSTRUCTIONS

Follow the guidelines given below in coding the CCS-P Mock Examination Cases.

1. Record up to four ICD-9-CM diagnoses and six CPT and/or HCPCS Level II procedural codes in the spaces provided at the end of the coding cases. Don't forget that points are deducted for inappropriate codes.
2. Select diagnoses, conditions, problems, or other reasons for care that require ICD-9-CM coding in a physician-based encounter/visit either in a physician's office, clinic, outpatient area, emergency room, ambulatory surgery, or other ambulatory care setting, apply ICD-9-CM instructional notations and conventions and current approved Basic Coding Guidelines for Outpatient Services and Diagnostic Coding and Reporting Requirements for Physician Billing. The new coding guidelines are in the back of this book
3. Sequencing is not required for the diagnoses or procedures.
4. Assign CPT/ HCPCS modifiers for hospital-based facilities if applicable.
5. To assign codes to secondary diagnoses, apply the following directions:
   - Code and report chronic diseases as many times as the patient is receiving treatment and care for the condition(s).
   - Code all documented conditions that coexist at the time of the visit and that require or affect patient care, treatment, or management.
   - Do not code conditions previously treated and no longer existing.
6. Code for professional services only and only for the designated physician for each individual case.
7. Assign CPT codes and/ HCPCS Level II codes for all appropriate procedures.
8. Assign CPT codes for anesthesia procedures listed in the anesthesia section only if applicable.
9. Assign CPT codes for medical procedures based on current CPT guidelines.
10. Confirm Evaluation and Management (E&M) codes based on the information provided in the box for each case. For the purposes of this examination, the levels of key components have been given. You will not be expected to assign the level of history, examinations, and medical decision making.
11. Assign CPT codes from the following: Medicine section, Radiology section, Laboratory and pathology section only when applicable.
12. Assign HCPCS Level II National (alphanumeric) codes as appropriate.
13. Do not assign:
    - HCPCS Level III Local codes
    - ICD-9-CM E codes
    - ICD-9-CM M codes
    - ICD-9-CM, Volume 3, procedure codes

## Mock Examination
## Part II Case 1

### Office Visit

| | |
|---|---|
| Patient's Name: | Fern Bishop |
| Date of Visit: | January 5, 2006 |
| Age: | 65 |
| Sex: | Female |
| Insurance: | Medicare |

**CCS-P Mock Examination**
**Part II Case 1**
**Office Visit**

HISTORY OF PRESENT ILLNESS: This is the third office visit for this 65-year-old female. For the past 4-5 weeks she has been having significant sharp stabbing pains in her anterior chest, primarily with movement, especially when lying down or sitting up. She does not have any palpitations or any significant shortness of breath, cough, wheezing, fever or chills. She does have a history of COPD with chronic mild exertional dyspnea.

PAST MEDICAL HISTORY: Pacemaker.

ALLERGIES: NKA.

MEDICATIONS: Lanoxin q day, inhaler as needed.

SOCIAL HISTORY: She quit smoking after 40 years. She is retired and lives with her husband.

FAMILY HISTORY: Father died of old age. Mother died from complications of open-heart surgery. Siblings are alive and well. One sister has diabetes and one brother has hypertension.

REVIEW OF SYSTEMS:

| | |
|---|---|
| HEENT: | No diplopia or new visual disturbance. No tinnitus, otalgia or sore throat. |
| Cardiac: | No sustained chest pain or palpitations. |
| Pulmonary: | COPD with chronic mild exertional dyspnea. |
| Gastrointestinal: | No melena, hematochezia, vomiting or diarrhea. |
| Musculoskeletal: | As per history of present illness. |

The remaining systems are negative.

PHYSICAL EXAMINATION:

| | |
|---|---|
| General: | Well-developed, well-nourished female in mild distress. Blood pressure 120/70. Temperature normal. Respirations 16. Pulse 68. |
| Skin: | No gross abnormalities. |
| HEENT: | Pupils are equal, round and reactive to light. Extraocular movements intact. Sclerae are clear. Conjunctivae are pink. Ears are normal. Pharynx is clear. Good occlusion of the teeth. |
| Neck: | Supple, no bruits. |
| Chest: | Anterior chest wall tenderness, primarily from the mid and lower left sternal border, extending laterally across the costal chondral cartilage. No associated deformity, swelling, erythema. No gross abnormalities. |
| Lungs: | Mildly diminished breath sounds bilaterally with no prominent rales, wheezing, rales or rhonchi. No rubs. |
| Heart: | Regular rate and rhythm. No murmurs, clicks or rubs. |
| Abdomen: | Soft and nontender. Bowel sounds are normal. No masses. |
| Back: | Appears normal with no tenderness. |
| Extremities: | Good color and warmth. |
| Vascular: | Pulses are present and symmetrical. |
| Neurological: | Alert, responds to questions. Cranial nerves grossly intact. Symmetrical strength and grasp bilaterally. No acute focal deficits. |
| Psychiatric: | No acute psychosis. |
| Pelvic/Genitalia: | Deferred as inappropriate. |
| Rectal: | Deferred as inappropriate |

## CCS-P Mock Examination
## Part II Case 1

### Office Visit

Continued:

ELECTROCARDIOGRAM: Dual chamber pacemaker, rate of 60. Rhythm - sinus. No significant ectopy noted.

IMPRESSION:
Chest wall pain. We will be placing her on anti-inflammatory drugs and will start her on the first dose of Motrin here. It is recommended that she start taking regular Motrin and limit activities that exacerbate her discomfort. Follow-up office visit is scheduled for two weeks from today.

| | |
|---|---|
| History: | Comprehensive |
| Examination: | Comprehensive |
| Medical Decision: | Moderate Complexity |

**Answer Sheet**
**CCS-P Mock Examination**
**Part II Case 1**

| DIAGNOSES | ICD-9-CM CODES | | | | | |
|---|---|---|---|---|---|---|
| Primary DX | | | | . | | |
| DX 2 | | | | . | | |
| DX 3 | | | | . | | |
| DX 4 | | | | . | | |

| PROCEDURES | CPT CODES | | | | | MODIFIERS (If Applicable) | | |
|---|---|---|---|---|---|---|---|---|
| PR 1 | | | | | | - | | |
| PR 2 | | | | | | - | | |
| PR 3 | | | | | | - | | |
| PR 4 | | | | | | - | | |
| PR 5 | | | | | | - | | |
| PR 6 | | | | | | - | | |
| PR 7 | | | | | | - | | |

**CCS-P Mock Examination**
**<u>Part II Case 2</u>**
**Office Visit**

| | |
|---|---|
| Patient's Name: | Alice Snook |
| Date of Visit: | January 16, 2006 |
| Age: | 25 |
| Sex: | Female |
| Insurance: | Workers' Compensation |

**CCS-P Mock Examination**
**<u>Part II Case 2</u>**
**Office Visit**

HISTORY OF PRESENT ILLNESS:
First visit for this 25-year-old female who was at home when she accidentally punched a door. She has had persistent pain in the left hand since yesterday. She describes the pain as severe. Left hand is swollen and sore to the touch in the knuckle area of the 5th digit.

PAST MEDICAL HISTORY: Noncontributory.

ALLERGIES: None.

PHYSICAL EXAMINATION:

| | |
|---|---|
| General: | Well-developed, well-nourished female in moderate distress. BP: 121/85 P: 88; R: 18; |
| Skin: | Warm and dry. |
| HEENT: | Unremarkable. |
| Chest: | Symmetrical. |
| Extremities: | The left hand is tender and mildly swollen with no gross deformity. Normal range of motion against resistance with moderate pain. No abrasions or lacerations. Normal distal neurosensory examination. The remainder of the extremity examination is within normal limits. |
| Neurological: | She is awake, alert, and oriented times three with no focal neurologic deficits. |

RADIOLOGY EXAMINATION:
The patient was taken to the office x-ray room where the left hand was x-rayed. Boxer's fracture shaft 5th finger appreciated in the AP and lateral views.

IMPRESSION:
Left 5th finger Boxer's fracture.
The patient was placed in an ulnar splint and was given a prescription for Darvocet p.r.n. pain and Motrin 800-mg t.i.d. She will follow up with me next week.

| | |
|---|---|
| History: | Expanded Problem Focused |
| Examination: | Expanded Problem Focused |
| Medical Decision: | Straightforward |

**Answer Sheet**
**CCS-P Mock Examination**
**Part II Case 2**

| DIAGNOSES | ICD-9-CM CODES | | | | | |
|---|---|---|---|---|---|---|
| Primary DX | | | | . | | |
| DX 2 | | | | . | | |
| DX 3 | | | | . | | |
| DX 4 | | | | . | | |

| PROCEDURES | CPT CODES | | | | | MODIFIERS (If Applicable) | | |
|---|---|---|---|---|---|---|---|---|
| PR 1 | | | | | | - | | |
| PR 2 | | | | | | - | | |
| PR 3 | | | | | | - | | |
| PR 4 | | | | | | - | | |
| PR 5 | | | | | | - | | |
| PR 6 | | | | | | - | | |
| PR 7 | | | | | | - | | |

**CCS-P Mock Examination**
**<u>Part II Case 3</u>**
**Office Visit**

| | |
|---|---|
| Date of Visit: | January 1, 2006 |
| Patient's Name: | Sadie Phillips |
| Age: | 70 |
| Sex: | Female |
| Insurance: | Medicare and AARP |

**CCS-P Mock Examination**
**Part II Case 3**
**Office Visit**

HISTORY OF PRESENT ILLNESS:
Patient has complaints of right-sided abdominal pain for one day. Experienced some dizziness today. No nausea/vomiting/diarrhea. No dysuria but has experienced frequent urination. Patient does have a history of UTI's that was documented in last office visit notes four years ago.

PAST MEDICAL HISTORY: Negative.

MEDICATIONS: None.

ALLERGIES: None known.

PHYSICAL EXAMINATION:

| | |
|---|---|
| Vitals: | BP: 96/69; P: 62; R: 18; T: 97.9 |
| HEENT: | ENT is normal. Pharynx is normal. |
| Neck: | Normal. Thyroid is normal. |
| Abdomen: | Normal bowel sounds. Non-tender and no organomegaly. Mild pain in right groin area. |
| Rectum: | Normal. |
| Urogenital: | Within normal limits. |

Automated microscopic urinalysis was performed in the office.
WBC: 11-25; RBC: 0; Epithelial cells: Moderate; Bacteria: >100,000.

IMPRESSION AND PLAN:
1. UTI
2. Bactrim 1 tab p.o. bid x 7 days.
3. Follow-up in office in one week.

| | |
|---|---|
| History: | Expanded Problem Focused |
| Examination: | Expanded Problem Focused |
| Medical Decision: | Straightforward |

**Answer Sheet**
**CCS-P Mock Examination**
**Part II Case 3**

| DIAGNOSES | ICD-9-CM CODES | | | | | |
|---|---|---|---|---|---|---|
| Primary DX | | | | . | | |
| DX 2 | | | | . | | |
| DX 3 | | | | . | | |
| DX 4 | | | | . | | |

| PROCEDURES | CPT CODES | | | | | MODIFIERS (If Applicable) | | |
|---|---|---|---|---|---|---|---|---|
| PR 1 | | | | | | - | | |
| PR 2 | | | | | | - | | |
| PR 3 | | | | | | - | | |
| PR 4 | | | | | | - | | |
| PR 5 | | | | | | - | | |
| PR 6 | | | | | | - | | |
| PR 7 | | | | | | - | | |

**Mock Examination**
**Part II Case 4**
**Office Visit**

| | |
|---|---|
| Patient's Name: | James Phillips |
| Date of Visit: | January 30, 2006 |
| Age: | 44 |
| Sex: | Male |
| Insurance: | Government |

**Mock Examination**
**Part II Case 4**
**Office Visit**

DATE OF OFFICE VISIT: 1-30-2006

HISTORY OF PRESENT ILLNESS
This is an established patient who complains of left elbow pain. The pain started about a month ago and has progressively gotten worse. It is exacerbated by rotation and flexion and extension of the elbow. Denies any trauma to the area. The patient is an avid tennis player and it seems that the pain is aggravated during play. He is in a tournament next week and is requesting help with pain relief. He has been on NSAIDs with very little effect.

PHYSICAL EXAMINATION:

| | |
|---|---|
| General: | Blood pressure 120/65. Pulse 68. Respirations 16. Temperature normal. |
| Extremities: | The left elbow has no swelling or ecchymosis. There is tenderness over the lateral epicondyle. Left shoulder and wrist are normal. Right upper extremity is normal. |
| CNS: | Intact sensation with equal strength. Ulnar and radial pulses are normal. |

IMPRESSION: Left lateral epicondylitis

The patient was given an injection of 10 mg. Aristospan and 4.0 cc of 2% Lidocaine into the area of tenderness on the left elbow. He was told to use Ibuprofen 600-mg q.i.d... Patient to follow-up in one week.

| | |
|---|---|
| History: | Expanded problem focused |
| Examination: | Expanded problem focused |
| Medical Decision: | Low complexity |

**Answer Sheet**
**Mock Examination**
**<u>Part II Case 4</u>**

| DIAGNOSES | ICD-9-CM CODES | | | | | |
|---|---|---|---|---|---|---|
| Primary DX | | | | . | | |
| DX 2 | | | | . | | |
| DX 3 | | | | . | | |
| DX 4 | | | | . | | |

| PROCEDURES | CPT CODES | | | | | MODIFIERS (If Applicable) | | |
|---|---|---|---|---|---|---|---|---|
| PR 1 | | | | | | - | | |
| PR 2 | | | | | | - | | |
| PR 3 | | | | | | - | | |
| PR 4 | | | | | | - | | |
| PR 5 | | | | | | - | | |
| PR 6 | | | | | | - | | |
| PR 7 | | | | | | - | | |

**Mock Examination**
**Part II Case 5**
**Office Visit**

| | |
|---|---|
| Patient's Name: | Lafayette Wilkinson |
| Date of Visit: | January 25, 2006 |
| Age: | 50 |
| Sex: | Male |
| Insurance: | Self Pay |

**Mock Examination**
**Part II Case 5**
**Office Visit**

HISTORY OF PRESENT ILLNESS:
Patient returns to the office one week following appendectomy. Patient is doing well and has no complaints of pain, bleeding, nor nausea and vomiting. Patient is taking Ampicillin 500-mg p.o. q 6 hr. and Tylenol for pain as needed. There are no complaints of chest pain, shortness of breath, or difficulty urinating.

ALLERGIES: No known allergies.

PHYSICAL EXAMINATION:

| | |
|---|---|
| Vital Signs: | Blood pressure 110/70. Temperature normal. Respirations 20. Pulse 66. |
| HEENT: | Normal. No masses. Eyes are equal and reactive. No thyroidomegaly. |
| Lungs: | Clear to auscultation and percussion. |
| Abdomen: | There is a healing surgical scar in the right lower quadrant. No redness or tenderness in that area noted. |

PLAN:
Patient is doing well from his surgery. To continue on Ampicillin for one more week and continue Tylenol for pain as needed. To follow up with us in two weeks.

| | |
|---|---|
| History: | Expanded Problem Focused |
| Examination: | Expanded Problem Focused |
| Medical Decision: | Straightforward |

**Answer Sheet**
**Mock Examination**
**Part II Case 5**

| DIAGNOSES | ICD-9-CM CODES | | | | | |
|---|---|---|---|---|---|---|
| Primary DX | | | | . | | |
| DX 2 | | | | . | | |
| DX 3 | | | | . | | |
| DX 4 | | | | . | | |

| PROCEDURES | CPT CODES | | | | | MODIFIERS (If Applicable) | | |
|---|---|---|---|---|---|---|---|---|
| PR 1 | | | | | | - | | |
| PR 2 | | | | | | - | | |
| PR 3 | | | | | | - | | |
| PR 4 | | | | | | - | | |
| PR 5 | | | | | | - | | |
| PR 6 | | | | | | - | | |
| PR 7 | | | | | | - | | |

**Mock Examination**
**Part II Case 6**
**Ambulatory Surgery**
**Face Sheet**

| | |
|---|---|
| Patient's Name: | Cora Law |
| Date of Visit: | January 4, 2006 |
| Age: | 58 |
| Sex: | Female |
| Insurance: | Commercial |

**Mock Examination**
**Part II Case 6**
**History and Physical**

DATE OF ADMISSION: 1-4-06

ADMITTING DIAGNOSIS: Scalp mass.

HISTORY OF PRESENT ILLNESS:
Patient is returning for recurrent scalp masses. She had one removed approximately one year ago and now has two more.

PAST MEDICAL HISTORY:
Scalp mass, one year ago. Patient has a history of hypertension and COPD.

ALLERGIES: Sulfa.

MEDICATIONS: Tenormin and Alupent.

SOCIAL HISTORY:
She smokes 1/2 pack a day; alcohol - social. She is retired and her hobbies include reading, gardening and bingo.

PHYSICAL EXAMINATION:

| | |
|---|---|
| General | Patient weighs 185. She is 5′ 6″ tall. BP 148/78. Pulse 80. Patient appears generally in good health considering her weight and history of COPD. |
| Head: | Mass on the vertex of the scalp with another mass located in the right posterior occipital region. |
| HEENT: | Pupils are equal, round and reactive to light and accommodation. Extraocular muscles are intact. Fundi are poorly visualized. |
| Neck: | Thyroid not palpable. No jugular venous distention. |
| Chest: | Lungs showed resonant breath sounds equally with left basilar rales. |
| Heart: | Regular rate and rhythm, no murmurs. |
| Abdomen: | No masses or rebound tenderness. |
| Extremities: | Normal with good reflexes. |

PLAN:
Admit to day surgery for removal of scalp masses.

**Mock Examination**
**Part Part II Case 6**

## Operative Report

| | |
|---|---|
| Date of Operation: | 1-4-06 |
| Preoperative Diagnosis: | Scalp mass x 2 |
| Postoperative Diagnosis: | Scalp mass x 2 |
| Operation: | Excision of scalp mass x 2 |
| Surgeon: | Linda Lee, MD |
| Anesthesia: | Monitored anesthesia care |
| Anesthesiologist: | James Allen, MD |
| Estimated Blood Loss: | Minimal |
| Drains: | None |
| Complications: | None |

PROCEDURE:
Patient is taken to the operating room with her informed consent. She is prepped and draped in the usual manner. IV sedation is administered, and then local, using one percent lidocaine.

The first mass measuring 2.0 cm was on the vertex of the scalp. There is a scar here from a previous excision and a mass just posterior to it. The scar was excised through a two-centimeter transverse incision with an elliptical incision, and she was found to have a sebaceous cyst which was adherent to the scar and also tracking posteriorly. This was excised in its entirety. The wound was closed with 2-0 Prolene in an interrupted fashion.

Next, a 2.5 cm mass is located in the right posterior occipital region, and this area was anesthetized with one percent lidocaine and a 2.5 cm transverse incision made over this through the skin and subcutaneous tissue, and the mass was circumferentially dissected and excised.

The wound was closed with 3-0 Vicryl in interrupted fashion for the subcu and we had a good skin closure with this. Steri-Strips and Benzoin applied.

The patient tolerated the procedure well. She was written a prescription for Vicodin one q 4 hr. p.r.n. for pain.

## Mock Examination
## Part II Case 6

**PATHOLOGY REPORT:**

| | |
|---|---|
| Date: | 1-4-06 |
| Physician: | Linda Lee, MD |
| Preoperative Diagnosis: | Scalp mass x 2 |
| Postoperative Diagnosis: | Scalp mass x 2 |
| Surgical Procedure: | Excision of scalp masses x 2 |

Specimen(s):
1. Scalp Mass
2. Scalp Mass

GROSS: There are two containers.

Container number one, labeled "scalp mass", consists of an ovoid firm mass of smooth surfaced tissue with overall dimensions of 2 x 1.5 x .5 cm. The specimen is marked with India ink, bisected and entirely submitted in cassette A1.

Container number two, labeled "scalp mass", consists of multiple portions of yellow-gray-white soft tissue in aggregate 3 x 1.5 x .3 cm and totally submitted in cassette A2.

GROSS AND MICROSCOPIC EXAMINATION:

| | | |
|---|---|---|
| Mass from scalp: | (Specimen #1) | Sebaceous Cyst |
| Mass from scalp: | (Specimen #2) | Sebaceous Cyst |

**Mock Examination**
**Part II Case 6**

**PROGRESS NOTES:**
Patient had removal of two scalp lesions. Tolerated procedure well. No complications. Will follow up in my office in two weeks. Normal diet, regular activities.

**ORDERS:**

STANDARD POSTOPERATIVE ORDERS

Discharge from Recovery Room when stable.
Urinary catherization if patient unable to void postop x 1; then call physician.
Vital signs q 15 minutes x 4; then q 30 minutes x 2; then q 1hour until discharge.
Tylenol 500mg q 4 hr. for pain.
Start on soft diet.

Discharge when patient is stable.

**Answer Sheet**
**Mock Examination**
**Part II Case 6**

| DIAGNOSES | ICD-9-CM CODES | | | | | |
|---|---|---|---|---|---|---|
| Primary DX | | | | . | | |
| DX 2 | | | | . | | |
| DX 3 | | | | . | | |
| DX 4 | | | | . | | |

| PROCEDURES | CPT CODES | | | | | MODIFIERS (If Applicable) | | |
|---|---|---|---|---|---|---|---|---|
| PR 1 | | | | | | - | | |
| PR 2 | | | | | | - | | |
| PR 3 | | | | | | - | | |
| PR 4 | | | | | | - | | |
| PR 5 | | | | | | - | | |
| PR 6 | | | | | | - | | |
| PR 7 | | | | | | - | | |

**Mock Examination**
**Part II Case 7**
**Emergency Room Visit**
**Face Sheet**

| | |
|---|---|
| Patient's Name: | Kris Keuren |
| Date of Visit: | January 19, 2006 |
| Age: | 35 |
| Sex: | Female |
| Insurance: | Commercial |

## Mock Examination
## Part II Case 7

DATE OF ADMISSION: 1-19-06

HISTORY:
This 35 year old female presents to the Emergency Room complaining of right wrist pain. Patient states she slipped and fell on an ice patch and used her right hand to break the fall. Right wrist is painful to the touch and quite painful with any movement. She has a contusion of her right hip.

PAST MEDICAL HISTORY: Non-contributory.

ALLERGIES: None.

PHYSICAL EXAMINATION:

| | |
|---|---|
| General: | Well developed female in acute distress. |
| HEENT: | Nose and throat clear. |
| Heart: | Regular rhythm. |
| Extremities: | Moves 3 extremities well. The right wrist is painful to touch. Unable to move wrist. Contusion right hip. |

PLAN:
Due to a massive accident, the radiological equipment is unavailable. Patient was given the option of waiting or going to a local orthopedic physician who has agreed to x-ray and treat the patient. The patient has opted to go to the physician's office. Wrist was wrapped in an ACE bandage and patient was discharged to the orthopedics' office.

IMPRESSION:
Sprain, right wrist. R/O fracture.

| | |
|---|---|
| History: | Expanded Problem Focused |
| Examination: | Expanded Problem Focused |
| Medical Decision: | Low |

**Mock Examination**
**Part II Case 7**
**Answer Sheet**

| DIAGNOSES | ICD-9-CM CODES | | | | | |
|---|---|---|---|---|---|---|
| Primary DX | | | | . | | |
| DX 2 | | | | . | | |
| DX 3 | | | | . | | |
| DX 4 | | | | . | | |

| PROCEDURES | CPT CODES | | | | | MODIFIERS (If Applicable) | | |
|---|---|---|---|---|---|---|---|---|
| PR 1 | | | | | | - | | |
| PR 2 | | | | | | - | | |
| PR 3 | | | | | | - | | |
| PR 4 | | | | | | - | | |
| PR 5 | | | | | | - | | |
| PR 6 | | | | | | - | | |
| PR 7 | | | | | | - | | |

**Mock Examination**
**Part II B Case 8**
**Nursing Home Visit**
**Face Sheet**

| | |
|---|---|
| Patient's Name: | Sheik Billy |
| Date of Visit: | January 13, 2006 |
| Age: | 35 |
| Sex: | Male |
| Insurance: | Commercial |

**Mock Examination**
**<u>Part II B Case 8</u>**
**Nursing Home Visit**

HISTORY OF PRESENT ILLNESS:
This 35 year old male patient is new to the Oakdale Nursing Home. He was admitted to this facility on 1/13/06 with the diagnoses of bilateral lower amputee, ruptured spleen, lacerated liver, and fractured pelvis sustained from a motor vehicle accident. The patient is admitted for therapy.

PAST MEDICAL HISTORY:
Patient was healthy prior to the accident. No history of diabetes, hypertension, cardiac or respiratory disease.

PAST SURGICAL HISTORY:
Patient has had both legs amputated below the knee. Splenectomy. Liver repair.

ALLERGIES:
No known allergies.

SOCIAL HISTORY:
Patient does not smoke or drink. Patient was an avid runner prior to the accident.

FAMILY HISTORY:
Noncontributory.

REVIEW OF SYSTEMS:

| | |
|---|---|
| HEENT: | Normal. |
| Respiratory: | Normal. |
| Cardiovascular: | Normal. |
| Hematologic: | Normal except for splenectomy and repair of lacerated liver. |
| Musculoskeletal: | Bilateral lower amputee. Healing pelvic fracture. Otherwise normal. |
| Neurological: | Normal. |
| Psychiatric: | Depressed. |

**Mock Examination**
**Part II B Case 8**
**Nursing Home Visit**

Continued:

PHYSICAL EXAMINATION:

| | |
|---|---|
| General: | Well developed, well nourished, depressed male in no acute distress. BP 128/75. Pulse: 80, regular and strong. Respirations: 12, unlabored and regular. Temperature: Normal. Height 5 foot 10 inches. |
| HEENT: | Pupils are reactive to light and accommodation. No vessel changes, exudates, or hemorrhages noted. Oral mucosa is normal. No lesions noted. |
| Neck: | Supple. No masses. Trachea is midline. |
| Respiratory: | Normal. No wheezes or rubs appreciated. |
| Cardiovascular: | Normal sinus rhythm. No murmurs. |
| Abdomen: | Laparotomy scar is healing well. No signs of infection. No evidence of masses or hernias. |
| Lymphatic: | No lymphadenopathy. |
| Genitourinary: | Normal. |
| Rectal Examination: | Deferred. |
| Musculoskeletal: | Patient is a bilateral lower amputee. Currently confined to wheelchair. Pelvic fracture is healing according to x-rays. Lower leg muscles have not been used since accident and are flaccid. Upper body is within normal limits. Range of motion is good. |
| Neurological: | Cranial nerves are intact. Moves all upper extremities on command without difficulty. Hand grips strong bilaterally. Lower extremities are flaccid and it is unsure if patient is unable to move stumps or will not move stumps. |
| Psychiatric: | Patient is depressed and this will be a concern which might hinder him in therapy. Patient is orientated to person, place and time. Judgment is impaired due to depression. Patient does have phantom leg syndrome. |

PLAN:
Patient will begin therapy to strengthen his lower stumps. He will be fitted with prostheses and will begin rehabilitative therapy. Psychologist will be obtained to help patient deal with depression and therapy.

Patient is on no special diet. Needs to become interactive with residents.

| | |
|---|---|
| History: | Comprehensive |
| Examination: | Comprehensive |
| Medical Decision: | Moderate Complexity |

**Answer Sheet**
**Mock Examination**
**Part II B Case 8**

| DIAGNOSES | ICD-9-CM CODES | | | | | |
|---|---|---|---|---|---|---|
| Primary DX | | | | . | | |
| DX 2 | | | | . | | |
| DX 3 | | | | . | | |
| DX 4 | | | | . | | |

| PROCEDURES | CPT CODES | | | | | MODIFIERS (If Applicable) | | |
|---|---|---|---|---|---|---|---|---|
| PR 1 | | | | | | - | | |
| PR 2 | | | | | | - | | |
| PR 3 | | | | | | - | | |
| PR 4 | | | | | | - | | |
| PR 5 | | | | | | - | | |
| PR 6 | | | | | | - | | |
| PR 7 | | | | | | - | | |

**Mock Examination**
**Part II Case 9**

## OFFICE VISIT
## Face Sheet

| | |
|---|---|
| Patient's Name: | J.W. Goldie |
| Date of Visit: | January 17, 2006 |
| Age: | 56 |
| Sex: | Male |
| Insurance: | Medicare |

**Mock Examination**
**Part II Case 9**

**Office Visit**

DATE OF OFFICE VISIT: 01-17-06

This is a repeat visit for this patient. He has complaints of indigestion for the past month. The indigestion occurs after eating heavy meals and/or physical exertion. The duration of pain lasts about 20 minutes. He states that he has had a previous cholecystectomy approximately two years ago.

There is no shortness of breath, nausea, vomiting, bloody stools or sweating. There is a family history of heart disease with his father having bypass surgery in his 60s. His mother died of a MI three years ago. The patient has a history of smoking, but is currently on the patch to help him stop. He does not exercise regularly. He denies any chest pains or cough. GU, Musc., Neuro, Skin, Eyes are negative.

Allergies: PCN and sulfa
Medications: Smoking patch.

PHYSICAL EXAMINATION:

| | |
|---|---|
| General: | Blood pressure 140/80, P 76, Resp. 16. Temperature is normal. |
| HEENT: | Head is normocephalic. No masses or lesions noted on the eyes. Oral mucosa is normal. Throat is normal. |
| Neck: | No distention of jugular vein. |
| Lungs: | Clear bilaterally to auscultation and percussion. No rubs, rales, or wheezing noted. |
| Heart: | Normal sinus rhythm. No rubs, gallops, or murmurs. Carotid arteries, abdominal artery and femoral arteries are normal. No bruits noted. Pedal pulses normal. No peripheral edema noted. |
| Abdomen: | No masses, tenderness, organomegaly. |
| Neurological: | Normal. |
| Extremities: | No clubbing, cyanosis, ischemia or edema noted. Gait is steady. Good range of motion in all extremities. |

Patient was taken to the office stress laboratory and the patient was placed on the treadmill.

PLAN:
Blood was drawn for cardiac profile and was sent to an outside lab. At this point, the patient will not be placed on prescriptions. It was suggested that he take an over the counter antacid like Pepcid or Axid to help prevent heart burn. It was recommended that the patient make an appointment with a gastroenterologist to rule out GI problems.

| | |
|---|---|
| History: | Detailed |
| Examination: | Detailed |
| Medical Decision: | Moderate Complexity |

**Mock Examination**
**Part II Case 9**

## Stress Test Report

The patient arrived in the stress lab and was placed on the ECG monitor and activated the treadmill. The patient was able to tolerate the treadmill for approximately 10 minutes and reached his desired heart rate. He did not develop any chest pains or signs of indigestion. There were no ECG changes.

RESULTS: Normal.

**Mock Examination**
**<u>Part II Case 9</u>**

**Answer Sheet**

| DIAGNOSES | ICD-9-CM CODES | | | | | |
|---|---|---|---|---|---|---|
| Primary DX | | | | . | | |
| DX 2 | | | | . | | |
| DX 3 | | | | . | | |
| DX 4 | | | | . | | |

| PROCEDURES | CPT CODES | | | | | MODIFIERS (If Applicable) | | |
|---|---|---|---|---|---|---|---|---|
| PR 1 | | | | | | - | | |
| PR 2 | | | | | | - | | |
| PR 3 | | | | | | - | | |
| PR 4 | | | | | | - | | |
| PR 5 | | | | | | - | | |
| PR 6 | | | | | | - | | |
| PR 7 | | | | | | - | | |

**Mock Examination**
**<u>Part II  Case 10</u>**
**Ambulatory Surgery**
**Face Sheet**

| | |
|---|---|
| Patient's Name: | Sally Hunter |
| Date of Visit: | January 16, 2006 |
| Age: | 45 |
| Sex: | Female |
| Insurance: | Commercial |

**Mock Examination**
**<u>Part II Case 10</u>**
**Ambulatory Surgery**
**History and Physical**

DATE OF ADMISSION: 1-16-06

ADMITTING DIAGNOSIS: Eyes turn out.

HISTORY OF PRESENT ILLNESS:
This is the first visit for this patient who is being admitted for ambulatory surgery. Patient will undergo eye muscle surgery in hopes of recapturing and maintaining binocular function.

PAST MEDICAL HISTORY:
The patient's eyes began to turn out in early childhood and underwent surgery for correction at the age of seven. Progression of the disease has now resulted in the patient only being able to use one eye at a time.
Allergies: None.
Medications: None.
Family History: No familial disorders known.

REVIEW OF SYSTEMS:
Review of systems in unremarkable.

PHYSICAL EXAMINATION:

| | |
|---|---|
| General: | Patient is alert, cooperative and in no acute distress. BP 120/80; Respirations 17; Pulse 77. |
| HEENT: | Head is normocephalic. Tympanic membranes clear. Nose, throat, and mouth are normal. No inflammation is noted. |
| Neck: | Supple with no masses palpated. |
| Eyes: | Visual acuity 20/20 OU with correction. Fundus is normal. Exotropia 30 prism diopters at distance, 20 prism diopters at near. Sensory testing reveals binocular function when the amount of strabismus is corrected with prisms, otherwise suppression OS. |
| Chest: | Clear to auscultation and percussion. |
| Heart: | Normal sinus rhythm without murmur, gallop or rub. |
| Skin: | Clear. |
| Extremities: | Full range of motion. Normal peripheral pulses. |
| Neurological: | Cranial nerves II through XII and deep tendon reflexes equal and symmetrical. |

PLAN: Strabismus surgery under general anesthesia.

**Mock Examination**
**Part II Case 10**
**Ambulatory Surgery**
**Operative Report**

| | |
|---|---|
| DATE OF OPERATION: | 1-16-06 |
| PREOPERATIVE DIAGNOSIS: | Exotropia |
| POSTOPERATIVE DIAGNOSIS: | Exotropia |
| PROCEDURE PERFORMED: | Recession, lateral rectus muscle, 6 mm O.U. |
| SURGEON: | E.B. Mannion, MD |
| ASSISTANT SURGEON: | Carlos Earl, III, MD |
| ANESTHESIOLOGIST: | Jim Wilkins, MD |

PROCEDURE:
Under general endotracheal anesthesia, the patient's adnex were prepped with Betadine. The patient was draped under sterile conditions. Forced ductions were performed and found to be negative, OU. A small wire lid speculum with solid teeth was applied OD. The right eye was rotated superonasally and an inferotemporal incision was made at the conjunctiva and tendon capsule in the cul-de-sac region with Westcott scissors. The right lateral rectus muscle was isolated on a muscle hook and brought out through the incision site. A double-arm suture of 6-0 Vicryl on a #29 spatula needle was placed through the muscle at its insertion and locked at both ends. The muscle was removed from the globe and reinserted into the sclera 6.0 mm from the original insertion site as measured with calipers. The conjunctiva was repositioned in its original position without suturing.

The lid speculum was transferred to the patient's left eye for an identical technique. The left lateral rectus muscle was recessed 6.0 mm.

At the completion of the surgery, several drops of Maxitrol were instilled OU and the patient left the operating room in good condition. No apparent complications noted.

**Mock Examination**
**Part II Case 10**

**Ambulatory Surgery**
**Progress Notes and Orders**

**PROGRESS NOTES:**

Patient was taken to the operating room for strabismus surgery. Patient tolerated the procedure well and no apparent complications were noted. The patient will be discharged when stable and when discharge criteria have been met. The patient is to follow up in my office tomorrow.

**PHYSICIAN ORDERS:**

A.M. admit on 1-16-06.
Patient to sign op permit

Postoperative Orders

Discharge when alert and stable.
IV orders per anesthesia.
Tylenol #3 q 4 h p.r.n.
Vistaril 50 mg q 4h for nausea
Cold moist compress to both eyes p.r.n. drainage

**Mock Examination**
**Part II Case 10**
**Answer Sheet**

| DIAGNOSES | ICD-9-CM CODES | | | | | |
|---|---|---|---|---|---|---|
| Primary DX | | | | . | | |
| DX 2 | | | | . | | |
| DX 3 | | | | . | | |
| DX 4 | | | | . | | |

| PROCEDURES | CPT CODES | | | | | MODIFIERS (If Applicable) | | |
|---|---|---|---|---|---|---|---|---|
| PR 1 | | | | | | - | | |
| PR 2 | | | | | | - | | |
| PR 3 | | | | | | - | | |
| PR 4 | | | | | | - | | |
| PR 5 | | | | | | - | | |
| PR 6 | | | | | | - | | |
| PR 7 | | | | | | - | | |

**Mock Examination**
**Part II Case 11**

**Ambulatory Surgery**
**Face Sheet**

| | |
|---|---|
| Patient's Name: | J. W. Brown |
| Date of Visit: | January 18, 2006 |
| Age: | 22 |
| Sex: | Male |
| Insurance: | Self Pay |

**Mock Examination**
**Part II Case 11**

**History and Physical**

DATE OF ADMISSION: 01-18-06

ADMITTING DIAGNOSIS: Twisting injury right knee.

HISTORY OF PRESENT ILLNESS:
This patient was playing baseball two weeks ago when he sustained an injury to his right knee while sliding into a base. Patient was seen in the Emergency Room where x-rays were negative for any fractures. Patient has been keeping his leg elevated and keeping weight off of it as much as possible.

PAST MEDICAL HISTORY: Negative.

ALLERGIES: None.

MEDICATIONS: None

SOCIAL HISTORY: Patient smokes 1 pack a day; alcohol - none.

PHYSICAL EXAMINATION:

| | |
|---|---|
| General: | Well-developed, well-nourished male. BP 120/70; Respirations 16; Pulse 75. |
| HEENT: | No gross lesions noted. Pupils round and equal. No icterus. No masses or thyroidomegaly. Oropharynx negative. Neck no masses or thyroidomegaly. |
| Chest: | Clear to auscultation and percussion. |
| Heart: | Normal sinus rhythm. |
| Abdomen: | No masses or rebound tenderness. |
| Extremities: | Right knee with recurrent swelling, locking and catching. 2+ effusion. Left knee is normal. |

PLAN:
Patient will be admitted for one-day surgery for arthroscopy of the right knee.

**Mock Examination**
**<u>Part II Case 11</u>**

**Operative Report**

Date of Operation: 01-18-06

Preoperative Diagnosis: Right knee medial meniscus tear

Postoperative Diagnosis: Right knee medical meniscus tear

Operation: Arthroscopic medial meniscectomy

Surgeon: D.D. Levers, MD

Anesthesia: General

Anesthesiologist: F.E. Godfrey, MD

INDICATIONS:
This patient has a twisting injury to the right knee. He has had swelling, locking, catching and involving the knee, 2+ effusion.

PROCEDURE:
The patient was taken to the operating room and general anesthesia was induced without complications. A well-padded pneumatic tourniquet was placed to the right upper thigh. The right leg was prepped and draped in the normal fashion. Diagnostic arthroscopy was performed. The findings are as listed below.

Under direct visualization, a medial portal was established. The posterior horn of the medial meniscus was debrided. A shaver was then introduced and taken back to a stable rim. The rest of the knee was then probed and the findings are listed below.

The scope was then withdrawn and the wound closed with #4-0 Vicryl. The patient tolerated the procedure well and was transferred to the recovery room.

FINDINGS:
1. Patello-femoral joint: No articular cartilage change.
2. Medial compartment: Grade 1 changes of the mediofemoral condyle, posterior horn meniscus tear.
3. Anterior cruciate ligament and posterior cruciate ligament intact.
4. Lateral compartment, no articular cartilage changes noted. Lateral meniscus is intact.

**Mock Examination**
**Part II Case 11**

## PROGRESS NOTES

Patient has a twisting injury to the right knee with swelling, locking, and catching.

Patient was taken to the operating room where an arthroscopic medial meniscectomy was performed.

Patient will be discharged with crutches and will make a follow-up appointment in two weeks.

## STANDARD POSTOPERATIVE ORDERS

1. Discharge from Recovery Room when stable.
2. Urinary catherization if patient unable to void postop x 1; then call physician.
3. Elevate right knee 20 degrees. Ice packs for 15 minutes then discontinue. Repeat x 1 hour.
4. Vital signs q 15 minutes x 4; then q 30 minutes x 2; then q 1 hour until discharge.
5. Tylenol 500mg q 4 hrs for pain.
6. Start on soft diet.
7. Discharge when patient is stable.

**Mock Examination**
**Part II Case 11**

**Answer Sheet**

| DIAGNOSES | ICD-9-CM CODES | | | | | |
|---|---|---|---|---|---|---|
| Primary DX | | | | . | | |
| DX 2 | | | | . | | |
| DX 3 | | | | . | | |
| DX 4 | | | | . | | |

| PROCEDURES | CPT CODES | | | | | MODIFIERS (If Applicable) | | |
|---|---|---|---|---|---|---|---|---|
| PR 1 | | | | | | - | | |
| PR 2 | | | | | | - | | |
| PR 3 | | | | | | - | | |
| PR 4 | | | | | | - | | |
| PR 5 | | | | | | - | | |
| PR 6 | | | | | | - | | |
| PR 7 | | | | | | - | | |

**Mock Examination**
**Part II Case 12**

**Ambulatory Care**
**Face Sheet**

| | |
|---|---|
| Date of Service: | January 15, 2006 |
| Age: | 62 |
| Sex: | Male |
| Admitting Diagnoses: | Urinary retention |
| Post Operative Diagnoses: | Benign prostatic hypertrophy |
| Procedure: | 1. Cystoscopy<br>2. Transurethral resection of the prostate |
| Discharge Disposition: | Home |

**Mock Examination**
**Part II Case 12**

**History and Physical**

DATE OF ADMISSION: 01/15/06

ADMITTING DIAGNOSIS: Urinary Retention

HISTORY OF PRESENT ILLNESS:
This is a 62-year-old male who has been experiencing increasing signs of urinary retention with urgency and difficulty with urination.

PAST MEDICAL HISTORY:
Positive for severe COPD, requiring home oxygen at 2.5 liters. Patient is also on steroids for COPD. Past history of myocardial infarction with coronary artery disease. Patient underwent cardiac catheterization, but is not considered a surgical candidate.

ALLERGIES: None known

MEDICATIONS:
Albuterol one dose four times a day; Theo-Dur 200 mg twice a day; Cardizem CD 120 mg once a day.

SOCIAL HISTORY: Significant for smoking 2 packs a day for 45 years. Occasional alcohol use.

FAMILY HISTORY: Non-contributory.

PHYSICAL EXAMINATION:

| | |
|---|---|
| General: | The patient is awake, alert and oriented. |
| HEENT: | Pupils are equal and react to light and accommodation. Extraocular muscles are intact. |
| Respiratory: | Prolonged expiratory phase. Scattered wheezes. |
| Cardiovascular: | Regular rate and rhythm. No murmurs, rubs or gallops. |
| Abdomen: | Soft, non-tender. Bowel sounds are present. No organomegaly. |
| Extremities: | No edema, cyanosis or clubbing. |
| Neurologic: | Nonfocal |

PLAN:
Patient is admitted to Ambulatory Surgery for Cystoscopy and possible Transurethral resection of the prostate.

## Mock Examination
## <u>Part II Case 12</u>

### Operative Report

| | |
|---|---|
| Date of Operation: | 01/15/06 |
| Preoperative Diagnosis: | Urinary Retention |
| Postoperative Diagnosis: | Benign Prostatic Hypertrophy<br>Incomplete Bladder Emptying |
| Operation: | Laser Coagulation of the Prostate |
| Surgeon: | Christopher Magee, Jr., MD |
| Anesthesiologist: | Leeland Kenna, MD |
| Anesthesia: | Spinal |

DESCRIPTION OF PROCEDURE:
The patient was placed on the operating table in the lithotomy position after spinal anesthesia was given. External genitalia was prepped and draped in the sterile manner.

A 21-French cystoscope was introduced within the bladder. The bladder was carefully inspected and there was no evidence of tumor. There was mild trabeculations in both ureteral orifices. At this time, the resectoscope was introduced and resection of the lateral lobes of the prostate was done allowing complete opening of the prostatic urethra. All of the prostatic chips were removed from the bladder. The bladder was coagulated and completely smoothed out with the VaporTrode. An 18-French Foley catheter was inserted into the bladder and left indwelling.

The patient tolerated the procedure well and was sent to the recovery room in satisfactory condition.

The patient will be discharged home when fully recovered with Foley in place. Patient will see me in my office tomorrow for removal of the Foley.

## Mock Examination
## Part II  Case 12

**PATHOLOGY REPORT**

TISSUES: Prostate Tissue

PRE-OPERATIVE DIAGNOSIS: Urinary Retention

POST- OPERATIVE DIAGNOSIS: Benign Prostatic Hypertrophy

GROSS DESCRIPTION:

Specimen received in formalin labeled "prostate tissue" consists of 9.0 x 9.0 x 2.5 cm. 40-gram aggregate of multiple irregular rubbery gray-white, tan-yellow, and tan-pink tissue. Representative sections (40 chips) are submitted.

MICROSCOPIC DIAGNOSIS:

Prostate tissue: Benign hyperplasia in 36 chips
Foci of adenocarcinoma in 4 chips

**Mock Examination**
**Part II Case 12**

---

**PROGRESS NOTE:**
The patient was taken to the OR where under spinal anesthesia a cystoscopy and transuretheral resection of the prostate was performed. The patient tolerated the procedure well and was transferred to the Recovery Room in satisfactory condition. Pathology report showed BPH and foci of adenocarcinoma in 4 chips.

---

**ORDERS:**
Standard Postoperative Orders

Discharge from the Recovery Room when stable.
Vital signs q 15 minutes x 4, q 30 minutes x 2, then q 1 hour until discharge
Vicodin, 40 mg one tablet p.r.n. for pain.
Macrobid b.i.d. for one week.
Discharge patient home when fully recovered and stable with Foley indwelling.
Patient is to return to my office tomorrow for follow-up and Foley removal.

---

**Mock Examination**
**Part II Case 12**

**Answer Sheet**

| DIAGNOSES | ICD-9-CM CODES | | | | | |
|---|---|---|---|---|---|---|
| Primary DX | | | | . | | |
| DX 2 | | | | . | | |
| DX 3 | | | | . | | |
| DX 4 | | | | . | | |

| PROCEDURES | CPT CODES | | | | | | MODIFIERS (If Applicable) | |
|---|---|---|---|---|---|---|---|---|
| PR 1 | | | | | | - | | |
| PR 2 | | | | | | - | | |
| PR 3 | | | | | | - | | |
| PR 4 | | | | | | - | | |
| PR 5 | | | | | | - | | |
| PR 6 | | | | | | - | | |
| PR 7 | | | | | | - | | |

**Mock Examination**
**Part II Case 13**

**Ambulatory Care**
**Face Sheet**

| | |
|---|---|
| Date of Service: | 01/17/06 |
| Age: | 52 |
| Sex: | Male |
| Admitting Diagnosis: | Chest pain |
| Discharge Diagnoses: | Coronary artery disease, native artery<br>Angina<br>History of coronary aorta bypass grafting |
| Procedures: | Left heart catheterization |
| Disposition: | Home |

**Mock Examination**
**Part II Case 13**

**History and Physical**

DATE OF ADMISSION: 1-17-06

HISTORY OF PRESENT ILLNESS:
This is a 52-year-old male with a history of angina for which he underwent four-vessel coronary surgical revascularization. This was performed last December. He had a left internal mammary artery to the left anterior descending coronary artery, sequential saphenous vein graft to the obtuse marginal and diagonal vessels and a saphenous vein graft to the right coronary artery. His left ventricular function was normal.

More recently he has been having problems with chest pain. For this reason he is now brought back to the cardiac catheterization laboratory for re-evaluation.

ALLERGIES: Demerol and Biaxin.

LABORATORY DATA:
His laboratory studies reveal normal electrolytes, BUN, creatinine and a mildly depressed hemoglobin and hematocrit of 13 and 38.8, respectively with normochromic, normocytic indices. The platelet count is normal. PT and PTT are normal.

ELECTROCARDIOGRAM: Demonstrates sinus bradycardia and otherwise is normal.

PHYSICAL EXAMINATION:

| | |
|---|---|
| Vital signs: | Stable. |
| General: | Well-developed, well-nourished male in no acute distress. Patient is oriented times three. Skin is warm and dry. Pupils round and equal. Neck supple; trachea is midline. |
| Chest: | Clear to auscultation and percussion. |
| Heart: | Normal sinus rhythm. No rubs, gallops appreciated. |
| Abdomen: | Soft without distention. There is no guarding or rebound. No organomegaly. |
| Extremities: | Unremarkable. |

Further decisions will be based on cardiac catheterization test results. He is agreeable to proceed. He is aware of the risks that include bleeding, infection, heart attack, rhythm disturbance, death, stroke, reaction to dye or damage to nerve or blood vessel.

He is aware of the alternatives of cardiac catheterization which would include medical therapy and possibly stress testing. He is agreeable to catheterization.

**Mock Examination**
**Part II Case 13**

**Cardiac Catheterization Report**

Date of Catherization: 01/17/06

Procedure: Cardiac Catheterization

Pre-operative Diagnosis: Chest pain
History of angina

Post-operative Diagnosis: Coronary artery disease

Surgeon: Cheryl Bottom, MD

Assistant: Sadie Phillips, MD

Cardiac Catherization Procedure:
The patient was brought to the cardiac catheterization laboratory n.p.o. with a peripheral intravenous line in place. The right groin was prepped and draped in the usual fashion. Local anesthesia was obtained with Xylocaine 2%.

Utilizing a modified Seldinger technique, the right femoral artery was entered percutaneously and a #5 French side-arm sheath was placed. Utilizing Judkins technique and left and right 4 bend Judkins catheters and a #5 French 110-cm pigtail catheter, left heart catherization was completed.

Upon completion, the arterial catheter and sheath were removed and hemostasis was achieved by direct pressure applied to the right groin. The patient tolerated the procedure well and left in stable condition.

IMPRESSION:
1. Severe native multi-vessel coronary arterial disease. Total occlusion of the proximal left anterior descending coronary artery after the first septal and first diagonal vessels.
2. Anatomically obstructive stenosis in the obtuse marginal vessel - 3 in its proximal and midportions.
3. Total occlusion of the mid right coronary artery.
4. Patent LIMA graft to the left anterior descending coronary artery.
5. Patent sequential saphenous vein graft to the diagonal vessel and OM-3 vessel. Small diseased diagonal vessel demonstrated.
6. Patent saphenous vein graft to the distal right coronary artery. Approximate 60-70% stenosis in the midportion of the posterior descending coronary artery.
7. Normal left ventricular size and systolic contractile pattern.
8. Mildly elevated left ventricular end-diastolic pressure 16 mmHg.

## Mock Examination
## Part II Case 13

**PROGRESS NOTE**

1/17/06 Patient admitted for left heart catherization. Aware of risks and benefits. Agreeable to proceed.

1/17/06 LHC completed via right femoral approach. Tolerated well. SVG to Diag./OM patent. Stenosis at level of Diagonal at SVG. SVG - RCA patent. LIMA to LAD patent. Normal LV. Severe native CAD. Films to be reviewed. D/C home today.

---

**PHYSICIAN ORDERS**

1/17/06
1. NPO - after MN except for meds
2. D5 1/2 NSS with 10 mEq. KCL/l at 75 cc/hr on admit
3. Pre op meds
4. Benadryl 50 mg p.o.
5. Tagamet 300 mg
6. Consent for right and left heart catherization
7. Diet: Cardiac

1/17/06
1. Darvocet –100 tab p.o. q 4-6 hr PRN pain
2. Tylenol #3 one tab p.o. q 4 hr PRN pain if unrelieved by Darvocet
3. Maintain IV at 150 cc/hr x 4 hr., then Heplock
4. Resume diet
5. Bed rest for 3 hours, then bathroom privileges
6. Blood pressure in right arm, pulse, respirations q 15 minutes x 2; q 30 minutes x2; q 1 hr x 2 or until stable; the q 4 hr. Call physician if heart rate 50 or >100 systolic B/P
7. Check pulses distal to catheterization site q 15 minutes x 2; q 30 minutes x 2; q 1 hr x 2; then q 4 hr. Notify physician of loss of palpable pulse, complaint or pain or coldness in distal extremity.
8. Check dressing for bleeding and hematoma q 15 minutes x 2; q 30 minutes x2; then q 1 hr x 2 and PRN.
9. Discharge when patient is stable.

**Mock Examination**
**Part II Case 13**

**Answer Sheet**

| DIAGNOSES | ICD-9-CM CODES | | | | | |
|---|---|---|---|---|---|---|
| Primary DX | | | | . | | |
| DX 2 | | | | . | | |
| DX 3 | | | | . | | |
| DX 4 | | | | . | | |

| PROCEDURES | CPT CODES | | | | | MODIFIERS (If Applicable) | | |
|---|---|---|---|---|---|---|---|---|
| PR 1 | | | | | | - | | |
| PR 2 | | | | | | - | | |
| PR 3 | | | | | | - | | |
| PR 4 | | | | | | - | | |
| PR 5 | | | | | | - | | |
| PR 6 | | | | | | - | | |
| PR 7 | | | | | | - | | |

## CCS-P Mock Examination
## Part II  Case  14

### Face Sheet

| | |
|---|---|
| Patient Name: | Nathan Jenkins |
| Date of Visit: | January 17, 2006 |
| Age: | 45 |
| Insurance: | HMO |

**CCS-P Mock Examination**
**Part II Case 14**

**History & Physical**

Date: January 17, 2006

Chief Complaint: Palpitations

Present Illness: This is a 45 year old male, who had visited the Emergency Room at Sun City Hospital on December 6, 2005, for rapid palpitations. He has had three episodes of sudden, rapid palpitations. Usually, they break on their own. The last episode lasted 18 hours. Patient was given Cardizem without any response. He usually is completely asymptomatic, although he feels poorly the day afterwards.

The arrhythmia seen on the electrocardiogram at Sun City Hospital was most consistent with classical flutter. Holter monitor was performed, which was normal. Ablation was recommended to the patient.

Past Medical History: Borderline hypertension, but he is not treated for it. No history of diabetes or pulmonary disease.

Family History: Negative.

Social History: Denies cigarette use.

Physical Examination:

| | |
|---|---|
| General: | Overweight male in no acute distress. Blood pressure is high at 138/80; pulse is regular at 160 beats per minute. |
| Neck: | Neck is supple without evidence of bruits. There is no thyromegaly. |
| Chest: | Clear to auscultation. |
| Heart: | Cardiac examination revealed a normal S1 S2 without murmurs. |
| Abdomen: | Benign. |
| Extremities: | No evidence of clubbing, cyanosis or edema. |

His electrocardiogram at Sun City Hospital showed classical atrial flutter at 104 beats per minute.

Impression: The patient's arrhythmia is fairly classic for atrial flutter.

Plan: Patient is to be admitted as an outpatient for ablation.

**CCS-P Mock Examination**
**Part II Case 14**

**Operative Report**

Date of Operation: January 17, 2006

Preoperative Diagnosis: Atrial Flutter

Postoperative Diagnosis:
1. Typical atrioventricular reentrant tachycardia
2. Classic type I atrial flutter

Operation:
1. Full electrophysiologic study with coronary sinus catheter
2. Follow up programmed stimulation with isoproterenol
3. Electrical cardioversion of atrial flutter
4. Radiofrequency catheter ablation of the slow A-V nodal pathway
5. Radiofrequency catheter ablation of the atrial flutter

Medications given:
Heparin 1000 units per hour
Isoproterenol 2 mcg per minute

Findings:

1. Baseline normal sinus nodal and His-Purkinje function. Ventricular function was not completely studied. The corrected sinus nodal recovery time measured 154 milliseconds at baseline. The H-V interval measured 53 milliseconds at baseline.
2. On isoproterenol 2 mcg per minute, reproducible induced typical AV nodal reentrant tachycardia with a cycle length of 260 milliseconds (231 beats per minute) was induced by double atrial electric stimuli at the high right atrium. This produces systolic blood pressure of 83 mmHg. The arrhythmia was terminated with ventricular burst pacing at 230 milliseconds. Dual AV nodal pathways were evident at baseline with a fast AV nodal effective refractory period measuring 500/310; the slow AV nodal effective refractory period measured 500/350/220.
3. Successful radiofrequency catheter ablation of the slow A-V nodal pathway was accomplished after 3 applications of radiofrequency energy of 50 watts/60 degrees centigrade to the roof of the coronary sinus os. Junctional tachycardia occurred within 6 seconds of radiofrequency application.
4. After slow AV nodal pathway ablation, antegrade AV nodal block measured 300 milliseconds. The AV nodal effective refractory period measured 400/240 and no slow AV nodal conduction could be seen. No inducible A-V nodal reentrant tachycardia despite double atrial electric stimuli on isoproterenol 2 mcg per minute AV nodal refractoriness.
5. Induced atrial fibrillation with rapid atrial pacing at 230 milliseconds at the high right atrium on isoproterenol 2 mcg per minute, this organized to classic type I atrial flutter.
6. Successful creation of bidirectional conduction block was accomplished across the isthmus of the tricuspid annulus and inferior vena cava, coronary sinus os of the inferior vena cava, coronary sinus os of the tricuspid annulus. Conduction block was proven using coronary sinus os and low right atrial pacing.

Impression:

1. Inducible typical atrioventricular nodal reentrant tachycardia.
2. Inducible atrial flutter, classic type I

**CCS-P Mock Examination**
**Part II Case 14**

**Progress Notes:**

Feels good.
BP 140/84
Groins healing well
Cardiac - normal
Will discharge home

---

**Physician Orders:**

1. Supine bed rest for 4 hours keeping left and right legs straight.
2. May elevate HOB no greater than 30 degrees
3. Vital signs every 15 minutes x 4, every 30 minutes x 4, every hour x 4.
4. Change IV to heplock.
5. 12 lead EKG
6. Percocet i-ii p.o q 6.

Discharge Instructions:

1. Discharge home when stable.
2. ASA 325 mg QD
3. Follow up with me in 1 month
4. Regular diet and activity

**CCS-P Mock Examination**

**Part II Case 14**

| Diagnoses | ICD-9-CM Codes | | | | | | | | |
|---|---|---|---|---|---|---|---|---|---|
| DX 1 | | | | . | | | - | | |
| DX 2 | | | | . | | | - | | |
| DX 3 | | | | . | | | - | | |
| DX 4 | | | | . | | | - | | |

| Procedures | CPT Codes | | | | | | | | | | |
|---|---|---|---|---|---|---|---|---|---|---|---|
| PP 1 | | | | | | | | | - | | |
| PP 2 | | | | | | | | | - | | |
| PP 3 | | | | | | | | | - | | |
| PP 4 | | | | | | | | | - | | |
| PP 5 | | | | | | | | | - | | |
| PP 6 | | | | | | | | | - | | |

**Mock Examination**
**Part II Case 15**

**Emergency Room**
**Facesheet**

| | |
|---|---|
| Name: | Charles Teal |
| Date: | January 4, 2006 |
| Age: | 50 |
| Insurance: | HMO |

**Mock Examination**
**Part II Case 15**

**Emergency Room Visit**

Date: 1/4/06

Chief Complaint: Cyst on groin area for several days

History of Present Illness: Patient complains of a tender swollen spot in the perirectal region. This has occurred for several days. It is painful and it is getting worse as time progresses.

Past Medical History: Negative for diabetes or hypertension.

Medications: None

Allergies: ASA

Social History: Patient smokes one pack per day.

Review of Systems: All negative.

Physical Examination:

General: Patient is alert and oriented x 3. Patient is in moderate distress.

Vitals: BP: 130/80; P: 111; R: 21; T: 100

Skin: There is a fluctuant abscess in the scrotal area which needs to be drained.

Procedure: Skin was prepped with Betadine and lidocaine 1% was given. The abscess was incised with a #11 knife and a large amount of pus drained. The area was irrigated with saline and packed with gauze.

Impression: Abscess of the scrotal wall.

Discharge instructions: Patient is to follow up in 3 days for removal of the gauze. Patient is to take Tylenol if needed for pain.

| | |
|---|---|
| History: | Problem focused |
| Physical Exam: | Problem focused |
| Medical Decision: | Straightforward |

**CCS-P Mock Examination**
**<u>Part II Case 15</u>**

| Diagnoses | ICD-9-CM Codes | | | | | | | | |
|---|---|---|---|---|---|---|---|---|---|
| DX 1 | | | | . | | | - | | |
| DX 2 | | | | . | | | - | | |
| DX 3 | | | | . | | | - | | |
| DX 4 | | | | . | | | - | | |

| Procedures | CPT Codes | | | | | | | | | | |
|---|---|---|---|---|---|---|---|---|---|---|---|
| PP 1 | | | | | | | | | - | | |
| PP 2 | | | | | | | | | - | | |
| PP 3 | | | | | | | | | - | | |
| PP 4 | | | | | | | | | - | | |
| PP 5 | | | | | | | | | - | | |
| PP 6 | | | | | | | | | - | | |

**Mock Examination**
**Part II Case 16**

**Face Sheet**

| | |
|---|---|
| Name: | Elizabeth Cooper |
| Date: | January 30, 2006 |
| Age: | 72 |
| Insurance: | Medicare |

**Mock Examination**
**Part II Case 16**

## HISTORY AND PHYSICAL

History of Present Illness:
Mrs. Cooper is returning to our office for follow up of lightheadedness. The patient has been doing well since her last visit. She has not experienced any syncope or near syncope. No chest pain or pressure, PND, orthopnea or dyspnea on exertion.

Medications: She is taking aspirin 81 mg q.d. and Celexa 10 mg q.d.

Review of Systems: General: No fevers or chills. Respiratory: No wheezing, cough or shortness of breath. GI: No complaints. GU: No complaints. Extremities: No edema or other problems.

Previous testing results: Stress nuclear study showed an area of septal and also apical thinning with improvements in counts on delay. There was some motion artifact, however, one has to be concerned about the possibility of ischemia in this region which would appear to be, if present, LAD. LV function was normal and there appears to be LVH. Of concern, the patient did not exercise a great distance, got about three minutes on Bruce protocol, and had a dip near her starting blood pressure at peak exercise.

Holter monitor showed short runs of paroxysmal SVT versus atrial fibrillation up to 150 beats per minute. Echocardiogram showed normal LV function, mild to moderate MR, mild TR. I am concerned with the stress nuclear study showing a question of LAD ischemia and the fact that her blood pressure at peak exercise dropped back near starting level.

Physical Examination:

| | |
|---|---|
| Vital signs: | BP: 144/60; P: 72 and regular. |
| Neck: | No JVD. |
| Lungs: | Clear bilaterally. |
| Cardiac: | Regular rate and rhythm. Grade 1/6 right upper sternal border systolic murmur and a positive S4. |
| Abdomen: | Soft, nontender and benign. |
| Extremities: | Femoral pulses appear to be 2+ without bruits. Distal extremities unremarkable.No significant edema. |
| Neurologic: | Alert and oriented, grossly appears nonfocal. |

Impression:
1. Coronary artery disease. Based on nuclear described above, I suspect there may be LAD coronary artery disease.
2. Mild to moderate MR by echo.
3. Probable hypertension

Plan:
1. Patient will be scheduled for outpatient cardiac catherization.
2. Continue aspirin at this point.

**Mock Examination**
**Part II Case 16**

**PROCEDURE**

| | |
|---|---|
| Date of Procedure: | January 30, 2006 |
| Preoperative Diagnosis: | Coronary artery disease |
| Postoperative Diagnosis: | Coronary artery disease of mid lateral anterior descending artery |
| Procedure: | Left heart catherization<br>Coronary arteriograms<br>Left venticulography<br>PTCA with stent |

Patient was taken to the cardiac catherization lab and was prepped and drapped in the usual sterile manner. The right femoral artery was entered using the percutaneous technique. Left coronary arteriograms were performed using 6 fr, JL4 catheters. Left ventriculography was performed using 6 fr, JR4 catheters. Right coronary arteriograms were performed using 6 fr JR4.

# 6 French sheath was sutured to right groin. Heparinized NaCl via pressure bag attached to 6 french sheath. The injection fraction was 79%.

Then 6 french RFA & FRV flex sheaths were placed. GFXB 3.5 guide & PT Graphix wire was used to cross lesion. IV NTG given. ACT baseline = 133. IV Heparin 3 units given. Mid left anterior descending lesion was predilated with 2.5 x 20 mm Maverick balloon. Stented with 2.5 x 18 mm Bx Velocity stent immediately distal to diagonal. Post dilated with 2.75 x 15 mm Maverick balloon with 14 bars with good opposition.

Results: Residual 0-5%. Side branch: Diagonal not jeopardized.

Complications: None.

**Mock Examination**
**Part II Case 16**

## Progress Notes

1/30/06 Heart catherization showed 90% stenosis of LAD. PTCA was performed with insertion of 2.5x18 mm BX Velocity stent. Patient tolerated procedure well.

1/31/06 No problems or complications from catherization. Pulses OK. Abdomen soft. No bleeding from femoral site.

---

## Physician Orders:

1/30/06
1. Right groin check, right DP pulse q 15 min x 4, then q 30 min x 4; then q4h.
2. Monitor femoral artery line, Swan if applicable.
3. NPO until fully alert, then liquids, then advance as tolerated to cardiac diet.
4. Bedrest with right leg extended; loose protective device right ankle. May elevate HOB 30 degrees while sheaths in.
5. Bedrest x eight hours after sheaths out, then out of bed with assistance.
6. IV D5 1/2 NS at 125 ml/hr x 8 hours.
7. Tridil 10 mcg/min. per standard concentration. Wean at 6 Am.
8. Uncoated ASA 325 mg PO q AM.
9. O2 at 2 L/min. via nasal cannula prn, SOB, or O2 sats <90%. Oximeter if O2 in use.

1/31/06
1. Discharge patient.
2. Script for Plavix 75 mg po OD x 1 month.
3. Follow up with me in 2 weeks.

**CCS-P Mock Examination**

**Part II Case 16**

| Diagnoses | ICD-9-CM Codes | | | | | | | | |
|---|---|---|---|---|---|---|---|---|---|
| DX 1 | | | | . | | | - | | |
| DX 2 | | | | . | | | - | | |
| DX 3 | | | | . | | | - | | |
| DX 4 | | | | . | | | - | | |

| Procedures | CPT Codes | | | | | | | | | | |
|---|---|---|---|---|---|---|---|---|---|---|---|
| PP 1 | | | | | | | | | - | | |
| PP 2 | | | | | | | | | - | | |
| PP 3 | | | | | | | | | - | | |
| PP 4 | | | | | | | | | - | | |
| PP 5 | | | | | | | | | - | | |
| PP 6 | | | | | | | | | - | | |

# CCS-P Mock Exam

## Coding Cases

## *Answer Key*

## CCS-P Mock Examination Answer Key

### Case 1

| Diagnoses | ICD-9-CM Codes | | | | | |
|---|---|---|---|---|---|---|
| DX 1 Chest Wall Pain | 7 | 8 | 6 | . | 5 | 2 |
| DX 2 Pacemaker status | V | 4 | 5 | . | 0 | 1 |
| DX 3 COPD | 4 | 9 | 6 | . | | |
| DX 4 History of tobacco use | V | 1 | 5 | . | 8 | 2 |

| Procedures | CPT Codes | | | | | | | |
|---|---|---|---|---|---|---|---|---|
| PP 1 Office Visit | 9 | 9 | 2 | 1 | 5 | - | | |
| PP 2 EKG - 12 Lead | 9 | 3 | 0 | 0 | 0 | - | | |
| PP 3 | | | | | | - | | |
| PP 4 | | | | | | - | | |
| PP 5 | | | | | | - | | |
| PP 6 | | | | | | - | | |

### Case 2

| Diagnoses | ICD-9-CM Codes | | | | | |
|---|---|---|---|---|---|---|
| DX 1 Boxer's Fracture Shaft 5th Finger | 8 | 1 | 5 | . | 0 | 3 |
| DX 2 | | | | . | | |
| DX 3 | | | | . | | |
| DX 4 | | | | . | | |

| Procedures | CPT Codes | | | | | | | |
|---|---|---|---|---|---|---|---|---|
| PP 1 Radiology hand 2 views | 7 | 3 | 1 | 2 | 0 | - | | |
| PP 2 Office visit | 9 | 9 | 2 | 0 | 2 | - | | |
| PP 3 Splint (Supplies) | A | 4 | 5 | 7 | 0 | - | | |
| PP 4 Application short arm splint | 2 | 9 | 1 | 2 | 5 | - | | |
| PP 5 | | | | | | - | | |
| PP 6 | | | | | | - | | |

## CCS-P Mock Examination Answer Key

### Case 3

| Diagnoses | ICD-9-CM Codes | | | | | |
|---|---|---|---|---|---|---|
| DX 1 Urinary Tract Infection | 5 | 9 | 9 | . | 0 | |
| DX 2 | | | | . | | |
| DX 3 | | | | . | | |
| DX 4 | | | | . | | |

| Procedures | CPT Codes | | | | | | | |
|---|---|---|---|---|---|---|---|---|
| PP 1 Office Visit | 9 | 9 | 2 | 0 | 2 | - | | |
| PP 2 Automated Microscopic Urinaylsis | 8 | 1 | 0 | 0 | 1 | - | | |
| PP 3 | | | | | | - | | |
| PP 4 | | | | | | - | | |
| PP 5 | | | | | | - | | |
| PP 6 | | | | | | - | | |

### Case 4

| Diagnoses | ICD-9-CM Codes | | | | | |
|---|---|---|---|---|---|---|
| DX 1 Left Lateral Epicondylitis | 7 | 2 | 6 | . | 3 | 2 |
| DX 2 | | | | . | | |
| DX 3 | | | | . | | |
| DX 4 | | | | . | | |

| Procedures | CPT Codes | | | | | | | |
|---|---|---|---|---|---|---|---|---|
| PP 1 Injection joint | 2 | 0 | 6 | 0 | 5 | - | | |
| PP 2 Injection Aristospan 5 mg | J | 3 | 3 | 0 | 3 | - | | |
| PP 3 Injection Aristospan 5 mg | J | 3 | 3 | 0 | 3 | - | | |
| PP 4 Office visit | 9 | 9 | 2 | 1 | 3 | - | | |
| PP 5 | | | | | | - | | |
| PP 6 | | | | | | - | | |

## CCS-P Mock Examination Answer Key

### Case 5

| Diagnoses | ICD-9-CM Codes | | | | | |
|---|---|---|---|---|---|---|
| DX 1 Postoperative Follow-up Surgery | V | 6 | 7 | . | 0 | 9 |
| DX 2 | | | | . | | |
| DX 3 | | | | . | | |
| DX 4 | | | | . | | |

| Procedures | CPT Codes | | | | | | | |
|---|---|---|---|---|---|---|---|---|
| PP 1 Office Visit (Postoperative Period) | 9 | 9 | 0 | 2 | 4 | - | | |
| PP 2 | | | | | | - | | |
| PP 3 | | | | | | - | | |
| PP 4 | | | | | | - | | |
| PP 5 | | | | | | - | | |
| PP 6 | | | | | | - | | |

### Case 6

| Diagnoses | ICD-9-CM Codes | | | | | |
|---|---|---|---|---|---|---|
| DX 1 Sebaceous Cyst | 7 | 0 | 6 | . | 2 | |
| DX 2 Hypertension | 4 | 0 | 1 | . | 9 | |
| DX 3 Chronic Obstructive Pulmonary Disease | 4 | 9 | 6 | . | | |
| DX 4 | | | | . | | |

| Procedures | CPT Codes | | | | | | | |
|---|---|---|---|---|---|---|---|---|
| PP 1 Excision of Cyst 2.0 cm | 1 | 1 | 4 | 2 | 2 | - | | |
| PP 2 Excision of Cyst 2.5 cm | 1 | 1 | 4 | 2 | 3 | - | 5 | 1 |
| PP 3 | | | | | | - | | |
| PP 4 | | | | | | - | | |
| PP 5 | | | | | | - | | |
| PP 6 | | | | | | - | | |

## CCS-P Mock Examination Answer Key

### Case 7

| Diagnoses | ICD-9-CM Codes | | | | | |
|---|---|---|---|---|---|---|
| DX 1 Wrist Sprain | 8 | 4 | 2 | . | 0 | 0 |
| DX 2 Hip Contusion | 9 | 2 | 4 | . | 0 | 1 |
| DX 3 | | | | . | | |
| DX 4 | | | | . | | |

| Procedures | CPT Codes | | | | | | | |
|---|---|---|---|---|---|---|---|---|
| PP 1 ER Visit | 9 | 9 | 2 | 8 | 2 | - | | |
| PP 2 | | | | | | - | | |
| PP 3 | | | | | | - | | |
| PP 4 | | | | | | - | | |
| PP 5 | | | | | | - | | |
| PP 6 | | | | | | - | | |

### Case 8

| Diagnoses | ICD-9-CM Codes | | | | | |
|---|---|---|---|---|---|---|
| DX 1 Rehabilitation | V | 5 | 7 | | 8 | 9 |
| DX 2 Status Post Amputee | V | 4 | 9 | . | 7 | 5 |
| DX 3 Depression | 3 | 1 | 1 | . | | |
| DX 4 | | | | . | | |

| Procedures | CPT Codes | | | | | | | |
|---|---|---|---|---|---|---|---|---|
| PP 1 Rehab Visit | 9 | 9 | 3 | 0 | 5 | - | | |
| PP 2 | | | | | | - | | |
| PP 3 | | | | | | - | | |
| PP 4 | | | | | | - | | |
| PP 5 | | | | | | - | | |
| PP 6 | | | | | | - | | |

## CCS-P Mock Examination Answer Key

### Case 9

| Diagnoses | ICD-9-CM Codes | | | | | |
|---|---|---|---|---|---|---|
| DX 1 Indigestion | 5 | 3 | 6 | . | 8 | |
| DX 2 Family history of ischemic heart disease | V | 1 | 7 | . | 3 | |
| DX 3 | | | | . | | |
| DX 4 | | | | . | | |

| Procedures | CPT Codes | | | | | | | |
|---|---|---|---|---|---|---|---|---|
| PP 1 Office Visit | 9 | 9 | 2 | 1 | 4 | - | | |
| PP 2 Stress Test | 9 | 3 | 0 | 1 | 5 | - | | |
| PP 3 Blood Draw | G | 0 | 0 | 0 | 1 | - | | |
| PP 4 Lab Handling | 9 | 9 | 0 | 0 | 0 | - | | |
| PP 5 | | | | | | - | | |
| PP 6 | | | | | | - | | |

### Case 10

| Diagnoses | ICD-9-CM Codes | | | | | |
|---|---|---|---|---|---|---|
| DX 1 Exotropia, unspecified | 3 | 7 | 8 | . | 1 | 0 |
| DX 2 | | | | . | | |
| DX 3 | | | | . | | |
| DX 4 | | | | . | | |

| Procedures | CPT Codes | | | | | | | |
|---|---|---|---|---|---|---|---|---|
| PP 1 Strabismus Surgery, Recession, lateral rectus muscle | 6 | 7 | 3 | 1 | 1 | - | 5 | 0 |
| PP 2 | | | | | | - | | |
| PP 3 | | | | | | - | | |
| PP 4 | | | | | | - | | |
| PP 5 | | | | | | - | | |
| PP 6 | | | | | | - | | |

**CCS-P Mock Examination Answer Key**

**Case 11**

| Diagnoses | ICD-9-CM Codes | | | | | |
|---|---|---|---|---|---|---|
| DX 1 Medial Meniscus Tear | 8 | 3 | 6 | . | 0 | |
| DX 2 | | | | . | | |
| DX 3 | | | | . | | |
| DX 4 | | | | . | | |

| Procedures | CPT Codes | | | | | | | |
|---|---|---|---|---|---|---|---|---|
| PP 1 Arthroscopic Medial Meninsectomy | 2 | 9 | 8 | 8 | 1 | - | R | T |
| PP 2 | | | | | | - | | |
| PP 3 | | | | | | - | | |
| PP 4 | | | | | | - | | |
| PP 5 | | | | | | - | | |
| PP 6 | | | | | | - | | |

**Case 12**

| Diagnoses | ICD-9-CM Codes | | | | | |
|---|---|---|---|---|---|---|
| DX 1 Benign prostatic hypertrophy | 6 | 0 | 0 | . | 0 | 0 |
| DX 2 Malignant neoplasm of prostate | 1 | 8 | 5 | . | | |
| DX 3 Coronary artery disease, native artery | 4 | 1 | 4 | . | 0 | 1 |
| DX 4 Chronic obstructive pulmonary disease | 4 | 9 | 6 | . | | |

| Procedures | CPT Codes | | | | | | | |
|---|---|---|---|---|---|---|---|---|
| PP 1 Laser coagulation of prostate | 5 | 2 | 6 | 4 | 7 | - | | |
| PP 2 | | | | | | - | | |
| PP 3 | | | | | | - | | |
| PP 4 | | | | | | - | | |
| PP 5 | | | | | | - | | |
| PP 6 | | | | | | - | | |

## CCS-P Mock Examination Answer Key

### Case 13

| Diagnoses | ICD-9-CM Codes | | | | | |
|---|---|---|---|---|---|---|
| DX 1 Coronary artery disease of native artery | 4 | 1 | 4 | . | 0 | 1 |
| DX 2 Angina pectoris | 4 | 1 | 3 | . | 9 | |
| DX 3 History of coronary artery bypass graft | V | 4 | 5 | . | 8 | 1 |
| DX 4 | | | | . | | |

| Procedures | CPT Codes | | | | | | | |
|---|---|---|---|---|---|---|---|---|
| PP 1 Left heart catheterization | 9 | 3 | 5 | 1 | 0 | - | | |
| PP 2 Injection for coronary artery | 9 | 3 | 5 | 3 | 9 | - | | |
| PP 3 Injection for grafts | 9 | 3 | 5 | 4 | 0 | - | | |
| PP 4 Left ventriculogram | 9 | 3 | 5 | 4 | 3 | - | | |
| PP 5 Imaging supervision, interpretation and report for injection procedure (s) during cardial catherization; ventricular | 9 | 3 | 5 | 5 | 5 | - | | |
| PP 6 Imaging supervision, interpretation and report for injection procedure(s) during cardial catherization; selective coronary angiography | 9 | 3 | 5 | 5 | 6 | - | | |

### Case 14

| Diagnoses | ICD-9-CM Codes | | | | | |
|---|---|---|---|---|---|---|
| DX 1 Conduction disorder unspecified | 4 | 2 | 6 | . | 8 | 9 |
| DX 2 Atrial flutter | 4 | 2 | 7 | . | 3 | 2 |
| DX 3 | | | | . | | |
| DX 4 | | | | . | | |

| Procedures | CPT Codes | | | | | | | |
|---|---|---|---|---|---|---|---|---|
| PP 1 Comprehensive EPS | 9 | 3 | 6 | 2 | 0 | - | | |
| PP 2 Ablation | 9 | 3 | 6 | 5 | 0 | - | | |
| PP 3 Programmed stimulation and pacing | 9 | 3 | 6 | 2 | 3 | - | | |
| PP 4 | | | | | | - | | |
| PP 5 | | | | | | - | | |
| PP 6 | | | | | | - | | |

**CCS-P Mock Examination Answer Key**

## Case 15

| Diagnoses | ICD-9-CM Codes | | | | | |
|---|---|---|---|---|---|---|
| DX 1 Abscess Scrotum | 6 | 0 | 8 | . | 4 | |
| DX 2 | | | | . | | |
| DX 3 | | | | . | | |
| DX 4 | | | | . | | |

| Procedures | CPT Codes | | | | | | | |
|---|---|---|---|---|---|---|---|---|
| PP 1 Incision and drainage scrotal wall | 5 | 5 | 1 | 0 | 0 | - | | |
| PP 2 Emergency Room Visit | 9 | 9 | 2 | 8 | 1 | - | 2 | 5 |
| PP 3 | | | | | | - | | |
| PP 4 | | | | | | - | | |
| PP 5 | | | | | | - | | |
| PP 6 | | | | | | - | | |

## B Case 16

| Diagnoses | ICD-9-CM Codes | | | | | |
|---|---|---|---|---|---|---|
| DX 1 CAD | 4 | 1 | 4 | . | 0 | 1 |
| DX 2 Mitral regurgitation | 4 | 2 | 4 | . | 0 | |
| DX 3 | | | | . | | |
| DX 4 | | | | . | | |

| Procedures | CPT Codes | | | | | | | |
|---|---|---|---|---|---|---|---|---|
| PP 1 LD Stent placement | 9 | 2 | 9 | 8 | 0 | - | L | D |
| PP 2 Left heart catheterization | 9 | 3 | 5 | 1 | 0 | - | 5 | 1 |
| PP 3 Coronary angiograms | 9 | 3 | 5 | 4 | 5 | - | | |
| PP 4 Left ventriculogram | 9 | 3 | 5 | 4 | 3 | - | | |
| PP 5 Imaging supervision, interpretation and report for injection procedure(s), ventricular angiography | 9 | 3 | 5 | 5 | 5 | - | | |
| PP 6 Imaging supervision, interpretation and report for selective coronary angiography | 9 | 3 | 5 | 5 | 6 | - | | |
| PP 7 | | | | | | | | |

## Appendix A

## PHARMACOLOGY OVERVIEW

### The most common prescription drugs with examples of diagnoses

#### Analgesics

**Acetaminophen w/codeine** (Tylenol #2, #3, #4) mild to moderate pain
**Advil** (ibuprofen) mild to moderate pain
**Bancap-HC (hydrocodone w/APAP)** moderate to severe pain, expectorant
**Darvon** (propoxyphene N/APAP)
**Demerol** (meperidine HC1)
**Dilaudid** (hydromorphine HC1)
**hydrocodone w/APAP** (Bancap-HC) pain, moderate to severe; antitussives/expectorants
**ibuprofen** (Advil, Motrin) NSAID, arthritis, osteoarthritis; rheumatoid arthritis, dysmenorrhea; mild to moderate pain, fever; gout
**Motrin** (ibuprofen)
**propoxyphene N/APAP** (Darvon) pain, narcotic
**Talwin** (pentazocine HC1)
**tramadol** (Ultram) moderate to severe pain
**Tylenol #2, #3, #4** (acetaminophen w/codeine
**Ultram** (tramadol)

#### Anti-inflammatory

**Anaprox** (naproxen)
**Celebrex** (celecoxib)
**celecoxib** (Celebrex) osteoarthritis and rheumatoid arthritis, adenomatous colorectal polyps
**Indocin** (indomethacin)
**Medrol** (methylprednisolone)
**methylprednisolone** (Medrol) inflammatory disorders
**Motrin** (naprosyn)
**Nalfon** (fenoprofen calcium)
**naproxen** (Anaprox) NSAID, mild to moderate pain, osteoarthritis, rheumatoid arthritis, dysmenorrhea, gout, ankylosing spondylitis, fever
**prednisone** inflammatory disorders, adrenal insufficiency, MS-relapsing, pneumocystic pneumonia, asthma
**rofecoxib** (Vioxx) NSAID, osteoarthritis, acute pain in adults, dysmenorrhea

#### Cardiovascular

**Accupril** (quinapril)
**Aldomet** (methyldopa) HTN
**amlodipidine** (Norvasc) angina, essential HTN, (calcium channel blocker)
**atenolol** angina pectoris, essential HTN, myocardial infarction
**atorvastatin** (Lipitor) hypercholesterolemia, hyperlipidemia; dysbetalipoproteinemia
**benazepril** (Lotensin) HTN, CHF
**Cardura** (doxazosin)
**Catapres** (clonidine HC1)
**Coumadin** (warfarin) anticoagulant
**Digoxin** (lanoxin)
**Doxazosin** (Cardura) HTN, BPH
**Dyazide** (triamterene/HCTZ)
**enalapril** (Vasotec) HTN, CHF, acute MI, nephropathy

## Cardiovascular Continued:

**Esidrix** (hydrochlorothiazide)
**furosemide** (Lasix) diuretic, peripheral & pulmonary edema, hypercalcemia
**hydrochlorothiazide** (Esidrix) HTN, diuretic
**Imdur** (isosorbide mononitrate)
**isosorbide mononitrate** (Imdur, ISMO) angina
**ISMO** (isosorbide mononitrate)
**lanoxin** (Digoxin) CHF, atrial fibrillation/flutter, paroxysmal atrial tachycardia
**Lasix** (furosemide)
**Lipitor** (atorvastatin)
**lisinopril** (Prinivil, Zestril) hypertension (HTN), congestive heart failure (CHF), acute MI
**Lopressor** (metoprolol) hypertension
**Lotensin** (benazepril)
**metoprolol** (Lopressor, Toprol XL) HTN, CHF, acute MI, angina
**Minipress** (prazosin HC1) HTN
**Norvasc** (amlodipine)
**Pravachol** (pravastatin) hypercholesterolemia, hyperlipidemia, dysbetalipoproteinemia
**Prinivil** (lisinopril)
**Quinapril** (Accupril) hypertension, CHF,
**simvastatin** (Zocor) hypercholesterolemia, hypertriglyceridemia, dysbetalipoproteinemia
**Toprol XL** (metoprolol)
**triamterene/HCTZ** (Dyazide) diuretic, hypertension, peripheral edema
**Vasotec** (enalapril)
**verapamil** angina, hypertension, supraventricular arrhythmia, atrial fibrillation/flutter, migraine prophylaxis
**Warfarin** (Coumadin) anticoagulation
**Zestril** (lisinopril)
**Zocor** (simvastatin

## Electrolytes

**K-Dur** (potassium chloride) hypokalemia, prevention of hypokalemia

## Endocrinology

**DiaBeta** (glyburide)
**Estrace** (estrogen)
**glipizide** (Glucotrol XL) DM Type 2
**Glucophage** (metformin)
**Glucotrol XL** (glipizide)
**glyburide** (DiaBeta, Micronase) DM Type 2
**levothyroxine** (Levoxyl, Synthroid) hypothyroidism, myxedema coma
**Levoxyl** (lecothyroxine)
**metformin** (Glucophage) DM, Type 2
**Micronase** (glyburide)
**Synthroid** (levothyroxine)

## Gastrointestinal

**lansoprazole** (Prevacid) GERD, esophagitis, gastric and duodenal ulcer, H. pylori
**Lomotil** (diphenoxylate) diarrhea
**omeprazole** (Prilosec) GERD, erosive esophagitis, gastric/duodenal ulcer, H. Pylori treatment
**Prilosec** (omeprazole)
**Prevacid** (lansoprazole)
**ranitidine** (Zantac) duodenal, gastric, peptic ulcer, esophagitis, dyspepsia, GERD

## Genitourinary

**allopurinol** (Zyloprim) prophylaxis for gout, urate nephropathy, calcium oxalate calculi
**conjugated estrogens** (Premarin, Prempro) antineoplastics; ca of breast and prostate, menopause; osteoporosis prevention; ovarian failure; primary atrophic vaginitis
**Diflucan** (fluconazole)
**Estrace** (estradiol)
**estradiol** (Estrace) vasomotor symptoms, atrophic vaginitis, osteoporosis prevention, palliative tx for breast ca and prostate ca
**fluconazole** (Diflucan) candidiasis
**medroxyprogesterone** (Provera) HRT, amenorrhea, dysfunctional uterine bleeding
**norgestimate/ethinyl estradiol** (Ortho Tri-Cyclen) oral contraceptive
**Ortho Tri-Cyclen** (norgestimate/ethinyl estradiol)
**Premarin** (conjugated estrogens)
**Prempro** (conjugated estrogens/medroxyprogesterone)
**Provera** (medroxyprogesterone)
**sildenafil citrate** (Viagra) erectile dysfunction
**Viagra** (sildenafil citrate)
**Zyloprim** (allopurinol)

## Immunology and Allergy

**Adrenalin** (epinephrine) allergies
**Allegra** (fexofenadine)
**Benadryl** (diphenhydramine) allergies
**Cetirizine** (Zyrtec)
**Chlor-Trimeton** (chlorapheneramine maleate) allergies
**Claritin** (loratadine)
**Dimetane** (brompheniramine maleate) allergies
**fexofenadine** (Allegra) allergic rhinitis, chronic urticaria
**Flonase** (fluticasone) allergic rhinitis
**fluticasone** (Flonase)
**loratadine** (Claritin) seasonal allergy, rhinitis, urticaria
**momentasone nasal** (Nasonex)
**Nasonex** (mometasone nasal)
**Zyrtec** (cetirizine) allergic rhinitis, chronic urticaria

## Musculoskeletal

**alendronate** (Fosamax) osteoporosis, Paget's disease
**carisoprodol** (Soma) muscle spasm
**cyclobenzaprine** (Flexeril) muscle spasm
**Flexeril** (cyclobenzaprine)
**Fosamax** (alendronate)
**Soma** (carisoprodol)

## Neurological

**clonazepam** (Klonopin) neuralgia, absence seizures
**Depakote** (divalproex)
**Dilantin** (phenytoin sodium) seizures
**divalproex** (Depakote) seizure disorder, mania, migraine prophylaxis
**gabapentin** (Neurontin) partial seizures, neuropathic pain
**Klonopin** (clonazepam)
**Neurontin** (gabapentin)

# Appendix A

## Psychiatric

**Ativan** (lorazepam)
**alprazolam** (Xanax) anxiety, panic disorder
**Ambien** (zolpidem)
**amitriptyline** (Elavil, Endep) depression, chronic pain
**bupropion HCL** (Wellbutrin SR)
**Celexa** (citalopram)
**Citalopram** (Celexa) depression
**Desyrel** (trazodone)
**Diazepam** (Valium) anxiety, alcohol withdrawal, muscle spasm, seizure disorder, status epilepticus
**Effexor XR** (venlafaxine)
**Elavil** (amitriptyline) depression
**Endep** (amitriptyline)
**fluoxetine** (Prozac) bulimia nervosa, depression, obsessive-compulsive disorder
**Halodol** (haloperidol)
**lorazepam** (Ativan) anxiety, insomnia, chemo-related nausea and vomiting, status epilepticus
**paroxetine** (Paxil) anxiety, panic disorder, depression; obsessive-compulsive disorder
**Paxil** (paroxetine)
**Prozac** (fluoxetine)
**sertraline** (Zoloft) anxiety, panic disorder, depression, obsessive-compulsive disorder
**trazodone** (Desyrel) depression
**Valium** (diazepam) anxiety
**venlafaxine** (Effexor EX) depression, anxiety
**Effexor XR** (venlafaxine)
**Wellbutrin SR** (bupropion HCL) depression
**Xanax** (alprazolam)
**Zoloft** (sertraline)
**zolpidem** (Ambien) insomnia

## Respiratory

**albuterol** (Proventil, Ventolin) asthma
**Flovent** (fluticasone propionate)
**fluticasone propionate** (Flovent) asthma
**montelukast** (Singulair) asthma
**Proventil** (albuterol) asthma
**Singulair** (montelukast) asthma
**Ventolin** (albuterol) asthma

## Appendix A

### Common Abbreviations

**Always use with caution! Abbreviations may have multiple meanings**

**a** ........ before
**ac** ........ before meals
**AD** ........ right ear
**Ad lib** ........ as desired
**alt dieb** ........ alternate days
**alt hr** ........ alternate hours
**alt noc** ........ alternate nights
**am, AM** ........ morning
**amt** ........ amount
**ante** ........ before
**aq** ........ aqueous (water)
**AS** ........ left ear
**AU** ........ both ears
**Ba** ........ barium
**bid** ........ two times a day
**bin** ........ two times a night
**C** ........ 100
**Cap(s)** ........ capusle(s)
**cc** ........ cubic centemeter
**CHF** ........ congestive heart failure
**d** ........ day
**Dx** ........ diagnosis
**D5W** ........ 5% dextrose in water
**D/C, dc** ........ discontinue
**dil** ........ dilute
**disp** ........ dispense
**DM** ........ diabetes mellitus
**dr** ........ dram
**elix** ........ elixir
**emul** ........ emulsion
**et** ........ and
**ext** ........ extract/external
**FDA** ........ Food and Drug Admin.
**Fe** ........ iron
**Fl** ........ fluid
**G** ........ gauge
**g. GM, gm** ........ gram(s)
**gal** ........ gallon
**gr** ........ gram
**gt, gtt** ........ drop(s)
**H** ........ hour/hypodermic
**HRT** ........ hormone replacement therapy
**Hs** ........ hour of sleep (bedtime)
**HTN** ........ hypertension
**IM** ........ intramuscular
**Inj** ........ injection
**IV** ........ intravenous
**IVPB** ........ IV piggy back (2nd line)
**IU** ........ international units
**K** ........ potassium
**Kg** ........ kilogram
**L** ........ liter
**Liq** ........ liquid
**mcg** ........ microgram
**mg** ........ milligram(s)
**ml, mL** ........ milliliter(s)
**mm** ........ millimeter
**NaCl 0.9%** ........ normal saline
**NKA** ........ no known allergy
**NKDA** ........ no known drug allergy
**noc, noct** ........ night
**non rep** ........ do not repeat
**NPO** ........ nothing by mouth
**NS** ........ normal saline
**NSAID** ........ non-steroidal anti-inflammatory drug(s)
**O** ........ pint
**od** ........ once day/daily
**OD** ........ right eye
**Om** ........ every morning
**OTC** ........ over the counter
**Oz, oz** ........ ounce
**pc** ........ after meals
**PCA** ........ patient-controlled analgesia
**PCN** ........ penicillin
**PDR** ........ Physican's Desk Reference
**per** ........ with
**PM, pm** ........ evening
**PRN, prn.** ........ as needed, as necessary
**PO, po** ........ by mouth
**pt** ........ pint
**pulv** ........ powder
**Q, q** ........ every
**q2h** ........ every two hours
**qd** ........ every day
**qh** ........ every hour
**qid** ........ four times a day
**qs** ........ as much as needed
**Rx** ........ prescription
**SC, sc, sq, subc, subq.** Subcutaneous
**Sig** ........ lable as follwows/directions
**SOB** ........ shortness of breath
**Susp** ........ suspension
**T, tbsp** ........ tablespoon
**tab** ........ tablet
**tid** ........ three times a day
**TO** ........ telephone order
**Top, top** ........ apply topically
**tsp** ........ teaspoon
**TX** ........ treatment
**ut, diet, UD** ........ as directed
**wt** ........ weight

## BE ALERT FOR SOUND ALIKES

Drug names may be similar in sound as well as spelling. It is important to be alert when referring to drugs. For Example:

Celebrex......................NSAID
vs
Cerebyx ...........anticonvulsant

DiaBeta.......oral hypoglycemic
vs
Zebeta beta-adrenergic blocker

Paxil. ............. .antidepressant
vs
Taxol.....................antineoplastic

## REFERENCE FOR PHARMACOLOGY

PRG Quick Note for Pharmacology

| | |
|---|---|
| Authors & Editors: | Mary Spivey Teslow, MLIS, RHIA<br>Patricia J. Schnering, RHIA, CCS<br>Toni Cade, MBA, RHIA, CCS |
| Produced & Copyright by: | PRG Publishing, Inc.<br>Phone: (888) 383-PRG1<br>E-mail: pjsprg@aol.com<br>www.prgpublishing.com |

| | |
|---|---|
| Web Sites for Pharmacology: | RxList.com, ePocrates.com<br>FDA.gov, DEA.gov, PDR.net<br>mayoclinic.com |

# APPENDIX B
# LABORATORY TESTING

## HEMATOLOGY/COAGULATION

**Complete Blood Count**
**Use:** basic blood evaluation
**AKA:** CBC
**Note:** usually includes Hct, Hgb, WBC counts and differential, platelet count and often RBC count

**Erythrocyte Count**
**AKA:** RBC Count (red blood cell)
**High:** acute hepatitis, acute MI, PID, rheumatoid arthritis
**Low:** anemias, leukemias and following severe hemorrhage

**Hematocrit**
**Use:** determines the % of whole blood composed of red blood cells
**AKA:** Hct, HCT
**High:** dehydration, Addison's disease, polycythemia due to dehydration and shock
**Low:** anemia, severe hemorrhage

**Hemoglobin**
**Use:** measures Hgb in the blood
**AKA:** Hb, Hgb
**High:** dehydration, pernicious anemia, sickle cell anemia, thalassemia, polycythemia, obstructive pulmonary diseases, CHF
**Low:** excessive fluid intake, iron deficiency anemia, pregnancy

**Hemoglobin, Glycated**
**Use:** monitors blood sugar control
**AKA:** HbA1C, GHb, DM control index
**Note:** Abnormal results over time indicate inadequate control.

**Leukocyte Count**
**AKA:** WBC Count (white blood cell)
**High:** acute infections, leukemias, acute hemorrhage
**Low:** chemotherapy, shock, cachexia

**Partial Thromboplastin Time**
**Use:** measures intrinsic clotting time
**AKA:** APTT, Activated
**High:** cirrhosis, leukemia, vitamin K deficiency, hemophilia
**Low:** extensive ca, early stages of disseminated intravascular coagulation

**Platelet Count**
**Use:** dx a bleeding disorder or bone marrow disease
**High:** iron deficiency anemia, post-op patients, malignancies, polycythemia
**Low:** acute leukemia, aplastic anemia, thrombocytopenic purpura

**Prothrombin Time**
**Use:** monitor blood-thinning medications used to prevent blood clots
**AKA:** PT, Pro Time
**Prolonged:** severe liver damage, heparin use, low vitamin K diet, colitis, chronic diarrhea

**Reticulocyte Count**
**Use:** measures % of reticulocytes (slightly immature red blood cells)
**High:** need for RBCs, hemolytic anemias, acute or severe bleeding
**Low:** bone marrow failure (toxicity, tumor, fibrosis, infection), cirrhosis, iron deficiency radiation therapy

# APPENDIX B
# LABORATORY TESTING

**Sedimentation Rate**
**Use:** monitors inflammatory and malignant diseases, and acute MI
**AKA:** erythrocyte sedimentation rate, sed rate, ESR
**High:** pregnancy, menstruation, infectious diseases, tissue damage

## SERUM ELECTROLYTES

**Note:** essential to normal metabolism, exists as acids, bases and salts
**AKA:** "Lytes"

**Calcium, Total**
**Use:** blood test to screen/monitor diseases of bone or calcium regulation (diseases of parathyroid and kidneys)
**AKA:** Ca+2, Ca++, serum calcium
**High:** metastatic ca of bone, lung, breast, Paget's disease, hyperparathyroidism, excess vitamin D
**Low:** severe pancreatitis, renal insufficiency, uremia, malabsorption, osteomalacia, hypoparathyroidism

**Chloride**
**AKA:** Cl
**High:** renal insufficiency, necrosis, dehydration, renal tubular acidosis, Cushing's syndrome, hyperventilation
**Low:** CHF, chronic renal failure, diabetic acidosis, diarrhea, excessive sweating, emphysema

**Magnesium**
**AKA:** Mg+2
**High:** renal insufficiency, use of antacids with magnesium
**Low:** chronic alcoholism, chronic diarrhea, hepatic insufficiency

**Phosphorus**
**AKA:** PO4
**High:** renal insufficiency, healing fx,hypoparathyroidism, excess vitamin D
**Low:** chronic alcoholism, ketoacidosis, hyperalimentation, hyperparathyroidism

**Potassium**
**AKA:** K
**High:** renal insufficiency, adrenal insufficiency, Addison's disease, hypoventilation
**Low:** chronic diarrhea, vomiting or malabsorption syndrome, diabetic acidosis, chronic kidney disease, use of thiazide diuretics

**Sodium**
**AKA:** NA
**High:** (hypernatremia) excessive dietary intake, Cushing's disease, excessive sweating, diabetes incipitus
**Low:** (hyponatremia): ascites, CHF, insufficient intake, diarrhea, vomiting, SIADH (syndrome of inappropriate diuretic hormone), diuretic use, chronic renal insufficiency, excessive water intake, peripheral edema, pleural effusion

## SERUM/URINE/STOOL

**Acid Phosphatase**
**High:** metastatic ca of bone, prostatic ca, some liver diseases, MI, pulmonary embolism, hepatobiliary diseases, hyperparathyroidism

**Alanine Aminotransferase**
**Use:** screens for liver disease
**AKA:** ALT, SGPT
**High:** acute hepatitis, liver necrosis

## SERUM/URINE/STOOL continued

### Albumin
**Use:** screen for liver or kidney disease or evaluate nutritional status
**AKA:** ALB
**Note:** albumin is a protein
**High:** shock, dehydration, multiple myeloma
**Low:** malnutrition, malabsorption, acute or chronic glomerulonephritis, cancers, leukemia, hepatitis, cirrhosis, hepatocellular necrosis

### Alkaline Phosphatase
**Use:** screen/monitor tx for liver or bone disorders
**AKA:** ALP, alk phos
**High:** biliary duct obstruction, hyperparathyroidism, healing fx, rickets, osteomalacia, neoplastic bone disorders, liver diseases

### Ammonia
**AKA:** NH4+
**Note:** particularly toxic to the brain, can cause confusion and lethargy
**High:** CHF, liver failure, GI bleed, leukemia, pericarditis

### Amylase
**Use:** blood test to diagnose/monitor pancreatic disease (blood)
**Note:** amylase is an enzyme that helps digest glycogen and starch
**High:** acute pancreatitis, ca of the pancreas, ovaries, or lungs, mumps,intestinal obstruction
**Low:** acute and chronic hepatitis, cirrhosis, toxemia of pregnancy

### Anion Gap
**Use:** dx and tx of acidosis
**High:** lactic acidosis, diabetic ketoacidosis, alcoholic ketoacidosis, starvation, renal failure
**Low:** multiple myeloma, chronic vomiting, hyperaldosteronism

### Arterial Blood Gases
**AKA:** ABGs
**Abnormal Results:** respiratory, metabolic or renal diseases, trauma

### Aspartate Aminotransferase
**Use:** detect liver damage
**AKA:** AST, SGOT
**High:** acute MI, liver disease, diseases of skeletal muscles

### Bilirubin, Total
**Use:** screen/monitor liver disorders
**Note:** bilirubin is a product of hemoglobin breakdown, causes jaundice
**High:** acute/chronic hepatitis, gallstones, toxic reaction to drugs/chemicals, infectious mononucleosis

### Blood Urea Nitrogen
**Use:** evaluate kidney function and dialysis effectiveness
**AKA:** BUN
**High:** GI hemorrhage, dehydration, renal insufficiency
**Low:** hepatic failure, cachexia

### Carbon Dioxide, Total
**AKA:** CO2
**High:** respiratory diseases, vomiting, intestinal obstruction
**Decreased:** acidosis, nephritis, diarrhea

**SERUM/URINE/STOOL continued**

**Carcinoembryonic Antigen**
**Use:** dx cancer and monitor tx
**AKA:** CEA
**High:** colon, breast, lung, pancreatic, thyroid ca, also heavy smoking

**Cholesterol, Total**
**Use:** screen for heart disease
**High:** MI, uncontrolled DM, hypothyroidism, atherosclerosis, hypercholesterolemia, hyperlipidemia
**Low:** acute MI, pernicious anemia, malnutrition, liver disease, sepsis, malabsorption.

**Creatinine**
**Use:** evaluate kidney function and tx
**High:** dehydration, diabetic nephropathy, kidney disease

**Creatine (Phospho)kinase**
**Use:** evaluate muscle damage
**AKA:** CPK, CK
**High:** acute MI, muscular dystrophies, muscle injury, CNS trauma and stroke

**Globulin**
**Use:** protein evaluation
**AKA:** CPK, CK
**High:** hepatic disease, plasma cell neoplasms, lupus, malaria

**Glucose**
**Use:** diagnose and manage DM
**AKA:** GTT glucose tolerance test
**High:** DM, IV therapy, hyperthyroidism, hyperpituitarism, liver diseases, nephritis
**Low:** hyperinsulinism, hyperthyroidism, Addison's disease.

**Iron**
**AKA:** Fe
**High:** anemias, liver disease.
**Low:** iron deficiency anemia, excessive fluid intake, pregnancy

**Lactose Dehydrogenase**
**AKA:** LDH
**High:** acute MI, infectious hepatitis, malignant tumors and widespread ca, hemolytic and pernicious anemias, acute leukemias
**Low:** x-ray irradiation

**Oxygen Saturation**
**AKA:** oximetry, O2
**High:** hyperventilation
**Low:** inadequate O2 inspiration, hypoxic lung diseases, hypoxic cardiac diseases, severe hypoventilation

**Prostate Specific Antigen**
**AKA:** PSA
**High:** BPH, prostate ca, prostatitism

**Stool Guaiac Test**
**Use:** detect hidden blood in stool
**AKA:** hemoccult
**Abnormal Results:** NSAIDs, colon polyps, colon ca, GI tumors, esophagitis, gastritis, inflammatory bowel disease, peptic ulcer

**Thyrotropin**
**AKA:** hTHS
**Abnormal Findings:** hyperthyroidism, hypothyroidism, depression, acute starvation, pregnancy, old age

**Thyroxine**
**AKA:** T4
**High:** Graves' disease, toxic thyroid adenoma, acute thyroiditis
**Low:** cretinism, myxedema, pituitary or idodine insufficiency, hypothalamic failure, renal failure, Cushing's disease, cirrhosis, advanced cancer

## SERUM/URINE/STOOL continued

**Triglycerides**
**AKA:** TG
**High:** hyperlipidemias, hypothyroidism, poorly controlled DM, nephrotic syndrome, hypertension, alcoholic cirrhosis, pregnancy, MI
**Low:** malabsorption syndrome, malnutrition, hyperthyroidism

**Uric Acid**
**High:** gout, leukemia, renal insufficiency, polycythemia, pneumonia
**Low:** acute hepatitis

**Viral Load**
**Use:** severity of immune system damage, monitor HIV status and tx
**AKA:** CD4 lymphocyte count
**Low below 350 ml:** herpes simplex, herpes zoster, TB
**Low below 200 ml:** pneumocystis carinii pneumonia,
**Low below 100 ml:** AIDS dementia
**Low below 50 ml:** cytomegalovirus

## COMMON ABBREVIATIONS

**AKA**........ also known as
**Ca**........ cancer, calcium
**CHF**........ congestive heart failure
**Dx**........ **d**iagnosis
**DM**........ diabetes mellitus
**Fx**........ fracture
**GI**........ gastrointestinal
**IV**........ intravenous
**MI**........ myocardial infarction
**NIDDM**........ non-insulin dependent DM
**NSAID**........ non-steroidal anti-inflammatory
**Tx**........ treatment

## REFERENCE FOR LABORATORY TESTING

**PRG Quick Note for Laboratory Testing**
Authors & Editors:
Mary Spivey Teslow, MLIS, RHIA
Patricia J. Schnering, RHIA, CCS
Produced & Copyright by: PRG Publishing, Inc.
Phone: (888) 383-PRG1
E-mail: pjsprg@aol.com
www.prgpublishing.com

For additional laboratory testing information, you may access:
http://www.labtestsonline.org/

ICD-9-CM Official Guidelines for Coding and Reporting
Effective December 1, 2005
Narrative changes appear in bold text
Items underlined have been moved within the guidelines since April 2005
The guidelines include the updated V Code Table

To obtain the guidelines online, visit the following web site:
http://www.cdc.gov/nchs/data/icd9/icdguide.pdf

The Centers for Medicare and Medicaid Services (CMS) and the National Center for Health Statistics (NCHS), two departments within the U. S. Federal Government's Department of Health and Human Services (DHHS) provide the following guidelines for coding and reporting using the International Classification of Diseases, 9th Revision, Clinical Modification (ICD-9-CM). These guidelines should be used as a companion document to the official version of the ICD-9-CM as published on CD-ROM by the U.S. Government Printing Office (GPO).

These guidelines have been approved by the four organizations that make up the Cooperating Parties for the ICD-9-CM: the American Hospital Association (AHA), the American Health Information Management Association (AHIMA), CMS, and NCHS. These guidelines are included on the official government version of the ICD-9-CM, and also appear in "*Coding Clinic for ICD-9-CM*" published by the AHA.

These guidelines are a set of rules that have been developed to accompany and complement the official conventions and instructions provided within the ICD-9-CM itself. These guidelines are based on the coding and sequencing instructions in Volumes I, II and III of ICD-9-CM, but provide additional instruction. Adherence to these guidelines when assigning ICD-9-CM diagnosis and procedure codes is required under the Health Insurance Portability and Accountability Act (HIPAA). The diagnosis codes (Volumes 1-2) have been adopted under HIPAA for all healthcare settings. Volume 3 procedure codes have been adopted for inpatient procedures reported by hospitals. A joint effort between the healthcare provider and the coder is essential to achieve complete and accurate documentation, code assignment, and reporting of diagnoses and procedures. These guidelines have been developed to assist both the healthcare provider and the coder in identifying those diagnoses and procedures that are to be reported. The importance of consistent, complete documentation in the medical record cannot be overemphasized. Without such documentation accurate coding cannot be achieved. The entire record should be reviewed to determine the specific reason for the encounter and the conditions treated.

The term encounter is used for all settings, including hospital admissions. In the context of these guidelines, the term provider is used throughout the guidelines to mean physician or any qualified health care practitioner who is legally accountable for establishing the patient's diagnosis. Only this set of guidelines, approved by the Cooperating Parties, is official.
The guidelines are organized into sections. Section I includes the structure and conventions of the classification and general guidelines that apply to the entire classification, and chapter-specific guidelines that correspond to the chapters as they are arranged in the classification. Section II includes guidelines for selection of principal diagnosis for non-outpatient settings. Section III includes guidelines for reporting additional diagnoses in non-outpatient settings. Section IV is for outpatient coding and reporting.

**ICD-9-CM Official Guidelines for Coding and Reporting**

**Section I. Conventions, general coding guidelines and chapter specific guidelines**

A. Conventions for the ICD-9-CM
   1. Format
   2. Abbreviations
      a. Index abbreviations
      b. Tabular abbreviations
   3. Punctuation
   4. Includes and Excludes Notes and Inclusion terms
   5. Other and Unspecified codes
      a. "Other" codes
      b. "Unspecified" codes
   6. Etiology/manifestation convention ("code first", "use additional code" and "in diseases classified elsewhere" notes)
   7. "And"
   8. "With"
   9. "See" and "See Also"

B. General Coding Guidelines
   1. Use of Both Alphabetic Index and Tabular List
   2. Locate each term in the Alphabetic Index
   3. Level of Detail in Coding
   4. Code or codes from 001.0 through V84.8
   5. Selection of codes 001.0 through 999.9
   6. Signs and symptoms
   7. Conditions that are an integral part of a disease process
   8. Conditions that are not an integral part of a disease process
   9. Multiple coding for a single condition
   10. Acute and Chronic Conditions
   11. Combination Code
   12. Late Effects
   13. Impending or Threatened Condition

C. Chapter-Specific Coding Guidelines
   1. Chapter 1: Infectious and Parasitic Diseases (001-139)
      a. Human Immunodeficiency Virus (HIV) Infections
      b. Septicemia, Systemic Inflammatory Response Syndrome (SIRS), Sepsis, Severe Sepsis, and Septic Shock
   2. Chapter 2: Neoplasms (140-239)
      a. Treatment directed at the malignancy
      b. Treatment of secondary site
      c. Coding and sequencing of complications
      d. Primary malignancy previously excised
      e. Admissions/Encounters involving chemotherapy, immunotherapy and radiation therapy
      f. Admission/encounter to determine extent of malignancy
      g. Symptoms, signs, and ill-defined conditions listed in Chapter 16
   3. Chapter 3: Endocrine, Nutritional, and Metabolic Diseases and Immunity Disorders (240-279)
      a. Diabetes mellitus
   4. Chapter 4: Diseases of Blood and Blood Forming Organs (280-289)
      **a. Anemia of chronic disease**
   5. Chapter 5: Mental Disorders (290-319)
      Reserved for future guideline expansion

6. Chapter 6: Diseases of Nervous System and Sense Organs (320-389)
   Reserved for future guideline expansion
7. Chapter 7: Diseases of Circulatory System (390-459)
   a. Hypertension
   b. Cerebral infarction/stroke/cerebrovascular accident (CVA)
   c. Postoperative cerebrovascular accident
   d. Late Effects of Cerebrovascular Disease
   **e. Acute myocardial infarction (AMI)**
8. Chapter 8: Diseases of Respiratory System (460-519)
   a. Chronic Obstructive Pulmonary Disease [COPD] and Asthma
   b. Chronic Obstructive Pulmonary Disease [COPD] and Bronchitis
9. Chapter 9: Diseases of Digestive System (520-579)
   Reserved for future guideline expansion
10. Chapter 10: Diseases of Genitourinary System (580-629)
    **a. Chronic kidney disease**
11. Chapter 11: Complications of Pregnancy, Childbirth, and the Puerperium (630-677)
    a. General Rules for Obstetric Cases
    b. Selection of OB Principal or First-listed Diagnosis
    c. Fetal Conditions Affecting the Management of the Mother
    d. HIV Infection in Pregnancy, Childbirth and the Puerperium
    e. Current Conditions Complicating Pregnancy
    f. Diabetes mellitus in pregnancy
    g. Gestational diabetes
    h. Normal Delivery, Code 650
    i. The Postpartum and Peripartum Periods
    j. Code 677, Late effect of complication of pregnancy
    k. Abortions
12. Chapter 12: Diseases Skin and Subcutaneous Tissue (680-709)
    Reserved for future guideline expansion
13. Chapter 13: Diseases of Musculoskeletal and Connective Tissue (710-739)
    Reserved for future guideline expansion
14. Chapter 14: Congenital Anomalies (740-759)
    a. Codes in categories 740-759, Congenital Anomalies
15. Chapter 15: Newborn (Perinatal) Guidelines (760-779)
    a. General Perinatal Rules
    b. Use of codes V30-V39
    c. Newborn transfers
    d. Use of category V29
    e. Use of other V codes on perinatal records
    f. Maternal Causes of Perinatal Morbidity
    g. Congenital Anomalies in Newborns
    h. Coding Additional Perinatal Diagnoses
    i. Prematurity and Fetal Growth Retardation
    j. Newborn sepsis
16. Chapter 16: Signs, Symptoms and Ill-Defined Conditions (780-799)
    Reserved for future guideline expansion
17. Chapter 17: Injury and Poisoning (800-999)
    a. Coding of Injuries
    b. Coding of Fracture
    c. Coding of Burns
    d. Coding of Debridement of Wound, Infection, or Burn
    e. Adverse Effects, Poisoning and Toxic Effects
    **f. Complications of care**

18. Classification of Factors Influencing Health Status and Contact with Health Service (Supplemental V01-V84)
    a. Introduction
    b. V codes use in any healthcare setting
    c. V Codes indicate a reason for an encounter
    d. Categories of V Codes
    **e. V Code Table 60**
19. Supplemental Classification of External Causes of Injury and Poisoning (E-codes, E800E999)
    a. General E Code Coding Guidelines
    b. Place of Occurrence Guideline
    c. Adverse Effects of Drugs, Medicinal and Biological Substances Guidelines
    d. Multiple Cause E Code Coding Guidelines
    e. Child and Adult Abuse Guideline
    **f.** Unknown or Suspected Intent Guideline
    g. Undetermined Cause
    h. Late Effects of External Cause Guidelines
    i. Misadventures and Complications of Care Guidelines
    j. Terrorism Guidelines

**Section II. Selection of Principal Diagnosis**
A. Codes for symptoms, signs, and ill-defined conditions
B. Two or more interrelated conditions, each potentially meeting the definition for principal diagnosis
C. Two or more diagnoses that equally meet the definition for principal diagnosis
D. Two or more comparative or contrasting conditions
E. A symptom(s) followed by contrasting/comparative diagnoses
F. Original treatment plan not carried out
G. Complications of surgery and other medical care
H. Uncertain Diagnosis
**I. Admission from Observation Unit**
    **1. Admission Following Medical Observation**
    **2. Admission Following Post-Operative Observation**
**J. Admission from Outpatient Surgery**

**Section III. Reporting Additional Diagnoses**
A. Previous conditions
B. Abnormal findings
C. Uncertain Diagnosis

**Section IV. Diagnostic Coding and Reporting Guidelines for Outpatient Services**
A. election of first-listed condition
    1. Outpatient Surgery
    2. Observation Stay
B. Codes from 001.0 through V84.8
C. Accurate reporting of ICD-9-CM diagnosis codes
D. Selection of codes 001.0 through 999.9
E. Codes that describe symptoms and signs
F. Encounters for circumstances other than a disease or injury
G. Level of Detail in Coding
    1. ICD-9-CM codes with 3, 4, or 5 digits
    2. Use of full number of digits required for a code
H. ICD-9-CM code for the diagnosis, condition, problem, or other reason for encounter/visit
I. "Probable", "suspected", "questionable", "rule out", or "working diagnosis"

J. Chronic diseases
K. Code all documented conditions that coexist
L. Patients receiving diagnostic services only
M. Patients receiving therapeutic services only
N. Patients receiving preoperative evaluations only
O. Ambulatory surgery
P. Routine outpatient prenatal visits

## Section I Conventions, general coding guidelines and chapter specific guidelines

The conventions, general guidelines and chapter-specific guidelines are applicable to all health care settings unless otherwise indicated.

### A. Conventions for the ICD-9-CM

The conventions for the ICD-9-CM are the general rules for use of the classification independent of the guidelines. These conventions are incorporated within the index and tabular of the ICD-9-CM as instructional notes. The conventions are as follows:

**1. Format:**

The ICD-9-CM uses an indented format for ease in reference

**2. Abbreviations**

**a. Index abbreviations**

NEC "Not elsewhere classifiable" This abbreviation in the index represents "other specified" when a specific code is not available for a condition the index directs the coder to the "other specified" code in the tabular.

**b. Tabular abbreviations**

NEC "Not elsewhere classifiable" This abbreviation in the tabular represents "other specified". When a specific code is not available for a condition the tabular includes an NEC entry under a code to identify the code as the "other specified" code (See Section I.A.5.a. "Other" codes").

NOS "Not otherwise specified" This abbreviation is the equivalent of unspecified. (See Section I.A.5.b., "Unspecified" codes)

**3. Punctuation**

**[ ]** Brackets are used in the tabular list to enclose synonyms, alternative wording or explanatory phrases. Brackets are used in the index to identify manifestation codes. (See Section I.A.6. "Etiology/manifestations")

**( )** Parentheses are used in both the index and tabular to enclose supplementary words that may be present or absent in the statement of a disease or procedure without affecting the code number to which it is assigned. The terms within the parentheses are referred to as nonessential modifiers.

: Colons are used in the Tabular list after an incomplete term which needs one or more of the modifiers following the colon to make it assignable to a given category.

**4. Includes and Excludes Notes and Inclusion terms**

**Includes:** This note appears immediately under a three-digit code title to further define, or give examples of, the content of the category.

**Excludes:** An excludes note under a code indicates that the terms excluded from the code are to be coded elsewhere. In some cases the codes for the excluded terms should not be used in conjunction with the code from which it is excluded. An example of this is a congenital condition excluded from an acquired form of the same condition. The congenital and acquired codes should not be used together. In other cases, the excluded terms may be used together with an excluded code. An example of this is when fractures of different bones are coded to different codes. Both codes may be used together if both types of fractures are present.

**Inclusion terms:** List of terms is included under certain four and five digit codes. These terms are the conditions for which that code number is to be used. The terms may be synonyms of the code title, or, in the case of "other specified" codes, the terms are a list of the various conditions assigned to that code. The inclusion terms are not necessarily exhaustive. Additional terms found only in the index may also be assigned to a code.

5. **Other and Unspecified codes**
   a. **"Other" codes**
      Codes titled "other" or "other specified" (usually a code with a 4th digit 8 or fifth-digit 9 for diagnosis codes) are for use when the information in the medical record provides detail for which a specific code does not exist. Index entries with NEC in the line designate "other" codes in the tabular. These index entries represent specific disease entities for which no specific code exists so the term is included within an "other" code.
   b. **"Unspecified" codes**
      Codes (usually a code with a 4th digit 9 or 5th digit 0 for diagnosis codes) titled "unspecified" are for use when the information in the medical record is insufficient to assign a more specific code.

6. **Etiology/manifestation convention ("code first", "use additional code" and "in diseases classified elsewhere" notes)**
   Certain conditions have both an underlying etiology and multiple body system manifestations due to the underlying etiology. For such conditions, the ICD-9-CM has a coding convention that requires the underlying condition be sequenced first followed by the manifestation. Wherever such a combination exists, there is a "use additional code" note at the etiology code, and a "code first" note at the manifestation code. These instructional notes indicate the proper sequencing order of the codes, etiology followed by manifestation.

   In most cases the manifestation codes will have in the code title, "in diseases classified elsewhere." Codes with this title are a component of the etiology/ manifestation convention. The code title indicates that it is a manifestation code. "In diseases classified elsewhere" codes are never permitted to be used as first listed or principal diagnosis codes. They must be used in conjunction with an underlying condition code and they must be listed following the underlying condition.

   There are manifestation codes that do not have "in diseases classified elsewhere" in the title. For such codes a "use additional code" note will still be present and the rules for sequencing apply.
   In addition to the notes in the tabular, these conditions also have a specific index entry structure. In the index both conditions are listed together with the etiology code first followed by the manifestation codes in brackets. The code in brackets is always to be sequenced second.

   The most commonly used etiology/manifestation combinations are the codes for Diabetes mellitus, category 250. For each code under category 250 there is a use additional code note for the manifestation that is specific for that particular diabetic manifestation. Should a patient have more than one manifestation of diabetes, more than one code from category 250 may be used with as many manifestation codes as are needed to fully describe the patient's complete diabetic condition. The **category** 250 diabetes codes should be sequenced first, followed by the manifestation codes.

   "Code first" and "Use additional code" notes are also used as sequencing rules in the classification for certain codes that are not part of an etiology/ manifestation combination. See - Section I.B.9. "Multiple coding for a single condition".

7. **"And"**
   The word "and" should be interpreted to mean either "and" or "or" when it appears in a title.

8. **"With"**

   The word "with" in the alphabetic index is sequenced immediately following the main term, not in alphabetical order.

9. **"See" and "See Also"**

   The "see" instruction following a main term in the index indicates that another term should be referenced. It is necessary to go to the main term referenced with the "see" note to locate the correct code.

   A "see also" instruction following a main term in the index instructs that there is another main term that may also be referenced that may provide additional index entries that may be useful. It is not necessary to follow the "see also" note when the original main term provides the necessary code.

**B. General Coding Guidelines**

1. **Use of Both Alphabetic Index and Tabular List**

   Use both the Alphabetic Index and the Tabular List when locating and assigning a code. Reliance on only the Alphabetic Index or the Tabular List leads to errors in code assignments and less specificity in code selection.

2. **Locate each term in the Alphabetic Index**

   Locate each term in the Alphabetic Index and verify the code selected in the Tabular List. Read and be guided by instructional notations that appear in both the Alphabetic Index and the Tabular List.

3. **Level of Detail in Coding**

   Diagnosis and procedure codes are to be used at their highest number of digits available.

   ICD-9-CM diagnosis codes are composed of codes with either 3, 4, or 5 digits. Codes with three digits are included in ICD-9-CM as the heading of a category of codes that may be further subdivided by the use of fourth and/or fifth digits, which provide greater detail.

   A three-digit code is to be used only if it is not further subdivided. Where fourth-digit subcategories and/or fifth-digit subclassifications are provided, they must be assigned. A code is invalid if it has not been coded to the full number of digits required for that code. For example, Acute myocardial infarction, code 410, has fourth digits that describe the location of the infarction (e.g., 410.2, Of inferolateral wall), and fifth digits that identify the episode of care. It would be incorrect to report a code in category 410 without a fourth and fifth digit

   ICD-9-CM Volume 3 procedure codes are composed of codes with either 3 or 4 digits. Codes with two digits are included in ICD-9-CM as the heading of a category of codes that may be further subdivided by the use of third and/or fourth digits, which provide greater detail.

4. **Code or codes from 001.0 through V84.8**

   The appropriate code or codes from 001.0 through V84.8 must be used to identify diagnoses, symptoms, conditions, problems, complaints or other reason(s) for the encounter/visit.

5. **Selection of codes 001.0 through 999.9**

   The selection of codes 001.0 through 999.9 will frequently be used to describe the reason for the admission/encounter. These codes are from the section of ICD-9-CM for the classification of diseases and injuries (e.g., infectious and parasitic diseases; neoplasms; symptoms, signs, and ill-defined conditions, etc.).

6. **Signs and symptoms**
   Codes that describe symptoms and signs, as opposed to diagnoses, are acceptable for reporting purposes when a related definitive diagnosis has not been established (confirmed) by the provider. Chapter 16 of ICD-9-CM, Symptoms, Signs, and Ill-defined conditions (codes 780.0 - 799.9) contain many, but not all codes for symptoms.
7. **Conditions that are an integral part of a disease process**
   Signs and symptoms that are integral to the disease process should not be assigned as additional codes.
8. **Conditions that are not an integral part of a disease process**
   Additional signs and symptoms that may not be associated routinely with a disease process should be coded when present.
9. **Multiple coding for a single condition**
   In addition to the etiology/manifestation convention that requires two codes to fully describe a single condition that affects multiple body systems, there are other single conditions that also require more than one code. "Use additional code" notes are found in the tabular at codes that are not part of an etiology/manifestation pair where a secondary code is useful to fully describe a condition. The sequencing rule is the same as the etiology/manifestation pair - , "use additional code" indicates that a secondary code should be added.

   For example, for infections that are not included in chapter 1, a secondary code from category 041, Bacterial infection in conditions classified elsewhere and of unspecified site, may be required to identify the bacterial organism causing the infection. A "use additional code" note will normally be found at the infectious disease code, indicating a need for the organism code to be added as a secondary code.
   "Code first" notes are also under certain codes that are not specifically manifestation codes but may be due to an underlying cause. When a "code first" note is present and an underlying condition is present the underlying condition should be sequenced first.
   "Code, if applicable, any causal condition first", notes indicate that this code may be assigned as a principal diagnosis when the causal condition is unknown or not applicable. If a causal condition is known, then the code for that condition should be sequenced as the principal or first-listed diagnosis.
   Multiple codes may be needed for late effects, complication codes and obstetric codes to more fully describe a condition. See the specific guidelines for these conditions for further instruction.
10. **Acute and Chronic Conditions**
    If the same condition is described as both acute (subacute) and chronic, and separate subentries exist in the Alphabetic Index at the same indentation level, code both and sequence the acute (subacute) code first.
11. **Combination Code**
    A combination code is a single code used to classify: Two diagnoses, or A diagnosis with an associated secondary process (manifestation) A diagnosis with an associated complication
    Combination codes are identified by referring to subterm entries in the Alphabetic Index and by reading the inclusion and exclusion notes in the Tabular List.

Assign only the combination code when that code fully identifies the diagnostic conditions involved or when the Alphabetic Index so directs. Multiple coding should not be used when the classification provides a combination code that clearly identifies all of the elements documented in the diagnosis. When the combination code lacks necessary specificity in describing the manifestation or complication, an additional code should be used as a secondary code.

12. **Late Effects**

A late effect is the residual effect (condition produced) after the acute phase of an illness or injury has terminated. There is no time limit on when a late effect code can be used. The residual may be apparent early, such as in cerebrovascular accident cases, or it may occur months or years later, such as that due to a previous injury. Coding of late effects generally requires two codes sequenced in the following order: The condition or nature of the late effect is sequenced first. The late effect code is sequenced second.

An exception to the above guidelines are those instances where the code for late effect is followed by a manifestation code identified in the Tabular List and title, or the late effect code has been expanded (at the fourth and fifth-digit levels) to include the manifestation(s). The code for the acute phase of an illness or injury that led to the late effect is never used with a code for the late effect.

13. **Impending or Threatened Condition**

Code any condition described at the time of discharge as "impending" or "threatened" as follows:
If it did occur, code as confirmed diagnosis.
If it did not occur, reference the Alphabetic Index to determine if the condition has a subentry term for "impending" or "threatened" and also reference main term entries for "Impending" and for "Threatened."
If the subterms are listed, assign the given code.
If the subterms are not listed, code the existing underlying condition(s) and not the condition described as impending or threatened.

## C. Chapter-Specific Coding Guidelines

In addition to general coding guidelines, there are guidelines for specific diagnoses and/or conditions in the classification. Unless otherwise indicated, these guidelines apply to all health care settings. Please refer to Section II for guidelines on the selection of principal diagnosis.

1. **Chapter 1: Infectious and Parasitic Diseases (001-139)**

   a. **Human Immunodeficiency Virus (HIV) Infections**

      1) **Code only confirmed cases**

      Code only confirmed cases of HIV infection/illness. This is an exception to the hospital inpatient guideline Section II, H.
      In this context, "confirmation" does not require documentation of positive serology or culture for HIV; the provider's diagnostic statement that the patient is HIV positive, or has an HIV-related illness is sufficient.

      2) **Selection and sequencing of HIV codes**

      **(a)Patient admitted for HIV-related condition**

      If a patient is admitted for an HIV-related condition principal diagnosis should be 042, followed by, additional diagnosis codes for all reported HIV-related conditions

      **(b)Patient with HIV disease admitted for unrelated condition**

If a patient with HIV disease is admitted for an unrelated condition (such as a traumatic injury), the code for the unrelated condition (e.g., the nature of injury code) should be the principal diagnosis. Other diagnoses would be 042 followed by additional diagnosis codes for all reported HIV-related conditions.

**(c) Whether the patient is newly diagnosed**

Whether the patient is newly diagnosed or has had previous admissions/encounters for HIV conditions is irrelevant to the sequencing decision

**(d) Asymptomatic human immunodeficiency virus**

V08 Asymptomatic human immunodeficiency virus [HIV] infection, is to be applied when the patient without any documentation of symptoms is listed as being "HIV positive," "known HIV," "HIV test positive," or similar terminology. Do not use this code if the term "AIDS" is used or if the patient is treated any HIV-related illness or is described as having any condition(s) resulting from his/her HIV positive status; use 042 in these cases.

**(e) Patients with inconclusive HIV serology**

Patients with inconclusive HIV serology, but no definitive diagnosis or manifestations of the illness, may be assigned code 795.71, Inconclusive serologic test for Human Immunodeficiency Virus [HIV].

**(f) Previously diagnosed HIV-related illness**

Patients with any known prior diagnosis of an HIV-related illness should be coded to 042. Once a patient has developed an HIV-related illness, the patient should always be assigned code 042 on every subsequent admission/encounter. Patients previously diagnosed with any HIV illness (042) should never be assigned to 795.71 or V08.

**(g) HIV Infection in Pregnancy, Childbirth and the Puerperium**

During pregnancy, childbirth or the puerperium, a patient admitted (or presenting for a health care encounter) because of an HIV-related illness should receive a principal diagnosis code of 647.6X, Other specified infectious and parasitic diseases in the mother classifiable elsewhere, but complicating the pregnancy, childbirth or the puerperium, followed by 042 and the code(s) for the HIV-related illness(es). Codes from Chapter 15 always take sequencing priority.

Patients with asymptomatic HIV infection status admitted (or presenting for a health care encounter) during pregnancy, childbirth, or the puerperium should receive codes of 647.6X and V08.

**(h) Encounters for testing for HIV**

If a patient is being seen to determine his/her HIV status, use code V73.89, Screening for other specified viral disease. Use code V69.8, Other problems related to lifestyle, as a secondary code if an asymptomatic patient is in a known high risk group for HIV. Should a patient with signs or symptoms or illness, or a confirmed HIV related diagnosis be tested for HIV, code the signs and symptoms or the diagnosis. An additional counseling code V65.44 may be used if counseling is provided during the encounter for the test.

When a patient returns to be informed of his/her HIV test results use code V65.44, HIV counseling, if the results of the test are negative.

If the results are positive but the patient is asymptomatic use code V08, Asymptomatic HIV infection. If the results are positive and the patient is symptomatic use code 042, HIV infection, with codes for the HIV related symptoms or diagnosis. The HIV counseling code may also be used if counseling is provided for patients with positive test results.

**b. Septicemia, Systemic Inflammatory Response Syndrome SIRS), Sepsis, Severe Sepsis, and Septic Shock**

**1) Sepsis as principal diagnosis or secondary diagnosis**

**(a) Sepsis as principal diagnosis**

If sepsis is present on admission, and meets the definition of principal diagnosis, the underlying systemic infection code (e.g., 038.xx, 112.5, etc) should be assigned as the principal diagnosis, followed by code 995.91, Systemic inflammatory response syndrome due to infectious process without organ dysfunction, as required by the sequencing rules in the Tabular List. Codes from subcategory 995.9 can never be assigned as a principal diagnosis.

**(b) Sepsis as secondary diagnoses**

When sepsis develops during the encounter (it was not present on admission), the sepsis codes may be assigned as secondary diagnoses, following the sequencing rules provided in the Tabular List.

**(c) Documentation unclear as to whether sepsis present on admission**

If the documentation is not clear whether the sepsis was present on admission, the provider should be queried. After provider query, if sepsis is determined at that point to have met the definition of principal diagnosis, the underlying systemic infection (038.xx, 112.5, etc) may be used as principal diagnosis along with code 995.91, Systemic inflammatory response syndrome due to infectious process without organ dysfunction.

**2) Septicemia/Sepsis**

In most cases, it will be a code from category 038, Septicemia, that will be used in conjunction with a code from subcategory 995.9 such as the following:

**(a) Streptococcal sepsis**

If the documentation in the record states streptococcal sepsis, codes 038.0 and code 995.91 should be used, in that sequence.

**(b) Streptococcal septicemia**

If the documentation states streptococcal septicemia, only code 038.0 should be assigned, however, the provider should be queried whether the patient has sepsis, an infection with SIRS.

**(c) Sepsis or SIRS must be documented**

Either the term sepsis or SIRS must be documented, to assign a code from subcategory 995.9.

**3) Terms sepsis, severe sepsis, or SIRS**

If the terms sepsis, severe sepsis, or SIRS are used with an underlying infection other than septicemia, such as pneumonia, cellulitis or a nonspecified urinary tract infection, a code from category 038 should be assigned first, then code 995.91, followed by the code for the initial infection. The use of the terms sepsis or SIRS indicates that the patient's infection has advanced to the point of a systemic infection so the systemic infection should be sequenced before the localized infection. The instructional note under subcategory 995.9 instructs to assign the underlying systemic infection first.

**Note:** The term urosepsis is a nonspecific term. If that is the only term documented then only code 599.0 should be assigned based on the default for the term in the ICD-9-CM index, in addition to the code for the causal organism if known.

**4) Severe sepsis**

For patients with severe sepsis, the code for the systemic infection (e.g., 038.xx, 112.5, etc) or trauma should be sequenced first, followed by either code 995.92, Systemic inflammatory response syndrome due to infectious process with organ dysfunction, or code 995.94, Systemic inflammatory response syndrome due to noninfectious process with organ dysfunction. Codes for the specific organ dysfunctions should also be assigned.

**5) Septic shock**

**(a) Sequencing of septic shock**

Septic shock is a form of organ dysfunction associated with severe sepsis. A code for the initiating underlying systemic infection followed by a code for SIRS (code 995.92) must be assigned before the code for septic shock. As noted in the sequencing instructions in the Tabular List, the code for septic shock cannot be assigned as a principal diagnosis.

**(b) Septic Shock without documentation of severe sepsis**

Septic shock cannot occur in the absence of severe sepsis. A code from subcategory 995.9 must be sequenced before the code for septic shock. The use additional code notes and the code first note provide sequencing instructions.

**6)** **Sepsis and septic shock associated with abortion** Sepsis and septic shock associated with abortion, ectopic pregnancy, and molar pregnancy are classified to category codes in Chapter 11 (630-639).

**7)** **Negative or inconclusive blood cultures** Negative or inconclusive blood cultures do not preclude a diagnosis of septicemia or sepsis in patients with clinical evidence of the condition, however, the provider should be queried.

**8)** **Newborn sepsis** See Section I.C.15.j for information on the coding of newborn sepsis.

**9)** **Sepsis due to a Postprocedural Infection** Sepsis resulting from a postprocedural infection is a complication of care. For such cases code 998.59, Other postoperative infections, should be coded first followed by the appropriate codes for the sepsis. The other guidelines for coding sepsis should then be followed for the assignment of additional codes.

**10)** **External cause of injury codes with SIRS** An external cause code is not needed with codes 995.91, Systemic inflammatory response syndrome due to infectious process without organ dysfunction, or code 995.92, Systemic inflammatory response syndrome due to infectious process with organ dysfunction. Refer to Section I.C.19.a.7 for instruction on the use of external cause of injury codes with codes for SIRS resulting from trauma.

2. **Chapter 2: Neoplasms (140-239) General guidelines** Chapter 2 of the ICD-9-CM contains the codes for most benign and all malignant neoplasms. Certain benign neoplasms, such as prostatic adenomas, may be found in the specific body system chapters. To properly code a neoplasm it is necessary to determine from the record if the neoplasm is benign, in-situ, malignant, or of uncertain histologic behavior. If malignant, any secondary (metastatic) sites should also be determined.

   The neoplasm table in the Alphabetic Index should be referenced first. However, if the histological term is documented, that term should be referenced first, rather than going immediately to the Neoplasm Table, in order to determine which column in the Neoplasm Table is appropriate. For example, if the documentation indicates "adenoma," refer to the term in the Alphabetic Index to review the entries under this term and the instructional note to "see also neoplasm, by site, benign." The table provides the proper code based on the type of neoplasm and the site. It is important to select the proper column in the table that corresponds to the type of neoplasm. The tabular should then be referenced to verify that the correct code has been selected from the table and that a more specific site code does not exist.

   See Section I. C. 18.d.4. for information regarding V codes for genetic susceptibility to cancer.

   a. **Treatment directed at the malignancy**
      If the treatment is directed at the malignancy, designate the malignancy as the principal diagnosis.
   b. **Treatment of secondary site**
      When a patient is admitted because of a primary neoplasm with metastasis and treatment is directed toward the secondary site only, the secondary neoplasm is designated as the principal diagnosis even though the primary malignancy is still present.
   c. **Coding and sequencing of complications**
      Coding and sequencing of complications associated with the malignancies or with the therapy thereof are subject to the following guidelines:
      1) **Anemia associated with malignancy**
         When admission/encounter is for management of an anemia associated with the malignancy, and the treatment is only for anemia, the **appropriate** anemia **code (such as code 285.22, Anemia in neoplastic disease)** is designated as the principal diagnosis and is followed by the appropriate code(s) for the malignancy.

         **Code 285.22 may also be used as a secondary code if the patient suffers from anemia and is being treated for the malignancy.**
      2) **Anemia associated with chemotherapy, immunotherapy and radiation therapy**
         When the admission/encounter is for management of an anemia associated with chemotherapy**, immunotherapy** or radiotherapy and the only treatment is for the anemia, the anemia is sequenced first followed by **code E933.1. The appropriate neoplasm code should be assigned as an additional code.**

3) **Management of dehydration due to the malignancy**
When the admission/encounter is for management of dehydration due to the malignancy or the therapy, or a combination of both, and only the dehydration is being treated (intravenous rehydration), the dehydration is sequenced first, followed by the code(s) for the malignancy.

4) **Treatment of a complication resulting from a surgical procedure**
When the admission/encounter is for treatment of a complication resulting from a surgical procedure, designate the complication as the principal or first-listed diagnosis if treatment is directed at resolving the complication.

d. **Primary malignancy previously excised**
When a primary malignancy has been previously excised or eradicated from its site and there is no further treatment directed to that site and there is no evidence of any existing primary malignancy, a code from category V10, Personal history of malignant neoplasm, should be used to indicate the former site of the malignancy. Any mention of extension, invasion, or metastasis to another site is coded as a secondary malignant neoplasm to that site. The secondary site may be the principal or first-listed with the V10 code used as a secondary code.

e. **Admissions/Encounters involving chemotherapy, immunotherapy and radiation therapy**

1) **Episode of care involves surgical removal of neoplasm**
When an episode of care involves the surgical removal of a neoplasm, primary or secondary site, followed by adjunct chemotherapy or radiation treatment **during the same episode of care**, the neoplasm code should be assigned as principal or first-listed diagnosis, using codes in the 140-198 series or where appropriate in the 200-203 series

2) **Patient admission/encounter solely for administration of chemotherapy, immunotherapy and radiation therapy**

If a patient admission/encounter is solely for the administration of chemotherapy, **immunotherapy** or radiation therapy **assign** code V58.0, Encounter for radiation therapy, or **V58.11**, Encounter for **antineoplastic** chemotherapy, **or V58.12, Encounter for antineoplastic immunotherapy as** the first-listed or principal diagnosis. If a patient receives **more than one of these therapies during the same admission more than one of these codes may be assigned, in any sequence.**

3) **Patient admitted for radiotherapy/chemotherapy and immunotherapy and develops complications**
When a patient is admitted for the purpose of radiotherapy**, immunotherapy** or chemotherapy and develops complications such as uncontrolled nausea and vomiting or dehydration, the principal or first-listed diagnosis is V58.0, Encounter for radiotherapy, or V58.1**1**, **Encounter for antineoplastic chemotherapy, or V58.12, Encounter for antineoplastic immunotherapy** followed by any codes for the complications.

See Section I.C.18.d.7. for additional information regarding aftercare V codes.

f. **Admission/encounter to determine extent of malignancy**
When the reason for admission/encounter is to determine the extent of the malignancy, or for a procedure such as paracentesis or thoracentesis, the primary malignancy or appropriate metastatic site is designated as the principal or first-listed diagnosis, even though chemotherapy or radiotherapy is administered.

**g. Symptoms, signs, and ill-defined conditions listed in Chapter 16**

Symptoms, signs, and ill-defined conditions listed in Chapter 16 characteristic of, or associated with, an existing primary or secondary site malignancy cannot be used to replace the malignancy as principal or first-listed diagnosis, regardless of the number of admissions or encounters for treatment and care of the neoplasm.

See section I.C.18.d.14, Encounter for prophylactic organ removal

**3. Chapter 3: Endocrine, Nutritional, and Metabolic Diseases and Immunity Disorders (240-279)**

**a. Diabetes mellitus**

Codes under category 250, Diabetes mellitus, identify complications/manifestations associated with diabetes mellitus. A fifth-digit is required for all category 250 codes to identify the type of diabetes mellitus and whether the diabetes is controlled or uncontrolled.

**1) Fifth-digits for category 250:**

The following are the fifth-digits for the codes under category 250:
0 type II or unspecified type, not stated as uncontrolled
1 type I, [juvenile type], not stated as uncontrolled
2 type II or unspecified type, uncontrolled
3 type I, [juvenile type], uncontrolled
The age of a patient is not the sole determining factor, though most type I diabetics develop the condition before reaching puberty. For this reason type I diabetes mellitus is also referred to as juvenile diabetes.

**2) Type of diabetes mellitus not documented**

If the type of diabetes mellitus is not documented in the medical record the default is type II.

**3) Diabetes mellitus and the use of insulin**

All type I diabetics must use insulin to replace what their bodies do not produce. However, the use of insulin does not mean that a patient is a type I diabetic. Some patients with type II diabetes mellitus are unable to control their blood sugar through diet and oral medication alone and do require insulin. If the documentation in a medical record does not indicate the type of diabetes but does indicate that the patient uses insulin, the appropriate fifth-digit for type II must be used. For type II patients who routinely use insulin, code V58.67, Long-term (current) use of insulin, should also be assigned to indicate that the patient uses insulin. Code V58.67 should not be assigned if insulin is given temporarily to bring a type II patient's blood sugar under control during an encounter.

**4) Assigning and sequencing diabetes codes and associated conditions**

When assigning codes for diabetes and its associated conditions, the code(s) from category 250 must be sequenced before the codes for the associated conditions. The diabetes codes and the secondary codes that correspond to them are paired codes that follow the etiology/manifestation convention of the classification (See Section I.A.6., Etiology/manifestation convention). Assign as many codes from category 250 as needed to identify all of the associated conditions that the patient has. The corresponding secondary codes are listed under each of the diabetes codes.

**(a) Diabetic retinopathy/diabetic macular edema Diabetic macular edema, code 362.07, is only present with diabetic retinopathy. Another code from subcategory 362.0, Diabetic retinopathy, must be used with code 362.07. Codes under subcategory 362.0 are diabetes manifestation codes, so they must be used following the appropriate diabetes code.**

**5) Diabetes mellitus in pregnancy and gestational diabetes**

(a) For diabetes mellitus complicating pregnancy, see Section I.C.11.f., Diabetes mellitus in pregnancy.

(b) For gestational diabetes, see Section I.C.11, g., Gestational diabetes.

**6) Insulin pump malfunction**

**(a) Underdose of insulin due insulin pump failure**

An underdose of insulin due to an insulin pump failure should be assigned 996.57, Mechanical complication due to insulin pump, as the principal or first listed code, followed by the appropriate diabetes mellitus code based on documentation.

**(b) Overdose of insulin due to insulin pump failure**

The principal or first listed code for an encounter due to an insulin pump malfunction resulting in an overdose of insulin, should also be 996.57, Mechanical complication due to insulin pump, followed by code 962.3, Poisoning by insulins and antidiabetic agents, and the appropriate diabetes mellitus code based on documentation.

**4. Chapter 4: Diseases of Blood and Blood Forming Organs (280-289)**

**a. Anemia of chronic disease Subcategory 285.2, Anemia in chronic illness, has codes for anemia in chronic kidney disease, code 285.21; anemia in neoplastic disease, code 285.22; and anemia in other chronic illness, code 285.29. These codes can be used as the principal/first listed code if the reason for the encounter is to treat the anemia. They may also be used as secondary codes if treatment of the anemia is a component of an encounter, but not the primary reason for the encounter.**

**When using a code from subcategory 285 it is also necessary to use the code for the chronic condition causing the anemia.**

**1) Anemia in chronic kidney disease When assigning code 285.21, Anemia in chronic kidney disease. It is also necessary to assign a code from category 585, Chronic kidney disease, to indicate the stage of chronic kidney disease. See I.C.10.a. Chronic kidney disease (CKD)**

**2) Anemia in neoplastic disease When assigning code 285.22, Anemia in neoplastic disease, it is also necessary to assign the neoplasm code that is responsible for the anemia. Code 285.22 is for use for anemia that is due to the malignancy, not for anemia due to antineoplastic chemotherapy drugs, which is an adverse effect. See I.C.2.c.1 Anemia associated with malignancy See I.C.2.c.2 Anemia associated with chemotherapy, immunotherapy and radiation therapy See I.C.17.e.1. Adverse effects**

**5. Chapter 5: Mental Disorders (290-319)**

Reserved for future guideline expansion

**6. Chapter 6: Diseases of Nervous System and Sense Organs (320-389)**

Reserved for future guideline expansion

7. **Chapter 7: Diseases of Circulatory System (390-459)**
   a. **Hypertension**

      **Hypertension Table**

      The Hypertension Table, found under the main term, "Hypertension", in the Alphabetic Index, contains a complete listing of all conditions due to or associated with hypertension and classifies them according to malignant, benign, and unspecified.

      1) **Hypertension, Essential, or NOS**

         Assign hypertension (arterial) (essential) (primary) (systemic) (NOS) to category code 401 with the appropriate fourth digit to indicate malignant (.0), benign (.1), or unspecified (.9). Do not use either .0 malignant or .1 benign unless medical record documentation supports such a designation.

      2) **Hypertension with Heart Disease**

         Heart conditions (425.8, 429.0-429.3, 429.8, 429.9) are assigned to a code from category 402 when a causal relationship is stated (due to hypertension) or implied (hypertensive). Use an additional code from category 428 to identify the type of heart failure in those patients with heart failure. More than one code from category 428 may be assigned if the patient has systolic or diastolic failure and congestive heart failure. The same heart conditions (425.8, 429.0-429.3, 429.8, 429.9) with hypertension, but without a stated causal relationship, are coded separately. Sequence according to the circumstances of the admission/encounter.

      3) **Hypertensive Kidney Disease**

         Assign codes from category 403, Hypertensive **kidney** disease, when conditions classified to categories 585-587 are present. Unlike hypertension with heart disease, ICD-9-CM presumes a cause-and-effect relationship and classifies renal failure with hypertension as hypertensive **kidney** disease.

      4) **Hypertensive Heart and Kidney Disease**

         Assign codes from combination category 404, Hypertensive heart and **kidney** disease, when both hypertensive **kidney** disease and hypertensive heart disease are stated in the diagnosis. Assume a relationship between the hypertension and the **kidney** disease, whether or not the condition is so designated. Assign an additional code from category 428, to identify the type of heart failure. More than one code from category 428 may be assigned if the patient has systolic or diastolic failure and congestive heart failure.

      5) **Hypertensive Cerebrovascular Disease**

         First assign codes from 430-438, Cerebrovascular disease, then the appropriate hypertension code from categories 401-405.

      6) **Hypertensive Retinopathy** Two codes are necessary to identify the condition. First assign the code from subcategory 362.11, Hypertensive retinopathy, then the appropriate code from categories 401-405 to indicate the type of hypertension.

      7) **Hypertension, Secondary**

         Two codes are required: one to identify the underlying etiology and one from category 405 to identify the hypertension. Sequencing of codes is determined by the reason for admission/encounter.

      8) **Hypertension, Transient**

         Assign code 796.2, Elevated blood pressure reading without diagnosis of hypertension, unless patient has an established diagnosis of hypertension. Assign code 642.3x for transient hypertension of pregnancy.

      9) **Hypertension, Controlled** Assign appropriate code from categories 401-405. This diagnostic statement usually refers to an existing state of hypertension under control by therapy.

**10) Hypertension, Uncontrolled**

Uncontrolled hypertension may refer to untreated hypertension or hypertension not responding to current therapeutic regimen. In either case, assign the appropriate code from categories 401-405 to designate the stage and type of hypertension. Code to the type of hypertension.

**11) Elevated Blood Pressure**

For a statement of elevated blood pressure without further specificity, assign code 796.2, Elevated blood pressure reading without diagnosis of hypertension, rather than a code from category 401.

**b. Cerebral infarction/stroke/cerebrovascular accident (CVA)**

The terms stroke and CVA are often used interchangeably to refer to a cerebral infarction. The terms stroke, CVA, and cerebral infarction NOS are all indexed to the default code 434.91, Cerebral artery occlusion, unspecified, with infarction. Code 436, Acute, but ill-defined, cerebrovascular disease, should not be used when the documentation states stroke or CVA.

**c. Postoperative cerebrovascular accident**

A cerebrovascular hemorrhage or infarction that occurs as a result of medical intervention is coded to 997.02, Iatrogenic cerebrovascular infarction or hemorrhage. Medical record documentation should clearly specify the cause-and-effect relationship between the medical intervention and the cerebrovascular accident in order to assign this code. A secondary code from the code range 430-432 or from a code from subcategories 433 or 434 with a fifth digit of "1" should also be used to identify the type of hemorrhage or infarct. This guideline conforms to the use additional code note instruction at category 997. Code 436, Acute, but ill-defined, cerebrovascular disease, should not be used as a secondary code with code 997.02.

**d. Late Effects of Cerebrovascular Disease**

**1) Category 438, Late Effects of Cerebrovascular disease**

Category 438 is used to indicate conditions classifiable to categories 430-437 as the causes of late effects (neurologic deficits), themselves classified elsewhere. These "late effects" include neurologic deficits that persist after initial onset of conditions classifiable to 430-437. The neurologic deficits caused by cerebrovascular disease may be present from the onset or may arise at any time after the onset of the condition classifiable to 430-437.

**2) Codes from category 438 with codes from 430-437**

Codes from category 438 may be assigned on a health care record with codes from 430-437, if the patient has a current cerebrovascular accident (CVA) and deficits from an old CVA.

**3) Code V12.59**

Assign code V12.59 (and not a code from category 438) as an additional code for history of cerebrovascular disease when no neurologic deficits are present.

**e. Acute myocardial infarction (AMI)**

**1) ST elevation myocardial infarction (STEMI) and non ST elevation myocardial infarction (NSTEMI) The ICD-9-CM codes for acute myocardial infarction (AMI) identify the site, such as anterolateral wall or true posterior wall. Subcategories 410.0-410.6 and 410.8 are used for ST elevation myocardial infarction (STEMI). Subcategory 410.7, Subendocardial infarction, is used for non ST elevation myocardial infarction (NSTEMI) and nontransmural MIs.**

**2) Acute myocardial infarction, unspecified Subcategory 410.9 is the default for the unspecified term acute myocardial infarction. If only STEMI or transmural MI without the site is documented, query the provider as to the site, or assign a code from subcategory 410.9.**

3) **AMI documented as nontransmural or subendocardial but site provided If an AMI is documented as nontransmural or subendocardial, but the site is provided, it is still coded as a subendocardial AMI. If NSTEMI evolves to STEMI, assign the STEMI code. If STEMI converts to NSTEMI due to thrombolytic therapy, it is still coded as STEMI.**

8. **Chapter 8: Diseases of Respiratory System (460-519)**
   a. **Chronic Obstructive Pulmonary Disease [COPD] and Asthma**
      1) **Conditions that comprise COPD and Asthma**
      The conditions that comprise COPD are obstructive chronic bronchitis, subcategory 491.2, and emphysema, category 492.

      All asthma codes are under category 493, Asthma. Code 496, Chronic airway obstruction, not elsewhere classified, is a nonspecific code that should only be used when the documentation in a medical record does not specify the type of COPD being treated.
      2) **Acute exacerbation of chronic obstructive bronchitis and asthma**
      The codes for chronic obstructive bronchitis and asthma distinguish between uncomplicated cases and those in acute exacerbation. An acute exacerbation is a worsening or a decompensation of a chronic condition. An acute exacerbation is not equivalent to an infection superimposed on a chronic condition, though an exacerbation may be triggered by an infection.
      3) **Overlapping nature of the conditions that comprise COPD and asthma**
      Due to the overlapping nature of the conditions that make up COPD and asthma, there are many variations in the way these conditions are documented. Code selection must be based on the terms as documented. When selecting the correct code for the documented type of COPD and asthma, it is essential to first review the index, and then verify the code in the tabular list. There are many instructional notes under the different COPD subcategories and codes. It is important that all such notes be reviewed to assure correct code assignment.
      4) **Acute exacerbation of asthma and status asthmaticus**
      An acute exacerbation of asthma is an increased severity of the asthma symptoms, such as wheezing and shortness of breath. Status asthmaticus refers to a patient's failure to respond to therapy administered during an asthmatic episode and is a life threatening complication that requires emergency care. If status asthmaticus is documented by the provider with any type of COPD or with acute bronchitis, the status asthmaticus should be sequenced first. It supersedes any type of COPD including that with acute exacerbation or acute bronchitis. It is inappropriate to assign an asthma code with $5^{th}$ digit 2, with acute exacerbation, together with an asthma code with $5^{th}$ digit 1, with status asthmatics. Only the $5^{th}$ digit 1 should be assigned.
   b. **Chronic Obstructive Pulmonary Disease [COPD] and Bronchitis**
      1) **Acute bronchitis with COPD**
      Acute bronchitis, code 466.0, is due to an infectious organism. When acute bronchitis is documented with COPD, code 491.22, Obstructive chronic bronchitis with acute bronchitis, should be assigned. It is not necessary to also assign code 466.0. If a medical record documents acute bronchitis with COPD with acute exacerbation, only code 491.22 should be assigned. The acute bronchitis included in code 491.22 supersedes the acute exacerbation. If a medical record documents COPD with acute exacerbation without mention of acute bronchitis, only code 491.21 should be assigned.

9. **Chapter 9: Diseases of Digestive System (520-579)**
   Reserved for future guideline expansion
10. **Chapter 10: Diseases of Genitourinary System (580-629)**
   a. **Chronic kidney disease**
      1) **Stages of chronic kidney disease (CKD) The ICD-9-CM classifies CKD based on severity. The severity of CKD is designated by stages I-V. Stage II, code 585.2, equates to mild CKD; stage III, code 585.3, equates to moderate CKD; and stage IV, code 585.4, equates to severe CKD. Code 585.6, End stage renal disease (ESRD), is assigned when the provider has documented end-stage-renal disease (ESRD).**

         **If both a stage of CKD and ESRD are documented, assign code 585.6 only.**
      2) **Chronic kidney disease and kidney transplant status Patients who have undergone kidney transplant may still have some form of CKD because the kidney transplant may not fully restore kidney function. Code V42.0 may be assigned with the appropriate CKD code for patients who are status post kidney transplant, based on the patient's post-transplant stage. The use additional code**

         **Use of a 585 code with V42.0 does not necessarily indicate transplant rejection or failure. Patients with mild or moderate CKD following a transplant should not be coded as having transplant failure, unless it is documented in the medical record. For patients with severe CKD or ESRD it is appropriate to assign code 996.81, Complications of transplanted organ, kidney transplant, when kidney transplant failure is documented. If a post kidney transplant patient has CKD and it is unclear from the documentation whether there is transplant failure or rejection it is necessary to query the provider.**
      3) **Chronic kidney disease with other conditions Patients with CKD may also suffer from other serious conditions, most commonly diabetes mellitus and hypertension. The sequencing of the CKD code in relationship to codes for other contributing conditions is based on the conventions in the tabular list. See I.C.3.a.4 for sequencing instructions for diabetes. See I.C.4.a.1. for anemia in CKD. See I.C.7.a.3 for hypertensive kidney disease. See I.C.17.f.1.b. Transplant complications, for instructions on coding of documented rejection or failure.**
11. **Chapter 11: Complications of Pregnancy, Childbirth, and the Puerperium (630-677)**
   a. **General Rules for Obstetric Cases**
      1) **Codes from chapter 11 and sequencing priority**
         Obstetric cases require codes from chapter 11, codes in the range 630-677, Complications of Pregnancy, Childbirth, and the Puerperium. Chapter 11 codes have sequencing priority over codes from other chapters. Additional codes from other chapters may be used in conjunction with chapter 11 codes to further specify conditions. Should the provider document that the pregnancy is incidental to the encounter, then code V22.2 should be used in place of any chapter 11 codes. It is the provider's responsibility to state that the condition being treated is not affecting the pregnancy.
      2) **Chapter 11 codes used only on the maternal record** Chapter 11 codes are to be used only on the maternal record, never on the record of the newborn.
      3) **Chapter 11 fifth-digits**
         Categories 640-648, 651-676 have required fifth-digits, which indicate whether the encounter is antepartum, postpartum and whether a delivery has also occurred.

4) **Fifth-digits, appropriate for each code**

The fifth-digits, which are appropriate for each code number, are listed in brackets under each code. The fifth-digits on each code should all be consistent with each other. That is, should a delivery occur all of the fifth-digits should indicate the delivery.

b. **Selection of OB Principal or First-listed Diagnosis**

1) **Routine outpatient prenatal visits**

For routine outpatient prenatal visits when no complications are present codes V22.0, Supervision of normal first pregnancy, and V22.1, Supervision of other normal pregnancy, should be used as the first-listed diagnoses. These codes should not be used in conjunction with chapter 11 codes.

2) **Prenatal outpatient visits for high-risk patients**

For prenatal outpatient visits for patients with high-risk pregnancies, a code from category V23, Supervision of high-risk pregnancy, should be used as the principal or first-listed diagnosis. Secondary chapter 11 codes may be used in conjunction with these codes if appropriate.

3) **Episodes when no delivery occurs**

In episodes when no delivery occurs, the principal diagnosis should correspond to the principal complication of the pregnancy, which necessitated the encounter. Should more than one complication exist, all of which are treated or monitored, any of the complications codes may be sequenced first.

4) **When a delivery occurs**

When a delivery occurs, the principal diagnosis should correspond to the main circumstances or complication of the delivery. In cases of cesarean delivery, the selection of the principal diagnosis should correspond to the reason the cesarean delivery was performed unless the reason for admission/encounter was unrelated to the condition resulting in the cesarean delivery.

5) **Outcome of delivery**

An outcome of delivery code, V27.0-V27.9, should be included on every maternal record when a delivery has occurred. These codes are not to be used on subsequent records or on the newborn record.

c. **Fetal Conditions Affecting the Management of the Mother**

1) **Codes from category 655**

Known or suspected fetal abnormality affecting management of the mother, and category 656, Other fetal and placental problems affecting the management of the mother, are assigned only when the fetal condition is actually responsible for modifying the management of the mother, i.e., by requiring diagnostic studies, additional observation, special care, or termination of pregnancy. The fact that the fetal condition exists does not justify assigning a code from this series to the mother's record.

2) **In utero surgery**

In cases when surgery is performed on the fetus, a diagnosis code from category 655, Known or suspected fetal abnormalities affecting management of the mother, should be assigned identifying the fetal condition. Procedure code 75.36, Correction of fetal defect, should be assigned on the hospital inpatient record. No code from Chapter 15, the perinatal codes, should be used on the mother's record to identify fetal conditions. Surgery performed in utero on a fetus is still to be coded as an obstetric encounter.

d. **HIV Infection in Pregnancy, Childbirth and the Puerperium** During pregnancy, childbirth or the puerperium, a patient admitted because of an HIV-related illness should receive a principal diagnosis of 647.6X, Other specified infectious and parasitic diseases in the mother classifiable elsewhere, but complicating the pregnancy, childbirth or the puerperium, followed by 042 and the code(s) for the HIV-related illness(es).

   Patients with asymptomatic HIV infection status admitted during pregnancy, childbirth, or the puerperium should receive codes of 647.6X and V08.

e. **Current Conditions Complicating Pregnancy**

   Assign a code from subcategory 648.x for patients that have current conditions when the condition affects the management of the pregnancy, childbirth, or the puerperium. Use additional secondary codes from other chapters to identify the conditions, as appropriate.

f. **Diabetes mellitus in pregnancy**

   Diabetes mellitus is a significant complicating factor in pregnancy. Pregnant women who are diabetic should be assigned code 648.0x, Diabetes mellitus complicating pregnancy, and a secondary code from category 250, Diabetes mellitus, to identify the type of diabetes.

   Code V58.67, Long-term (current) use of insulin, should also be assigned if the diabetes mellitus is being treated with insulin.

g. **Gestational diabetes**

   Gestational diabetes can occur during the second and third trimester of pregnancy in women who were not diabetic prior to pregnancy. Gestational diabetes can cause complications in the pregnancy similar to those of pre-existing diabetes mellitus. It also puts the woman at greater risk of developing diabetes after the pregnancy. Gestational diabetes is coded to 648.8x, Abnormal glucose tolerance. Codes 648.0x and 648.8x should never be used together on the same record.

   Code V58.67, Long-term (current) use of insulin, should also be assigned if the gestational diabetes is being treated with insulin.

h. **Normal Delivery, Code 650**

   1) **Normal delivery**

      Code 650 is for use in cases when a woman is admitted for a full-term normal delivery and delivers a single, healthy infant without any complications antepartum, during the delivery, or postpartum during the delivery episode. Code 650 is always a principal diagnosis. It is not to be used if any other code from chapter 11 is needed to describe a current complication of the antenatal, delivery, or perinatal period. Additional codes from other chapters may be used with code 650 if they are not related to or are in any way complicating the pregnancy.

   2) **Normal delivery with resolved antepartum complication**

      Code 650 may be used if the patient had a complication at some point during her pregnancy, but the complication is not present at the time of the admission for delivery.

   3) **V27.0, Single liveborn, outcome of delivery**

      V27.0, Single liveborn, is the only outcome of delivery code appropriate for use with 650.

i. **The Postpartum and Peripartum Periods**

1) **Postpartum and peripartum periods**
The postpartum period begins immediately after delivery and continues for six weeks following delivery. The peripartum period is defined as the last month of pregnancy to five months postpartum.

2) **Postpartum complication**
A postpartum complication is any complication occurring within the six-week period.

3) **Pregnancy-related complications after 6 week period**
Chapter 11 codes may also be used to describe pregnancy-related complications after the six-week period should the provider document that a condition is pregnancy related.

4) **Postpartum complications occurring during the same admission as delivery**
Postpartum complications that occur during the same admission as the delivery are identified with a fifth digit of "2." Subsequent admissions/encounters for postpartum complications should be identified with a fifth digit of "4."

5) **Admission for routine postpartum care following delivery outside hospital**
When the mother delivers outside the hospital prior to admission and is admitted for routine postpartum care and no complications are noted, code V24.0, Postpartum care and examination immediately after delivery, should be assigned as the principal diagnosis.

6) **Admission following delivery outside hospital with postpartum conditions**
A delivery diagnosis code should not be used for a woman who has delivered prior to admission to the hospital. Any postpartum conditions and/or postpartum procedures should be coded.

j. **Code 677, Late effect of complication of pregnancy**

1) **Code 677**
Code 677, Late effect of complication of pregnancy, childbirth, and the puerperium is for use in those cases when an initial complication of a pregnancy develops a sequelae requiring care or treatment at a future date.

2) **After the initial postpartum period**
This code may be used at any time after the initial postpartum period.

3) **Sequencing of Code 677**
This code, like all late effect codes, is to be sequenced following the code describing the sequelae of the complication.

k. **Abortions**

1) **Fifth-digits required for abortion categories**
Fifth-digits are required for abortion categories 634-637. Fifth-digit 1, incomplete, indicates that all of the products of conception have not been expelled from the uterus. Fifth-digit 2, complete, indicates that all products of conception have been expelled from the uterus prior to the episode of care.

2) **Code from categories 640-648 and 651-659**
A code from categories 640-648 and 651-659 may be used as additional codes with an abortion code to indicate the complication leading to the abortion.

Fifth digit 3 is assigned with codes from these categories when used with an abortion code because the other fifth digits will not apply. Codes from the 660-669 series are not to be used for complications of abortion.

3) **Code 639 for complications**
Code 639 is to be used for all complications following abortion. Code 639 cannot be assigned with codes from categories 634-638.

4) **Abortion with Liveborn Fetus**
When an attempted termination of pregnancy results in a liveborn fetus assign code 644.21, Early onset of delivery, with an appropriate code from category V27, Outcome of Delivery. The procedure code for the attempted termination of pregnancy should also be assigned.

5) **Retained Products of Conception following an abortion**
Subsequent admissions for retained products of conception following a spontaneous or legally induced abortion are assigned the appropriate code from category 634, Spontaneous abortion, or 635 Legally induced abortion, with a fifth digit of "1" (incomplete). This advice is appropriate even when the patient was discharged previously with a discharge diagnosis of complete abortion.

**12.Chapter 12: Diseases Skin and Subcutaneous Tissue (680-709)**
Reserved for future guideline expansion

**13. Chapter 13: Diseases of Musculoskeletal and Connective Tissue (710-739)**
Reserved for future guideline expansion

**14.Chapter 14: Congenital Anomalies (740-759)**

a. **Codes in categories 740-759, Congenital Anomalies**
Assign an appropriate code(s) from categories 740-759, Congenital Anomalies, when an anomaly is documented. A congenital anomaly may be the principal/first listed diagnosis on a record or a secondary diagnosis.

**When a congenital anomaly does not have a unique code assignment, assign additional code(s) for any manifestations that may be present. When the code assignment specifically identifies the congenital anomaly, manifestations that are an inherent component of theanomaly should not be coded separately. Additional codes should be assigned for manifestations that are not an inherent component.**

Codes from Chapter 14 may be used throughout the life of the patient. If a congenital anomaly has been corrected, a personal history code should be used to identify the history of the anomaly. **Although present at birth, a congenital anomaly may not be identified until later in life. Whenever the condition is diagnosed by the physician, it is appropriate to assign a code from codes 740-759.**

For the birth admission, the appropriate code from category V30, Liveborn infants, according to type of birth should be sequenced as the principal diagnosis, followed by any congenital anomaly codes, 740759.

**15.Chapter 15: Newborn (Perinatal) Guidelines (760-779)**
For coding and reporting purposes the perinatal period is defined as **before** birth through the 28th day following birth. The following guidelines are provided for reporting purposes. Hospitals may record other diagnoses as needed for internal data use.

a. **General Perinatal Rules 1) Chapter 15 Codes**
They are never for use on the maternal record. Codes from Chapter 11, the obstetric chapter, are never permitted on the newborn record. Chapter 15 code may be used throughout the life of the patient if the condition is still present.

2) **Sequencing of perinatal codes**
Generally, codes from Chapter 15 should be sequenced as the principal/first-listed diagnosis on the newborn record, with the exception of the appropriate V30 code for the birth episode, followed by codes from any other chapter that provide additional detail. The "use additional code" note at the beginning of the chapter supports this guideline. If the index does not provide a specific code for a perinatal condition, assign code 779.89, Other specified conditions originating in the perinatal period, followed by the code from another chapter that specifies the condition. Codes for signs and symptoms may be assigned when a definitive diagnosis has not been established.

3) **Birth process or community acquired conditions**
If a newborn has a condition that may be either due to the birth process or community acquired and the documentation does not indicate which it is, the default is due to the birth process and the code from Chapter 15 should be used. If the condition is community-acquired, a code from Chapter 15 should not be assigned.

4) **Code all clinically significant conditions**
All clinically significant conditions noted on routine newborn examination should be coded. A condition is clinically significant if it requires:
- clinical evaluation; or
- therapeutic treatment; or
- diagnostic procedures; or
- extended length of hospital stay; or
- increased nursing care and/or monitoring; or
- has implications for future health care needs

**Note:** The perinatal guidelines listed above are the same as the general coding guidelines for "additional diagnoses", except for the final point regarding implications for future health care needs. Codes should be assigned for conditions that have been specified by the provider as having implications for future health care needs. Codes from the perinatal chapter should not be assigned unless the provider has established a definitive diagnosis.

**b. Use of codes V30-V39**
When coding the birth of an infant, assign a code from categories V30-V39, according to the type of birth. A code from this series is assigned as a principal diagnosis, and assigned only once to a newborn at the time of birth.

**c. Newborn transfers**
If the newborn is transferred to another institution, the V30 series is not used at the receiving hospital.

**d. Use of category V29 1) Assigning a code from category V29**
Assign a code from category V29, Observation and evaluation of newborns and infants for suspected conditions not found, to identify those instances when a healthy newborn is evaluated for a suspected condition that is determined after study not to be present. Do not use a code from category V29 when the patient has identified signs or symptoms of a suspected problem; in such cases, code the sign or symptom. A code from category V29 may also be assigned as a principal code for readmissions or encounters when the V30 code no longer applies. Codes from category V29 are for use only for healthy newborns and infants for which no condition after study is found to be present.

2) **V29 code on a birth record**
A V29 code is to be used as a secondary code after the V30, Outcome of delivery, code.

**e. Use of other V codes on perinatal records**

V codes other than V30 and V29 may be assigned on a perinatal or newborn record code. The codes may be used as a principal or first-listed diagnosis for specific types of encounters or for readmissions or encounters when the V30 code no longer applies. See Section I.C.18 for information regarding the assignment of V codes.

**f. Maternal Causes of Perinatal Morbidity**

Codes from categories 760-763, Maternal causes of perinatal morbidity and mortality, are assigned only when the maternal condition has actually affected the fetus or newborn. The fact that the mother has an associated medical condition or experiences some complication of pregnancy, labor or delivery does not justify the routine assignment of codes from these categories to the newborn record.

**g. Congenital Anomalies in Newborns**

For the birth admission, the appropriate code from category V30, Liveborn infants according to type of birth, should be used, followed by any congenital anomaly codes, categories 740-759. Use additional secondary codes from other chapters to specify conditions associated with the anomaly, if applicable. Also, see Section I.C.14 for information on the coding of congenital anomalies.

**h. Coding Additional Perinatal Diagnoses**

**1) Assigning codes for conditions that require treatment**

Assign codes for conditions that require treatment or further investigation, prolong the length of stay, or require resource utilization.

**2) Codes for conditions specified as having implications for future health care needs**

Assign codes for conditions that have been specified by the provider as having implications for future health care needs.

**Note:** This guideline should not be used for adult patients.

**3) Codes for newborn conditions originating in the perinatal period**

Assign a code for newborn conditions originating in the perinatal period (categories 760-779), as well as complications arising during the current episode of care classified in other chapters, only if the diagnoses have been documented by the responsible provider at the time of transfer or discharge as having affected the fetus or newborn.

**i. Prematurity and Fetal Growth Retardation**

Providers utilize different criteria in determining prematurity. A code for prematurity should not be assigned unless it is documented. The 5th digit assignment for codes from category 764 and subcategories 765.0 and 765.1 should be based on the recorded birth weight and estimated gestational age. A code from subcategory 765.2, Weeks of gestation, should be assigned as an additional code with category 764 and codes from 765.0 and 765.1 to specify weeks of gestation as documented by the provider in the record.

**j. Newborn sepsis**

Code 771.81, Septicemia [sepsis] of newborn, should be assigned with a secondary code from category 041, Bacterial infections in conditions classified elsewhere and of unspecified site, to identify the organism. It is not necessary to use a code from subcategory 995.9, Systemic inflammatory response syndrome (SIRS), on a newborn record. A code from category 038, Septicemia, should not be used on a newborn record. Code 771.81 describes the sepsis.

## 16. Chapter 16: Signs, Symptoms and Ill-Defined Conditions (780-799)

Reserved for future guideline expansion

## 17. Chapter 17: Injury and Poisoning (800-999)

### a. Coding of Injuries

When coding injuries, assign separate codes for each injury unless a combination code is provided, in which case the combination code is assigned. Multiple injury codes are provided in ICD-9-CM, but should not be assigned unless information for a more specific code is not available. These codes are not to be used for normal, healing surgical wounds or to identify complications of surgical wounds.

The code for the most serious injury, as determined by the provider and the focus of treatment, is sequenced first.

1) **Superficial injuries**

Superficial injuries such as abrasions or contusions are not coded when associated with more severe injuries of the same site.

2) **Primary injury with damage to nerves/blood vessels**

When a primary injury results in minor damage to peripheral nerves or blood vessels, the primary injury is sequenced first with additional code(s) from categories 950-957, Injury to nerves and spinal cord, and/or 900-904, Injury to blood vessels. When the primary injury is to the blood vessels or nerves, that injury should be sequenced first.

b. **Coding of Fractures**

The principles of multiple coding of injuries should be followed in coding fractures. Fractures of specified sites are coded individually by site in accordance with both the provisions within categories 800-829 and the level of detail furnished by medical record content. Combination categories for multiple fractures are provided for use when there is insufficient detail in the medical record (such as trauma cases transferred to another hospital), when the reporting form limits the number of codes that can be used in reporting pertinent clinical data, or when there is insufficient specificity at the fourth-digit or fifth-digit level. More specific guidelines are as follows:

1) **Multiple fractures of same limb**

Multiple fractures of same limb classifiable to the same three-digit or four-digit category are coded to that category.

2) **Multiple unilateral or bilateral fractures of same bone**

Multiple unilateral or bilateral fractures of same bone(s) but classified to different fourth-digit subdivisions (bone part) within the same three-digit category are coded individually by site.

3) **Multiple fracture categories 819 and 828**

Multiple fracture categories 819 and 828 classify bilateral fractures of both upper limbs (819) and both lower limbs (828), but without any detail at the fourth-digit level other than open and closed type of fractures.

4) **Multiple fractures sequencing**

Multiple fractures are sequenced in accordance with the severity of the fracture. The provider should be asked to list the fracture diagnoses in the order of severity.

c. **Coding of Burns**

Current burns (940-948) are classified by depth, extent and by agent (E code). Burns are classified by depth as first degree (erythema), second degree (blistering), and third degree (full-thickness involvement).

1) **Sequencing of burn and related condition codes**

Sequence first the code that reflects the highest degree of burn when more than one burn is present.

a. **When the reason for the admission or encounter is for treatment of external multiple burns, sequence first the code that reflects the burn of the highest degree.**

b. **When a patient has both internal and external burns, the circumstances of admission govern the selection of the principal diagnosis or first-listed diagnosis.**

c. **When a patient is admitted for burn injuries and other related conditions such as smoke inhalation and/or respiratory failure, the circumstances of admission govern the selection of the principal or first-listed diagnosis.**

2) **Burns of the same local site**

Classify burns of the same local site (three-digit category level, 940-947) but of different degrees to the subcategory identifying the highest degree recorded in the diagnosis.

3) **Non-healing burns**
Non-healing burns are coded as acute burns. Necrosis of burned skin should be coded as a non-healed burn.

4) **Code 958.3, Posttraumatic wound infection**
Assign code 958.3, Posttraumatic wound infection, not elsewhere classified, as an additional code for any documented infected burn site.

5) **Assign separate codes for each burn site**
When coding burns, assign separate codes for each burn site. Category 946 Burns of Multiple specified sites, should only be used if the location of the burns are not documented. Category 949, Burn, unspecified, is extremely vague and should rarely be used.

6) **Assign codes from category 948, Burns**
Burns classified according to extent of body surface involved, when the site of the burn is not specified or when there is a need for additional data. It is advisable to use category 948 as additional coding when needed to provide data for evaluating burn mortality, such as that needed by burn units. It is also advisable to use category 948 as an additional code for reporting purposes when there is mention of a third-degree burn involving 20 percent or more of the body surface.

In assigning a code from category 948:

- Fourth-digit codes are used to identify the percentage of total body surface involved in a burn (all degree).
- Fifth-digits are assigned to identify the percentage of body surface involved in third-degree burn.
- Fifth-digit zero (0) is assigned when less than 10 percent or when no body surface is involved in a third-degree burn.
  Category 948 is based on the classic "rule of nines" in estimating body surface involved: head and neck are 18 percent, the anterior trunk 18 percent, posterior trunk 18 percent, and genitalia one percent. Providers may change these percentage assignments where necessary to accommodate infants and children who have proportionately larger heads than adults and patients who have large buttocks, thighs, or abdomen that involve burns.

7) **Encounters for treatment of late effects of burns**
Encounters for the treatment of the late effects of burns (i.e., scars or joint contractures) should be coded to the residual condition (sequelae) followed by the appropriate late effect code (906.5-906.9). A late effect E code may also be used, if desired.

8) **Sequelae with a late effect code and current burn** When appropriate, both a sequelae with a late effect code, and a current burn code may be assigned on the same record (when both a current burn and sequelae of an old burn exist).

**d. Coding of Debridement of Wound, Infection, or Burn**
Excisional debridement involves surgical removal or cutting away, as opposed to a mechanical (brushing, scrubbing, washing) debridement. For coding purposes, excisional debridement is assigned to code 86.22. Nonexcisional debridement is assigned to code 86.28.

**e. Adverse Effects, Poisoning and Toxic Effects**
The properties of certain drugs, medicinal and biological substances or combinations of such substances, may cause toxic reactions. The occurrence of drug toxicity is classified in ICD-9-CM as follows:

1) **Adverse Effect** When the drug was correctly prescribed and properly administered, code the reaction plus the appropriate code from the E930-E949 series. Codes from the E930-E949 series must be used to identify the causative substance for an adverse effect of drug, medicinal and biological substances,

correctly prescribed and properly administered. The effect, such as tachycardia, delirium, gastrointestinal hemorrhaging, vomiting, hypokalemia, hepatitis, renal failure, or respiratory failure, is coded and followed by the appropriate code from the E930-E949 series.

Adverse effects of therapeutic substances correctly prescribed and properly administered (toxicity, synergistic reaction, side effect, and idiosyncratic reaction) may be due to (1) differences among patients, such as age, sex, disease, and genetic factors, and (2) drug-related factors, such as type of drug, route of administration, duration of therapy, dosage, and bioavailability.

**2) Poisoning**

**(a) Error was made in drug prescription**

Errors made in drug prescription or in the administration of the drug by provider, nurse, patient, or other person, use the appropriate poisoning code from the 960-979 series.

**(b) Overdose of a drug intentionally taken**

If an overdose of a drug was intentionally taken or administered and resulted in drug toxicity, it would be coded as a poisoning (960-979 series).

**(c) Nonprescribed drug taken with correctly prescribed and properly administered drug**

If a nonprescribed drug or medicinal agent was taken in combination with a correctly prescribed and properly administered drug, any drug toxicity or other reaction resulting from the interaction of the two drugs would be classified as a poisoning.

**(d) Sequencing of poisoning**

When coding a poisoning or reaction to the improper use of a medication (e.g., wrong dose, wrong substance, wrong route of administration) the poisoning code is sequenced first, followed by a code for the manifestation. If there is also a diagnosis of drug abuse or dependence to the substance, the abuse or dependence is coded as an additional code. See Section I.C.3.a.6.b. if poisoning is the result of insulin pump malfunctions and Section I.C.19 for general use of E-codes.

**3) Toxic Effects**

**(a) Toxic effect codes**

When a harmful substance is ingested or comes in contact with a person, this is classified as a toxic effect. The toxic effect codes are in categories 980-989.

**(b) Sequencing toxic effect codes**

A toxic effect code should be sequenced first, followed by the code(s) that identify the result of the toxic effect.

**(c) External cause codes for toxic effects**

An external cause code from categories E860-E869 for accidental exposure, codes E950.6 or E950.7 for intentional self-harm, category E962 for assault, or categories E980-E982, for undetermined, should also be assigned to indicate intent.

**f. Complications of care**

**1) Transplant complications**

**(a) Transplant complications other than kidney Codes under subcategory 996.8, Complications of transplanted organ, are for use for both complications and rejection of transplanted organs. A transplant complication code is only assigned if the complication affects the function of the transplanted organ. Two codes are required to fully describe a transplant complication, the appropriate code from**

**subcategory 996.8 and a secondary code that identifies the complication.**

**Pre-existing conditions or conditions that develop after the transplant are not coded as complications unless they affect the function of the transplanted organs.**

**Post-transplants surgical complications that do not relate to the function of the transplanted organ are classified to the specific complication. For example, a surgical wound dehiscence would be coded to the wound dehiscence, not as a transplant complication.**

Post-transplant patients who are seen for treatment unrelated to the transplanted organ should be assigned a code from category V42, Organ or tissue **replaced by transplant, to identify the transplant status of the patient. A code from category V42 should never be used with a code from subcategory 996.8.**

**(b) Kidney transplant and chronic kidney disease Patients with chronic kidney disease (CKD) following a transplant should not be assumed to have transplant failure or rejection unless it is documented by the provider. If documentation supports the presence of failure or rejection, then it is appropriate to assign code 996.81, Complications of transplanted organs, kidney followed by the appropriate CKD code.**

**18. Classification of Factors Influencing Health Status and Contact with Health Service (Supplemental V01-V84) Note: The chapter specific guidelines provide additional information about the use of V codes for specified encounters.**

**a. Introduction**

ICD-9-CM provides codes to deal with encounters for circumstances other than a disease or injury. The Supplementary Classification of Factors Influencing Health Status and Contact with Health Services (V01.0 - V84.8) is provided to deal with occasions when circumstances other than a disease or injury (codes 001-999) are recorded as a diagnosis or problem. There are four primary circumstances for the use of V codes:

**1)** A person who is not currently sick encounters the health services for some specific reason, such as to act as an organ donor, to receive prophylactic care, such as inoculations or health screenings, or to receive counseling on health related issues.

**2)** A person with a resolving disease or injury, or a chronic, long-term condition requiring continuous care, encounters the health care system for specific aftercare of that disease or injury (e.g., dialysis for renal disease; chemotherapy for malignancy; cast change). A diagnosis/symptom code should be used whenever a current, acute, diagnosis is being treated or a sign or symptom is being studied.

**3)** Circumstances or problems influence a person's health status but are not in themselves a current illness or injury.

**4)** Newborns, to indicate birth status

**b. V codes use in any healthcare setting**

V codes are for use in any healthcare setting. V codes may be used as either a first listed (principal diagnosis code in the inpatient setting) or secondary code, depending on the circumstances of the encounter. Certain V codes may only be used as first listed, others only as secondary codes. See Section I.C.18.e**, V Code Table.**

**c. V Codes indicate a reason for an encounter**

They are not procedure codes. A corresponding procedure code must accompany a V code to describe the procedure performed.

**d. Categories of V Codes**

**1) Contact/Exposure**

Category V01 indicates contact with or exposure to communicable diseases. These codes are for patients who do not show any sign or symptom of a disease but have been exposed to it by close personal contact with an infected individual or are in an area where a disease is epidemic. These codes may be used as a first listed code to explain an encounter for testing, or, more commonly, as a secondary code to identify a potential risk.

**2) Inoculations and vaccinations**

Categories V03-V06 are for encounters for inoculations and vaccinations. They indicate that a patient is being seen to receive a prophylactic inoculation against a disease. The injection itself must be represented by the appropriate procedure code. A code from V03-V06 may be used as a secondary code if the inoculation is given as a routine part of preventive health care, such as a well-baby visit.

**3) Status**

Status codes indicate that a patient is either a carrier of a disease or has the sequelae or residual of a past disease or condition. This includes such things as the presence of prosthetic or mechanical devices resulting from past treatment. A status code is informative, because the status may affect the course of treatment and its outcome. A status code is distinct from a history code. The history code indicates that the patient no longer has the condition.

A status code should not be used with a diagnosis code from one of the body system chapters, if the diagnosis code includes the information provided by the status code. For example, code V42.1, Heart transplant status, should not be used with code 996.83, Complications of transplanted heart. The status code does not provide additional information. The complication code indicates that the patient is a heart transplant patient.

The status V codes/categories are:

V02 Carrier or suspected carrier of infectious diseases Carrier status indicates that a person harbors the specific organisms of a disease without manifest symptoms and is capable of transmitting the infection.

V08 Asymptomatic HIV infection status This code indicates that a patient has tested positive for HIV but has manifested no signs or symptoms of the disease.

V09 Infection with drug-resistant microorganisms This category indicates that a patient has an infection that is resistant to drug treatment. Sequence the infection code first.

V21 Constitutional states in development

V22.2 Pregnant state, incidental This code is a secondary code only for use when the pregnancy is in no way complicating the reason for visit. Otherwise, a code from the obstetric chapter is required.

V26.5x Sterilization status

V42 Organ or tissue replaced by transplant

V43 Organ or tissue replaced by other means

V44 Artificial opening status
V45 Other postsurgical states
V46 Other dependence on machines
V49.6 Upper limb amputation status
V49.7 Lower limb amputation status
V49.81 Postmenopausal status
V49.82 Dental sealant status
V49.83 Awaiting organ transplant status
V58.6 Long-term (current) drug use This subcategory indicates a patient's continuous use of a prescribed drug (including such things as aspirin therapy) for the long-term treatment of a condition or for prophylactic use. It is not for use for patients who have addictions to drugs.

**Assign a code from subcategory V58.6, Long-term (current) drug use, if the patient is receiving a medication for an extended period as a prophylactic measure (such as for the prevention of deep vein thrombosis) or as treatment of a chronic condition (such as arthritis) or a disease requiring a lengthy course of treatment (such as cancer). Do not assign a code from subcategory V58.6 for medication being administered for a brief period of time to treat an acute illness or injury (such as a course of antibiotics to treat acute bronchitis).**

V83 Genetic carrier status
Genetic carrier status indicates that a person carries a gene, associated with a particular disease, which may be passed to offspring who may develop that disease. The person does not have the disease and is not at risk of developing the disease.

V84 Genetic susceptibility status
Genetic susceptibility indicates that a person has a gene that increases the risk of that person developing the disease.

**Codes from category V84, Genetic susceptibility to disease, should not be used as principal or first-listed codes. If the patient has the condition to which he/she is susceptible, and that condition is the reason for the encounter, the code for the current condition should be sequenced first. If the patient is being seen for follow-up after completed treatment for this condition, and the condition no longer exists, a follow-up code should be sequenced first, followed by the appropriate personal history and genetic susceptibility codes. If the purpose of the encounter is genetic counseling associated with procreative management, a code from subcategory V26.3, Genetic counseling and testing, should be assigned as the first-listed code, followed by a code from category V84. Additional codes should be assigned for any applicable family or personal history. <u>See Section I.C. 18.d.14 for information on prophylactic organ removal due to a genetic susceptibility.</u>**

Note: Categories V42-V46, and subcategories V49.6, V49.7 are for use only if there are no complications or malfunctions of the organ or tissue replaced, the amputation site or the equipment on which the patient is dependent. These are always secondary codes.

**4) History (of)**

There are two types of history V codes, personal and family. Personal history codes explain a patient's past medical condition that no longer exists and is not receiving any treatment, but that has the potential for recurrence, and therefore may require continued monitoring. The exceptions to this general rule are category V14, Personal history of allergy to medicinal agents, and subcategory V15.0, Allergy, other than to medicinal agents. A person who has had an allergic episode to a substance or food in the past should always be considered allergic to the substance.

Family history codes are for use when a patient has a family member(s) who has had a particular disease that causes the patient to be at higher risk of also contracting the disease.

Personal history codes may be used in conjunction with follow-up codes and family history codes may be used in conjunction with screening codes to explain the need for a test or procedure. History codes are also acceptable on any medical record regardless of the reason for visit. A history of an illness, even if no longer present, is important information that may alter the type of treatment ordered.

The history V code categories are:

V10 Personal history of malignant neoplasm
V12 Personal history of certain other diseases
V13 Personal history of other diseases
Except: V13.4, Personal history of arthritis, and V13.6, Personal history of congenital malformations. These conditions are life-long so are not true history codes.
V14 Personal history of allergy to medicinal agents
V15 Other personal history presenting hazards to health
Except: V15.7, Personal history of contraception.
V16 Family history of malignant neoplasm
V17 Family history of certain chronic disabling diseases
V18 Family history of certain other specific diseases
V19 Family history of other conditions

**5) Screening**

Screening is the testing for disease or disease precursors in seemingly well individuals so that early detection and treatment can be provided for those who test positive for the disease. Screenings that are recommended for many subgroups in a population include: routine mammograms for women over 40, a fecal occult blood test for everyone over 50, an amniocentesis to rule out a fetal anomaly for pregnant women over 35, because the incidence of breast cancer and colon cancer in these subgroups is higher than in the general population, as is the incidence of Down's syndrome in older mothers.

The testing of a person to rule out or confirm a suspected diagnosis because the patient has some sign or symptom is a diagnostic examination, not a screening. In these cases, the sign or symptom is used to explain the reason for the test.

A screening code may be a first listed code if the reason for the visit is specifically the screening exam. It may also be used as an additional code if the screening is done during an office visit for other health problems. A screening code is not necessary if the screening is inherent to a routine examination, such as a pap smear done during a routine pelvic examination.

Should a condition be discovered during the screening then the code for the condition may be assigned as an additional diagnosis.
The V code indicates that a screening exam is planned. A procedure code is required to confirm that the screening was performed.

The screening V code categories:

| | |
|---|---|
| V28 | Antenatal screening |
| V73-V82 | Special screening examinations |

**6) Observation**

There are two observation V code categories. They are for use in very limited circumstances when a person is being observed for a suspected condition that is ruled out. The observation codes are not for use if an injury or illness or any signs or symptoms related to the suspected condition are present. In such cases the diagnosis/symptom code is used with the corresponding E code to identify any external cause.

The observation codes are to be used as principal diagnosis only. The only exception to this is when the principal diagnosis is required to be a code from the V30, Live born infant, category. Then the V29 observation code is sequenced after the V30 code. Additional codes may be used in addition to the observation code but only if they are unrelated to the suspected condition being observed.

The observation V code categories:

| | |
|---|---|
| V29 | Observation and evaluation of newborns for suspected condition not found For the birth encounter, a code from category V30 should be sequenced before the V29 code. |
| V71 | Observation and evaluation for suspected condition not found |

**7) Aftercare**

Aftercare visit codes cover situations when the initial treatment of a disease or injury has been performed and the patient requires continued care during the healing or recovery phase, or for the long-term consequences of the disease. The aftercare V code should not be used if treatment is directed at a current, acute disease or injury. The diagnosis code is to be used in these cases. Exceptions to this rule are codes V58.0, Radiotherapy, and **codes from subcategory** V58.1, **Encounter for c**hemotherapy **and immunotherapy for neoplastic conditions**. These codes are to be first listed, followed by the diagnosis code when a patient's encounter is solely to receive radiation therapy or chemotherapy for the treatment of a neoplasm.

Should a patient receive both chemotherapy and radiation therapy during the same encounter code V58.0 and V58.1 may be used together on a record with either one being sequenced first.

The aftercare codes are generally first listed to explain the specific reason for the encounter. An aftercare code may be used as an additional code when some type of aftercare is provided in addition to the reason for admission and no diagnosis code is applicable. An example of this would be the closure of a colostomy during an encounter for treatment of another condition.

Certain aftercare V code categories need a secondary diagnosis code to describe the resolving condition or sequelae, for others, the condition is inherent in the code title.
Additional V code aftercare category terms include, fitting and adjustment, and attention to artificial openings.

Status V codes may be used with aftercare V codes to indicate the nature of the aftercare. For example code V45.81, Aortocoronary bypass status, may be used with code V58.73, Aftercare following surgery of the circulatory system, NEC, to indicate the surgery for which the aftercare is being performed. Also, a transplant status code may be used following code V58.44, Aftercare following organ transplant, to identify the organ transplanted. A status code should not be used when the aftercare code indicates the type of status, such as using V55.0, Attention to tracheostomy with V44.0, Tracheostomy status.

The aftercare V category/codes:

| | |
|---|---|
| V52 | Fitting and adjustment of prosthetic device and implant |
| V53 | Fitting and adjustment of other device |
| V54 | Other orthopedic aftercare |
| V55 | Attention to artificial openings |
| V56 | Encounter for dialysis and dialysis catheter care |
| V57 | Care involving the use of rehabilitation procedures |
| V58.0 | Radiotherapy |
| **V58.11** | **Encounter for antineoplastic chemotherapy** |
| **V58.12** | **Encounter for antineoplastic immunotherapy** |
| V58.3 | Attention to surgical dressings and sutures |
| V58.41 | Encounter for planned post-operative wound closure |
| V58.42 | Aftercare, surgery, neoplasm |
| V58.43 | Aftercare, surgery, trauma |
| V58.44 | Aftercare involving organ transplant |
| V58.49 | Other specified aftercare following surgery |
| V58.7x | Aftercare following surgery |
| V58.81 | Fitting and adjustment of vascular catheter |
| V58.82 | Fitting and adjustment of non-vascular catheter |
| V58.83 | Monitoring therapeutic drug |
| V58.89 | Other specified aftercare |

**8) Follow-up**

The follow-up codes are used to explain continuing surveillance following completed treatment of a disease, condition, or injury. They imply that the condition has been fully treated and no longer exists. They should not be confused with aftercare codes that explain current treatment for a healing condition or its sequelae. Follow-up codes may be used in conjunction with history codes to provide the full picture of the healed condition and its treatment. The follow-up code is sequenced first, followed by the history code.

A follow-up code may be used to explain repeated visits. Should a condition be found to have recurred on the follow-up visit, then the diagnosis code should be used in place of the follow-up code.

The follow-up V code categories:

V24 Postpartum care and evaluation
V67 Follow-up examination

**9) Donor**

Category V59 is the donor codes. They are used for living individuals who are donating blood or other body tissue. These codes are only for individuals donating for others, not for self donations. They are not for use to identify cadaveric donations.

**10) Counseling**

Counseling V codes are used when a patient or family member receives assistance in the aftermath of an illness or injury, or when support is required in coping with family or social problems. They are not necessary for use in conjunction with a diagnosis code when the counseling component of care is considered integral to standard treatment.

The counseling V categories/codes:

V25.0 General counseling and advice for contraceptive management
V26.3 Genetic counseling
V26.4 General counseling and advice for procreative management V61 Other family circumstances
V65.1 Person consulted on behalf of another person
V65.3 Dietary surveillance and counseling V65.4 Other counseling, not elsewhere classified

**11) Obstetrics and related conditions**

See Section I.C.11., the Obstetrics guidelines for further instruction on the use of these codes.

V codes for pregnancy are for use in those circumstances when none of the problems or complications included in the codes from the Obstetrics chapter exist (a routine prenatal visit or postpartum care). Codes V22.0, Supervision of normal first pregnancy, and V22.1, Supervision of other normal pregnancy, are always first listed and are not to be used with any other code from the OB chapter.

The outcome of delivery, category V27, should be included on all maternal delivery records. It is always a secondary code.

V codes for family planning (contraceptive) or procreative management and counseling should be included on an obstetric record either during the pregnancy or the postpartum stage, if applicable.

Obstetrics and related conditions V code categories:

V22 Normal pregnancy

V23 Supervision of high-risk pregnancy
Except: V23.2, Pregnancy with history of abortion. Code 646.3, Habitual aborter, from the OB chapter is required to indicate a history of abortion during a pregnancy.

V24 Postpartum care and evaluation

V25 Encounter for contraceptive management
Except V25.0x (See Section I.C.18.d.11, Counseling)

V26 Procreative management
Except V26.5x, Sterilization status, V26.3 and V26.4 (See Section I.C.18.d.11., Counseling)

V27 Outcome of delivery V28 Antenatal screening (See Section I.C.18.d.6., Screening)

**12) Newborn, infant and child**

See Section I.C.15, the Newborn guidelines for further instruction on the use of these codes.

Newborn V code categories:

V20 Health supervision of infant or child

V29 Observation and evaluation of newborns for suspected condition not found (See Section I.C.18.d.7, Observation).

V30-V39 Liveborn infant according to type of birth

**13) Routine and administrative examinations**

The V codes allow for the description of encounters for routine examinations, such as, a general check-up, or, examinations for administrative purposes, such as, a pre-employment physical. The codes are for use as first listed codes only, and are not to be used if the examination is for diagnosis of a suspected condition or for treatment purposes. In such cases the diagnosis code is used. During a routine exam, should a diagnosis or condition be discovered, it should be coded as an additional code. Pre-existing and chronic conditions and history codes may also be included as additional codes as long as the examination is for administrative purposes and not focused on any particular condition.

Pre-operative examination V codes are for use only in those situations when a patient is being cleared for surgery and no treatment is given.

The V codes categories/code for routine and administrative examinations:

V20.2 Routine infant or child health check
Any injections given should have a corresponding procedure code.

V70 General medical examination V72 Special investigations and examinations. Except V72.5 and V72.6

**14) Miscellaneous V codes**

The miscellaneous V codes capture a number of other health care encounters that do not fall into one of the other categories. Certain of these codes identify the reason for the encounter, others are for use as additional codes that provide useful information on circumstances that may affect a patient's care and treatment.

<u>**Prophylactic Organ Removal**</u>

<u>For encounters specifically for prophylactic removal of breasts, ovaries, or another organ due to a genetic susceptibility to cancer or a family history of</u>

cancer, the principal or first listed code should be a code from subcategory V50.4, Prophylactic organ removal, followed by the appropriate genetic susceptibility code and the appropriate family history code.

If the patient has a malignancy of one site and is having prophylactic removal at another site to prevent either a new primary malignancy or metastatic disease, a code for the malignancy should also be assigned in addition to a code from subcategory V50.4. A V50.4 code should not be assigned if the patient is having organ removal for treatment of a malignancy, such as the removal of the testes for the treatment of prostate cancer.

Miscellaneous V code categories/codes:

V07 Need for isolation and other prophylactic measures
V50 Elective surgery for purposes other than remedying health states
V58.5 Orthodontics V60 Housing, household, and economic circumstances
V62 Other psychosocial circumstances V63 Unavailability of other medical facilities for care
V64 Persons encountering health services for specific procedures, not carried out
V66 Convalescence and Palliative Care
V68 Encounters for administrative purposes V69 Problems related to lifestyle

**15) Nonspecific V codes**

Certain V codes are so non-specific, or potentially redundant with other codes in the classification, that there can be little justification for their use in the inpatient setting. Their use in the outpatient setting should be limited to those instances when there is no further documentation to permit more precise coding. Otherwise, any sign or symptom or any other reason for visit that is captured in another code should be used.

Nonspecific V code categories/codes:

V11 Personal history of mental disorder A code from the mental disorders chapter, with an in remission fifth-digit, should be used.
V13.4 Personal history of arthritis V13.6 Personal history of congenital malformations
V15.7 Personal history of contraception
V23.2 Pregnancy with history of abortion V40 Mental and behavioral problems
V41 Problems with special senses and other special functions
V47 Other problems with internal organs
V48 Problems with head, neck, and trunk
V49 Problems with limbs and other problems Exceptions:
V49.6 Upper limb amputation status
V49.7 Lower limb amputation status
V49.81 Postmenopausal status
V49.82 Dental sealant status
49.83 Awaiting organ transplant status
V51 Aftercare involving the use of plastic surgery
V58.2 Blood transfusion, without reported diagnosis
V58.9 Unspecified aftercare
V72.5 Radiological examination, NEC
V72.6 Laboratory examination

Codes V72.5 and V72.6 are not to be used if any sign or symptoms, or reason for a test is documented. See Section IV.K. and Section IV.L. of the Outpatient guidelines.

**V Code Table**

**Items in bold indicate a change from the April 2005 table Items underlined have been moved within the table since April 2005**

**FIRST LISTED:** V codes/categories/subcategories which are only acceptable as principal/first listed.

**Codes:**

| | |
|---|---|
| V22.0 | Supervision of normal first pregnancy |
| V22.1 | Supervision of other normal pregnancy |
| V46.12 | Encounter for respirator dependence during power failure |
| **V46.13** | **Encounter for weaning from respirator [ventilator]** |
| V56.0 | Extracorporeal dialysis |
| V58.0 | Radiotherapy<br>**V58.0 and V58.11 may be used together on a record with either one being sequenced first, when a patient receives both chemotherapy and radiation therapy during the same encounter code.** |
| **V58.11** | **Encounter for antineoplastic chemotherapy**<br>V58.0 and **V58.11** may be used together on a record with either one being sequenced first, when a patient receives both chemotherapy and radiation therapy during the same encounter code. |
| **V58.12** | **Encounter for antineoplastic immunotherapy** |

**Categories/Subcategories:**

| | |
|---|---|
| V20 | Health supervision of infant or child |
| V24 | Postpartum care and examination |
| V29 | Observation and evaluation of newborns for suspected condition not found<br>Exception: A code from the V30-V39 may be sequenced before the V29 if it is the newborn record. V30-V39 Liveborn infants according to type of birth |
| <u>V57</u> | <u>Care involving use of rehabilitation procedures</u> |
| V59 | Donors |
| V66 | Convalescence and palliative care<br>Exception: V66.7 Palliative care |
| V68 | Encounters for administrative purposes |
| V70 | General medical examination<br>Exception: V70.7 Examination of participant in clinical trial |
| V71 | Observation and evaluation for suspected conditions not found |
| V72 | Special investigations and examinations<br>Exceptions:<br>**V72.4 Pregnancy examination or test**<br>V72.5 Radiological examination, NEC<br>V72.6 Laboratory examination<br>V72.86 Encounter for blood typing |

**FIRST OR ADDITIONAL:** V code categories/subcategories which may be either principal/first listed or additional codes

**Codes:**

| | |
|---|---|
| **V15.88** | **History of fall** |
| V43.22 | Fully implantable artificial heart status |
| **V46.14** | **Mechanical complication of respirator [ventilator]** |
| V49.81 | Asymptomatic postmenopausal status (age-related) (natural) |
| **V49.84** | **Bed confinement status** |

V49.89 Other specified conditions influencing health status
V70.7 Examination of participant in clinical trial
V72.5 Radiological examination, NEC
V72.6 Laboratory examination
**V72.86 Encounter for blood typing**

**Categories/Subcategories:**

| | |
|---|---|
| V01 | Contact with or exposure to communicable diseases |
| V02 | Carrier or suspected carrier of infectious diseases |
| V03-06 | Need for prophylactic vaccination and inoculations |
| V07 | Need for isolation and other prophylactic measures |
| V08 | Asymptomatic HIV infection status |
| V10 | Personal history of malignant neoplasm |
| V12 | Personal history of certain other diseases |
| V13 | Personal history of other diseases<br>Exception:<br>V13.4 Personal history of arthritis<br>V13.69 Personal history of other congenital malformations |
| V16-V19 | Family history of disease |
| V23 | Supervision of high-risk pregnancy |
| V25 | Encounter for contraceptive management |
| V26 | Procreative management<br>Exception: V26.5 Sterilization status |
| V28 | Antenatal screening |
| V45.7 | Acquired absence of organ |
| V49.6x | Upper limb amputation status V49.7x Lower limb amputation status |
| V50 | Elective surgery for purposes other than remedying health states |
| V52 | Fitting and adjustment of prosthetic device and implant |
| V53 | Fitting and adjustment of other device |
| V54 | Other orthopedic aftercare |
| V55 | Attention to artificial openings |
| V56 | Encounter for dialysis and dialysis catheter care<br>Exception: V56.0 Extracorporeal dialysis |
| ~~V57~~ | ~~Care involving use of rehabilitation procedures~~ |
| V58.3 | Attention to surgical dressings and sutures |
| V58.4 | Other aftercare following surgery |
| ~~V58.6~~ | ~~Long-term (current) drug use~~ |
| V58.7 | Aftercare following surgery to specified body systems, not elsewhere classified |
| V58.8 | Other specified procedures and aftercare |
| V61 | Other family circumstances |
| V63 | Unavailability of other medical facilities for care |
| V65 | Other persons seeking consultation without complaint or sickness |
| V67 | Follow-up examination |
| V69 | Problems related to lifestyle |
| **V72.4** | **Pregnancy examination or test** |
| V73-V82 | Special screening examinations |
| V83 | Genetic carrier status |

**ADDITIONAL ONLY:** V code categories/subcategories which may only be used as additional codes, not principal/first listed

**Codes:**

V13.61 Personal history of hypospadias

V22.2 Pregnancy state, incidental
**V46.11 Dependence on respirator, status**
V49.82 Dental sealant status
V49.83 Awaiting organ transplant status
V66.7 Palliative care

**Categories/Subcategories:**
V09 Infection with drug-resistant microorganisms
V14 Personal history of allergy to medicinal agents
V15 Other personal history presenting hazards to health
Exception:
V15.7 Personal history of contraception
**V15.88 History of fall**
V21 Constitutional states in development
V26.5 Sterilization status
V27 Outcome of delivery
V42 Organ or tissue replaced by transplant
V43 Organ or tissue replaced by other means
Exception: V43.22 Fully implantable artificial heart status
V44 Artificial opening status
V45 Other postsurgical states
Exception: Subcategory V45.7 Acquired absence of organ
V46 Other dependence on machines
**Exception:**
**V46.12 Encounter for respirator dependence during power failure V46.13 Encounter for weaning from respirator [ventilator]**
V49.6x Upper limb amputation status
V49.7x Lower limb amputation status
~~V58.6 Long-term (current) drug use~~
V58.7 Aftercare following surgery to specified body systems, not elsewhere classified
V58.8 Other specified procedures and aftercare
V61 Other family circumstances
V63 Unavailability of other medical facilities for care
V65 Other persons seeking consultation without complaint or sickness
V67 Follow-up examination V69 Problems related to lifestyle
**V72.4 Pregnancy examination or test**
V73-V82 Special screening examinations
V83 Genetic carrier status

**ADDITIONAL ONLY:** V code categories/subcategories which may only be used as additional codes, not principal/first listed
**Codes:**
V13.61 Personal history of hypospadias V22.2 Pregnancy state, incidental
**V46.11 Dependence on respirator, status**
V49.82 Dental sealant status V49.83 Awaiting organ transplant status
V66.7 Palliative care

**Categories/Subcategories:**
V09 Infection with drug-resistant microorganisms
V14 Personal history of allergy to medicinal agents
V15 Other personal history presenting hazards to health
Exception:
V15.7 Personal history of contraception

**V15.88 History of fall**
V21 Constitutional states in development
V26.5 Sterilization status
V27 Outcome of delivery
V42 Organ or tissue replaced by transplant
V43 Organ or tissue replaced by other means
Exception:
V43.22 Fully implantable artificial heart status
V44 Artificial opening status
V45 Other postsurgical states
Exception: Subcategory V45.7 Acquired absence of organ
V46 Other dependence on machines
**Exception:**
**V46.12 Encounter for respirator dependence during power failure**
**V46.13 Encounter for weaning from respirator [ventilator]**
V49.6x Upper limb amputation status
V49.7x Lower limb amputation status
V58.6 Long-term current drug use
V60 Housing, household, and economic circumstances
V62 Other psychosocial circumstances
V64 Persons encountering health services for specified procedure, not carried out
V84 Genetic susceptibility to disease
**V85 Body Mass Index**

**NONSPECIFIC CODES AND CATEGORIES:**
V11 Personal history of mental disorder
V13.4 Personal history of arthritis
V13.69 Personal history of congenital malformations
V15.7 Personal history of contraception
V40 Mental and behavioral problems
V41 Problems with special senses and other special functions
V47 Other problems with internal organs
V48 Problems with head, neck, and trunk
**V49.0 Deficiencies of limbs**
**V49.1 Mechanical problems with limbs**
**V49.2 Motor problems with limbs**
**V49.3 Sensory problems with limbs**
**V49.4 Disfigurements in limbs**
**V49.5 Other problems with limbs**
**V49.9 Unspecified condition influencing health status**
~~V49 Problems with limbs and other problems~~
~~Exceptions:~~
~~V49.6 Upper limb amputation status~~
~~V49.7 Lower limb amputation status~~
~~V49.81 Postmenopausal status (age-related) (natural)~~
~~V49.82 Dental sealant status~~
~~V49.83 Awaiting organ transplant status~~
V51 Aftercare involving the use of plastic surgery
V58.2 Blood transfusion, without reported diagnosis
V58.5 Orthodontics
V58.9 Unspecified aftercare
V72.5 Radiological examination, NEC
V72.6 Laboratory examination

**19. Supplemental Classification of External Causes of Injury and Poisoning (E-codes, E800-E999)**

Introduction: These guidelines are provided for those who are currently collecting E codes in order that there will be standardization in the process. If your institution plans to begin collecting E codes, these guidelines are to be applied. The use of E codes is supplemental to the application of ICD-9-CM diagnosis codes. E codes are never to be recorded as principal diagnoses (first-listed in non-inpatient setting) and are not required for reporting to CMS.

External causes of injury and poisoning codes (E codes) are intended to provide data for injury research and evaluation of injury prevention strategies. E codes capture how the injury or poisoning happened (cause), the intent (unintentional or accidental; or intentional, such as suicide or assault), and the place where the event occurred.

Some major categories of E codes include:

transport accidents
poisoning and adverse effects of drugs, medicinal substances and biologicals
accidental falls
accidents caused by fire and flames
accidents due to natural and environmental factors
late effects of accidents, assaults or self injury
assaults or purposely inflicted injury
suicide or self inflicted injury

These guidelines apply for the coding and collection of E codes from records in hospitals, outpatient clinics, emergency departments, other ambulatory care settings and provider offices, and nonacute care settings, except when other specific guidelines apply.

**a. General E Code Coding Guidelines**

**1) Used with any code in the range of 001-V84.8**

An E code may be used with any code in the range of 001-V84.8, which indicates an injury, poisoning, or adverse effect due to an external cause.

**2) Assign the appropriate E code for all initial treatments**

Assign the appropriate E code for the initial encounter of an injury, poisoning, or adverse effect of drugs, **not for subsequent treatment.**

**3) Use the full range of E codes**

Use the full range of E codes to completely describe the cause, the intent and the place of occurrence, if applicable, for all injuries, poisonings, and adverse effects of drugs.

**4) Assign as many E codes as necessary**

Assign as many E codes as necessary to fully explain each cause. If only one E code can be recorded, assign the E code most related to the principal diagnosis.

**5) The selection of the appropriate E code**

The selection of the appropriate E code is guided by the Index to External Causes, which is located after the alphabetical index to diseases and by Inclusion and Exclusion notes in the Tabular List.

**6) E code can never be a principal diagnosis**

An E code can never be a principal (first listed) diagnosis.

**7) External cause code(s) with systemic inflammatory response syndrome (SIRS)**

An external cause code(s) may be used with codes 995.93, Systemic inflammatory response syndrome due to noninfectious process without organ dysfunction, and 995.94, Systemic inflammatory response syndrome due to noninfectious process with organ dysfunction, if trauma was the initiating insult that precipitated the SIRS.

The external cause(s) code should correspond to the most serious injury resulting from the trauma. The external cause code(s) should only be assigned if the trauma necessitated the admission in which the patient also developed SIRS. If a patient is admitted with SIRS but the trauma has been treated previously, the external cause codes should not be used.

**b. Place of Occurrence Guideline**

Use an additional code from category E849 to indicate the Place of Occurrence for injuries and poisonings. The Place of Occurrence describes the place where the event occurred and not the patient's activity at the time of the event.

Do not use E849.9 if the place of occurrence is not stated.

**c. Adverse Effects of Drugs, Medicinal and Biological Substances Guidelines**

**1) Do not code directly from the Table of Drugs**

Do not code directly from the Table of Drugs and Chemicals Always refer back to the Tabular List..

**2) Use as many codes as necessary to describe**

Use as many codes as necessary to describe completely all drugs, medicinal or biological substances

**3) If the same E code would describe the causative agent**

If the same E code would describe the causative agent for more than one adverse reaction, assign the code only once

**4) If two or more drugs, medicinal or biological substances**

If two or more drugs, medicinal or biological substances are reported, code each individually unless the combination code is listed in the Table of Drugs and Chemicals. In that case, assign the E code for the combination

**5) When a reaction results from the interaction of a drug(s)** When a reaction results from the interaction of a drug(s) and alcohol, use poisoning codes and E codes for both

**6) If the reporting format limits the number of E codes**

If the reporting format limits the number of E codes that can be used in reporting clinical data, code the one most related to the principal diagnosis. Include at least one from each category(cause, intent, place) if possible

If there are different fourth digit codes in the same three digit category, use the code for "Other specified" of that category

If there is no "Other specified" code in that category, use the appropriate "Unspecified" code in that category.

If the codes are in different three digit categories, assign the appropriate E code for other multiple drugs and medicinal substances.

**7) Codes from the E930-E949 series**

Codes from the E930-E949 series must be used to identify the causative substance for an adverse effect of drug, medicinal and biological substances, correctly prescribed and properly administered. The effect, such as tachycardia, delirium, gastrointestinal hemorrhaging, vomiting, hypokalemia, hepatitis, renal failure, or respiratory failure, is coded and followed by the appropriate code from the E930-E949 series.

**d. Multiple Cause E Code Coding Guidelines**

If two or more events cause separate injuries, an E code should be assigned for each cause. The first listed E code will be selected in the following order: E codes for child and adult abuse take priority over all other E codes. See Section I.C.19.e., Child and Adult abuse guidelines E codes for terrorism events take priority over all other E codes except child and adult abuse E codes for cataclysmic events take priority over all other E codes except child and adult abuse and terrorism. E codes for transport accidents take priority over all other E codes except cataclysmic events and child and adult abuse and terrorism. The first-listed E code should correspond to the cause of the most serious diagnosis due to an assault, accident, or self-harm, following the order of hierarchy listed above.

**e. Child and Adult Abuse Guideline**

**1) Intentional injury**

When the cause of an injury or neglect is intentional child or adult abuse, the first listed E code should be assigned from categories E960-E968, Homicide and injury purposely inflicted by other persons, (except category E967). An E code from category E967, Child and adult battering and other maltreatment, should be added as an additional code to identify the perpetrator, if known.

**2) Accidental intent**

In cases of neglect when the intent is determined to be accidental E code E904.0, Abandonment or neglect of infant and helpless person, should be the first listed E code.

**f. Unknown or Suspected Intent Guideline**

**1) If the intent (accident, self-harm, assault) of the cause of an injury or poisoning is unknown**

If the intent (accident, self-harm, assault) of the cause of an injury or poisoning is unknown or unspecified, code the intent as undetermined E980-E989.

**2) If the intent (accident, self-harm, assault) of the cause of an injury or poisoning is questionable**

If the intent (accident, self-harm, assault) of the cause of an injury or poisoning is questionable, probable or suspected, code the intent as undetermined E980-E989.

**g. Undetermined Cause**

When the intent of an injury or poisoning is known, but the cause is unknown, use codes: E928.9, Unspecified accident, E958.9, Suicide and self-inflicted injury by unspecified means, and E968.9, Assault by unspecified means. These E codes should rarely be used, as the documentation in the medical record, in both the inpatient outpatient and other settings, should normally provide sufficient detail to determine the cause of the injury.

**h. Late Effects of External Cause Guidelines**

**1) Late effect E codes**

Late effect E codes exist for injuries and poisonings but not for adverse effects of drugs, misadventures and surgical complications.

**2) Late effect E codes (E929, E959, E969, E977, E989, or E999.1)**

A late effect E code (E929, E959, E969, E977, E989, or E999.1) should be used with any report of a late effect or sequela resulting from a previous injury or poisoning (905-909).

**3) Late effect E code with a related current injury**

A late effect E code should never be used with a related current nature of injury code.

**4) Use of late effect E codes for subsequent visits**

Use a late effect E code for subsequent visits when a late effect of the initial injury or poisoning is being treated. There is no late effect E code for adverse effects of drugs. Do not use a late effect E code for subsequent visits for follow-up care (e.g., to assess healing, to receive rehabilitative therapy) of the injury or poisoning when no late effect of the injury has been documented.

**i. Misadventures and Complications of Care Guidelines**

**1) Code range E870-E876**

Assign a code in the range of E870-E876 if misadventures are stated by the provider.

**2) Code range E878-E879**

Assign a code in the range of E878-E879 if the provider attributes an abnormal reaction or later complication to a surgical or medical procedure, but does not mention misadventure at the time of the procedure as the cause of the reaction.

**j. Terrorism Guidelines**

**1) Cause of injury identified by the Federal Government (FBI) as terrorism**

When the cause of an injury is identified by the Federal Government (FBI) as terrorism, the first-listed E-code should be a code from category E979, Terrorism. The definition of terrorism employed by the FBI is found at the inclusion note at E979. The terrorism E-code is the only E-code that should be assigned. Additional E codes from the assault categories should not be assigned.

**2) Cause of an injury is suspected to be the result of terrorism**

When the cause of an injury is suspected to be the result of terrorism a code from category E979 should not be assigned. Assign a code in the range of E codes based circumstances on the documentation of intent and mechanism.

**3) Code E979.9, Terrorism, secondary effects**

Assign code E979.9, Terrorism, secondary effects, for conditions occurring subsequent to the terrorist event. This code should not be assigned for conditions that are due to the initial terrorist act.

**4) Statistical tabulation of terrorism codes** For statistical purposes these codes will be tabulated within the category for assault, expanding the current category from E960-E969 to include E979 and E999.1.

## Section II. Selection of Principal Diagnosis

The circumstances of inpatient admission always govern the selection of principal diagnosis. The principal diagnosis is defined in the Uniform Hospital Discharge Data Set (UHDDS) as "that condition established after study to be chiefly responsible for occasioning the admission of the patient to the hospital for care."

The UHDDS definitions are used by hospitals to report inpatient data elements in a standardized manner. These data elements and their definitions can be found in the July 31, 1985, Federal Register (Vol. 50, No, 147), pp. 31038-40.
Since that time the application of the UHDDS definitions has been expanded to include all non-outpatient settings (acute care, short term, long term care and psychiatric hospitals; home health agencies; rehab facilities; nursing homes, etc).

In determining principal diagnosis the coding conventions in the ICD-9-CM, Volumes I and II take precedence over these official coding guidelines. (See Section I.A., Conventions for the ICD-9-CM).

The importance of consistent, complete documentation in the medical record cannot be overemphasized. Without such documentation the application of all coding guidelines is a difficult, if not impossible, task.

**A. Codes for symptoms, signs, and ill-defined conditions**

Codes for symptoms, signs, and ill-defined conditions from Chapter 16 are not to be used as principal diagnosis when a related definitive diagnosis has been established.

**B. Two or more interrelated conditions, each potentially meeting the definition for principal diagnosis.**

When there are two or more interrelated conditions (such as diseases in the same ICD-9-CM chapter or manifestations characteristically associated with a certain disease) potentially meeting the definition of principal diagnosis, either condition may be sequenced first, unless the circumstances of the admission, the therapy provided, the Tabular List, or the Alphabetic Index indicate otherwise.

**C. Two or more diagnoses that equally meet the definition for principal diagnosis**

In the unusual instance when two or more diagnoses equally meet the criteria for principal diagnosis as determined by the circumstances of admission, diagnostic workup and/or therapy provided, and the Alphabetic Index, Tabular List, or another coding guidelines does not provide sequencing direction, any one of the diagnoses may be sequenced first.

**D. Two or more comparative or contrasting conditions.**

In those rare instances when two or more contrasting or comparative diagnoses are documented as "either/or" (or similar terminology), they are coded as if the diagnoses were confirmed and the diagnoses are sequenced according to the circumstances of the admission. If no further determination can be made as to which diagnosis should be principal, either diagnosis may be sequenced first.

**E. A symptom(s) followed by contrasting/comparative diagnoses**

When a symptom(s) is followed by contrasting/comparative diagnoses, the symptom code is sequenced first. All the contrasting/comparative diagnoses should be coded as additional diagnoses.

**F. Original treatment plan not carried out**

Sequence as the principal diagnosis the condition, which after study occasioned the admission to the hospital, even though treatment may not have been carried out due to unforeseen circumstances.

**G. Complications of surgery and other medical care**

When the admission is for treatment of a complication resulting from surgery or other medical care, the complication code is sequenced as the principal diagnosis. If the complication is classified to the 996-999 series and the code lacks the necessary specificity in describing the complication, an additional code for the specific complication should be assigned.

**H. Uncertain Diagnosis**

If the diagnosis documented at the time of discharge is qualified as "probable", "suspected", "likely", "questionable", "possible", or "still to be ruled out", code the condition as if it existed or was established. The bases for these guidelines are the diagnostic workup, arrangements for further workup or observation, and initial therapeutic approach that correspond most closely with the established diagnosis.

**Note: This guideline is applicable only to short-term, acute, long-term care and psychiatric hospitals.**

**I. Admission from Observation Unit**

**1. Admission Following Medical Observation**

**When a patient is admitted to an observation unit for a medical condition, which either worsens or does not improve, and is subsequently admitted as an inpatient of the same hospital for this same medical condition, the principal diagnosis would be the medical condition which led to the hospital admission.**

**2. Admission Following Post-Operative Observation**
**When a patient is admitted to an observation unit to monitor a condition (or complication) that develops following outpatient surgery, and then is subsequently admitted as an inpatient of the same hospital, hospitals should apply the Uniform Hospital Discharge Data Set (UHDDS) definition of principal diagnosis as "that condition established after study to be chiefly responsible for occasioning the admission of the patient to the hospital for care."**

**J. Admission from Outpatient Surgery**
**When a patient receives surgery in the hospital's outpatient surgery department and is subsequently admitted for continuing inpatient care at the same hospital, the following guidelines should be followed in selecting the principal diagnosis for the inpatient admission:**

- **If the reason for the inpatient admission is a complication, assign the complication as the principal diagnosis.**
- **If no complication, or other condition, is documented as the reason for the inpatient admission, assign the reason for the outpatient surgery as the principal diagnosis.**
- **If the reason for the inpatient admission is another condition unrelated to the surgery, assign the unrelated condition as the principal diagnosis.**

## Section III. Reporting Additional Diagnoses

GENERAL RULES FOR OTHER (ADDITIONAL) DIAGNOSES
For reporting purposes the definition for "other diagnoses" is interpreted as additional conditions that affect patient care in terms of requiring:

clinical evaluation; or
therapeutic treatment; or
diagnostic procedures; or
extended length of hospital stay; or
increased nursing care and/or monitoring.

The UHDDS item #11-b defines Other Diagnoses as "all conditions that coexist at the time of admission, that develop subsequently, or that affect the treatment received and/or the length of stay. Diagnoses that relate to an earlier episode which have no bearing on the current hospital stay are to be excluded." UHDDS definitions apply to inpatients in acute care, short-term, long term care and psychiatric hospital setting. The UHDDS definitions are used by acute care short-term hospitals to report inpatient data elements in a standardized manner. These data elements and their definitions can be found in the July 31, 1985, Federal Register (Vol. 50, No, 147), pp. 31038-40.

Since that time the application of the UHDDS definitions has been expanded to include all non-outpatient settings (acute care, short term, long term care and psychiatric hospitals; home health agencies; rehab facilities; nursing homes, etc).

The following guidelines are to be applied in designating "other diagnoses" when neither the Alphabetic Index nor the Tabular List in ICD-9-CM provide direction. The listing of the diagnoses in the patient record is the responsibility of the attending provider.

**A. Previousconditions**
If the provider has included a diagnosis in the final diagnostic statement, such as the discharge summary or the face sheet, it should ordinarily be coded. Some providers include in the diagnostic statement resolved conditions or diagnoses and status-post

procedures from previous admission that have no bearing on the current stay. Such conditions are not to be reported and are coded only if required by hospital policy. However, history codes (V10-V19) may be used as secondary codes if the historical condition or family history has an impact on current care or influences treatment.

**B. Abnormal findings**

Abnormal findings (laboratory, x-ray, pathologic, and other diagnostic results) are not coded and reported unless the provider indicates their clinical significance. If the findings are outside the normal range and the attending provider has ordered other tests to evaluate the condition or prescribed treatment, it is appropriate to ask the provider whether the abnormal finding should be added.

**Please note:** This differs from the coding practices in the outpatient setting for coding encounters for diagnostic tests that have been interpreted by a provider.

**C. Uncertain Diagnosis**

If the diagnosis documented at the time of discharge is qualified as "probable", "suspected", "likely", "questionable", "possible", or "still to be ruled out", code the condition as if it existed or was established. The bases for these guidelines are the diagnostic workup, arrangements for further workup or observation, and initial therapeutic approach that correspond most closely with the established diagnosis.
**Note: This guideline is applicable only to short-term, acute, long-term care and psychiatric hospitals.**

## Section IV. Diagnostic Coding and Reporting Guidelines for Outpatient Services

These coding guidelines for outpatient diagnoses have been approved for use by hospitals/ providers in coding and reporting hospital-based outpatient services and provider-based office visits.

Information about the use of certain abbreviations, punctuation, symbols, and other conventions used in the ICD-9-CM Tabular List (code numbers and titles), can be found in Section IA of these guidelines, under "Conventions Used in the Tabular List." Information about the correct sequence to use in finding a code is also described in Section I.

The terms encounter and visit are often used interchangeably in describing outpatient service contacts and, therefore, appear together in these guidelines without distinguishing one from the other.

Though the conventions and general guidelines apply to all settings, coding guidelines for outpatient and provider reporting of diagnoses will vary in a number of instances from those for inpatient diagnoses, recognizing that:

The Uniform Hospital Discharge Data Set (UHDDS) definition of principal diagnosis applies only to inpatients in acute, short-term, long-term care and psychiatric hospitals.

Coding guidelines for inconclusive diagnoses (probable, suspected, rule out, etc.) were developed for inpatient reporting and do not apply to outpatients.

**A. Selection of first-listed condition**

In the outpatient setting, the term first-listed diagnosis is used in lieu of principal diagnosis. In determining the first-listed diagnosis the coding conventions of ICD-9-CM, as well as the general and disease specific guidelines take precedence over the outpatient guidelines.

Diagnoses often are not established at the time of the initial encounter/visit. It may take two or more visits before the diagnosis is confirmed.

The most critical rule involves beginning the search for the correct code assignment through the Alphabetic Index. Never begin searching initially in the Tabular List as this will lead to coding errors.

1. **Outpatient Surgery**
   **When a patient presents for outpatient surgery, code the reason for the surgery as the first-listed diagnosis (reason for the encounter), even if the surgery is not performed due to a contraindication.**
2. **Observation Stay**
   **When a patient is admitted for observation for a medical condition, assign a code for the medical condition as the first-listed diagnosis. When a patient presents for outpatient surgery and develops complications requiring admission to observation, code the reason for the surgery as the first reported diagnosis (reason for the encounter), followed by codes for the complications as secondary diagnoses.**

**B. Codes from 001.0 through V84.8**

The appropriate code or codes from 001.0 through V84.8 must be used to identify diagnoses, symptoms, conditions, problems, complaints, or other reason(s) for the encounter/visit.

**C. Accurate reporting of ICD-9-CM diagnosis codes**

For accurate reporting of ICD-9-CM diagnosis codes, the documentation should describe the patient's condition, using terminology which includes specific diagnoses as well as symptoms, problems, or reasons for the encounter. There are ICD-9-CM codes to describe all of these.

**D. Selection of codes 001.0 through 999.9**

The selection of codes 001.0 through 999.9 will frequently be used to describe the reason for the encounter. These codes are from the section of ICD-9-CM for the classification of diseases and injuries (e.g. infectious and parasitic diseases; neoplasms; symptoms, signs, and ill-defined conditions, etc.).

**E. Codes that describe symptoms and signs**

Codes that describe symptoms and signs, as opposed to diagnoses, are acceptable for reporting purposes when a diagnosis has not been established (confirmed) by the provider. Chapter 16 of ICD-9-CM, Symptoms, Signs, and Ill-defined conditions (codes 780.0 - 799.9) contain many, but not all codes for symptoms.

**F. Encounters for circumstances other than a disease or injury**

ICD-9-CM provides codes to deal with encounters for circumstances other than a disease or injury. The Supplementary Classification of factors Influencing Health Status and Contact with Health Services (V01.0- V84.8) is provided to deal with occasions when circumstances other than a disease or injury are recorded as diagnosis or problems.

**G. Level of Detail in Coding**

1. **ICD-9-CM codes with 3, 4, or 5 digits**
   ICD-9-CM is composed of codes with either 3, 4, or 5 digits. Codes with three digits are included in ICD-9-CM as the heading of a category of codes that may be further subdivided by the use of fourth and/or fifth digits, which provide greater specificity.
2. **Use of full number of digits required for a code** A three-digit code is to be used only if it is not further subdivided. Where fourth-digit subcategories and/or fifth-digit subclassifications are provided, they must be assigned. A code is invalid if it has not been coded to the full number of digits required for that code. See also discussion under Section I.b.3., General Coding Guidelines, Level of Detail in Coding.

**H. ICD-9-CM code for the diagnosis, condition, problem, or other reason for encounter/visit**

List first the ICD-9-CM code for the diagnosis, condition, problem, or other reason for encounter/visit shown in the medical record to be chiefly responsible for the services provided. List additional codes that describe any coexisting conditions. In some cases the first-listed diagnosis may be a symptom when a diagnosis has not been established (confirmed) by the physician.

**I. "Probable", "suspected", "questionable", "rule out", or "working diagnosis"**

Do not code diagnoses documented as "probable", "suspected," "questionable," "rule out," or "working diagnosis". Rather, code the condition(s) to the highest degree of certainty for that encounter/visit, such as symptoms, signs, abnormal test results, or other reason for the visit. **Please note:** This differs from the coding practices used by short-term, acute care, long-term care and psychiatric hospitals.

**J. Chronic diseases**

Chronic diseases treated on an ongoing basis may be coded and reported as many times as the patient receives treatment and care for the condition(s)

**K. Code all documented conditions that coexist**

Code all documented conditions that coexist at the time of the encounter/visit, and require or affect patient care treatment or management. Do not code conditions that were previously treated and no longer exist. However, history codes (V10-V19) may be used as secondary codes if the historical condition or family history has an impact on current care or influences treatment.

**L. Patients receiving diagnostic services only**

For patients receiving diagnostic services only during an encounter/visit, sequence first the diagnosis, condition, problem, or other reason for encounter/visit shown in the medical record to be chiefly responsible for the outpatient services provided during the encounter/visit. Codes for other diagnoses (e.g., chronic conditions) may be sequenced as additional diagnoses.

For outpatient encounters for diagnostic tests that have been interpreted by a physician, and the final report is available at the time of coding, code any confirmed or definitive diagnosis(es) documented in the interpretation. Do not code related signs and symptoms as additional diagnoses.

**Please note:** This differs from the coding practice in the hospital inpatient setting regarding abnormal findings on test results.

**M. Patients receiving therapeutic services only**

For patients receiving therapeutic services only during an encounter/visit, sequence first the diagnosis, condition, problem, or other reason for encounter/visit shown in the medical record to be chiefly responsible for the outpatient services provided during the encounter/visit. Codes for other diagnoses (e.g., chronic conditions) may be sequenced as additional diagnoses.

The only exception to this rule is that when the primary reason for the admission/encounter is chemotherapy, radiation therapy, or rehabilitation, the appropriate V code for the service is listed first, and the diagnosis or problem for which the service is being performed listed second.

**N. Patients receiving preoperative evaluations only**

For patients receiving preoperative evaluations only, sequence **first** a code from category V72.8, Other specified examinations, to describe the pre-op consultations. Assign a code for the condition to describe the reason for the surgery as an additional diagnosis. Code also any findings related to the pre-op evaluation.

**O. Ambulatorysurgery**

For ambulatory surgery, code the diagnosis for which the surgery was performed. If the postoperative diagnosis is known to be different from the preoperative diagnosis at the time the diagnosis is confirmed, select the postoperative diagnosis for coding, since it is the most definitive.

**P. Routine outpatient prenatal visits**

For routine outpatient prenatal visits when no complications are present, codes V22.0, Supervision of normal first pregnancy, or V22.1, Supervision of other normal pregnancy, should be used as the principal diagnosis. These codes should not be used in conjunction with chapter 11 codes.

## Conversion Table of New ICD-9-CM Codes
October 2005

The National Center for Health Statistics (NCHS) and the Centers for Medicare & Medicaid Services (CMS), have issued new diagnosis and procedure codes for the International Classification of Diseases, 9th Revision, Clinical Modification (ICD-9-CM). The effective date for new codes is October 1. For each new code the table shows its previously assigned code equivalent. The code equivalents were used for reporting diagnosis and procedure information up to the time the new codes were issued.

| **Current Assignment** | **Previous Assignment** | **Diagnosis Codes Text** |
|---|---|---|
| **259** | **Category** | **Other endocrine disorders** |
| 259.5 | 257.8 | Androgen insensitivity syndrome<br>Partial androgen insensitivity<br>Reifenstein syndrome |
| **276** | **Category** | **Disorders of fluid, electrolyte, and acid-base balance** |
| **576.5** | **Sub category** | **Volume depletion** |
| 276.50 | 276.5 | Volume depletion, unspecified |
| 276.51 | 276.5 | Dehydration |
| 276.52 | 276.5 | Hypovolemia<br>Depletion of volume of plasma |
| **278** | **Category** | **Obesity and other hyperalimentation** |
| **278.0** | **Subcategory** | **Overweight and obesity**<br>**Use additional code to identify Body Mass Index (BMI, if known (V85.21-85.4)** |
| 278.02 | 278.00 | Overweight |
| **287** | **Category** | **Purpura and other hemorrhagic conditions** |
| **287.3** | **Subcategory** | **Primary thrombocytopenia** |
| 287.30 | 287.3 | Primary thrombocytopenia, unspecified<br>Megakaryocytic hypoplasia |
| 287.31 | 287.3 | Immune thrombocytopenic purpura<br>Idiopathic thrombocytopenic purpura<br>Tidal platelet dysgenesis |
| 287.32 | 287.3 | Evans' syndrome |
| 287.33 | 287.3 | Congenital and hereditary thrombocytopenic purpura<br>Congenital and hereditary thrombocytopenia<br>Thrombocytopenia with absent radii (TAR) syndrome<br>Excludes: Wiskott-Aldrich syndrome (279.12) |
| 287.39 | 287.3 | Other primary thrombocytopenia |
| **291** | **Category** | **Alcohol induced mental disorders** |
| **291.8** | **Subcategory** | **Other specified alcohol induced mental disorders** |
| 291.82 | 291.89 | Alcohol induced sleep disorders<br>Alcohol induced circadian rhythm sleep disorders<br>Alcohol induced hypersomnia<br>Alcohol induced insomnia<br>Alcohol induced parasomnia |

Conversion Table of New ICD-9-CM Codes
October 2005

| Current Assignment | Previous Assignment | Diagnosis Codes Text |
|---|---|---|
| **292** | **Category** | **Drug induced mental disorders** |
| **292.8** | **Subcategory** | **Other specified drug induced mental disorders** |
| 292.85 | 292.89 | Drug induced sleep disorders<br>Drug induced circadian rhythm sleep disorder<br>Drug induced hypersomnia<br>Drug induced insomnia<br>Drug induced parasomnia |
| **327** | **NEW Category** | **Organic sleep disorders** |
| **327.0** | **New SubCategory** | Organic disorders of initiating and maintaining sleep category<br>[Organic insomnia]<br>Excludes: insomnia NOS (780.52)<br>insomnia not due to a substance or known physiological condition (307.41-307.42)<br>insomnia with sleep apnea NOS (780.51) |
| 327.00 | 780.51; 780.52 | Organic insomnia, unspecified |
| 327.01 | 780.51; 780.52 | Insomnia due to medical condition classified elsewhere<br>Code first underlying condition<br>Excludes: insomnia due to mental disorder (3 |
| 327.02 | 307.41 | Insomnia due to mental disorder<br>Code first mental disorder<br>Excludes: alcohol induced insomnia (291.82)<br>drug induced insomnia (292.85) |
| 327.09 | 780.51; 780.52 | Other organic insomnia |
| **327.1** | **New Subcategory** | Organic disorder of excessive somnolence [Organic hypersomnia]<br>Excludes: hypersomnia NOS (780.54)<br>hypersomnia not due to a substance or known physiological condition (307.43-307.44)<br>hypersomnia with sleep apnea NOS (780.53) |
| 327.10 | 780.53; 780.54 | Organic hypersomnia, unspecified |
| 327.11 | 780.53; 780.54 | Idiopathic hypersomnia with long sleep time |
| 327.12 | 780.53; 780.54 | Idiopathic hypersomnia without long sleep time |
| 327.13 | 780.53; 780.54 | Recurrent hypersomnia<br>Kleine-Levin syndrome<br>Menstrual related hypersomnia |
| 327.14 | 780.53; 780.54 | Hypersomnia due to medical condition classified elsewhere<br>Code first underlying condition<br>Excludes: hypersomnia due to mental disorder (327.15) |

Conversion Table of New ICD-9-CM Codes
October 2005

| Current Assignment | Previous Assignment | Diagnosis Codes Text |
|---|---|---|
| 327.15 | 307.43 | Hypersomnia due to mental disorder<br>Code first mental disorder<br>Excludes: alcohol induced hypersomnia (291.82)<br>drug induced hypersomnia (292.85) |
| 327.19 | 780.53; 780.54 | Other organic hypersomnia |
| **327.2** | **New Subcategory** | Organic sleep apnea<br>Excludes: Cheyne-Stokes breathing (786.04)<br>hypersomnia with sleep apnea NOS (780.53)<br>insomnia with sleep apnea NOS (780.51)<br>sleep apnea in newborn (770.81-770.82)<br>sleep apnea NOS (780.57 |
| 327.20 | 780.57 | Organic sleep apnea, unspecified |
| 327.21 | 780.57 | Primary central sleep apnea |
| 327.22 | 780.57 | High altitude periodic breathing |
| 327.23 | 780.57 | Obstructive sleep apnea (adult) (pediatric) |
| 327.24 | 780.57 | Idiopathic sleep related nonobstructive alveolar hypoventilation<br>Sleep related hypoxia |
| 327.25 | 780.57 | Congenital central alveolar hypoventilation syndrome |
| 327.26 | 780.57 | Sleep related hypoventilation/hypoxemia in conditions classifiable elsewhere<br>Code first underlying condition |
| 327.27 | 780.57 | Central sleep apnea in conditions classified elsewhere<br>Code first underlying condition |
| 327.29 | 780.51; 780.53; 780.57 | Other organic sleep apnea |
| **327.3** | **New Subcategory** | Circadian rhythm sleep disorder<br>Organic disorder of sleep wake cycle<br>Organic disorder of sleep wake schedule<br>Excludes: alcohol induced circadian rhythm sleep disorder (291.82)<br>circadian rhythm sleep disorder of nonorganic origin (307.45)<br>disruption of 24 hour sleep wake cycle NOS (780.55)<br>drug induced circadian rhythm sleep disorder (292.85) |
| 327.30 | 307.45 | Circadian rhythm sleep disorder, unspecified |
| 327.31 | 307.45 | Circadian rhythm sleep disorder, delayed sleep phase type |
| 327.32 | 307.45 | Circadian rhythm sleep disorder, advanced sleep phase type |
| 327.33 | 307.45 | Circadian rhythm sleep disorder, irregular sleep-wake type |
| 327.34 | 307.45 | Circadian rhythm sleep disorder, free-running type |

| Current Assignment | Previous Assignment | Diagnosis Codes Text |
|---|---|---|
| 327.35 | 307.45 | Circadian rhythm sleep disorder, jet lag type |
| 327.36 | 307.45 | Circadian rhythm sleep disorder, shift work type |
| 327.37 | 307.45 | Circadian rhythm sleep disorder in conditions classified elsewhere<br>Code first underlying condition |
| 327.39 | 307.45 | Other circadian rhythm sleep disorder |
| **327.4** | **New Subcategory** | Organic parasomnia<br>Excludes: alcohol induced parasomnia (291.82)<br>rug induced parasomnia (292.85)<br>parasomnia not due to a known physiological conditions (307.47) |
| 327.40 | 780.59 | Organic parasomnia, unspecified |
| 327.41 | 780.59 | Confusional arousals |
| 327.42 | 780.59 | REM sleep behavior disorder |
| 327.43 | 780.59 | Recurrent isolated sleep paralysis |
| 327.44 | 780.59 | Parasomnia in conditions classified elsewhere<br>Code first underlying condition |
| 327.49 | 780.59 | Other organic parasomnia |
| **327.5** | **New Subcategory** | Organic sleep related movement disorders<br>Excludes: restless leg syndrome (333.99)<br>sleep related movement disorder NOS (780.58) |
| 327.51 | 780.59 | Periodic limb movement disorder<br>Periodic limb movement sleep disorder |
| 327.52 | 729.82 | Sleep related leg cramps |
| 327.53 | 306.8 | Sleep related bruxism |
| 327.59 | 780.58 | Other organic sleep related movement disorders |
| 327.8 | 780.50 | Other organic sleep disorders |
| **362** | **Category** | **Other retinal disorders** |
| **362.0** | **Subcategory** | **Diabetic retinopathy** |
| 362.03 | 362.02 | Nonproliferative diabetic retinopathy NOS |
| 362.04 | 362.02 | Mild nonproliferative diabetic retinopathy |
| 362.05 | 362.02 | Moderate nonproliferative diabetic retinopathy |
| 362.06 | 362.02 | Severe nonproliferative diabetic retinopathy |
| 362.07 | 362.02 | Diabetic macular edema<br>Diabetic retinal edema<br>Note: Code 362.07 must be used with a code for diabetic retinopathy (362.01-362.06) |
| **426** | **Category** | **Conduction disorders** |
| **426.8** | **Subcategory** | **Other specified conduction disorders** |
| 426.82 | 794.31 | Long QT syndrome |

Conversion Table of New ICD-9-CM Codes
October 2005

| Current Assignment | Previous Assignment | Diagnosis Codes Text |
|---|---|---|
| **443** | **Category** | **Other peripheral vascular disease** |
| **443.8** | **Subcategory** | **Other specified peripheral vascular diseases** |
| 443.82 | 443.89 | Erythromelalgia |
| **525** | **Category** | Other diseases and conditions of the teeth and supporting structures |
| **525.4** | **New Subcategory** | Complete edentulism<br>Use additional code to identify cause of edentulism (525.10- 525.19) |
| 525.40 | 525.10 | Complete edentulism, unspecified Edentulism NO |
| 525.41 | 525.10 | Complete edentulism, class I |
| 525.42 | 525.10 | Complete edentulism, class II |
| 525.43 | 525.10 | Complete edentulism, class III |
| 525.44 | 525.10 | Complete edentulism, class IV |
| **525.5** | **New Subcategory** | Partial edentulism<br>Use additional code to identify cause of edentulism (525.10- 525.19 |
| 525.50 | 525.10 | Partial edentulism, unspecified |
| 525.51 | 525.10 | Partial edentulism, class I |
| 525.52 | 525.10 | Partial edentulism, class II |
| 525.53 | 525.10 | Partial edentulism, class III |
| 525.54 | 525.10 | Partial edentulism, class IV |
| **567** | | Peritonitis and retroperitoneal infections |
| 567.21 | 567.2 | Peritonitis (acute) generalized<br>Pelvic peritonitis, male |
| 567.22 | 567.2 | Peritoneal abscess Abscess (of):<br>abdominopelvic<br>mesenteric<br>omentum<br>peritoneum<br>retrocecal<br>subdiaphragmatic<br>subhepatic<br>subphrenic |
| 567.23 | 567.2 | Spontaneous bacterial peritonitis |
| 567.29 | 567.2 | Other suppurative peritonitis<br>Subphrenic peritonitis |
| **567.3** | **New Subcategory** | Retroperitoneal infections |
| 567.31 | 728.89 | Psoas muscle abscess |
| 567.38 | 567.2 | Other retroperitoneal abscess |
| 567.39 | 567.9 | Other retroperitoneal infections |
| **Current Assignment** | **Previous Assignment** | **Diagnosis Codes Text** |

| | | |
|---|---|---|
| 567.81 | 567.8 | Choleperitonitis<br>Peritonitis due to bile |
| 567.82 | 567.8 | Sclerosing mesenteritis<br>Fat necrosis of peritoneum<br>(Idiopathic) sclerosing mesenteric fibrosis<br>Mesenteric lipodystrophy<br>Mesenteric panniculitis<br>Retractile mesenteritis |
| 567.89 | 567.8 | Other specified peritonitis<br>Chronic proliferative peritonitis<br>Mesenteric saponification<br>Peritonitis due to urine |
| **585** | **Category** | **Chronic kidney disease (CKD)**<br>**Use additional code to identify kidney transplant status, if applicable (V42.0)** |
| 585.1 | 585 | Chronic kidney disease, Stage I |
| 585.2 | 585 | Chronic kidney disease, Stage II (mild) |
| 585.3 | 585 | Chronic kidney disease, Stage III (moderate) |
| 585.4 | 585 | Chronic kidney disease, Stage IV (severe) |
| 585.5 | 585 | Chronic kidney disease, Stage V |
| 585.6 | 585 | End stage renal disease |
| 585.9 | 585 | Chronic kidney disease, unspecified<br>Chronic renal disease<br>Chronic renal failure NOS<br>Chronic renal insufficiency |
| **599** | **Category** | **Other disorders of urethra and urinary tract** |
| **599.6** | **Subcategory** | **Urinary obstruction**<br>**Excludes: urinary obstruction die to hyperplasia of prostate (600.0-600.9 with fifth-digit 1** |
| 599.60 | 599.6 | Urinary obstruction, unspecified<br>Obstructive uropathy NOS<br>Urinary (tract) obstruction NOS |
| 599.69 | 599.6 | Urinary obstruction, not elsewhere classified |

| Current Assignment | Previous Assignment | Diagnosis Codes Text |
|---|---|---|
| **651** | **Category** | **Multiple gestation** |
| 651.70 | 651.8 | Multiple gestation following (elective) fetal reduction<br>Fetal reduction of multiple fetuses reduced to single fetus<br>Unspecified as to episode of care or not applicable |
| 651.71 | 651.8 | Multiple gestation following (elective) fetal reduction<br>Fetal reduction of multiple fetuses reduced to single fetus<br>Delivered, with or without mention of antepartum condition |
| 651.73 | 651.8 | Multiple gestation following (elective) fetal reduction<br>Fetal reduction of multiple fetuses reduced to single fetus<br>Antepartum condition or complication |
| | | **CERTAIN CONDITIONS ORIGINATING IN THE PERINATAL PERIOD (760-779)**<br>**Includes: conditions which have their origin in the perinatal period, before birth through he first 28 days after birth, even though death or morbidity occurs later** |
| **760** | **Category** | **Fetus or newborn affected by maternal conditions which may be unrelated to present pregnancy** |
| **760.7** | **Subcategory** | **Noxious influences affection fetus aor newborn via placenta or breast milk** |
| 760.77 | 760.79 | Anticonvulsants<br>Carbamazepine<br>Phenobarbital<br>Phenytoin<br>Valproic acid |
| 760.78 | 760.79 | Antimetabolic agents<br>Methotrexate<br>Retinoic acid<br>Statins |
| **763** | **Category** | **Fetus or newborn affected by other complications of labor and delivery** |
| **763.8** | **Subcategory** | **Other specified complications of labor and delivery affection fetus or newborn** |
| 763.84 | 770.1 | Meconium passage during delivery<br>Excludes: meconium aspiration (770.11, 770.12)<br>meconium staining (779.84) |
| **770** | **Category** | **Other respiratory conditions of fetus and newborn** |
| **771** | **Subcategory** | **Fetal and newborn aspiration** |
| 770.10 | 770.1 | Fetal and newborn aspiration, unspecified |
| 770.11 | 770.1 | Meconium aspiration without respiratory symptoms<br>Meconium aspiration NOS |

| Current Assignment | Previous Assignment | Diagnosis Codes Text |
|---|---|---|
| 770.12 | 770.1 | Meconium aspiration with respiratory symptoms<br>Meconium aspiration pneumonia<br>Meconium aspiration pneumonitis<br>Meconium aspiration syndrome NOS<br>Use additional code to identify any secondary pulmonary hypertension (416.8), if applicable |
| 770.13 | 770.1 | Aspiration of clear amniotic fluid without respiratory symptoms Aspiration of clear amniotic fluid NOS |
| 770.14 | 770.1 | Aspiration of clear amniotic fluid with respiratory symptoms<br>Aspiration of clear amniotic fluid with pneumonia<br>Aspiration of clear amniotic fluid with pneumonitis<br>Use additional code to identify any secondary pulmonary hypertension (416.8), if applicable |
| 770.15 | 770.1 | Aspiration of blood without respiratory symptoms<br>Aspiration of blood NOS |
| 770.16 | 770.1 | Aspiration of blood with respiratory symptoms<br>Aspiration of blood with pneumonia<br>Aspiration of blood with pneumonitis<br>Use additional code to identify any secondary pulmonary hypertension (416.8), if applicable |
| 770.17 | 770.1 | Other fetal and newborn aspiration without respiratory symptoms |
| 770.18 | 770.1 | Other fetal and newborn aspiration with respiratory symptoms<br>Other aspiration pneumonia<br>Other aspiration pneumonitis<br>Use additional code to identify any secondary pulmonary hypertension (416.8), if applicable |
| **770.8** | **subcategory** | **Other respiratory problems after birth** |
| 770.85 | 770.1 | Aspiration of postnatal stomach contents without respiratory symptoms Aspiration of postnatal stomach contents NOS |
| 770.86 | 770.1 | Aspiration of postnatal stomach contents with respiratory symptoms<br>Aspiration of postnatal stomach contents with pneumonia<br>Aspiration of postnatal stomach contents with pneumonitis<br>Use additional code to identify any secondary pulmonary hypertension (416.8), if applicable |
| **779** | **Category** | **Other and ill-defined conditions originating in the perinatal period** |
| **779.8** | **Sub category** | **Other specified conditions originating in the perinatal period** |
| 779.84 | None | Meconium staining<br>Excludes: meconium aspiration (770.11, 770.12)<br>meconium passage during delivery (763.84) |

Conversion Table of New ICD-9-CM Codes
October 2005

| Current Assignment | Previous Assignment | Diagnosis Codes Text |
|---|---|---|
| **780** | **Category** | **General symptoms** |
| **780.9** | **Sub category** | **Sleep disturbances** |
| 780.95 | 780.99 | Other excessive crying<br>Excludes: excessive crying of infant (baby) (780.92) |
| **799** | **Category** | **Other ill-defined and unknown causes of morbidity and mortality** |
| **799.0** | **Sub category** | **Asphyxia and hypoxemia** |
| 799.01-799.02 | 799.0 | Asphyxia |
| 799.02 | 799.0 | Hypoxemia |
| **996** | **Category** | **Complications peculiar to certain specified procedures** |
| **996.4** | **Sub category** | **Mechanical complication of internal orthopedic device, implant, and graft** |
| 996.40 | 996.4 | Unspecified mechanical complication of internal orthopedic device, implant, and graft |
| 996.41 | 996.4 | Mechanical loosening of prosthetic joint<br>Aseptic loosening |
| 996.42 | 996.4 | Dislocation of prosthetic joint<br>Instability of prosthetic joint<br>Subluxation of prosthetic joint |
| 996.43 | 996.4 | Prosthetic joint implant failure<br>Breakage (fracture) of prosthetic joint |
| 996.44 | 996.4 | Peri-prosthetic fracture around prosthetic joint |
| 996.45 | 996.4 | Peri-prosthetic osteolysis |
| 996.46 | 996.4 | Articular bearing surface wear of prosthetic joint |
| 996.47 | 996.4 | Other mechanical complication of prosthetic joint implant<br>Mechanical complication of prosthetic joint NOS |
| 996.49 | 996.4 | Other mechanical complication of other internal orthopedic device, implant, and graft<br>Excludes: mechanical complication of prosthetic joint implant (996.41-996.47) |

Conversion Table of New ICD-9-CM Codes
October 2005

| Current Assignment | Previous Assignment | V CODES<br>Text |
|---|---|---|
| **V12** | | **Personal history of certain other diseases** |
| **V12.4** | | **Disorders of nervous system and sense organs** |
| V12.42 | V12.49 | Infections of the central nervous system Encephalitis Meningitis |
| **V12.6** | | **Diseases of respiratory system** |
| V12.60- | V12.6 | Unspecified disease of respiratory system |
| V12.61 | V12.6 | Pneumonia (recurrent) |
| V12.69 | V12.6 | Other diseases of respiratory system |
| **V13** | | **Person history of other diseases** |
| **V13.0** | | **Disorders of urinary system** |
| V13.02 | V13.09 | Urinary (tract) infection |
| V13.03 | V13.09 | Nephrotic syndrome |
| **V15** | | **Other personal history presenting hazards to health** |
| **V15.8** | | Other specified personal history presenting hazards to health |
| V15.88 | V15.49 | History of fall<br>At risk for falling |
| **V17** | | **Family history of certain chronic disabling diseases** |
| **V17.8** | | **Other musculoskeletal diseases** |
| V17.81 | V17.8 | Osteoporosis |
| V17.89 | V17.8 | Other musculoskeletal diseases |
| **V18** | | **Family history of certain other specific conditions** |
| V18.9 | V19.8 | Genetic disease carrier |
| **V26** | | **Procreative management** |
| **V26.3** | | **Genetic counseling and testing** |
| V26.31 | V26.3 | Testing for genetic disease carrier status |
| V26.32 | V26.3 | Other genetic testing |
| V26.33 | V26.3 | Genetic counseling |
| **V46** | | **Other dependence on machines** |
| V46.13 | V46.11 | Encounter for weaning from respirator [ventilator] |
| V46.14 | V46.11 | Mechanical complication of respirator [ventilator]<br>Mechanical failure of respirator [ventilator] |
| **V49** | | **Other conditions influencing health status** |
| **V49.8** | | **Encounter for other and unspecified procedures and aftercare** |
| V49.84 | V49.89 | Bed confinement status |

Conversion Table of New ICD-9-CM Codes
October 2005

| Current Assignment | Previous Assignment | V CODES<br>Text |
|---|---|---|
| **V58** | | **Encounter for other and unspecified procedures and aftercare** |
| **V58.1** | | **Encounter for antineoplastic chemotherapy and immunotherapy** |
| V58.11 | V58.1 | Encounter for antineoplastic chemotherapy |
| V58.12 | 140-208;230-239 | Encounter for antineoplastic immunotherapy |
| **V59.7** | **New Subcategory** | Donors, Egg (oocyte) (ovum) |
| V59.70 | V59.8 | Egg (oocyte) (ovum) donor, unspecified |
| V59.71 | V59.8 | Egg (oocyte) (ovum) donor, under age 35, anonymous recipient<br>Egg donor, under age 35 NOS |
| V59.72 | V59.8 | Egg (oocyte) (ovum) donor, under age 35, designated recipient |
| V59.73 | V59.8 | Egg (oocyte) (ovum) donor, age 35 and over, anonymous recipient<br>Egg donor, age 35 and over NOS |
| V59.74 | V59.5 | Egg (oocyte) (ovum) donor, age 35 and over, designated recipient |
| **V62** | | **Other psychosocial circumstances** |
| V62.84 | V62.89 | Suicidal ideation<br>Excludes: suicidal tendencies (300.9) |
| **V64** | | **Persons encountering health services for specific procedures, not carried out** |
| **V64.0** | | **Vaccination not carried out** |
| V64.00 | V64.0 | Vaccination not carried out, unspecified reason |
| V64.01 | V64.0 | Vaccination not carried out because of acute illness |
| V64.02 | V64.0 | Vaccination not carried out because of chronic illness or condition |
| V64.03 | V64.0 | Vaccination not carried out because of immune compromised state |
| V64.04 | V64.0 | Vaccination not carried out because of allergy to vaccine or component |
| V64.05 | V64.0 | Vaccination not carried out because of caregiver refusal |
| V64.06 | V64.2 | Vaccination not carried out because of patient refusal |
| V64.07 | V64.0 | Vaccination not carried out for religious reasons |
| V64.08 | V64.02 | Vaccination not carried out because patient had disease being vaccinated against |
| V64.09 | V64.02 | Vaccination not carried out for other reason |
| **V69** | | **Problems related to lifestyle** |
| V69.5 | V69.8 | Behavioral insomnia of childhood |
| **V72** | | **Special investigations and examinations** |
| **V72.4** | | **Pregnancy examination or test** |
| V72.42 | V22.0-V22.1 | Pregnancy examination or test, positive result |
| **V72.8** | | **Other specified examinations** |
| V72.86 | V72.83 | Encounter for blood typing |

| Current Assignment | Previous Assignment | V CODES Text |
|---|---|---|
| **V85** | **New Category** | Body Mass Index<br>Kilograms per meters squared<br>Note: BMI adult codes are for use for persons over 20 years old |
| V85.0 | None | Body Mass Index less than 19, adult |
| V85.1 | None | Body Mass Index between 19-24, adult |
| **V85.2** | **New Subcategory** | Body Mass Index between 25-29, adult |
| V85.21 | None | Body Mass Index 25.0-25.9, adult |
| V85.22 | None | Body Mass Index 26.0-26.9, adult |
| V85.23 | None | Body Mass Index 27.0-27.9, adult |
| V85.24 | None | Body Mass Index 28.0-28.9, adult |
| V85.25 | None | Body Mass Index 29.0-29.9, adults |
| **V85.3** | **New Subcategory** | Body Mass Index between 30-39, adult |
| V85.30- | None | Body Mass Index 30.0-30.9, adult |
| V85.31 | None | Body Mass Index 31.0-31.9, adult |
| V85.32 | None | Body Mass Index 32.0-32.9, adult |
| V85.33 | None | Body Mass Index 33.0-33.9, adult |
| V85.34 | None | Body Mass Index 34.0-34.9, adult |
| V89.35 | None | Body Mass Index 35.0-35.9, adult |
| V89.36 | None | Body Mass Index 36.0-36.9, adult |
| V85.37 | None | Body Mass Index 37.0-37.9, adult |
| V85.38 | None | Body Mass Index 38.0-38.9, adult |
| V85.39 | None | Body Mass Index 39.0-39.9, adults |
| V85.4 | None | Body Mass Index 40 and over, adult |

Conversion Table of New ICD-9-CM Codes
October 2005

| Current Assignment | Previous Assignment | Procedure Codes<br>TEXT |
|---|---|---|
| **00.1** | **Subcategory** | Procedures and interventions not elsewhere classified |
| 00.18 | 99.29 | 00.18 Infusion of immunosuppressive antibody therapy during induction phase of solid organ transplantation<br>monoclonal antibody therapy<br>polyclonal antibody therapy |
| **00.4** | **New Subcategory** | **Adjunct Vascular System Procedures**<br>**Note: These codes can apply to both coronary and peripheral vessels. These codes are to be used in conjunction with other therapeutic procedure codes to provide additional information on the number of vessels upon which a procedure was performed and/or the number of stents inserted. As appropriate, code both the number of vessels operated on (00.40-00.43), and the number of stents inserted (00.45-00.48).**<br>**Code also any:**<br>**angioplasty or atherectomy (00.61- 00.62, 00.66, 39.50)**<br>**endarterectomy (38.10 – 38.18)**<br>**insertion of vascular stent(s) (00.55, 00.63-00.65, 36.06 -36.07, 39.90)**<br>**other removal of coronary artery obstruction (36.09)** |
| 00.40 | None | Procedure on single vessel<br>Number of vessels, unspecified<br>Excludes: (aorto)coronary bypass (36.10 – 36.19)<br>intravascular imaging of blood vessels (00.21-00.29) |
| 0.41 | None | Procedure on two vessels<br>Excludes: (aorto) coronary bypass (36.10 – 36.19)<br>intravascular imaging of blood vessels (00.21-00.29) |
| 00.42 | None | Procedure on three vessels<br>Excludes: (aorto) coronary bypass (36.10 – 36.19)<br>intravascular imaging of blood vessels (00.21-00.29) |
| 00.43 | None | Procedure on four or more vessels<br>Excludes: (aorto) coronary bypass (36.10 – 36.19)<br>intravascular imaging of blood vessels (00.21-00.29) |
| 00.45 | None | Insertion of one vascular stent<br>Number of stents, unspecified |
| 00.46 | None | Insertion of two vascular stents |
| 00.47 | None | Insertion of three vascular stents |
| 00.48 | None | Insertion of four or more vascular stents |

| **Current Assignment** | **Previous Assignment** | **Procedure Codes TEXT** |
|---|---|---|
| **00.6** | **subcategory** | **Procedures on blood vessels** |
| 00.66 | 36.01 (deleted),<br>36.02 (deleted),<br>36.05 (deleted | Percutaneous transluminal coronary angioplasty [PTCA] or coronary atherectomy<br>Balloon angioplasty of coronary artery<br>Coronary atherectomy<br>Percutaneous coronary angioplasty NOS<br>TCA NOS<br>Code also any:<br>injection or infusion of thrombolytic agent (99.10)<br>insertion of coronary artery stent(s) (36.06- 36.07)<br>intracoronary artery thrombolytic infusion (36.04)<br>number of vascular stents inserted (00.45 - 00.48)<br>number of vessels treated (00.40 – 00.43) |
| **007** | **New subcategory** | **Other hip procedures** |
| 00.70 | 81.53 | Revision of hip replacement, both acetabular and femoral components<br>Total hip revision<br>Code also any:<br>removal of (cement) (joint) spacer (84.57)<br>type of bearing surface, if known (00.74 – 00.76)<br>Excludes:<br>revision of hip replacement, acetabular component only (00.71)<br>revision of hip replacement, femoral component only (00.72)<br>revision of hip replacement, Not Otherwise Specified (81.53)<br>revision with replacement of acetabular liner and/or femoral head only (00.73) |
| 00.71 | 81.53 | Revision of hip replacement, femoral component<br>Partial, femoral component only<br>That with:<br>exchange of acetabular liner<br>exchange of femoral stem and head<br>Code also any type of bearing surface, if known (00.74 - 00.76)<br>Excludes:<br>revision of hip replacement, acetabular component (00.71)<br>revision of hip replacement, both acetabular and femoral components (00.70)<br>revision of hip replacement, not otherwise specified (81.53)<br>revision with replacement of acetabular liner and/or femoral head only (00.73) |

Conversion Table of New ICD-9-CM Codes
October 2005

| **Current Assignment** | **Previous Assignment** | **Procedure Codes TEXT** |
|---|---|---|
| 00.72 | 81.53 | Revision of hip replacement, femoral component<br>Partial, femoral component only<br>That with:<br>exchange of acetabular liner<br>exchange of femoral stem and head<br>Code also any type of bearing surface, if known (00.74 - 00.76)<br>Excludes:<br>revision of hip replacement, acetabular component (00.71)<br>revision of hip replacement, both acetabular and femoral components (00.70)<br>revision of hip replacement, not otherwise specified (81.53)<br>revision with replacement of acetabular liner and/or femoral head only (00.73) |
| 00.73 | 81.53 | Revision of hip replacement, acetabular liner and/or femoral head only<br>Code also any type of bearing surface, if known (00.74 – 00.76) |
| 00.74 | None | Hip replacement bearing surface, metal on polyethylene |
| 00.75 | None | Hip replacement bearing surface, metal-on-metal |
| 00.76 | None | Hip replacement bearing surface, ceramic-on-ceramic |
| **00.8** | **New sub category** | Other knee procedures<br>Note: Report up to two components using 00.81 – 00.83 to describe revision of knee replacements.<br>If all three components are revised, report 00.80. |
| 00.80 | 81.55 | Revision of knee replacement, total (all components)<br>Replacement of femoral, tibial, and patellar components (all components)<br>Code also any removal of (cement) (joint) spacer (84.57)<br>Excludes:<br>revision of only one or two components (tibial, femoral or patellar component) (00.81 – 00.84) |
| 00.81 | 81.55 | Revision of knee replacement, tibial component<br>Replacement of tibial baseplate and tibial insert (liner)<br>Excludes:<br>revision of knee replacement, total (all components) (00.80) |
| 00.82 | 81.55 | Revision of knee replacement, femoral component<br>That with replacement of tibial insert (liner)<br>Excludes:<br>revision of knee replacement, total (all components) (00.80) |
| 00.83 | 81.55 | Revision of knee replacement, patellar component<br>Excludes:<br>revision of knee replacement, total (all components) (00.80) |

| **Current Assignment** | **Previous Assignment** | **Procedure Codes TEXT** |
|---|---|---|
| 00.84 | 81.55 | Revision of total knee replacement, tibial insert (liner)<br>   Replacement of tibial insert (liner)<br>Excludes:<br>   that with replacement of tibial component (tibial baseplate and liner) (00.81) |
| **01.** | **Category** | **Incision and excision of skull, brain, and cerebral meninges** |
| **01.2** | **Subcategory** | **Craniotomy and Craniectomy**<br>**Excludes: decompression of skull fracture (02.02)**<br>   **Exploration of orbit (16.01-16.09)**<br>   **That as operative approach – omit code** |
| 01.26 | None | Insertion of catheter into cranial cavity<br>Code also any concomitant procedure (e.g. resection (01.59)) |
| 01.27 | None | Removal of catheter from cranial cavity |
| **37** | | **Other operations on heart and pericardium**<br>**Code also any injection or infusion of platelet inhibitor (99.200** |
| **37.4** | **New Subcategory** | Repair of heart and pericardium |
| 37.41 | 37.99 | Implantation of prosthetic cardiac support device around the heart<br>   Cardiac support device (CSD)<br>   Epicardial support device<br>   Fabric (textile) (mesh) device<br>   Ventricular support device on surface of heart<br>Code also any:<br>   cardiopulmonary bypass [extracorporeal circulation] [heartlung machine] if performed (39.61)<br>   mitral valve repair (35.02, 35.12)<br>   mitral valve replacement (35.23 -35.24)<br>   transesophageal echocardiography (88.72)<br>Excludes: circulatory assist systems (37.61 – 37.68) |
| 37.49 | 37.99 | Other repair of heart and pericardium |
| **39.7** | **Subcategory** | **Endovascular repair of vessel** |
| 39.73 | | Endovascular implantation of graft in thoracic aorta<br>   Endograft(s)<br>   Endovascular graft(s)<br>   Endovascular repair of defect of thoracic aorta with graft(s) or device(s)<br>   Stent graft(s) or device(s)<br>   That for repair of aneurysm, dissection, or injury<br>Excludes: fenestration of dissecting aneurysm of thoracic aorta (39.54) |

Conversion Table of New ICD-9-CM Codes
October 2005

| Current Assignment | Previous Assignment | Procedure Codes TEXT |
|---|---|---|
| **81.** | **Category** | **Repair and plastic operations on joint structures** |
| **81.1** | **Subcategory** | **Arthrodesis and arthroereisis of foot and ankle** |
| 81.18 | 81.99 | Subtalar joint arthroereisis |
| **84** | **Category** | **Other procedures on musculoskeletal system** |
| **84.5** | **Subcategory** | **Implantation of other musculoskeletal devices and substances**<br>**Excludes: Insertion of (non-fusion) spinal disc replacement device (84.60-84.69)** |
| 84.56 | None | Insertion of (cement) spacer<br>Insertion of joint spacer |
| 84.57 | None | Removal of (cement) spacer<br>Removal of joint spacer |
| 84.58 | 84.59 | Implantation of interspinous process decompression device<br>Excludes: fusion of spine (81.00-81.08, 81.30-81.39) |
| **84.7** | **New subcategory** | Adjunct codes for external fixator devices<br>Code also any primary procedure performed:<br>application of external fixator device (78.10, 78.12-78.13, 78.15, 78.17-78.19)<br>reduction of fracture and dislocation (79.00-79.89) |
| 84.71 | None | Application of external fixator device, monoplanar system<br>Excludes:<br>other hybrid device or system (84.73)<br>ring device or system (84.72) |
| 84.72 | None | Application of external fixator device, ring system<br>Ilizarov type<br>Sheffield type<br>Excludes:<br>monoplanar device or system (84.71)<br>other hybrid device or system (84.73) |
| 84.73 | None | Application of hybrid external fixator device<br>Hybrid system using both ring and monoplanar devices<br>Excludes:<br>monoplanar device or system, when used alone (84.71)<br>ring device or system, when used alone (84.72) |

Conversion Table of New ICD-9-CM Codes
October 2005

| **Current Assignment** | **Previous Assignment** | **Procedure Codes TEXT** |
|---|---|---|
| **86.9** | **Subcategory** | **Other operations on skin and subcutaneous tissue** |
| 86.97 | 86.94 | Insertion or replacement of single array rechargeable neurostimulator pulse generator<br>Rechargeable pulse generator (single array, single channel) for intracranial, spinal, and peripheral neurostimulator<br>Code also any associated lead implantation (02.93,03.93,04.9 |
| 86.98 | 86.95 | Insertion or replacement of dual array rechargeable neurostimulator pulse generator<br>Rechargeable pulse generator (dual array, dual channel) for intracranial, spinal, and peripheral neurostimulator<br>Code also any associated lead implantation (02.93,03.93,04.92) |
| **92.2** | **Subcategory** | **Therapeutic radiology and nuclear medicine**<br>**Excludes that for:**<br>**Ablation of pituitary gland (07.64-07.69)**<br>**Destruction of chorioetinal leasion (14.26-14.27)** |
| 92.20 | 92.28 | Infusion of liquid brachytherapy radioisotope<br>I-125 radioisotope<br>Intracavitary brachytherapy<br>Includes: removal of radioisotope |

## EVALUATION FORM FOR THE BOOK AND INTERACTIVE CD-ROM

As we have learned through quality improvement concepts, there is always the opportunity to do something better. Therefore, if you have suggestions for improving the book and CD-ROM, please let us know. We invite your input and feedback.

Please rate each of the following aspects of this book on a scale of 1 to 5, where: **5 is excellent, 4 is above average, 3 is average, 2 is below average, and 1 is poor**

| | | | | | |
|---|---|---|---|---|---|
| Depth/completeness of coverage | 5 | 4 | 3 | 2 | 1 |
| Organization of material | 5 | 4 | 3 | 2 | 1 |
| Study tips | 5 | 4 | 3 | 2 | 1 |
| Appropriate level of writing | 5 | 4 | 3 | 2 | 1 |
| Cover design and attractiveness | 5 | 4 | 3 | 2 | 1 |
| Overall design and layout of book | 5 | 4 | 3 | 2 | 1 |
| Overall satisfaction with book | 5 | 4 | 3 | 2 | 1 |

Would you recommend this book to future candidates preparing for the AHIMA Certified Coding Specialist - Physician Based Examination?

☐ Yes ☐ No

Please indicate whether you are ☐ Student ☐ Educator

Would you recommend the CD-ROM to:

CCS-P Exam Candidates ☐ Yes ☐ No

HIM Educators ☐ Yes ☐ No

What can we do to make this book better for you to use?______________________________

Thank you!


**Mail to:** **Professional Review Guides, Inc.**
**P. O. Box 528**
**St. Petersburg, Florida 33731**

**Phone:** **(727) 526-3163**

**Toll Free: (888) 383-PRG1 ~ or ~ 1- (888) 383-7741**

**FAX:** **(727) 526-4474**

**E-mail:** **pjsprg@aol.com**